FROM THE COMMAND P[...]

demonstrate how some companies are i[...] sales concepts and practices. Each of these boxes is directed toward students gaining enhanced knowledge of the practice of personal selling.

CHAPTER

1 Cemex—High-Tech Cement Marketer
2 Carrier Corporation—Keeping Things Cool
3 Betrayal from the Top
4 Getting a Grip on the Market
5 Online Information System for Salespeople
6 Being Different Can Be an Advantage
7 Charge of the Lilliputians
8 Web Auction Sites Just Keep on Selling More and More
9 Service-Oriented Wholesaler
9 Better Service Through Partnership
12 Surveying Customers Via Email
13 It's All in the Palm of My Hand

KEEPING UP ONLINE boxes provide students with a web address to log on to for special insights. Each box will include questions related to the website noted in the box.

CHAPTER

1 Salesautopsy.com
2 Sales and Marketing Executives International
3 E-Center for Business Ethics
3 TRUSTe
3 U.S. Equal Employment Opportunity Commission
3 Federal Trade Commission
4 DuPont Company
5 Procter & Gamble Company
6 *Journal of Personal Selling & Sales Management* (JPSSM)
7 *Sales and Marketing Management* (S&MM)
8 E-mail
9 The Digital Route to Sales and Service
10 General Electric Corporation
11 U.S. Census Bureau
12 Bizjournals.com
13 Radvision
13 Instant Yellow Pages
13 Empower Geographics

PERSONAL SELLING

Second Edition

PERSONAL SELLING

Building Customer Relationships and Partnerships

ROLPH E. ANDERSON
Drexel University

ALAN J. DUBINSKY
Purdue University

RAJIV MEHTA
New Jersey Institute of Technology

Houghton Mifflin Company
Boston *New York*

To my talented and supportive wife, Sallie, and our wonderful children, Rachel and Stuart.—Rolph Anderson

To the memory of a loving father, Elliott S. Dubinsky, and to three especially caring and supportive individuals—Caron Rodman, David Dubinsky, and Deborah Tulman.—Alan Dubinsky

To the memory of a wonderful father, R.K.—for his unconditional love; to my mother, Kamlesh—for her love and sacrifice; they made it all possible.—Rajiv Mehta

Publisher: George T. Hoffman
Senior Development Editor: Chere Bemelmans
Editorial Assistant: Amy Galvin
Project Editor: Shelley Dickerson
Editorial Assistant: Sarah Driver
Senior Art/Design Coordinator: Jill Haber
Senior Photo Editor: Jennifer Meyer Dare
Composition Buyer: Chuck Dutton
Manufacturing Manager: Priscilla Manchester
Marketing Manager: Mike Schenk
Marketing Specialist: Lisa E. Boden

Cover image: Digital Vision/Getty Images, Stockbyte Photography/Veer

Printed in the U.S.A.

Library of Congress Control Number: 2005938686

Student Edition (use for ordering) –
ISBN 13: 978-0-618-64570-1
ISBN 10: 0-618-64570-5

Exam Copy –
ISBN 13: 978-0-618-73101-5
ISBN 10: 0-618-73101-6

1 2 3 4 5 6 7 8 9–DOW–10 09 08 07 06

BRIEF CONTENTS

CONTENTS

PART 2
The Personal Selling Process

CHAPTER 4
Prospecting and Qualifying: Filling the Salesperson's "Pot of Gold" 99

CHAPTER 5
Planning the Sales Call: Steps to a Successful Approach 134

CHAPTER 9
Following Up and Servicing the Account: Building Strategic Partnerships by Keeping Customers Satisfied and Loyal 281

PART 3
Understanding and Communicating with Customers

CHAPTER 10
Understanding and Negotiating with Organizational Buyers 320

PREFACE

Nearly twenty percent of all college graduates, regardless of major, will start their careers in professional sales. Professional personal selling offers a career opportunity that can be personally satisfying as well as financially rewarding for highly motivated men and women. According to the most recent *Occupational Outlook Handbook* published by the U.S. Department of Labor, demand for sales jobs is expected to grow by 10 to 20 percent through the year 2012. Moreover, a national compensation study reported in *Sales & Marketing Management* found that the average annual income across all levels of salespeople exceeds $100,000. For entry-level salespersons with one to three years of sales experience, the average earnings were approximately $50,000. In addition, opportunities for advancement are excellent as many CEOs of major corporations started their careers in sales.

Now is an especially exciting and challenging time to study professional selling. Rapid growth in telecommunication technologies and global markets has propelled personal selling into one of the most dynamic, fast changing, and rewarding of all the business professions. Organizations in business-to-business markets are using innovative approaches, sales channels, and technologies to profitably sell their products and services in the global market. Several behavioral, technological, and managerial forces are influencing buyer-seller relationships, and they are changing the way sales activities are carried out and how salespeople understand, prepare for, and accomplish their jobs. With advances in telecommunications technology, salespeople are becoming increasingly independent of sales managers and moving away from merely "selling" to "serving" their customers more like consultants and business partners. Successful salespeople consult regularly with customers to determine the best combination of products and services to satisfy their customers' business needs. Innovative strategies are explored to provide greater value-added service and to build mutually profitable, ongoing relationships and partnerships with customers.

Students interested in pursuing careers in professional selling today must be superbly prepared to assume sales positions after college graduation. They must be forearmed with the requisite knowledge, skills, and attitude because many sales recruiters will hire only those students who manifest stellar professional selling qualities. Much of this preparation will occur in college courses, particularly those involving personal selling. Therefore, a major goal in writing this text was to create diverse "real-world" experiences for students in each chapter through experiential learning such as Internet exercises, role plays, case studies, and self-assessment tools.

As the ultimate revenue generators, salespeople are critical to the well being of their companies and to their country's economy, especially in an era of intense global competition. Unless products and services are profitably sold, companies cannot stay in business and their employees will lose their jobs. Thus, in many ways, every business and nearly everyone—from customers to employees—depend on the success of salespeople.

Features of the Book

Personal Selling: Building Customer Relationships and Partnerships, Second Edition, uses a pragmatic, up-to-date, realistic, upbeat, and professional approach to the study of personal selling. Our writing style is conversational, and we talk one-to-one with students. Although we present considerable theoretical material, we use non-technical language in our analyses and always try to show the practical application of the theory. We give many "real world" company examples that allow students to further enhance their understanding of the concepts. Other important features of the second edition are as follows:

- The text focuses exclusively on professional *business-to-business* selling, not on retail or door-to-door selling to consumers. Why? Because most college students today begin their sales careers after college graduation and view a job in retail sales or selling direct to consumers as unsuitable for a college-trained professional. Focusing on business-to-business selling helps students understand that personal selling is a respected, well-paid professional career with abundant opportunities and rewards for those who are qualified and motivated. Moreover, it reinforces the need for salespeople to help customers become more profitable by helping them develop successful strategies for "selling through" to their customers.
- Emphasizing the increased importance of ethics and legal issues in personal selling and business in general, we address this complex area early in the book—now in Chapter 3. Topics include the ethical concerns of salespeople, treatment of coworkers and competitors, and behaving ethically every day. In addition, the chapter includes self-assessment exercises to determine your level of moral and ethical standards.
- To support and complement the comprehension of crucial concepts and issues, we cite and report current research findings in useful, understandable, and interesting ways that provide students with insights for their sales careers. When research is cited, we explain and illustrate how students can use the findings to increase their own sales performance.
- Timeliness and keeping up-to-date with "real world" best practices in personal selling are critical. To enhance students' understanding of how salespeople in today's progressive companies do their jobs, we use current examples (from both the online and offline business press) taken from the best business practices.

- Sales positions are becoming more and more high-tech. This requires students to become intimately familiar with the high-tech tools and services that facilitate salespeople's jobs. Our text describes the pragmatic use of high-tech tools and the advantages (and a few disadvantages from excessive use) in skillfully using such tools to sell more efficiently and effectively.
- Long-term customer loyalty, not merely customer satisfaction, leads to the highest profitability for both salespeople and their organizations. Our mantra throughout the book is the significance of attracting, cultivating, and retaining satisfied and loyal customers and developing mutually profitable partnerships with selected buyer organizations. Chapter 9 focuses on building strategic partnerships.

Chapter Pedagogy

Personal Selling: *Building Customer Relationships and Partnerships* offers several special features to facilitate student learning, including the following:

- Each chapter begins with a set of chapter goals. These goals address those areas most important in the chapter. After studying the chapter, students can review the chapter goals to assess whether they have indeed achieved them.
- Following each chapter's goals, we profile a successful salesperson in the *"Inside Personal Selling"* feature. These profiles present salespeople from diverse backgrounds who sell diverse products for various types of organizations. By reading these profiles, students will discover that there is no stereotypical successful salesperson. Individuals from all "walks of life"—with various demographic and psychographic characteristics—can be highly successful in sales.
- We present the personal selling process (PSP) as a revolving cycle of seven interacting, overlapping stages centered on prospects and customers in each of the chapters of Part II. The stage dealt with in that particular chapter is highlighted on the wheel. This wheel reinforces the interconnectedness and relationships among the seven stages by illustrating that the wheel keeps revolving so that there is really no precise beginning or end to the personal selling process.
- Today's salespeople need to be able to discern their strengths and weaknesses themselves without depending solely on feedback from their sales managers. Our textbook includes several *personal assessment tools*, including those on ethics and communication styles, that students will be able to use for purposes of self-appraisal and skill building.
- Six new chapter vignettes entitled *"On the Frontlines: The Life of a Salesperson"* follow the "real-world" personal selling experiences of a recent college graduate, Jason Smyczynski. Jason's perceptions and description of his day-to-day activities as a professional salesperson will help students relate more realistically to a business-to-business sales career.

- Other *"On the Frontlines"* boxes demonstrate the activities of "real world" salespeople working with prospects and customers before, during, and after the sale.
- *"It's Up to You"* boxes stimulate student thinking. These boxes pose a problem to students and ask how they would handle a particular "live" selling situation.
- *"From the Command Post"* boxes demonstrate how some companies are implementing the latest sales concepts and practices. Each of these boxes is directed toward students' gaining enhanced knowledge of real-world practices in personal selling.
- *"Keeping Up Online"* boxes provide students with a web address to log on to for special insights. Each box includes questions related to the website noted in the box.
- In each chapter of the text, we provide several websites where students can find additional resources that amplify the chapter material.
- Chapter Review Questions in the margin of the text provide material for class discussion or student review.
- All chapters conclude with a chapter Summary, Key Terms, Topics for Thought and Class Discussion, Projects for Personal Growth, and a Case. New to this edition are Internet Exercises and two Role-Play Exercises in each chapter. Fourteen additional case studies—one for each chapter—can be found at the Online Learning Center. All of these pedagogical tools are designed to ensure that students understand and can apply the chapter material effectively.

Text Content and Organization

In reading this text, there are five basic goals that we want our readers to achieve. Specifically, we want you to

1. Understand and appreciate the multifaceted roles that salespeople play in progressive organizations.
2. Obtain a solid conceptual background and understanding of the dynamic environment in which today's professional salespeople function.
3. Develop a comprehensive and in-depth, practical knowledge of how to apply the steps involved in the personal selling process (PSP) skillfully.
4. Utilize an array of proven, effective tools and techniques for assessing and enhancing your abilities for personal selling.
5. Feel fully confident to assume a position in business-to-business sales.

To accomplish these objectives, we first provide an overview of personal selling. Then, we discuss, illustrate, and analyze the personal selling process. In each of the chapters on the PSP, we depict the process as a revolving wheel of seven interacting, overlapping steps, and highlight the step or steps covered in that particular chapter. Next, we direct our attention to topics related to enhancing students' understanding of customers and persuasively communicating with them. Finally, we offer advice and suggestions on how to achieve success in the sales field by developing long-term, mutually satisfying relationships and partnerships with customers that lead to mutual profits.

Personal Selling: Building Customer Relationships and Partnerships is divided into four parts covering fourteen chapters:

Part 1. Overview of Personal Selling Part 1, "Overview of Personal Selling," introduces the career field of personal selling to students and describes the dynamic selling environment in which modern salespeople operate. Chapter 1, "Introduction to Personal Selling: It's a Great Career!" discusses such topics as the differences between yesterday's and today's salesperson, customer-oriented selling vis-à-vis the marketing concept, sales job opportunities and advantages, telecommunication advances in selling, and salespeople's career paths. In Chapter 2, "Adjusting to the Dynamic Personal Selling Environment," we analyze the key evolutionary and revolutionary factors influencing personal selling. These include *behavioral* forces (e.g., more expert and demanding buyers, rising customer expectations, internationalization of markets), *technological* forces (e.g., sales force automation, virtual sales offices, electronic commerce), and *managerial* forces (e.g., selling cost reduction efforts, shift to direct marketing alternatives, professional salesperson certification). All three of these megatrends are relentlessly and irrevocably changing the way that salespeople understand, prepare for, and accomplish their jobs. Chapter 3 addresses "Ethical and Legal Considerations in Personal Selling." Ethical issues confronting salespeople include their interactions with prospects and customers, competitors, peers, and employers. We also describe various local, national, and international laws that affect the performance of salespeople, and then offer an approach to ethical decision-making.

Part 2. The Personal Selling Process We believe that the heart of personal selling, as well as its most exciting part, is the *personal selling process (PSP)*. This process entails seven basic steps that salespeople carry out to ultimately make a sale and engender long-run customer satisfaction and loyalty. Therefore, Part 2 contains six chapters that address the PSP in detail. Chapter 4, "Prospecting and Qualifying Prospects: Filling the Salesperson's 'Pot of Gold,'" describes the importance of prospecting, how to qualify sales leads, various kinds of prospecting sources, and basic steps in a prospecting plan. In Chapter 5, "Planning the Sales Call: Steps to a Successful Approach," we focus on key issues in the preapproach and approach steps of the personal selling process. In particular, attention is paid to several useful techniques and methods for effectively executing these two steps, as well as how to deal with sales call reluctance—a bane of many salespeople.

We then move on to a discussion about preparing for and making a sales presentation and demonstration in Chapter 6, "Sales Presentation and

Demonstration: The Pivotal Exchange." Extensive attention is given to alternate kinds of demonstrations, preparation of written presentations (sales proposals), adaptive versus canned presentations, and making sales presentations to buyer groups. In Chapter 7, "Negotiating Sales Resistance and Objections for 'Win-Win' Agreements," students learn how to deal with prospect and customer resistance or objections to buying. Major issues covered include how to plan for objections, how to handle objections, how to overcome price resistance, and how to ensure a "win-win" outcome for both buyer and seller.

The last two chapters of this section of the text—Chapter 8, "Confirming and Closing the Sale: Start of the Long Term Relationship," and Chapter 9, "Following Up and Servicing the Account: Building Strategic Partnerships by Keeping Customers Satisfied and Loyal"—pertain to consummating the sale and attending to post-sale activities. Chapter 8 analyzes why some salespeople fail to close, important closing signals, when to close, effective techniques for closing, and handling rejection. Chapter 9 addresses, among other issues, the importance of customer satisfaction and loyalty, customer service expectations, assessing customer satisfaction, critical post-sale activities, the 8Cs of customer loyalty, and strategies for building long-term relationships and partnerships with selected customers.

Part 3. Understanding and Communicating with Customers Part 3, "Understanding and Communicating with Customers," contains three chapters, the topics of which will enhance students' abilities to carry out effectively the steps in the personal selling process. Chapter 10, "Understanding and Negotiating with Organizational Buyers," describes the various kinds of organizational customers that business-to-business salespeople must understand, the different negotiation styles of buyers, decision-making styles of buyers, and selling in international markets. In "Strategic Understanding of Your Company, Products, Competition, and Markets" (Chapter 11), we discuss the various kinds of knowledge salespeople require to do their job effectively. Chapter 12, "Communicating Effectively with Diverse Customers," describes the different dimensions of effective listening, alternative formats and types of questions to ask prospects, the use of body language and space, the four communication styles of buyers, and building trust in buyer-seller relationships.

Part 4. Achieving Success in Personal Selling In Part 4 we focus on topics for "Achieving Success in Personal Selling." In Chapter 13, "Managing Your Time and Your Territory," we address the importance of salesperson effectiveness and efficiency, methods for using time wisely, how to avoid time traps, efficient routing alternatives, and how to prioritize accounts. In Chapter 14, "Starting Your Personal Selling Career," we show students how to use the personal selling process to obtain their initial sales job following college graduation. In addition, we discuss what employers are looking for, how they will screen applicants for jobs, and how to follow-up the interview or employment decision with an appropriate letter.

A Fully Integrated Package

Personal Selling: Building Customer Relationships and Partnerships offers a comprehensive package of ancillary materials, including PowerPoint slides for each chapter and a video series to assist instructors and students. An instructor website as well as an Instructor's Resource Manual with Test Bank contain a variety of tools tied to the text and designed to facilitate instructor-led classes as well as online learning environments. The student website includes text-specific content to support and enhance the textbook.

Instructor's Resource Manual with Test Bank

The Instructor's Resource Manual with Test Bank is designed to be the basic source of information to support text material in each chapter of *Personal Selling: Building Customer Relationships and Partnerships*. The Instructor's Resource Manual includes suggested class schedules and detailed teaching notes for each chapter of the text; suggested responses to end-of-chapter questions, exercises, and cases; and in-class role-playing exercises. The comprehensive Test Bank includes almost 1,200 multiple-choice, true-false, and essay questions, each identified with the corresponding learning objective and page numbers for reference.

Instructor Website

The Anderson Online Teaching Center at **http://college.hmco.com/pic/andersonPS2e** offers valuable information for instructors including PowerPoint slides, classroom response system ("Clicker") content, lecture outlines, sample syllabi, and solutions for end-of-chapter material. The variety of information included on the site is designed to enhance the learning and teaching experience. The complete Instructor's Resource Manual with Test Bank is also available for download on the website.

HMClassPrep CD-ROM with HMTesting

The HMClassPrep Instructor CD-ROM includes a wide variety of instructor resources such as HMTesting, the complete Instructor's Resource Manual with Test Bank, and PowerPoint slides. With HMTesting, the computerized testing program, an instructor can select questions and produce test masters for easy duplication. Instructors can select their own questions or have the program select them. They can also customize tests by creating new questions, editing existing ones, and generating multiple versions of the tests. A call-in service is also available.

PowerPoint Slides

Included on the HMClassPrep CD-ROM and the Anderson Online Teaching Center, an extensive set of PowerPoint slides provides instructors with lecture presentations, including key figures from the text. Instructors can use the slides as is for display on computer-based projection systems, edit them to suit personal course objectives, or print them out for use in making transparency acetates or handouts for student note taking.

Videos

A video program accompanies *Personal Selling: Building Customer Relationships and Partnerships* to illustrate important concepts from the text. Each video is designed to demonstrate and emphasize key personal selling concepts by the use of real-world sales situations.

Student Website

The Anderson Online Study Center provides additional information, guidance, and activities that will help enhance the concepts presented in this text. The site offers students ACE self-test questions, Ready Notes, Flashcards, Web Resources, Learning Objectives, Outlines, and company links. In addition, the site will feature links to important job and career sites.

Acknowledgements

Preparing a college textbook is a long-term team effort that depends on contributions from many talented people. First, we are deeply indebted for the insightful comments and suggestions of our reviewers: A.E. Beatty, Northern Arizona University; Richard Bethel, Ferris State University; Thomas F. Cannon, University of Texas at San Antonio; Bobby Cutler, Cleveland State University; Philip Gonsher, Johnson County Community College; Susan Meyer, Colorado State University; Henry Noel, College of the Southwest; C. David Shepherd, Kennessaw State University; Jeff Totten, Bemidji State University; Gary Walk, Lima Technical College; Jack Forrest, Cumberland University; Kevin Feldt, The University of Akron; Karl Sooder, University of Southwest Florida; Robert McMurrian, University of Tampa; John Lanasa, Duquesne University; and Pravin Kamdar, Cardinal Stritch University.

For writing several excellent case studies, our special appreciation and recognition goes to Paul F. Christ, Director of the MBA Program at West Chester State University, and James T. Strong, Dean of the College of Business Administration and Public Policy at California State University, Dominguez Hills.

Unwavering support and encouragement from our deans and chairs at our respective universities—Dean George P. Tsetsekos and Marketing Department Chair Trina Larsen Andras at Drexel University, Dean Dennis Savaiano and Department Chair Richard Widdows at Purdue University, and Acting Dean David Hawk and Associate Dean Barbara Tedesco at New Jersey Institute of Technology—were invaluable in enabling us to complete the second edition of *Personal Selling: Building Customer Relationships and Partnerships.*

Several colleagues have contributed greatly to our understanding of personal selling and to our development as teachers, researchers, and writers. Although a comprehensive list is not possible here, we would like to thank the following university professors for sharing their knowledge and perspectives with us: Mark Somers, Asokan Anandarajan, Ken Kirchhoff, Shanthi Golapakrishnan, William Rudelius, Lucette Comer, Lawrence Chonko, Rajan Nataraajan, Jeffrey Sager, Chae Un Lim, Steven Skinner, Francis Yammarino, Srini Swaminathan, Burt Brodo, Stan Kligman, Larry Colfer, Joe Rocereto, Mary Shoemaker, and Khalid Dubas.

Most important to initiating and completing *Personal Selling: Building Customer Relationships and Partnerships* was the guidance and motivation provided by the professional team at Houghton Mifflin. Never have we worked with a more talented, dedicated, and congenial group of people. In particular, we want to thank George Hoffman, Publisher, for giving us the opportunity to prepare this second edition. Chere Bemelmans, Senior Development Editor, and Shelley Dickerson, Project Editor, both provided many excellent ideas to improve the book.

All of the above mentioned people and many others have facilitated our work and helped make what is usually an arduous task almost fun. It is our fervent hope that our combined efforts represented by this text will give students many enjoyable and rewarding learning experiences that prepare them for a successful career in professional personal selling.

Rolph E. Anderson
Alan J. Dubinsky
Rajiv Mehta

ROLPH E. ANDERSON, PH.D.

Rolph Anderson is the Royal H. Gibson Sr. Professor of Business Administration and former Head of the Department of Marketing at Drexel University. He earned his Ph.D. from the University of Florida and his MBA and BA degrees from Michigan State University. His primary research and publication areas are personal selling and sales management, customer relationship management, and customer loyalty. He is author or co-author of twenty textbooks, including *Multivariate Data Analysis*, Sixth Edition, the most frequently cited text in academic marketing.

Dr. Anderson's research has been widely published in the major refereed journals in his field, including articles in the *Journal of Marketing Research, Journal of Marketing, Journal of Retailing, Journal of the Academy of Marketing Science, Journal of Experimental Education, Business Horizons, European Journal of Marketing, Psychology & Marketing, Journal of Global Marketing, Journal of Marketing Education, Journal of Business-to-Business Marketing, Marketing Education Review, Journal of Managerial Issues, Industrial Marketing Management, Journal of Business & Industrial Marketing,* and *Journal of Personal Selling & Sales Management.* His classic *Journal of Marketing Research* article on "Consumer Dissatisfaction: The Effect of Disconfirmed Expectations on Perceived Product Performance" was one of the pioneering articles in the study of customer satisfaction. In 1988, he won the national Mu Kappa Tau award for the best article published in the *Journal of Personal Selling & Sales Management.* In 1992, Dr. Anderson was selected for the second time by the Drexel College of Business & Administration students to receive the Faculty Appreciation Award. In 1995, he was recipient of the national "Excellence in Reviewing Award" from the editor of the *Journal of Personal Selling & Sales Management.* In 1998, he received the American Marketing Association Sales Special Interest Group inaugural "Excellence in Sales Scholarship Award." He received Drexel University's LeBow College of Business "Research Achievement" award in 2000–2001, and its "Academic Leadership in Textbook Publishing" award in 2003.

Dr. Anderson has served several professional organizations as an officer, including President, Southeast Institute for Decision Sciences (IDS); Board of Directors, American Marketing Association (Philadelphia Chapter); Secretary and Board of Directors, Academy of Marketing Science; Vice-President for Programming, AMA (Philadelphia Chapter); National Council, Institute for Decision Sciences; Board of Directors, Northeast IDS; and Co-Chairman, 61st International American Marketing Association Conference. Dr. Anderson is a member of the Editorial Boards of five academic journals. He also serves on the Faculty Advisory Board of the Fisher Institute for Professional Selling and on the national Sales Committee for *Financial Services Advisor* magazine.

Prior to entering academia, Dr. Anderson worked in sales and managerial positions for three *Fortune* 500 companies. Active as a business and government consultant, he is also a retired U.S. Navy Supply Corps Captain. With wife, Sallie, they are parents of two college students, Rachel and Stuart. Professor Anderson's biographical sketch appears in *Who's Who in America* and *Who's Who in American Education.*

ALAN J. DUBINSKY, PH.D.

Alan Dubinsky is a Professor in the College of Family and Consumer Sciences at Purdue University. He earned his Ph.D. from the University of Minnesota, as well as his MBA and BS degrees. He is a former editor of the *Journal of Personal Selling & Sales Management,* the leading academic journal that focuses on selling and sales management. He has authored *Sales Training: An Analysis of Field Sales Techniques* and co-authored *Managing the Successful Sales Force and High Performers: Recruiting and Retaining Top Employees.* Additionally, he has given selling skills sales training seminars to industrial salespeople, as well as marketing seminars to executives.

Dr. Dubinsky has published over 150 research articles in personal selling and sales management. They have appeared in the major journals in his field, including the *Journal of Marketing Research, Journal of Marketing, Journal of Retailing, Journal of the Academy of Marketing Science, European Journal of Marketing, Journal of Business Research, Journal of Business-to-Business Marketing, Industrial Marketing Management, Journal of Personal Selling & Sales Management, Psychology & Marketing, Academy of Management Journal, Journal of Applied Psychology, Personnel Psychology, Sloan Management Review, Business Horizons,* and *Journal of Marketing Education.*

He is co-recipient of the national Mu Kappa Tau award for the best article of the year published in the *Journal of Personal Selling & Sales Management.* His co-authored article titled "A Path-Analytic Study of a Model of Salesperson Performance" was designated as the best article of the year in the *Journal of the Academy of Marketing Science.* His article "Salesperson Failure: Sales Management is the Key," which appeared in *Industrial Marketing Management,* was selected for the Annual Excellence in Research Award by the American Marketing Association Selling and Sales Management Special Interest Group. In addition, his co-authored article "Transformational and Contingent Reward Leadership: Individual, Dyad, and Group Levels of Analysis" won the outstanding article of the year award in *Leadership Quarterly.* His co-authored article "Sales Force Socialization" that appeared in the *Journal of Marketing* was voted by the AMA Sales SIG as one of the top ten most influential articles in the selling and sales management literature in the twentieth century. Furthermore, he has received the Excellence in Reviewing Award from the *Journal of Personal Selling & Sales Management.* He is on the Editorial Board of four academic journals.

Dr. Dubinsky has served on the faculty of seven universities. Prior to entering academia, he was a territory manager for Burroughs Corporation (now Unisys). He also spent a year in Volunteers in Service to America (VISTA), the United States' domestic Peace Corps, as a full-time volunteer, where he coordinated volunteer programs in public elementary schools to assist at-risk students in enhancing their literacy skills.

RAJIV MEHTA, PH.D.

Rajiv Mehta is an Associate Professor of Marketing at New Jersey Institute of Technology. Previously, he served on the faculty of Loyola University New Orleans. He earned his Ph.D. in Marketing from Drexel University in 1994.

Dr. Mehta's research has been widely published in major academic journals and presented at national and international academic conferences. His research, which focuses on the areas of personal selling and sales management, marketing channels, and global marketing, has appeared in *Industrial Marketing Management, Journal of Personal Selling and Sales Management, Business Horizons, European Journal of Marketing, International Marketing Review, Journal of Business to Business Marketing, Journal of Business and Industrial Marketing, Journal of Marketing Channels, Journal of Global Marketing, International Journal of Physical Distribution and Logistics Management, Journal of Managerial Issues, Journal of Services Marketing, Management Bibliographies and Reviews, Journal of Shopping Center Research*, and others.

In 2001, his co-authored article "Leadership and Cooperation in Marketing Channels: A Comparative Empirical Analysis of the United States, Finland, and Poland" received the award for excellence as the outstanding paper in *International Marketing Review*. He also received the Stanley Hollander Best Retail Research Paper Award for another co-authored article entitled "Leadership Styles, Culture, and Cooperation in Global Marketing Channels," which was published in the *Journal of Shopping Center Research.*

At New Jersey Institute of Technology, his contributions to teaching were recognized by the alumni when he has awarded the university-wide Robert W. Van Houten award for Teaching Excellence in 2005. He also received the University Award for Excellence in the Category of Teaching in Upper Division Undergraduate Instruction in 2005. While at Loyola University New Orleans, its College of Business Administration chose him three straight years to receive the Excellence in Research award.

Prior to entering academia, Dr. Mehta worked in sales and marketing for a major international manufacturer of steel wire ropes and cables.

CHAPTER 1

Introduction to Personal Selling: It's a Great Career!

"Everybody lives by selling something!"

Robert Louis Stevenson (1850–1894), Scottish novelist

After reading this chapter, you should understand:

- How the concept of marketing is evolving.
- Why and how salespeople are being empowered.
- The differences between yesterday's salesperson and today's professional salesperson.
- What roles professional salespeople play in providing customer satisfaction within the framework of the marketing concept and customer-oriented selling.
- Many of the opportunities and advantages offered by a professional sales career.
- How telecommunications advances can help salespeople.
- The multiple career paths branching out from an initial job in personal selling.

INSIDE PERSONAL SELLING:

Meet Anne Hubbell of Kodak

Anne Hubbell never expected to be in sales: "I went to art school!" Now an account executive in Kodak's entertainment imaging group, she sells motion picture negative film stock to independent filmmakers from Maine to Virginia. Hubbell loves movies, and after college she ran a nonprofit media center, organizing film festivals that showcased independent films. Later, she produced for television and made a documentary that went into theatrical release. Then she joined Kodak and began calling on filmmakers who are not part of the big movie studios–a customer base she understands well because of her background.

Hubbell spends much of her time building and maintaining relationships with prospects and customers. "One of the nice things about my job is that I go to a lot of film festivals and industry events," she says. Not only does she increase awareness of Kodak's diverse line of imaging products, but she is also always available to consult with filmmakers about their needs as they prepare for production. She usually reads the scripts to understand what each movie is about and what each customer wants to achieve.

In fact, she says, "I do more educating than selling. If a prospect calls to say, 'I have $100,000 to make a feature film,'

I'll explain what can be done within that budget." Product knowledge is critical, Hubbell observes: "I need to know exactly how our film stock is going to perform under specific conditions." For example, filmmakers who shoot outdoors at night must use a different stock from those who shoot indoors, where the lighting can be controlled. "I have to be able to advise customers, especially low-budget filmmakers, on what will work best for their situation–not simply for the best look for their film, but also how to work within their budget," she notes.

Because Hubbell travels extensively throughout her territory, often visiting movie sets where Kodak stock is being used, she depends on her cell phone and personal digital assistant to stay in touch and on schedule. She uses database software to organize the complete contact information for every sales lead and every customer, adding links to previous projects that these filmmakers have worked on so she can refresh her memory before a meeting or phone call. To track sales opportunities, she follows the progress of dozens of upcoming productions and makes detailed notes about communications with customers and prospects. Whenever she finds out that a production is about to begin (and Kodak is making the sale), Hubbell updates the database "so there is a record of the entire sales process."

MARKETING AND PERSONAL SELLING: CHANGING WITH THE TIMES

Chapter Review Question

How does the new concept of marketing differ from the old one?

For almost two decades, the official AMA definition of marketing was *the process of planning and executing the conception, pricing, promotion, and distribution of ideas, goods and services to create exchanges that satisfy individual and organizational objectives.* In mid-2004, however, the board of directors of the American Marketing Association approved a new definition: *"Marketing is an organizational function and a set of processes for creating, communicating, and delivering value to customers and for managing customer relationships in ways that benefit the organization and its stakeholders."*

The old definition viewed marketing largely from the seller perspective by emphasizing management of the marketing mix and creating exchanges. But the new definition shifts the perspective more to the customer side by focusing on delivering value and managing customer relationships. As Kotler succinctly states, "Current marketing is moving from a transaction-orientation to a customer-relationship-building orientation"[1]

Empowerment of Salespeople

Like the overall marketing process, personal selling—the most important and costly part of the marketing communication mix for many companies—also is changing with the times. Thanks largely to continuous innovations in telecommunication technologies, salespeople are becoming increasingly empowered and independent of their sales managers. With instant Internet access to up-to-the-minute information that customers want (such as price changes, inventory levels, product shortages, and new products), many salespeople function almost like mobile offices for their companies in serving customers.

Today's business-to-business salespeople are moving away from merely "selling" toward "serving" customers by becoming more like customer consultants and business partners. They are being trained to go beyond thinking narrowly about a single sales transaction to building long-term relationships and partnerships with customers. What's more, as companies recognize the value of customer relationship management (CRM) in achieving customer loyalty and higher profitability, they are requiring salespeople to play expanding roles in carrying out CRM strategies at the critical customer interface. Expanding responsibilities for salespeople need not make you feel uneasy! Many exciting benefits come along with these changes, as we will see in chapter 2.

Chapter Review Question
Why and how are salespeople being empowered?

PERSONAL SELLING: A FRESH LOOK

Personal selling is one of the most exciting, challenging, rewarding, and dynamic of all possible careers. Yet, ironically, it's also one of the most misunderstood, overlooked, and underrated career fields. What thoughts come to your mind when you hear the term *salesperson*? Do you think of fast-talking caricatures in comic strips or television shows? Or does the term conjure up pathetic Willy Loman in Arthur Miller's play *Death of a Salesman*? Do you think of door-to-door salespeople with their foot in the door spouting sales spiels about encyclopedias or cosmetics? If these are some of the images you have in your mind, you're in for a real awakening as you learn about the exciting career opportunities and rewards offered in personal selling today.

Today's successful professional salespeople are among the highest paid people in their organizations and among those most likely to be promoted to senior management. This should not be surprising, because salespeople are the direct revenue generators for their companies, and they know their company's customers best. Salespeople serve as the essential liaisons or "boundary spanners" who facilitate communication, negotiations, transactions, and relationships between buyers and sellers. Without its salespeople successfully selling products and services, no organization could survive for long. Ultimately, everybody's job in an organization depends largely on the success of its salespeople. Intensifying global competition in selling products that are so alike that many customers view them as commodities only makes the salesperson's job more important.

Contemporary salespeople are being presented with greater opportunities, challenges, and rewards than ever, and they will need to be well educated, comprehensively trained, culturally sensitive, and highly professional to succeed in this evolving new sales environment. In carrying out their customer-relationship-building roles, this new breed of salespeople must make skillful use of the latest technology, develop innovative selling strategies, make effective sales presentations and demonstrations, negotiate "win-win" agreements, and build profitable long-term relationships based on customer satisfaction and loyalty.

About now, you may be thinking, "Wow! Salespeople have some heavy responsibilities." "Am I really cut out to be a salesperson?" "Aren't topnotch salespeople just born that way?" "Do I really need a degree to become a salesperson?" "Will I have to pressure customers to buy products in which I don't believe?" By the time you finish reading this book, you will have answers to all these questions, as well as many fresh insights and perspectives on the sales profession. You may be uncertain at this point whether the selling profession is for you, but just keep your mind open. You may be surprised and delighted by the possibilities you encounter.[2]

We strongly believe that professional personal selling is one of the most beneficial and satisfying of all possible careers. Many who think of salespeople in negative ways have not encountered the professional business-to-business salespeople who are the focus of this book. Instead, they interact with telemarketers and door-to-door salespeople who may call at inconvenient hours to aggressively pitch unwanted products or services, or with retail store clerks who are typically order takers working for low hourly wages. These sales jobs are considered low-level by most college students because they do not offer the career opportunities desired, so we will seldom mention salespeople who sell primarily to consumer households. Our goal throughout this book is to prepare students for successful professional careers in business-to-business sales, where potential earnings and career opportunities are virtually unlimited.

Professional Salespeople

By frequently placing the word *professional* in front of *personal selling, selling,* or *salespeople* in our discussions, we are emphasizing that today's successful salespeople are generally well-educated, highly trained, customer-relationship-oriented career professionals. Sales professionals understand the "lifetime value" of loyal customers, so they focus on long-run relationships rather than merely single-transaction profitability. They understand that keeping current customers loyal is even more important than attracting new customers because nearly 70 percent of sales for most companies come from the repeat purchases of loyal customers.[3] Loyal customers usually are the most profitable for the following reasons:

- They buy the largest dollar volume.
- They cost less to serve because they are further up the relationship learning curve with your company.
- They refer other customers and generate positive word-of-mouth promotion for your products and services.
- They readily purchase new products introduced by your company.
- They are receptive to *upselling* (buying higher-priced versions of products) and *cross-selling* (buying other types of products).
- They are the most forgiving when problems occur.[4]

For these reasons, we consistently stress that professional salespeople must strive not only to satisfy customers fully in each and every transaction, but also to go that extra mile by providing pre- and post-sale customer service that bestows added value and helps achieve customer loyalty. Later in this chapter and in the chapters ahead, we'll discuss what it means to be a professional salesperson. Now, let's begin our journey into the world of professional personal selling.[5]

Who Sells? Virtually Everyone!

Personal selling, whether one considers it an art or a discipline, involves the use of persuasive communication to negotiate mutually beneficial agreements. Selling is at the heart of nearly all our relationships with other people. Although we will concentrate on *business-to-business* selling situations, the concepts and techniques we will examine apply to negotiating agreements in business, school, social, and family settings—and almost anywhere there are relationships with people. Perhaps, this weekend, you will be making a personal "sales presentation" to persuade a special person to agree to a date with you. Maybe, this term, you'll try to convince your professor to let you take the final exam early. During an upcoming election, you may endeavor to persuade your friends to vote for your favorite candidate. Early in your career, you may attempt to sell your boss on giving you a raise or a few days off. In diverse settings with all kinds of people, you are continually negotiating mutually beneficial agreements or commitments through persuasive communication. In other words, you're selling!

Learning the principles of selling will improve anyone's chances for success in virtually any field.[6] It's been observed that top professionals (in most career fields) are good salespeople and that top salespeople are professional. For example, a story at SellingPower.com reveals that famous comedian Jay Leno, host of "The Tonight Show" since 1992, planned from early childhood to become a salesperson, and he attributes much of his success as a standup comedian and a much-in-demand corporate speaker to his knowledge of selling techniques.[7]

There are tens of millions of salespeople in the world working in virtually all types of profit-oriented and not-for-profit organizations. Many are called by more euphemistic-sounding names; thus we encounter salespeople known as account representatives, sales engineers, marketing representatives, account executives, customer representatives, institutional advancement officers, stockbrokers, and customer relationship managers. Virtually every occupation involves an element of personal selling—from a trial lawyer making a case in front of a jury to a politician making a speech to win voter support to an entertainer trying to win over an audience.

What's Sold? Nearly Everything!

At one or more stages in the distribution process from manufacturer or service provider to ultimate user, professional salespeople are needed to sell nearly everything used by every organization and every person in the world. The products and services that salespeople sell to different types of customers can range almost endlessly: from desktop computers sold to purchasing agents for companies . . . to heavy construction equipment sold to building contractors . . . to cosmetics sold to major retail chains . . . to jet aircraft sold to foreign governments . . . to consulting services sold to corporations. Every product or service you can think of is probably sold by a business-to-business salesperson at some point in the supply chain. Our focus, throughout the book, will be on those salespeople who sell their companies' products and services to other organizations—including diverse business enterprises, not-for-profit institutions, and government agencies. These salespeople are respected, highly paid professionals who consider personal selling either a lifelong career or vital experience leading to higher-level management positions.

New Professionalism Required

Contemporary salespeople must develop a new level of professionalism and sensitivity to customer concerns as they face increasingly diverse, multicultural, and sophisticated customers whose expectations continue to rise. The old "door-to-door" salesperson has essentially been replaced by various forms of direct marketing (such as telemarketing, e-mail, and direct-mail letters and catalogs) aided by advanced communication methods and technology. Revolutionary developments in telecommunication technologies have led customers to expect greater value at lower prices and faster, better service. Today's salespeople must be more educated and better trained than ever because they frequently call on professional purchasing agents who themselves are well-educated and highly trained in skillful buying for their companies. Salespeople need to use innovative selling strategies and tactics to negotiate "win-win" agreements with these expert buyers, who are generally equipped with computerized systems and thus can continuously monitor and analyze purchasing alternatives, product turnover, and supplier performance. Professional buyers often know at least as much as the salesperson about the products and services offered by various suppliers, so today's salespeople must be well-prepared professionals to succeed in increasingly demanding and competitive markets. While domestic buyers are becoming more expert and demanding, foreign competition for domestic and global markets continues to intensify. Only those companies that provide truly world-class product quality, professional personal selling, and superior customer service will thrive in the future.[8]

Whew! We have a lot to discuss, so let's get started. In this first chapter, we begin by refuting some stereotypes and myths about salespeople. Then we'll look at how personal selling continues to evolve and what it's like to be a professional salesperson today.

Myth of the Born Salesperson

"Salespeople are born, not made" is an oft-heard remark that's dead wrong. Research suggests that personal characteristics (those traits with which one is born) do have some influence on sales performance, but not nearly so much as a determined individual has in developing his or her own skills or as a sales manager has in training recruits.[9] A bubbly personality, quick wit, and a few clever sales techniques are not enough for a successful career in business-to-business sales. Moreover, pushiness, brashness, and puffery have no lasting place in professional selling. Today's customer wants to deal with salespeople who are knowledgeable, honest, trustworthy, competent, and service oriented. Many of today's sales practitioners and scholars view personal selling as a mixture of art *and* disciplined skills. Some observers, however, express strong opinions one way or another about the nature of personal selling:

> Some people have more natural ability than others, but selling is not an art. It's a discipline. There's a specific selling process you have to go through, and anyone can learn it. It involves taking all the different steps, reducing them to a checklist, and then executing them one by one. There's no magic to it, and you don't need a lot of natural talent. What you need is a disciplined, organized approach to selling. If you have that, you'll outperform the great salesperson who doesn't understand the process every time. Selling can definitely be learned.[10]

Chapter Review Question
Discuss the myth of the "born" salesperson.

Salesperson Commitment

Salesperson commitment to job and company can vary widely and can dramatically affect performance. Some salespeople are almost apathetic about their daily work and exert little effort to improve their sales productivity or more fully satisfy their customers. Others are intensely involved with their jobs but feel no bond with their organization. These "lone wolves" put forth high personal effort and show concern for their customers but are ever vigilant about seeking alternative employment where the "grass looks greener." Still other salespeople care little for their sales job but feel a high degree of commitment to their employer. They often seek close attachments to the firm but fail to perform their selling job either efficiently or effectively.

Successful professional salespeople, unlike the foregoing three types of underachievers, display a high degree of commitment to their jobs, their customers, and their companies. They are determined to satisfy customers while achieving both personal and organizational selling objectives. Moreover, they feel a meaningful bond with the firm—its management, staff, values, philosophies, and practices—and see themselves as team players. Such "super salespeople" are the bulwark of the most successful organizations. They seek to generate sales revenue in win-win sales agreements that benefit *both* buyer and seller over the short and long term.[11]

The Marketing Concept and Customer-Oriented Selling

Professional salespeople today tend to adopt two interrelated business philosophies. One is known as the *marketing concept.* According to Kotler and Armstrong, "The marketing concept holds that achieving organizational goals depends on determining the needs and wants of target markets and delivering the desired satisfactions more effectively and efficiently than competitors."[12]

Customer-Oriented Selling Focus on identifying customers' needs and engaging in selling and servicing behaviors that help build and maintain a high level of customer satisfaction and loyalty in the long run.

Professional Salesperson Salesperson who sees a sales career as a true profession for which he or she must be well educated, well prepared, and thoroughly professional in order to negotiate successfully with professional buyers.

An organization that adheres to this philosophy knows that successful implementation requires not only its sales force but also its entire administrative and sales support staff to be focused on customer satisfaction. In fact, a company-wide customer orientation is needed, as described by Frank "Buck" Rodgers, legendary former marketing vice president for IBM and author of *The IBM Way*:

> At IBM, everybody sells! . . . Every employee has been trained to think that the customer comes first—everybody from the CEO, to the people in finance, to the receptionists, to those who work in manufacturing. . . . 'IBM doesn't sell products. It sells solutions.' . . . An IBM marketing rep's success depends totally on his ability to understand a prospect's business so well that he can identify and analyze its problems and then come up with a solution that makes sense to the customer.[13]

Chapter Review Question

Explain the relationship among personal selling, the marketing concept, and customer-oriented selling.

Closely related to the marketing concept is **customer-oriented selling**. Salespeople who practice customer-oriented selling focus on identifying their customers' needs accurately and on engaging in selling and servicing behaviors that help build and maintain a high level of customer satisfaction. The focus is on building mutually profitable, long-lasting customer relationships or partnerships.[14] Extensive information collection and processing facilitate this outcome.[15] Customer-oriented salespeople put heavy emphasis on uncovering and addressing their customers' needs. They know their customers, and they understand their customers' customers as well. Thus they can help customers develop strategies for "selling through" to their own customers. Such efforts enhance the buyer-seller relationship and augment customer satisfaction and loyalty.[16] These top-performing salespeople make satisfying customers their major focus. Consequently, their customers respect and trust them . . . and expect to continue interacting with them in the future.[17] Even if you have no sales experience, assume that you are about to start a sales career and honestly answer the questions in the exercise on the next page to see how customer oriented you are. Then evaluate yourself to see how you might increase your customer-oriented attitude and behavior.

The salesperson who practices customer-oriented selling identifies customer needs accurately, and engages in selling and servicing behaviors that build and maintain customer satisfaction.
Royalty Free/Corbis

How well did you do on the self-assessment of your customer orientation? Do you need to change some attitudes or behaviors? Development of marketing and customer-oriented selling concepts has changed the focus of professional personal selling from a short-run emphasis on sellers' needs to a long-run emphasis on customers' needs. Contrasts between yesterday's salesperson and today's **professional salesperson** are summarized in Table 1.1.

HOW CUSTOMER ORIENTED ARE YOU?

Determine how customer oriented you are by responding to the statements below, using the following scale:

5-Strongly Agree 4-Agree 3-Neither Agree nor Disagree 2-Disagree 1-Strongly Disagree

1. I want to help my customers achieve their goals. ____
2. I want to serve my customers so well that they will come back to buy more from me. ____
3. It's more important to satisfy a customer than to make a big sales commission on a product that won't satisfy the customer. ____
4. I use a canned sales pitch for most sales. ____
5. I try to influence customers by providing information rather than by applying pressure. ____
6. I try to sell the product best suited to my customer's problem even if my commission is lower on that product. ____
7. I listen to customers more than I talk to them so I can understand their needs. ____
8. I try to answer a customer's questions about products as honestly as I can. ____
9. I try to help customers solve their problems even if I occasionally have to recommend a competitor's product. ____
10. I am willing to politely disagree with a customer in order to help him or her make a better decision. ____
11. I try to give customers accurate expectations about what the product will do for them. ____
12. I try to resolve customers' complaints promptly so that they want to remain my customers. ____
13. I want customers to be fully satisfied so they will become repeat buyers from me. ____
14. I try to sell customers all I can convince them to buy, even if it's more than they really need. ____
15. I keep alert to spot weaknesses in a customer's personality so I can use them to apply buying pressure at the right time. ____
16. If I'm not sure whether a product is right for a customer, I still pressure him or her to buy because it's not my job to figure out whether or not the product's right for the customer. ____
17. I usually try to persuade customers to buy the product on which I make the most commission. ____
18. I sometimes paint too rosy a picture of my products to make them sound as good as possible to customers. ____
19. If a customer doesn't ask about a particular product weakness, I don't think it's my job to mention it. ____
20. It's sometimes necessary to stretch the truth a little in describing a product to a customer. ____
21. Even when I know they're wrong, I generally pretend to agree with customers in order to please them. ____
22. I sometimes imply to a customer that something is beyond my control when it's not. ____
23. When customers come back to complain about a product I sold them, I often try to avoid them. ____
24. In negotiating with customers, my main focus is on winning the sale. ____
25. I never let customers assume something that's incorrect because over the long run, my integrity and honesty are among my best sales tools.

The higher your score for items 1 through 3, 5 through 13, and 25, the more customer oriented you are. Total scores of 52 or higher on these items indicate a strong customer orientation; a score of less than 39 indicates a weak customer orientation.

The lower your score for items 4 and items 14 through 24, the more customer oriented you are. Total scores of 24 or less indicate a strong customer orientation; a score of over 36 indicates a weak customer orientation.

Source: *Adapted from Robert Saxe and Barton A. Weitz, "The SOCO Scale: A Measure of the Customer Orientation of Salespeople,"* Journal of Marketing Research, *19 (August 1982): 343–351. Reprinted with permission of the American Marketing Association.*

TABLE 1.1

Contrasting Yesterday's and Today's Salespeople

Yesterday's Salesperson	Today's Professional Salesperson
Product oriented	Customer oriented
Thinks mainly about *selling* customers	Thinks mainly about *serving* customers
Does little sales call planning	Develops sales call strategy to achieve specific objectives
Makes sales pitches without listening much to customers	Listens to and communicates meaningfully with customers
Sales presentation focuses on product features and price	Sales presentation focuses on customer benefits
Thinks in terms of manipulative selling techniques	Thinks in terms of helping customers solve problems
Goal is to make immediate sales	Goal is to develop long-term, mutually beneficial relationships
Disappears once a sale is made	Follows up with customers to provide service and ensure satisfaction leading to customer loyalty
Works alone and has little interest in understanding customers' problems	Works as a member of a team of specialists to serve customers

WHAT IS A CUSTOMER?

A customer may have many names: client, account, patron, patient, parishioner, member, fan, or voter. Whatever the name, every organization thrives, survives, or dies on the basis of how well it satisfies its customers. After all, customers are the lifeblood of both salespeople and the organizations for which they work because they provide the sales revenues on which the entire organization depends. The two basic categories of customers or markets are *consumers* and *organizations*. In order to sell successfully to consumers or organizations, sales representatives must understand how these markets buy.

Consumer markets consist of individuals who purchase goods and services for their own personal consumption. All customers other than ultimate consumers are organizational customers. There are three types of *organizational markets:* producers, resellers, and governments.

The *producer market* consists of both manufacturing firms and nonprofit organizations that purchase goods and services for the production of additional goods and services to sell, rent, or supply. For example, General Motors (www.gm.com) may purchase sheet steel from USX (www.ussteel.com) and automobile tires from Goodyear (www.goodyear.com) to manufacture its automobiles for sale to its dealer customers. An example of a *nonprofit* producer market is a church that buys a Hammond organ to "produce" music at Sunday services.

The *reseller market* includes individuals and organizations that purchase goods to resell, rent, or use in their own business operations. Resellers are "middlemen" (also called intermediaries) who facilitate the flow of goods from producers to ultimate users and consumers. Three common types of resellers are industrial distributors, wholesalers, and retailers. Each serve specific types of customers. *Industrial distributors* sell primarily to manufacturers or producers of goods and services. *Wholesalers* sell chiefly to retailers. And *retailers* sell to consumers. For example, an industrial distributor might sell drill bits to a garage door manufacturer. A large wholesaler may buy Godiva (www.godiva.com) chocolates from the Campbell Soup Company (a producer; www.campbellsoup.com) to sell to Bloomingdale's (a retailer; www.bloomingdales.com) for sale to its department store shoppers. A public library may become a nonprofit reseller by purchasing a Xerox (www.xerox.com) copier for its patrons to use, thus providing better services to its patrons.

Finally, the *government market* includes all local, state, and federal governmental units that purchase or rent products and services to carry out the functions of government. At the national level, the Defense Logistics Agency (DLA) buys for all the armed services, and the General Services Administration (GSA) (www.gsa.gov) buys for the civilian branches and agencies of the federal government. State and local governments also have buying functions conducted by various governmental units.

Chapter Review Question
List and briefly describe the three kinds of profit and nonprofit organizational markets.

WHAT IS A PRODUCT?

A *product* is anything offered to a market to satisfy customer needs and wants. It can be a *tangible product*, such as a forklift, or an *intangible service*, such as professional advice from an estate planner. Note, however, that this distinction between tangible products and intangible services lacks precision because nearly all products have intangible aspects and all services have tangible aspects. A computer usually comes with a warranty and may include a service contract (intangibles). And professional advice may include a detailed written financial analysis and investment plan (tangibles).

Customers buy products for *benefits or solutions to their problems*. They do not seek laser printers as such but, rather, want "attractive financial reports." Salespeople can never assume that the most obvious or functional benefit is the one the customer wants. And salespeople should always be thinking past their immediate customers to their customers' customers. For example, an alert salesperson noticed that many women owned several wristwatches because they sought the watch's benefit as an ornament or accessory to match their clothes rather than as a timepiece. With this information, the maker of Swatches, whose customers are wholesalers and retailers, developed and profitably sold stylish, multicolored plastic watches for their customers to sell through to consumers.

Augmented Product Complete bundle of benefits offered by a product, including its core function, various enhancing characteristics, and supplemental benefits and services.

The actual problem-solving benefit a customer seeks is called the *core product.* For example, a company may want a corporate airplane for its executives' convenience in attending meetings across the country and internationally. Product characteristics such as safety features, interior styling, comfort level, range, cruising speed, fuel capacity, and a respected brand name turn this core product into something tangible such as a Cessna Citation Jet (www.cessna.com). We call the combination of a core product and product characteristics the *tangible product.* Many customers want additional tangible and intangible benefits, such as credit, product use training, repair service, replacement guarantees, and warranties. The **augmented product** is the complete bundle of benefits offered by a product, including its core function, various enhancing characteristics, and supplemental benefits and services.[18] We can see that tangible and intangible benefits and services blend together to form every product. We will therefore use the term *product* to refer to both products and services.

Chapter Review Questions

What is a product? How do core products, tangible products, and augmented products differ?

DIVERSE ROLES OF THE PROFESSIONAL SALESPERSON

As products and services have become more technical, competition more intense, buyers more sophisticated, and purchase decisions more widely shared (by several levels of management and technical experts in organizations), personal selling has grown in complexity. Behind the basic job of the professional salesperson today lie a great many different types of selling roles, tasks, and responsibilities.

Selling Roles Vary Across Organizations

Retailers, wholesalers, industrial distributors, manufacturers, service firms, and nonprofit organizations are some examples of employers who need salespeople. Each of these organizations employs different types of salespeople for different selling roles. For example, an IBM (www.ibm.com) marketing representative who calls on large manufacturers to sell complex mainframe computers has a role different from that of the Procter & Gamble (www.pg.com) salesperson who sells laundry soap to wholesalers. Similarly, the Microsoft (www.microsoft.com) salesperson who sells Windows software to large legal firms has tasks and responsibilities different from those of the Caterpillar Tractor (www.cat.com) salesperson who sells construction equipment to state highway departments. If a customer's organization has a large and intricate structure, several salespeople from the same firm may be required to sell to various levels within that buyer organization. Out of necessity, smaller firms often train their salespeople to handle a broad range of customers and customer needs. Factors that influence the numbers and kinds of salespeople a firm may hire include the following:

- Size and characteristics of potential buyers
- Price, complexity, and type of products
- Types and number of distribution channels
- Geographic location and relative dispersion of customers
- Level of marketing and technical support required

Selling Positions and Jobs

Selling entails an array of different activities and tasks. One researcher identified ten key categories of salesperson activities: basic selling activities, order-related tasks, product service, information/communication management, account service, conferences/meetings, training/recruitment for the firm, entertainment, out-of-town travel, and middlemen tasks.[19] Furthermore, selling can be divided into three basic roles, or jobs: (1) order taking, (2) order supporting, and (3) order creating. These sales activities reflect the following continuum of complexity from mere response selling to the highly creative selling necessary to obtain new business:

Order Taking
- Response selling
  - Inside order taker
  - Outside order taker

Order Supporting
- Missionary selling

Order Creating
- Trade selling
- Technical selling
- Creative selling

Order Taking Processing routine orders or reorders for products that have been sold previously to the buying firm.

Order Supporting The process of having minimal involvement in sales generation but instead providing assistance to customers.

Order Taking. **Order taking** entails processing routine orders or reorders for products that have already been sold to the buying firm. The major goal is to continue the ongoing relationship with existing customers and maintain sales revenue. *Response selling* requires the salesperson simply to respond to customer requests. Response salespersons are either *inside order takers*—such as retail clerks in department stores or telephone salespersons in wholesaler organizations—or *outside order takers* who work outside of the firm's offices. These include truck driver-salespeople who travel a regular route to replenish inventories (e.g., Frito-Lay snacks or Coca-Cola soft drinks) for customers such as retail grocery stores.

Missionary Selling Educating, building goodwill, and providing services to customers (e.g., doctors and dentists) by giving them samples and information about products and services (such as new pharmaceuticals and medicines to prescribe or recommend for their patients).

Order Supporting. **Order-supporting** salespeople do minimal sales generation but instead serve to provide customers with assistance. **Missionary selling** requires the salesperson to educate customers, build goodwill, and provide services. The missionary salesperson seldom takes sales orders from customers directly but instead furnishes information about products to middlemen or "deciders," who in turn sell or recommend the products to their own customers. For example, the pharmaceutical company's "detail person"—a missionary salesperson—introduces physicians to new drugs and related products in hopes that the physicians will prescribe these products for their patients. Distilleries, pharmaceutical companies, food manufacturers, and transportation firms commonly employ missionary salespeople to help their wholesale and retail customers sell through to their own customers.

Order Creating The process of identifying prospective buyers, providing them with information, motivating them to buy, confirming the sale, and following up after the sale has been made to ensure customer satisfaction. Trade, technical, and creative salespeople all do order creating in varying degrees.

Major pharmaceutical firms, such as Merck (www.merck.com) and Pfizer (www.pfizer.com), have sharply boosted their total sales staff in recent years because of the large number of new product introductions. In many instances, physicians needed pharmaceutical company "detail reps" to help them understand the benefits and possible side effects of new drugs before prescribing these products for their patients. As the number of new drugs on the market continues to explode, more and more pharmaceutical companies have increased their missionary sales calls on doctors.

Trade Selling Creative field service to wholesale and distributor customers, such as expediting orders, taking reorders, restocking shelves, setting up displays, providing in-store demonstrations, and distributing samples to store customers.

Order Creating. Order-creating salespeople identify prospective buyers, offer them information, stimulate them to buy, close the sale, and follow up to provide services after the sale. Trade, technical, and creative salespeople engage in order creating to varying degrees. **Trade selling** generally occurs when a manufacturer sells to a distributor wholesaler—a business that resells the product rather than using it in its own business operations. As in response selling, the salesperson responds to customer requests. Field service, however, is more important in trade selling. The trade-selling representative expedites orders, takes reorders, restocks shelves, sets up displays, provides in-store demonstrations, and distributes samples to store customers. Trade sellers are usually discouraged from hard selling to customers.

Technical selling requires a specifically trained salesperson, often called a sales engineer, to help customers solve technical problems. Technical selling resembles professional consulting and is common in such industries as steel, chemicals, heavy machinery, and computers, where product offerings tend to be complex. A sales engineer typically helps customers understand the proper use of complex products, system design, and product installation and maintenance procedures.

Chapter Review Questions

Name the three basic selling roles, and describe the continuum of sales jobs ranging from simple response selling to complex creative selling.

What types of creative salespeople are discussed in this chapter?

Creative selling calls upon the salesperson to stimulate product demand among present and potential customers. Creative selling includes sales development and sales maintenance. *Sales development* attempts to generate new customers. *Sales maintenance* tries to ensure a continuous flow of sales from present customers. Salespeople required to do both tasks tend to spend more time on maintenance work, because developing new prospects takes more time and may be less rewarding in the short run.

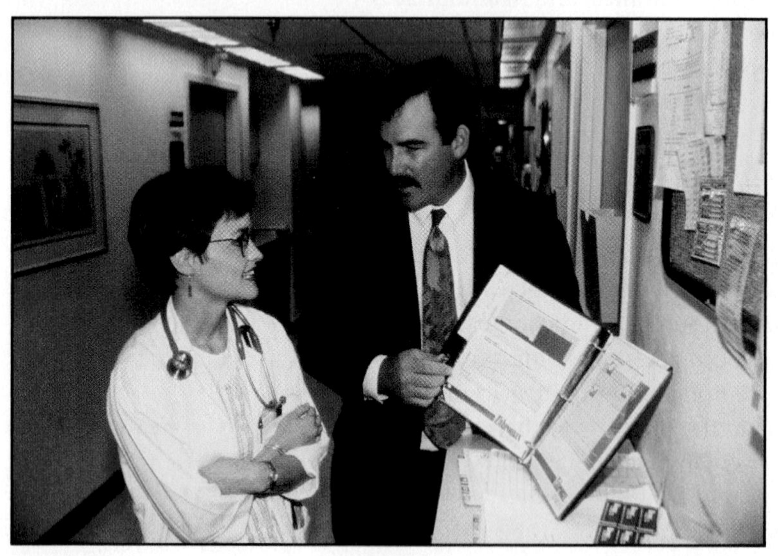

Missionary salespeople educate deciders like doctors and pharmacists about products and services to recommend to their patients or customers.
David J. Sams/Getty Images

Although we have talked about selling positions as though each job consisted of a definite set of tasks, it is important to realize that every selling job may include all three essential characteristics of order taking, order supporting, and order creating. An outside order taker dealing with a demanding and indecisive customer might give a convincing product explanation and create an order. And some kinds of missionary salespeople might actually "take" an order (a publisher's book representative, for example, may write out and deliver a professor's textbook order to the bookstore manager). No matter what the selling role, however, the bottom-line goal of all selling is to obtain the order. And *that* usually involves a certain amount of creativity. Read the following *On the Frontlines* to see how one salesperson had to alter his selling approach to create sales.

ON THE FRONTLINES

Using "Insiders" to Get the Sale

Simon Perez is a successful missionary salesperson for a large pharmaceutical company whose territory covers the Miami area. Simon's job is not to sell his company's new medicines and drugs directly to doctors but to educate them about these products' benefits and side effects and, in so doing, convince them to prescribe the products for their patients. Although Simon earns a good base salary, he also receives a quarterly bonus depending on the total dollar amount of his company's products sold in his territory. Simon heard that some of the top missionary salespeople in his company earned bonuses larger than their base salaries. During his first few weeks as a missionary salesperson, Simon found that the doctors in his territory were often unavailable to talk to him, and even when they became available for a few minutes, there was seldom enough time to tell the doctors all that he wanted them to know.

Feeling frustrated by his inability to secure much time with the doctors, Simon began to wonder whether there might be something wrong with his approach. After one late Friday evening sales meeting at his company's regional headquarters, Simon asked Susan Hankens, one of his fellow missionary salespeople, how she managed to speak to doctors about the company's products. Susan told Simon that all missionary salespeople have the same problem. Doctors are very busy people who seldom have much time to sit down with sales representatives of any kind. "What I do," Susan said, "is work with the office staff—the nurses, receptionists, or medical assistants—who interact with the doctor daily. They do most of my job for me. First, I make sure that they're glad to see me because I bring in special snacks, pastries, cookies, sandwiches, or soft drinks, every time I call on them. I learn the birthdays of everybody in the office and make sure that I remember to give them a little something on that special occasion, usually a birthday cake and small gift. Sometimes I'll hang around the medical office for an hour or more talking to them about their families and telling them a little more about our products each time they get a break from their work with patients. Of course, I stay out of their way, but I continue to engage them in conversation about a myriad of things of interest to them. And I always try to tell them everything they need to know about our company's new products and answer all their questions. Then, before leaving, I make sure that I've left lots of product samples for everyone, along with our product brochures. I also leave my telephone number and e-mail address in case a doctor or anyone has any more questions. My experience is that the office staff probably does a better job of educating the doctors about our products than I could do, especially since they work together and trust one another. It's great having all these busy, talented people help me do my job."

After talking with Susan, Simon tried her approach by working closely with the office staff, nurses, and medical assistants in his territory's medical offices. Although he still was unable to meet with the doctors as often as he liked, Simon felt that he had done his job when he had managed to educate the doctor's support team about his company's products. As a missionary salesperson, he realized that you don't really know how effectively you have educated prospects and customers about your company's products until quarterly sales figures come out. But Simon feels he must be doing something right because last quarter, for the first time, his bonus was larger than his base salary.

WHAT DOES A PROFESSIONAL SALESPERSON DO?

Personal Selling Process (PSP) The seven interacting, overlapping stages that every salesperson, no matter what the product or service being sold, must carry out.

The many different types of sales situations and jobs all tend to involve seven basic stages that form the **personal selling process (PSP)**. In order of completion, they are

1. prospecting and qualifying
2. planning the sales call (the preapproach)
3. approaching the prospect
4. making the sales presentation and demonstration
5. negotiating sales resistance or objections
6. confirming and closing the sale
7. following up and servicing the account[20]

Salespeople must work through all seven interrelated stages while trying to negotiate sales agreements with prospects or customers. Not all activities in the PSP stages require direct interaction with the prospect or customer, but both activities that require customer interaction and those that do not can have a dramatic impact on success with a given buyer.[21]

Continuous Cycle or Wheel

Wheel of Personal Selling Depiction of the seven stages of the PSP as a continuous cycle of stages carried out by professionals in the field of sales.

The seven stages of the PSP are best depicted as a continuous cycle or wheel of overlapping stages, as shown in Figure 1.1. Note that once the **wheel of personal selling** is set in motion, it continues to revolve from one stage to the next. Thus it is easy to see that stage 7 is not the end of the cycle but rather a new beginning, for the salesperson's follow-up and service activities generate repeat sales and purchases of new products as customer needs change over time. The wheel is not a rigid, inexorable mechanism that can't be stopped, changed, or reversed if necessary. Sometimes, the salesperson must return to, skip over, or redesign a stage in the PSP when an initial approach or turn of the wheel fails to work. Flexibility in responding to feedback about customers' wants and needs is critical in making the most effective and efficient use of the PSP concept.

The PSP Wheel Revolves Around Prospects and Customers

As you examine Figure 1.1, keep in mind that the *center* or focus of the wheel—prospects and customers—is its most important part. Without prospects and customers, the wheel would have nothing around which to revolve! In addition, present customers are good sources of new leads—or potentially qualified prospects. Below is a brief overview; we will discuss each of the seven stages in depth later, beginning in chapter 4.

Prospecting and Qualifying. Current-customer rosters continuously shrink through death, bankruptcy, relocation, or switches to other suppliers. In order to increase or even maintain sales volume, salespeople must unceasingly

FIGURE 1.1

THE PERSONAL SELLING PROCESS (PSP)

search for new customers. Potential new customers are called *prospects*. Most salespeople spend more time on prospecting than on any other selling activity. **Prospecting** requires salespeople to obtain *leads*. A lead is basically the name and address or telephone number of a person or organization that may have a need for the company's product or service. Before a *lead* can be considered a genuine prospect, it must be qualified in terms of *need or want, authority to buy, money to buy*, and *eligibility to buy*. An easy way to remember these four qualifiers is the acronym "NAME," which consists of the first initial of each phrase. When companies or individuals pass all four of these screens, they become "prospects" on which to make a sales call.

Prospecting First step in the PSP, wherein salespeople find leads and qualify them on four criteria: need, authority, money, and eligibility (NAME) to buy.

Planning the Sales Call (the Preapproach). In the preapproach or planning stage, the salesperson obtains detailed information about the prospective buyer and the buying situation and then develops a strategy for ensuring a favorable reception. Information sources include trade associations, chambers of commerce, credit bureaus, mailing list companies, government and public libraries, investment firms, and the Internet (via search engines such as www.google.com or www.yahoo.com). Perhaps the most direct source of information is a low-profile preliminary call at the prospect's business site. While at the prospect's company site, salespeople can talk subtly to receptionists or other employees, gather company brochures and materials, and simply observe the way the business operates. Such efforts must be undertaken diplomatically and graciously, though, to avoid being viewed as spying or snooping. One means of doing this is to inform a prospect's personnel of your intentions for the visit and then ask for permission to gather information.

Approaching the Prospect. The salesperson makes his or her vital first impression in the approach stage. Salespeople must quickly gain and hold a prospect's attention and interest. Depending on the situation, numerous methods for approaching the prospect can succeed, ranging from referral by a mutual acquaintance to the customer-benefit approach. Probably the approach salespeople most often use is a *sales letter* to introduce themselves, their company, and its products, followed up by a telephone call to obtain more information and arrange a sales call appointment. In chapter 5, we'll discuss variations of the classic sales letter approach, including "seeding" (becoming a kind of "pen pal" with a company manager) and "prenotification" (obtaining permission to send sales materials). For now, keep in mind that successful salespeople learn to tailor their approach to suit each new prospect.

Making the Sales Presentation and Demonstration. The sales presentation is the persuasive communication at the heart of the selling process. After asking the customer qualifying questions to uncover specific needs, the salesperson proposes the products and services that will best satisfy those needs; highlights their features, advantages, and benefits; and stimulates desire for the offerings with a skillful demonstration. Success in this stage demands carefully planned strategies and tactics, followed by anticipation and rehearsal of probable interactions between buyer and seller. Like the approach stage, each sales presentation must be tailored to the prospect and the selling situation. A practical sales presentation combined with a convincing product demonstration can help secure a favorable outcome. Mere "dog and pony shows," no matter how elaborate, seldom succeed. A salesperson who employs skillful questioning and reactive listening as prospects describe their needs stands a far better chance of thoroughly understanding the exact nature of the customer's problem, so that the sales presentation and demonstration "speak" directly to providing a solution. An effective sales presentation and demonstration must make it clear to prospects that you are not just selling products but also solving their problems.

Negotiating Sales Resistance or Objections. Seldom do prospects or customers automatically accept the salesperson's sales proposal and sign a purchase agreement. Instead, salespeople are likely to confront customer resistance. However, do not be discouraged by prospect resistance or objections. These are usually positive signs of interest and involvement. In fact, experienced salespeople often say, "The sale doesn't begin until the prospect says 'No.'" View such objections, then, as positive requests for more information so that the prospect can justify a purchase decision. If you anticipate the customer's possible objections and prepare responses before making the sales call, you will be better able to counter buyer objections with information that will confirm the sale.

Confirming and Closing the Sale. In order to increase their *closing ratio* (number of orders/number of sales calls), salespeople must become skillful closers. The close is the crowning moment of the sales process, the moment for which the salesperson has worked so hard, when the customer agrees to order the product. Typically, new salespeople are shy about asking for the order. No closing question is more decisive than "Shall we write up the order?" but it need not be that blatant. Often, you can accomplish the same result with an indirect closing question such as "When do you need the product delivered?" In chapter 8 we'll describe effective ways to close a sale.

"When do I close the sale?" is another question new salespeople often ask. There is no perfect time to close the sale. An old adage says that salespeople need to know their ABCs (that is, "Always be closing"). This means you should attempt "trial closes" throughout your interaction with the prospect. Trial closes are simply attempts to make prospects show their *readiness to buy*. Here are some examples of "trial closes": "Is this the kind of solution you're looking for?" or "Do you think this product will meet your needs?" or "How do you like it so far?" or "So, what do you think?"

Involving prospects directly in demonstrating the product or "trying it out" can help prospects gain confidence in the product and move them toward the close. Nonverbal trial closes can also be effective. Even a small physical act such as moving the order form and pen in front of prospects may generate a reflex action to pick up the pen and sign the order. Savvy salespeople also learn to read and closely observe body language to spot an opportune time for a close. The close can happen at any time during the sales process—in the first few minutes of the first sales call, or in the last few seconds of the sixth. Skillful salespeople learn a variety of closing techniques, discussed in chapter 8, to help prospects make decisions in the buying process.

Following Up and Servicing the Account. Generally, it is far easier—and less costly—to keep present customers satisfied than to search out and acquire new customers. That is why, after making the sale, top-performing salespeople maintain close contact with the customer to handle any complaints and to provide customer service such as installation, repair, or credit approvals. Satisfied customers are more likely to become loyal repeat buyers. Loyal customers, as we noted earlier, usually are the most profitable: They buy the most, cost less to serve, refer others, and are usually the most forgiving when problems occur.[22] And these loyal customers over their lifetimes can be worth up to ten times as much as the average customer. Companies as diverse as Pizza Hut (www.pizzahut.com), Home Depot (www.homedepot.com), and General Motors (www.gm.com) are working not only to satisfy customers but also to keep their loyalty. Pizza Hut estimates that the lifetime value of its regular customers is over $8,000,

The personal selling process (PSP) can involve selling to individual buyers or a team of buyers.
Jeff Zarud/Corbis

IT'S UP TO YOU

You are a salesperson for Herculon, Inc., a manufacturer of industrial equipment. You have received extensive sales training for three months, especially in product knowledge, competition, and selling skills. Today is your first day in your new territory. You know little about the territory or who are the most likely prospects. You have, however, the names, addresses, and telephone numbers, of key people at companies that have inquired about Herculon products or purchased from the company in the past. How will you begin working in your newly assigned territory?

Chapter Review Question

Describe the seven stages in the professional personal selling process (PSP). Why do we depict them as a wheel?

Home Depot (www.homedepot.com) figures $23,000, Cadillac (www.cadillac.com) division of General Motors reports $332,000, and Lexus (www.lexus.com) calculates over $600,000.[23] The message seems clear: Loyal customers mean big profits!

Follow-up calls can also produce sales of ancillary items or new products, as well as referrals to new prospects. Frequent and comprehensive follow-up is a primary means of securing long-run, satisfied, and loyal customers . . . and of keeping the *personal selling process wheel* revolving. Using what you've learned so far in this chapter, consider the situation described in the accompanying *It's Up to You* feature.

USING TECHNOLOGY TO SELL BETTER

Extranets Corporate networks that allow communication between a company and selected customers, suppliers, and business partners.

Intranets Internal corporate networks that allow salespeople and other employees within a company to obtain information and communicate with each other.

Today's professional salespeople can enhance their productivity and customer satisfaction levels by making skillful use of the latest technologies in carrying out each of the seven steps of personal selling. For example, some salespeople use the Internet and e-mail to prospect for customers, to notify their customers about upcoming price changes or product shortages, to introduce new products, and to ask for referrals to new prospects. **Extranets**—corporate networks that allow communication between a company and selected customers, suppliers, and business partners—often yield prospects, too. Most companies also have **intranets**—internal corporate networks that allow salespeople and other employees within a company to obtain information and communicate with each other. For instance, salespeople use their company intranets to gain quick access to the latest product prices, inventories, or delivery dates.

En route to customers' offices, salespeople often use cellular phones or car phones to let customers know about any traffic problems that might delay their arrival for a sales call appointment. Portable fax machines, pagers, video cell phones with Internet capabilities, and handheld or pocket computers all help salespeople communicate with and serve their prospects and customers more efficiently and effectively.

Some companies and salespeople include impressive full-color video sales presentations and product demonstrations on their websites. During long-term negotiations, salespeople can respond to customers' questions either by e-mail or at a website that provides answers to the most frequently asked questions (FAQs). Customer service (e.g., installation, maintenance, and warranty information) also can be furnished on a website. Starting in chapter 4 with our in-depth discussion of each stage in the **PSP,** we will further describe and provide examples of salespeople using the latest technologies. Who knows what future innovations will help salespeople do their jobs better? Read this chapter's *From the Command Post* feature to learn how a cement marketer has employed technology to enhance customer service.

Chapter Review Question

Give some examples of how salespeople can use different technologies to improve their efficiency and better serve prospects and customers.

FROM THE COMMAND POST: CEMEX—HIGH-TECH CEMENT MARKETER

Cemex (www.cemex.com) is a highly successful international marketer of cement based in Monterrey, Mexico. It established an information technology department in the mid-1980s and its first e-mail system in 1991. It has provided a wealth of internal and external information to its employees in efforts to enhance corporate efficiency and effectiveness. In fact, the company places computers with Internet access in its employees' homes.

Concrete must be poured within ninety minutes of mixing. Ensuring that trucks travel from plants to building sites on schedule has always been a problem. Cemex now installs computers and global positioning receivers in all of its ready-mix concrete trucks. The current system calculates which truck should go where and also enables dispatchers to redirect trucks en route to a given construction site. As a result, delivery time has dropped on average from three hours to less than twenty minutes in crowded Mexico City! The system has also allowed trucks to deliver many more orders per day.

Cemex is also planning to use Construmix (the construction industry portal) to provide other services for customers who already purchase Cemex concrete online. For instance, the company is considering creating an online meeting place for all parties involved in a construction project. Blueprints would be placed on the Internet and updated online, allowing contractors and suppliers to consult a current version of the blueprints at all times.

Cemex management believes its high-tech approach frees up employees' imagination and fosters a healthy degree of competition among company units. The company's financial success is a tribute to its efforts: Cemex has an operating margin twice that of its two largest rivals and a 5 percent greater return on assets.

Source: *From "The Cemex Way,"* The Economist *(June 16, 2001). Copyright © 2001 The Economist Newspaper Ltd. All rights reserved. Reprinted with permission. Further reproduction prohibited. www.economist.com.*

BENEFITS OF PROFESSIONAL PERSONAL SELLING AS A CAREER

Selling is one of the entry-level positions most accessible to college graduates. About 15 to 20 percent of all college graduates, regardless of major, start out in selling jobs. Some companies require sales experience as a prerequisite for advancement into managerial ranks. Many chief executive officers of Fortune 500 corporations began their careers as sales representatives. H. Ross Perot, self-made billionaire and former candidate for U.S. president, who was a salesman for IBM (www.ibm.com) before quitting to start Electronic Data Systems (www.eds.com), says, "I sold Christmas cards and garden seeds in Texarkana, Texas. At the age of 12, I peddled newspapers in a poor section of town filled with flophouses. I never thought of doing anything besides selling."[24]

A sales career offers many benefits, particularly its initial availability to just about anyone interested in a challenging career with unlimited opportunities where there are nearly always job openings. In the United States, more than one million new or experienced salespeople are needed annually by new and expanding businesses, so there is frequently a shortage of qualified salespeople. Sales is a great place to start for almost any managerial career. Newly promoted executives often say that the entry field they would choose if they had to start over would be sales, because of the opportunity it offers to work directly with customers and learn the business from the ground up. Let's take a look at some of the other benefits a salesperson can expect to share in once he or she has started a career in professional selling.

Financial Rewards

Salespeople are among the best-paid employees in business. Almost nothing limits earnings in sales, other than the salesperson's drive and ability, especially in business-to-business selling. Earning more than one hundred thousand dollars yearly is not unusual, and some salespeople earn more than one million dollars annually. Unlike most jobs that offer small annual raises based on a boss's subjective performance evaluation or on increases in the cost of living, the sales profession offers commissions, bonuses, and sales contest money and prizes in addition to a regular salary. Commissions are typically paid promptly on order size or profitability; individual and group bonuses are often awarded when salespeople exceed their annual sales quotas; and winners of sales contests may receive all kinds of booty (sailboats, exotic vacations, and entertainment packages), as well as prize money. People accustomed to being paid a regular salary may not like the idea of being paid partially in commissions, but they shouldn't worry. Salespeople paid solely in commissions usually earn the most money.

Perks

In addition to potentially high earnings, sales positions include various perquisites, or "perks." Expense account benefits, for example, permit salespeople to enjoy the "good life" while doing business with customers. Dinners at top restaurants, tickets to ball games and concerts, and health club and golf club memberships are some examples of legitimate business entertainment. Other perks may include use of a company credit card, company car, cell phone, or a computer for home use, and low-interest loans. Some benefits play the dual roles of recognizing and rewarding successful salespeople while allowing them to entertain and better serve their prospects and customers.

Visibility

Beyond tangible rewards, most sales careers offer a high degree of recognition. Top-performing salespeople can become in-house celebrities known to high-level management and virtually everyone else in the company. Senior managers often give personal recognition to their highest-achieving salespeople by interacting with them during special celebrations, vacation trips, or leadership seminars. For instance, at a payroll-processing company with sales of more than $100 million a year, the top ten salespeople are invited to spend a day discussing organizational issues with the CEO. At one meeting, the top ten salespeople drafted a new compensation plan for the entire sales force.

High Demand

Despite the many opportunities and high compensation in selling, shortages of qualified salespeople often arise. For example, when IBM announced that it would have to lay off twelve thousand employees, it simultaneously reassigned three thousand people to its sales force. Mobility tends to be higher for salespeople than for most professionals because selling skills are highly transferable to other products, and virtually every organization needs quality salespeople. As key generators of sales revenue—the lifeblood of any organization—salespeople are among the first to be hired and the last to be fired.

The Internet carries many sources for sales jobs. *Sales and Marketing Management* magazine offers a special careers section at its website, www.salesandmarketing.com. At several popular employment sites (e.g., www.monster.com) job seekers post their resumés and look for sales opportunities by geographic areas. Opportunities for people entering sales careers are nearly always good, because sales force turnover across all industries exceeds 20 percent a year. Turnover is so high partially because sales managers must often hire marginal people just to cover their territories. Many talented people never consider a sales career because they have negative ideas about selling, often including the following misconceptions:

- Most salespeople are dishonest and unethical.
- All sales jobs require overnight traveling.
- Most sales jobs involve door-to-door selling.
- Most customers treat salespeople with contempt.

- Few salespeople hold college degrees.
- Salespeople must push unneeded products on people.
- Most salespeople suffer humiliating personal rejection.

Although these exaggerated negative perceptions stem from outmoded tales about traveling and door-to-door salespeople, they are so widely held that many potentially good salespeople fail to even consider sales as a career. Admittedly, some sales jobs *do* require regular travel away from home, long working hours, continual pressure to achieve, interaction with difficult customers, frequent rejection, and constant self-management. These same conditions, however, apply to many other jobs as well.

Job Freedom and Independence

Salespeople are like entrepreneurs or independent businesspeople in that they largely manage themselves. Essentially, they are empowered to carry out a particular array of responsibilities delegated to them by their sales managers.[25] They set their own working hours and develop unique personal selling styles, yet they still enjoy the security of working for an organization that provides medical coverage, vacation pay, and retirement benefits. Compared to the cost of starting one's own business, a sales career offers tremendous leverage for a small monetary investment.

Outside salespeople seldom have a supervisor looking over their shoulders or timing their coffee breaks. In fact, if they do an outstanding job, salespeople can become somewhat like talented professional baseball or basketball players whose worth to the organization is often greater than that of their coaches. Top salespeople, like top athletes, are less likely to suffer from unfair or capricious actions on the part of a sales manager who doesn't like them. Still, salespeople cannot afford to slack off. Although job freedom and independence attract many people to sales, the pressure is always on, even if only self-imposed, to make a sales quota and earn higher commissions, bonuses, and other incentives. Competitive salespeople who expend great amounts of effort are likely to be better producers.[26] They are also the ones who receive the rewards. Being your own boss means working for the most demanding person of all—yourself.

Adventure and Satisfaction

Selling is adventurous because it challenges you to grow personally and professionally. It can be an invigorating experience to deal every day with people from diverse backgrounds and frames of reference. Many nonselling jobs are so routine and narrowly defined that they seldom present the employee with a challenge and may actually limit his or her personal and professional growth. Any limits on creativity and growth in selling tend to be self-imposed.

Selling can also give you more personal satisfaction than most jobs because the essence of your job is helping others solve their problems and achieve their goals. The better salesperson you are, the more benefits you will

KEEPING UP ONLINE: SALESAUTOPSY.COM

Salespeople the world over make numerous errors—some traumatic and some only mildly upsetting. Regardless of the seriousness of the mistake, though, salespeople can learn from their errors. Now salespeople can visit a website designed to help professional salespeople avoid certain kinds of mistakes, or at least stop making them. Sales Autopsy (www.salesautopsy.com) provides numerous examples of mistakes made by real salespeople and offers an analysis of why each mistake occurred. How might you currently make use of this website? What do you see as this website's strengths? What are its weaknesses?

provide to others—your customers, company, and family and the nation's economy. And for this you are well paid.

Reprinted by permission of Dan Seidman, SalesAutopsy.com

Objective Performance Evaluation

A salesperson who shows ability will be spotted quickly. In many fields, the seniority system or office politics seems to determine how much pay an employee receives. This is not the case in sales. Sales performance is highly visible and quantifiable. The salesperson is generally rewarded in relation to his or her sales productivity (e.g,, sales revenue, percent of quota achieved, and profitability). In fact, if the salesperson works strictly on commission, earnings are directly proportional to sales. Few jobs offer such objective performance appraisals.

Contribution to Society

Salespeople make many valuable contributions to society. They improve the quality of people's lives by identifying their needs and wants, helping solve their problems, adding value to products and services, and introducing new products. By generating income for their companies, salespeople provide jobs for many other people. With intensifying worldwide competition, the success of America's professional salespeople in domestic and world markets will become increasingly important to the health of our economy.

Chapter Review Question

Discuss the benefits and drawbacks of a career in personal selling.

CAREERS FOR DIFFERENT TYPES OF INDIVIDUALS

No single background, cultural heritage, ethnic group, gender, age, or personality type ensures success in selling to diverse customer types. On the contrary, some research has found that salespeople are most successful when selling to buyers who are the same gender, age, and personality type as they are;[27] that if they have more positive thoughts about the buyer and enhanced confidence, they are more likely to make the sale;[28] and that the sales effectiveness of a salesperson is related to the degree of similarity between the customer and salesperson[29]—especially with respect to their thinking alike.[30] As a result, sales managers have been advised to try to match their salespeople with similar customer types.[31] For instance, women and minorities may be especially appropriate sales reps to call on customers who are women and minorities, particularly when they are similar in other characteristics relevant to the buying situation.

Which Career Paths Begin with Personal Selling?

Many companies offer multiple career paths to newly hired salespeople: (1) professional selling, (2) sales management, and (3) marketing management. Figure 1.2 shows how the sales track branches out into multiple career path alternatives. Regardless of which path you take, your work challenges, desires, attitudes, and concerns will evolve as you pass through the various stages of your career.[32] And the longer you stay on your chosen path, the better prepared you will become to assume greater job responsibilities and advancement.[33]

Choosing the Right Career Path

Following completion of an initial training program, the trainee is promoted to sales representative and, depending on the industry and company, given a title similar to one of these: marketing representative, account representative, account executive, account manager, sales representative, sales engineer, sales associate, sales coordinator, sales consultant, market specialist, territory manager, or salesperson. Typically, newly designated salespeople spend a year or

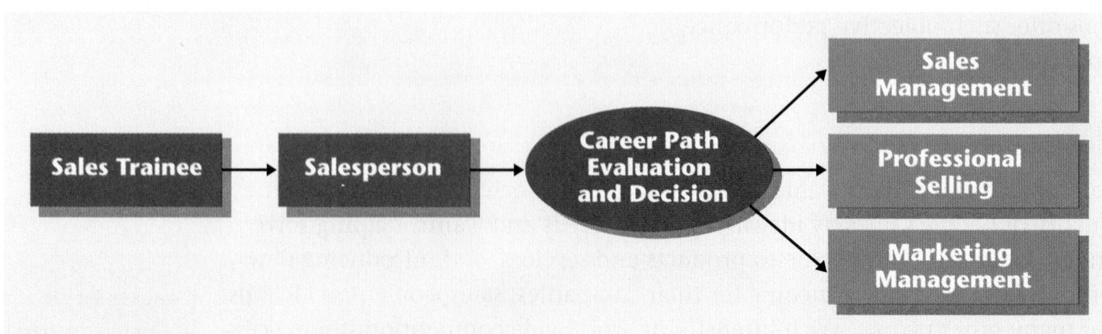

FIGURE 1.2

MULTIPLE CAREER PATHS IN PERSONAL SELLING

two in the field gaining essential experience before a decision is made regarding their long-term career with the company. The length of this field-selling experience varies with the industry, company, product, market complexities, and, of course, the individual. After the salesperson has achieved success in field-selling assignments, he or she meets with the sales manager, and perhaps a human resources manager, to examine the salesperson's skills and performance record. This in-depth evaluation provides the basis for deciding the individual's best career path.

Many experienced salespeople move on to sales management or marketing management, but not everyone has the ability and desire to become a manager. Yet most salespeople want to advance in their sales career. The good news is that excellent opportunities exist for advancement into higher levels of personal selling.

Professional Selling. If you choose the professional selling career path, you may spend three to five years as a *sales representative* before promotion to *senior sales representative*. After five to seven years in this capacity, a senior salesperson will be promoted to *master sales representative*. Top-performing master sales reps may be named *national or key account sales representatives* with responsibility for selling to a few major customers-for example, national retail chains such as Target (www.target.com) and Home Depot (www.homedepot.com) or large manufacturers such as Procter & Gamble (www.pg.com) and DuPont (www.dupont.com).

Sales Management. If you choose the sales management career path, you will probably be promoted from salesperson to sales supervisor or field sales manager, with responsibility for day-to-day guidance of a few salespeople in a given sales branch. Next comes promotion to *branch sales manager*, then *district manager*, with successively larger territorial responsibilities as a manager. From district sales manager, the successive promotion steps would be *zone, division,* and *regional sales manager,* although these hierarchical titles may vary from one company to another. Then comes promotion to *national sales manager* and, in some companies, *vice president of sales*. Finally, a few talented people who started in sales have an opportunity to become *CEO*.

A close alternative to the sales management career path is the *sales management staff* route. Here, you might serve as a *sales analyst, sales training manager*, or *assistant to the sales manager*. Staff people work at every organizational level and may hold positions in sales planning, sales promotion, sales recruiting, sales analysis, or sales training. Although people in sales management staff positions have no line authority over the sales force, they frequently hold impressive titles, such as *assistant national sales manager*, and they often switch over to top positions in line management after demonstrating success in their staff positions.

Marketing Management. Following success in field sales, you might be selected for the marketing management career path. This path often starts with promotion to a position as a *product* or *brand manager* for a product category (e.g., Pillsbury's Hungry Jack biscuits). Success in product management leads to promotion to *director of product management*, then *vice president of marketing*, and maybe eventually company *president and CEO*. In sum, sales is a great place to start, no matter what direction your future career takes.

SUMMARY

Selling is a universal activity. At one time or another, everyone uses persuasive communication to "sell" products, services, ideas, opinions, or points of views. The new AMA definition of marketing, along with the marketing concept and customer-oriented selling, are working together to change the focus of professional personal selling from a short-run focus on transactions and the needs of sellers to a long-run focus on relationships and the needs of customers. Salespeople, as the critical boundary spanners between buyer and seller companies are playing ever-larger roles in implementing customer relationship management (CRM) strategies. All organizations, whether profit oriented or not, are recognizing that achieving full customer satisfaction and loyalty provides the largest payoff over the long-run. Hence, salespeople are being trained and motivated to concentrate not so much on individual transactions as on building long-term relationships and partnerships with customers.

Consumers and *organizations* form the two basic categories of customers or markets. Organizational markets, which can be either profit-oriented or nonprofit, include *producers, resellers,* and *governments*. A *product* is anything offered to a market to satisfy customer needs and wants. Every product is an amalgam of a *core product*, a *tangible product*, and an *augmented product*.

Selling roles include order taking, order supporting, and order creating. Regardless of the sales position, professional salespeople carry out seven basic stages in the personal selling process, from prospecting and qualifying to following up and servicing the account to achieve customer satisfaction and loyalty. Each of these steps benefits from applying technological resources, including hand-held computers, the Internet, extranets, intranets, cell phones, beepers, and portable fax machines.

Sales careers offer opportunities for virtually anyone who is motivated to learn and earn by helping others solve their problems. Benefits include financial rewards, perquisites, a fast track to the top of an organization, job freedom and independence, personal satisfaction, objective performance evaluation, and the opportunity to make a contribution to society. Career paths that begin in personal selling tend to offer three routes: *professional personal selling, sales management,* and *marketing management*. The latter two paths can lead to senior executive positions in the company.

KEY TERMS

Customer-Oriented Selling	Order Creating	Extranets	Intranets
Missionary Selling	Prospecting	Order Taking	Order Supporting
Wheel of Personal Selling	Augmented Product	Personal Selling Process (PSP)	
Professional Salesperson	Trade Selling		

TOPICS FOR THOUGHT AND CLASS DISCUSSION

1. Have you ever known or met a person who appeared to be a "natural born" salesperson? What made you think he or she was a good salesperson? Given what you now know about professional personal selling, do you think you could call this person a truly professional salesperson? Why or why not?
2. What kind of selling might you like to do? With what products and what customers would you prefer to work? What do you think would be some advantages and disadvantages of each kind of selling for you personally?
3. Think about why you would want a career in professional personal selling. What would motivate you best? Money? Job independence? Opportunities to help people? Discuss your thoughts and feelings with classmates.

INTERNET EXERCISES

1. Assume that you are graduating from college soon with a dual major in marketing and finance and that you are interested in learning about different career opportunities for salespeople. Using your college's online database resources, develop general descriptions for sales jobs in the following types of organizations (remember that "salesperson" may not necessarily be the job title advertised). What are the similarities and differences among the "sales" jobs?
   - Financial services firm (e.g., Fidelity or Merrill Lynch)
   - Food manufacturer (e.g., Pillsbury or Kellogg)
   - Not-for-profit institution (e.g., Kimmel Center for the Performing Arts in Philadelphia or a large private university)
   - Major sports team (e.g., Chicago Bears or Los Angeles Lakers)
2. As a soon-to-be college graduate, you plan to start your career in sales, and you have interviews set up with the four companies, named below. Prior to the interviews, you feel that it would be to your advantage to talk with the interviewer about the career advancement opportunities available to those who start out in sales. To prepare for your interviews, go to the websites for these four companies and anywhere else you can think of to learn more about the career paths leading up from sales at these companies.
   - Black & Decker
   - Kimberly Clark
   - Nestlé Foods
   - Xerox

PROJECTS FOR PERSONAL GROWTH

1. You have just inherited a pencil-manufacturing business. Pencils are hardly a glamorous product, but they enjoy a large and competitive market. See if you can develop a description of your product that would help your sales staff sell the core, tangible, and augmented product.
2. Use what you have learned about what professional salespeople do to "sell" one of your classmates something in your classroom—a pen, chair, book, pair of shoes, or the like. Once you've successfully sold to the classmate, try selling to your instructor.

ROLE-PLAY EXERCISE 1.1

Guest Lecturers Answer Questions About Sales Careers

Situation

Kay Burke and Dave Simpson are both 28-year-old marketing employees for a large food manufacturer. They have been invited to speak to a group of seniors from the College of Business at a local university about career opportunities in sales. Even though most of the students are marketing majors, Kay and Dave know from their own college days that the students probably have a poor image of sales as a career.

Upon earning her degree in marketing from a southeastern university, Kay accepted a job with National Foods Corporation, where she completed a two-month sales training program before being assigned a sales territory of her own. After three successful years as a field sales rep selling grocery products to wholesalers and retailers, she was promoted to branch sales manager. Then came an opportunity to become product manager for the Contented Canine brand of dry dog food, and Kay grabbed it. Having been in this job for two years, Kay has been performing well and may be in line for another promotion soon to a more important assignment as product manager for the Colonel Crunchy line of ready-to-eat breakfast cereals. Kay hopes eventually to earn promotion to director of product management and aspires to become the vice president of marketing someday.

Dave Simpson also accepted a job with National Foods right after graduating from college and completed National's training program before being assigned to a sales territory. Dave was a solid performer in field sales for four years before being promoted to senior sales representative. At the time of his promotion, Dave was also given an opportunity to become a branch sales manager or an assistant product manager, but he chose to remain in sales, which he loves. His next promotion in the professional selling career path he has chosen will be to master sales representative. Then, after performing well in that job, he expects to be promoted to national sales representative.

Roles

Kay Burke and Dave Simpson Students chosen to play the roles of Kay Burke and Dave Simpson have a very challenging assignment, so these role players should be among the most confident and most articulate students in class. Ms. Burke and Mr. Simpson are both bright, confident people who are able to provide candid and professional-sounding answers to virtually any student question. They are genuinely interested in helping students develop a positive attitude toward sales careers. In particular, they want to illustrate the advantages of starting one's career in sales and to dispel the various myths about professional personal selling. An unstated but important part of this campus visit is to identify and attract some high potential candidates for National Food's grocery products sales force. Both Ms. Burke and Mr. Simpson should present a short introductory talk to the students before opening up the meeting to student questions.

Senior Students Several students, or even the entire class, can play the role of the graduating seniors who show varying degrees of interest and skepticism about sales as a career. These students should feel free to politely ask Ms. Burke and Mr. Simpson virtually anything they would like to know about sales careers. Student role players should remain professional at all times in asking their questions, but they should not hesitate to ask sensitive questions about such concerns as career opportunities for minorities and women in sales, drug testing, potential monetary rewards, and the criteria for performance evaluations.

Professor Someone, probably the instructor in the course, should play the role of the professor who invited Kay Burke and Dave Simpson to speak to his or her class. Some background should be presented about both Ms. Burke and Mr. Simpson, and the instructor is encouraged to ad-lib beyond the information provided in the role-play scenario. For example, the professor may have had both guest speakers as students about six years ago, and he or she may want to provide a favorable insight or two about each.

ROLE-PLAY EXERCISE 1.2

Panel Discussion on "Whether Salespeople Manipulate or Satisfy Customers"

Situation

Bernie Rubio, radio host of the regular weekly talk show "Business Today," has invited two businesspeople, George Newman and Wanda Hernandez, and a business writer, Carolyn Mack, to be guests on today's show. Mr. Newman is sales manager for television station WBCM, and Ms. Hernandez is national sales manager for Celestial Cosmetics. Carolyn Mack, a writer for *Buyer Beware*—a monthly magazine that rates the quality of brands within product categories—has authored a newly published book titled *Market Manipulation and Your Money*.

The three have been asked to discuss "Customer Seduction or Satisfaction in Today's Marketplace?" with host Bernie Rubio. A week ahead of the scheduled airing of the show, Mr. Rubio provided each of his guests with the following list of potential discussion topics.

- Are salespeople manipulators or satisfiers of customer needs?
- What is a product?
- What is a customer?
- What are people usually looking for when they buy products and services?
- Do people buy rationally or emotionally?
- What should be the role of the professional salesperson?

Roles

George Newman Sales manager for television station WBCM for the past four years, Mr. Newman spends most of his time preparing sales presentation strategies and coaching his four-person sales force on how to prospect, set up appointments, and make sales presentations and demonstrations. One of his favorite expressions is "Customers don't buy products and services, they buy people! If prospects believe in your honesty, reliability, and professionalism, they'll buy our television advertising time." Mr. Newman requires all his salespeople to spend at least one day a week telemarketing to generate and set up appointments with new prospects. Each of his salespeople has a laptop computer, cell phone, and electronic pager to obtain instant market information and communicate with customers and the sales office.

Wanda Hernandez National sales manager for Celestial Cosmetics for over five years, Ms. Hernandez feels strongly that you must give people a rational reason for buying emotionally. She believes that people often buy for reasons that they are embarrassed to state or sometimes are even unaware of themselves. "Ask anyone why they don't like prunes," she says, "and they'll always say 'because I don't like the taste'; but if you probe deeper, you'll learn that they associate prunes with old age and laxatives." She feels that marketing mixes and salespeople must create positive images for products and services that are compatible with customers' self-concepts.

Carolyn Mack An outspoken critic of what she sees as widespread customer manipulation by misleading advertising and deceptive salespeople, Ms. Mack says that many advertisers and salespeople create demand for products that people don't need. Salespeople, she says, are taught clever negotiating strategies and closing techniques that seduce people into buying products and services of poor quality. She would like to see state licensing of all salespeople operating within designated state boundaries. Licensing of salespeople, she believes, will force them to satisfy minimum professional standards in order to continue selling within that state.

Bernie Rubio As host of the radio talk show, his job is to fill the airways with interesting conversation from his guests or himself. Whenever the discussion gets bogged down or boring, he steps in to switch topics or to ask a provocative question.

Radio Audience All remaining students in the class can serve as the radio audience, who, from time to time, will be invited to "call in" questions for the panel. Host Bernie Rubio will have to take the initiative in getting the radio audience involved, perhaps at around the halfway point of the panel discussion.

CASE 1.1 DECISIONS! DECISIONS! WHICH CAREER PATH SHOULD I CHOOSE?

Nearing completion of his third year as a sales representative for Admiralty Food Company in Chicago, John Drain had just received notice that his sales manager had scheduled John's annual performance evaluation for the coming Monday at 9 A.M. John felt confident about meeting with his boss for his evaluation because he was having an outstanding year and had a good shot at winning the company's "Salesperson of the Year" award. Only two other salespeople out of forty-three in the Midwest region were selling at John's pace this year.

Admiralty Food sold most of its products through wholesalers or direct to large supermarket buying centers. John had more than one hundred customers, most of whom he called on about every two weeks. He believed that his track record with Admiralty was impressive by anybody's standards. He sold 105 percent of his assigned quota the first year, 115 percent the second year, and nearly 135 percent the third year, and he was on track this year to reach 140 percent of quota. During each of the past three years, John had made the "CEO's Sales Club" and, along with other top-performing Admiralty salespeople from around the country, had won an exciting vacation. John was proud to work for Admiralty because the company had an excellent reputation for quality products and superior service.

(continued)

Beginning with the fourth year in field selling for Admiralty, the annual performance evaluation for all salespeople included a discussion of their desired career path. Although salespeople were not required to declare a career path in their fourth year, the sales manager had to indicate the salesperson's seeming preference at that time. John didn't feel quite ready to make a career path decision, but he had given serious thought to the different options.

With a degree in marketing from Central Michigan University and halfway through an evening M.B.A. program at Roosevelt University, John believed all three sales/marketing career paths at Admiralty were open to him. He could continue on the *personal selling track*—progressing from field sales representative to senior sales rep to master sales rep. Or he could switch to the *sales management track,* which leads from field sales rep to branch sales manager, to district sales manager, to regional sales manager, to national sales manager, and perhaps senior vice president for sales. Finally, he could move into *marketing management* by becoming a brand manager for one of the company's product lines and then seek promotion first to director of product management and next to vice president of marketing; on this track, he might eventually have a chance to become CEO. John recognized that each of these career paths had their pluses and minuses, depending on one's personal needs, lifestyle, and goals.

John was engaged to be married that summer to Sylvia Maplewood, a public relations manager for Admiralty. He considered how this might affect his career strategy. Although the company had no nepotism rule, he decided it would be awkward to work in headquarters marketing and interact on a daily business basis with his wife.

John's thoughts about each of the possible career tracks are summarized below.

Professional Personal Selling Track

John loved the freedom and independence of personal selling. He wasn't sure that he could stand being cooped up in an office all day long. By remaining in personal selling, John felt sure that he would maximize his income over the next five to seven years. He knew his commissions from his continuing top performance put his earnings ahead of nearly everyone in the sales organization except for regional sales managers and above. However, John didn't think he could maintain his torrid selling pace for more than about five years. He figured his earnings would peak after that, and he would probably be shifted to a large national account or two where sales maintenance was most important. At that point, it might be nice to become a sales manager to guide the career development of younger salespeople, or to take on new challenges in marketing management. If he waited another five years or so to choose a career path, however, his chances of success in it would be diminished.

Sales Management Track

John feared that the pressure of traveling and meeting sales quotas might eventually become nerve racking instead of challenging and exciting as it was now. He and Sylvia planned to have a couple of children, and John wanted to watch them grow up. He wanted time to take them to dance classes or soccer games and be home in the morning when they got up, as well as at night to tuck them in bed. Sales managers were really like field marketing managers in that they spent most of their time in the office forecasting sales; preparing sales plans and budgets; setting sales goals and sales quotas; recruiting, selecting, and training new salespeople; designing sales territories; developing compensation plans; motivating and leading the salespeople; analyzing sales volume, costs, and profits by territory, product, customer, and salesperson; evaluating sales performance; and monitoring the ethical conduct of the sales force.

Marketing Management Track

John recognized that if he became a brand manager, he might be moving into a more risky field; a brand manager's career success or failure seemed to depend on successful new products. At the annual sales meeting last year, he remembered the comments of one of the company's brand managers at dinner:

Brand managers have a lot of responsibility but little authority. Our job is to develop marketing strategies, improve present products, develop new

(continued)

products, and manage the marketing mixes for all of them within a fiercely competitive and changing marketing environment. If a new product is successful, you can just hang onto its coat tails and let it pull you to success. But if you get identified with a product failure, you'd better get your résumé up to date. When you're a salesperson, you can always blame unsuccessful products on headquarters marketing, but brand managers can't blame product failures on the sales force.

In moving from the sales force to brand management, John feared that he might be trading in the day-to-day pressures of selling for career-threatening pressures. In addition, John had heard from his fiancée that politics could be subtle at headquarters, and he would probably have to tone down his natural tendency toward candor. Moreover, he noticed that the top marketing positions seemed to be filled disproportionately by people with Ivy League M.B.A.s. All in all, though, John believed that moving into marketing management was the best way to go if you wanted to become one of the top officers in the company.

Reviewing his own strengths and weaknesses, John listed the following strengths: *communication skills, analytical ability, product knowledge, drive, ambition, extroverted personality, well organized, results oriented, competitive*. Under weaknesses, he listed *impatient, nonpolitical, distaste for tedious paperwork,* and *too honest for own good.*

Questions

1. Do you think John should declare a career path now? If not, why not?
2. Taking into account John's attitudes, strengths, and weaknesses, what advice would you give John about the suitability of each of the three career paths for him? If forced to choose, which career path would you judge best for John? Explain your answer.

CASE 1.2 WHAT? YOU WANT TO BE A SALESPERSON?

CASE 1.2 "WHAT? YOU WANT TO BE A SALESPERSON?" CAN BE FOUND ONLINE AT HTTP://COLLEGE.HMCO.COM/PIC/ANDERSONPS2E

CHAPTER 2

Adjusting to the Dynamic Personal Selling Environment

After reading this chapter, you should understand:

- What megatrends are affecting personal selling now and what megatrends will affect personal selling in the foreseeable future.
- How "online" sales channels are empowering customers, especially giant retailers.
- How developments in telecommunications technology are dramatically changing personal selling.
- Why rising personal selling costs are encouraging salespeople and their companies to make increasing use of alternative direct-marketing techniques.
- What current trends in information management will affect how salespeople do their jobs.
- Why today's professional salespeople need to be much like micro-marketing managers in their expanding roles.

"If today's salespeople don't innovate and automate, they'll evaporate."

Anonymous

INSIDE PERSONAL SELLING

Meet Julie Wroblewski of eFunds

Julie Wroblewski obtains most of her sales leads from a technology that barely existed ten years ago—and some of the services she sells are even newer. Wroblewski is an account executive for eFunds, which provides electronic payment software and processing solutions, as well as both the data and the analysis tools to help companies make decisions about financial risk (fraud, for example). Customers include banks, financial services firms, retailers, electronic funds networks, government agencies, and e-commerce firms.

Technology is a vital part of the personal selling environment for eFunds. "I get most of my leads through our website," Wroblewski says. Prospects visit the site (www.efunds.com) and then call or e-mail the company for more information. A group at eFunds headquarters screens these requests and sends them on to reps for personal contact.

Because they've browsed the website, prospects usually have a general idea of what eFunds can do for them. Still, Wroblewski carefully investigates each prospect's unique needs and situation. To save time and money, she schedules as many as ten conference calls per week so that various eFunds technical specialists can discuss solutions to prospects' problems. For a typical conference call, she says, "I learn about the prospect's needs and expectations ahead of time, gather a pool of eFunds experts, and we work through the agenda with the prospect's business

people." A growing number of prospects do business globally, which means people in other countries sometimes participate in these conference calls.

To spot sales opportunities, Wroblewski reads the *Wall Street Journal, Fast Company,* and several technology magazines. "But what is really new for sales folks in today's environment are Internet sources like *Wall Street Journal Online* and online newsletters," she observes. "I can have news about particular firms forwarded to my e-mail inbox. This keeps me up-to-date about prospects and companies where I'm trying to make an appointment."

Technology also affects what Wroblewski sells. One of eFunds's newest offerings is a service that allows online shoppers to pay with electronic checks that look much like ordinary bank checks. Consumers without credit cards like the convenience, and merchants pay lower fees than they would for processing credit card payments.

Not long ago, Wroblewski began talking with an education company that wanted to start accepting Internet checks. After an initial phone call to discuss the prospect's situation, "We set up a time for eFunds experts to meet face-to-face with their management," she says, "and we presented our proposal using a PowerPoint electronic presentation." She followed up with periodic conference calls to address technical issues, supplemented by e-mails to provide additional details. After nine months, she closed the deal—and now eFunds powers the electronic checks on this customer's website.

What an exciting and challenging time it is to be—or to plan on being—a salesperson! Salespeople today face an incredibly dynamic selling environment that offers them enormous opportunities but also some major challenges. Marketplace changes are occurring at such a breakneck pace that some salespeople feel as though they are trapped on a high-tech treadmill going faster and faster. While performing their challenging jobs, modern salespeople also must cope with revolutionary and evolutionary developments in telecommunications, increasingly expert and demanding buyers, and continuously rising customer expectations for product quality and service. Change is inevitable in every field, of course, but several dramatic megatrends make personal selling one of today's most volatile—yet exciting and rewarding—careers.

MEGATRENDS AFFECTING PERSONAL SELLING

To become successful or maintain their success, today's salespeople must recognize and adapt to several *megatrends* in order to enhance their effectiveness and efficiency. Three major forces—*behavioral, technological,* and *managerial*—are influencing buyer-seller relationships and how salespeople do their jobs.[1] Outlined in Table 2.1 are the key elements of each of these three forces. In this

TABLE 2.1

MEGATRENDS AFFECTING PERSONAL SELLING

BEHAVIORAL FORCES	
• **More Expert and Demanding Buyers**	• **Empowerment of Customers**
• **Rising Customer Expectations**	• **Globalization of Markets**
• **Micro-Segmentation of Domestic Markets**	• **Expanding Power of Giant Retailers**
TECHNOLOGICAL FORCES	
• **Sales Force Automation** • Portable Computers (notebook, handheld, and pocket PCs) • Electronic Data Interchange • Videoconferencing (via desktop, laptop, or handheld computers) • Multi-function Cell Phones and Satellite Pagers • Voice Mail, E-mail, and Instant Messaging	• **Mobile Virtual Sales Offices** • **Electronic Commerce** • Internet Blogs Podcasting Screen Sharing WebEx • Extranets • Intranets
MANAGERIAL FORCES	
• **Selling Cost Reduction Efforts** • **Shift to Direct-Marketing Alternatives** • Direct Mail • Telemarketing • Teleselling • Personalized E-mail • Kiosks • Facsimile	• **Certification of Salespeople**

Sales Megatrends Major behavioral, technological, and managerial trends that influence how salespeople perform their jobs.

chapter, we will discuss the nature of these inexorable forces—or **sales megatrends**—and their probable effects on salespeople and their work.

Behavioral Forces

Buyers' attitudes, preferences, and behaviors, as well as competitors' efforts, are changing frequently, so salespeople must stay alert and flexible enough to modify their selling strategies and approaches quickly. Let's briefly discuss some of these factors.

More Expert and Demanding Buyers. Organizational buyers are becoming increasingly skillful at obtaining value for their expenditures. Companies are developing more efficient purchasing processes and using professional buying committees composed of purchasing, engineering, finance, marketing, legal, and operations management. Sales presentations to these diverse expert buying committees and to all other customers who treat purchases like long-term investments require a talented new type of professional salesperson. Most sales organizations are providing intensified training to help salespeople work effectively in these complex selling situations where the customer often knows as much as they do about the products and services available from various suppliers.

Rising Customer Expectations. Salespeople must reconcile themselves to the fact that customer expectations for products and services will probably continue to rise. What was satisfactory yesterday may not fill the bill tomorrow. Organizational buyers are less and less tolerant of inferior products. Japanese automobile manufacturers, for example, are pushing quality and service to such high levels that one American manufacturer of auto parts found that it could not compete successfully in the international market. After marketing automobile gaskets for years in the United States, the company assumed it could also become a major player in the world market. It set its initial sights on Japan. Unfortunately, it had limited success because, even though its gaskets exceeded all U.S. auto manufacturers' requirements, they weren't good enough for the Japanese producers. Why? Although U.S. car owners are used to seeing an occasional drop of oil on the garage floor—especially from a car with over 50,000 miles—a single drop of oil in Japan is ample justification for a complaint to the manufacturer.

Today's and tomorrow's customers will expect products and services of ever-higher quality. Successful sales representatives must never become defensive about the limitations of their company's products or services. Instead, they must be willing and able to look at their offerings from the perspectives of their most critical customers to see what improvements are needed. As the company's "eyes and ears in the field," salespeople should promptly report competitors' innovations or customer complaints to their sales managers. By readily accepting this role of gathering market information, alert salespeople can help their companies develop new products or services and improve current offerings to achieve higher levels of customer satisfaction.

Micro-Segmentation of Domestic Markets. The United States has become increasingly multicultural and multilingual. Selling in major parts of Miami, New York City, Los Angeles, Chicago, Philadelphia, Detroit, and San Antonio—in fact, in most large cities—will increasingly require salespeople to understand different cultures, languages, tastes, and preferences for everything from food and clothing to cosmetics. Sales forces that do not understand and adapt to this rich mix of wants and needs will fail to reach several large, fast-growing markets.

Some companies have responded to this multicultural mosaic by dividing the United States into distinct markets based on unique cultural and ethnic tastes and preferences. These companies then allocate a percentage of their advertising budget to regional promotion, and in some instances the regional ad budget may be elevated in response to regional sales growth. Many organizational sellers are also developing and marketing specialized products that exemplify their regional sales approach; for example, product variations—for everything from food to clothing to music—sold in the Southwest differ from those sold in the Northwest. Goya

Foods (www.goya.com), which employs a Spanish-speaking sales force that serves both large retailers and the *bodegas* (Hispanic mom-and-pop stores), has already won a major share of the diverse Hispanic market by catering to the special tastes and preferences of consumers who have immigrated to the United States from Mexico, Puerto Rico, Venezuela, and Cuba.

Empowerment of Customers. Like salespeople, customers too are experiencing dramatic changes. Advances in telecommunication technologies are empowering them as they use computers (whether desktop, notebook, handheld, or pocket versions), multi-function cell phones, kiosks, desktop videoconferencing, and who knows what forthcoming electronic devices to go back and forth (online and off-line) between the Internet and traditional brick-and-mortar vendors to do research before purchasing products and services. Sometimes customers—whether consumers or businesses—do their product comparison research online and then purchase off-line. At other times, they do their research at conventional stores or outlets then buy online. Not long ago, General Electric (www.ge.com) told its numerous suppliers that it would stop purchasing from them if they did not offer GE the option of buying products and services online. In response to these empowered customers, progressive sellers are trying to smoothly integrate their online and off-line businesses, so that they can readily recognize and offer appropriate product and service packages no matter which sales channel customers enter. With their new empowerment, customers are becoming more knowledgeable, expert, and demanding in their purchasing. The Internet and other "online" sales channels have empowered customers in various ways, as shown in Table 2.2.

TABLE 2.2

EMPOWERMENT OF CUSTOMERS

"Off-line" Sales Channels	"Online" Sales Channels
Static, Dated Information	Dynamic "Real-Time" Information
Many Place, Time, and Space Barriers (limited hours open)	No Place, Time, or Space Barriers (open 24/7/365)
Few Customer Alliances or Communities	Many Customer Alliances and Communities
Few Customized Products	Many Customized Products
Narrow Selection of Products	Large Selection of Products
Limited Price Sensitivity	High Price Sensitivity
Limited Access to Competitors' Offerings	Instant Access to Competitors' Offerings
High Switching Costs	Low Switching Costs
Seller Initiates the Offer	Customer May Initiate the Offer, e.g., *e-Bay.com* and *PriceLine.com*
Slow Negotiations	Fast Negotiations
Hard to Get Away from a Salesperson	Easy to Click Out of an Electronic Sales Presentation

Expanding Power of Giant Retailers. One particular group of customers has seen its relative negotiating power vis-à-vis salespeople and their companies grow dramatically: giant retailers. Only a few retailers today account for more than half of total retail sales. Large retail organizations—such as Wal-Mart (www.walmart.com), Target (www.target.com), Home Depot, (www.homedepot.com) and Best Buy (www.bestbuy.com)—have gained and continue to gain an increasing share of the consumer's dollar. As these giant retailers grow bigger and exceed the size and power of the manufacturers that supply them, they dictate the buyer-seller relationship. For instance, several dominant retailers are bypassing wholesalers and distributors to buy directly from manufacturers who give them "key account" (large account) status and special attention. Also, large retailers such as Wal-Mart are leveraging electronic data interchange (EDI) technology to force out middlemen and to require manufacturers' direct sales organizations to assume the functions and administrative costs of "just-in-time" inventory control, order billing, and sales promotion.

Radio Frequency Identification (RFID). Changing demands of giant retailers and methods of serving them are bringing about dramatic change in the relationship between suppliers and giant retailers. For instance, Wal-Mart, Target, and the U.S. Department of Defense (www.dod.gov) have notified their large suppliers that they must switch from identifying products with the tradition UPC bar codes to using radio frequency identification (RFID) tags.[2] Unlike UPCs, which are limited to a single code for all products of a similar type, RFID tags are unique so that individual products can be identified and tracked. RFIDs offer large cost savings by enabling fast, accurate inventories of products, quickly locating a specific pallet of goods in a huge warehouse, and reducing theft. RFID technology is already used widely. Family pets are often embedded with small RFID chips to prevent their being lost, highway toll booths use them for electronic toll collection, airlines track passenger baggage, and even library books may have them. Perhaps the most immediate concern for some salespeople is the potential lost of privacy, because RFID technology can be used to monitor the whereabouts of company vehicles throughout the day. Nevertheless, to continue selling to these giant customers today and (probably) to smaller customers tomorrow, companies have no choice but to affix an RFID to all their products. In some cases, salespeople may need to push for prompt adoption of these new customer requirements within their own companies.

To meet the demands of giant retailers, large manufacturers such as Procter & Gamble (www.pg.com) have set up sales offices near, or sometimes even within, the retailer's headquarters. The growing dominance of these giant retailers has led to establishing single-sourcing, multi-year contracts with manufacturers. In such instances, an agreement between the buyer and the seller allows one manufacturer to be the single supplier for a given product (or array of products); in return, though, the manufacturer must provide an extremely high level of service and support to the large retailer. Giant supermarkets have gained so much leverage over producers that they often charge "slotting fees" to allow manufacturers to place their products on the retail shelves. For example, if a cereal manufacturer wants a large grocery chain to

IT'S UP TO YOU

You have just been assigned to your territory, which has many potential organizational customers. Competition is keen, however, and customers tend to buy chiefly on price—they want the best value for their money. Concomitantly, prospects and customers in your territory have increasing expectations of their suppliers and the service they should provide. Knowing that price is the major driver of prospects and customers and that your firm is not the lowest-priced seller, you are stumped about how you can succeed in this territory. How will you begin to build your sales program? What resources will you call on within your organization and outside it? What technologies and tools might come to your aid?

stock a newly launched cereal, the retailer may demand that the seller pay a fee *up front* for filling precious shelf space with the new product. Doing so reduces the grocery retailer's financial risk associated with taking on a new product. As giant retailers have gained power, many small manufacturers and suppliers, either unable or unwilling to meet their costly demands, have simply stopped calling on them. However, for many larger companies, giant retail customers are too critical to their businesses to lose. Therefore, their salespeople must remain alert to skillfully and nimbly respond to the growing needs and demands of these powerful customers. Keeping in mind the megatrends we have discussed so far, consider the personal selling situation presented in the accompanying *It's Up to You* feature.

Globalization of Markets. With its large population, high discretionary income levels, and political stability, the United States is the world's most attractive market. Companies based in Asia (particularly those in Japan, South Korea, Hong Kong, and Taiwan), as well as many from the European Union (especially those in Germany, France, and Great Britain), have worked hard to capture huge market shares of the most basic U.S. industries: automobiles, steel, electronic components, televisions, home appliances, industrial chemicals, textiles, and machine tools. Many foreign manufacturers and service companies are also establishing operations in the United States, particularly in the automobile and electronic appliances markets.

As larger shares of the U.S. domestic market are gobbled up by companies from around the globe, U.S. firms are seeking sales growth by becoming major exporters of their products and services. Numerous U.S.-based firms, such as Colgate-Palmolive (www.colgate.com), Apple Computer (www.apple.com), Coca-Cola (www.cocacola.com), and IBM (www.ibm.com) already generate more than half their annual sales revenue from exports. For global sales growth, many U.S. salespeople must learn how to sell in foreign countries. Language, customs, culture, politics, ethics, laws, economies, market information, and distribution channels are just a few of the areas where differences can make international selling much more challenging but also potentially

ON THE FRONTLINES

Even "IT" Managers Want to Have Fun

Security on the Web is a major headache for information technology (IT) managers and customers alike. Hackers bent on creating mischief or perpetrating actual theft of data or money keep many IT managers awake at night. After all, if a website is not secure, the potential for rampant harm to the site's organization and its customers looms large. Consequently, numerous firms have sprung up to sell safeguards against hacker invaders. A major problem for security service companies, however, is how to get their names and service offerings in front of target markets.

Web advertising is frequently used by network security service providers to reach target adopters who are usually "heavy users" of the Web. These promotional efforts, though, are often obscured by the plethora of competing advertisements. One creative solution has been to develop and install an intriguing game (similar to popular video games) on a security provider's website aimed directly at IT managers. When IT managers and their subordinates click on the banner ad for the game, they are whisked to the security provider's website, where they download and play the game. Although the game revolves around computer security issues, it is fun to play and specifically designed to capture the attention and interest of IT professionals.

While enjoying the game, IT players also learn how the security protection provider's products can protect a website. Given the complexity of security products, several levels in a buying firm (including IT) tend to be involved in their purchase. Clever and challenging games can garner a large following of potential security service buyers, especially when augmented by promotional activities such as game contests, publicity, and referrals. Bottom line: Even when you're selling a serious product to business professionals, it can be done successfully in a fun way.

more rewarding for salespeople willing to make the extra effort. The future economic health of the United States depends partially on how well salespeople and sales managers do their jobs as competition from foreign products and services intensifies. Fortunately, many organizational sellers are preparing their salespeople to sell in foreign cultures.[3] (In subsequent chapters in this book, we will discuss selling in foreign markets.)

Chapter Review Questions

What specific market and competitive forces are changing personal selling and buyer-seller relationships? What are their effects?

Why do some companies see selling in the United States as increasingly like selling internationally?

Technological Forces

Probably the most obvious and dramatic influences on personal selling today are technological innovations, especially in telecommunications. Today's most successful salespeople are those who make skillful and efficient use of technology to increase their productivity in serving customers. Sales force automation, mobile virtual sales offices, and electronic commerce using the Internet, extranets, and intranets are some dominant technological forces driving changes in the way personal selling is conducted. Before we examine these topics, read the accompanying *On the Frontlines* feature and see how technology is being used in creative and fun ways to capture the attention of business prospects.

Sales Force Automation. Sales force automation (SFA) is the use of high-tech tools that help salespeople work effectively and efficiently. Salespeople now employ a host of SFA innovations, including portable (notebook or handheld) computers, electronic data interchange, videoconferencing, multi-function cellular phones, satellite pagers, voice mail, and electronic mail. SFA tools provide a cornucopia of benefits for resourceful and creative organizational sales personnel. One study found that the more strategic, administrative, and operating issues that management considered prior to purchasing SFA technology, the greater the benefits realized from its use.[4] Let's briefly discuss the most widely applied SFA technologies.

Portable Computers. Some of the most exciting changes in the buyer-seller relationship are coming about via sophisticated portable computers that range in size from notebook to handheld to pocket PCs. Combined with creative software, these tools have empowered salespeople and helped reduce or eliminate much of their tedious paperwork (for example, filling out sales call reports, order forms, and expense reports). Other software is assisting salespeople in the management of their customer accounts (organizing accounts, targeting e-promotions, timing sales calls), thus enhancing their productivity. Many salespeople regularly use e-mail with attachments to send pamphlets, brochures, or preformatted sales letters tailored to the needs of prospects and customers. Most important, salespeople use computers and other handheld telecommunication devices to instantly tap in to huge data banks of information about credit, prices, inventory, production, and shipping instead of requesting data from their sales manager or other home office sources.

Salespeople also use their computers to develop and improve customer relationships. For example, some salespeople keep their prospects and customers informed by e-mailing them a monthly newsletter that provides important information about new products, upcoming price changes, or early alerts about possible product shortages. Instead of relying on traditional hardcopy sales materials, CD-ROM technology allows salespeople to customize sales presentations on their portable computers and then promptly e-mail them (with attachments) to customers. Resourceful and creative salespeople are finding many ways to use technology to better serve their customers and their companies.

Electronic Data Interchange (EDI). Electronic data interchange is the linking together of channel member computer systems to allow real-time exchanges of information between manufacturers and resellers (that is, retailers, wholesalers, or distributors). For instance, a retailer's computers can be linked to the manufacturer's computers so that real-time retail sales automatically update the retailer's product mix and the manufacturer's production schedules. The EDI linkage automatically transmits purchase orders, invoices, price quotations, shipping dates, reports, and promotional information to the manufacturer. Similarly, EDI provides retailers with product sales data, consumer purchasing patterns, customer-tailored promotions and merchandising, product profitability analyses, and demand forecasts based on sales trends. To illustrate, independent retailers who sell Hallmark (www.hallmark.com) greeting cards at locations throughout the United States use EDI to transmit orders and receive acknowledgment and delivery dates within seconds from Hallmark's Kansas City, Missouri, headquarters. Not only are orders filled faster, thereby reducing store "out-of-stocks"; they also are no longer lost in the mail.

As more business buying is handled by EDI systems, the role of the salesperson continues to evolve. No longer are routine price, inventory levels, shipment confirmations, and technical information communicated to prospects and customers via salespeople. Instead, they are automatically transmitted via EDI systems. Because of the reduction in routine, labor-intensive order processing, today's salespeople can devote more time to serving customers in a consulting role. Salespeople who excel at this consultative role will build higher levels of trust with customers and thereby enhance development of mutually profitable buying and selling relationships. Ideally, all salespeople should strive to serve their prospects and customers as knowledgeable consultants who help them "sell through" to their own customers. Helping customers grow and improve their profitability over the long run gives salespeople and their companies opportunities to sell more. Savvy salespeople recognize the truth in the saying "If your customers prosper, so will you." EDI is a key technological tool that can facilitate a mutually beneficially partnership between buyers and sellers.

Videoconferencing. This tool is usually a corporate (internal) satellite television system that makes possible simulated face-to-face interaction among geographically separated individuals. Individual salespeople can videoconference using desktop, laptop, or handheld computers, and large rooms of people at different locations can communicate via huge monitors. For example, if you have a video camera on your computer, Apple Computer's Tiger operating system enables you to hold a video conference via an instant-messaging program with up to three other people simultaneously.[5] Conference participants appear in a virtual meeting room that is so realistic that their reflections bounce off the table.

Many companies have cut the cost of travel and employee "downtime" by substituting videoconferencing—or teleconferencing, as it's sometimes called—for national and regional conferences. In fact, one study found that technology has decreased the amount of travel for 63 percent of executives, as videoconferencing has become one of their major alternatives.[6] Widely dispersed salespeople (and their managers) can use desktop videoconferences for sales meetings, training, and customer interaction without leaving their individual virtual offices. General Electric (www.ge.com) managers stay in touch with their different sales forces and markets through an internal communication system. Once a week, field salespeople conduct a videoconference with personnel in various corporate divisions around the world to talk about market opportunities and challenges and to decide on prompt action.

Salespeople generally are able to spend less than a third of their time in face-to-face selling. If videoconferencing can convert part of the time salespeople spend traveling, waiting to see customers, and attending internal sales meetings to time spent with customers, then sales and customer satisfaction may experience significant gains.

Videoconferencing is only one of many technological tools that salespeople use to improve their productivity.
Thinkstock/Getty Images

Multi-Function Cell Phones and Satellite Pagers. Mobile communications innovations, especially cellular phones and satellite pagers (beepers), are helping salespeople keep in touch with customers, their managers, and the home office even when hundreds or thousands of miles away. Beyond the ability to make and receive phone calls anywhere in the world, modern multifunction cell phones also enable you to snap pictures, run simulations, play games, listen to music, and organize your activities. Many companies supply their sales forces with cell phones and pagers to enhance their salespeople's customer orientation and improve productivity. Cell phones enable salespeople to obtain the latest customer information or relevant home office information en route to a customer's place of business; to alert customers about unavoidable delays, such as a car breakdown or traffic jam; to speak with drivers in company delivery trucks who can check on customer orders; and to instantly send pictures to customers or the home office. Whenever a cell phone is stuck temporarily in a dead spot, beepers can be used as a backup device to provide salespeople with timely information or alert them that prospects, customers, management, or other company personnel are trying to reach them.

Voice Mail. Voice mail—various electronic methods of sending and receiving voice messages—is dramatically improving the efficiency of sales force communications. AT&T has determined that 75 percent of all business communications are not completed on the first try. Staying in touch with office support people, answering customer inquiries, keeping distributors informed about product availability and delivery dates, and carrying out numerous other telephone communications consume a lot of a salesperson's time. Voice mail ensures that the salesperson connects every time to leave a message.

Many salespeople use voice mail to keep in touch with their sales managers while on the road calling on wholesalers, distributors, or independent retailers. Before they used voice mail, most of these salespeople were on the phone every night updating their managers on their daily activities and discussing problems. Now their evenings are freer because they can dial into the system whenever they like to leave messages and retrieve information left by their sales managers.

Electronic Mail (E-mail). The Internet has changed the way people communicate. Electronic mail (e-mail) has virtually replaced letters and even telephone calls as our preferred medium for corresponding with others. Billions of e-mail messages are sent daily. Electronic messages can be sent to a single receiver's e-mail address or written on an electronic "bulletin board" for hundreds or even thousands of computer users to see at the same time. Instead of enduring the frustration of playing telephone tag with a customer, sales peer, or sales manager, salespeople can always leave electronic mail for prospects and customers, who can read the messages when convenient. E-mail is as fast as a phone call and usually less subject to misunderstanding because the message is in text format for the receiver to read several times if necessary. A company can cut its information-handling costs by 60 percent or more by replacing regular mail and filing cabinets with electronic mail and storage.[7] One popular handheld device for managing e-mail is Research in Motion's (www.rim.com) "BlackBerry," which includes a tiny keyboard that enables salespeople to read, write, forward, reply to, delete, or file their messages while keeping only one e-mail address and mailbox.

Courtesy of Research In Motion Limited

Instant Messaging (IM). Sometimes even e-mails are not fast enough. For instance, when you send an e-mail, you don't know when the customer you are trying to reach will check his or her e-mail "Inbox" and get back to you. Also, if you and a customer engage in a conversation by sending several e-mails back and forth, both of you have to repeatedly click through some steps (e.g., open, read, reply, and send). With instant messaging (IM), however, you can get around these steps by using a previously set-up contact list of customers, co-workers, or others. Instant messaging allows you to send messages back and forth in conversational style with any of the people on your list who are online. Most of the popular instant-messaging programs provide a variety of features that salespeople might use, including

- Sending Instant Messages: communicate back and forth with anyone on your list while you're both online
- Using Chat Rooms: set up special chat rooms for customers and/or co-workers
- Sharing Files: instantly share websites, pictures, sounds, and files.

Virtual Sales Offices. More than ten million U.S. employees conduct business from virtual offices (for example, one's home or car). As one salesperson explained, "With all the technology I carry around in my briefcase, I'm almost like the mobile world headquarters for my company." At *BusinessWeek Online* (www.bwcourses.com), various courses on business and technology are offered free to registrants. Many salespeople would find a course titled "The Wireless Mobile Office" particularly valuable.

Salespeople are more empowered today than ever before. Powerful portable computers, telecommunication software, handheld fax machines, satellite pagers, multi-use cell phones, and voice mail are among the many tools that enable salespeople to have mobile virtual offices. While driving in their cars, having lunch at a restaurant, or virtually anywhere else, salespeople can keep in contact with customers, sales managers, and co-workers almost anywhere in the world. Companies are also assigning more decision-making authority to field salespeople, making it unnecessary for them to report to a sales manager for authorization. Electronic automation is enabling field salespeople to become increasingly self-sufficient, thereby eliminating the need for many branch sales offices. To illustrate, IBM (www.ibm.com) has a telecommuting program in two of its divisions. The company asked salespeople not to come into the office except to deliver sales presentations, pick up their mail, or take a break from working at home. IBM saved millions of dollars in overhead costs from this initiative, and most of those participating preferred it to working at the office. Virtual sales offices also give salespeople the opportunity to teach customers how to access their suppliers' communication technologies, such as EDI or extranets, to get answers to their questions or obtain the latest information on products and prices. Clearly, more and more of the actual products that today's salespeople offer customers have become consulting and professional advice.

Electronic Commerce. Electronic commerce includes all the activities of companies and other organizations that use the Internet. These activities consist largely of using the Internet and proprietary networks such as intranets and extranets to sell products and services and expedite communication.

Internet. The Internet may be one of the most important technological tools of all time for sales transactions. It makes possible virtually instantaneous interactions among manufacturers, intermediaries or middlemen, and households. More than 97 percent of large businesses have established websites, and worldwide business-to-business (B2B) Internet purchases are expanding rapidly, having quadrupled from $1.9 trillion in 2002 to over $8 trillion in 2005.[8] Salespeople frequently use this electronic channel for prospecting. Some salespeople use the Internet somewhat like a worldwide electronic yellow pages. For instance, a salesperson planning cold calls on companies in a suburb of a major city can utilize an online database service to develop a list of the suburb's businesses, along with their addresses, telephone numbers, sales volume, and names of key executives. Using information from online databases, enterprising salespeople have developed networks or centers of influence by setting up special online forums and inviting prospects to log on. Other salespeople have established their own website communities for prospects and customers to exchange opinions and views on products and services. For business-to-business sales, the Internet continues to offer innovative ways to reach prospects and customers rapidly, effectively, and inexpensively. Among the technologies that salespeople are using creatively are blogs, podcasting, screen-sharing software, and WebEx.

Blogs. A phenomenon called blogs (short for *weblogs*) is becoming a huge part of the Internet scene and offers many opportunities for salespeople and their companies. Blogs are essentially personal or corporate "journals" where information, opinions, pictures, and videos can be posted. Blogs require very little technical ability to set up, update, and maintain, so they have quickly become immensely popular, and many sell advertising space. Over 9 million blogs already exist, and about 40,000 are being created daily. Even many giant companies have blogs. Microsoft (www.microsoft.com), for example, set up its Channel 9 Video blog to communicate with its software developers. Some salespeople post their PowerPoint sales presentations, along with pictures and videos for their company's product or services, on customized blogs for prospects and customers to access. Instead of reading newspapers and magazines or watching television, many young people receive their news and other information largely from blogs, so it's a phenomenon that salespeople, sooner or later, may need to incorporate into their sales and customer relationship strategies.[9]

Podcasting. Among business-to-business salespeople, the use of Web-based broadcasting is rising rapidly. Podcasting (a word coined from *iPods* and *broadcasting*) enables audio programs to be delivered via the Internet to prospects who can listen to the message at any time on a portable music player, such as an iPod. Thus podcasting allows salespeople to provide their own radio show for prospects and customers. Sales presentations, new-product demonstrations, the latest information on pricing or delivery dates, technical advice, or any other messages can be sent via podcasting. In early 2005, General Motors (www.gm.com) introduced its own company podcast to promote its new automobiles. As a personalized radio show, the possibilities for podcasting in personal selling and customer relationship management seem endless.

Screen-Sharing. For less than about $100 a month, individuals or companies can install computer software that allows them to share sales presentations over the Internet without having to download anything. Using screen-sharing software instead of making an in-person sales call, the salespeople can call or e-mail prospects and give them a password to instantly view whatever is on the salesperson's computer screen. Complex or in-depth sales presentations, which might not be appropriate for the typical time-constrained sales call, can often be made via screen-sharing. Companies such as Disney, Safeway, T-Mobile, Forbes, and Whole Foods Market are achieving large cost savings through use of the technology for sales presentations. Screen-sharing can be especially valuable for smaller companies. For instance, San Francisco-based Philippe Becker Design sent two salespeople to make a presentation to an East Coast snack food Fortune 500 prospect at a cost of about $5,000. With a screen-sharing program, these sales presentations could have been made at a fraction of the cost.[10]

WebEx. Many companies are using WebEx Communications (www.webex.com) services for online meetings, Web conferencing and videoconferencing with employees, suppliers, prospects, and customers. More specifically, WebEx services are being used across these companies in sales, support, training, marketing, engineering, and other functions. WebEx fits seamlessly with sales force automation and customer relationship management strategies. Using WebEx, for example, salespeople can make online sales calls and share comprehensive sales presentations and demonstrations. AstraZeneca (www.astrazeneca.com), one of the world's leading pharmaceutical companies, uses WebEx to connect its network of 10,000 employees, hundreds of suppliers, and over 5,800 corporate customers. With the cost of promoting and selling branded drugs already as much as 30 percent and rising, AstraZeneca has found WebEx to be an important way to improve communication with physicians, employees, and suppliers, while reducing travel costs.[11]

Intranets. An intranet is an *internal* company network that looks and feels like the Internet because it uses the same tools, such as *Netscape Navigator, Microsoft Explorer,* or *Mozilla Firefox* browsers. But intranets are proprietary company networks that link salespeople, other employees, and business affiliates through personal computers and other devices. Organizations use intranets for diverse functions, including e-mail, team projects, and desktop publishing. Intranets are an ideal solution for a mobile sales force or a diverse sales force that needs instant access to a lot of rapidly changing information. For instance, a California software-solutions provider uses an intranet system as the primary information supplier for its sales force of two hundred. Instead of using dated manuals and countless photocopies and memos, the firm simply posts its sales-related data—everything from information about sales processes to news about competitors and product specifications—on its internal intranet server.

Extranets. Another important business use of electronic channels is a corporate-maintained extranet to provide customer support and service. Transferring customer support information to a website is a labor-efficient and cost-effective way of distributing information to thousands of current and potential customers. Extranets can offer prospects and customers an array of product and technical information, design guides, videos, and graphics. Beyond prospecting and customer support, some companies use their extranets as direct sales channels. For example, Ernst & Young (www.ey.com) provides online consulting services for small companies, and Vanguard Group (www.vanguard.com), one of the world's largest mutual fund sellers, uses an extranet to provide education on financial topics for its different tiers of customers who log on with their passwords.

For B2B sales, the Internet and its related electronic variations offer powerful, low-cost ways to locate high-quality prospects, conduct research on prospects and customers, sell to organizational buyers, support sales channels, provide customer service, and facilitate ongoing communications. Research has found that the amount a firm spends on the Internet (budget allocation) and the extent to which the firm uses the Internet (usage) can positively influence sales performance and overall efficiency.[12] Thus salespeople need to know how to use the Internet, intranets, and extranets to their advantage and for the benefit of their prospects and customers. Read *From the Command Post,* on p. 49, to see how one firm has used e-commerce beneficially.

Chapter Review Question

Name some major advances in telecommunications and computer technology that are affecting personal selling. Describe briefly how salespeople can use each to improve their effectiveness and efficiency.

Managerial Forces

In response to the dynamic behavioral and technological megatrends, sales organizations are trying various strategies to achieve profitable sales growth and closer customer relationships. Among these strategies are (1) cost reduction efforts, (2) a shift from field selling to direct-marketing alternatives, and (3) certification of salespeople.

FROM THE COMMAND POST: CARRIER CORPORATION—KEEPING THINGS COOL

Carrier Corporation (www.carrier.com) is the largest producer of air conditioning, heating, and refrigeration equipment in the world. Its products are used primarily in commercial and residential buildings, as well as in trucks. In an effort to boost sales, Carrier turned to the Web, and its success has been phenomenal.

Carrier has been able to identify and target website visitors with the products they are most likely to purchase by offering visitors a discount on shipping if they provide their zip code. With zip code information, Carrier can determine the characteristics of a particular visitor's zip code area and match those characteristics with the kinds of products most likely to be needed by individuals in that zip code. For instance, website ads offer visitors with zip codes in wealthy areas air conditioning systems with remote controls. Visitors living in zip code areas with many multiple-family dwellings are offered window unit air conditioners. Carrier's technology allows it to offer the right product to the right site visitor in twenty milliseconds!

Returns from this system have been overwhelming. Revenues per visitor have increased from $1.47 to $37.42. And the number of individuals who have visited the site *and* made a purchase has increased 2,673 percent! How's that for a cool number?

Source: *From SellingPower.com,* CRM Newsletter *(October 8, 2001). Reprinted with permission.*

Efforts to Reduce Selling Costs. The median cost of a business-to-business sales call—although it varies widely by industry and company—is now more than $250. For some large industrial companies, unusual complexity of both the selling process and the product itself can lead to sales call costs of $400 to $1,000 or more.

To reduce selling costs, many manufacturers and service providers are aggressively seeking alternatives to large national sales forces. Some large manufacturers are cutting costs by reaching customers through distributors and other kinds of middlemen (for example, independent brokers and manufacturers' agents). Other companies are turning to part-time salespeople to help call on reseller customers such as wholesalers and retailers. Still others are using the techniques of **direct marketing,** such as direct mail, inbound and outbound **telemarketing,** and **teleselling** (conducting the entire sales process on "fast-forward" via telephone). Rather than fight or fear these additional sales methods, field salespeople should jump on the bandwagon and cooperate with these hybrid approaches to better serve customers and improve their companies' efficiency and effectiveness. The end result should be an increasing sales pie for all sales force members, no matter what the selling channel used to reach prospects and customers.

Direct Marketing Selling alternatives that bypass or partially substitute for field salespeople, including *direct mail, telemarketing, teleselling, kiosks, facsimile,* and *electronic mail.*

Telemarketing Use of telephone by support staff to help salespeople identify prospects, gather information, and answer inquiries.

Teleselling Conducting the entire personal selling process via telephone.

Shift to Direct-Marketing Alternatives. Several direct-marketing alternatives for selling to organizational buyers either support or bypass field salespeople. These include *direct mail, telemarketing, teleselling, kiosks, facsimile,* and *electronic mail.* The speed with which some direct-marketing methods, such as facsimile and e-mail, reach the customer has produced the nickname "salespeople on wings."

Direct Mail. "Snail mail" (or postal mail) remains an effective direct sales channel for many organizational buyers. With national "do-not-call" telephone lists and misleading e-mails that too often turn out to be spam, direct mail is one of the few ways to break through all the promotional clutter to reach customers at work or home. The fastest-growing segment of direct mail is catalog sales. Applying database marketing techniques, mailing list companies use computers to generate the names and addresses of prospects based on company demographics (for example, annual sales volume, type of products sold, number of employees, geographical location). For instance, a large office-products manufacturer restructured its sales force to reach approximately three million small businesses that it believed needed its products. Instead of making field sales calls on each prospect, though, it employed advertising and direct mail for many of the smallest businesses.

Telemarketing. A marketing strategy conducted by telephone to support or sometimes substitute for personal, face-to-face customer interactions is called *telemarketing.* Most often sellers use telemarketing to generate leads and qualify prospects. More than 250,000 U.S. businesses use either outbound or inbound telemarketing. *Outbound telemarketing* places telephone calls to customers at their businesses instead of making costly sales calls in person. Whereas a sales representative can average five face-to-face calls per day, a telemarketer can make up to fifteen phone contacts per hour. Although the final sale may not be closed over the telephone, telemarketers can qualify prospects for the field sales force to call upon. *Inbound telemarketing* uses an organization's inside sales personnel to respond to customers who call a toll-free number to obtain information or place orders. Such call-in leads from promotional campaigns can be targeted and prioritized for timely follow-up by the field sales force. Larger firms are using telemarketing to prospect and work with marginally profitable accounts. Smaller firms that cannot afford large field sales forces use telemarketing to expand their geographic markets. As shown in Figure 2.1, telemarketing has many applications, but it also has its strengths and weaknesses.

Teleselling. Teleselling represents a fundamental shift in buyer-seller relationships. Whereas telemarketing generally has the limited objective of generating *warm leads* to pass on to the field sales force, teleselling handles the *entire* selling process from beginning to end via telephone. Although the teleselling process resembles the traditional PSP steps, teleselling switches over to "fast-forward." Instead of being tightly scripted, as telemarketing is, teleselling uses a flexible but systematic approach much like a salesperson making a face-to-face sales call. Sophisticated database marketing allows telesellers to contact targeted prospects efficiently. IBM has moved many of its former field salespeople into teleselling cubicles, where some of the salespeople have sharply increased their annual sales and incomes by phoning prospects and customers considered too small for the field sales force to call on. Telesellers typically have high repeat-sales ratios because they provide customers with

APPLICATIONS	ADVANTAGES	DISADVANTAGES
• Prospecting • Setting sales appointments • Taking customer orders • Maintaining goodwill • Informing customers about new products and services • Notifying customers about special offers • Handling customer complaints • Reactivating past customers • Keeping contact with marginal accounts • Providing service • Answering customer inquiries	• Saves time • Low cost • Flexible • Convenient • Can reach almost anyone • Yields higher profits	• Lacks multisensory appeal (sight, touch, smell) • Obscures observable demographic information (age, sex, race) • Makes refusals easier • Incurs cost of telephone calls • Requires brief persuasive messages

FIGURE 2.1

TELEMARKETING APPLICATIONS, ADVANTAGES, AND DISADVANTAGES

buying convenience and prompt service. Teleselling is a cost-effective supplement or alternative to field sales. In organizational markets where large, complex sales and long negotiations require personal contact, numerous companies are using hybrid selling teams by combining telesales reps with field reps and telemarketers to achieve better market penetration and customer support. The accompanying *From the Command Post* feature discusses a company that has had great success in using a "talking" computer salesperson, which is featured on our textbook website, **http://college.hmco.com/pic/andersonps2e**.

Online Study Center
Improve Your Grade

Kiosks. In a growing number of organizations, kiosks (or "computer salespeople") are replacing their human counterparts. Many customers have become comfortable with self-service automated systems at banks, airports, and elsewhere, so they are increasingly willing to use interactive kiosks to make purchases. Kiosks are very efficient, low-cost salespeople when strategically placed and regularly monitored. Kiosks can also provide customers with the latest product availability information, calculate product operating costs, compare product price and features across models and with competitors' products, write up an order that reflects the customer's specific preferences, and instantly transmit the order to the factory for accelerated delivery. Toyota (www.toyota.com) and other automobile manufacturers have experienced considerable success with kiosk ordering of new vehicles at their dealerships.

Facsimile. Faxing is an increasingly popular and inexpensive way to deliver sales promotions and other information to prospects and customers, while avoiding wasteful unopened junk mail. A page of text or a chart can be faxed in about twenty seconds at the cost of a short long-distance phone call. Faxes overcome problems of delayed transportation, unreliable couriers, and frustrating games of telephone tag. A fax can be sent virtually anywhere in the world at any time, whether the receiving office is open or not, and the information will await the addressee's arrival. Some salespeople have successfully sold products and services by sending special offers to selected prospects and customers via fax, but this approach must be used with caution because it can turn prospects off, much as junk mail and spam do.

Personalized E-mail. Although it was discussed as one of the major technological megatrends, e-mail is such a low-cost yet effective form of direct marketing that it deserves to be discussed further as a key managerial megatrend. As part of their e-mail prospecting or sales presentations, some salespeople use embedded one-minute video info-commercial messages, personalized for different prospects. If called in advance or left voice mails to let them know that a customized video e-mail is coming, about 40 percent of prospects will open it. One marketing executive calls video mail the best prospecting tool his company has ever used.[13]

The prevalence of personal computers in U.S. businesses makes e-mail the least expensive way to contact prospects and customers at their offices or homes with minimal interruption. Although it can be extremely difficult to break through the clutter of unwanted spam, e-mails from a respected company or one familiar to the prospect will often be opened. But "phishing" scams—fraudulent e-mails or websites meant to trick people into supplying personal information—are making people less confident about opening e-mails from readily recognized companies. Even if only a small percentage of the e-mails are opened, however, it's still a very cost-effective from of communication. Applying this logic, many companies use e-mail—sometimes along with telemarketing and direct mail—as part of a sales campaign to reach prospects and customers. Salespeople who send e-mails to large numbers of prospects or customers simultaneously must be careful to obtain prior permission or use a carefully targeted e-mail address list. Most spam is commercial advertising, often for dubious products or get-rich-quick schemes, and few people are receptive to unwanted e-mail sales pitches. When sending a large volume of e-mails, therefore, astute salespeople first contact their Internet service provider (ISP) to ensure that the e-mails aren't seen as spam and electronically blocked. Even Harvard University (www.harvard.edu) fell into this trap once when their e-mail acceptance notifications to several hundred students were erroneously blocked by an Internet service provider (ISP) because they looked like spam. Since the mid-1990s, AOL (www.aol.com) and EarthLink (www.earthlink.com) have won millions of dollars in judgments and settlements against purveyors of spam under trespass, computer fraud, and specific anti-spam laws passed by nineteen states.

Despite its limitations, e-mailing is a powerful tool for simultaneously reaching many prospects and customers. E-mails have encouraged millions of people to go to websites for a vast array of both industrial and consumer products and services. Creative direct marketers will keep coming up with innovative approaches to contact prospects and customers electronically.

Certification of Salespeople. One way in which many companies and national sales organizations are trying to overcome negative stereotypes and gain status for salespeople is through professional certification. Professionals in other areas, such as finance and accounting, convey accomplishment and status with certifications such as CPA, CFA, or CFP. Two professional sales organizations—Sales and Marketing Executives International (SME-I) and the National Association of Sales Professionals (NASP)—have been in the vanguard of promoting salesperson certification. A salesperson, for example, who completes the NASP program and earns sufficient points (based on experience, training, professional involvement, and testing) receives designation as a Certified Professional Salesperson (CPSP). For more information about NASP professional sales certification, see: www.nasp.com/SiteFiles/Certification/certifcont.html. Sales certification is a positive response to customer demands for increased quality, trust, and professionalism in sales. Certification can identify someone as a respected sales professional who has met high standards of knowledge, skills, and ethics—thus enhancing the salesperson's professionalism and credibility. A salesperson who applies for certification usually must have a certain amount of practical experience, enroll in educational seminars and courses, pass a sales competency exam, provide some professional references, and agree to comply with a code of conduct. You may wish to consider becoming a certified professional salesperson to enhance your image with prospects and customers and to further your development for a successful, long-term sales career. Ask sales managers at your company for opinions about professional sales certification before contacting one of the aforementioned two professional sales organizations for more information. After earning certification as a professional salesperson, you might want to consider working next for American Marketing Association (AMA) certification as a *professional certified markete* (PCM). The expanding roles of salespeople are requiring them increasingly to perform like field marketing managers. For more information about PCM certification, see the following AMA website: *www.marketingpower.com/content591.php*. Read *Keeping Up Online* to obtain further insights into how you might benefit from becoming a member of Sales and Marketing Executives International.

Chapter Review Questions

Describe the three broad megatrends affecting personal selling.

What are some companies doing to reduce selling costs?

In your own words, define the term *direct marketing*. Describe some tools and techniques used in direct marketing.

Describe the type of assistance that salespeople may receive from the company's telemarketing staff. What can field salespeople do to increase the benefits they derive from telemarketers?

What is teleselling? How have many former field salespeople who were transferred to teleselling increased their incomes?

KEEPING UP ONLINE: SALES AND MARKETING EXECUTIVES INTERNATIONAL

Sales and Marketing Executives International (SME-I) is dedicated to enhancing the profession of sales and marketing. Its many members throughout the world network, learn, and socialize at regular meetings in their respective geographic locations. SME-I is especially focused on offering educational opportunities for its members. Members who have already graduated from college or even hold graduate degrees find that learning can never formally end in the fast-paced, ever-changing world of professional personal selling.

Investigate the SME-I website at www.smei.org to see how you might use SME-I right now. What benefits might SME-I offer you in your selling career? What other professional sales organizations might provide help as you advance in your selling career?

ADAPTING TO MEGATRENDS

Flexible and resourceful salespeople need not fear the proliferation of selling alternatives to sales reps. Successful selling still requires interpersonal skills and flexible sensitivity to design and carry out major parts of the sales and customer service process. Some telecommunication and computer innovations will partially substitute for salespeople in fulfilling certain sales activities, such as prospecting or routine order taking. Their more significant role, however, will be to help professional salespeople do their jobs more effectively and efficiently, especially in selling to organizations.

Many progressive sales organizations are spending millions of dollars each year preparing their salespeople through education, training, and the latest telecommunication equipment to deal with and fully exploit this dynamism. Top-performing salespeople, however, must remain vigilant to spot trends that will affect them and become early adopters of new technologies and selling tools to better serve their customers, their companies, and themselves. These confident, professional salespeople know that the changes unfolding can confer many benefits as well as challenges.

Not only do virtually all salespeople use technology; they also sell it. For example, U.S. companies and consumers spend over $400 billion annually on computer hardware, software, and technology services. Despite earnings that range between $110,000 and $200,000 when they meet quota and can exceed $1,000,000 for top performers, skilled technology salespeople are hard to find.[14] In fact, there will be a significant shortage of technology salespeople by 2010.[15] The selling world is indeed a 'changin'—and sales professionals who are flexible and adaptable can become a productive part of it.

Trends in Information Management

Behind the megatrends that influence salespeople and how they operate are key trends in information management. Four of these trends are database marketing, data warehousing, data mining, and push technology. Each of these can influence the way salespeople do their jobs. Let's briefly discuss each.

Database Marketing Computerized analysis of sales transaction databases to identify customer purchase patterns and profiles to better serve target markets.

Database Marketing. Most companies collect massive amounts of information from diverse sources about prospects and customers for their computerized database. The sheer size of some of these databases is astounding; for example, Ford Motor Company (www.ford.com) has 50 million names, Citicorp (www.citicorp.com) 30 million, Kimberly Clark (www.kimberly-clark.com) 10 million, and Kraft General Foods (www.kraft.com) 2.5 million. General Motors (www.gm.com) has a database of 12 million GM credit card holders, giving it ready access to detailed data on their buying habits. **Database marketing** is a computerized process for analyzing these databases to identify customer purchase patterns and profiles that will enable the company to develop customized products, sales strategies, and personalized service for profitable target customer groups. Database marketing can provide insightful analyses, including

- Determining the most profitable and least profitable customers
- Identifying the best-selling and most profitable products and services
- Targeting sales efforts with greater efficiency and effectiveness
- Developing creative ways to repackage and re-price products and services to better satisfy market segments
- Evaluating opportunities for developing profitable new products and services.

Database marketing relies on sales and marketing information systems that collect the details of individual or company purchase transactions. For example, when a customer makes a purchase using a credit card or loyalty card, a database simultaneously records the store or vendor name, location, date of the purchase, product type, and purchase price, and all of this information is associated with an identified purchaser. Over time, a transaction history and profile are created for every customer.

Database marketing also offers tremendous opportunities for cross-selling related products. For instance, after doing an analysis of its database of 1.3 million customers, Canon Computer Systems (www.usa.canon.com) conducted a direct-mail campaign that asked computer printer owners whether they would like information on a new color scanner. Buyers of the scanners were offered four ink cartridges free for their printers. Canon obtained a whopping 50 percent response rate. Such complementary insights into product purchase patterns can also be translated into more effective strategies for field salespeople.

Data Warehouse Corporate-wide database built from information systems already in place in the company.

Data Warehousing. A **data warehouse** (or information warehouse) is essentially an immense corporate-wide customer database, built with data from diverse information systems already in place in the company that can be shared across all functional departments. American Airlines (www.aa.com) gathers customer information from all its customer touch points. The data collected includes demographics, take-off points and destinations, prices paid, and hotel accommodations. When customers call, e-mail, or connect to the American Airlines website, they are immediately recognized and classified as to their relative profitability to AA. Then, on the basis of their past purchase preferences, they are offered a customized package that might include recommendations for hotels, car rentals, and vacation packages in addition to flight options. Data warehouses facilitate customization of product and service to match preanalyzed customer desires, thereby increasing customer satisfaction and long-term relationships.

Using a company's computer database, salespeople can instantly access the latest information on inventory levels, price changes, product shortages, delivery schedules, and the like.
Corbis

Smaller *data marts* group information from the data warehouse into formats pertaining to specific strategic initiatives. A company, for instance, may have one data mart for market segmentation, another for ad campaign management, and a third for forecasting product sales. Each data mart is continually optimized for its designated task.

A data warehouse can be enhanced with information obtained from third-party suppliers. For example, lifestyle classifications or demographic information such as estimated household income and educational level added to customer profiles can aid decision making. Similarly, demographic data such as company size, annual sales, geographic locations, growth rates, typical purchase order size, and the like can be collected and analyzed for business customers.

Push Technology Combination of data warehousing and e-mail to retrieve and send relevant information to prospects and customers.

Push Technology. Using data warehousing along with the latest iteration of e-mail to automatically send relevant information to prospects and customers is called **push technology**.

E-mail is considered push technology because the salesperson proactively arranges for the message to be *pushed* out to recipients. Once push technology is set in motion, the desired information is automatically delivered to designated customers. Without requiring any additional effort after the initial setup, push technology enables salespeople to continually provide their customers with timely information and services. Many salespeople who own handheld multi-function devices such as the BlackBerry, use push technology to have their personal e-mails automatically forwarded to them, along with discreet notification that a new message has arrived.

The key to a successful push strategy is knowing exactly what your customers need and exactly when they want it. Among the first applications of push technology were news retrieval services that delivered, via e-mail, news articles containing user-specified key words. For example, if Dell (www.dell.com), a business customer, depends on Microsoft (www.microsoft.com) for key software products such as Windows, lawsuits filed against Microsoft might force changes in its software products, thereby changing what Dell could promote as prepackaged software with its computers. By submitting keywords, such as “Microsoft, lawsuits, Windows,” Dell would receive via e-mail any news articles containing these three words, in any order. Companies can use this same technology to keep track of how they’re being written about and perceived in news articles.

Another application of push technology is in the sale, distribution, and upgrade of software applications. When the software vendor completes the latest upgrade, it can electronically upgrade its customer’s computers, with minimal or no customer involvement. Whether a breaking news article concerning a customer, an alert about an unexpected increase in the price of a product, or notification that your computer software has been updated while you were at a meeting, push technology provides the precise type of information you specified for receipt and delivery.

Success in personal selling depends on close relationships with customers and “selling through” by understanding the changing wants and needs of your customers’ customers. Push technology, skillfully employed, can enhance those relationships by making sure customers have the latest, relevant information. When the right information is supplied at the right time, customers and salespeople are more likely to enter communication and negotiations with the benefit of shared understandings. Push technology will become an increasingly valuable tool for salespeople in keeping their customers informed.

Data Mining. Insights about markets and customers can be obtained through sophisticated analytical techniques collectively known as data mining. More precisely, data mining is the process of using statistical analysis to detect relevant hidden patterns in a customer database. Data mining software accesses the data warehouse and uses quantitative tools such as decision trees, cluster analysis, neural networks, and regression analysis to detect underlying relationships between and among variables. To illustrate, researchers found through data mining that fathers often buy beer as an impulse purchase when buying baby diapers. Displaying beer close to the diapers increased sales of both products. Wal-Mart (www.walmart.com) uses data mining to identify customer purchasing patterns, such as what products are typically bought together (for example, bananas and read-to-eat cereals, or tissues and nonprescription cold medicines). Through data mining, Wal-Mart controls inventory costs, boosts sales, and improves shoppers' satisfaction.

Data Mining Using statistical tools, such as decision trees, cluster analysis, and regression analysis, to detect relevant customer purchase patterns between and among variables in a database.

Many other companies are using data mining techniques to create customer profiles; analyze the potential return for different pricing, promotion, and direct-mail strategies; forecast sales; and generally improve customer satisfaction and loyalty. Salespeople can further their long-term customer relationships by sharing data mining insights that help their customers profitably sell through to their own customers.

Information management reports can help salespeople better assess, analyze, anticipate, and serve customer needs.
José Luis Pelaez, Inc./CORBIS

Information Management and Relationship Selling

As we have seen, information management includes various forms of database technology, all of which are readily available to salespeople for assessing, analyzing, anticipating, and serving customer needs. Resourceful salespeople will make use of these systematically designed and implemented database technologies to develop long-term, personalized, and profitable relationships with each of their customers. Information management and relationship selling go hand in hand as part of the evolutionary development of a marketing strategy called one-to-one marketing.

One-to-One Marketing. **One-to-one marketing** represents a sharp philosophical change from the traditional view of customers as a mass market to seeing them as individuals. Instead of trying to increase market share by selling more goods to more customers, one-to-one marketing concentrates on selling more goods, more profitably to selected customers. It seeks a larger share of individual customers' wallets or expenditures, rather than a larger share of some mass market. Rather than finding customers for products, one-to-one marketing focuses on developing ongoing relationships

One-to-One Marketing A philosophical change from the traditional approach of looking at customers as a mass market to viewing customers as individuals. One-to-one marketing seeks to sell more products to fewer (selected) customers, rather than more products to more customers.

with individual customers by providing them with exactly the products and services they want.

One-to-one marketing is not new by any means. General store owners back in the 1800s were one-to-one marketers because they knew and served the exact tastes and preferences of their relatively few customers. In this era of giant sellers with thousands of customers, it was nearly impossible to meet the tastes and preferences of individual customers until database technologies emerged. Today, marketing strategists and salespeople use database technologies to identify the specific customers they want to cultivate; then they tailor products, services, and communications to meet the customer's precise expectations. One of the nation's largest financial services companies, KeyCorp (www.keycorp.net), achieved a more than 350 percent return on investment by implementing one-to-one marketing. By collecting customer profiles, interests, activities, and goals on its website and integrating these profiles into its database, KeyCorp dramatically increased its ability to meet the financial expectations of its customers and cross-sell them other products via direct mail, teleselling, and the Internet.[16]

Salespeople: One-to-One Relationship Builders. Ultimately, the quality of individual relationships that salespeople develop with customers will determine the success of one-to-one marketing strategies, especially in business-to-business markets. Salespeople are the companies' real one-to-one customer relationship builders and sustainers. Tampering with these long-term customer relationships can be disastrous. To illustrate, Xerox (www.xerox.com) management almost bankrupted the company when it too hastily reorganized its various sales forces and, in the process, severed many long-term customer-salesperson relationships and lost countless sales.

By taking full advantage of the customized information that database technologies provide, resourceful salespeople can better learn and even better anticipate their individual customers' exact needs and expectations—and then provide them with the products and services and positive relationship experiences that contribute to cumulative customer satisfaction and loyalty. Today's professional salespeople are empowered like no previous generation of salespeople to effectively and efficiently do their sales jobs for themselves and their companies. As database technologies and applications increase in sophistication, they will no doubt continue to enhance salespeople's abilities to further long-term, trusting, satisfying, and profitable one-to-one relationships with customers.

Chapter Review Question
How are information management trends affecting salespeople?

PROFESSIONAL SALESPEOPLE AS CUSTOMER RELATIONSHIP MANAGERS

As the aforementioned megatrends and information trends continue to evolve and influence personal selling and buyer-seller relationships, the role of salespeople will continue to expand and change. Instead of merely selling products, today's business-to-business salespeople are expected to function as customer relationship managers, serving a wide variety of customer needs and offering customers expert advice on making their business operations more profitable. Their expanding CRM responsibilities to provide cumulative full customer satisfaction and sustain customer loyalty require them to perform diverse, expanding roles, including the following:

- *Customer Partners:* Today's salespeople cannot merely know their own company's business; they must also thoroughly understand their customers' businesses—as well as the businesses of their customers' customers. They must develop partnerships with customers and help them "sell-through" to their customers in order to achieve competitive advantages and increased profitability.
- *Buyer-Seller Team Coordinators:* Modern salespeople must know how to use backup organizational specialists from both seller and buyer teams in marketing research, traffic management, engineering, finance, operations, and customer services to solve customer problems.
- *Market Analysts and Planners:* Salespeople must monitor changes in the marketing environment, especially competitive actions, and help devise strategies and tactics to adjust to these changes and satisfy customers.
- *Customer Service Providers:* Today's prospects and customers generally expect a high level of service. They want problem-solving advice, technical assistance, financing information, and expedited deliveries. After making a sale, salespeople must continually follow up with customers to ensure that the product is fully meeting customer expectations.
- *Buyer Behavior Experts:* Salespeople must study customer purchase decision processes and buyer motivations in order to better communicate with and serve customers.
- *Opportunity Spotters:* Salespeople who remain alert to unsatisfied or unrecognized customer needs and potential problems are able to recommend new products, new markets, or innovative marketing mixes to their own companies.
- *Intelligence Gatherers:* Providing informational feedback from the field to headquarters marketing for use in strategic and tactical planning is an important part of the salesperson's job. Salespeople are still the frontline "eyes and ears" of their companies.
- *Sales Forecasters:* Sales managers need salespeople's help in estimating future sales and setting sales quotas for territorial assignments and markets.
- *Marketing Cost Analysts:* Professional salespeople should concentrate on profitable sales rather than merely on sales volume or quotas. To accomplish this objective, companies first need to share profit information with their salespeople, and many now do so because it can lead to more profitable sales.
- *Allocators of Scarce Products:* Periodically, products are in short supply and are demanded by competing customers; oil and gas products are a good example. Customer relationships can become especially difficult during these times. Many customers will become resentful and even switch suppliers if they believe salespeople have treated them unfairly in allocating scarce products.
- *Field Public Relations People:* Because they deal with customers on a daily basis, salespeople must handle many customer problems, concerns, and

complaints that require sensitivity and public relations skills. Professional salespeople recognize that long-term relationships with customers matter more than profit on any one transaction.

- *Adopters of Advanced Sales Technology:* Rising personal selling costs are requiring sales reps to adopt new technologies to improve their efficiency and effectiveness in serving customers.

Today's salespeople must perform these multiple roles while serving customers in dynamic world markets that are continuously changing in response to the inexorable behavioral, technological, and managerial forces we have discussed in this chapter. In order to keep their professional edge, salespeople must remain alert to rapidly emerging market opportunities and challenges that significantly affect how they serve their customers and represent their companies. Their daily interactions with customers put salespeople in the best position to inform their companies' management about recent competitors' actions, changing customer needs, and the latest market developments. Just like professional athletes who never stop trying their hardest whether they are far behind or far ahead in a game, professional salespeople strive to do their best every day for their customers, their companies, their families, and themselves.

Chapter Review Question

Why must today's professional salesperson learn to function more like a micro-marketing manager in the field?

SUMMARY

Several megatrends are changing the way salespeople engage in their job tasks and carry out their responsibilities. These trends can be categorized as behavioral, technological, and managerial. First, several market or customer developments are having a profound impact on how field salespeople function. Second, revolutionary advances in telecommunication technology are helping salespeople do their jobs better but, in some cases, partially replacing salespeople. Third, sales organizations' efforts at cost reduction, their increasing use of direct-marketing alternatives, and salesperson certification are affecting buyer-seller interactions and relationships. Given these major forces, today's salespeople work in dramatically changing selling environments and must increasingly operate like micro-marketing managers in their territories.

KEY TERMS

Sales Megatrends
Teleselling
Data Mining
Direct Marketing
Database Marketing
Push Technology
Telemarketing
Data Warehouse
One-to-One Marketing

TOPICS FOR THOUGHT AND CLASS DISCUSSION

1. Which of the advances in telecommunications and computer technology do you think will provide the most help to salespeople over the next decade?
2. Discuss how you think salespeople can take advantage of each of the phenomena taking place under the managerial megatrend.
3. How do you think the rising cost of personal selling and the growth of direct-marketing techniques will affect salespeople?

INTERNET EXERCISES

1. Many major companies sell more products and services online via e-commerce than they do in traditional brick-and-mortar stores or outlets. Check out the websites of each of the following companies and see whether they offer purchasing options online. Also, try to find out their dollar sales volumes online and off-line to compare.
   - Cisco Systems (www.cisco.com)
   - Williams-Sonoma (www.williams-sonoma.com)
   - Pitney Bowes (www.pitneybowes.com)
   - Staples (www.staples.com)
2. Salespeople need to keep up with the latest technologies (including computer software) that might affect how they do their sales jobs. Go to the following websites, or to other professional selling-related websites, and find three innovations that you think will help salespeople become more effective and efficient. Describe these innovations, and explain why you feel each will increase salesperson productivity.
   - Sales and Marketing Management (www.salesandmarketing.com/smm/index.jsp)
   - Siebel Systems (www.siebel.com)
   - SalesForce.com (www.salesforce.com)
   - SellingPower.com (www.sellingpower.com)

PROJECTS FOR PERSONAL GROWTH

1. Assume that a firm has divided the United States into ten regional markets based on need for its products—industrial lawn mowers, lawn sweepers, watering equipment, and garden tools. Also assume that the company's CEO has asked you to prepare a map of the United States showing these regional markets. Clearly label each region according to how you identify it. For example, perhaps part of the southwestern United States has different needs owing to the terrain and desert-like environment of the area, whereas part of Florida may be identified with abundant moisture, humidity, and tropical plants. Do any library research necessary to complete your map.
2. Ask two business-to-business salespeople about telecommunication use in their sales work. What SFA equipment has been most helpful to them? Why? How have their companies assisted them in selling and in serving prospects and customers? What other equipment would they like? What other support would they like from their companies in helping them work with prospects and customers?

ROLE-PLAY EXERCISE 2.1

Considering Alternatives To Door-to-Door Selling

Situation

For the past sixteen years, Nina Sanchez has been the major owner of a small manufacturing firm, Lovely Look Cosmetics, Inc., that makes and sells a line of women's cosmetics to small retail outlets. Company sales have declined about 15 percent a year in each of the past four years in the three states where Lovely Look products are sold: Delaware, Pennsylvania, and New Jersey. All 35 employees own part of the private company and participate in a profit-sharing plan. There are 15 salespeople, 12 production workers, and 8 managers.

Ms. Sanchez scheduled an emergency company meeting this weekend for all employees to discuss strategies and tactics for dealing with declining sales. After a half-hour continental breakfast for all attendees, Ms. Sanchez outlined some of the problems that the company was facing:

- Increased price competition from other cosmetics manufacturers.
- High costs of selling (salespeople receive a small salary but a 30 percent commission on sales as an incentive and to cover their automobile expenses). Several salespeople have already complained that the 30 percent commission on sales is too low even to cover their travel costs fully, so there is nothing left over as an incentive to make cold calls.

Ms. Sanchez said that they need to focus on the possibility of switching out of field selling to some other way of reaching prospects and customers, such as

- Direct mail (catalogs and flyers)
- Telemarketing
- Party-plans during lunch at business offices
- Selling to some large retailers

Roles

Nina Sanchez This role calls for a student who can project the confidence, leadership, and diplomacy to solicit input from her employees without making snap judgments. It should be left up to her employees to make favorable or unfavorable comments about the ideas of others. However, Ms. Sanchez can point out potential problems that need to be worked out regarding each strategy—for example, "As a very small manufacturer, how would we obtain distribution through large retail stores in competition with national cosmetics brands?"

Owner-Employees of Lovely Look, Inc. One student should be assigned to try to make a succinct case at the meeting for each of the options for selling to prospects and customers, including the option of continuing to sell "door-to-door." Other innovative alternatives to field selling should be encouraged.

ROLE-PLAY EXERCISE 2.2

Personal and Professional Concerns of Saleswomen

Situation

Susan Dunmeyer, who will graduate this year with a bachelor's degree in business from Western Michigan University, is interviewing for a job with Farley Industries, Inc., a medium-sized office furniture manufacturer, that sells through industrial distributors and direct to some large companies. Susan is a B+ student who has been active in campus activities, although she has not held any offices. Susan has a boyfriend, Bruce Dusinberre, who will be graduating at the same time with a degree in engineering. They expect to be married within about two years, after they have gotten their careers under way.

Only five feet tall and weighing exactly 100 pounds, Susan is not sure that sales is right for her, but she wanted to take the interview to get some more perspectives on sales as a possible career choice. Susan is concerned about several things in selecting a career:

- Traveling away from home, especially after she begins having children
- Whether her small size will be a disadvantage in sales
- Dealing with sexual overtures from customers and colleagues
- Taking male customers to dinner as part of her sales job
- How to get male buyers to take her seriously if she is selling a complex, technical product
- How Bruce, her future husband, might react if she were eventually to make more money than he does

Susan is being interviewed by Esther Edmunds, district sales manager for Farley Industries. Esther Edmunds graduated from Western Michigan eight years ago. A standout on the women's basketball team at WMU, Esther exhibits great confidence and a "can-do" spirit that seems contagious to others interacting with her. She thinks personal selling is a great career, especially for women and minorities, because performance evaluations in this field are so much more objective than in many other jobs.

Roles

Susan Dunmeyer Susan is seeking more information to help her make up her mind about sales as a career choice. Although most people don't think she's particularly shy, Susan is concerned about her lack of aggressiveness and believes her small size may make it difficult for her to be successful in sales. She once read that tall people tend to be more successful than short people in personal selling. Susan is also worried about traveling overnight, staying alone in hotels, and having her car break down at night in a strange area. Finally, she has heard that jobs in sales pay well, and she's not sure how her future husband will take it if she out-earns him.

Esther Edmunds Ms. Edmunds has interviewed many female applicants for sales jobs over the years, and she can remember her own concerns. She likes to reassure women about personal selling as a career by telling about her concerns and actual experiences. She feels that there is no other career where she could be making as much money and enjoying as much freedom as she does in sales. An African-American, she feels that her own best chance for a top management position is through the personal selling and sales management career path. She believes so strongly in sales for women and minorities that she considers it a personal failure if she is unable to convince a woman or member of a minority group that the advantages in personal selling far outweigh the disadvantages.

CASE 2.1 SAVORING SUCCESS AND CONTEMPLATING THE FUTURE

Gloria Pattengale was eating dinner with two of her United Business Technologies (UBT) colleagues, Vickie Brodo and Deborah Coyle, at one of the best restaurants in Los Angeles. The three had just finished three weeks of training as new sales representatives, and the dinner was part of their reward from UBT for finishing at the top of their training class. Out of twenty new sales trainees participating in the program—eight women and twelve men—Vickie had finished third, Deborah second, and Gloria first in overall scores on the six training categories: (1) role-plays, (2) product demonstrations, (3) case analyses, (4) written exams, (5) use of sales force automation (SFA) equipment, and (6) peer ratings. Now, for the first time in weeks, they could relax and reflect on their experiences and what might be ahead for them at UBT. They all knew UBT quickly assigns newly trained sales representatives to individual sales territories.

While sipping their drinks and waiting for dinner, the three friends talked about the rigorous training they had just completed. They had had almost no time for relaxation, not even on weekends, because each Friday night instructors assigned time-consuming projects, such as preparing PowerPoint sales proposals or sales presentations for hypothetical customers, for completion by Monday morning. None of the three could remember ever undergoing such sustained pressure. Let's listen in on their conversation.

GLORIA PATTENGALE: I'm sure glad I took that selling and sales management course in college. I'd done a lot of this stuff before—like role-playing and preparing sales presentations and case analyses using PowerPoint—but the UBT sales training was still the most intense pressure I've ever been under. I worked a lot harder here than I did in college. Bet some of the guys are mad because none of them ranked in the top three. They're probably having pizza tonight while we dine in the style I'd like to become accustomed to.

(continued)

VICKIE BRODO: Earning 98 percent on that last exam made the difference for me. I just barely beat out Tom Bajier, who came up strong on the final exam, too.

DEBORAH COYLE: Well, we all made it. Let's drink a toast to UBT's next three superstar salespeople.

VICKIE BRODO: It feels great to be a winner!

GLORIA PATTENGALE: It sure does. But to be honest, I get a little nervous just thinking about going out into my own territory within a few days. We didn't have any training about what it's like for a woman traveling a sales territory. I wish we'd had some women trainers. I'm not sure men really understand some of the problems we can run into.

DEBORAH COYLE: I agree. What are we going to do when we stay overnight at a hotel? I don't want to go down to the hotel lounge alone, and I know I'm going to get bored sitting around in the room. Guess I'll just watch a movie on television or read some good books.

VICKIE BRODO: You know what really worries me? Trying to do everything they expect of us *besides* selling. Did you see that list of salesperson duties the national sales manager put up during his lecture? Wow! All that talk about "selling through" to our customers' customers, and about serving as business partners and consultants to our customers, was too much. I just want to sell products to my customers and keep them satisfied. I'm not going to know enough about my customers' customers or their businesses to offer them consulting advice. They'd probably resent it anyway . . . coming from a 23-year old woman on her first full-time job.

GLORIA PATTENGALE: Yeah, I agree. And that wasn't all. Do you remember he said that we had to be the company's "eyes and ears" in the field by gathering intelligence about competitors' actions and changing customer needs? Won't the customers tell us their needs? I'm sure not going to spend valuable selling time trying to gather "intelligence"—whatever that means. Isn't that supposed to be the job of marketing research?

DEBORAH COYLE: What worried me was when he said we need to ensure that we allocate our time to those customers and products that are most profitable. We didn't really cover that in our training. We don't even have access to total sales and profit information for our customers. Boy, if we do all the stuff they're talking about, what's left for the sales managers to do? All I'm interested in is making my sales quota and winning one of those exotic overseas trips.

VICKIE BRODO: It's great being assigned a company car with a phone plus a nice laptop computer. One of the guys said the car and computer could be picked up as early as Monday if we go into the office. With my new laptop, I plan to stay in touch with my customers weekly by sending them e-mails. Maybe I'll even prepare a monthly newsletter to let my customers know about stuff like upcoming price changes, inventory shortages, and new-product introductions. I think I'll call it Vickie's News and Views. I could send it as an e-mail attachment.

DEBORAH COYLE: Hey, I like that idea, Vickie! Maybe, we won't have to make so many sales calls if we handle more stuff by e-mail. Nobody said we had to make all our sales calls in person, did they?

GLORIA PATTENGALE: Say, maybe we could do a lot of the personal selling process on the Internet. I might set up a website for my prospects and customers that will show them our product line and give them all kinds of information that they would usually ask me about. In fact, I'll bet somebody in the Information Technology (IT) Department would put a video on my website demonstrating how each of our products works. I know we've got a videotape like that because the CEO shows it to the financial community to promote our company and keep its stock price up. You know if we used our heads and the Internet, we could spend a lot less time doing all the paperwork involved in working with customers.

VICKIE BRODO: Sorry, gals, but I've got to go. Let's plan on meeting next week around this time to discuss some more of our brilliant ideas about how to make our jobs easier. Let's each bring at least five ideas to discuss next time, Okay? Well, gotta run. See ya!

Questions

1. In their conversation, do the women seem unnecessarily concerned about taking on their new territorial assignments? Do you think any special issues arise for saleswomen but not for salesmen? Why or why not?
2. Do the women have an accurate understanding of what many salespeople are expected to do today? Why or why not? What can the company do to help its salespeople handle their expanded roles?
3. Are the women's ideas about making their sales jobs easier realistic? Which ones make the most sense? Which ones make the least sense? Could the company provide a lot of this information for customers on an extranet or on the Internet?
4. Assume you are a friend of one of the women. What five ideas would you give her about using the Internet and other telecommunication tools to make her more effective and efficient in her sales assignments?
5. Do you think the use of high-tech equipment—laptop computers, cell phones, pagers, and the like—will help the young saleswomen appear more professional?

CASE 2.2 WE'RE TRYING TO CUT COSTS . . . WE CAN'T AFFORD LAPTOPS NOW!

CASE 2.2 "WE'RE TRYING TO CUT COSTS . . . WE CAN'T AFFORD LAPTOPS NOW!" CAN BE FOUND ONLINE AT HTTP://COLLEGE.HMCO.COM/PIC/ANDERSONPS2E

CHAPTER 3

Ethical and Legal Considerations in Personal Selling

After reading this chapter, you should understand:

- What ethics are and why there is no universally accepted standard for ethics.
- Ethical concerns of salespeople in dealing with customers, competitors, employers, and co-workers.
- Behavior that salespeople have a right to expect from their employers.
- Legal and ethical issues in foreign markets.
- How to approach ethical decisions.

"The reputation of a thousand years is determined by the conduct of one hour."

Japanese proverb

INSIDE PERSONAL SELLING

Meet Renata Bitoy of Houghton Mifflin

Ethical questions can arise in any personal selling situation, even when the product is a college textbook. Just ask Renata Bitoy, a sales representative for the College Division of Boston-based Houghton Mifflin Company. Bitoy travels to campuses in the Midwest, visiting with professors to discuss their needs and presenting her company's textbooks and educational materials.

During the comprehensive training all new sales reps receive, Bitoy and her colleagues were introduced to Houghton Mifflin's standards of ethical behavior and its Code of Employee Conduct. The code lays out company policies and procedures related to payments and gift giving, discrimination, sexual harassment, conflict of interest, privacy and confidentiality, fraudulent behavior, and other workplace issues.

"In our training course, we discussed relationship building with the professors and the administrative support staff," remembers Bitoy. "We are in this business for the long term, and if you want to build strong relationships, you must earn the customer's respect and show you are genuinely interested in improving how students learn."

Misrepresentation, for example, is inappropriate and unprofessional: "You have to be honest with the professors to gain

their trust and keep their business year after year," she says. For this reason, she is careful never to disparage another publisher's books or mislead professors about the availability of a textbook.

When professors are trying to decide which textbook to assign, they frequently request a free review copy of each text under consideration. But what happens to review copies after the decision has been made? Most unadopted textbooks are placed in the department library as a resource for students and faculty. Bitoy prefers this because the text is in use and visible, which means the department may consider it later.

"Some departments don't have the space and ask that I pick up the texts," she says. "Then I can place them at another school for consideration. On occasion, however, a text will be sold to a used-book vendor. This is problematic because books sold to used-book vendors will ultimately increase the price that students pay for textbooks in the future. In my tenure at Houghton Mifflin I have come across only one instructor who abused the system." Her solution to this ethical question, therefore, is to discover as much as possible about her customers, their teaching needs, and their patterns.

"The more you learn about your customers, the better you can determine how to proceed in a particular situation," says Bitoy. "Some situations have the potential for higher value over time. You have to determine how much service to provide in each case." This is a delicate balancing act, because the actions Bitoy takes today will influence the future course of her relationship with her customers.

Throughout your life, you've undoubtedly faced difficult issues that forced you to make decisions concerning what's right and what's wrong. In a few instances, you may have experienced tremendous conflict about the issue; in others, you made your decision without hesitation. Some situations probably provided no guidelines for decision making; in others, some general policies or philosophies were available to guide you. Ethical issues confront all of us every day, and dealing with them can be fraught with great uncertainty and uneasiness. As you move into your professional selling career, ethical issues will abound in great variety and complexity. Your successful attention to ethical concerns will contribute significantly to your ultimate effectiveness as a salesperson—as well as to your satisfaction with your career choice.

Some people seem to have developed almost an immunity or insensitivity to high ethical standards. Individuals cheat in school and on their income tax returns, their resumés, their insurance claims, and almost anywhere the chances of detection are low. Don't despair, though, there is some good news. People seem to be getting fed up with such ethical decay, and many are calling for adherence to higher standards of conduct by politicians, businesspeople—and perhaps even ourselves.

WHAT ARE ETHICS?

Ethics Moral code of conduct and principles that govern individuals and societies in determining what is right or wrong.

Ethics may be defined as the study of what is good and bad or right and wrong. Conceptually, ethics comprise a moral code of conduct and principles governing individuals and societies that deals with matters as they *should* be, not necessarily as they are. For hundreds and even thousands of years, different societies have measured human conduct by rigorous standards set forth in such religious sources as the Bible, the Torah, or the Qur'an. In modern industrial society, however, there has been a trend toward accepting more secular guidance, where there is no universally reognized or consistent code of conduct. Misconduct that is not illegal is seldom clearly defined or agreed upon.[1] People may differ widely about what constitutes ethical or unethical behavior, especially in complex, competitive societies. For example, a recent study found that somewhere between 70 and 85 percent of today's college students cheat on their exams.[2] Thus, thorough analysis and evaluation must precede the development of ethical standards for business decision making. And perhaps we should keep in mind the view of the great humanitarian Dr. Albert Schweitzer, who described ethics as "an obligation to consider not only our own personal well-being, but also that of other human beings."

Business Ethics Build Trust in Relationships

In business, a decision that is "right" or "wrong" has too often been made on the basis of *economic* criteria. Arthur Andersen, Enron, Global Crossing, MCI World Com, Adelphia, and HealthSouth are some of the companies whose downfall in recent years has been attributed to executive behavior based largely on economic criteria that overstepped the boundaries of ethical conduct into illegality. Beyond breaking their company's bonds of trust in their relationships with customers, suppliers, shareholders, and employees, these business scandals have brought about new government scrutiny and legislation affecting salespeople, which we will discuss later in this chapter.

A relationship of most any kind, and certainly a business relationship, must be built on a foundation of *mutual trust* between the buyer and seller. In a sales context, trust has been defined as "one party's belief that its needs will be met in the future by actions undertaken by the other party."[3] In other words, trust is a mutual belief, shared by parties in a relationship, that each will live up to the obligations it has assumed. Trust requires confidence in another party's reliability and integrity in situations where vulnerability and risk are often present.[4] How is trust manifested and built over time? Only by consistent ethical behavior by the parties developing a relationship can mutual trust be established and maintained. Ethical behaviors are the critical building blocks in bringing about a trustful relationship that both buyer and seller perceive as "win-win." However, like a fine vase, trust can be very fragile and must be handled with forethought and care at all times. Trust may take years to build, but it can be broken by one careless decision or action. We will discuss trust in more depth as a critical element in building relationships in chapter 8.

KEEPING UP ONLINE: E-CENTER FOR BUSINESS ETHICS

At the *E-Center for Business Ethics,* you can find insightful information and perspectives about business ethics and corporate codes of conduct. You can also enroll in a ten-week online program leading to an "Ethics Certificate." Visit the center's website at **www.e-businessethics.com.** How might salespeople benefit from earning an ethics certificate?

Salesperson Ethics Must Go Beyond Legal Requirements

Some salespeople have the idea that if it's legal, it's ethical. But people are not ethical simply because they stay within the law. Ethical behavior and legal behavior are not the same. A salesperson can be dishonest, unprincipled, untrustworthy, unfair, and uncaring without breaking the law.[5] In fact, some businesspeople have two sets of ethical standards—one that they use in their personal life and one that they employ in the office. And the set that guides their personal conduct is likely to be on a higher moral plane than their "office ethics." Many U.S. companies recognize this problem; indeed, more than 38 percent offer ethics training,[6] and about 20 percent of large corporations have appointed ethics officers.[7]

Most of us would probably agree that doing what we personally believe is wrong is unethical. Thus a salesperson who believes that it's wrong to pressure prospects to buy a product that they don't really need, yet does so anyway, is acting unethically. Salespeople must work assiduously at being ethical at all times. Why? Because it's the right thing to do, and because a salesperson's reputation for ethical behavior and integrity is one of the most valuable assets he or she can bring to negotiations with prospects and customers. Shakespeare described the importance of guarding one's reputation in act 3, scene 3 of *Othello:*

> Who steals my purse steals trash; 'tis something, nothing;
> 'Twas mine, 'tis his, and has been slave to thousands;
> But he that filches from me my good name
> Robs me of that which not enriches him
> And makes me poor indeed.

Once a salesperson's reputation is damaged, it is extremely hard to repair, and at the very least, doing so takes a long, long time. Don't ever allow yourself to be tempted to do anything unethical, because nothing will destroy your career faster. Read *Keeping Up Online* to see how you can add to your knowledge of ethical issues.

Ethical Image of Salespeople

By far, the vast majority of sales reps are strongly ethical. However, largely because of its persuasive nature, high visibility, direct contact with customers—

ON THE FRONTLINES

Honesty Is Not for Sale

Salespeople constantly face ethical dilemmas. These dilemmas may occur between sales managers and salespeople, between salespeople, and (most likely) between salespeople and their customers. Because money is involved in selling to customers, this interaction is especially ripe for ethical conflicts. How salespeople choose to react to each ethical situation will have a long-term effect on their company and their personal success.

Some buyers may try to "bait" salespeople to determine how they will react to a questionable request. Their intent is to separate ethical salespeople from unethical ones, remaining a customer of the former and removing the latter from further consideration.

To illustrate, a salesperson may be calling on a prospective company that could become a major account. As the initial sales interview approaches its conclusion, the buyer, in what appears to be an earnest question, asks the salesperson, "How much of a kickback (i.e., bribe) will I receive, given the unusually large size of my order?" How the salesperson responds to this question will probably affect subsequent business with the individual. Assuming, of course, that the buyer is ethical, which is generally the case, the buyer is seeking a response that demonstrates high ethical conduct on the part of the salesperson. A reply such as "If this is what it takes to do business here, I don't want anything to do with it" is the kind of response that the honest purchaser is looking for. Any response that indicates that the salesperson is not honest will probably result in the loss of this sale and of any future purchases from the buyer. As a guiding principle, salespeople must never compromise their integrity or let anyone intimidate them by asking for "special favors." In the rare case where the buyer is dishonest, it's better to lose that business than to compete unethically for it. And, too, remember the old adage: "Even crooks like to do business with people they can trust."

and a few people who call themselves salespeople but are really more like con artists—personal selling unfortunately continues to attract criticism about low ethical standards. Door-to-door salespeople and automobile salespeople have borne much of this criticism. Because of the number of complaints about their salespeople, some car dealerships have resorted to videotaping final sales transactions. But, apparently, not just these salespeople are suspect. Even business-to-business sales personnel, through questionable conduct, have served to tarnish the image of professional salespeople. In a survey of two hundred sales managers—ranging from major corporations to privately held companies—nearly half admitted that their salespeople had lied on a sales call.[8] To counter this negative image, today's salespeople must hold themselves and their companies to a high standard of ethics and avoid even the appearance of questionable ethics. They must be paragons of trustworthiness; that is, their conduct must demonstrate to their customers that their word is "golden." Indeed, research has found that customers are more trusting of salespeople if they perceive that salespeople are behaving ethically.[9] Trustworthiness in salespeople has a strong positive impact on the ways in which salespeople and their customers interact.[10] As Warren Buffett, CEO of Berkshire-Hathaway (www.berkshirehathaway.com), has said, "It takes years to build customer trust, but it can be lost in a moment." Read *On the Frontlines* for a sense of how salespeople must sometimes make ethical decisions under extreme pressure.

Chapter Review Question
What are ethics?

ETHICAL CONCERNS OF SALESPEOPLE

Salespeople work in a business environment "ideal" for ethical conflict:

> The sales organization is unique . . . its members work apart from each other, experiencing little daily contact with supervisors, subordinates, or peers. . . . The resulting impact on ethical decision making can be negative, since individuals interacting in a group produce decisions at higher levels of moral reasoning than when acting alone . . . instances of role stress which [provide] many unique opportunities for ethical issues and dilemmas [can] arise. The central nature of selling—a negotiation between buyer and seller—is inherently a laboratory of ethical scenarios.[11]

Therefore, professional salespeople must be ethically sensitive in their interactions with a variety of people and organizations, including customers, co-workers, competitors, and their own companies. One's ethical sensitivity is partially a function of one's moral philosophy, which is an overall guiding ideology of what is considered to be right and wrong. Salespeople's moral philosophy has been shown to influence their perceptions of the appropriateness of questionable selling activities.[12] Furthermore, how right or wrong sales managers perceive salespeople's behavior toward others to be can influence the rewards or discipline managers recommend.[13] Moreover, companies have ethical obligations toward their employees.

Customer Relationships

It is never smart to engage in unethical practices with customers, even when the customer is the instigator. Even dishonest and unethical customers don't trust unethical salespeople and will eventually stop dealing with them. Losing such customers in the short run may simply be the price an ethical salesperson must pay for long-run success in selling. Professional salespeople build long-run relationships of mutual trust, respect, and confidence with customers. Any loss of personal or company integrity in the eyes of customers jeopardizes these relationships. Read *It's Up to You* on the next page to try your hand at dealing with an ethical issue in selling. Next, we discuss some areas in which ethical problems can arise with customers.

Special Gifts. Bribes, payoffs, and kickbacks are clearly illegal and can bring about serious legal problems for violators. Nevertheless, some salespeople insist on "showing their appreciation" to customers by giving them *expensive* gifts. Sometimes, especially around the holiday seasons, some customers will drop subtle hints that they expect a nice gift for all the business they've been giving you. One survey of sales managers revealed that almost nine out of ten

IT'S UP TO YOU

You are a salesperson for Atlas Sporting Goods, Inc., a manufacturer of sports equipment and apparel. While you are trying to negotiate a $125,000 sale with a buyer for one of the largest retailers in your territory, the buyer says to you, "You know what, young man? Our deal would be a lot sweeter if you could see your way to getting me a complete set of your company's titanium golf clubs with a pro bag and pull cart. What do you think, partner?" If you negotiate this sale, your commission will be $5,000, and you will surpass your annual quota by $1,500 and receive a $5,000 bonus. The golf clubs, bag, and cart would cost you about $900 because you, as an employee of Atlas, can buy them at cost. At retail, they would sell for about $2,500. What factors will influence your decision? If you choose to say no, how will you attempt to salvage the sale?

believed that not paying bribes would put their companies at a competitive disadvantage.[14] Such ambivalence on the part of sales managers places salespeople in an awkward position unless companies have established clear policies that address the issue of gift giving—something most salespeople want.[15] Numerous companies have solved this problem for salespeople by refusing to allow their employees to accept any gifts from suppliers. What's more, many supplier companies have stopped giving holiday gifts to customers, offering instead to contribute to the customer's favorite charity.[16]

Entertainment. Taking a customer or prospect to dinner, to play golf, or to a ball game or special event is generally an acceptable and often expected part of doing business. Moreover, it can provide additional time for the buyer and seller to discuss business and impart much important information in a relaxed setting. But lavishly entertaining a prospect or customer may well be a disguised bribe to influence a purchase. For example, pharmaceutical company salespeople have been roundly criticized for treating doctors to fine meals at expensive restaurants, supplying free tickets to Broadway shows and sporting events, offering cash payment for listening to sales presentations, and even providing free trips to expensive resorts to influence the most intimate and important of medical decisions: selection of drugs to prescribe for patients.[17]

Entertainment is a part of doing business, but it can be misinterpreted as a bribe.
Ken Fisher/Getty Images

Overpromising. In order to win the sale, some salespeople will promise much more than they can deliver. Later, they think that the customer will accept some reasonable excuse. Promising an unrealistic delivery date in order to make a sale is not only an ethical violation but also poor business practice. Customers prefer to buy from salespeople whose word and promises can be relied on. A maxim to follow as a salesperson is "Promise only what you can deliver."

Misrepresenting or Covering Up the Facts. A few salespeople try to cover up the facts or distort the truth to make a quick sale. For example, pharmaceutical sales reps for Purdue Pharma (www.pharma.com) touted the advantages of a powerful painkilling medication that costs more than $300 for a bottle of one hundred pills. Simultaneously, law enforcement personnel had been warning pharmacists about the hazards of this morphine-like drug, which has the capacity to induce addiction. Yet for some time, Purdue Pharma's sales reps failed to rectify this catastrophic weakness in their sales presentations to pharmacists. In fact, 120 users of the drug died over a four-year period, and several other users became severely addicted to it. The salespeople's allegedly unethical conduct resulted in many pharmacists deciding not to stock the drug. Once salespeople have started down the slippery slope of misrepresentation (or lying), "reconstituting integrity is next to impossible."[18]

Another, more interesting example of disinformation used as a sales tactic has recently come to light. Merck (www.merck.com)—a premier pharmaceutical firm that manufactures the blockbuster, multibillion-dollar painkiller Vioxx—has come under congressional investigation because taking Vioxx is associated with increased risk of heart attack. Even though senior management was aware of the heart attacks risk and Food and Drug Administration warnings were imminent, an army of 3,000 salespersons were offered $2,000 bonuses for meeting sales goals. They worked in campaigns with such codenames as "Project Offense" for aggressively boosting sales. Confidential Merck memos advised salespeople not to discuss heart risks. Sales tactics were so detailed that they even included the "correct" length of time to shake a physician's hand—three seconds—and how to eat bread when dining with doctors—"one small bite-sized piece at a time." During the congressional hearings, a lawmaker asserted, "When it comes to the one thing doctors most needed to know about Vioxx—its health risks—Merck's answer seems to be disinformation and censorship . . . emphasizing the positive in selling the painkiller is disinformation designed to deflect safety concerns."[19]

To assess your own level of moral and ethical standards, answer the thirty questions on page 74.

Manipulating Order Forms. During sales contests or as sales quota deadlines loom, some salespeople are tempted to finagle their actual sales records by shifting orders from one period to another or overselling some products. Customers are not always aware of how much inventory they need, so the unethical salesperson may try to persuade them to overbuy. Overselling and order manipulation not only cheat customers but also are unfair to colleagues competing in the sales contest or striving to make quotas. In one Fortune 500 data-processing firm, sales reps who had already exceeded their annual quota by December would hold orders and submit them at the start of the new year. Doing so would allow them to jumpstart their quota drive for the new year.

Disclosing Confidential Information. In an effort to ingratiate themselves with important customers, some salespeople reveal confidential and potentially harmful information about their customers' competitors. Customers who receive such

DETERMINE YOUR LEVEL OF MORAL AND ETHICAL STANDARDS

Assume that you are a sales manager, and respond to each of the following actions that salespersons exhibit in dealing with their customers, co-workers, and company. Use the following scale when responding to each statement:

Extremely Ethical	Ethical	Neutral	Unethical	Extremely Unethical
1	2	3	4	5

1. Routinely pays money to customers as incentives for purchasing products. ____
2. Frequently takes clients out for meals at expensive restaurants. ____
3. Gives expensive presents to clients during the holiday season. ____
4. Sometimes knowingly sells defective products to customers. ____
5. Pushes customers to buy products they don't need. ____
6. Tries to sell higher-cost products to customers when lower-cost products are more appropriate for their needs. ____
7. Does not inform buyers about negative aspects of the product. ____
8. Sells returned or used merchandise as new. ____
9. Presents misleading information about how the product will benefit the buyer. ____
10. Makes false promises about delivery dates to get the sales contract. ____
11. Makes exaggerated claims about product features, advantages, or benefits. ____
12. Often promises customers more than can be delivered. ____
13. Misleads customers about product availability to close the deal. ____
14. Frequently calls in sick to take a day off. ____
15. Blames co-workers for her or his own mistakes. ____
16. Tries to take personal credit when a co-worker lands a new customer. ____
17. Makes sexual advances to co-workers. ____
18. Makes sexually suggestive comments and creates an uncomfortable work environment for co-workers. ____
19. Makes racially disparaging comments about customers or co-workers. ____
20. Flirts with customers to land the sale. ____
21. Overstates expenses on reimbursement reports. ____
22. Makes personal charges on a company credit card. ____
23. Does personal business on company time. ____
24. Misrepresents or covers up negative facts about his or her company's products. ____
25. Does not take responsibility for mistakes. ____
26. Uses a company phone for personal long-distance calls. ____
27. Takes sales promotion samples meant for buyers. ____
28. Disparages and mocks the competition during sales presentations. ____
29. Discloses confidential information about the competition. ____
30. Spreads misinformation about the competition. ____

Add up your scores for the thirty questions. A score higher than 130 indicates that you are an extremely ethical person with high moral standards; a score between 100 and 130 indicates that you have reasonably high ethical standards; a score below 100 indicates that your ethical sensitivity may need further development.

KEEPING UP ONLINE: TRUSTe

Do you believe that organizations such as TRUSTe help or hinder salespeople in doing their jobs? Why? Take a look at the TRUSTe website at **www.TRUSTe.org** to see how it might be useful to a salesperson, prospect, customer, or competitor.

information have to wonder whether these salespeople are also leaking confidential information about *their* companies. This seed of mistrust is likely to inhibit future communication with customers. Ethical salespeople play it straight with all their customers and earn a reputation for being honest and trustworthy.

With more sophisticated computer technology and software and Internet-based buying, large amounts of data—for example, product preferences, purchase patterns, and customer demographics and psychographics—can be subtly collected and analyzed for use by salespeople or for sale to other companies. A Federal Trade Commission (FTC) study found that more than 90 percent of commercial websites collect at least one type of personally identifying information from visitors, and 57 percent gather some type of demographic information.[20] Yet the FTC found that only 14 percent of the sites surveyed reveal what they do with the personal information they collect.[21] "Cookies"—small files placed on computer hard drives when a prospect or customer visits certain websites—are the most common means of obtaining this information. Because they can track users' movement on the Web, they pose a threat to privacy. With few regulations on business use of this information, companies can buy and sell information about customers to gain competitive advantage. Companies who want to be both ethical and socially responsible should clearly post their privacy policies on their websites for browsers to read. TRUSTe is a nonprofit organization, supported by a network of corporate, industry, and nonprofit sponsors, that works to advance global trust in the Internet through its seal and certification program. It grants TRUSTe awards to websites that subscribe to its established privacy principles and agree to comply with its oversight and resolution process. Websites that display the trustmark must disclose their information collection and privacy policies in a straightforward privacy statement. Anyone who believes that his or her privacy has been compromised can file a complaint at the TRUSTe website (www.TRUSTe.org). Take a closer look at the TRUSTe website in *Keeping Up Online*.

Reprinted by permission of TRUSTe.org

Showing Favoritism. Salespeople nearly always like some customers more than others, but the ethical salesperson cannot afford to show favoritism by, say, moving a favored customer's deliveries ahead of others' orders or making sure preferred customers receive scarce products when others do not. One study found that more than 50 percent of salespeople surveyed believed that showing favoritism toward a customer creates an ethical conflict.[22] In addition, customers who are discriminated against will deeply resent such unequal treatment and may refuse to buy from salespeople even suspected of such behavior.

Treatment of Co-workers

A few excessively aggressive salespeople will behave unethically even in competing with their own company sales colleagues. Unethical behavior among co-workers can destroy employee morale, work against company goals and objectives, and ruin the reputation of the company. In fact, the kind of feedback that salespeople give their sales peers influences peer job satisfaction and even performance.[23] Let's look at some examples of what would generally be considered unethical behavior in dealing with one's colleagues.

Sexual harassment violates both ethical and legal codes of conduct.
GunGuntmar Fritz/Zefa/CORBIS

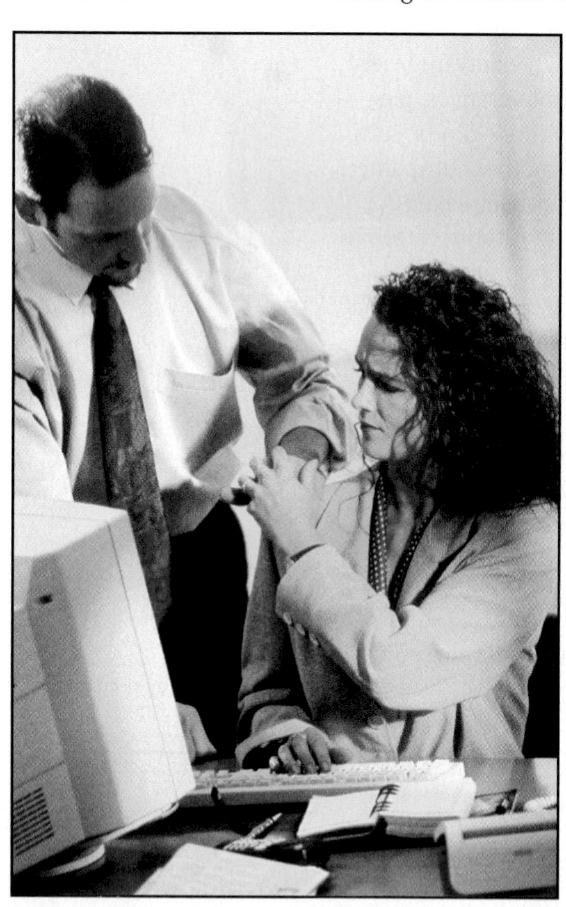

Sexual Harassment. Salespeople, whether males or females, may become perpetrators or victims of sexual harassment that violates both ethical and legal codes of conduct. In 1980, the Equal Employment Opportunity Commission wrote its guidelines defining sexual harassment as a form of sex discrimination and, therefore, illegal under Title VII of the Civil Rights Act of 1964. The EEOC definition follows:

> Unwelcome sexual advances, requests for sexual favors, and other verbal or physical conduct of a sexual nature constitutes sexual harassment when (1) submission to such conduct is either explicitly or implicitly a term or condition of an individual's employment, (2) submission to or a rejection of such conduct by an individual is used as a basis for employment decisions affecting such individual, or (3) such conduct has the purpose or effect of unreasonably interfering with an individual's work performance or creating an intimidating, hostile, or offensive working environment.[24]

Quid Pro Quo Harassment A person in authority's demand for sexual favors from an employee in exchange for a job advantage, such as being hired or promoted.

As indicated in the EEOC definition, the law recognizes two types of employment-related sexual harassment: (1) **quid pro quo harassment,** where a person in authority demands sexual favors from an employee in exchange for a job advantage, such as being hired or promoted, and (2) creation

IT'S UP TO YOU

You are a 23-year-old saleswoman for an office equipment company who has just finished making a sales presentation to the purchasing agent of a large manufacturer. It seemed to go well. But then the purchasing agent (a middle-aged male) says, "I liked your sales presentation and maybe we'll be able to do business. But there are many suppliers, so I prefer to buy from someone with whom I have a special relationship. How about dinner tonight so we can start developing that relationship?"

of a **hostile environment,** where a pattern of sexual behavior makes the job so unpleasant that the victim's work is adversely affected. An open demand for job-related sexual favors is clearly recognized as illegal. But with respect to *hostile environment harassment*—for example, hazing, joking, and sexually suggestive talk—interpretation of the law becomes fuzzy. Where does good-humored kidding cease and harassment begin?

Hostile Environment A pattern of sexual behavior that makes the job so unpleasant that the victim's work is adversely affected.

Experiencing sexual harassment is much more common for women than for men.[25] Some women fear filing a sexual harassment case because it may lead to public humiliation, possible job loss, and threats to their family happiness. Many, therefore, opt to leave the job or suffer in silence. Nevertheless, many women have filed lawsuits, and some have received substantial awards from juries. In a recent study of salespeople, half reported having been involved in office romances.[26] This statistic may portend increased sexual harassment in sales offices.[27]

Stealing Customers from Colleagues. Both encroaching on another salesperson's territory and trying to convince a customer doing business in two different territories to make all purchases from your territory are unethical practices. Salespeople found guilty of poaching on other salespeople's territories may face reprimands from management and possible loss of their jobs. One Fortune 500 company took a unique approach when one of its saleswomen crossed over into a colleague's sales territory to make a sale. Rather than censuring the errant salesperson, management decided to give both salespeople credit for the sale and one-half of the commission, as well as requiring both sales personnel to install and service the computer at the new account.

Undermining Co-workers. Occasionally, salespeople become so obsessed with their own lust for success that they deliberately undercut their co-workers. Failing to relay a customer's telephone message to a sales colleague is an unethical activity. So is telling the boss's secretary some disparaging remark made by another salesperson about the boss. Such viciously self-serving salespeople usually underestimate other people, who will quickly size them up and begin to shun them. Few salespeople succeed for long by disparaging colleagues. Remember this old saying: "To hold someone else down, a part of you has to stay down, too."

Chapter Review Question

Can you explain the difference between *quid pro quo* *harrassment and hostile environment harassment?*

Treatment of Competitors

Perhaps it can be argued that "all's fair in love and war," but this is certainly not the case for ethical salespeople in dealing with competitors. Initiating unethical practices against competitors can stimulate unethical retaliatory action from them and lead to accelerating aggressive activity that soon crosses the line into legal violations. Let's consider potential problems that could arise.

Disparaging Competitors. Making negative, exaggerated statements about competing products and companies is an unethical practice that may prompt retaliation from competitors. Even the best companies are sometimes guilty of disparaging competitors. One Fortune 500 company was accused of using sales demonstrations that "unfairly" denigrated the competition by purposely misusing materials and devices to assess the effectiveness of the competitor's product. Describing the weaknesses of a competitor's offerings relative to yours is acceptable, but going to excessive lengths to impugn the integrity of those offerings is simply unfair and unethical.

Tampering with Competitors' Products. It is unethical and illegal for salespeople to damage competitors' products, tamper with their displays and point-of-sale materials, or reduce their product shelf space in retail stores or elsewhere. Salespeople who stoop to such activities may also anger retailers and wholesalers, who naturally resent any unauthorized tampering with their displays. A small producer of cereal was set upon by its behemoth competitors in efforts to get its product off grocery shelves. Its competitors slashed open the small producer's cereal boxes on the shelves; the small manufacturer, angered by the attack, responded in kind! This open warfare hurt all parties involved, including the retailers, until such futile and infantile activities ceased.

Competitive Snooping. Salespeople use many ruses to obtain valuable information about competitors. To obtain competitive pricing information, for instance, some salespeople ask customers to solicit bids from competitors. Some pretend to be customers at professional conferences, trade shows, and exhibits or on plant tours of the competition. These practices are neither uncommon nor illegal, and some would argue that such behavior is okay because "nearly everybody does it." But salespeople who are trying to maintain the highest ethical standards will see such practices as questionable at best.

Salespeople Ethics and Their Company

Salespeople and other employees sometimes believe that standards of ethics don't fully apply when dealing not with an individual but with an organization, be it the Internal Revenue Service, an insurance firm, or their own company. After all, they reason, it's not human, it's just a big bureaucratic organization with lots of money. But when large numbers of people start taking home a few ballpoint pens or paper tablets, padding expense accounts, or doing personal business on company time, the costs of doing business can go up dramatically. Eventually, these abuses translate into higher prices to customers, lower profits, lower wages and salaries, and fewer company employees as the company loses sales to more efficient competitors. Let's discuss some of the more obvious and problematic tactics.

Expense Account Padding. Salespeople can easily pad their expense accounts by taking friends out to dinner and claiming they were entertaining customers or by submitting excess claims for meal expenses, mileage, taxi fares, tips, and the like. Padding one's expense account, however, may be viewed as stealing by sales managers and can lead to dismissal if discovered. An expense account should *not* be considered a supplement to or extension of your salary. It is provided by the company to assist you in the performance of your job (so don't bite the hand that feeds you!).

Unauthorized Use of Company Resources. Making personal telephone calls on company phones, using company copying machines for personal purposes, keeping company promotional premiums intended for customers, taking home supplies from the office for personal use, and driving a company car on unauthorized personal trips are unethical activities that can significantly add to company costs. U.S. businesses lose billions of dollars yearly to thefts committed by employees. One study found that approximately one-third of job applicants claim to have stolen merchandise, ranging in value from $25 to $1,500, from an employer.[28] Some employees rationalize stealing from their own companies by claiming that the company owes it to them for underpaying them, or that they're just borrowing something that they will pay back later, or that "everybody else does it," so it must be all right.

Personal Use of Company Time. U.S. workers steal more than $120 billion worth of time each year from their companies. Some employees go beyond long lunch hours, personal telephone calls, and excessive socializing to actually "moonlighting" on part-time jobs during the same hours that they are supposed to be working for their primary employer. Because of their independence and freedom, salespeople have many opportunities to convert company time to personal use, but ethical sales reps will give their companies a full day's work even if they have made all of their scheduled sales calls for the day. There is always some customer servicing or paperwork to be done. In the Midwest sales branch office of a major manufacturer, many salespeople took off Friday afternoons for socializing. Branch management, after getting wind of this behavior, started scheduling mandatory in-branch sales training for Friday afternoons!

Fabrication of Sales Records. Because many companies base their performance evaluations of salespeople at least partially on their sales *activities* as well as their sales *results*, some salespeople are tempted to falsify their numbers of sales calls, service calls, or promotional mailings to customers. Smart salespeople realize that activity quotas are guides designed to help them learn what it takes to achieve top performance. Falsifying sales activity records may become a habit that causes salespeople to become lazy, and soon there are adverse effects on their sales performance. One Fortune 500 company required sales reps to submit their daily call reports from the previous week to their manager every Monday morning. One of their less productive salespeople completed the call reports each Monday morning by obtaining company names and addresses from a phone book. What he recorded appeared to be a call on a legitimate prospect but was in reality a fabrication. Eventually, the salesperson was terminated for sub-par performance.

Manipulation of Customer Orders. To win sales contests or meet their annual quotas, salespeople may persuade customers to over-order products with the promise that they can return them after the contest or end of the year. Not only does this unethical practice harm sales colleagues who are competing fairly in the contest, but it also creates unnecessary costs for the company and hurts the image of the company and its salespeople with customers.

Employer Ethics with Their Salespeople

Ethical salespeople have a right to expect ethical treatment from their companies, especially with regard to compensation, sales territories, sales quotas, and hiring, promoting, and firing policies.

Compensation. Prompt, accurate payment of salary, commissions, and bonuses, and timely reimbursement of selling expenses, are basic requirements for any ethical company in dealing with its salespeople. Any company that tries to delay payments or cheat salespeople out of their fair commissions or reimbursement for selling expenses will see its sales force turnover skyrocket.

Sales Territories. Sales managers must ensure that salespeople are involved in the fair assignment of sales territories. Ideally, all salespeople should receive territories that are equal in sales potential. Whenever territories must be reassigned, split up, or moved to national accounts, the salespeople should receive early warning of the impending change and should be given an opportunity to negotiate a new territorial assignment. This is especially important because salespeople's satisfaction with their sales territory affects their performance.[29]

Sales Quotas. Setting unrealistically high sales quotas for salespeople, and then applying constant pressure to produce sales, is unfair and unethical. Moreover, it destroys motivation. Salespeople should be involved in setting their own quotas, so that they will view the quotas as fair. An important aspect of sales force motivation and loyalty to the company is the salespeople's perception that they are being treated fairly and ethically. This may not always be the case, though, because some sales managers tend to play favorites. Research has found that salespeople whom their sales managers view as desirable work partners, as well as desirable social partners and friends, are evaluated more favorably than those who are not perceived in such a way.[30]

Chapter Review Question

Discuss some of the more common ethical concerns of salespeople.

Hiring, Promoting, and Firing. Although all forms of discrimination have been legally prohibited since the 1964 Civil Rights Act (which was made even more powerful by the Equal Employment Opportunity Act of 1972), continuing evidence suggests that *sexism, racism,* and *ageism* still influence managerial decisions in hiring, promoting, and firing salespeople. Over the long run, the most successful companies are those that provide equal opportunities for all employees and base decisions on job performance.[31] Read the accompanying *Keeping Up Online* feature to find out more about the EEOC.

KEEPING UP ONLINE: U.S. EQUAL EMPLOYMENT OPPORTUNITY COMMISSION

The EEOC works to ensure that companies provide equal employment opportunities for all applicants. Visit the EEOC online at **www.eeoc.gov.** Have the actions of the EEOC helped or hurt sales forces in the United States? Justify your answer.

THE COMPANY'S ETHICAL EYES AND EARS IN THE FIELD

Misguided managers sometimes employ unethical means to achieve short-run sales and profit levels. Read *From the Command Post* on page 82 to see how managers in some large firms have pushed their salespeople too far. To counter unethical behavior, some companies (e.g., Texas Instruments) have an ethics officer who answers anonymous employee questions in the monthly company magazine or in weekly online news columns on ethics. Professional salespeople should accept the role of customer representative or spokesperson whenever they spot questionable marketing activities, such as those discussed below.[32]

Product Quality and Service

Poor product quality, unsafe products, unreasonable return policies, and poor servicing of products after the sale are examples of unethical practices that salespeople should not have to tolerate from their companies. If the company persists in shady activities, a salesperson would probably be better off seeking a job with a more ethical company. Over the long run, unethical companies are unlikely to prosper competing against ethical companies.

Pricing

Some companies or salespeople routinely inflate list prices so they can appear to offer customers a discount. And salespeople are often accused of taking advantage of uninformed customers or those less aggressive in negotiating. Ethical salespeople, however, will not resort to price gouging or taking advantage of a naïve customer. Though you may make the sale now, customers will eventually find out that they paid too much and refuse to buy from you again.

Salespeople can legitimately offer price and quantity discounts, but such discounts must be made available on an equal basis to all customers. One aggrieved customer called a salesperson from a large computer manufacturer, complaining that he had been charged a higher price than a colleague at another firm for exactly the same computer system. The customer demanded a refund for the difference between what he paid and what his colleague paid, or he would remove the system from his office and cancel the sale. The salesperson's management quickly agreed to the customer's demands.

FROM THE COMMAND POST: BETRAYAL FROM THE TOP

Financial statements aren't what they used to be! Although financial statements presumably represent an objective appraisal of an organization's financial condition at a given point in time, an increasing number of companies have been hauled into court for alleged accounting malfeasance. High-ranking executives from Enron, Global Crossing, Adelphia, Tyco, ImClone Systems, WorldCom, and several other companies have been accused by the federal government of illegal activities, such as "cooking the company books" to report inflated earnings. Millions of company employees and shareholders feel betrayed and angry by such apparent dishonesty in the executive suites of several U.S. corporations. What's more, many employees trusted the integrity of top management at their companies and kept their 401(k) retirement money invested in their employer's stock. Now, some of these companies have declared bankruptcy and virtually wiped out employee retirement funds.

What caused these egregious lapses in ethical and legal standards by formerly honored and trusted executives? Many set increasingly ambitious and eventually impossible sales and earnings objectives for their companies. Struggling to increase or maintain sales and earnings projections in a declining economy caused some senior executives to resort to financial manipulation in efforts to shore up the stock price of their companies. By engaging in highly questionable, if not outright illegal, accounting practices (e.g., recording product shipments to channel members as actual sales and recording routine operating expenses as capital assets to be written off over several years), these executives have badly damaged faith in business leadership. Without ethical leadership from the top on down, no organization can expect to develop the healthy, profitable relationships with prospects and customers that are essential to company success. No short-run payoff is ever worth the devastation that such behavior inflicts on individual companies and industry in general. Despite any glib or cynical comments to the contrary, "honesty is always the best policy," whether you're a salesperson or a CEO.

Distribution

Some unethical salespeople will sell lower-quality products and inferior services to young people, the elderly, non-English-speaking Americans, and poorly informed people, often at prices as high as or higher than those charged for better products and services.[33] Unscrupulous firms and salespeople tend to prey on customers who are undereducated, dependent on credit, unaware of their legal rights, or unable to read or speak English.

Promotion

Chapter Review Question

Describe some of the ways in which professional salespeople can be the ethical "eyes and ears" of their companies.

Deceptive advertising, misleading product warranties, phony promotional contests, and dishonest fund-raising activities are unethical and often illegal. Unfair or stereotypical representation of gender, racial and ethnic minorities, sexual orientation, the disabled, or senior citizens may be viewed as merely insensitive instead of unethical, but such promotions can upset major customer groups. Whenever salespeople hear customers commenting negatively about the company's promotional efforts, they should relay this information to sales and marketing management. No salesperson should be expected to work under the cloud of unethical advertising.

BEHAVING ETHICALLY, EVERY DAY

When you interact with prospects and customers, you represent yourself and your firm. Your conduct will send them strong signals regarding what kind of person you are and for what kind of company you work. Furthermore, how you behave on the job will affect how your management, colleagues, and peers perceive you. And research has revealed that more ethically sensitive salespeople perform better and have greater success than their less ethically sensitive counterparts.[34] When performing your sales job, it may be helpful to reflect on the ideas presented in Table 3.1.

In efforts to assist employees, some firms have established codes of ethics or codes of conduct that describe behavior considered acceptable and unacceptable in the execution of their jobs. Some codes are detailed and strict, and others are more general in nature. Their purpose is to provide guidelines for employees about appropriate job deportment. The mere existence of such codes may lead sales personnel to view their company as supporting an ethical climate,[35] thus requiring exemplary selling behavior. Studies have found that salespeople want their firms to provide ethical policies to assist them in doing their jobs.[36] Furthermore, the ethical climate of an organization may have an impact on salespeople's performance.[37] Some professional associations have created codes of conduct, and following them is a requirement for membership. The American Marketing Association (AMA) has developed a code that even includes behavior on the Internet, as shown on page 84.

TABLE 3.1

ETHICAL IDEAS FOR SALESPEOPLE

1. Ethical conflicts and choices are inherent in personal selling.
2. The law is the lowest common denominator of ethical behavior.
3. No single satisfactory standard of ethical action agreeable to everyone exists to assist you in making on-the-job decisions.
4. Ethical action has diverse and sometimes conflicting determinants (for example, the customer, management, your peers, industry standards, competition).
5. Your value system will have a dramatic effect on your ethical conduct.
6. The lower you are in the corporate hierarchy, the greater the likelihood that you will feel pressure to engage in unethical conduct.
7. Your company's top management will set the tone for its ethical conduct.

Source: *Adapted from Clarke L. Caywood and Gene R. Laczniak, "Ethics and Personal Selling:* Death of a Salesman *as an Ethical Primer,"* Journal of Personal Selling and Sales Management *5 (August 1986): 81–88.*

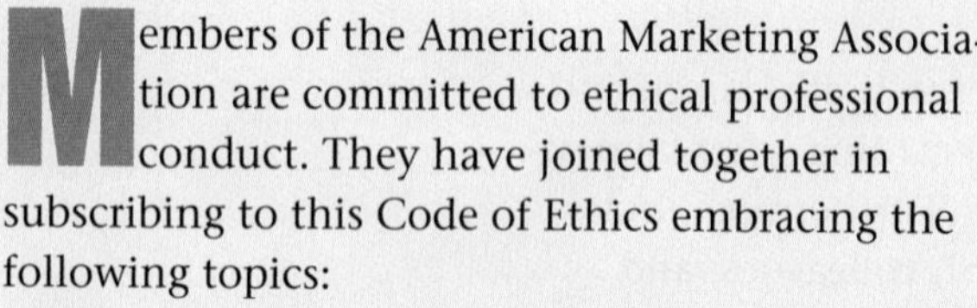

AMA CODE OF ETHICS

Members of the American Marketing Association are committed to ethical professional conduct. They have joined together in subscribing to this Code of Ethics embracing the following topics:

Responsibilities of the Marketer

Marketers must accept responsibility for the consequences of their activities and make every effort to ensure that their decisions, recommendations and actions function to identify, serve and satisfy all relevant publics: customers, organizations and society.

Marketers' Professional Conduct must be guided by:

1. The basic rule of professional ethics: not knowingly to do harm;
2. The adherence to all applicable laws and regulations;
3. The accurate representation of their education, training and experience; and
4. The active support, practice and promotion of this Code of Ethics.

Honesty and Fairness

Marketers shall uphold and advance the integrity, honor and dignity of the marketing profession by:

1. Being honest in serving consumers, clients, employees, suppliers, distributors, and the public;
2. Not knowingly participating in conflict of interest without prior notice to all parties involved; and
3. Establishing equitable fee schedules including the payment or receipt of usual, customary and/or legal compensation for marketing exchanges.

Rights and Duties of Parties in the Marketing Exchange Process

Participants in the marketing exchange process should be able to expect that:

1. Products and services offered are safe and fit for their intended uses;
2. Communications about offered products and services are not deceptive;
3. All parties intend to discharge their obligations, financial and otherwise, in good faith; and
4. Appropriate internal methods exist for equitable adjustment and/or redress of grievances concerning purchases.

It is understood that the above would include, but is not limited to, the following responsibilities of the marketer:

In the area of product development and management:

- disclosure of all substantial risks associated with product or service usage;
- identification of any product component substitution that might materially change the product or impact on the buyer's purchase decision;
- identification of extra cost-added features.

In the area of promotions:

- avoidance of false and misleading advertising;
- rejection of high-pressure manipulations, or misleading sales tactics;
- avoidance of sales promotions that use deception or manipulation.

In the area of distribution:

- not manipulating the availability of a product for the purpose of exploitation;
- not using coercion in the marketing channel;

(continued)

- not exerting undue influence over the reseller's choice to handle a product.

In the area of pricing:

- not engaging in price fixing;
- not practicing predatory pricing;
- disclosing the full price associated with any purchase.

In the area of marketing research:

- prohibiting selling or fundraising under the guise of conducting research;
- maintaining research integrity by avoiding misrepresentation and omission of pertinent research data;
- treating outside clients and suppliers fairly.

Organizational Relationships

Marketers should be aware of how their behavior may influence or impact the behavior of others in organizational relationships. They should not demand, encourage or apply coercion to obtain unethical behavior in their relationships with others, such as employees, suppliers, or customers.

1. Apply confidentiality and anonymity in professional relationships with regard to privileged information;
2. Meet their obligations and responsibilities in contracts and mutual agreements in a timely manner;
3. Avoid taking the work of others, in whole, or in part, and representing this work as their own or directly benefiting from it without compensation or consent of the originator or owner; and
4. Avoid manipulation to take advantage of situations to maximize personal welfare in a way that unfairly deprives or damages the organization of others.

Any AMA member found to be in violation of any provision of this Code of Ethics may have his or her Association membership suspended or revoked.

American Marketing Association Code of Ethics for Marketing on the Internet

Preamble The Internet, including online computer communications, has become increasingly important to marketers' activities, as they provide exchanges and access to markets worldwide. The ability to interact with stakeholders has created new marketing opportunities and risks that are not currently specifically addressed in the American Marketing Association Code of Ethics. The American Marketing Association Code of Ethics for Marketing on the Internet provides additional guidance and direction for ethical responsibility in this dynamic area of marketing. The American Marketing Association is committed to ethical professional conduct and has adopted these principles for using the Internet, including online marketing activities utilizing network computers.

General Responsibilities Internet marketers must assess the risks and take responsibility for the consequences of their activities. Internet marketers' professional conduct must be guided by:

1. Support of professional ethics to avoid harm by protecting the rights of privacy, ownership and access.
2. Adherence to all applicable laws and regulations with no use of Internet marketing that would be illegal if conducted by mail, telephone, fax or other media.
3. Awareness of changes in regulations related to Internet marketing.
4. Effective communication to organizational members on risks and policies related to Internet marketing, when appropriate.
5. Organizational commitment to ethical Internet practices communicated to employees, customers and relevant stakeholders.

Privacy Information collected from customers should be confidential and used only for expressed purposes. All data, especially confidential customer data, should be safeguarded against unauthorized access. The expressed wishes of others should be respected with regard to the receipt of unsolicited e-mail messages.

(continued)

AMA CODE OF ETHICS (CONTINUED)

Ownership Information obtained from the Internet sources should be properly authorized and documented. Information ownership should be safeguarded and respected. Marketers should respect the integrity and ownership of computer and network systems.

Access Marketers should treat access to accounts, passwords, and other information as confidential, and only examine or disclose content when authorized by a responsible party. The integrity of others' information systems should be respected with regard to placement of information, advertising or messages.

GOING BEYOND ETHICS: LAWS AFFECTING BUSINESS-TO-BUSINESS PERSONAL SELLING

Among the most important federal laws for business-to-business salespeople to understand are the Robinson-Patman Act, the Sherman Act, and the Clayton Act. These acts cover price discrimination, collusion, price fixing, restraint of trade, exclusive dealing, reciprocity, tie-in sales, business and product descriptions, orders and terms of sale, unordered goods, secret rebates, customer coercion, and business defamation. It may be surprising to learn that one of the most important recent laws affecting personal selling is the Sarbanes-Oxley Act (SOX) of 2002. SOX requires higher standards and executive responsibility for accuracy in financial reports. And the most important financial report for a company usually is its profit and loss (P&L) statement, which focuses on sales revenue. Typically, sales revenue is the highest dollar amount on a company's P&L statement, and salespeople often contribute directly to this figure. Many salespeople have some discretion over pricing, discounts, rebates, and the reporting of sales revenue up the line. Salesperson errors in reporting sales data, such as claiming shipments into the supply chain as final user sales, can lead to violations of the Sarbanes-Oxley Act.

Price Discrimination

The Clayton Act prohibits a seller (salesperson) from discriminating on price or terms of sale among different customers when the discrimination would injure competition. It also makes it illegal for a buyer to knowingly induce or accept a discriminatory price.

Under the Robinson-Patman Act, a seller (salesperson) cannot sell at different prices in different markets, or charge different prices to different purchasers for the same quality and quantity of goods. Differences in price or terms of sale can be successfully defended only if (1) the price differential was given in good faith to match, not beat, a price offered by a competitor; or (2) the price differential represents a cost saving resulting from different manufacturing techniques or quantities in which the products are sold or delivered. Price reductions are permissible when based on quantity ordered, closeout sales, lower shipping and selling costs, good-faith meeting of competition, and lower commissions paid to salespeople. For their own legal protection, sellers should establish accounting procedures that can certify cost differences in selling to certain customers.

Price Fixing

If two or more competing sellers conspire to set or maintain uniform prices and profit margins, they are involved in **price fixing.** Even an informal exchange of price information between competitors or discussion of pricing policies at trade shows has been found to be illegal by the courts.

Price Fixing Two or more competing sellers conspiring to set or maintain uniform prices and profit margins.

Collusion

Competing sellers who agree to set prices, divide up markets or territories, or act to the detriment of a third competitor are involved in an illegal arrangement called **collusion.**

Collusion An illegal arrangement in which competing sellers agree to set prices, divide up markets or territories, or act to the detriment of a third competitor.

Exclusive Dealing

Exclusive dealing consists of agreements in which a manufacturer or wholesaler grants one dealer exclusive rights to sell a product in a certain trading area and insists that the dealer not carry competing lines. These actions are illegal under the Clayton Act.

Exclusive Dealing Agreements in which a manufacturer or wholesaler grants one dealer exclusive rights to sell a product in a certain trading area and insists that the dealer not carry competing lines. Illegal under the Clayton Act.

Restraint of Trade

Dealers cannot be prohibited from selling competitors' products as a condition of receiving the right to sell the manufacturer's product. Under both the Sherman Act and the Clayton Act, agreements made between competitors to divide a market into noncompetitive territories or to restrict competition are acts in restraint of trade.

Reciprocity

Reciprocity, or purchasing from suppliers who buy from your company, is a controversial but not uncommon practice. Reciprocity agreements that eliminate competition are illegal, and the Department of Justice and the Federal Trade Commission (FTC) will intervene to stop systematic reciprocal buying practices deemed to be anticompetitive.

Tie-In Sales

A **tie-in** occurs when a seller (salesperson) requires a customer to buy an unwanted product along with the desired product. Such requirements are prohibited.

Tie-In An often-illegal seller's requirement that a customer purchase an unwanted product along with the desired product.

Unordered Goods

Section 5 of the FTC Act prohibits companies from shipping unordered goods or shipping larger quantities than customers ordered.

Orders and Terms of Sale

It is illegal for sellers to substitute goods different from those ordered, to misrepresent delivery dates, or to fail to fill an order within a reasonable time. Key terms of sale, such as warranties or guarantees, the ability of the buyer to cancel a contract or obtain a refund, and important facts in a credit or financing transaction cannot be concealed or misrepresented.

Business Descriptions

Salespeople must never misrepresent their company's financial strength, length of time in business, reputation, or particulars about its plant, equipment, and facilities.

Product Descriptions

It is illegal to lie about how a product is made. A salesperson may not state that a product is "custom-made" or "tailor-made" when it is actually ready-made. In addition, no statements can be made about "proven" claims unless scientific or empirical evidence is available to substantiate the truth of the claims.

Secret Rebates

Salespeople cannot secretly reward a dealer's salespeople for pushing sales of their company's products. Even if the dealer's management approves such an incentive plan for their employees, this practice may violate the Sherman Act if it results in unfair discrimination among competing dealers.

Customer Coercion

Salespeople cannot make fictitious inquiries that harass a competitor or pressure anyone into buying a product through scare tactics, coercion, or intimidation.

Business Defamation Any action or utterance that slanders, libels, or disparages a competitor, causing the competitor financial damage, lost customers, unemployment, or lost sales.

Business Slander Unfair and untrue *oral* statements made about competitors that damage the reputation of the competitor or the personal reputation of an individual in that business.

Business Defamation

Many companies and their salespeople have been sued by competitors for making slanderous statements about them that caused financial damage, lost customers, unemployment, or lost sales. The Federal Trade Commission can impose cease-and-desist orders or obtain an injunction against companies that engage in unfair or deceptive practices through their salespeople. What's more, private lawsuits may be brought against the offenders. **Business defamation** can include the following offenses:

1. **Business slander** occurs when unfair and untrue *oral* statements are made about competitors that damage the reputation of the competitor or the personal reputation of an individual in that business.

2. **Business libel** occurs when unfair and untrue statements are made about a competitor *in writing* (usually a letter, sales literature, advertisement, or company brochure), damaging the competitor's reputation or the personal reputation of an individual in that business.
3. **Product disparagement** occurs when false or deceptive comparisons or distorted claims are *made during or after a sales presentation* about a competitor's products, services, or properties. These statements are considered defamatory *per se;* that is, a defamed company or individual need not prove actual damages to win a favorable verdict, only that the statement is untrue. Below are the kinds of statements that may be judged defamatory:
   - Untrue comments that a competitor is engaging in illegal or unfair business practices
   - Untrue remarks that a competitor fails to live up to its contractual obligations and responsibilities
   - Untrue statements regarding a competitor's financial condition
   - Untrue statements that a principal in the competitor's business is incompetent, of poor moral character, unreliable, or dishonest

Business Libel Unfair and untrue statements made about a competitor *in writing* (usually a letter, sales literature, advertisement, or company brochure), damaging the competitor's reputation or the personal reputation of an individual in that business.

Product Disparagement False or deceptive comparisons or distorted claims *made during or after a sales presentation* about a competitor's products, services, or properties. These statements are considered defamatory *per se.*

When the FTC receives a complaint or believes that a company is violating a law, it issues a complaint to the company stating that it is in violation. If the company persists in the questionable practice, the FTC can issue a cease-and-desist order demanding that the business stop the practice or risk civil penalties in court of $10,000 per day for each infraction. Read the accompanying *Keeping Up Online* feature to find out more about the FTC.

A reputation for integrity and high ethical standards in dealing with all people at all times is one of the most valuable possessions of the professional salesperson. Ethics will pay off in the long run because nearly all customers—even those who are not ethical themselves—prefer to do business with a salesperson who is ethical.

Chapter Review Questions

Name and briefly describe several of the most important federal laws affecting business-to-business selling.

What are the three most common kinds of business defamation?

Why should salespeople be especially careful about business defamation during or after the sales presentation?

KEEPING UP ONLINE: FEDERAL TRADE COMMISSION

The Federal Trade Commission (FTC) is the agency most involved in regulating U.S. business practices. Sometimes, however, the FTC encourages firms within an industry to establish their own set of trade practices. If businesses could agree on their own set of trade practices, do you think it still would be necessary to have a Federal Trade Commission? Why? Go to the FTC website at **www.ftc.gov** to see the wide range of business practices, both online and off-line, that come under its regulatory authority.

ETHICS AND REGULATION IN INTERNATIONAL SALES

Professional salespeople must avoid unethical and illegal activities such as bribes, payoffs, or kickbacks.
David Pollack/Corbis

Salespeople in international selling face shifting ethical standards and accepted modes of behavior as they go from one country to another. Selling practices that are illegal or unethical in one country may be accepted ways of doing business in another. Yet salespeople who engage in some practices that are acceptable abroad may be criticized or even prosecuted for violation of U.S. law. International salespeople are restrained by three laws.

1. U.S. law prohibits American companies from trading with some foreign countries—which vary depending on our political relationships.
2. Salespeople must obey the *laws of the host country* where they operate, even though these may differ sharply from U.S. laws. Some foreign countries actually have more restrictive business laws than the United States. For example, Greece sued Colgate-Palmolive (www.colgatepalmolive.com) for giving away razor blades with its shaving cream. France and Sweden regulate across-border flows of mailing lists and data about citizens. Japan restricts compilation of computerized mailing lists. More often, however, U.S. companies and their salespeople face particularly difficult moral and ethical issues in foreign countries with less restrictive business laws. For instance, in some countries, payment of bribes to high-level military officials in order to sell weapons to their government is the expected way of doing business.
3. The multinational firm is subject to *international laws* that are enforced across national boundaries. Gifts, bribes, and payoffs have consistently been identified as the major abuses in international personal selling. One case, for example, involved payments of nearly $38,000,000 made by Lockheed Martin (www.lockheedmartin.com) to government officials in Japan, Italy, and the Netherlands to win sales for its L1011 Tri Star and F-104 Starfighter jet airplanes. The Foreign Corrupt Practices Act prohibits U.S. firms from giving such bribes to host country personnel. Both the United Nations and the European Economic Community are standardizing commercial codes that deal with such issues as product safety and environmental standards and are making them binding on all companies whose nations endorse the codes. Eventually, perhaps, ethical standards can be established among trading partners.

Sales representatives planning to sell products or services in a foreign country should check with the U.S. Department of Commerce (www.commerce.gov) for information about each country's legal restrictions on imports and about U.S. restrictions on exports. For example, sales of some categories of technological equipment and processes are restricted by U.S. law or by edict of the Department of State (www.state.gov) or

Department of Defense (www.dod.gov), and such items are not allowed to leave the country. Then, before beginning any transaction within the foreign country, sales representatives should contact the commercial attaché at the U.S. embassy for information on the specific legal requirements in conducting business there.

In international negotiations, salespeople must not confuse ethical standards and the law. Ethical practices vary greatly from one country to another. "Lubrication bribery," or the payment of small amounts of money to grease the wheels of bureaucracy, is deeply entrenched in some parts of the world. A lubrication bribe, or *baksheesh*, is often the accepted and expected way of doing business in the Middle East and Far East. In Italy, a *bustarella* (an envelope stuffed with lire notes) persuades a particular license clerk to do his job. By contrast, *mordida* ("the bite") ensures that a Mexican government inspector will not do his job. *Whitemail bribery* buys influence at high levels.

Even though payoffs and bribes sometimes seem necessary to do business in some countries, a study of sixty-five major American corporations (forty of which admitted to making questionable payments abroad) found that these payments usually just shift orders from one American company to another. If both companies follow the same ethical standards, no payment is needed. Interestingly, though, a study of eight hundred senior executives in fifteen developing countries determined that, out of twenty-one major trading nations, firms in the United States (as well as in Russia and Asia) are *most likely* to pay bribes when seeking business in emerging nations. This is occurring despite the U.S. government's ratification of the *1999 Anti-Bribery Convention of the Organization for Economic Development and Cooperation*, which is aimed at prosecuting U.S. companies that foster corruption in international markets.[38] Table 3.2 provides useful propositions concerning doing business in foreign countries.

Chapter Review Question
What are three different sets of laws that international salespeople must abide by?

TABLE 3.2

Doing Business in Foreign Countries

1. When one is operating in foreign markets, no single standard of ethical behavior applies to all business decisions. A wide range of standards and modes of ethical conduct will confront salespeople selling in international markets.
2. In developing countries, not the laws of the country but, rather, the degree of enforcement of those laws is likely to determine the lower limit of acceptable business behavior of sales personnel.
3. The upper level of ethical conduct pertaining to doing business in foreign markets is not clearly defined.
4. Flagrant unethical behavior by salespeople may attract substantial attention in foreign countries and might lead to regulatory action aimed at the offending company.
5. Salespeople must be intimately familiar with the foreign country in which they are operating to avoid an ethnocentric posture and ethical misjudgments.

Source: *Adapted from Gene R. Laczniak and Jacob Naor, "Global Ethics: Wrestling with the Corporate Conscience,"* Business *(July-September 1985): 3–10.*

MAKING ETHICAL DECISIONS

In both the domestic and international arenas, ethical standards must be a part of the salesperson's individual value system and incorporated into his or her decision making. Table 3.3 suggests a five-step process for ethical decision making.

A salesperson's reputation for ethical conduct is an invaluable advantage in developing and maintaining long-term relationships with customers. It makes good economic sense to be known as a salesperson who can be trusted to do the right thing in all situations. Thus, whether you're a naturally ethical person or someone who simply wants to be as successful as possible in your career, remember that people with many years of experience in sales have discovered that behaving ethically pays big dividends in the long run.

TABLE 3.3

ETHICAL DECISION-MAKING CHECKLIST

1. General Questions

- Who is responsible to act?
- What are the consequences of the action? (Benefits-Harm Analysis)
- What rights, and whose rights, are affected? (Rights-Principles Analysis)
- What is fair treatment in this case? (Social Justice Analysis)

2. Solution Development

- What solutions are available to me?
- Have I considered all of the creative solutions that might permit me to reduce harm, maximize benefits, respect more rights, or be fair to more parties?

3. Selection of the Optimum Solution

- What are the potential consequences of my solutions?
- Which of the options I have considered does the most to maximize benefits, reduce harm, respect rights, and increase fairness?
- Are all parties treated fairly in my proposed decision?

4. Implementation

- Who should be consulted and informed?
- What actions will ensure that my decision achieves the intended outcome?
- Implement the decision.

5. Follow-Up

- Was the decision implemented correctly?
- Did the decision maximize benefits, reduce harm, respect rights, and treat all parties fairly?

Source: *Adapted from Patrick E. Murphy, "Implementing Business Ethics,"* Journal of Business Ethics *(December 1988): 913.*

SUMMARY

Ethics is the study of what's right and wrong and serves as the basis for a code of conduct for interactions among people. Salespeople need training in ethical conduct for dealing with customers, competitors, co-workers, and their own companies. In addition, companies have a responsibility to act ethically with their salespeople. International selling is affected by U.S. laws, laws of the host country, and international laws enforced across national boundaries, as well as by varying ethical expectations in different countries. Salespeople and their companies should bear in mind that what is legal or ethical in the host country may not be in the United States. But even so, the salesperson and his or her company will be held responsible for their conduct in both countries. Cultural differences make it critical that salespeople understand the legal, ethical, and social climate of any countries in which they are attempting to sell their company's products.

KEY TERMS

Ethics	Price Fixing	Tie-In	Business Libel
Quid Pro Quo Harassment	Collusion	Business Defamation	Product Disparagement
Hostile Environment	Exclusive Dealing	Business Slander	

TOPICS FOR THOUGHT AND CLASS DISCUSSION

1. How do you think your ethical values were formed? Who had the most influence on you? Why?
2. Why must salespeople concern themselves with ethical issues? Isn't it enough to understand and operate within the law?
3. Do you believe that ethical standards in the United States are relatively stable or changing? Do you think U.S. ethical standards are becoming higher or lower? Why?
4. Why do countries differ so sharply about what is ethical or unethical behavior? Do you think that all countries would ever adopt an international code of ethical behavior in business?
5. How do you think you would handle a situation in which you were trying to make a multimillion-dollar sale to a foreign country and that country's trade representative made it clear that he expected a substantial bride?
6. Have you ever been a victim of sexual harassment? If so, how did you deal with it?
7. What do you think are today's major ethical issues?
8. Do you have any personal guidelines for what is ethical or unethical behavior? Would you like to see everyone use your guidelines?

INTERNET EXERCISES

1. Go online to find the ethical codes or codes of business conduct for three different companies (e.g., Coca-Cola, Haliburton, and DuPont). You can find various companies' business codes at websites such as *infomgmt.homestead.com/files/ethcod_f.htm.*

Compare the three codes. How do they vary in length, specificity, and content? What does each code have to say about salesperson or selling behavior?

2. Using your college's electronic database, find three articles on "business ethics" in business journals or magazines. In what journals or magazines did you find the articles? Do the articles mention ethics in personal selling? What guidelines, if any, do the articles provide for ethical conduct? If you were to start up a small business, what would your one-page ethical code or code of business conduct say to your employees?

PROJECTS FOR PERSONAL GROWTH

1. Locate and interview two salespeople. Ask them how they decide whether a particular behavior is ethical or unethical. Did they receive any instruction in ethics during their sales training program? Do their companies have codes of ethics? What punishments or penalties accompany ethical violations?
2. Write down two ethical dilemmas that you have personally faced. How did you decide what to do in each case? In retrospect, do you think your decisions were the right ones? Who was affected by your decision? How? Would you be willing to tell your friends the total truth about the dilemma and how you resolved it? How do you think they would react?
3. Go to your college or public library and look through issues from the 1940s or 1950s of popular magazines such as *Life* or *Time* and compare them with recent issues. Do the advertisements seem more or less ethical than those of today? Why do you think so, and what might account for the differences?

ROLE-PLAY EXERCISE 3.1

Overpromising

Situation

For six months, 23-year-old Homer Swisher has been a field sales representative for Dayton-Clark Corporation, a small automobile parts manufacturer based in Alabama. Because they were to attend a trade show together later in the day, Homer got the chance to go on a sales call with his boss, John Wright. Homer quietly observed as Mr. Wright made one of the largest sales of the year. Much to Homer's surprise, before signing the contract, John verbally promised the customer a delivery date that Homer was quite sure Dayton-Clark could not meet.

BOSS (JOHN WRIGHT): Well, Homer, did you learn anything by watching me in action? You give a customer what he wants and you'll nearly always make the sale.

HOMER: Yes sir, you made a great sales presentation. But I wasn't aware that we could get five weeks delivery on that new equipment.

BOSS: It's not important whether we can deliver in five weeks or not, Homer. If I had told him that delivery would take eight weeks, I'd have lost the sale. When we get back to the office, I'll go over to production and tell them we need delivery in five weeks. If they don't make it, it's not my fault. At the end of five weeks, I'll tell the customer that I don't know what the problem is, but I'll find out and get back to him. Then, after a couple of days, I'll call the customer back and tell him that production messed up. To smooth things over, I'll write the customer a note and enclose a couple of tickets to a ballgame or something.

HOMER: Doesn't the production manager get angry when he's blamed for missing the delivery date?

BOSS: Naw, I just keep him out of the picture. I don't complain to him when the product isn't delivered in five weeks and he never finds out what I told the customer.

HOMER: I don't think I can deliberately mislead customers on something as important as delivery dates. Don't customers stop buying from you when you don't keep your promises?

BOSS: Homer, in this business, it's a daily fight for survival and you say and do what you must to get the order when you have the opportunity. Tomorrow's another day. Customers understand that you can't control everything, and they don't blame you personally for mistakes at the home office. Haven't you ever promised something to someone that you knew you couldn't deliver on?

Roles

Homer Swisher A conscientious young man who would like to do the right things in his career, Homer wants to question his boss further about the effect that overpromising has on future business with those customers. He's not really trying to judge his boss but, rather, wants to learn what a salesperson has to do to compete in this industry. Homer is concerned that he may have to adopt this questionable practice of overpromising because his boss is advocating it. It is difficult for a salesperson to reject the selling techniques of his or her sales manager, but Homer wants to know whether overpromising is something he will have to do in order to compete. He knows that he may be treading on thin ice in discussing what may be an ethical issue, so he tries to be careful not to irritate his boss.

John Wright A smooth-talking, very confident young man who is only three years older than Homer, John was promoted to sales supervisor last year after two years with Dayton-Clark. John's original sales territory was in the northern part of the state, but since his promotion, he has been assigned a new territory in the southern part of the state. Three other salespeople besides Homer Swisher report to John.

ROLE-PLAY EXERCISE 3.2

Dealing with Sexual Harassment

Situation

Renée Mathieson works as a field sales representative for Lady Smyth Company, a manufacturer of women's hosiery and undergarments. Ms. Mathieson makes sales calls on the buying offices of retail store chains and a few large independent department stores. Renée loves the freedom and challenge her job offers, but after three years covering a territory, she hopes to be promoted to branch sales manager after her annual performance evaluation in two months. Without this promotion, she is afraid that the sales management career path may become closed to her. Her district sales manager, Anthony Bizzarri, is a 42-year-old, recently divorced man, who has been in his present job for seven years. Renée realizes, as do most of the other sales reps, that Mr. Bizzarri's career has probably peaked because people are generally promoted after only four or five years in that job.

Today, Mr. Bizzarri (or Tony, as everyone calls him) is spending the day with Renée calling on customers and getting an idea of the level of customer satisfaction in her territory. At the end of the day, Tony tells Renée that he is pleased with what he has seen in her territory and that she certainly seems in line to be promoted to branch manager. However, he adds, there are four other strong candidates for the job as well, and he must make a decision within four weeks to forward to the regional manager, George Bishop, for approval. As they are drinking their coffee after an early-evening meal in an excellent restaurant, Tony takes Renée's hand and says, "Renée, let me put it to you this way. I can choose anyone I want to be branch manager, and I'd like to choose you, but what's in for me if I choose you? As you know, I've been divorced for over a year now, and I'd like some steady companionship. You're a single woman with an active social life. Do you think you could fit me in for a date at least once a week? If you can, the branch manager job is yours."

Renée is stunned by Tony's proposition, and she is certainly not attracted to him, even if he weren't seventeen years older. Besides, she has a steady boyfriend who will be finishing law school next year, and she has no interest in dating anyone else. Nevertheless, Renée doesn't want to insult Tony or make him mad, so she's desperately looking for some way to put him off.

Roles

Renée Mathieson Charming and enthusiastic, Renée has had to find a way to discourage several men who have approached her over the years, but she's never had to deal with an amorous boss before. She wants to find a way to discourage Tony without jeopardizing her promotion or causing him to lose face. She is reluctant to report Tony to his boss because she thinks that could lead to some serious trouble for her. It would be difficult to substantiate her allegations, and she might get labeled as a trouble-maker.

Tony Bizzarri Ever since his divorce and recognition that his career is going nowhere, Tony has invested most of his energy in the active pursuit of young women. It's almost like a challenge for him to win them over, and he seems to feel better about himself whenever he is successful. He knows that he's taking a chance in propositioning Renée, but he figures that she's fair game because she's an ambitious, single woman. "Moreover," he thinks, "what can she do to hurt my career? I've already peaked out. Besides, who's going to believe her if she tells on me after failing to get the promotion? People will think it's just sour grapes."

CASE 3.1 IT'S THE SHORT RUN THAT MATTERS MOST!

After graduating from Eastern Michigan University, Stewart Dickinson accepted a sales position with Spearhead Technologies, Inc., a small, fast-growing measuring instruments firm in Kalamazoo, Michigan. After completing his first year on the job, Stewart felt a little disappointed because he didn't make his annual sales quota. Although the sales manager, Sylvia Ambers, did not express any disappointment at Stewart's year-end performance review, she did tell him that she thought he could do better. And she suggested that Stewart talk with some top-performing salespeople in the company to see if he could pick up some sales tips. In fact, she said that she had arranged for Stewart to meet next Wednesday with George Fagus, who had been with the company only two years but had exceeded his sales quota each year.

Stewart was a little apprehensive when he met George for lunch at a popular Kalamazoo restaurant. George was a smooth-talking, former varsity football player at the University of Nebraska who exhibited supreme confidence. The two had met only casually and had never really talked. What's more, Stewart knew that Sylvia had probably asked George to give him some selling advice. After exchanging some pleasantries and other small talk about sports, George said, "Stew, let me level with you. Sylvia has asked me to help you out. I understand that you had an okay year, but you're a bright, energetic guy who can do better."

(*continued*)

"George," responded Stewart, "I've worked really hard this year but it's been tough selling measuring instruments in this down market, especially when our competitors are offering better deals than we are."

"I hear you, Stew. But to play in the big leagues, you've got to be aggressive and creative! Let me give you a personal example. At the beginning of last quarter, it didn't look like I was going to make my sales quota this year, either. So I shifted to a creative strategy. I told a couple of my biggest customers that I'd heard rumors about a big price increase in our line of measuring instruments next quarter, and I advised them to stock up now. Both of these big customers doubled their orders for the month. On another one of my sales calls, the prospect said that he was about to place a big order with a major competitor, Midas Measures, because he needed some measuring devices specially tailored to some new equipment his company had recently purchased. His company's production manager needed the new instruments within two weeks, so he wasn't even considering buying from Spearhead because he had heard that it took us nearly a month to deliver. Well, between you and me, Stew, he was right, but why should I just give up and let some competitor take that business? I told the prospect that if he would sign the order form today, I'd put a rush on his order, fax it in immediately, and have it delivered within nine days. Of course, it ain't goin' to happen, but I got the order instead of the competitor, who probably wouldn't have delivered on time either. When the prospect doesn't get the instruments within nine days, I'll just give him an excuse about a screw-up in production. 'Hey, it's not my fault,' I'll tell him . . ., 'I did my best!'"

Stewart thought for a moment and replied, shaking his head, "George, I'm not comfortable misleading customers or lying to them about delivery dates."

"I don't like it either, Stew, but I've found if you don't use every weapon in your arsenal to make a sale, you're going to lose it. Remember the trainers told us never to be negative about competitors before, during, or after a sales presentation? Well, that advice is for wimps. If I subtly plant a little negative information about a competitor during the sales presentation or afterward, it helps me win the sale. Besides, our competitors are always badmouthing our products. You gotta fight fire with fire!"

George winked at Stewart. "Stew, I've found that if I can bring my biggest customers a little insider information about their competitors, they reward me with a big order. Just the other day, I told the purchasing manager at Giant Gears, Inc., that their major competitor, Pitt Manufacturing, was upgrading their warranties to five years on all their products. That little bit of information got me a 25 percent larger order than usual. What's the harm in telling them something that they're going to find out about soon anyway?"

"But, George," said Stewart, sitting back and crossing his arms, "Aren't you concerned that when you don't deliver an order on time, you'll lose that customer's future business? And if you reveal confidential information to one customer about another one, won't that lead to mistrust in your long-run relationships with customers?"

George split a roll, buttered it generously, and took a large bite. "The game is making sales, not developing relationships. Furthermore, all this talk about customer relationship management is just that—so much talk. I'm not going to be in sales long enough to see any long-run pay off. After another year in field selling, I expect to be a sales manager. Right now, I'm looking good because my sales volume is great. If customers start complaining later, who cares? That's going to be the problem of whoever has taken over my old territory. I'll have moved on. Stew, it's all about doing what's best for you right now. No matter what anyone says, it's all about the short run . . . today's transaction . . . even top management turns over about every three years, so who's ever around for the long run? In the long run, we're all dead!"

Questions

1. What do you think about George Fagus's approach to personal selling? Why do you think he's viewed as a top performer at Spearhead Technologies?
2. Do you think that Stewart should follow George's advice, at least for the next year or so, so that he can make his sales quotas? Why? If you don't agree with George's advice, what advice would you give Stewart? What should Stewart do next year at this

(*continued*)

time if he hasn't made his sales quota? What should he say to his sales manager, Sylvia Ambers?

3. Do you think Spearhead Technologies has any problems in its performance evaluation system? For example, do you think the company is giving equal weight to qualitative performance and quantitative performance? What can the company do to ensure a better balance in its performance evaluation for salespeople? How might an improved performance evaluation system help Spearhead Technologies?

CASE 3.2 AFFABLE, OR OVERLY AFFECTIONATE?

CASE 3.2 "AFFABLE, OR OVERLY AFFECTIONATE?" CAN BE FOUND ONLINE AT HTTP://COLLEGE.HMCO.COM/PIC/ANDERSONPS2E

CHAPTER 4

Prospecting and Qualifying: Filling the Salesperson's "Pot of Gold"

After reading this chapter, you should understand:

- The steps in the personal selling process.
- The importance of prospecting.
- How to qualify leads as prospects.
- Several prospecting methods.
- The steps in developing a prospecting plan.

"Concentrate on the activities of prospecting, presenting and following-up; the sales will take care of themselves."

Brian Tracy, nationally known sales consultant

INSIDE PERSONAL SELLING

Meet Jenn Berdis of DHL

"Prospecting," says Jenn Berdis, "is a huge part of my day-to-day job." Berdis is an account representative for DHL, the leading global express delivery and logistics company. She attracts new customers and keeps current customers satisfied by improving DHL's small-parcel shipping programs, covering everything from letters to packages weighing as much as 150 pounds.

Berdis averages twenty new business calls a week and spends about 40 percent of her time looking for leads as well as following up on promising prospects. She identifies potential customers in a variety of ways, such as looking at Internet sites, folowing up on lead campaigns generated through DHL's customer relationship management system, and using DHL's database tools. In addition, she uses telemarketing, area-specific canvassing, and cold calling—visiting businesses without an appointment.

Leads from DHL drivers are particularly valuable, because the drivers often develop relationships with employees of the companies where they make deliveries. Berdis tracks the results "to determine which methods have proved most successful in obtaining appointments with prospects and which have resulted in new business. Over time, this has

allowed me to understand where my energy should be spent," she notes.

To qualify a prospect, Berdis visits the company's website, studies its brochures, and reads its annual report. "We're looking for two things," she explains. "We want to identify a company's need for transportation and shipping. We also want to understand its organizational structure. Is this a multi-location account or a single site? Who are the key players within that organization, and what are their concerns?" Berdis's research helps her identify not only the people in the company who use shipping services but also the person who actually has the authority to make buying decisions about shipping.

Not long ago, one of DHL's drivers returned from a delivery with a lead. He had learned that a beauty products distributor was unhappy with its current shipping company. Next, Berdis says, "I visited the distributor's website to learn more about its business, customer base, and distribution network." Armed with this background information, she phoned the company's president and asked a number of qualifying questions.

As a result of that phone call, "I was able to schedule a meeting with the president and his key managers," Berdis remembers. "It also helped me plan my sales call." During her visit with the shipping manager and other executives, she developed a more detailed understanding of the company's requirements and expectations. Then she presented a couple of specific alternatives for solving the current problem—and closed the sale. "If you can position yourself as a consultant, someone who wants to understand the customer's business and help address the challenges that keep its managers awake at night, you will be viewed as a real partner."

With the globalization of trade, the current business environment can be characterized as intensely competitive. Firms from all over the world are vying with each other for survival or a bigger piece of the pie. Indeed, some leading business philosophers have adopted a rather unconventional way of viewing competition. They observe that the traditional perspective is to view companies as competing against one another, but more realistically, many firms are waging economic war against one another.[1] Although manufacturing high-quality products has become imperative for survival, it's hard to differentiate, for long, one company's offerings from those of other companies. Even innovative products such as Apple's iPod (www.apple.com) are quickly copied by other manufacturers. Commonplace high-tech products, such as computers, are widely considered little more than commodities by customers today, so most buyers just search for the best price. With companies marketing commodity-like products to most of the same customer groups, fierce competitive battles are waged, not so much on the production line but in the marketing arena. To win these ongoing battles, some business thinkers advise firms to develop guerilla marketing tactics based on militaristic concepts of strategic planning to overpower competitors.[2]

To craft successful marketing strategies, managers need to make timely and effective product, pricing, distribution, and promotion mix decisions. Nested within the promotion mix, which also encompasses advertising, sales promotion, and public relations, is personal selling. There are exceptions, but personal selling is usually the most expensive and most emphasized component of the promotion mix for companies marketing high-priced, technologically complex, high-involvement products targeted at business-to-business markets. Thus, if you subscribe to the economic warfare view, then winning "marketing battles" requires development and implementation of marketing strategies where salespeople serve as the frontline infantry soldiers who do the hand-to-hand combat. To illustrate, GlaxoSmithKline P.L.C. (www.gsk.com/worldwide.htm), the world's second-largest drug manufacturer, recently called for a "cease-fire in the arms race" of pharmaceutical companies continually increasing the size of their sales forces.[3] Spurred by fierce competition to generate blockbuster sales, drug companies increased their full-time and part-time sales representatives calling on physicians by nearly 100,000 in 2004, while cutting back on research and hiring other employees. There is now more than one sales rep for every two doctors.

Even if you feel that the warfare analogy is a bit overstated, the preceding paragraphs should help you appreciate how crucial personal selling is to company success. Unless salespeople are successful in doing their jobs as direct revenue generators, the company cannot thrive or even survive for long. Thus it is imperative to explore the many activities that professional salespeople carry out in generating prospects, confirming sales, building trust, nurturing relationships, increasing customer satisfaction, and augmenting customer loyalty. In chapters 4 through 9, our discussion centers on the **personal selling process (PSP),** which encompasses seven stages through which salespeople must progress. Each of these stages will be described separately to make it clear how the PSP can foster selling success.

Personal Selling Process (PSP) The seven-stage process of professional personal selling, from prospecting and qualifying prospects to following up and servicing customers.

For years salespeople have used the PSP to achieve success for themselves, their companies, and their customers. In a sense, salesperson efforts to facilitate purchases and engender customer satisfaction resemble ways in which effective managers (or leaders) deal with their employees (or followers):

> Leadership and selling are both forms of influence. . . . Like leadership, the sales influence may be a matter of persuasion or it can derive from a participative or consensual decision. . . . In the sales-customer and the leader-follower situations, the salesperson and the leader make the attempt to change and influence the perceptions, cognitions, decisions, and behaviors of the customer and the follower. If the customer and the follower are influenced, both the selling and the leadership are *successful*. . . . If the customer and the follower are influenced *and* their needs and expectations are fulfilled, then the selling and the leadership are successful and *effective*. The selling and the leadership are successful and effective when the needs of the customers are met by a sale as a consequence of the efforts of the salesperson and when the goals of followers are achieved as a consequence of the efforts of the leader.[4]

STAGES IN THE PERSONAL SELLING PROCESS

Professional salespeople need to master basic selling strategies and tactics and then develop their own styles in adapting to specific customer types and selling situations. As we learned in chapter 1, countless small tasks in the PSP may be organized into seven major stages[5]:

1. Prospecting and qualifying
2. Planning the sales call (preapproach)
3. Approaching the prospect
4. Making the sales presentation and demonstration
5. Negotiating resistance and objections
6. Confirming and closing the sale
7. Following up and servicing customers

Although we have sequentially numbered the PSP stages above, it is more accurate to think of them as interacting, overlapping, and continuous stages, depicted as the revolving cycle or wheel shown in Figure 4.1. Successful selling relies on retaining *good* customers through post-sale service and relationship development, which leads to repeat sales and referrals to new prospects whom you hope to turn into customers—and so the wheel keeps turning. We will present this wheel at the beginning of the next six chapters to trace our discussion of the PSP. "Prospecting and Qualifying," the first stage of the PSP and the subject of this chapter, is highlighted on this chapter's wheel.

FIGURE 4.1

THE PERSONAL SELLING PROCESS (PSP)

It is strongly suggested that you read each of the personal selling process chapters multiple times and that you look for opportunities to use the information you learn and the insights you attain here as soon as possible. You might find opportunities to do this by joining a student marketing or sales organization, taking a part-time job, role-playing with friends or fellow students, or participating in class discussions. Using the PSP early on will have the following three important and near-term benefits for you:

1. It will acquaint you with principles and methods of *real-world selling.*
2. It will help you decide whether professional personal selling is the right career choice for you.
3. It will give you more confidence in interviewing for jobs, whether in personal selling or in other fields.

Chapter Review Question
Identify and describe the seven basic stages in the selling process.

THE IMPORTANCE OF PROSPECTING

As depicted by the wheel of personal selling, the selling process can be viewed as a continually revolving cycle, each stage of which connects with—and overlaps—adjoining stages. The entire wheel turns around its *most important* part: its "axis" of *prospects* and *customers*. Although every stage of the PSP is crucial, the central importance of prospects and customers makes the first and seventh stages of the process especially significant. After all, the promise of potential customers and the security of satisfied current customers give the wheel its initial forward movement—and its continuous momentum. The initial push of the PSP wheel comes in the Prospecting and Qualifying stage.

Prospecting is the process of searching for leads—people and organizations that might need your product—and then qualifying them as prospects or potential customers. (We discuss *qualifying* later in this chapter.) It is an essential, future-oriented task in that the payoff in sales comes later. It is not done, however, without certain costs (e.g., salesperson time, out-of-pocket costs, opportunity costs of failing to further develop another satisfied account). Despite its costs, prospecting must be a continuous part of the selling job. Many salespeople think of prospects as their "pot of gold" from which they can draw whenever sales are slow. To increase or even maintain sales volume, sales reps must *continually* seek out and prospect for new customers for several reasons:

Prospecting The process of searching for leads—people and organizations that might need your product—and then qualifying them as prospects or potential customers.

- The need to increase total sales.
- Customers switch to other suppliers.
- Customers move out of your territory.
- Customers go out of business.
- Customers die.
- Customers' businesses are taken over by another company.
- Customers have only a one-time need for the product.
- Relationships with some customers deteriorate, and they stop buying from you.
- Your buying contacts are promoted, demoted, transferred, or fired, or they retire or resign.

Prospecting can produce significant benefits. Salespeople who continually prospect can generate a steady flow of sales (future sources of sales revenue come from prospects) and offset customer attrition. Also, prospecting can help create a more productive selling environment because the likelihood of your making a sale increases when you are dealing with a legitimate, or "qualified," prospect. In addition, prospecting helps create a more enjoyable sales call atmosphere because you know before making the initial contact that the prospect needs the product.

Chapter Review Question

Give several reasons why a salesperson's present customers stop buying.

In the next section, we discuss many different ways to prospect for leads. Later in the chapter, we'll talk about how to qualify those leads. And, in *The Life of a Salesperson*, you'll see how Jason Smyczynski, who has recently embarked on a career as a salesperson, prospects for and qualifies leads.

PROSPECTING FOR LEADS

Random-Lead Searching Generation of leads by randomly calling on organizations. Sometimes called "blind" searching.

Selective-Lead Searching Application of systematic strategies to generate leads from predetermined target markets.

The two basic ways to search for leads are random searching and selective searching.[6] **Random-lead searching,** sometimes called blind searching, generates leads by randomly calling on organizations (door-to-door canvassing) or by mass promotional appeals (advertising) to which organizations respond and thereby identify themselves as leads. Because randomly searching for leads can be inefficient, most salespeople prefer to employ more planned strategies. The application of systematic strategies to generate leads from predetermined target markets is called **selective-lead searching.**

Table 4.1 shows several random searching methods and selective searching methods; we can further divide the latter into direct and indirect sources. Leads can also be categorized as effort and non-effort leads. *Non-effort leads* are supplied by the company or from an individual's voluntary inquiry or response to advertising. An *effort lead* is generated solely by the salesperson. Most leads come from diligent efforts, whereas non-effort leads are considered serendipitous.[7] *Direct sources* allow leads to be identified by name or approached directly by salespeople, whereas *indirect sources* require leads to identify themselves by responding to a general call. Each of the random and selective searching methods can be useful to professional salespeople, depending on the product and the customer mix in a given situation. Let's discuss several methods for obtaining leads.

Random-Lead Searching

Door-to-Door Canvassing Knocking on doors in a commercial area without an appointment to locate prospects.

Cold Calling Approaching or calling a business without an appointment for the purpose of prospecting or selling.

Random-lead searching includes door-to-door canvassing and cold calls, territory blitz of organizations, advertising, electronic mail, and websites.

Door-to-Door Canvassing and Cold Calls. **Door-to-door canvassing** requires knocking on many doors in a given area, without an appointment, and introducing yourself in search of leads. This approach is usually not very efficient or effective, but it can supplement other methods for obtaining leads. For instance, if you are between scheduled sales calls, **cold calling** can be a valuable use of

TABLE 4.1

Looking for Leads

Random-Lead Searching Methods	
Door-to-door canvassing of organizations	Advertising
Territory blitz of organizations	Print media
Cold calls on organizations	Broadcast media
E-mails to organizations	Websites
Selective-Lead Searching Methods	
Direct Sources	**Indirect Sources**
Friends, neighbors, and acquaintances	Direct mail or e-mail
Personal observation	Trade shows, fairs, and exhibitions
Spotters, or "bird dogs"	Professional seminars and conferences
Satisfied customers and former customers	Contests
Endless chain	Free gifts
Networking	Unsolicited inquiries
Centers of influence	Telemarketing
Internet (World Wide Web)	
Junior salespeople and sales associates	
Professional sales organizations	
Company records	
Directories and mailing lists	
Newsletters	
Surveys	

what might otherwise be down-time. You should use door-to-door canvassing, which can be very time-consuming and unproductive, only when other lead-generating approaches are unavailable or don't seem to be working. To reduce the frustration of cold calls that produce few shows of interest, precede your visit with some research on the company (e.g., nature of the business, size, problems, key contact individuals) to maximize the effectiveness of the call.

A great deal of face-to-face canvassing has been replaced by telephoning, faxing, or e-mailing initial sales messages to potential customers and then following up with face-to-face calls if the prospect responds favorably. The best salespeople develop excellent telephone skills and can fearlessly call prospective new accounts. A slow afternoon's paperwork can be enlivened by making a few telephone cold calls, and they often yield at least a few appointments, if not an actual sale. Because of the growing number of "no-call telephone lists," telephoning leads is becoming much less effective in the business-to-consumer

ON THE FRONTLINES: THE LIFE OF A SALESPERSON

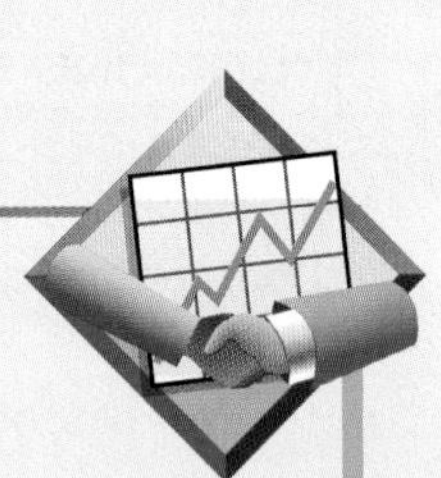

Jason Smyczynski: Manufacturers' Sales Representative

Jason Smyczynski graduated from Loyola University in New Orleans, Louisiana, with a B.A. in marketing. Even prior to college, Jason knew that he wanted to follow in his father's footsteps and embark on a career as a sales representative. Thus Jason majored in marketing and took keen interest in all his marketing classes, especially the personal selling course.

A brain-child of his father's, Chris-Jay Marketing is a family-run small business that essentially operates as a manufacturers' agent and sales representative for many firms that focus on the industrial, welding, and safety markets. Robert Smyczynski, along with his hard-working sons Jason and Chris, has built Chris-Jay Marketing into a thriving small business with yearly revenues upwards of $6 million and an annual growth rate of approximately 12 percent.

As a manufacturers' agent and sales representative, Chris-Jay Marketing represents a number of small to medium-sized firms, including Norton Abrasives, the Danaher Tool Group (Armstrong Hand Tools, Allen Hand Tools, and Craftsman Industrial Hand Tools), and American Insulated Wire. These firms manufacture a wide array of industrial products, such as sandpaper, wrenches, sockets, ratchets, welding gloves, extension cords, halogen lights, and measuring tapes. These products are sold mainly to industrial distributors, which resell them to diverse other businesses.

Instead of incurring the expense of hiring and managing their own direct sales forces, these small manufacturers employ Chris-Jay Marketing as their sales representatives and agents to cover four states: Louisiana, Mississippi, Alabama, and Florida. In these states, Robert, Chris, and Jason call on industrial distributors such as Industrial Welding Supply and Turner Supply (but not the big-box retail stores such as Ace Hardware, Home Depot, and Lowe's that market to consumers).

Because Chris-Jay Marketing is a small company, its salespeople must be very creative, professional, and service oriented to carry out the personal selling process successfully in highly competitive markets dominated by a few large businesses. Day-to-day motivation of the Chris-Jay Marketing salespeople is not a problem because they are paid strictly on commission—no salary. "So, if we don't sell, we don't eat," quips Jason.

We will follow Jason's personal selling activities throughout several chapters in this book via special *On the Frontlines* boxes titled "The Life of a Salesperson."

ON THE FRONTLINES: THE LIFE OF A SALESPERSON

Prospecting for and Qualifying Leads

"Prospecting and qualifying is probably the most important, ongoing part of my sales job," declares Jason. On behalf of Chris-Jay Marketing, he prospects for new business customers by using several standard sources, including the Thomas Register of National Manufacturers, Dun & Bradstreet, the Yellow Pages, and the Internet. Together, these sources provide most of the information he needs about potential prospects, including company names, addresses, business type, products, key managers, and financial data. As a member of Specialty Tools and Fastener Distributors Association, he obtains leads from their directory on distributors. Jason also regularly networks with businesspeople and other professionals whom he meets at conferences, trade shows, and meetings—always asking for business cards, on which he makes notations to help him remember important information about the contact. Another valuable source of leads and referrals is satisfied current and former customers. Jason feels that the most direct and easiest way to collect the names of new prospects is to ask current prospects and customers for referrals. "People won't give you the name of a potential customer unless they respect that company and its people and they feel that you and your company personnel are professional and trustworthy. Referrals from current customers are nearly always prequalified in terms of the need for our products, person who has the authority to make purchase decisions, the company's overall credit worthiness, and its eligibility to buy from us. Of course, I do go through my usual qualifying checklist, but it's nearly always just a formality to confirm the reliability of the referral." Traveling across several states to meet industrial hand tools distributors, Jason always makes sales call appointments in advance and notifies his prospects and customers a few days before his arrival at their office. Because his clients are small industrial distributor-resellers, Jason typically is able to meet with the owners who have the ultimate authority to make purchase decisions.

"Being a sales rep is a great way to make a good living and enjoy a pleasant lifestyle," says Jason. "Basically, all you do is travel around meeting and talking with people. How hard is that, especially if you genuinely like people, as I do?" *Bottom line:* "If I do the upfront work in prospecting and qualifying, my sales calls are highly productive and my sales job flows smoothly along," explains Jason.

market and can even be illegal, but calling customers in the business-to-business setting is still a viable strategy for making initial contacts.

One highly successful industrial salesperson calls prequalified companies and asks a key manager for an opportunity to meet with him or her for breakfast or lunch. He says something like this: "I'd like the opportunity to meet you and have you meet me. I've just found it's a good business practice to expand your network to share ideas." As this creative salesperson explains, "It's very hard for most people to be so insensitive as to turn down an invitation to meet a fellow human being who has not talked about selling products of any kind." Once he gets the breakfast or luncheon appointment, his focus is on building rapport by mainly listening to the other person, while avoiding the temptation to talk about his own company's products. Later, after the business relationship has been established, he asks for permission to make a sales call. "It's easy," he explains, "to turn down someone who mentions a product or service in the initial contact with a prospect who can simply say, 'I'm not interested in your product or service.' But it's much more difficult to say, 'I'm not interested in meeting you.'"

Territory Blitz An intensified version of door-to-door canvassing in which several salespeople join efforts to call on every organization in a given territory or area.

Territory Blitz of Organizations. A version of door-to-door canvassing is the **territory blitz** (or area blitz), in which several salespeople join efforts to call on every organization within a given territory. Any leads developed during this blitz are turned over to the *regular* territory salesperson for follow-up. This often inefficient approach is seldom used today, because it can be perceived as unprofessional and a "turn-off" if businesspeople detect and resent this all-out invasion of their home turf.

Advertising. Various forms of *print media* (newspapers, magazines, telephone book directories, billboards, and posters) exposure can stimulate people to inquire about the product or service and thus identify themselves as good leads. *Broadcast media* (television, radio, the Internet) exposure can generate leads among audiences less likely to view print media. Some companies prepare leads for the salesperson's call by mailing DVDs and videocassettes or sending e-mails that demonstrate the product or service to make more efficient use of the salesperson's selling time during the actual sales call.

Electronic Mail and Websites. Some salespeople and their companies send unsolicited e-mails over the Internet to large numbers of people. But mass e-mailing requires special care and consideration for the privacy of organizations and their people. Such e-mails may turn off more customers than they attract, especially if the subject lines are viewed as misleading or deceptive. E-mails should target only those companies and people most likely to need the promoted products and services. Some legitimate online marketing research firms will sell you the e-mail addresses of companies and people who have given permission to be solicited for certain categories of products and services. Another, safer approach is to establish a company website that requires or encourages those who visit the site to provide basic qualifying information and then asks them to check a box indicating whether they would grant permission to be contacted by e-mail about products of interest.

Sending out unsolicited, mass commercial e-mails may be considered "spamming" and can cause Internet providers such as AOL to cut off the e-mailer's access. Internet providers will cut off even highly desirable e-mails if they appear to be spam. Harvard University tried to send several hundred e-mails at the same time to high school students, notifying them that they had been accepted for admission. But AOL blocked all these e-mails because they looked like a spamming operation. It's always a good idea to let your Internet provider know in advance before you undertake any mass mailings.

Many recipients of frequent commercial e-mails quickly delete them or set up "filters" to block e-mails from that source in the future. The American Marketing Association has developed a code of ethics, presented in chapter 3, that outlines a set of principles for using the Internet for online selling activities. All salespeople should be familiar with these principles before attempting to prospect online. *TRUSTe,* another nonprofit organization, has developed a "trust-mark" that it awards only to websites that strictly adhere to its privacy principles. E-mail can be an effective tool for prospecting and qualifying, but it is best used only with permission to send such messages, and only if they are not sent so frequently and repetitively as to irritate recipients.

Selective Searching: Direct Sources

In selective searching for leads, the salesperson generates leads from predetermined target markets such as acquaintances, prospects and former customers, other salespeople, and company letters.

Friends, Neighbors, and Acquaintances. Probably the easiest sources of leads for new salespeople are people they already know. It's hard to say "no" to friends, neighbors, and acquaintances, and these sources generally are willing to help you get your sales career started. Many life insurance companies and other direct sellers tell new salespeople to write down the names and addresses of all their neighbors, friends, and acquaintances who might buy the product and then make a telephone or personal sales call to each.

Technical sales personnel and other business-to-business salespeople can find this approach valuable. Perhaps you sell printing services to small businesses, and your best friend's husband just opened his own flower shop. Or maybe, while chatting with people at church or temple services, you learn that one of them is planning to open up a new business location. A low-key style usually works best in approaching friends, neighbors, and acquaintances. If you come on too strong as a salesperson, even friends will start to avoid you.

Personal Observation. This approach is also called the "railroad crossing technique." At a rail crossing you stop, look, and listen. You do the same with personal observation. All successful salespeople pick up leads from personal observations made during their daily routines. While pleasurably reading newspapers and magazines, listening to the radio, taking a ride in their car, overhearing a conversation while dining at a restaurant, or watching television in their easy chairs, they spot leads. For instance, announcements of a company relocating to your city, expanding its operations, or replacing its vice president of purchasing all provide leads for products and services ranging from construction to communications and computer equipment. Or while driving through a given area, you may see numerous signs and billboards with the names of companies (potential prospects) on them.

Spotters. Sometimes called "bird dogs," people who work in ordinary people-contact jobs for other companies are often excellent **spotters** who can help you obtain good leads. Bartenders, doormen, taxi drivers, and service people such as hair stylists hear the intimate conversations of many people.

Spotters People who work in jobs where they meet many other people and who can help salespeople obtain business leads. Also called "bird dogs."

They learn who is looking for financial advice, larger office space, a new fleet of company cars, landscaping, office furniture, or personal computers. Within organizations, secretaries, receiving dock workers, maintenance people, and even mailroom personnel can be valuable "bird dogs" for leads.

Satisfied Customers and Former Customers. A valuable source for leads is information elicited from your recently satisfied customers and even your former customers. They can often refer you to people in other organizations who might be interested in your product or service. This referral strategy provides you with leads already qualified, at least partially, by your customers.[8] Research has indicated that one referral can be as valuable as up to twelve cold calls.[9] One recent survey found that 80 percent of satisfied customers are willing to provide referrals, but only 20 percent are requested to do so.[10] A study of four hundred marketing managers whose companies advertise in trade publications to generate leads revealed that almost 40 percent of the leads produced went completely unanswered.[11] Salespeople might ask their satisfied customers to contact leads for them, including writing personal reference letters of introduction that can help them "break the ice" when meeting leads. Some salespeople make a point of giving inexpensive but nice gifts to customers who refer prospects to them. By showing their appreciation in this tangible and memorable way, these salespeople provide an incentive for their customers to provide additional referrals.

Even when prospects decide not to buy or discontinue buying from you, they may still give you leads to other potential customers. All you have to do is *ask!* Former prospects often appreciate your honest efforts to sell to them and generally feel a little guilty about not buying from you. So, like many nice people, they may try to "make it up to you" by supplying names of other potential customers. It is essential, however, that you retain each prospect's trust and respect if you expect referrals to potential customers. Former customers often will give you referrals if asked—provided that your relationship with them ended on good terms. But never try to "guilt-trip" former prospects or customers into giving you referrals; they will resent such an attitude and probably will not accommodate you. When you approach former prospects or customers for referrals, first politely remind them who you are, and then simply ask whether they know of any other people or organizations that might be interested in your product. In the *On the Frontlines* feature found on our website **http://college.hmco.com/pic/andersonPS2e,** you'll discover how one industrious salesman succeeds with this approach.

Online Study Center
Improve Your Grade

Endless Chain A classic method of prospecting in which the salesperson simply asks recent prospects for further prospect referrals.

Endless Chain. Somewhat similar to obtaining leads from satisfied customers is the **endless chain** approach, in which salespeople obtain leads and referrals from each prospect they meet, whether they make a sale or not. This prospecting approach generates what are called "referred leads" and can be highly successful.[12] One former podiatrist, who sold life insurance on the side, got to know well-known athletes in the Philadelphia area who came to him with their foot problems. After their medical treatment was complete, he would ask them about their life insurance coverage. Many were young and had little or no coverage, so he convinced a few to purchase life insurance through him.

Following each discussion of life insurance, whether he made a sale or not, the podiatrist-salesperson asked for referrals to other celebrity athletes. By forming this endless chain, the podiatrist was so successful that he quit his practice in a few years and retired to the beaches in Florida, where he continues to collect large annual royalties from the life insurance renewals of his policyholders.

Networking Meeting others in social or business settings to talk informally, establish rapport, and build relationships with people who can be contacted later for referrals or as potential prospects.

Networking. The strategy of using interpersonal relationships for achieving objectives is known as **networking**. It involves meeting others in social or business settings to talk informally, establish rapport, and build relationships with people who can be contacted later for referrals or as potential prospects. Several organizations—for example, local chapters of the American Marketing Association (AMA) and Sales & Marketing Executives International (SME-I)—usually provide excellent networking opportunities at their monthly meetings.

Centers of Influence. Salespeople from many kinds of organizational settings, as well as professionals such as dentists, accountants, and lawyers, subtly cultivate potential customers by joining professional, social, and civic organizations whose members are potential customers and *opinion leaders*. From such organizations, whether formal or informal, salespeople can develop **centers of influence**—individuals or groups of people whose opinions, professional activities, and lifestyles are respected in the salespeople's target market. Health clubs, country clubs, university alumni associations, hobby groups, professional associations, and civic organizations offer the salesperson opportunities to develop contacts and centers of influence that can lead to many potential customers. For example, a pharmaceutical salesperson may socialize at a club with a physician who agrees to prescribe his company's latest drug. Because doctors interact with one another, other physicians are likely to decide to prescribe the same drug for their patients. Or you may sell your firm's services to a large, highly regarded company and then inform other leads in the center of influence about this firm's use of your product. Their reaction may be "Gee, if your service is good enough for them, then it's probably good enough for us."

Networking and centers of influence can be powerful ways to prospect for leads.
Age Fotostock/SuperStock

Centers of Influence Individuals or groups of people whose opinions, professional activities, and lifestyles are respected among people in the salesperson's target markets.

Internet (World Wide Web). One of the most pervasive and rapidly growing means of prospecting is via the Internet, or World Wide Web. Some salespeople view the Internet as a worldwide electronic directory. For instance, a salesperson planning to make cold calls in a large office building in another city might use an online database service to develop a list of the building's corporate tenants, along with their sales volume and the names of their key executives. Salespeople also prospect by developing networks or centers of influence through online forums where leads for their products are likely to log

Chapter Review Question
What is the centers-of-influence approach to finding potential customers?

on. With growth of the Internet, many salespeople are using their own and others' websites, discussion boards, newsgroups, e-mail, and listservs to transmit information on the products they market. Websites (e.g., simoncells.com/scripts/default.asp) embedded with audio and streaming video demonstrations that provide data on product specifications and ways to contact the salesperson can be a very cost-effective way to generate leads.

Junior Salespeople and Sales Associates. When junior salespeople or "sales associates" take on much of the responsibility for developing leads and qualifying them, senior salespeople can spend their time more profitably in developing sales presentation strategies and actually selling to prospects. For instance, one salesperson for a vegetable processor made profitable use of a "quasi-sales associate." He hired and paid a high school student to place brochures and product samples in the hands of all supermarket produce managers in a southeastern state and then request permission for the sales representative to call on them. Out of 500 produce managers contacted, 180 managers agreed to meet with the sales rep, and 140 out of those 180 prospects bought!

You might ask other salespeople in your company who sell products different from yours which of their customers might be likely prospects for you. Or you might set up a "buddy system" whereby each company salesperson helps out the others with names of leads. A variation on this approach is to ask *non-competing* salespeople in other companies for leads. For example, sitting in a customer's office with another sales rep gives you the opportunity to ask him or her for the name of a lead, and you can reciprocate in kind. Also, you can identify what other products are used along with yours (e.g., corrugated boxes and wine bottles go together) and then contact the salespeople selling those companion products for leads.

Professional Sales Organizations. Today's professional salespeople may join Sales & Marketing Executives International (www.smei.org), the National Association of Sales Professionals (www.nasp.com), or less formal *tip clubs* that meet regularly over breakfast, lunch, or dinner for a short program and to share information, ideas, and perspectives on selling. Both the SME-I and tip clubs provide opportunities to gather information on leads, exchange referrals, cross-sell, and learn new selling techniques.

Company Records. As a salesperson, always remember to look for—and use—possibilities right in front of you. Information available on internal company records, such as warranty cards, repair service logs, and even complaint letters, often indicates who can use a related product or service, who hasn't bought anything for a long time, or whose dissatisfaction with a current product might be solved with a new product. Timely follow-ups on these leads can be profitable.

Mailing Lists and Directories. Any person or organization that has ever ordered anything by mail or telephone, requested product or service information, obtained a credit card, or applied for a mortgage or loan is probably on one or more lists. Compilation of mailing lists is big business because *targeting*—reaching the highest-potential customers—is the name of the prospecting game. Professional salespeople frequently use targeted lists purchased from mailing list providers. In addition, online or off-line directories (phone books, trade association directories, users' lists, manufacturing directories, service industry guides, organization directories, membership lists) provide a wealth of information. A medical products supply sales rep, for example, can make a quick sweep through a metropolitan area telephone directory and compile the office telephone numbers of oral surgeons and their locations. A selective inventory of directories and websites that contain archival information for prospecting is provided in Table 4.2.

TABLE 4.2

SELECTED INTERNET SOURCES OF INFORMATION FOR PROSPECTING

Name	Type of Information	Website
Thomas Register of American Manufacturers	Listing of manufacturers based on product classifications	http://thomasnet.com/
Yellow Pages	Listing of more than 10 million businesses	www.yellowpages.com
Fortune Magazine	Fortune 500 firms	www.fortune.com
Forbes Magazine	Forbes 500 firms	www.forbes.com
Inc. Magazine	Inc. fastest-growing small firms	www.inc.com
U. S. Census Bureau	Information on industrial activity	www.census.gov/cir/www/
Dun & Bradstreet	Information on small and large firms	www.dnb.com/us/
Moody's Industrial Manuals	Data on over 10,000 corporations	www.moodys.com/cust/default.asp
Hoover's Online	Information on small and large businesses	www.hoovers.com

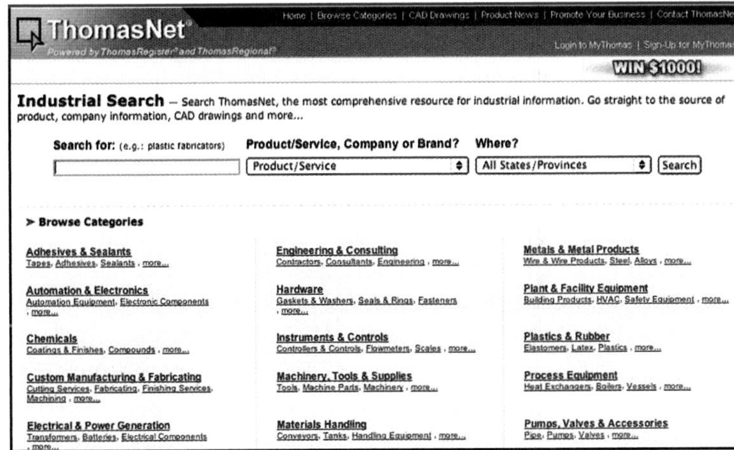

Newsletters. In this age of personal computers and desktop publishing programs, some enterprising salespeople prepare periodic newsletters to mail or e-mail to their prospects. Newsletters can keep prospects up to date on new products, upcoming price changes, seasonal discounts, special services, and newsworthy information about the industry. A page or two will do, but give your newsletter a first-class look and provide valuable, relevant information that reflects well on your integrity and professionalism. Be sure to identify yourself clearly as the sender by including your name, business address, e-mail address, and telephone number in the newsletter.

If a newsletter doesn't seem right for you, simply cut out articles from magazines and newspapers and mail or e-mail them to prospects with a note attached: "Mary, Thought you'd be interested in seeing the attached article. Best regards, Sally." In this way, you can develop a kind of pen-pal relationship with your prospects and customers.

Surveys. Although legitimate pollsters and marketing researchers dislike it, many companies generate leads by conducting so-called surveys by mail, telephone, e-mail, or personal interview. Some pretend to want to know a respondent's opinion on some issue when, in reality, the questions are asked in an effort to qualify the individual. To screen out non-prospects, surveys often use opening questions such as "Do you use oil to heat your business offices?" or "Does your company maintain a jet aircraft for executive use?" or "Do you use conveyor belts in your warehouse?" If the answer to the question is "no," then typically the survey promptly ends with the caller saying, "Thank you for your time."

Chapter Review Question

Describe the survey approach to generating leads.

Some surveys are conducted mechanically by using computers that randomly dial offices and play preprogrammed messages (sometimes from celebrities). Virtually anyone who has a telephone number, listed or unlisted, can be reached this way. Those people who complete the survey have usually qualified themselves as prospects for a salesperson to call later. An Internet variation is to send out thousands of e-mails seeking responses to a "survey." Respondents are considered prospects and receive follow-up e-mails and perhaps a telephone call or two. Salespeople who use the survey method deceptively should be prepared for angry reactions from people who resent the intrusion on their privacy.

Selective Searching: Indirect Sources

An indirect source of leads requires leads to identify themselves by responding to direct mail, making contact at a trade show or professional seminar, entering a contest, or responding to the offer of a free gift.

Direct Mail. Direct mail offers many subtle ways to prospect for new customers, including sales letters, catalogs, invitations, samples, new-product mailings, advertising reprints, and e-mails. Given the proliferation of telephone "Do Not Call" lists and of Internet "spam" that causes people to quickly delete many unsolicited e-mail messages, direct mail remains the most reliable way to reach people in their homes and offices. Although businesspeople and householders receive a lot of "junk mail," they will open mail that they perceive as interesting or possibly important. Accordingly, direct mailers use many techniques—such as plain white or brown envelopes without company logos, stamps placed crookedly, and no return address—to avoid looking like unwanted junk mail. Salespeople or their companies can use a lead directory to do one-time mailings (via the Internet or the Post Office) to obtain quick responses, or they can conduct strategic mail campaigns to steadily convince more people to become prospects (see the accompanying *Example of Direct Mail*). Prospecting via regular mail or e-mail is part science and part art form, but an effective sales letter can bring in many leads. In preparing a direct-mail piece, consider the following general guidelines:

- If possible, avoid using an envelope or stamp that makes it obvious that this could be what some recipients would consider "junk mail." Some creative direct mailers use various techniques (plain white or brown envelopes, crookedly placed stamps, and computer fonts that make the address look like handwriting) to make their letter stand out from the clutter of direct mail that most people receive.
- Address your letter to an individual by name and position.
- Where appropriate, use an attention-grabbing opening statement or headline.
- Make the format attractive but not too flamboyant.
- Keep the promotion straightforward and simple to understand.
- Stress *customer benefits*, not product features.
- Provide customer testimonials or independent research as proof for the quality of your product and the benefits stressed.
- Ask for action after the recipient has read the material (e.g., call a toll-free number, mail in a coupon, or click a box on the e-mail).
- Personalize the direct-mail piece by adding a written postscript (use a special writing font if you are doing a mass letter mailing). Studies show that a P.S. is the most frequently read and remembered part of a letter.
- Follow your mailing with a prompt response to recipients—for example, "May I come by to show you how our product can save you hundreds of dollars a year?"
- Keep records of the mailing results (e.g., calculate the return on your mailing by comparing mailing cost to sales generated from the mailing). Not all mailings are equal. Two or three different versions of the mailing might be sent out and compared in terms of their effectiveness at generating leads.

Chapter Review Question

Provide some basic guidelines for preparing a direct-mail piece to obtain leads on potential customers.

Trade Shows, Fairs, and Exhibitions. Trade shows have proved especially effective for prospecting as well as for determining prospect needs.[13] At fairs, trade shows, and exhibitions, many organizations from the automotive, boat, and computer industries, and even from the aircraft manufacturing industry, display and demonstrate their products. These special displays of new products in diverse categories attract many visitors from diverse companies. Some may just be looking, but most are interested in the products. In essence, they select themselves as potential prospects. Names and addresses of attendees can be obtained in various ways—requests to mail product literature, registrations for prizes, participation in contests, or business card drawings. At the show or exhibit, video presentations and product demonstrations can move attendees

EXAMPLE OF DIRECT MAIL

Johnson & Williams Investment Planning, Inc.
916 W. Touhy Avenue, Suite 34
Chicago, IL 34790

September 8, 2005

Ms. Susan Brophy, CEO
Brophy Manufacturing
1407 S. Washington Street
Arlington Heights, IL 47401

Dear Ms. Brophy:

Congratulations on the recent establishment of Brophy Manufacturing in Chicago. Your company no doubt is on the road to an exciting and rewarding future. As your firm travels that profitable road, we would like to offer our services as investment portfolio managers as a way to increase your employee benefits and morale while cutting overall costs.

In business since 1974, Johnson & Williams has earned a reputation for sound, shrewd investments and for friendly, attentive client service among leaders in the Chicago business community. We offer a wide variety of services and specialize in tailoring investment plans to meet the individualized needs of each of our clients.

Perhaps you are thinking, "But I've just started out and am not really ready to begin thinking about investment or pension options for my employees." We sincerely believe that it is never too soon to begin assisting your employees in planning their financial future. Their loyalty and productivity can be significantly enhanced by the products and services we offer.

We would be pleased if you would accept our invitation for a corporate investment consultation. This consultation is absolutely free of any charge or obligation and is intended to help you assess (1) your firm's financial readiness for employee investment/pension options and (2) the kinds of investments your employees would like to make. To schedule a consultation and receive more information about Johnson & Williams, please use the enclosed reply card and postage-paid envelope to indicate where and when you prefer to be reached by telephone, or simply call us at 1-800-368-PLAN. You can also visit our website at www.J&Winvestplanning.com to contact us or learn more about the services we provide.

As soon as we hear from you, one of our senior investment managers will be assigned promptly to work with your company in developing a precisely customized plan to meet your needs.

With thanks for your attention, I am

Very truly yours,

Cynthia Johnson, President

IT'S UP TO YOU

As a salesperson for Megadisc Software Corporation, you have been assigned to work two days at one of the biggest trade shows of the year. Your company has invested a small fortune in display and demonstration equipment for the show. The Megadisc exhibit features a bank of five computers set up so that interested prospects can run demo versions of Megadisc's newest product offerings. In addition, two large laser-disc-driven video monitors allow passersby to play their choice of thirty specialized file segments that describe different aspects of the Megadisc programs, which help businesses streamline computer and telecommunications hookups. Your company has sent along plenty of brochures and a sign-up sheet for exhibit visitors who would like more information. During your first day at the exhibit, dozens of people stopped by to look at your video segments and to try out the demo programs, but only two put their names on the sign-up sheet. It is now the morning of your second and last day of handling the exhibit. You are worried that Megadisc management will think you did a poor job of generating prospects. How will you generate more sign-ups today?

through part of the selling process. One caveat about trade shows: Prompt follow-up after the show is essential, before your prospect goes "cold." Try your hand at working a trade show exhibit in *It's Up to You.*

Professional Seminars, Workshops, and Conferences. Seminars, workshops, and conferences or conventions that many potential customers are likely to attend can be lead-generating "supermarkets." For example, a cell phone manufacturer may advertise, in a local newspaper, a seminar at which area businesspeople will see a demonstration of the firm's latest innovations in telecommunications. At the conclusion of the seminar, the presenter might say something like "This seminar was sponsored by XYZ Manufacturing. We have more information available, so if you'd like to talk with us now or want a representative to stop by your office to show you how we can cut your costs and increase your profits, we'll be happy to do so. Several of our company's people (with big red badges) will remain in the room for the next hour to answer your questions. If you must leave now, please drop your business card into the box near the door or complete one of the information sheets. Thanks again for coming."

Attend as many workshops, seminars, luncheons, special sessions,

Heavy security surrounding an American fighter aircraft on static display at Farnborough Airfield, England, Monday July 19, 2004. The biannual Farnborough International Air Show attracts visitors and exhibitors from around the world.
AP/Wide World Photos

and coffee breaks as you can to circulate with the members and chat with them about themselves (where they work, what they do, their special interests, and so on). Exchange business cards with them and take some notes on the cards following your conversations. Obtain a list of attendees and collect all the literature, programs, brochures, and handouts that seem relevant. After the conference, call or write to the most promising leads and prospects, remind them how you met, recall a few pleasantries, and then try to set up an appointment.

Contests. Who among us hasn't excitedly opened a letter from Publishers' Clearing House or Readers' Digest that says, "You may have won ten million dollars!" Many of us do the tearing, scraping, and pasting tasks necessary to enter these contests even though our chances of winning anything are slim. Few people, even business managers, can resist a contest, especially if entering requires little effort. Contests are nearly always going on at trade shows and exhibits and in newspapers and magazines. Typically, all people need to do to enter is submit their name and address on a simple form and answer a few questions about themselves or their company. People who enter the contest are presumed to be interested in the prize offered, so they may be good prospects to buy it if they don't win. Even the lucky winners may not win all the ancillary products needed to use the prize, or they may see that their company could benefit from other employees having the product, too. For example, a CEO might win a video cell phone. Then later, she may realize that salespeople in her firm could increase their effectiveness and efficiency if her company supplied them with video cell phones to take on sales calls.

Free Gifts. Many companies offer inexpensive free gifts, such as a dozen golf balls or small tool sets, to people who respond to an advertisement. Although few people who see the ad actually respond to it, many of those who do will eventually buy the advertised product for themselves or their companies. Another method of attracting potential customers is to offer them a special prize to visit your company facility for a product demonstration. An animal-breeding service used an innovative adaptation of the free gift approach to obtain the names of prospects interested in its unique service, as described in the following *From the Command Post.*

Unsolicited Inquiries. Such inquiries usually come from individuals who see a telephone directory advertisement, receive an e-mail, browse a website, read an article about the firm, return a magazine tear-out postcard, or respond to some other promotional campaign. Unsolicited telephone calls and letters from people asking for information are usually excellent leads, because the inquirers often have prequalified themselves or their companies in terms of need, authority, money, and eligibility to buy the product or service. In essence, such non-effort leads are "freebies"—they cost you nothing, yet you can benefit from them handsomely. Inside telemarketing salespeople should respond promptly to these calls and letters, find out how soon the prospects are planning to make a purchase, and then turn the names of prospects (ranked according to buying intentions) over to the territorial salesperson. Surprisingly, some salespeople and their companies have no system for tracking such call-ins, nor do they follow up on telephone and letter inquiries.

FROM THE COMMAND POST: GETTING A GRIP ON THE MARKET

A large animal-breeding service in the Midwest mailed a single leather glove to each of 3,700 farmers and cattle breeders who might be interested in an artificial insemination service. The glove was imprinted with the company logo and came with a brochure entitled *Get a Better Grip on Beef A.I.* (artificial insemination). To receive the matching glove, prospects only had to mail in the reply card. A sales rep, bearing the other glove, called on each respondent. A follow-up mailing to those who didn't respond advised prospects, "You still have time to get a better grip on Beef A.I." The ingenious company reported a 47 percent total response to the two mailings and more than $110,000 in additional sales!

Another kind of unsolicited inquiry is generated via Internet or extranet prospecting. Many sales professionals secure valuable leads from their firm's website or extranets for current customers. Customers who visit a company's extranet, for instance, might be offered monetary or product incentives for referring other potential customers. Web surfers visiting a firm's site frequently request more product or service information, which opens an opportunity for a salesperson to follow up with a phone call. A company that knows what other websites potential customers visit can gather more leads by setting up a hot link or advertisement in those areas, linking Internet surfers directly to the firm's site.[14]

Telemarketing for Prospects. Companies can amass numerous leads via outbound calls to leads by the firm's telemarketers and from inbound toll-free telephone responses to advertisements in magazines and newspapers or on billboards, radio, or television. For example, one large data processing firm uses telemarketing to call leads and ask if and when they expect to be ready to make a purchase decision. If the prospect says in three months, the lead receives a higher priority than if the prospect answers six months. Sometimes, telemarketing generates more leads than the company's salespeople can handle. The same company ran a special lead-generating program that obtained 13,000 computer sales leads for seventy salespeople over a ten-month period!

A Fortune 500 manufacturer generates more than 30,000 leads a year by providing a toll-free number at which prospective customers can obtain product literature, repair service, or a sales contract. Useful information yielded in those incoming calls goes to the company's inquiry center, which mails a questionnaire to each inquirer. Those who return their questionnaires become prospects to be called on by salespeople. The accompanying *Keeping Up Online* feature describes a well-known company that few people would associate with the use of telemarketing.

Chapter Review Question

Distinguish between random searching and selective searching for leads. Give some examples of each.

KEEPING UP ONLINE: DUPONT COMPANY

DuPont, the chemical giant, employs former field salespeople as telemarketing reps to identify "hot prospects" for their field sales force, answer customers' technical questions, help resolve distribution problems, and even sell some products. More than 50 percent of the leads passed on to the field sales force by the telemarketers become DuPont customers. Explore DuPont's website at **www.DuPont.com** and think of innovative ways in which the company might use it to generate more leads for their field sales force.

Marketing Information Systems, Customer Relationship Management, and Data Mining Systems

Marketing Information System (MIS) Any systematized, continuous process of gathering, sorting, analyzing, evaluating, and distributing market information. Can be helpful to salespeople in obtaining leads and prospects.

Many industrial companies find that they need a continuous computerized marketing information system (MIS) to develop leads. A **marketing information system (MIS)** which is a systematized, continuous process of gathering, sorting, analyzing, evaluating, and distributing market information, can be useful in prospecting. For instance, an MIS has provided great prospecting assistance at a large and successful mechanical contractor that designs, manufactures, and installs plumbing, instrumentation, heating, ventilation, air conditioning, and fire protection equipment. The company's major sales opportunities come from construction projects, such as high-rise office buildings, commercial complexes, manufacturing and processing plants, wastewater treatment plants, and nuclear generating plants. Usually, the company would wait until specific job bid lists were published and then submit a bid, along with numerous other competitors. Under such conditions, bidding amounts to a price war. In addition, successful bids wind up having to conform to job specifications determined without the contractor's input. To overcome these disadvantages of straight-bid work, the firm began promoting its engineering and construction management capabilities to customers via mail, e-mail, and a website. By proactively promoting its expertise, the company now generates advance information about construction projects and becomes involved early in project development, which generally assures the firm of sales.

Customer Relationship Management A business strategy designed to augment revenues and increase the profitability of companies by better understanding their customers' needs and buying behaviors—and, in that process, developing a stronger relationship with their customers.

Another noteworthy trend is the use of **customer relationship management** (CRM) and sophisticated data mining software systems to help identify prospects. Customer relationship management is a business strategy designed to augment revenues and increase the profitability of companies through better understanding of their customers' needs and buying behaviors—and, in that process, to develop a stronger relationship with their customers. CRM puts customers at the center of a company's business activities and decision-making processes. It brings together diverse information (compiled from data sources within and outside the organization) about customers, sales, and marketing in order to develop a holistic view of each customer. CRM provides precise computerized information about individual customers to help company employees (sales, customer service, or marketing representatives) assist them in making fully satisfying purchases, create up-selling and cross-selling opportunities, develop target marketing strategies, and use successful competitive positioning tactics. According to Nykamp, "CRM suggests that a consistent, positive customer experience across all channels and media and across all sales, marketing, and service functions can increase customer loyalty and advocacy."[16]

CRM software developed by firms such as Siebel Systems (www.siebel.com) and Dendrite, Inc. (www.dendrite.com) is used by pharmaceutical sales representatives to track information on drug samples provided to physicians and pharmacists and to gather information on the types of prescriptions written. These data-based systems can be used to manage customer relationships effectively, identify new prospects, and help missionary salespeople in the field provide better product education and sales support.

Companies such as RadioShack (www.radioshack.com) and Wal-Mart (www.walmart.com) are using statistical software to mine volumes of data to identify "hidden" interrelationships among buyers and the products they purchase, along with associated complementary products.[17] **Data mining** can be used to identify which new home buyers are most likely to purchase complementary products such as home security systems, lawn care equipment, and swimming pools.

Data Mining A procedure that uses statistical software to mine volumes of data to identify "hidden" interrelationships among buyers and the products they purchase, along with associated complementary products.

Chapter Review Questions

Why is the centers-of-influence approach the preferred method for seeking leads among professionals such as doctors, lawyers, insurance agents, financial advisers, and accountants?

How can internal company records, such as warranty cards, be of value in developing lists of prospects?

What is a marketing information system (MIS) and how can it help manage leads?

Define customer relationship management and discuss how it can be used to manage relationships with customers.

Describe data mining.

Sales and Marketing Executives Marketing Library

For prospecting or any other stage in the PSP, *Sales and Marketing Executives Marketing Library* at *www.smei.org/displayindustrynews.cfm* is an outstanding source of information and help for salespeople. The library offers:

1. More than 200,000 searchable articles on sales and marketing.
2. Discussions by top marketing/sales leaders about their latest strategies and ideas.
3. Access to the world's first knowledgebase in sales and marketing.
4. Company and industry profiles.
5. The latest compensation data for salespeople, sales managers, and marketing managers, plus much more.

THE PROSPECTING PLAN

Based on the above discussion, we hope it is now evident that professional salespeople consider prospecting a critical function, not a hit-or-miss affair. Therefore, to maximize prospecting activities, you must develop and execute a comprehensive prospecting plan that should cover the following six stages:

1. *Set objectives for prospecting.* What do you hope to achieve when you prospect? To answer this question, establish specific, reasonable, quantitative goals, rather than vague ones that provide no direction. Rather than "I want to significantly increase the leads I gain through prospecting," make your goal specific: "Through prospecting I will make sales calls for two hours per day and add five new accounts by June 1."
2. *Allocate time for prospecting.* Prospecting is too important an activity to leave until you have time left over, perhaps at the end of the day. Prospecting demands hard work, initiative, time, resourcefulness, and creativity. Its end results should be your lifeblood as a salesperson. To approach it casually may leave you bereft of future sales.
3. *Become familiar with prospecting techniques.* You will want to become conversant with the various prospecting methods that we have discussed. Evaluate when to use which methods and which ones seem best suited to your industry and customer types.
4. *Choose one or more prospecting techniques.* Study these prospecting approaches over and over again and test them out. Determine which you feel comfortable with and which really work for you. As time goes by, you may opt to use some new prospecting techniques, omit ones you've been employing, and modify others.
5. *Systematize the prospecting plan.* Successful professional salespeople classify prospects and keep up-to-date prospect records. You should maintain accurate and detailed information about each prospect (e.g., company name, contact person(s), address, phone number, type of business, products needed by the prospect, and company size). You could classify prospects by product, by customer type, by geographic area, by size, or by potential. You could even categorize them by call priority: on whom you should call first, second, third, and so forth.
6. *Evaluate the results.* Carefully analyze your prospecting performance against the prospecting objectives that you set in step 1. In other words, compare your outcomes with your objectives. Where your results are below goal, try to identify the barriers to your success. Where your results are above goal, determine why you exceeded your expectations. These two analyses will help you set your prospecting goals for the next period as well as your prospecting strategies and tactics. In addition, you will want to determine which prospecting techniques worked best for you. Figure 4.2 illustrates how you can assess the effectiveness of the various prospecting methods you employ. In this example, the salesperson approached ten firms (under the "Prospect" column) using seven different prospecting methods (cold calls, influence centers, direct mail, e-mail, Internet website, spotters, and newsletters). The salesperson determined each method's effectiveness by whether it led to a qualified prospect (under the "Results: Qualified prospect?" column). The method was deemed *effective* if it resulted in a bona fide prospect (a "yes") and *ineffective* if it did not. Of course, you may want to personalize this basic format by adding more columns (e.g., actual dollar results, reasons for success or failure, and suggestions for the next call).

Chapter Review Question

Describe the different elements of a prospecting plan.

FIGURE 4.2

PROSPECTING METHODS FORM

	PROSPECTING METHODS							
Prospect	Cold calls	Centers of influence	Direct mail	E-mail	Internet website	Spotters	Newsletter	Results: Qualified prospect?
Jones Co.	X							No
Pearson				X				No
Fox, Inc.			X					Yes
Simpson						X		Yes
Ace Mfg.					X			Yes
G&G Ltd.		X						No
Apex Inc.							X	Yes
Genus	X							No
Hyperon			X					Yes
Excelco							X	Yes

PROSPECTS: THE SALESPERSON'S POT OF GOLD

Without prospects, the personal selling process can't begin. Prospects are essential to the continuing health of any sales organization. Consciously or unconsciously, whether making sales calls on present customers, listening to the car radio while driving to their next sales appointment, relaxing at home reading the evening newspaper, or attending a party with friends and acquaintances, professional salespeople are *always* prospecting. In fact, an old maxim for salespeople is "Apply your ABP's" (i.e., *Always Be Prospecting*).

Prospects not only provide every selling organization with the promise of future business but also furnish special solace for individual salespeople who must deal with the occasional rejection and frustration that accompany every selling job. When a salesperson hasn't made a sale in some time, a long list of prospects looks like a shining "pot of gold" at the end of the faint rainbow on an otherwise rainy day. It also provides the motivation to make the next sales call that may lead to that big sale—and a beautiful, bright, sunny day.

Although we have discussed many approaches to generating leads through prospecting, most professional salespeople have their favorite methods and adapt each to their own individual styles. For example, some of the best make greater use of centers of influence, existing records, seminars, and trade shows than do their lower-performing counterparts.[18] You may discover that some prospecting methods work best with certain products in certain markets at certain times. Thus, like professional golfers who choose the precise club for each situation—whether near the green or in the rough or a sand trap—you must become increasingly skilled at selecting the best approach for your selling situation. Finally, even when you think that you've done "enough" prospecting for the day or week or year, remember: Skillful, diligent prospecting efforts and professional selling success usually go hand-in-hand. Always try for that next prospect. After all, that next prospect could become your best customer ever.

QUALIFYING: HOW A LEAD BECOMES A PROSPECT

Lead Anything—a name, address, or telephone number—that points to a potential prospect.

Prospect A lead that has been qualified as a definite potential buyer.

Now that you have some understanding of how to prospect for customers, let's turn our attention to qualifying prospects. Prospecting typically requires more salesperson time than any other PSP activity. In prospecting, you must first obtain leads to people whose firms seemingly could benefit from your company's product or service. Essentially, a **lead** is a possible buyer (sometimes called a *suspect*). The most basic lead information usually consists of a name, phone number, and address. It is necessary to *qualify* the lead or suspect to create a **prospect**. Salespeople contact and call on four groups of people:

1. Leads qualified as prospects and called on;
2. Leads improperly judged as qualified and called on in error;
3. Qualified non-suspects contacted by a cold call; and
4. Unqualified non-suspects contacted by a cold call (those who reject the sales overture).[19]

Clearly, as a salesperson your goal is to reduce time wasted in dealing with individuals who fall into the second and fourth categories. Therefore, you first must qualify the lead in terms of the following criteria:

- **N**eed or want
- **A**uthority to buy
- **M**oney to buy
- **E**ligibility to buy

NAME An abbreviation for the process of qualifying a lead in terms of *need* for the product, *authority* to buy, *money* to buy, and overall *eligibility* to buy.

The lead becomes a prospect only when the potential buyer meets all four of the qualifying criteria. As noted in chapter 1, it is easy to remember this qualifying process: Think of adding another **NAME** to your "pot of gold." But before adding this name to your list of prospects, you must determine that the lead qualifies on all four criteria: **N**eed, **A**uthority, **M**oney, and **E**ligibility to buy. Let's discuss each of these criteria now.

Need or Want. Savvy salespeople avoid wasting time and effort trying to sell products and services to people who neither need nor want them. Not only are such efforts usually not productive, but many salespeople also consider it unethical to try selling products to unqualified people. It's better to sell products to customers in such a way that the customers—not the products—keep coming back! Most often, in your initial contact you can quickly determine which leads have a *genuine* need or want for your products and services. Sometimes, however, you may see that the customer has an unrecognized need or is unaware of a product that can satisfy a latent need. That unrecognized need is your opportunity to explain and demonstrate your product's benefits. For example, until you point them out, an office manager may not appreciate the cost and time-saving advantages of having the latest-model fax machine to communicate with customers and suppliers.

Authority to Buy. One of the biggest mistakes that novice salespeople make is spending too much time with people who lack sufficient purchase decision-making authority. The industrial sales rep who tries to sell the drill press to the purchasing agent in the office but doesn't bother to see the machine operator and his supervisor in the factory has failed to grasp the concept of authority to buy. Whether presenting to an individual or a group of people, the alert salesperson finds out who will influence the purchase and whose approval is necessary. Sometimes you can qualify the prospect's authority to buy by merely asking, "Whose approval is needed for this purchase?" and "What individuals in your firm have an influence on this decision?"

Organizations such as Japan Airlines and Singapore Airlines periodically purchase capital-intensive products such as the state-of-the art Boeing 787 (www.boeing.com) or the double-decker Airbus 380 (www.airbus.com) that are being considered in their fleet expansion plans. The decision to purchase these airplanes, which cost over of $250 million apiece, does not reside in one individual but with a group of managers, who must collectively decide to (or not to) purchase products after all the pros and cons of buying them are carefully considered. In such instances, no single manager in Japan Airlines or Singapore Airlines has the authority to make the purchase decisions, so the salesperson must persuasively interact with several members in the customer buying center.

To reduce administrative costs and, in the process, increase profits, many firms are outsourcing the purchase decisions to system integrators who have been delegated the authority to purchase products on behalf of their principals. These outside agencies are given the responsibility of carefully negotiating the purchase decision and arranging follow-up and post-sale service.

Money to Buy. Prospects must have the money or credit to buy before they can be qualified. Selling products and services to a company that has little or no chance of paying wastes your time and your own company's resources, especially if the products must be repossessed later or even written off as bad debts.

Ensuring that a prospect has sufficient capital with which to make the purchase should be a "no-brainer" for salespeople. That isn't always the case, however. For example, a salesperson at a Fortune 500 computer manufacturer spent months closing a computer sale, only to have the buyer declare bankruptcy shortly after installation. This unfortunate selling situation could have been avoided had the salesperson done his homework and discovered that his prospect was not financially sound. Sales to buyers who cannot pay are especially detrimental to a service organization, because services performed cannot be repossessed. Services are intangible and perishable in that they are simultaneously produced and consumed, so service organizations often demand payment prior to performing services.

National credit-rating services such as Dun & Bradstreet (www.dnb.com/us/) provide financial information about organizational buyers. For smaller companies, Better Business Bureaus, commercial banks, or local credit-rating services can provide information about the lead's ability to buy. Of course, if it's just a matter of temporary cash flow, a resourceful sales rep may be able to arrange an installment or time payment plan that allows the lead to be qualified as a prospect. Lee Iacocca, former top Ford executive and CEO of Chrysler, became, in his words, "an overnight success" when he came up with an innovative idea to help people and organizations buy automobiles. He explains in his book *Iacocca: An Autobiography:*

> While sales of 1956 Fords were poor everywhere, our district was the weakest in the entire country. I decided that any customer who bought a new 1956 Ford should be able to do so for a modest down payment of 20 percent, followed by three years of monthly payments of $56. This was a payment schedule that almost anyone could afford, and I hoped that it would stimulate sales in our district. I called my idea "56 for '56." At that time, financing for new cars was just coming into its own. "56 for '56" took off like a rocket. Within a period of only three months, the Philadelphia district moved from last place in the country all the way to first. In Dearborn, [Michigan,] Robert S. McNamara, vice president in charge of the Ford Division—later he would become secretary of defense in the Kennedy administration—admired the plan so much that he made it part of the company's national marketing strategy. He later estimated it was responsible for selling 75,000 cars. And so, after ten years of preparation, I became an overnight success. Suddenly I was known and even talked about in national headquarters. I had toiled in the pits for a good decade, but now I had a big break. My future suddenly looked a lot brighter. As a reward, I was promoted to district manager of Washington, D.C.[20]

Eligibility to Buy. Many organizations seek to buy products and services when they are ineligible to do so. It would be a mistake, for instance, for some manufacturers to bypass their wholesalers to sell to retailers. Feeling threatened by the manufacturer, the alienated wholesalers might retaliate and refuse to carry the manufacturers' line for distribution to other retailers.

Some small electronics retailers bypass their electronics wholesalers and purchase some of their stock from large electronics retailers who buy directly from electronics manufacturers in large quantities (thus receiving substantial trade discounts). The small retailers receive a better price from the large retailer than they would from their wholesalers. Technically, though, the small retailer is supposed to buy from the electronics wholesaler. This "gray market" type of buying and selling can undermine the effectiveness and efficiency of the marketing channel, as well as lead to conflict among the manufacturers, wholesalers, and large and small retailers. Screening out these ineligible people in the qualifying process will provide your sales manager with solid evidence of your judgment, thoroughness, and commitment to ethical practices.

You must also be certain that your prospect is in *your* territory and not in that of one of your sales peers. If the account is outside your territory, the prospect is ineligible to make the purchase from you. "Stealing" an account or accidentally crossing into a sales associate's territory can create tremendous ill will and poor morale among sales force members. Therefore, when in doubt, always confirm that a prospect is indeed within your territory; if not, turn it over to the appropriate salesperson.

Targeting large accounts that are sometimes handled solely by senior managers in their corporate offices is also not encouraged. Salespeople should make every effort to find out if large customers, which are often referred to as house accounts, are being serviced by corporate executives and, if so, avoid targeting them.

Even if your sales territory and customer base appear to be stable now, you would be wise to do some prospecting and qualifying activities every workday.
Chuck Savage/Corbis

Chapter Review Question
What four criteria determine whether a lead becomes a prospect?

SUMMARY

The seven basic stages in the personal selling process should be viewed not as separate, mutually exclusive steps toward a sale but, rather, as a process in which stages overlap and integrate and continuously revolve like a wheel with no definite end or beginning once it has started rotating.

Several prospecting methods are available, and they can be categorized as either *random searching* or *selective searching* approaches. Prospecting is a never-ending process for professional salespeople, because new prospects must constantly replace current customers who stop buying for various reasons. To be effective in prospecting, salespeople should employ a six-step prospecting plan that starts with establishing prospecting objectives and concludes with evaluating prospecting results.

Skillful and ethical use of websites, extranets, and e-mails can generate leads who often qualify themselves in answers to log-on requests. Because of the volume of leads they generate, large industrial firms often handle leads with computerized marketing information systems (MIS). In general, the most successful salespeople are those who are the most resourceful, energetic, and skillful in finding new sources of prospects and more efficient ways to qualify them. With continuous innovations in telecommunication technology, creative and alert salespeople will identify many new opportunities for prospecting and qualifying—and filling up their "pots of gold."

Whether a prospect buys or not, the salesperson should always ask for referrals, because these start the PSP wheel rotating again. Leads qualified on the basis of *need, authority, money,* and *eligibility* to buy are called prospects.

KEY TERMS

Personal Selling Process (PSP)
Prospecting
Random-Lead Searching
Selective-Lead Searching
Door-to-Door Canvassing
Cold Calling
Territory Blitz
Spotters
Endless Chain
Networking
Centers of Influence
Marketing Information System (MIS)
Customer Relationship Management
Data Mining
Lead
Prospect
NAME

TOPICS FOR THOUGHT AND CLASS DISCUSSION

1. Why is prospecting and qualifying prospects such a crucial stage in the selling process? Do you think innovations in telecommunications will necessitate more or less prospecting and qualifying of prospects? Why?
2. If you were hired by Fidelity Investments to contact businesses and non-profit organizations to sell them retirement plans, which prospecting methods do you think you would use? Why?
3. In making a cold call on a medium-sized manufacturing company to sell a contract building maintenance service, how would you go about qualifying the company?
4. It's October 1 and your first day on the job as a salesperson for a central air conditioning firm in a town of about 65,000 people. Your boss, the owner of Stibb's Commercial Air Conditioning, has said, "Go out and get some business customers." Until now, Mr. Stibb has relied on a small advertisement in the local telephone directory to generate sales, but because sales are particularly slow during the fall and winter months, he has hired you as his first salesperson. Your earnings will come solely from commissions. How will you prospect for potential customers?
5. Your sister and two of her female colleagues have recently graduated from business school, pooled their limited resources, and opened up an accounting firm in three rooms on the sixteenth floor of an office building in Los Angeles. The three partners want to audit the financial statements and annual reports of small- to medium-sized companies in the metropolitan area. They all attended the same East Coast high school and college, and none of them has any long-time friends or acquaintances in Los Angeles. Although you know little about selling accounting services, you promise to come up with a strategy. What prospecting methods do you think might best help the three accountants generate potential business clients?
6. What student prospecting strategies would you recommend to a market research firm that specializes in carrying out research projects and developing marketing plans for colleges and universities?

INTERNET EXERCISES

1. Assume that you work as a sales representative of a Fortune 100 pharmaceutical company that manufactures various drugs for the treatment of heart disease. Use the appropriate Internet websites identified in Table 4.2 and conduct a Web-based search to locate the following leads in your zip code and/or county:
   - Cardiovascular physicians at hospitals who perform heart surgery and prescribe drugs for the heart

- Doctors associated with an HMO who prescribe drugs for preventing heart disease
- Doctors associated with a private practice who prescribe drugs for preventing heart disease

2. As a newly recruited salesperson, you need to find leads you can call upon to carry your Fortune 500 company's line of household products and kitchen appliances (windows, blinds, convection and microwave ovens, dish washers, cooking ranges, and so on). Use the appropriate Internet websites identified in Table 4.2 and conduct a Web-based search to find the following leads:
   - Giant retailers such as Sears, Wal-Mart, Home Depot, Lowe's, and Ace Appliances located in your state
   - Small- and mid-sized retail stores found in small-town USA
   - Home remodelers located in your state
   - Interior designers located in your state
3. In your job as a textbook salesperson working for a Fortune 500 publishing company, use the Internet websites identified in Table 4.2 and conduct a Web-based search to locate the following leads in your state:
   - Professors, in community colleges and universities that offer architecture, business, and engineering courses, who can use books on these fields in their classes
   - Bookstores located on the campuses that will sell textbooks on architecture, business, and engineering
   - Stores (such as Barnes & Noble, Borders, and Walden Book Stores) that sell books

PROJECTS FOR PERSONAL GROWTH

1. Develop a direct-mail or e-mail letter to send to generate business prospects for a new video cell phone for salespeople to take on sales calls. In your prospecting letter, be sure to specify the benefits the cell phone will offer the company, translate them into financial terms, provide proof of those benefits, request specific action, and supply an incentive to act promptly.
2. Prepare a list of ten organizations in your area that you think would be good prospects for the products listed below. Describe your sources and criteria for selecting the organizations, and explain how you would go about qualifying them.
   - Automobile leasing
   - Overnight package or freight delivery
   - Professional nursing uniform supplies
   - Bottled water for offices
3. In newspapers or trade magazines, find five examples of companies using (a) telemarketing, (b) mail-in response cards, (c) toll-free telephone numbers, (d) websites, or (e) a combination of two or more of these to generate leads. Explain the reasoning behind the lead-generating strategy of each approach.
4. Research and prepare a report on the trade show or exhibit marketing industry. In your report, cover the following points:
   - What is a trade show or exhibition?
   - Who attends trade shows?
   - How can a company generate leads or prospects by participating in a trade show?
   - What industries hold the largest shows?
   - What cities hold the most?
   - Is the number of trade shows increasing or decreasing each year? Why?
5. While reading your local newspaper or browsing the Internet over the next few days, find two industrial firms, two non-profit organizations (such as a church, university, or museum), and two professional service firms (such as consulting or landscaping) that are prospecting through advertising, either online or off-line. Critique the effectiveness of the six advertisements in accomplishing their objectives. How would you change each?

ROLE-PLAY EXERCISE 4.1

Prospecting by Telemarketing

Situation

Cathy Macowitz is a telemarketer for a business news magazine called *Progress*. Her job requires her to call area businesses and determine whether they would be interested in placing an advertisement in one of the magazine's upcoming monthly issues. Her leads come from such basic sources as the Chamber of Commerce Directory and the business Yellow Pages for the area. Although few sales are made over the phone, Cathy is generally able to reject or qualify leads as prospects efficiently. *Progress* is read by approximately 20 percent of the area's business executives, and the cost of a full-page, color advertisement is $20,000. A black-and-white ad costs $12,000. Half-page and quarter-page ads cost one-half and one-quarter as much as full-page ads, respectively. For example, a half-page color ad would be $10,000, and a one-quarter page color ad would be $5,000. Ms. Macowitz uses a standardized opening and qualifying questions to determine up front whether the business may be interested in placing an ad. Moments ago, Ms. Macowitz called Samstone Luggage Company, gave the name of her company's magazine, and asked to speak to the advertising manager. Within 20 seconds, Anne Byrd picks up her phone and says, "Yes, this is the advertising manager for Samstone Luggage."

Roles

Cathy Macowitz With a degree in English from one of the small colleges in the area, Cathy is very articulate and enjoys being a telemarketer. She likes the attractive compensation but also enjoys meeting a lot of new people over the phone each day. Most businesspeople are very nice and willingly answer her questions.

Anne Byrd Very professional at all times on the job, Anne has been advertising manager for Samstone for the past six years. Her company sells executive briefcases and quality luggage for business or pleasure travel.

ROLE-PLAY EXERCISE 4.2

Prospecting at the Trade Show

Situation

At the annual American Power Tools Association trade show, Gordon Moffa—a buyer for a regional chain of hardware stores—stops in front of the impressive exhibit of the Hercules Power Tools Corporation. The exhibit simultaneously shows eight videotapes of different home projects (ranging from refinishing a basement to converting an attic into office space) on eight giant television monitors. In front of each television monitor are the power tools used in completing that particular project.

On duty at the exhibit is Domenic Sollica, one of Hercules's top field sales representatives. Domenic's job is to prospect for new customers at the trade show by engaging in purposeful conversation with those people who stop at the Hercules exhibit. Then, after qualifying them, he asks them to sign the register book, entering their name, position, and company address and the Hercules products in which they're most interested. Watching Mr. Moffa out of the corner of his eye, Domenic says good-bye to two people to whom he had been talking for several minutes and walks over to Mr. Moffa.

Roles

Gordon Moffa In addition to its spectacular appearance, the Hercules exhibit has attracted Mr. Moffa's attention because it focuses on the type of power tools that many hardware store customers ask about and buy. Mr. Moffa buys power tools from several companies for each of the eight stores in the *Dad's Toolbox* hardware chain, and he has often thought that he would prefer to buy a complete line from one supplier. But he's concerned about becoming a captive of one manufacturer and about several other things, including the suggested retail price for Hercules power tools, the trade discount for relatively small-quantity buyers, delivery responsiveness on short notice, warranties, and exchange policies for defective products.

Domenic Sollica An outstanding field sales rep, Domenic feels a little uncomfortable playing host at the Hercules exhibit, but his sales manager thought it would be good for him to meet the broad range of Hercules customers, especially since Domenic may be promoted to district sales manager in a year or two. Domenic uses non-threatening, probing questions to find out everything he can about Mr. Moffa and his buying needs.

CASE 4.1 PROSPECTING BY DRIVING AROUND

When the phone rings, Charlie Preston knows exactly who is on the other end. It is eight o'-clock Wednesday evening, and his sales manager, Melinda White, punctual as always, is making her weekly checkup call to see how Charlie did last week. Charlie and Melinda work for RealVoice Corporation, a distributor of electronic communications equipment. One of the company's exciting new products, a portable e-mail/cell phone device called the *InTouch 200,* is about the size of a pack of cards, weighs only five ounces, and can be carried in a suit coat pocket. RealVoice is a small player in this growing but highly competitive market, and it seeks to carve out a niche by marketing its products mainly to small and medium-sized companies. Customers and prospects for RealVoice products include companies that have many salespeople and other employees (e.g., delivery, installation, and maintenance people) who spend little time at the central headquarters office.

Charlie, who has been with RealVoice for less than four months, is not looking forward to this conversation with Melinda, because he had a rather lackluster week. He completed only one sale to a small account with limited long-term profit potential for RealVoice. Although the three-day company training program for new salespeople covered many different prospecting methods, Charlie prefers to drive his company car out into his territory near Portland, Oregon, and become familiar with the companies and people in it. Business growth is exploding in the area, so the telephone directories are always out of date. Only by driving around his territory can Charlie be one of the first salespeople to locate and make calls on the new companies that have recently opened for business.

During his first three months on the job, Charlie had considerable success by merely driving around until he spotted an industrial park or a company whose parking lot contained a lot of look-alike, middle-range cars—the kind usually purchased in large numbers as company cars for salespeople. Even during his daily routine of putting gas in his car, eating meals, and doing personal errands, Charlie makes it a point to subtly prospect for business by starting conversations with people. Charlie used this technique to find four prospects during his first four months with RealVoice, and he turned two of them into customers after only a few sales calls. But this past month his sales have really slowed, probably because many area companies are cutting costs during the current economic slow-down. Charlie picks up the phone and tries to put himself into a positive, upbeat frame of mind before he speaks.

CHARLIE: Hello.

MELINDA: Hi Charlie, this is Melinda. How are you doing? Just calling to see how your week went.

CHARLIE: Well, it was not one of my best weeks, but I've got a lot of pots heating up on the old stove. [Charlie has a few accounts that he is working on that hold promise, but he knows Melinda is really interested in how many sales he made this week.]

MELINDA: That's good, Charlie, but first, tell me about your week. How many sales did you make?

CHARLIE: Unfortunately, I sold only one account last week, but I'm only about one sales call away on two others. [Charlie fears Melinda's notorious wrath. Another rep in the company has told him about how upset Melinda becomes when a salesperson has poor weekly numbers. Instead, Charlie is surprised to hear her reply in a mild, comforting tone.]

(*continued*)

MELINDA: Well, why don't you give me an idea of what happened on each call, and maybe we can figure out a way to change your luck. [Feeling relieved by Melinda's approach, Charlie proceeds to describe the past week on the road.]

CHARLIE: Let me start on a positive note. I did find three prospects this week that should turn into customers eventually. Last Thursday, while I was having coffee in a doughnut shop down in Salem, I met a guy named Carl Avery, who turned out to be the sales manager of Lixon Wholesale Foods. He's a high-energy guy who has ten sales reps located throughout the state. He said that one of his frustrations is that he has a hard time reaching his sales reps during the day and has been thinking about equipping each with a portable e-mail or cell phone device. I told him that our new *In-Touch 200* did both jobs, and he was interested. So I followed him back to his office and showed him some of our latest product brochures and let him play with my own *In-Touch 200* for a few minutes. He seemed impressed. He even called to ask Joe Lixon, the company president, to come down for a look, but Mr. Lixon had gone for the day. Anyway, I tried to close Carl and get him to buy a few for his sales force on a trial basis, but he said he wasn't quite sure he was ready. He asked me to call him back in about three weeks, after he's had a chance to educate himself more about competitive products.

On Monday I had an appointment to see the president of Waller Rubber Company. I found out about this company through a friend of mine who buys tires from them for his bicycle repair business. The president told me that they sell products throughout the United States and Canada and that they have a twenty-five-member direct sales force. I told him that his company sounded just right for our RealVoice *In-Touch 200*. He told me that he didn't have the budget this year, but he was pretty sure that he would be interested about a year from now. Just then his secretary buzzed to remind him of a meeting. So he quickly thanked me for my time and walked me to the door. As he was leaving, he yelled back to me, "Why don't you see Pete over in MR? He might be interested." I didn't know what he meant by MR, and he was gone before I could ask. I waited for a few minutes by the secretary's desk to see if she knew what MR meant, but she was so engrossed in her phone conversation, I don't think she even noticed I was standing nearby. She's kind of an airhead, so she probably wouldn't have known anyway. So I headed on out for my next appointment.

MELINDA: Have you checked out Lixon Wholesale Foods and Waller Rubber Company with our credit department for advance approval of sales to them?

CHARLIE: I haven't had a chance yet, but I'll do that as soon as I'm close to a sale. They're good-sized companies with nice facilities, so I'm sure there won't be any problems with either of them.

MELINDA: You're probably right, but it's a good idea to check them out credit-wise before you spend any more time with them.

CHARLIE: You're right. I'll call my friend, Bob Cammarota, in the credit department tomorrow to check both companies out. Before I forget, Melinda, I want to tell you what happened today while I was having a flat tire fixed at a service station. I struck up a conversation with a guy named Walt Stauffer who turns out to be the sales manager for a company that sells auto parts to service stations. He told me that they currently sell in twenty states and have thirty-five sales reps but are planning to cut back in the near future. He wasn't sure how many reps they are going to keep, but he liked the idea of a combination e-mail and cell phone in one device. He looked over my *In-Touch 200* and our brochures for several minutes; so I know he's interested. He especially liked the size and design of our product, although he thought the price was a little high. He asked whether the payments could be spread out over a longer period of time, and I told him I would get back to him on that. I got his business card, and I'll call him on Monday to set up an appointment. I think this account offers good potential.

Overall, I averaged about six in-person calls a day last week, but most of my contacts were pretty much up-front flat rejections due to budget cutbacks. I didn't even see about a third of my prospects because they were in meetings. Guess I should have used my *In-Touch 200* to call or e-mail ahead of time to reconfirm. Times are tough in my territory now, but I'll keep charging until things turn up again.

Reprinted with permission of Paul Christ, West Chester University of Pennsylvania.

Questions

1. After hearing Charlie describe his week, what do you think his sales manager, Melinda, will say to him?
2. Do Charlie's prospecting strategies sound effective and efficient for his territory? Why? Can you offer Charlie any suggestions to improve his prospecting strategies and tactics?
3. Do you think RealVoice should help Charlie develop leads? What prospecting methods could RealVoice use to help Charlie and other company salespeople?
4. With the company's new product, the *In-Touch 200*, what can Charlie and/or RealVoice management do to generate leads and stimulate sales?
5. How do you think Charlie is performing in qualifying the leads he finds? What could he do better?

CASE 4.2 WHEN COLD CALLING TURNS COLD

CASE 4.2 "WHEN COLD CALLING TURNS COLD" CAN BE FOUND ONLINE AT HTTP://COLLEGE.HMCO.COM/PIC/ANDERSONPS2E

CHAPTER 5

Planning the Sales Call: Steps to a Successful Approach

"Failing to prepare is preparing to fail."

John Wooden,
legendary former UCLA basketball coach

After reading this chapter, you should understand:

- Why it's important to plan and prepare for the sales call.
- How to plan the sales call.
- How to prepare prospects for the initial sales call.
- The causes of sales call reluctance.
- Which strategies to use in approaching the prospect.
- Necessary steps in greeting the prospect.
- How to interact with the prospect's receptionist.

INSIDE PERSONAL SELLING

Meet Glenda Blake of Houghton Mifflin

Selling a college textbook requires homework. Before meeting with a professor, Glenda Blake, a senior sales representative for Houghton Mifflin Company, finds out what courses he or she teaches, checks course enrollment, and learns what texts are currently assigned. She also researches copyright dates, because professors using a new text are unlikely to switch to another text right away.

Much of the information Blake needs to plan a sales call—the courses, the number of sections, and the instructor's name, in many cases—comes from the class schedule and college catalog. "I do as much research as I can before I knock on the door of the people making the buying decision," she says. She often asks the department secretary for information and always visits the college bookstore to see what texts are currently being used.

Blake keeps detailed files on every account and reviews her notes before every sales call. If, for example, an instructor is interested in technology, she comes prepared to talk about the technological tools and enhancements available for a particular book. Armed with all this information, she is ready to meet the professor.

Because she may visit dozens of instructors on one campus, Blake does not make individual appointments. She investigates

office hours, and if a professor is not immediately available, she sets a time to meet or returns after class. Blake always begins by reintroducing herself and her company, "because instructors don't see me every day." Then, drawing on what she has learned through her homework, she will inquire about the instructor's textbook needs.

Although her job performance is assessed on the basis of sales, Blake says customers "really see me more as a consultant, someone who lets them know what is going on in the textbook business. They have so much to do: teaching, research, seeing students, grading papers, preparing for class. If I can give them information to help them make a decision, they see me as an asset rather than a nuisance."

Blake had to overcome some nervousness when she first began in sales. However, because she was a reporter for her college newspaper, she knew how to get in to see and talk with all kinds of people. She also learned from her colleagues. "Early on, I was able to observe my manager and follow an experienced rep," she says. "Even now, if I see a colleague do something that works really well, I have no problem borrowing it."

Rather than rehearse a sales pitch—"I don't think it would come across as natural," Blake explains—she concentrates on understanding the customer. "I believe that if you are prepared and go in with a professional attitude and a polite personality," she says, "people will talk to you. They will help you do your job. I listen carefully and tailor what I say based on customer needs."

In chapter 4, we discussed the initial step of the Personal Selling Process (PSP), which encompasses a wide array of methods to prospect for and qualify leads. Well, now that you have your list of potential prospects on whom to call, you're probably eager to start calling on them. After all, "time is money." However, before you rush out to make your first sales call, it might be wise to consider a few additional steps to help ensure that your efforts will be successful. Making sales calls on customers, especially first-time calls, takes careful preparation. Just as a professional baseball player takes batting practice to prepare for the game, professional salespeople must plan and prepare for the sales call by "practicing," preferably with someone knowledgeable playing the role of the prospect. Planning and repeated practice can be hard work, but it is crucial to your success. If you don't relate to the sports analogy, perhaps you can think of your preparation for the initial sales call as similar to a dress rehearsal for the opening of a play. If you are thoroughly prepared for the play or your sales call, you will generally be able to "Do it once . . . and do it right." There are no chances for a replay before a live audience.

Planning is no more or less than developing a strategy, or game plan, if you will, for achieving an objective. It involves identifying your goals and charting a course of action or "road map" to help you achieve the desired results. Planning the sales call approach—often referred to as the **preapproach** stage of the PSP—is considered by sales managers to be even more important

Preapproach The approach-planning stage of the selling process.

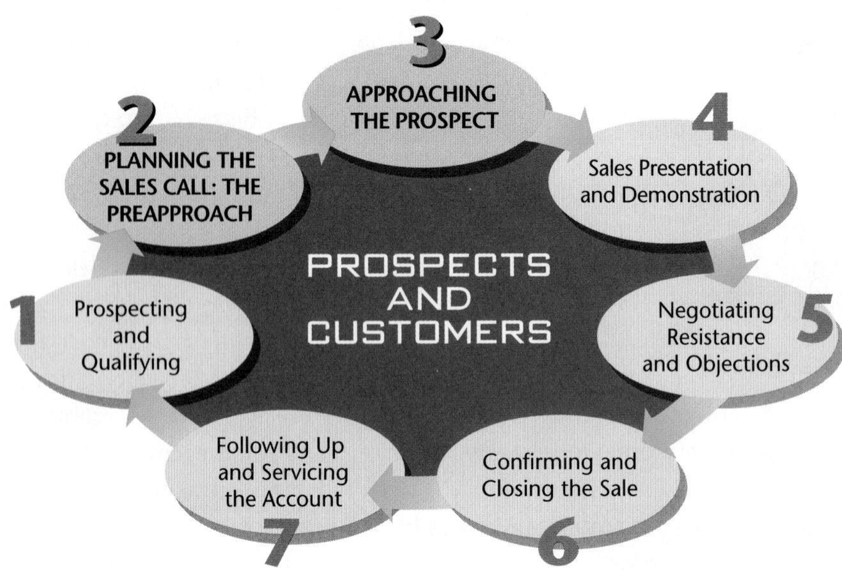

FIGURE 5.1

THE PERSONAL SELLING PROCESS (PSP)

Approach The first face-to-face contact with the prospect.

than the next stage of the PSP, which is the **approach** itself. Preapproach planning provides salespeople with an overall framework for negotiating and decision making, not only *before* the sales call but *during* and *after* the sales call. Careful planning and repeated practice help quell nervousness and build confidence in what and how you communicate while meeting with your customers. In this chapter we will discuss both the preapproach and the approach stages of the PSP,[1] which is shown in Figure 5.1.

IMPORTANCE OF PLANNING THE SALES CALL

Successful salespeople have several important reasons to carefully deliberate their approaches to prospects and customers. Thorough planning helps ensure success, so let's focus our discussion now on the major reasons for planning sales calls.

Establishing Sales Call Objectives

Each sales call should have realistic, meaningful, and measurable objectives. These objectives provide direction and focus for the sales call. Without direction, sales reps will be unfocused in their interaction with the prospect and thus will squander precious time and risk incurring the prospect's displeasure for wasting his or her time. Clear-cut objectives enable salespeople to determine after the sales call whether they were effective (met their goals) or not, and then to analyze why they obtained the results they did. When establishing objectives for a sales call, some sales personnel set a *primary objective* (targeted outcome), a minimum objective (lowest acceptable outcome), and an optimal objective (best possible outcome).

Some salespeople use **"SMART"** steps to set their objectives:[2]

SMART A method of setting sales call objectives that are **S**pecific, **M**easurable, **A**chievable, **R**elational, and **T**emporal.

- ***Specific:*** Establish a specific, major objective for the sales call.
- ***Measurable:*** Ensure that your major objective is measurable or quantifiable—for example, a certain number of units or dollar sales volume.
- ***Achievable:*** Make sure the goals you set are realistic and achievable.
- ***Relational:*** Always try to further a positive long-term relationship with the prospect whether you achieve your major objective on this sales call or not.
- ***Temporal:*** If you can, establish with the prospect a specific timeframe for achieving the major objective. For instance, arrange for trial use of the product or service for a designated time period, with the prospect's purchase decision to follow.

Ultimately, most sales calls should achieve one or more of three overall objectives:

1. *Generate sales*—sell particular products or services to target customers on designated sales calls.
2. *Develop the market*—lay the groundwork for generating new business by educating customers, gaining visibility, and developing relationships with prospective buyers.
3. *Protect the market*—learn competitors' strategies and tactics and protect relationships with current customers to keep them satisfied and loyal.

Improving Effectiveness and Efficiency

Salespeople must consider not only how quickly and directly they accomplish their sales call goals—*effectiveness*—but also how many resources they use in the process—*efficiency*. Inefficient use of such resources as a salesperson's time, expense account, and promotional materials can make sales unprofitable. In planning the sales call, the salesperson must determine the desired specific goal and the exact steps necessary to reach that goal at minimal cost.

Preparing for Customer Reaction

Top salespeople prepare for sales calls by anticipating prospects' possible responses to each step and statement in the selling process. Prospects lose confidence and respect for a salesperson whose responses to questions are not clear or are misleading. It's better to respond to the prospect's question with "I don't know" than to make up an answer. But it's far better for establishing your credibility as a professional to have the necessary information *before* you see the prospect. Establishing credibility can augment your persuasiveness[3] and strengthen the buyer-seller relationship.[4] It's a good idea to go through every step of the planned sales presentation from the perspective of an inquisitive and demanding potential *customer*. Putting yourself in the customer's shoes in a sales call rehearsal will enhance the success of subsequent buyer-seller interactions and ultimately boost your selling effectiveness.[5]

Enhancing Self-Confidence and Professionalism

Planning is preparing for the future, and the best-prepared salesperson is usually the most confident, professional, and successful. Establishing sales call objectives, determining the most effective and efficient methods to accomplish those objectives, anticipating and preparing for prospect reactions, and rehearsing the sales call are all part of an overall strategy that will help build your confidence on the sales call. In addition, you significantly add to your perceived professionalism when prospects see that you have an organized, confident sales presentation that demonstrates in-depth understanding of their needs and perspectives. When prospects sense your confidence and professionalism, their own confidence in your knowledge is enhanced, and they typically become more receptive to sales negotiations. Thus preplanning is a valuable forerunner to successful sales calls.

Determining Which Selling Strategies to Use

Sometimes the sales call objective is simply to introduce yourself, to gather more information about the prospect's needs, or to develop a closer relationship. At other times the objective may be to win a large order. Each objective, depending on the stage in the selling process and on the prospect's needs and personality, requires a different sales presentation strategy.

Chapter Review Questions

Give some basic reasons for planning sales calls.

Identify and explain different reasons for establishing sales call objectives.

With respect to sales call objectives, explain the difference between a primary, a minimum, and an optimal objective, and then provide examples of each.

What do the letters in *SMART* stand for? How can *SMART* help a salesperson set sales call objectives?

Avoiding Errors

Gathering prospect information ahead of the sales call helps salespeople reduce their chances of making serious errors in front of the prospect. The information obtained can be woven into the approach, the sales presentation, and each of the other remaining steps in the PSP. A sales rep who has the requisite knowledge is unlikely to say or do something that will annoy or upset the prospect. For example, if you discover that the prospect is reluctant to use the latest technology in his firm because of his lack of technical knowledge, you will not want to exacerbate those feelings or risk embarrassing the prospect during the sales call. Similarly, if you know that the prospect has had a good relationship with her current vendor for years, you won't want to disparage the competitor. In fact, nearly all top professional salespeople agree that it's never a good idea to put down any competitor; this tactic will only make you look negative and unconstructive.

PLANNING FOR THE SALES CALL: SEVEN STEPS TO PREAPPROACH SUCCESS

Different types of sales situations, customers, and products can cause preapproach planning and even sales presentation strategies to vary widely. Some salespeople call on hundreds of small accounts, whereas others call on only a few big ones. Some salespeople are sales team coordinators; others operate largely on their own. Some salespeople spend weeks or months gathering preapproach information about large potential customers. Others must size up

TABLE 5.1

Seven Steps in Preapproach Planning
1. Prepare the prospect for the initial sales call.
2. "Sell" the sales call appointment to the prospect.
3. Gather and analyze information about the prospect.
4. Conduct a Problems and Needs Assessment for the prospect.
5. Identify the product *features, advantages, and benefits* likely to be of most interest to the prospect, with major focus on the benefits.
6. Select the best sales presentation and demonstration strategy for the prospect.
7. Plan and rehearse your approach to the prospect.

a prospect quickly in the showroom or at an industrial trade show, rapidly plan and make an approach, qualify the prospect by asking questions and interpreting verbal and nonverbal responses, and then tailor an impromptu sales presentation to meet the prospect's most obvious needs.

Although sales call planning is always essential, it *increases* in importance when

- the customer's decision is complex, high-involvement, and high-risk;
- future interactions and negotiations with the customer are expected;
- the customer's needs are unique;
- the customer has access to a range of alternatives; and
- the sale is critical to the salesperson.

Although the planning and preparation steps differ for initial sales calls and subsequent sales calls, seven basic steps lead to preapproach success, as outlined in Table 5.1.

Prepare the Prospect for the Initial Sales Call

A salesperson who fails to warm up a prospect before making that first *cold call* may meet with an icy reception. One approach for favorably preparing a prospect for the sales call is **seeding.**

Seeding Prospect-focused activities, such as mailing pertinent news articles, carried out several weeks or months before a sales call.

Seeding. Sowing seeds for a potential future sales harvest requires prospect-focused activities carried out well in advance of a sales call. The process of seeding includes the following four preliminary steps:

1. First, identify industries or customer categories that offer high sales potential and make a file folder for each.
2. Second, learn as much as possible about the most important concerns of these industries, such as needs in the areas of new-product development, product quality, return on investment, or raw material supplies.
3. Third, keep these needs in mind while browsing through newspapers, trade journals, or general business magazines, and copy pertinent articles.

4. Fourth, select specific companies with high sales potential from each of the industries and find out the names of one or more key people in the buying center at each company.

After you have completed those four steps, the "seeding" campaign can begin. Several times prior to the initial sales call, the salesperson should find relevant articles and mail them to one of the prospects,[6] along with a business card (but no sales literature, because this is a *prospecting* not a *selling* stage) and a handwritten note saying something like "Hope you'll find the attached article interesting." Many salespeople also use *push technology* (discussed in chapter 2) to deliver news articles to prospects via e-mail. Using key words pertinent to a given prospect, a salesperson can quickly identify relevant articles *or let the push technology do it.* After mailing four to six articles to a prospect over a period of several weeks ("seeding"), the salesperson has created a relationship that will probably ensure a positive reception for the initial call. An often overlooked but important point is to enclose the articles in distinctive envelopes to ensure that each prospect remembers receiving your mailings.

Chapter Review Questions

What are the steps to preapproach success?

Define *seeding* and briefly explain how this technique can be used.

"Sell" the Sales Call Appointment

No one wants his or her time wasted, so the salesperson must develop a persuasive strategy to sell the prospect on the initial sales appointment. This effort is directed at piquing the prospect's interest before making a face-to-face sales call. In essence, you must "sell" the idea that the prospect's time will be well spent talking with you about your product or service. One way of doing this is to *prenotify* prospects of your intention to call on them.

Prenotification The use of an in-person cold call, a mailing, or a telephone call to send a strong signal to the prospect that the salesperson would like to schedule a sales call appointment.

Prenotification. One step beyond seeding and sales promotion is the technique of **prenotification,** which successful salespeople have found to be an effective approach for making an appointment. Whereas the aforementioned techniques simply make a prospect aware of you and your company, prenotification sends a strong signal to the prospect that you would like to make the initial sales call soon. To prenotify the prospect, the salesperson uses the *telephone*, a *letter*, a *fax*, an *e-mail*, or an *in-person cold call* indicating the intention to make the first sales call and persuading the prospect to set a specific date, time, and place for the appointment.

Cold Call Initial face-to-face contact with a prospect who is not expecting the salesperson to call.

Prenotification by Cold Call. The term **cold call** refers to a salesperson's first-time attempt to obtain a face-to-face contact with a prospect without an appointment. Such efforts may lead to an actual meeting with the prospect or to the arrangement of a subsequent appointment (the "prenotification" part of the cold call). For instance, one resourceful salesperson for a large office equipment supplier often sets up appointments by making an in-person cold call on the prospect's business. If the prospect is willing to see her on the cold call, great. But if the prospect is unavailable, this salesperson writes a date and time on her business card, hands it to the prospect's secretary, and says, "I've written a day and time on my business card to meet with Mr. Barley. Would you please ask him to call me if that time is inconvenient so we can schedule another time?" This technique might not work for everyone, but this saleswoman has such a friendly personality that she readily wins over secretaries, who then help "sell" the appointments to their bosses.

Prenotification by Letter, Fax, or E-mail. Salespeople for one marketer of industrial sealing devices use written prenotifications to obtain their first sales appointment with a prospect. A week before they call on a prospect, they mail (or sometimes fax) a postcard with a list of the types of products the company sells and a message saying that they look forward to visiting the prospect next week at a certain time. This way, when they arrive at the prospect's office, they can honestly tell the secretary that the prospect has been informed about the sales call. Customers generally feel obliged to accept a sales call that has been announced in advance. This technique makes the salespeople seem much more professional than salespeople who show up unexpectedly at the prospect's office. Many sales reps use a similar procedure by e-mailing prospects (the e-mail addresses can often be obtained by calling the firm or using a search engine such as Google (www.google.com), Lycos (www.lycos.com), Yahoo! (www.yahoo.com), AltaVista (www.altavista.com), or HotBot (www.hotbot.com).

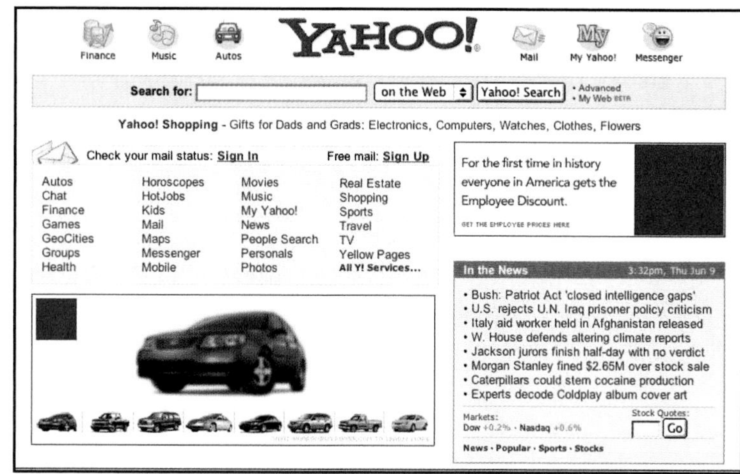

Prenotification by Telephone. One marketing researcher has found an effective three-stage approach to telephone prenotification.[7] First, you introduce yourself, your company, and your product to the prospect and obtain the prospect's permission to send product literature. Second, you mail the product literature and any product samples. Third, after allowing the prospect a short time to "digest" your mailing, you make a follow-up phone call and request a personal appointment. An illustration of this process appears in Table 5.2.

Like most telephone prenotification strategies, this three-stage approach works because it requires commitment from the prospect on three different occasions. At the first stage, the prospect is obliged to provide feedback expressing at least some interest in you, your company, and/or your product by granting you permission to mail product information. At the second stage, the prospect receives and, you hope, has reviewed the material you mailed. At the third stage, during the follow-up phone call, you attempt to (1) discover whether the prospect read the product literature, (2) determine the prospect's reactions to the literature, (3) encourage questions because they are the best indicators of interest in the product, and (4) arrange a day and time for a personal visit.

TABLE 5.2

Prenotification by Telephone to Obtain a Sales Call Appointment

After learning the name of the purchasing agent or key decision maker, the salesperson using the prenotification phone call approach to obtain an appointment might continue along the following lines.

When the prospect's receptionist answers the call, the salesperson can say: *Hello! My name is ______, and I'm trying to reach Mr. ______ to tell him some exciting news. Is he in?*

When the prospect answers the phone, the salesperson can say:

Hello, Mr. ______, my name is ______, and I'm a marketing representative for ______ Company. We've developed some outstanding new materials-handling equipment and customer service concepts that can save your company many thousands of dollars yearly. Several of our current customers have already increased their profits by 10 to 20 percent using our products. Because yours is a progressive company, you might be interested in seeing our latest literature on these products. I didn't want to clutter up your mailbox with something you might discard as junk mail, so I thought it best to call first and get your permission to mail the literature. May I send you this information?

Good! I'll mail it today. I'll put it in a large blue folder with our company name and red horse trademark on the outside, so you'll be able to readily identify it. Is there any special department code I should type on the folder to make sure that it is routed to you as fast as possible? I'll give you a call in a few days, after you've had a chance to review the literature, to see what questions you have. Will that be okay? Good! I'll put the information in the mail today. I think you'll be pleased to see what we can offer you. I look forward to talking with you again soon, Mr. ______. Thank you for your time!

Possible Prospect Resistance

"Our company is not interested in any materials-handling equipment at this time."

"We're perfectly happy with the equipment we've got now."

"We don't do business over the phone."

Responses:

Mr. ______, I'm calling purely in the spirit of "there's no harm in asking." You've got absolutely nothing to lose—and possibly a lot to gain—by looking over the literature I'll send you. I'm confident that you'll find our new equipment offers you substantial potential savings, while providing better service to your customers. We're getting very positive testimonials from other customers. Two companies in your area, ______ and ______, are using the equipment and are very pleased. I'd be delighted to visit your office to answer any questions you may have about the specific benefits you can expect. And I'll also give you a videotaped demonstration in your office or a live demonstration at our local plant, whichever you prefer. So you can't lose Mr. ______. May I mail you the literature today?

Tactical Hints

Don't try to hard-sell prospects. Talk to them like a friend or neighbor. Make reassuring statements like "Some of our satisfied customers were initially skeptical about the materials-handling equipment until they observed it in action and saw how it improved their company profits."

Gather and Analyze Information About the Prospect

Today's and tomorrow's successful salespeople will be those who have the best information about their targeted customers. Although some basic information about prospects is gathered in the prospecting stage, the salesperson usually must acquire more in-depth information for the actual sales call. Information gathered about a prospect prepares the salesperson to handle both routine and unanticipated situations during a sales call. Valuable data include (1) the prospect's name and its pronunciation, (2) nickname if preferred, (3) job title, (4) duties, (5) superior, (6) education, (7) work experience, (8) level of technical expertise, (9) purchasing authority, (10) buying behavior, (11) personality, (12) after-work activities, and (13) hobbies and interests, as well as (14) the size of the prospect's family and the approximate ages of family members.

Using a basic format like the one shown in Table 5.3, salespeople can keep up-to-date records on each of their industrial prospects and customers. As relevant information emerges, it can be added to the *"Insights and Comments"* section of this form. Ideally, all of this information can be maintained on the salesperson's laptop or handheld computer so that it can be called up for review just prior to seeing the prospect.

Chapter Review Questions

Describe the prenotification phone call approach to obtaining the initial sales appointment.

One caveat is in order when collecting preapproach information. You must assess the information with caution. There is always a chance that the information you collect will be inaccurate, dated, or misinterpreted. Misinterpreting the information can be costly, leading to the loss of a sale or even a customer. One study found that many salespeople have relatively inaccurate perceptions of their customers. Specifically, salespeople tend to estimate inaccurately the performance, price, and service levels that customers want.[8] Such erroneous beliefs will lead salespeople to behave in ways that irritate the buyer and restrict a successful sales call outcome.

Numerous sources of information can help salespeople strategically plan their approach to organizational prospects (businesses, not-for-profit institutions, and government agencies). Similar to those used in prospecting, major sources include (1) information available in various departments in the salesperson's company—marketing, accounting, credit, purchasing, and data processing; (2) federal, state, and local government reports; (3) trade association newsletters, brochures, and literature from trade shows and exhibits; (4) trade journals; (5) online and offline directories, indexes, and bibliographies; (6) mailing lists bought from commercial companies; (7) the prospect and the prospect's business (through observation); and (8) current customers of the seller. Let's discuss two sources that can be especially helpful: in-house purchasing agents and electronic directories and databases.

The more information a salesperson has regarding a prospect, the better prepared he or she will be to handle any situation during a sales call.
Steve Prezant/Corbis

TABLE 5.3

Organizational Customer/Prospect Profile: Summary Information

CONTACT INFORMATION

Company Name ____________________

Address ____________________

Telephone Number __________ **Fax Number** __________

E-mail address __________ **Company Website** __________

Prenotification by: ____ **Cold Call** ____ **Letter** ____ **Fax** ____ **Telephone** ____ **E-mail**

COMPANY INFORMATION

Type of Business: ____ Manufacturer ____ Wholesaler ____ Retailer ____ Service ____ Government ____ Petroleum ____ Not-for-Profit ____ Utility ____Mine/Quarry ____Other (specify __________)

Buying Pattern: ____ Weekly ____ Monthly ____ Semiannually ____Yearly ____ Seasonal ____ As needed ____ Other (specify __________)

Number of Locations: __________

Number of Employees: __________

Annual Sales Revenues: __________

Prospect's Customers: ____________________

Prospect's Competitors: ____________________

PURCHASING PATTERNS

	Products Purchased	Annual $ Amount	Company Share	Brand Preferred	Competitive Suppliers
1.					
2.					
3.					
4.					
5.					
6.					
7.					
8.					
Totals					

Historical Buying Patterns: ____________________

CUSTOMER CONTACTS

INITIATORS:

	Name/Responsibilities	Department	Calling Hours
1.			
2.			

Contacts	Dates	Results

(*continued*)

TABLE 5.3

Organizational Customer/Prospect Profile: Summary Information [continued]

GATEKEEPERS:

	Name/Responsibilities	Department	Calling Hours
1.	______	______	______
2.	______	______	______

Contacts	Dates	Results

INFLUENCERS:

	Name/Responsibilities	Department	Calling Hours
1.	______	______	______
2.	______	______	______

Contacts	Dates	Results

DECIDERS:

	Name/Responsibilities	Department	Calling Hours
1.	______	______	______
2.	______	______	______

Contacts	Dates	Results

BUYERS:

	Name/Responsibilities	Department	Calling Hours
1.	______	______	______
2.	______	______	______

Contacts	Dates	Results

USERS:

	Name/Responsibilities	Department	Calling Hours
1.	______	______	______
2.	______	______	______

	Contacts	Dates	Results
1.	______	______	______
2.	______	______	______

PERSONAL SELLING STRATEGIES

Sales Call Objectives:

1. ______ 3. ______ 5. ______

2. ______ 4. ______ 6. ______

Prospect's Problems Assessment:

1. ______ 3. ______ 5. ______

2. ______ 4. ______ 6. ______

(*continued*)

TABLE 5.3

Organizational Customer/Prospect Profile: Summary Information [continued]

Prospect's Needs Assessment:

1. ______ 3. ______ 5. ______
2. ______ 4. ______ 6. ______

Product *Features* to Emphasize:

1. ______ 3. ______ 5. ______
2. ______ 4. ______ 6. ______

Product *Advantages* to Emphasize:

1. ______ 3. ______ 5. ______
2. ______ 4. ______ 6. ______

Product *Benefits* and *Value* to Emphasize:

1. ______ 3. ______ 5. ______
2. ______ 4. ______ 6. ______

Best Demonstration/Sales Presentation Strategy:

1. ______ 3. ______ 5. ______
2. ______ 4. ______ 6. ______

Expected Resistance/Objections:

1. ______ 3. ______ 5. ______
2. ______ 4. ______ 6. ______

Suggested Methods for Handling Objections:

1. ______ 3. ______ 5. ______
2. ______ 4. ______ 6. ______

Confirming and Closing Approach:

1. ______ 3. ______ 5. ______
2. ______ 4. ______ 6. ______

Follow-Up and Servicing Activities:

1. ______ 3. ______ 5. ______
2. ______ 4. ______ 6. ______

Insights and Comments: ______

In-House Purchasing Agents. Buyers in the *seller's* purchasing department are a good source of information on business prospects because they may be procuring products and services from these companies. Because *reciprocity* (you buy from me and I'll buy from you) is a widespread business practice, it's always a good idea to see whether your company is a buyer from, as well as a seller to, the company you're calling on. This can be especially valuable if your company is large and has many different departments or groups that individually buy and sell.

Electronic Directories and Databases. Business data can also be purchased for computer analysis (see Table 5.4). The *Electronic Yellow Pages,* containing listings from nearly all the nation's 4,800 phone books, is the largest directory of American companies available. *ABI/Inform* presents background data on industries, companies, products, and current business topics from 550 publications. Standard & Poor's *Compustat* provides detailed balance sheet and income statement information for more than 5,000 companies. *Industry Data Sources* compiles information on 65 major industries from trade association reports, government publications, and industry studies by brokerage firms. *Economic Information Systems (EIS)* maintains data on about 400,000 establishments. Another valuable online source is the *Definitive Database,* which contains 15 million mailing and telemarketing records from over 250 well-known business-to-business and high-technology publications.

Dun & Bradstreet's *Harris Infosource* provides comprehensive coverage of the most significant segments of U.S. businesses. It has more than 2 million records to help locate prospects, find new customers, and qualify sales leads in minutes. *Dun's Market Identifiers* reports information on more than 2 million U.S. businesses with ten or more employees, including address, product, financial, and marketing information.

Hundreds of online database vendors, including Compuserve, Inc., Bibliographic Retrieval Service (BRS), Dow Jones News Retrieval, and Dialog Information Services, Inc., provide access to more than two hundred databases in a variety of business and scientific fields. Some provide electronic access to hundreds of business databases, newsletters, company annual reports, and investment firm reports. As computer databanks continue to proliferate and computer software increases in versatility, salespeople will be able to obtain instant access to prospect data organized in any way desired. Only a few minutes before meeting the prospect, perhaps while waiting in the car or reception area, the salesperson will be able to electronically review relevant information about the prospect, including the objectives and strategy for this particular sales call. Some companies have made rapid progress toward this scenario, as described in the accompanying *From the Command Post* feature (on page 150). And in *On the Frontlines: The Life of a Salesperson* (on page 149), you'll see how Jason Smyczynski, who has recently embarked on a career as a salesperson, plans his sales call and approaches the prospect.

TABLE 5.4

Selective Electronic Directories and Databases

Directories and Databases	Type of Information	Website
Yellow Pages	Listing of more than 10 million businesses	www.yellowpages.com
ABI/Inform	Data on industries, companies, products, and current business topics from 550 publications	www.proquest.com
COMPUSTAT (Standard & Poor's)	Detailed balance sheet and income statement information for more than 5,000 firms	www.compustat.com
Industry Data Sources	Trade association reports, government publications, and industry studies by brokerage firms on 65 major industries	www.virtualpet.com /industry/data/data.htm
Economic Information Systems	Data on about 400,000 establishments	fisher.lib.virginia.edu
The Definitive Database	Contains 15 million mailing and telemarketing records from over 250 well-known business-to-business and high-technology publications	www.definitivedatabase .com
Harris Infosource (Dun & Bradstreet)	With more than 2 million records, this online database can help find prospects. It provides comprehensive coverage of the most significant segments of U.S. businesses.	www.harrisinfo.com
Dun's Market Identifiers (Dun & Bradstreet)	Reports on more than 2 million U.S. businesses with ten or more employees, including market research, mailing and telemarketing lists, industry statistics, and financial and marketing information	library.dialog.com /bluesheets/html /bl0516.html

ON THE FRONTLINES: THE LIFE OF A SALESPERSON

Planning the Sales Call and Approaching the Prospect

In the previous chapter we introduced Jason, a young manufacturer's sales representative for Chris-Jay Marketing. Upon meeting Jason, one of the first things you notice is his friendly, extraverted personality. "I'm truly 'in my element' when I'm meeting and learning about new people. Sales is one of the few professions I can think of where you get paid handsomely for introducing yourself to people," enthuses Jason.

"In sales, you don't make money by staying in the office, but you always have to do your homework," Jason stresses. "So, even though I hate being tied to a desk, I take time to carefully 'prep' for each of my sales calls." These *prep steps*, as Jason calls them, are designed to gather information about each prospect before making the sales call. Jason is very resourceful and creative in digging for information. Although he usually checks online and off-line financial databases, such as Dun & Bradstreet, Standard and Poor's, and Value Line, Jason also "Googles" the prospect company to find pertinent news items. "Basically, I want to be as knowledgeable as possible before calling on my prospect. My preparation gives me extra confidence in our first meeting. With background information, I can better understand 'where the prospect is coming from,' and this helps break the ice in our initial contact. Often, my prospects tell me they're impressed by my knowledge of their industry and company, and I think my thorough preparation enables me to come across as more professional than many competitive salespeople."

In calling to make the first sales call appointment, Jason nearly always encounters a "gatekeeper," usually a receptionist or administrative assistant. "Administrative assistants and receptionists have tremendous influence," explains Jason. "Unless you get them on your side, you're going to have a hard time obtaining an appointment with their boss. So, my first job is to sell the gatekeeper on letting me talk to his or her manager. I'm usually successful in doing this by being professional yet courteous. My typical approach is straightforward: 'Hello, my name is Jason Smyczynski from Chris-Jay Marketing. May I talk to Mr. Johnson?' If the administrative assistant asks me, 'What about?' then I reply with something like 'It's to arrange an appointment to talk about some mutual benefits.'" As Jason explains, "This usually conveys the impression that it's somewhat personal but important for Mr. Johnson to talk with me." After getting by the gatekeeper, Jason still has to "sell" his prospect on the appointment, usually by presenting a way in which the meeting will benefit the prospect. Depending on the prospect, the benefit can be many different things: a solution to a company problem that Jason knows about, a new product that can do something more efficiently for the prospect, or a way to reduce costs for part of the company's operations. The day before the actual appointment, Jason calls the prospect to reconfirm the place and time. If the prospect is not available by phone or voice mail, he sends out an e-mail remainder.

On the day of the sales call, Jason reminds himself, "You only have one chance to make a great first impression and it's a lasting one." He always makes a point to arrive several minutes ahead of his appointment so he can go over his summary sheet to refresh himself on his sales call strategy and the key points he wants to make. "I also try to 'dress for success' by looking appropriately professional," Jason points out. "On meeting the prospect, I warmly smile and offer a friendly, firm handshake while introducing myself, and then I give the prospect my business card." In the

(continued)

early part of the call, Jason tries to quickly size up his prospect's personality and communication style. "Normally, I try to make some friendly small talk first, maybe about some picture or object in the prospect's office, before turning to business, unless the prospect's style dictates otherwise."

During the initial sales call, Jason keeps in mind that this is the time to gather more in-depth information about the prospect instead of trying to make a sales pitch. Patiently listening and asking probing questions to uncover the prospect's perceived problems and needs generally pay off in future sales, affirms Jason. "Too many salespeople are so anxious to get the sale that they start selling before they know the prospect's needs," he observes. Learning to listen on sales calls has paid off for him. He believes that there's a direct correlation between his growing ability to listen and ask incisive questions and the rise in his earnings.

When first meeting with prospects, Jason doesn't hesitate to ask whether he can take notes. After getting permission, he makes his notations on a summary sheet, somewhat like the one in Table 5.3. "Even though I may already know many of the answers, I still probe my prospects for information about their company to make sure that I understand their perspectives and have the latest information. My primary purpose on the first sales call with a new prospect is not to sell but to learn and start developing our relationship," states Jason. Once the initial sales call is completed, Jason often goes somewhere quiet—perhaps a library, a park, or his car—to put his game plan together, while his thoughts are still fresh, for the next sales call on that prospect. "I want to make sure that I always have my ducks in a row," emphasizes Jason, "because I really hate to lose a sale."

FROM THE COMMAND POST: ONLINE INFORMATION SYSTEM FOR SALESPEOPLE

At one chemical producer, sales representatives obtain needed information from an online automated information system. The system updates the salespeople daily on their accounts, products, and performance. Once a field salesperson signs on at a terminal, menus appear on the screen that present different options, depending on the type of information sought. Before making a sales call, the salesperson can obtain an order status report summarizing shipments, along with an explanation of the reasons for unfilled orders. Data can also be secured on specific products that the customer bought this month, the previous month, and for the year to date. After obtaining data on buying activity, the salesperson can switch to another menu that shows sales forecasts for each product and the progress toward those objectives. The system was designed to make the terminals as user-friendly as possible. After less than four hours of training, 95 percent of the time salespeople can locate the information they want with just two keystrokes. Salespeople are assured of the latest data because the system is hooked into the company's automated order-billing system. The database is updated constantly as new orders come in and shipments go out. Thus salespeople can obtain data on everything that occurred up to 6 o'clock the previous afternoon.

KEEPING UP ONLINE: PROCTER & GAMBLE COMPANY

Procter & Gamble (www.pg.com) maintains a wealth of sales information on its database. How might a salesperson who sells packaging materials use this website to learn more about P&G's packaging needs?

Identify the Prospect's Problems and Needs

Prior to the initial sales call, it is difficult to know the prospect's *specific* needs. However, by carefully analyzing the preapproach information gathered, you can often identify basic problems the prospect is facing and get a general sense of that prospect's needs. An obvious place to learn more about a prospect company's problems and needs is its website. Consider the situation in *Keeping Up Online*, and then go to Procter & Gamble's website to gather appropriate preapproach information.

Uncovering specific organizational problems and conducting a needs assessment for a business prospect usually requires an initial sales call. During the call, some salespeople use a technique referred to as SPIN to zero in quickly on the prospect's needs. Successfully used for many years by Xerox salespeople, **SPIN** is a powerful technique that enables a salesperson to conduct a needs assessment in the initial interaction with a prospect. On the basis of this assessment, the salesperson can determine which of her or his firm's products can best solve the prospect's problems. More important, the SPIN technique allows the salesperson to identify how the prospect's firm will be able to benefit from purchasing a particular product or service. Here's what SPIN stands for and how it can be used:

SPIN A selling technique that enables the salesperson to identify a prospect's major needs quickly. The acronym stands for **S**ituation, **P**roblem, **I**mplications, and **N**eeds payoff.

- ***Situation:*** First, the salesperson tries to learn about the prospect's situation. For example, a photocopier salesperson might ask, "How many copies do you make a month in your office?" "What kinds of documents do you most often copy?" "Who usually makes the decision to buy copier equipment?" Note that the sales rep is keying in on the specific work environment in which the product (copier) is used by the prospect.
- ***Problem:*** Second, the salesperson identifies a problem that the prospect regularly encounters with products presently in use. For example, the copier sales rep might ask, "Do you have problems copying blue ink, like on blueprints?" "Do you find that your present copier is so complex that only a few people use it?" "Does your present copier break down frequently?" All three inquiries focus on difficulties the prospect might be having with her present copier—difficulties for which the salesperson knows his product provides a solution.
- ***Implication:*** Third, the salesperson learns the implications, or results, of the problem. For example, the copier salesperson could ask, "Do you

have to go to the trouble of changing the copier setting or have to do the messy job of changing the copier's ink supply in order to copy blue ink?" "Do you have to do other people's photocopying because they don't know how to use your complex copier?" "Do you have to go to another department to try to get your copying done when your copier breaks down?" Here, the salesperson examines the consequences of the prospect's using the current competitive product.

- ***N**eeds Payoff:* Finally, the salesperson proposes a solution to the problem and asks for some kind of commitment from the prospect. For example, the sales rep might inquire, "If I could provide you with a machine that would copy blue ink, would you be interested?" "If I could supply you with a copier so simple to operate that even the CEO can use it, would you be interested?" "If I had a copier for you that seldom breaks down, would you be interested?" In this final step, the sales rep is set on arriving at a sound solution to the prospect's problem and then obtaining the prospect's commitment to making the purchase or, at least, agreement to try the product.

Chapter Review Questions

What do the letters in *SPIN* stand for? Give an example of the SPIN approach.

Note that in all of these sample questions, the first commitment asked for is simply one of "interest." In most organizational selling situations, the initial sales call mainly allows the salesperson and prospect to meet and learn about each other. Pushing too hard for a close at this early point might alienate the prospect. Once the prospect has indicated that he or she is interested, however, it's usually easy to convince the prospect to commit to another sales call—and a full sales presentation.

Identify Product Features, Advantages, and Benefits

After conducting an appraisal of the prospect's problems and needs, the next step in succeeding in the preapproach phase is to identify and develop a list of (1) features, (2) advantages, and (3) benefits offered by your company's products as tailored to the prospect's needs. To do so correctly, first identify the features of the products being considered for this sale. Second, enumerate the advantages of your products relative to competitors' products. And third, determine as exhaustively as possible the observable value and benefits of each product that will be sold to the customer's firm. This aspect of sales demonstration strategies will be described more fully in the next chapter, but contemplating these issues early in the game will give you a head start in designing your presentation.

Choose the Sales Presentation Strategy

The next step to preapproach success is to select the best sales presentation strategy for your prospect. Here again, although we will discuss various sales presentation strategies in detail in the next chapter, this is a good time to mention two concepts. Together, they provide an excellent guide for choosing the most appropriate sales presentation strategy for each prospect. First, the truly customer-oriented salesperson (recall chapter 1) strives at all times to identify and solve customer problems by skillfully observing, listening, and asking probing questions. Second, the most successful salespeople learn how

IT'S UP TO YOU

You notice in your company's records that a customer in your new territory, Excelsior Parts, bought one of your firm's heavy-duty photocopiers for small businesses about five years ago. You hope that Excelsior might be ready to replace that old copier with one of the new, much faster models that offers higher print quality. Unfortunately, the last salesperson for your territory is long gone, and she left behind no information about the account. In fact, internal records show only the address and telephone number for Excelsior Parts—nothing about what the firm does, who its principals are, how large it is, or the last time one of your firm's salespeople called there. Surprisingly, there is no record of any service calls for Excelsior either. Your company sells high-quality photocopiers, but they would be unlikely not to need servicing for five years. Perhaps Excelsior has already replaced the old copier with a competitor's brand. However, the old copier was a top-of-the-line portable model costing about $4,000, so Excelsior may still have it but may be obtaining service elsewhere. How do you prepare for and rehearse a sales call on a former customer that hasn't been contacted by your company in nearly five years? If your company is going to reestablish a relationship with Excelsior, it seems clear that it's up to you.

to "flex" (adapt) their communication styles in accordance with their prospects' communication styles (which we'll discuss in chapter 12). For now, keep these key concepts in mind as you soon prepare your sales presentation.

Rehearse Your Approach

As top athletes, public speakers, and professional entertainers know, the more they practice their skills, the more successful they become. You should rehearse, rehearse, rehearse until you have mastered your total sales presentation and feel comfortable and confident about it. Do not memorize a canned spiel, but keep in mind the key points you want to make in each part of the sales presentation and other stages of the selling process. Carefully planning, preparing, and rehearsing each sales call will spell success, and it is especially important when approaching a new customer or a former customer who no longer purchases products from your company. This latter situation is described in *It's Up to You*.

INITIAL CALL RELUCTANCE—SALES "STAGE FRIGHT"

Once you have marched up the steps to preapproach success, you may have yet another barrier to overcome, especially if you are a new sales rep. One of the biggest problems new salespeople face is picking up the phone and initiating contact with prospects. Many salespeople, both experienced and novice, suffer from *sales call reluctance*. It is a kind of sales stage fright that can persist regardless of what they sell, how well they have been trained, or how much they believe in the product and the company.

Sales call reluctance can be attributed to *sales call anxiety* (SCA)—the fear of being negatively evaluated and rejected by customers. SCA has four components. One dimension is *negative evaluation of the self.* The salesperson is insecure about his or her ability to perform well and make a favorable impression on the customer. The second element of SCA is *imagined negative evaluations from customers.* Salespeople with SCA wish to convey a strong and positive impression of themselves, yet they perceive that customers think ill of them. A third aspect of SCA is *physiological symptoms.* That is, salespeople with SCA have adverse physical reactions to making sales calls (e.g., sweating, shaky hands, dizziness, and an unsteady voice). The fourth component of SCA consists of urges to engage in *protective actions.* Salespeople with SCA tend to employ self-protective responses during a sales call (avoiding eye contact with the prospect, speaking quickly, fiddling with the hands). All of these elements of SCA have a detrimental impact on salespeople's performance unless they can be overcome.[9]

Sales call reluctance can take many forms. Most new salespeople suffer some of its symptoms at one time or another. One salesperson who earns in the high six figures was so worried about making sales calls that she almost dropped out of a sales career after her first year selling Samuel Adams beer to nightclubs and restaurants. She was especially reluctant to make cold calls. In her words, "My mother always taught me to be polite, and I felt that making sales calls on prospects was like showing up for dinner without being invited." Not until this young woman began to use some of the sales techniques that she had learned in school to turn cold calls into warm calls—prenotification and obtaining referrals—did her fears begin to go away. After a while, she learned that most of her prospects and customers were pleased to see her and to talk about their business needs. Don't worry that you might exhibit some of the fears shown in Table 5.5. If you persevere in using the techniques and skills you'll learn from this text and in your classroom exercises, such fears will be groundless.

Many of the barriers to making sales calls can be gradually or even readily overcome through the following techniques:

- Listen carefully to the excuses other salespeople use to justify call reluctance and learn to analyze your own excuses objectively.
- Use supportive role-playing and discussions with sales colleagues to overcome fear.
- Make some initial prospect contacts with a partner for support; then make calls without partner support.
- Review and reenact recent sales calls with sales colleagues to critique your performance constructively for signs of progress.
- Shift the focus from individual prospect personalities to sales objectives by writing the latter down before making a sales call.
- Rehearse sales calls with sales colleagues to reinforce positive behaviors.
- Observe and emulate the behavior of successful salespeople.

Keep in mind that even the top professionals become nervous before important initial sales calls. Think of your discomfort this way: Your nervousness

TABLE 5.5

KINDS OF SALES CALL RELUCTANCE

Social or Self-Image Threat—Belief that sales calls are sure to go wrong, resulting in personal humiliation.

Intrusion Sensitivity—Fear of upsetting prospects by interrupting and intruding on them.

Analysis Paralysis—Overanalyzing and over-preparing for the sales call and then becoming too petrified to take action.

Group Fright—Fear of making presentations before groups of people; this fear is akin to the widespread dread of public speaking.

Social Class or Celebrity Intimidation—Fear of contacting affluent or prominent prospects.

Role Ambivalence—Embarrassment about the negative image of selling as a career choice.

Exploitation Guilt—Apprehension that family, relatives, and friends will consider sales approaches exploitive, resulting in such "close" prospects being overlooked.

shows that you really care about your prospect and your selling performance. In fact, it would probably be more worrisome if you were *never* nervous before an important initial sales call!

Chapter Review Question

List several kinds of sales-call stage fright. What would you do to overcome these fears?

INTERACTION WITH THE RECEPTIONIST

As you enter the prospect's outer office, you will meet the receptionist. Receptionists are also called "buffers" or "gatekeepers" because part of their role is to keep you (and other salespeople) away from their bosses. After all, bosses are busy, and their time is important. Thus receptionists can significantly help or hinder your selling efforts.

What determines whether you win the receptionist's assistance or incur his or her wrath? Usually, it is the behavior you exhibit with that person. Are you soft spoken, well mannered, and polite? Or are you boisterous, insincerely flattering or flirtatious, and ill mannered? The first way of presenting yourself encourages the receptionist to cooperate with your efforts to see the prospect. The latter style may lead to stumbling blocks being placed between you and the prospect.

Buyers often complain that salespeople are rude, particularly to receptionists. As one company executive says, "What really bothers me is when they treat my receptionist like trash."[10] Any salesperson who would be this inconsiderate and stupid probably won't succeed in sales. To gain a receptionist's help, you should be sure to do the following:

- Give the receptionist your business card.
- Speak clearly and audibly to help the receptionist pronounce and spell your name correctly.
- Be friendly but not fresh.
- Don't try to wheedle confidential information about the prospect or the firm out of the receptionist.
- Act like a guest, because that's what you are.
- Be patient. Many delays are unavoidable, so don't fume about them.
- Be courteous and respectful.
- Don't ignore the receptionist on your way out. Always thank the receptionist for his or her cooperation before leaving the premises.

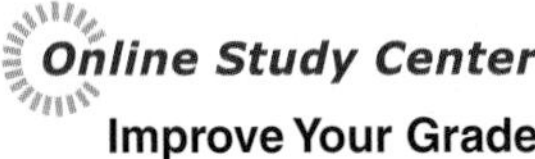

Improve Your Grade

An example of a salesperson's using a unique approach to deal successfully with a receptionist is provided in the *On the Frontlines* story online at **http://college.hmco.com/pic/andersonPS2e.**

APPROACHING THE PROSPECT

Although a letter, a telephone call, an e-mail, or a brief cold call is often perfectly acceptable for arranging an initial sales call, most professional selling situations absolutely require that the actual approach be a well-planned, face-to-face meeting with the prospect. Despite all that we have said about the usefulness of computer and telecommunications technologies, most prospects are still most impressed—and best persuaded—by an *in-person* visit from a salesperson. And the old saying "You never get a second chance to make a first impression" suggests how important that first contact with the prospect can be.

When we meet new people, we tend to size them up or categorize them in some way. In essence, people start to make up their minds about others within seconds after meeting them. We tend to think, "Boy, this guy is pushy" or "She really seems bright and nice." Clothes and accessories (glasses, briefcase, umbrella, jewelry, pen), general grooming, facial expressions, body postures, voice tones and inflections, and choice of words all send messages. This is why it is often advocated that you "dress for success." However, it might be better to think in terms of "dressing the part," which can vary with the prospect on whom you're calling. For example, it might be appropriate for you to call on a prospect who's working at a dusty construction site wearing your best overalls. Taking into account the prospect and the setting for the sales call, dress appropriately so that you will feel comfortable with each other. Indeed, a study has reported that salesperson attractiveness can have an impact on a buyer's intention to purchase products.[11]

The first few minutes of interaction between the salesperson and the prospect are crucial in creating an impression that may be quite resistant to modification later. In fact, a prospect may decide whether to buy from the salesperson within minutes of the initial interaction. Thus all salespeople need to make sure that the prospect's first impression of them is a positive one.[12]

The approach must attract and hold the prospect's attention and interest. Business prospects are busy people, so you must convince them that meeting with you is worth their time and offers a significant potential benefit. Therefore, just as companies try to differentiate their products to gain a competitive advantage, you want to positively distinguish yourself from the competitive salespeople who call on your prospect.

Depending on the selling situation, you can choose among several effective methods for approaching the prospect, as outlined in Table 5.6. These methods can be divided into non-product-related approaches, piquing-interest approaches, consumer-directed approaches, and product-related approaches.[13]

Gatekeepers can help or hinder selling efforts, and salespeople should always treat them with respect.
Kwame Zikomo/Superstock

TABLE 5.6

Strategies for Approaching Prospects

	Non-Product-Related Approaches
Self-Introduction	Smoothly and professionally greet prospect.
Mutual Acquaintance or Reference	Mention the names of satisfied customers whom the prospect respects.
Free Gift or Sample	Offer a free gift, sample, or luncheon invitation.
Dramatic Act	Do something dramatic or memorable in a positive way to capture the prospect's attention.
	Piquing-Interest Approaches
Customer Benefit	Offer the customer a benefit immediately.
Curiosity	Offer the prospect a benefit that appeals to the prospect's curiosity.
	Consumer-Directed Approaches
Compliment or Praise	Subtly but sincerely compliment the prospect.
Survey	Ask permission to obtain information about whether the prospect might need your product.
Question	Involve the prospect in two-way communication early on by asking a question.
	Product-Related Approaches
Product or Ingredient	Show the customer the product or a model of the product.
Product Demonstration	Begin demonstrating the product upon first meeting the prospect.

Non-Product-Related Approaches

Self-Introduction. A warm smile and firm handshake are the important beginnings and endings of sales calls. In the self-introduction approach, sales reps greet prospects by name and give their own name and company: "Good morning, Mr. Stevens. I'm Marie Potts from IBM, here for our ten o'clock appointment." Stating the prospect's name is a means of acknowledging the uniqueness of the prospect and potentially reducing invisible barriers between the salesperson and the prospect. Most salespeople present their business card at this point, but some prefer to wait until the close of the interview for emphasis.

Mutual Acquaintance or Reference. Mentioning the names of satisfied customers respected by the prospect (even if they are competitors) can be a compelling approach. For example, "Your colleague, George Ferguson at Monsanto, has just switched to our process, and so have four of the top five chemical companies in the area." This kind of statement can impel prospects to think, "Gee, if they bought it, maybe I should, too." Testimonial letters from satisfied customers can be especially valuable when selling high-investment or high-risk products or services (e.g., major capital expenditures on an office building or a company jet aircraft). Salespeople must avoid mere name dropping, however, because prospects will often contact the referenced person before buying. Therefore, be sure that the individual will verify your testimonial.

Free Gift or Sample. Door-to-door salespeople long ago discovered that a cosmetics sample, key chain, or free toothbrush can help them establish good will and gain entry to a prospect's home. Similarly, professional salespeople can offer prospects a luncheon invitation, a free seminar, trial use of a product, or a limited sample of services (e.g., a basic estate-planning analysis for a firm's managers). When a buyer who relished lemon drops kept stonewalling, one enterprising salesperson sent the buyer ten pounds of lemon drops. After receiving the candy, the buyer was so touched by such thoughtfulness that he immediately called the salesperson, arranged an appointment for the next day, and became the salesperson's best account.[14] A chemical products firm uses free gifts as an especially effective approach with its prospects. Its sales reps, who sell industrial-strength cleaning solvents for use in factories, offer prospects (typically purchasing personnel or heads of custodial services) small gifts (e.g., fishing lures or screwdriver kits) in return for a sales presentation. Although the gifts are not expensive, they have a favorable impact on the targeted prospects. Remember, however, that salespeople need to be sure not to violate legal and ethical guidelines in using this approach.

Dramatic Act. Infrequently, the salesperson might attempt dramatic or attention-getting efforts if he or she seems to be running up against a brick wall. Some salespeople, for instance, have placed twenty dollars on the prospect's desk and announced, "If I can't show you in the next twenty minutes how our product does everything I claim it will, you can keep the twenty dollars." Often, they let the prospect keep the money whatever the outcome, because it's a relatively inexpensive way of ensuring that they have the prospect's attention. Even more dramatic approaches include "accidentally" dropping the product on the floor to show its durability or holding a cigarette lighter flame under a piece of packaging material to demonstrate its fire resistance. Any dramatic approach, though, should be used with caution. Why? Because the prospect, if offended by such blatant showmanship, may become defensive. Nevertheless, dramatics are sometimes beneficial in capturing a prospect's full attention and memorably demonstrating your product's benefits.

Piquing-Interest Approaches

Customer Benefit. Prospects seek to solve problems or obtain benefits from their purchases. Why else would they buy? The **customer benefit approach** is designed to demonstrate vividly how the sales rep's product can provide that benefit for the prospect. Here are some examples of the customer benefit approach:

Customer Benefit Approach An approach whereby the salesperson offers the prospect a specific benefit that can be realized from using the salesperson's product.

- "Would you like to learn how to save 20 percent or more on your fleet automobile expenses by using our leasing plan?"
- "Our new, high-speed mainframe computer can cut your MIS costs by up to 30 percent."
- "Independent research companies have judged our compact Baby Bull bulldozer to be the best value on the market for construction firms with annual sales volume below fifty million dollars."
- "By converting your 'key person' insurance policy to our new all-business plan, you will have a million dollars more coverage at the same price you're paying now."

Note that in each of these illustrations, the salesperson emphasizes the product's *benefits* (the motive for buying), not its features or characteristics (qualities that can be seen, touched, smelled, and so on). Why? Because individuals buy a product for the benefits it offers, not for the characteristics or features that it possesses. Features are important only if they directly translate into benefits for the buyer, as illustrated in the following example: "All of our new computers come with flat-panel monitors (feature) that take up 50 percent less space on office desks (benefit), giving each employee more working space (benefit), which studies show will improve efficiency (benefit). In addition, employees will experience less eye strain (benefit), which should increase productivity and reduce absenteeism from eye-related health problems (benefits)."

Curiosity. As we have noted, your goal in this type of approach is to set yourself apart in a favorable way from other salespeople. When you use creativity in an offbeat but still business-like way, the prospect may become interested in seeing you because you have stimulated his or her curiosity. For example, a computer salesperson has asked prospects the following question with positive results: "May I please have three hundred seconds of your time?" Many prospects have smiled after hearing the question and have granted the salesperson an interview simply because the approach is unusual. A salesperson whose prospect wouldn't return his phone calls sent a telephone equipped with large numbers to the prospect, along with directions about how to call him and the benefits of doing so. This audacious approach resulted in the prospect finally agreeing to see the salesperson.[15]

Consumer-Directed Approaches

Compliment or Praise. A subtly and sincerely delivered compliment can be a positive approach to a prospect that sets a pleasant atmosphere for the interview. In fact, research has found that using praise can enhance one's persuasive ability.[16] Most prospects (or, for that matter, people in general) want positive feedback or praise. An indirect compliment is often more effective than a direct one, which may be dismissed as flattery. Some examples of the compliment approach follow.

- "I can't help but ask you about that beautiful antique clock you have on your wall. Would you tell me something about it?"
- "Your secretary is really efficient and thoughtful. She called me at eight o'clock this morning to let me know that you needed to change our appointment to 3 this afternoon."
- "Congratulations on your company's recent award as one of Pittsburgh's top ten corporate 'good citizens.' That's an honor that any company would like to win."

Survey Approach An approach whereby the salesperson asks the prospect to answer a few survey questions, the responses to which establish quickly whether the prospect has a need for the salesperson's product.

Survey. Whether over the telephone or in person, the **survey approach** is widely used by salespeople selling business insurance, security systems, computerized information services, or any product where a potential need cannot be established without obtaining basic information about the prospect. Simply requesting the prospect's permission to ask a few survey questions is usually an inoffensive and nonthreatening way to begin a sales call. For example, "Mr. Peters, may I ask you a few questions about your information needs? Your answers will help us determine whether you can substantially benefit by subscribing to one of our electronic information services." After receiving a yes answer, the salesperson can probe further to learn the exact nature and intensity of the prospect's needs.

Question. Asking questions is a good way to involve prospects in two-way communication. Prospects often disclose other useful information (such as the level of their interest) when they respond to salespeople's questions. One type of question that helps qualify prospects, for example, is "If I could show you how your organization can increase profits by 10 percent or more by using our new desktop publishing software, would you be willing to give me half an hour of your time?" Such a question necessitates the prospect's thoughtful consideration and quickly separates the "lookers" from the "buyers." Furthermore, the salesperson moves along the path to an early sales close if the subsequent sales presentation meets the prospect's expectations. Most salespeople avoid asking questions that prospects are likely to answer negatively. The classic example of this poor approach is the retail store clerk's old standby "May I help you?" which nearly always earns the response "No thanks, I'm just looking." The salesperson essentially has nowhere to go from there . . . but away.

Product-Related Approaches

Product or Ingredient. Most sales reps on calls like to carry a sample, model, or picture of the product. This approach allows prospects to see exactly what you are selling and permits a smooth transition into the sales presentation and demonstration. Producing a cutaway cross section of a new type of heavy-duty truck battery or hydraulic pump or a customized computer printout can significantly enhance the impact of your first contact.

Chapter Review Question

Name as many different approach strategies as you can, and briefly give a sales example of each.

Product Demonstration. Demonstrating the product upon first approaching the prospect can be an excellent way to show the benefits offered and immediately involve the prospect. For example, a company that sells coffeemaker systems has outfitted a van as a traveling salesroom to introduce its coffeemaker system in supermarkets. The firm's salespeople drive the van to wholesale and retail chain headquarters and invite everyone from purchasing agents to top management to come out to the van for a cup of fresh coffee and pastry. This approach enables the sales reps to talk to the buyers in a relaxed atmosphere, free from telephone interruptions, with all the facilities needed for a demonstration. As this organization's sales manager reports, "Frequently, six or seven top company executives visit the van, rather than the one or two we would have been able to see during ordinary office calls. They stay longer too—and they buy."

GREETING THE PROSPECT

Some professional salespeople will tell you that the first twenty seconds with a new prospect are critical. What the prospect observes and perceives in you may have a lasting impact. Your first face-to-face contact can set the tone for the entire sales call and may also affect your long-term relationship. Therefore, something as fleeting as the handshake requires practice because it is the physical greeting that accompanies your verbal greeting. Several aspects of your approach, as discussed below, will have a discernible effect on your success with the prospect.

During the first few minutes, interactions between the salesperson and prospect create an impression that may be difficult to change.
Ken Reid/Getty Images

Mood

Your mood, or psychological state, when you call on a prospect will have a marked impact on the end result of that sales call. In fact, your mood is likely to affect how customer oriented you are and how helpful you will be with the prospect.[17] We all have bad days, but if you carry that negativity into the sales call, the end result will be less than satisfactory. Negative thinking begets more negative thinking, which leads to negative behavior and adverse results. Conversely, positive thoughts lead to positive behavior that further reinforces the positive thoughts and positive behavior, thus producing favorable outcomes. Successful sales personnel learn to bounce back from a setback and go on to the next call with positive energy and optimism.

You *can* learn to be optimistic—to overcome adversity and develop a positive mood state.[18] The technique involves three steps:

1. *Identify self-defeating beliefs and the events that trigger those beliefs.* For example, perhaps you are reluctant to make cold calls. Such activities (or events) can create self-defeating beliefs within you (e.g., "I always do poorly when making cold calls.").
2. *Gather evidence to assess the accuracy of your self-defeating beliefs.* For example, what evidence supports your belief that you cannot make effective cold calls?
3. *Replace the negativity (self-defeating beliefs) with constructive and accurate beliefs.* For example, you might say to yourself, "So what if I'm not the best salesperson in the world? That doesn't mean I can't make effective cold calls. Why, even the best salespeople make bad cold calls at times. With enough practice, I will learn how to make effective cold calls and fine-tune my own methods."

Facial Expression

Nearly all of us like to see a pleasant, smiling face, even when we're a bit down ourselves. Salespeople should practice the art of warmly smiling with their eyes as well as their mouths, while simultaneously greeting prospects. As simple as this sounds, we all know people who smile only with their mouths while their eyes remain cold or dull. Although nothing is said, many people notice this lack of harmony between the mouth and eyes. Stir up genuinely positive feelings for the prospect, and your smile and eyes will project enthusiasm and a warm, gracious disposition. And by looking the prospect in the eye, you will show respectful attention to what he or she is saying.

Body Posture

Salespeople are usually advised to maintain a comfortable, erect posture in greeting prospects in order to project a positive attitude. In general, this is sound advice. In some cases, however, it might be better for the salesperson to bend slightly at the waist or gently bow or nod the head when greeting and shaking hands with the prospect, because a "stiff" posture might imply feelings of superiority. This is especially true when greeting prospects and customers from Japan or China. Also, when a salesperson is much taller than a prospect, it is impolite to maintain an erect posture that forces the prospect to look and reach too far upward for the greeting! Courtesy, consideration for others, and common sense will help you determine the appropriate body posture for greeting a prospect. Many experiments have shown that virtually all salespeople can increase their attractiveness and communication effectiveness with others if they maintain good eye contact, act upbeat, dress well, listen well, and maintain a good body posture.[19]

Shaking Hands

We often unconsciously judge others, and are judged by them, by the way we shake hands. Some top salespeople will tell you that it's best to let the prospect decide whether or not to shake hands. A friendly extended hand can be a positive way to begin a sales call, but it can also turn off some prospects,

TABLE 5.7

Appropriate and Inappropriate Handshakes

Seal-the-Deal—A firm and warm handshake with smiling eye contact communicates "trust me," particularly in U.S. culture. It says that you are confident and have nothing to hide.

The Fish—Extending a limp hand to someone is somewhat like handing him or her a lifeless fish. Failure to firmly grasp the prospect's hand shows a lack of warmth and sends a negative message about your self-confidence.

Three-Fingered Claw—Closing too quickly on the handshake will often result in your shaking only two or three fingers of the other person, or vice versa. It's an awkward situation that both of you want to exit from as quickly as possible, and it certainly isn't a good start with a prospect.

Bone Crusher—Some salespeople, thinking that a powerful handshake sends a positive, confident message, almost crush the prospect's hand. This handshake will probably turn off many prospects because it makes them think you're trying to dominate.

The Pumper—A few salespeople pump the prospect's hand like they're drawing water up from a well. If you are this boorish up front, the prospect may wonder about your long-run sensitivity to his or her needs.

The Death Grip—Some salespeople keep shaking hands for an interminable length of time and seem unwilling to let go. A handshake is a greeting, not an embrace! Any salesperson who hangs on too long to either a man's or a woman's hand may inadvertently send an off-putting sexual message.

The Dish Rag—Salespeople who are nervous about meeting a prospect or customer may present a wet hand for shaking and reveal their nervousness. Even when you don't feel nervous, it's wise to take a few seconds to dry your hands on your handkerchief before going in to see the prospect.

especially on cold calls. Of course, you must use your common sense and size up the situation. If a prospect is seated behind her desk when you put out your hand, you're forcing her to stand up, and this may not be a good way to begin. In social settings, good etiquette calls for the person in the superior position to decide whether or not to shake hands, and men have generally been taught to let women initiate handshakes. Because most communication takes place between people who lack definite superior-inferior relationships, salespeople should not force a handshake on a prospect but should be ready to extend a hand whenever the situation warrants. A handshake sends a silent message about the salesperson, as illustrated in Table 5.7. Most all of us have experienced each of these kinds of handshakes at one time or another. How did you feel at the time? How about your own handshake? Is it ever one of these inappropriate kinds?

Presenting Your Business Card

Usually, presenting your business card shortly after shaking hands with a prospect will help keep your name and that of your company in front of him or her as you talk. It's a good idea to present your business card each time you call on a prospect until you're sure that he or she knows your name and your company. Because prospects see many salespeople only once or twice a year, it is presumptuous to take it for granted that prospects will remember you from one sales call to the next. When a sales supervisor or manager travels in your territory with you, presenting your business card to each prospect will help prevent you from being embarrassed in front of your boss should the prospect forget your name. In some cultures, such as Japan, exchanging business cards and carefully examining them is a fundamental rule of business etiquette and mutual respect.

IMPROVING ONE'S SELF-IMAGE

Even though all of the foregoing discussion is sound, positive advice for salespeople in their daily approaches and interactions with prospects and customers, some salespeople have found that they need to go much further to solve the long-run problem of *self-image*. They feel that they must change their self-image before they can really live out a daily mood of optimism. Dr. Maxwell Maltz, the plastic surgeon who wrote *Psycho-Cybernetics*, found that although he could improve people's physical appearances dramatically, many of his patients retained their old, negative self-images.[20] He realized that unless a patient's mental self-image was changed, plastic surgery was of little avail in improving the patient's overall attitude.

Viewed as a magnificent computer, the human mind is "programmed" daily by whatever thoughts are allowed to enter. As you go through life, you accumulate many "files" containing life experiences. How you interpret those files of experiences continually writes new programs for your mental computer. Over time, you develop a subconscious pattern of loading the stored file automatically whenever you encounter a new situation that resembles a previous one. Thus, to break out of the pattern of running the same old programs over and over again, we need to rewrite some of the files that go into our mind-computers. Even though much of our self-image was formed in childhood, it is never too late to repair or change a damaged self-image. In fact, any successful person has undoubtedly rewritten some mental files. Many top performers in sales and other competitive fields work diligently at programming themselves to view every failure as a kind of success. Every failure is, after all, at least a learning experience. To reprogram your self-image, Maltz suggests counting all the positive experiences in your life each night before you fall asleep. Start at the earliest age you can remember, and recall every positive event you can: the time you won the school playground race, the praise your teacher gave you for the picture you drew, the compliment you received from your coach about the game you played, a grade you earned, praise you received on a school project, the promotion you earned on your part-time job, or the time a classmate called you "smart," "cute," or "nice." These recollections, no matter how small they seem, are worth storing in your mind as you replace your old negative files with fresh, positive ones. You may not accomplish a self-transformation overnight, or even in a few weeks, but each day you will make some progress, and before you know it you will have a more positive self-image. Greater success will surely follow.

One of the best pieces of advice for new or discouraged salespeople is first to accept yourself as you are now and then slowly move from there toward self-improvement. After all, as a famous poster says, "God Don't Make No Junk." You are a worthy human being who has something valuable to contribute to others. Dr. Maxwell Maltz sums up the case for self-acceptance in this way:

> Accept yourself as you are—and start from there. Learn to emotionally tolerate imperfection in yourself. It is necessary to intellectually recognize our shortcomings, but disastrous to hate ourselves because of them. Differentiate between your "self" and your behavior. . . . Don't hate yourself because you're not perfect. You have lots of company.

Chapter Review Question
How might a salesperson overcome a poor self-image?

SUMMARY

In planning the approach or preapproach stage of the PSP, the salesperson must carefully plan the sales call and establish specific goals for achievement. The level of planning depends on the particular selling situation, but planning is always essential. Seeding and prenotification often are effective and efficient ways to prepare a prospect for the sales call. Demographic and psychographic information about organizational (business, not-for-profit, and government) prospects can be obtained from either internal or external sources. Selling the prospect on the appointment is a preliminary step that can help ensure a favorable reception for the sales call. Sales call reluctance, which is common among new salespeople, can prove an impediment to sales success until it's overcome by putting into practice good sales techniques and philosophy.

Approach strategies must be matched with the type of prospect and the selling situation. Even the salesperson's initial greeting during the approach can be critical in establishing rapport with a prospect. Always treat receptionists with the utmost courtesy and respect, not only because that's the way you should treat everyone but also because these gatekeepers can have great influence on the salesperson's success in the approach stage. Finally, a salesperson has several ways to improve his or her daily mood—and even long-run self-image—in order to present a more favorable personality to prospects and customers.

KEY TERMS

Preapproach	Seeding	Cold Call	Customer Benefit Approach
Approach	Prenotification	SPIN	Survey Approach
SMART			

TOPICS FOR THOUGHT AND CLASS DISCUSSION

1. What strategy would you use to arrange a sales appointment for each of the following situations?
   - Selling a corporate jet to a CEO of a large company
   - Selling lighting fixtures to the chief administrator of a large city hospital
   - Selling the arrangements committee of the American Marketing Association on choosing your resort hotel for the AMA's annual summer educators' conference three years from now
2. You have a salesperson friend who fears calling prospects on the phone to arrange sales appointments. You'd like to help him or her overcome this fear. What's your advice?
3. You've tried many different approaches with an organizational prospect who seems nice enough but just isn't impressed with you. Finally, you decide to risk a dramatic approach. Describe some dramatic acts you might use. What risks accompany this approach?

INTERNET EXERCISES

1. You have been appointed to work as a U.S. sales representative for Airbus Industrie, which has just developed the Airbus 380, a state-of-the-art double-decker aircraft that carries between 550 and 900 passengers. Conduct a Web-based search for detailed information about the airline industry. More specifically, to help you plan the sales call and make your approach successful, find the following information:
   - The addresses and locations of the headquarters of the major players in the airline industry (passenger airlines and cargo carriers)
   - The sales, market share, profits, and size of each of the major competitors
   - The regions of the United States and of the world where they operate
   - What type of aircraft they currently use
   - The names, addresses, e-mail addresses, and telephone numbers of purchasing managers for all of the airlines and cargo carriers
2. As a freshly recruited salesperson for a dental supply company that has developed a revolutionary, less expensive compound for filling dental cavities, you need to quickly find detailed information about dentists in your county whom you can contact—information that will help you plan a successful sales call and approach. Conduct a Web-based search for the following information on dentists in your county:
   - Names, addresses, e-mail addresses, and telephone numbers of dentists in private practice
   - Names, addresses, e-mail addresses, and telephone numbers of dentists in large dental clinics
   - Owner names, addresses, e-mail addresses, and telephone numbers of dental supply stores
3. In your job as a sales rep for a health maintenance organization (HMO), you need to contact small, medium-sized, and large organizations to sell a better employee health insurance plan. Use the Internet websites identified in Table 5.4 or any others to conduct a search for the following information, which will help you plan your sales call to organizations in your county:
   - Addresses and locations of small, medium-sized, and large organizations
   - Sales, market share, profits, and size of each of the firms
   - Names, addresses, e-mail addresses, and telephone numbers of human resource department managers that make decisions on employee health insurance plans

PROJECTS FOR PERSONAL GROWTH

1. Choose two companies in your hometown, one large and one small, and plan an approach (preapproach) strategy for each of them.
2. Assume a selling scenario in which you are the salesperson. Then develop the best approach strategy you can for a designated prospect, using the seven steps to preapproach success.
3. Using the mutual acquaintance or reference approach and the customer-benefit approach strategies, role-play how you would execute each one in these two situations: (a) You are a textbook salesperson for a large publisher calling on the chair of the marketing department at a state university. (b) You are a salesperson for a security guard company calling on a large retail store manager.
4. With a classmate, demonstrate each of the types of handshakes listed here. Describe your feelings as you perform each handshake. (a) Seal-the-Deal, (b) Fish, (c) Three-Fingered Claw, (d) Bone Crusher, (e) Pumper, (f) Death Grip, (g) Dish Rag.
5. Develop an organizational prospect profile on your favorite company. You might start by going online using a basic search engine such as Google and then requesting an annual report or other descriptive materials from the company. Use sources at your school library such as Standard and Poor's, Dun & Bradstreet, or Value Line to learn more about the company and its financial situation. *Note*: You might want to practice cold calling by contacting representatives within the company itself, but be sure to indicate that you are a student working on a project before requesting pamphlets and other materials or information. Otherwise, you may be assumed to be snooping on behalf of a competitor and may hear a quick "hang-up"!

ROLE-PLAY EXERCISE 5.1

Prenotifying a Prospect by Telephone

Situation

Two months after graduating from college, Paul Canfield has just completed a four-week sales training program for Commercial Security Systems (CSS). CSS provides security guards, guard dogs, and electronic surveillance devices for business organizations and large nonprofit institutions such as colleges, libraries, and museums. After completing initial training, all future field sales reps are assigned to one month's work as telemarketers setting up appointments for the field sales reps. Prenotification by telephone is one of the major techniques used by CSS to help set up sales call appointments for field sales reps. The approach used by CSS is to call a likely prospect, such as a new or growing business or a recently burglarized or vandalized one, and ask permission to send some CSS product brochures and other information on security systems. Then, about two days after the prospect should have received the mailer, the telemarketer calls back, asks whether the brochures were received, and suggests an in-person sales call to explain more about the benefits and advantages of the security systems offered by CSS. Paul Canfield has just called Faithful Battery Corporation (FBC) to start the process, and he has been put through to Mike Burke, manager of company security.

Roles

Paul Canfield It is Paul's task to obtain permission to send CSS's security brochures and promotional materials even if the prospect organization does not seem particularly interested. After receiving the mailed materials, the prospect may become more receptive to an appointment with a field sales rep that Paul will try to set up.

Steve Hammer Mr. Hammer became head of security only six months ago, so he may be more receptive to a new look at security than someone who has more of a stake in the present system.

ROLE-PLAY EXERCISE 5.2

Applying the SPIN Technique

Situation

John Lambert sells portable photocopying machines to small and moderate-sized businesses and nonprofit organizations. His company, Lavin-Biccoh, has trained him and other salespeople to use the SPIN approach to identify organizational problems and needs.

On a cold sales call to a medium-sized insurance company with eight departments of thirty or more people and five old-style copiers that tend to break down frequently, John is talking to Regina Flores, the office manager responsible for maintenance of all company photocopying machines.

Roles

John Lambert Thoroughly trained in the SPIN approach to identifying prospect problems and needs, John puts the technique into practice in this cold call situation.

Regina Flores Ms. Flores has received several complaints from secretaries and other employees about the frequent problems with the photocopying machines. Each time one breaks down, the employee has to run around to find one that's working and doesn't have too long a queue.

CASE 5.1 THE REALLY COLD INITIAL SALES CALL

John Gibbons smiles as he drives past the college library. He remembers the many long nights he spent there cramming for tests and finishing reports. But all that is finally over, and now he has his first job. It feels good. Since his graduation eight months ago, he has been a salesperson for Electronic Business Communications Company (EBCC), and his old college town is part of his territory. John is driving by the campus on his way to the east side of town, where industrial parks and business campuses have sprouted over the past five years. He believes this area of town holds great sales potential, and he tells his passenger, Matt Block, that he is eager to "press the flesh and sell some EBCC machines."

Matt Block has been a sales manager for ten years and is respected and liked by his sales reps. One of the reasons why his people like him is his low-key management style. He rarely tells his reps how to run their territories unless they are in trouble or ask for his advice. Matt hired John and likes his enthusiasm, but over the past few months he has become concerned with John's performance. His sales are not rising as rapidly as those of other new EBCC salespeople. Matt understands that new reps often have problems, but experience has taught him that new reps should begin to show substantial signs of improvement by their sixth month in a sales territory. Because John is still finding it difficult to make sales in his eighth month, Matt is going along on his calls today to try to find out why.

MATT: Where are we headed?

JOHN: We're going over to the east side of town. That's where the growth seems to be happening. Several new businesses have moved in, and a few big companies have started branch offices there.

MATT: What kind of businesses?

JOHN: I'm not really sure. I just remember when I was in college here, my business professors kept talking about this section of town being a booming area, so I thought we should make sure that EBCC is in on the ground floor.

[They enter the east side of town and quickly come upon an industrial park.]

JOHN: Look over there, Matt. There's Marshall Company. I think I've heard of that company before.

Don't they sell insurance or some type of financial service?

MATT: I really don't know. Can't say that I've heard of them.

JOHN: Well, if they are an insurance or financial services company, they sure can use some EBCC machines.

[John pulls the car into the parking lot, and both men get out. John carries a briefcase containing his selling aids. They enter the building and approach the receptionist.]

RECEPTIONIST: Good morning. May I help you?

JOHN: Yes, we're here to see the person who handles the ordering of electronic office equipment.

RECEPTIONIST: I'm not sure who that is. Do you know the name?

JOHN: No, I don't. Do you think you could call someone to find out who it is?

RECEPTIONIST: *[Looking a little annoyed.]* Let me see.

[The receptionist picks up the phone and dials a number. After explaining to the person on the other end of the line what John wants, she waits a moment, thanks the person, and hangs up.]

RECEPTIONIST: You want to go to Personnel. Go down the hallway and make the first right. Then it's the first office on the right.

JOHN: Okay, thanks.

[When John and Matt reach the Personnel office, they come to the desk of Margaret Page, the front desk secretary.]

MARGARET: Yes, sir. What can I do for you?

JOHN: *[Handing his business card to her.]* I would like to see the person who orders your office equipment, please.

MARGARET: Do you have an appointment?

JOHN: No, I didn't know that one was required.

MARGARET: Mr. Ford sees sales representatives only by appointment.

JOHN: Well, could you just tell him that two representatives from EBCC are here?

MARGARET: *[Sounding impatient.]* I'm sorry, but he is busy now. In fact, his schedule is booked tight all day.

JOHN: All right, would you tell him that we dropped by, and that I'll try another time? Thank you.

[John and Matt leave the building and head to the car. As they get into the car, John turns to Matt.]

JOHN: Well, no luck on the first one. You know, that has happened to me a lot lately. I've been having bad luck getting in to see buyers. Do you have any advice that might help me?

MATT: *[Thinking to himself, "This guy needs some serious help."]* Maybe I do. Let's drive over to that coffee place we passed on the way here and talk.

Questions

1. What do you think are John's major problems as a salesperson?
2. Outline a strategy for John to follow in making initial sales call appointments so that he won't be turned away so often.
3. What first-meeting approach might John use to win over "gatekeepers" such as receptionists and administrative secretaries?
4. What kind of training program do you think EBCC has for new salespeople? What would you suggest that the program include?

CASE 5.2 APPROACHING PROSPECTS TO SELL A "GOTTA HAVE IT" PRODUCT

CASE 5.2 "APPROACHING PROSPECTS TO SELL A 'GOTTA HAVE IT' PRODUCT" CAN BE FOUND ONLINE AT HTTP://COLLEGE.HMCO.COM/PIC/ANDERSONPS2E

CHAPTER 6

Sales Presentation and Demonstration: The Pivotal Exchange

After reading this chapter, you should understand:

- Alternative sales presentation strategies.
- Guidelines for effective sales presentations and demonstrations to organizational prospects.
- Preparation of written sales presentations.
- Sales presentation strategies for different prospect categories.
- Use of adaptive and canned sales presentations.
- Sales presentations to prospect groups.
- How to make a sales presentation memorable.

"There are always three speeches, for every one you actually give. The one you practiced, the one you gave, and the one you wish you'd given."

Dale Carnegie

INSIDE PERSONAL SELLING

Meet Greg Genova of Kennametal

As a senior metal-working systems engineer for Kennametal, Inc., Greg Genova has to speak two languages. He has to know the language of management—to talk about cash flow and return on investment—as well as the language of machine operators on the shop floor—to discuss set-up ease and cutting rates. Kennametal is the largest marketer of metal-cutting tools in America, with annual sales of approximately $1.8 billion. Its customers are companies in aerospace, automotive, construction and farm machinery, power generation and transmission equipment, and home appliances.

Early in the sales process, Genova learns as much as he can about a prospect's business so he can demonstrate how Kennametal products will enhance productivity. "I look for opportunities where our products can have a significant impact in a short time," he says. "If you can improve the bottom line immediately, that wins the customer over. In some cases, I had a product in my car that made a productivity increase while I was still in the customer's plant."

Showing prospects what Kennametal's products will do is essential, stresses Genova. Although he can talk about a product's

features and benefits, companies are sometimes skeptical until they see results. Moreover, Genova must convince both management and machine operators of his products' value. Otherwise, the operators might sabotage the demonstration and tell management that the new product does not work. Because Genova has operated factory equipment—"and I have the scars on my hands to prove it"—he has the credibility to enlist the operators' trust and cooperation during a demonstration.

On occasion, Genova has the opportunity to unseat an entrenched competitor by demonstrating the superior advantages and benefits of Kennametal products. He recently heard from an aerospace company that had a contract to manufacture jet engine mounts. The company had previously made the part from a different steel alloy but had not allowed for the use of a new government-mandated alloy that was more difficult to cut. As a result, the company was spending thousands of dollars more than expected to fulfill the contract.

Despite an existing relationship with a Kennametal competitor, the company put out a call to anybody who could help solve the problem. Genova visited the plant and analyzed the situation. He found that the company's machines were removing 1 to 3 cubic inches of metal per minute in cutting the alloy. "I was able to go in and show that Kennametal's tools could remove 33 cubic inches of metal per minute," Genova recalls. This dramatic demonstration of product speed and superiority won the account for Kennametal. "We ended up saving the company over a million dollars on the contract," he says. "They actually made me supplier of the year!"

Congratulations, you've successfully completed your approach and soon you'll be starting your sales presentation and demonstration. Are you a little nervous? Good! That's totally natural because most everyone is apprehensive before making a speech or presentation of any kind. A little anxiety can be helpful. The late, great comedian Bob Hope said that he was always nervous before going on stage—and he became even *more* nervous if he didn't feel that his anxiety level was high enough, because he knew a good performance depended on high energy.

Stage 4, as shown in Figure 6.1, is the pivotal point of the Personal Selling Process (PSP) for two reasons. First, the sales presentation is halfway through the PSP. So far, a qualified prospect has been identified, preliminary information about the prospect has been collected, and you have approached the prospect to pique his or her interest. Second, it is at this point that you must attempt to arouse the prospect's desire for and conviction to buy the product, ultimately making a transition toward closing the sale. Some people think of a sales presentation as a situation in which a product or service is described and demonstrated to a passive person or group of people. However, successful salespeople see the sales presentation and demonstration as the *pivotal*

FIGURE 6.1

THE PERSONAL SELLING PROCESS

exchange between seller and buyer in the long sequence of progressive exchanges that make up the selling process. When planning sales presentation strategies, savvy salespeople make room for buyers to elaborate on their perceptions of problems and needs, actively soliciting their participation at every phase of the presentation and demonstration. This approach to sales presentations is best exemplified in the *consultative problem-solving strategy,* which is preferred by most professional salespeople. However, other strategies covered in this chapter may be more appropriate in some situations.

Chapter Review Question

Why are the sales presentation and demonstration so important in the Personal Selling Process?

THE FIRST SALES CALL AND THE SALES PRESENTATION

After you've established initial contact with a prospect, when does the sales presentation begin? The answer to this question depends on the industry in which you're selling and on the selling situation itself. If you're a paper company sales representative trying to dislodge a competitor, and the buyer—who may have seen six other salespeople that day—gives you exactly five minutes of her time, you will be wise to minimize the usual "ice-breaking" conversation and begin your presentation, or offer to come back another day. But if you represent a large computer company and are trying to convince a prospect corporation that it would benefit from installing a multimillion-dollar mainframe computer, it may take several sales calls just to gather information from various people within the buyer organization before you are ready to make a sales presentation to a key decision maker or committee.

Remember this, however: In a sense, whenever you interact with the prospect or his or her company colleagues, you are on stage making a presentation. Although you may not actually be presenting and demonstrating your product or service that day, you are still representing your company and yourself. Therefore, your behavior—both verbal and nonverbal—*is* a personal sales presentation of sorts. Many experienced salespeople say that you have to sell yourself before you can make the product sale. Thus the information that you gathered in the preapproach stage about the company's culture, dress code, or preferred communication style can prove especially valuable in this PSP stage to guide your ongoing "presentation" conduct.

PLANNING THE SALES PRESENTATION

An active, participatory exchange during a sales presentation may become routine once you have established a good relationship with your buyer. But how do you plan that first big presentation with a new prospect so that you're not the only one doing the talking? Before planning the sales presentation tactics, the professional salesperson first develops an overall strategy for handling the chain of interactions with the prospect. In planning the sales presentation and demonstration strategy for organizational prospects, salespeople often find it helpful to think in terms of the five basic, sequential stages denoted in Table 6.1: (1) *gathering information,* (2) *identifying the prospect's problems and needs,* (3) *preparing and presenting the sales proposal,* (4) *confirming the sale and/or the relationship,* and (5) *building relationships and achieving customer satisfaction.*

Gathering Information

Even a well-prepared sales presentation may contain some tentative data and information based on assumptions or opinions. Oftentimes, you can use small talk to verify some of this information, while simultaneously sizing up the prospect: *What type of person is this? What kind of mood is he or she in? What communication style should I use? Which persuasive appeals might work best?* Too much small talk, however, can be detrimental to the sales process. A chronic complaint of organizational buyers is that salespeople talk too much, fail to ask the right questions, and do not really listen to the buyer. Such inconsiderate salespeople dominate the conversation and ignore the specific and unique concerns of their prospects. If you're not actively listening, you probably won't be able to identify or understand prospect problems and needs and thereby arrive at a sound solution.

TABLE 6.1

PLANNING THE SALES PRESENTATION AND DEMONSTRATION
1. Gathering information
2. Identifying the prospect's problems and needs
3. Preparing and presenting the sales proposal
4. Confirming the sale and/or the relationship
5. Building relationships and achieving customer satisfaction

Top-performing salespeople understand that the first step in the sales presentation is to gather all the relevant information they can about prospects and their perceived problems. First, they make sure they're talking to decision-makers (those with authority to buy) or key influencers, so neither party's time is wasted. Next, they ask probing questions to encourage prospects to provide information on perceived problems, objectives, financial issues, needs, and personal feelings. Like a doctor's patient, sometimes prospects know that they have a problem, but not what it is, so they describe the symptoms. In such cases, even after talking with the prospect, salespeople may need to play the role of a doctor—or even of Sherlock Holmes, whose observations, probing questions, and insightful analyses always enable him to discover the underlying facts that lead to the correct solution.

Identifying the Prospect's Problems and Needs

Using a consultative, problem-solving approach, the professional salesperson can efficiently uncover the prospect's perceived problems and needs by skillful questioning and careful listening. "What led you to switch suppliers in the past?" "How do you currently deal with this situation?" "How long has this problem been occurring?" Note that the emphasis is *always* on the prospect's perceptions of his or her needs, *not* the salesperson's. Each of the foregoing questions deals solely with the prospect's needs. It matters little what the salesperson thinks he or she is selling; what really matters is what the prospect thinks he or she is buying. People and companies buy for their own unique reasons, and the salesperson must understand those reasons in order to focus on the appropriate product benefits. Today's professional salespeople spend more time defining client needs than on any other part of the sales presentation process.

Preparing and Presenting the Sales Proposal

Before you "go on stage" (make a sales presentation), take the time and effort to prepare yourself to give a superb performance.

Professional Approach to Sales Presentations. A traditional salesperson makes a standard product-oriented presentation and sales proposal to all prospects, regardless of their individual needs. In contrast, the professional salesperson customizes the sales presentation and proposal to the client's specific business situation, needs, and individual communication style.[1] Furthermore, the salesperson must adapt sales presentation terminology to the buyer. For instance, technical language is appropriate for technically well-versed buyers but inappropriate for prospects with sketchy technical sophistication. Many times, salespeople must identify and quickly adjust their sales presentation strategy and tactics to some particularly challenging prospects, as shown in Table 6.2.

FAB A memory-aid acronym that stands for a product's **F**eatures, **A**dvantages, and **B**enefits that will appeal most to a salesperson's customer.

FAB Leads to SELLS. Salespeople must first uncover each customer's needs and wants and then present the product features, advantages, and benefits (FAB) that will appeal *most* to that customer. Let's describe the three parts of the **FAB** selling approach.

TABLE 6.2

Prospect Categories and Sales Presentation Strategies

Skeptical Sid and Sally. Be conservative in the sales presentation. Avoid puffery; stay with the facts. Understate a little, especially in areas where the prospect is knowledgeable.

Silent Sam and Sue. To encourage Silent Sam or Sue to talk, ask questions and be more personal than usual. Encourage them to tell you about some of their interests, problems, and successes.

Paula and Pete Procrastinator. Summarize benefits that will be lost if they don't act quickly. Reassure them that they have the authority and the ability to make decisions. Use a little showmanship, where appropriate, to overcome their indecision.

Gussy and Garfield Grouch. Ask questions to uncover any underlying problems. Encourage them to tell their story. Many salespeople are put off and even intimidated by grouchy people, but by keeping a positive attitude and patiently asking questions, you can oftentimes draw them out and begin talking on a more congenial level.

Edith Ego and Ollie Opinionated. Listen attentively to whatever they say, agree or at least accept their views, cater to their wishes, and subtly flatter their egos.

Irma and Irwin Impulsive. Speed up the sales presentation, omit unneeded details, and hit the high points. Try to come to a sales agreement early by using *trial closes* whenever the situation seems right.

Mary and Melvin Methodical. Slow down the sales presentation to adjust your tempo to theirs. Provide additional explanations for each key point, and include many details.

Teresa and Tim Timid or Carol and Corey Cautious. Speak at a gentle, comfortable, deliberate pace. Use a simple, straightforward, logical presentation. Reassure them on each key point.

Tom and Thelma Talkative. Don't allow their continuous "small talk" to take your sales presentation off on a tangent. Listen politely, but move back on track as quickly as possible. Say something like "That reminds me that our product has . . . ." Then wrap up the sales presentation as quickly as you can.

Cathy and Charlie Chip-on-the-Shoulder. Don't argue or become defensive with them. Remain calm, sincere, and friendly. Agree with them as much as you can. Show respect for them and their viewpoints.

Source: *Adapted from Rolph E. Anderson, Joseph F. Hair, and Alan J. Bush,* Professional Sales Management, *1988. Copyright © 1998 The McGraw-Hill Companies. Reproduced with permission of The McGraw-Hill Companies.*

1. *Features* are a product or service's relatively obvious characteristics: what the customer can see, touch, hear, taste, or smell. In the case of a laptop computer for office use, some of its features may be a rich-looking carrying case, light weight, large memory capacity, internal modem, noiseless keys, multicolored screen projection, and built-in alarm clock. As we noted in Chapter 4, it's important to keep in mind that features matter little to prospects unless they can be translated into customer benefits.
2. *Advantages* are performance characteristics that show how the product can help the customer solve a problem better than present products do. A

salesperson may inform the customer that this laptop is the most reliable on the market and that it is completely shock resistant. Claims like this, however, must be provable. For example, the salesperson could roughly drop the laptop on a table and then show that the computer is still at the same point in the word-processing program as it was prior to the shock. Although somewhat dramatic, this type of live demonstration might be needed to prove the laptop's durability.

3. *Benefits* are what the customer wants from the product, and they must be demonstrated with the prospect involved as much as possible. The salesperson who discovers that a prospect wants to buy pocket PCs to encourage company managers to pose more "what if" questions for the marketing database system might invite the prospect to run a simulation on the pocket PC. Likewise, if the prospect's sales force wants handheld PCs because they are easy to carry and lightweight, the salesperson can show how they fit into a shirt or coat pocket. These invitations to experience the product sharply increase the impact of a demonstration.

Although the three aspects of the FAB selling approach need not be covered in any particular order, it's usually best to present the customer benefit early because that's the customer's "hot button" and reason for buying. Consider the following illustrations of the FAB selling formula:

- "You'll be able to produce dazzling, professional, full-color reports and memos *(benefit)* with this new portable *(advantage)* Hewlett-Packard inkjet printer with its interface kit for Apple computers *(feature)*."
- "Your team's win-loss record should quickly improve *(benefit)* with this new lightweight but incredibly strong titanium baseball bat *(features)* because it enables the batter to swing faster and hit the ball up to 50 percent harder *(advantage)*, thus changing many former soft line outs into smashing line drives *(benefit)*."

These two examples illustrate the presentation and demonstration possibilities in using the FAB selling approach. Low-tech or high-tech, all products have features, advantages, and benefits that can be presented. But remember that it's the *benefits* that make prospects and customers want to buy.

It's always important to include *trial closes*, or subtle attempts to move toward the close whenever appropriate in the sales presentation. The acronym **SELLS** will help you remember to cover FAB and include trial closes:

SELLS A memory-aid acronym: **S**how your product's key features; **E**xplain its major advantages; **L**ead into specific benefits for the prospect; **L**et the prospect do most of the talking; and **S**tart a trial close, and use more throughout the presentation.

- **S**how your product's key features.
- **E**xplain its major advantages.
- **L**ead into specific benefits for the prospect.
- **L**et the prospect do most of the talking.
- **S**tart a trial close, and use more throughout the presentation.

When you make a sales presentation, concentrate on the benefits that customers want and on how best they can use the product to achieve those benefits. When you make sales presentations to business resellers such as distributors, wholesalers, or retailers, always include financial information and a marketing strategy that show how to profitably *resell* the product to the customers of these middlemen. Finally, you must sell the prospect on the product's benefits relative to its cost over the product's typical usage life.

Value-Added Selling. Although FAB selling—as described above—is a long-standing and useful professional sales presentation approach, a more comprehensive strategy is **value-added selling (VAS),** which focuses on providing customers with extra, or added-value, benefits over and above those offered by competitors.[2] Nearly all customers want to get the highest overall value they can for their dollar expenditures. The underlying concept for VAS can be seen in the following equation:

Value-Added Selling Providing customers more extra or added-value benefits than offered by competitors.

$$\text{VALUE} = \frac{\text{BENEFITS}}{\text{COSTS}}$$

Many consumers tend to make these calculations almost intuitively, in their heads. For professional organizational buyers, however, maximizing the value received for their company's purchase dollars is a critical part of their jobs. Therefore, they generally prefer to compare the bundle of benefits offered by competitive sellers side-by-side. Savvy professional salespeople realize that it is to their advantage to facilitate this process. However, they also realize that value—like beauty and many other things—is in the eye of the beholder, so customers—even corporate buyers—perceive diverse benefits differently. Therefore, it is more realistic to think of the foregoing equation with "perceived" placed in front of each of the three variables, as follows:

$$\text{Perceived VALUE} = \frac{\text{Perceived BENEFITS}}{\text{Perceived COSTS}}$$

It is up to the value-added salesperson to understand what perceived benefits are most important to each customer and then to present an optimal combination of the highest perceived benefits and lowest perceived costs—that is, the best overall perceived value. For instance, some customers may value styling more highly than durability in certain products (such as company cars that are replaced every three years), and they may perceive inconvenience in the purchase procedure or subsequent use of the products (such as a lack of nearby service centers for routine maintenance of those company cars) as adding to the perceived costs. VAS strives to show customers that the extra overall perceived value the salesperson is offering is greater than that which competitors are offering. In value-added sales presentations, salespeople must go beyond the FAB approach to convincingly present and demonstrate the overall added value (benefits) that the customer will receive from purchasing from their company. One of the major value-added benefits that some salespeople forthrightly point to in their sales presentations is their own personal, professional post-purchase service. Everyone is familiar with one effective approach to using VAS in sales presentations: providing customers with a chart designed to show that the salesperson's company offers more added value benefits than competitors across four VAS categories: (1) product, (2) relationship, (3) company, and (4) salesperson. An example of a *Value-Added Benefit Comparison Chart* is provided in Table 6.3.

TABLE 6.3

Value-Added Benefit Comparison Chart

1. Value-Added *Product* Benefits	Your Firm	Firm A	Firm B	Firm C
Brand reputation (or brand recognition)	✓			
Brand loyalty from customers		✓		
Brand quality as perceived by customers	✓			
Warranty coverage	✓			
Durability of products over usage life	✓			
Low cost of operation over usage life	✓			
Low customer complaints and returns	✓			
High customer satisfaction levels	✓			
2. Value-Added *Relationship* Benefits	**Your Firm**	**Firm A**	**Firm B**	**Firm C**
Commitment to the relationship	✓			
Relationship integrity	✓			
Communication openness in the relationship	✓			
Level of relationship cooperation	✓			
Mutual compatibility of relationship goals			✓	
Viability of long-run relationship				✓
Relationship learning and development orientation	✓			
Confidentiality in relationship	✓			
Emphasis on "win-win" relationship outcomes		✓		
Relationship help in "selling through" channels	✓			
3. Value-Added *Company* Benefits	**Your Firm**	**Firm A**	**Firm B**	**Firm C**
Overall reputation within the industry	✓			
Customer service reputation	✓			
New-product development and innovation		✓		
Ethical behavior	✓			

(continued)

TABLE 6.3

Value-Added Benefit Comparison Chart [continued]

Availability of technical support			✓	
Reliability in supply chain distribution	✓			
Exchange and return policy		✓		
4. Value-Added *Salesperson* Benefits	**Your Firm**	**Firm A**	**Firm B**	**Firm C**
Overall professionalism	✓			
Knowledge and expertise	✓			
Dependability	✓			
Initiative and follow-up	✓			
Resourcefulness in solving customer problems		✓		
Ethical and principled behavior	✓			
Customer advocacy in resolving customer complaints	✓			
"Can do" attitude			✓	
Trustworthiness	✓			

Value-Added Sales Presentation. During the sales presentation, a salesperson using the VAS strategy shows the bundle of value-added benefits included in his offer versus that of competitors. For example, using a *Value-Added Benefit Comparison Chart* like that depicted in Table 6.3, a salesperson for an imaging technologies firm can point out the added value for the customer that derives from his product's brand reputation for quality and superior customer service. Additionally, the salesperson might point out that his firm adds value to its diagnostic ultrasound equipment by providing a free two-year warranty, whereas competitors offer only the standard one-year warranty. As he continues with his sales presentation, the salesperson illustrates the comparative added value offered the customer under each of the other three categories (company, relationship, and salesperson). Note that a check mark is assigned only to the perceived top ranked company in the category, so that the salesperson can readily see those categories where competitors offer higher value to customers.

Before preparing a Value-Added Benefit Comparison Chart, it is important for the salesperson to find out what benefits the prospect or customer perceives as most important under each of the major benefit categories. One straightforward approach would be simply to ask purchasing agents and other members of the buyer center what specific benefit criteria are likely to be used to make their purchase decision. Many professional buyers have developed their own comparison form or chart—not unlike the Value-Added Benefit Comparison Chart—to make their purchase decisions. Perhaps you can ask for a copy of the form to help you prepare for your sales presentation. Some buyers may be impressed that you want to learn how they make their decisions and readily give you a copy.

In their purchasing process, organizations across the board—whether manufacturers, resellers, not-for-profit institutions, or governments—are continually seeking higher benefits while reducing costs. Closer supplier relationships, longer-term contracts, and fewer suppliers are indicators of an ever-growing trend toward achieving these goals. As the director of purchasing at a major automotive manufacturer puts it, "We're no longer just asking who should supply this particular part for the production of a given vehicle brand. Instead, we're asking ourselves who should be our long-run supplier for this product line in multiple production programs." Selling customers on a long-term partnership based on providing added value across the product, company, relationship, and salesperson dimensions is not just another sales strategy; it is fast becoming the *only* viable sales strategy. Unless customers can be continuously convinced that they are obtaining the best overall value for their money, they are not going to remain satisfied or loyal. Thus no salesperson can afford to become complacent about customer perceptions of their value-added bundle of benefits. Soliciting regular customer feedback about satisfaction levels, either formally in surveys or informally by asking probing questions on sales calls, is essential for early detection of any perceived problems in the relationship. And because customer expectations are continuously rising, so must your value-added offerings.

Confirming the Relationship and the Sale

In traditional sales negotiations, the salesperson spends the most time working to overcome buyer resistance and to close the sale by prevailing over the "stubborn" customer. Such salespeople see prospects as adversaries or challengers to be hustled into early purchase commitments. Professional salespeople, on the other hand, see their prospects as *business partners*. They uncover the problems and needs of their prospect partners through attentive listening and by serving as a trusted adviser and friend. Only when they fully understand a prospect's needs, and believe that they have the best product to satisfy those needs, should sales reps start their trial closes: "Are these benefits the ones you're seeking?" "How do you feel about this product's ability to solve the problems you've outlined?"

Chapter Review Question

What is the value-added selling approach to sales presentations? Identify and discuss the four value dimensions.

Building Relationships and Achieving Customer Satisfaction

Some underperforming salespeople neglect post-purchase customer service. Immediately after the sale, their interest, contact, and relationship with the customer fall off rapidly. Such shortsightedness or indifference is a "relationship killer," and these salespeople may later have to work doubly hard to reestablish rapport and rebuild the relationship with that customer. Truly professional salespeople never let the relationship with the customer wither. Their commitment to providing totally satisfying service continues throughout the long-run relationship—before, during, and after the sale. Professional salespeople understand that fully satisfying current customers generates repeat

KEEPING UP ONLINE: *JOURNAL OF PERSONAL SELLING AND SALES MANAGEMENT [JPSSM]*

JPSSM, a research-based journal in the fields of personal selling and sales management, serves a diverse readership that includes sales professionals, professors, researchers, trainers, and students. Readers of *JPSSM* do so chiefly to (1) gain a broader perspective on selling and sales management beyond the boundaries of personal experience and (2) stay abreast of the knowledge explosion in selling and sales management, including the latest research findings and evolving concepts. How might salespeople make use of *JPSSM* to assist them in their selling positions? Visit the journal's website and view some of its offerings at *mkt.cba.cmich.edu/jpssm* and try to find answers to this question.

sales, referrals to other prospects, and increased sales as customer needs grow.[3] Xerox found that its totally satisfied customers are six times more like to repurchase Xerox products than customers who are merely satisfied.[4] In this context, it is important to keep in mind the underlying principle for contemporary customer relationship selling: "The cost of finding and selling to new customers is much higher than [that of] reselling to your current customers."[5]

Top-performing salespeople are continually seeking new ways to better serve their customers. They join sales organizations such as *Sales and Marketing Executives International* (www.smei.org) attend sales and marketing seminars, compare notes with other salespeople, and make a habit of reading sales books, journals, newspapers like the *Wall Street Journal* (www.wsj.com), and business magazines such as *Sales and Marketing Management* (www.salesandmarketing.com). A quarterly academic publication, with a sizable salesperson and sales manager readership, is the *Journal of Personal Selling and Sales Management* (JPSSM), described in the accompanying *Keeping Up Online* feature.

Chapter Review Question
What are the basic steps in planning the sales presentation?

GENERAL GUIDELINES FOR EFFECTIVE SALES PRESENTATIONS

As you now know, making a presentation is not a haphazard activity. Much thought and care must go into your sales presentation if you are to be successful in your selling efforts. Highly effective communication with prospects and customers during sales presentations encompasses the following four principles:

1. *Participation:* Prospects who actively participate in the sales presentation and demonstration retain more information and tend to develop more favorable attitudes toward the product.
2. *Association:* Prospects remember new information better if they can connect it to their personal knowledge, past experiences, and frames of reference.

FROM THE COMMAND POST: BEING DIFFERENT CAN BE AN ADVANTAGE

Did you ever wonder how companies and their salespeople fight through all the promotional "clutter" so that their messages are seen or heard by their target markets? With great difficulty, that's how! Competition tends to be keen in most industries, so promotional messages are numerous and frequent. In fact, these competitive promotions often seem to have little impact other than to cancel or offset each other. Consequently, many marketing communication programs and salespeople's selling efforts are ineffective. Thus the onus often falls on field salespeople to develop communication and sales programs that truly "awaken" awareness and interest in the target audience.

Perhaps you don't want to wear a chicken suit unless you're calling on Perdue Farms (www.perdue.com), but sometimes getting in the door with prospects and extant customers requires creativity and a willingness to try something unusual that will clearly differentiate the firm from its competitors. Some firms have discovered that custom-designing of invitations (a type of sales presentation) for fundraisers, promotional events, and other gatherings can have a positive effect on their recipients. Using arresting mailers can generate significantly higher response rates.

Several factors contribute to high response rates. For instance, a vendor's style is as significant as a person's style. Designing a mailer with a new twist that grabs the reader's attention can project a stimulating, innovative image. Also, crafting eye-catching pieces that strike readers' senses by being unusual (in size, for example, or personalization) rather than having a mass-produced tenor is advantageous. Third, elaborate mailers incorporating unusual materials (such as three-dimensional cut-outs or pieces of cloth or plastic) can set the supplier apart from competitors. Finally, mailers that reflect clearly the event being promoted set the tone and start people talking about the activity.

In sum, a successful communication program that supports the sales force's efforts is one that offers uniqueness, not "me-tooism."

3. *Transfer:* Prospects who see the product being used in situations similar to their own can better visualize the benefits they will derive from the product.
4. *Insight:* Product demonstrations should weave the facts and figures from the sales presentation into the prospect's own experience because this often leads to special insights that favorably impress the prospect.[6]

Some salespeople have found success by being somewhat flamboyant in their sales presentations and demonstrations. Never be reluctant to develop your own style, because this uniqueness can be an effective sales tool that sets you apart from the competition, as illustrated in the accompanying *From the Command Post* feature.

Effective Sales Demonstrations

"One picture is worth a thousand words, and one demonstration is worth a thousand pictures" is a well-known axiom among professional salespeople. To bring their sales presentations to life, most successful salespeople try to make realistic—often dramatic—product *demonstrations*. It is said that prospects want to "see, hear, feel, smell, and taste" a product before making a purchase decision. Hence the best salespeople work to involve as many of the prospect's senses as possible in their demonstrations. One sales rep for a shatterproof glass producer led his company's sales force year after year in sales by using a creative demonstration strategy: aggressively hitting the shatterproof glass with a hammer in front of prospects. But he became an even bigger success when he handed the hammer to prospects and invited *them* to hit the glass. Few other tactics could so effectively increase their direct involvement in and understanding of the product.

The demonstration can be a powerful selling tool, but it calls for careful planning and practice. Strategic planning of the demonstration enables the salesperson to prepare in advance for all of the eventualities. The eight basic steps for preparing demonstrations follow.

1. Select benefits to demonstrate that fit the prospect's needs.
2. Decide what to say about the benefits from the prospect's perspective.
3. Select sales aids that involve the most human senses possible and have the most positive impact.
4. Pre-check all sales aids to make sure everything is working smoothly.
5. Decide when and where to make the demonstration. Usually a controlled environment is best.
6. Figure out how to involve the prospect. Remember: "If they try it, they'll buy it."
7. Prepare a written demonstration outline. Include three columns: (a) Benefit to demonstrate, (b) what to say, and (c) what to do.
8. Rehearse the demonstration many times until you have the right wording and timing of actions—but don't try to memorize the *entire* demonstration; if you do, it will come across as canned and perfunctory.

Appropriate dress and appearance can facilitate salesperson success.
Stockdisc/Getty Images

Dressing for Selling Success

An important part of any sales presentation is the salesperson's personal appearance. Many companies hire consultants to conduct seminars for their salespeople on personal grooming, selecting clothing and accessories, and using body language. A few salespeople have been successful despite dressing in bizarre ways, but most professional salespeople make sure that their appearance helps them makes sales. What's the best way to dress? As with many other facets of professional selling, the answer depends on the prospects, selling situations, and products, but we offer some general advice in Table 6.4.

TABLE 6.4

Dressing for Sales Presentation Success

- **Goal:** Your goal is to convey professionalism, confidence, trustworthiness, and integrity.
- **Clothes:** Wear conservatively cut clothes in muted or neutral colors that make little obvious impression but subliminally speak of power, confidence, and success. Avoid bright hues, intricate patterns, or anything that's trendy or showy. Dark blue is nearly always safe.
- **Makeup:** Saleswomen should wear only moderate makeup unless they represent a cosmetics company and are showing off a new line. If your makeup says, "I'd rather be partying than doing business," securing your prospect's serious attention will be an uphill battle.
- **Jewelry:** Neither salesmen nor saleswomen should wear ostentatious or noisy jewelry that can suggest a preoccupation with appearance. Salesmen are safest wearing no jewelry at all, and saleswomen should wear only conservative jewelry.
- **Briefcase:** Choose a conservative, unobtrusive briefcase in dark brown or cordovan. A flat zipper case is a good choice because it helps you look organized and like someone who deals only with important matters. Replace your case when it starts to show wear.
- **Business Cards:** Choose simple, dignified business cards without gaudy logos or emblems. Always carry them in a special metal or leather business card case to keep them from becoming dirty or dog-eared.
- **Writing Pen:** Never ask a customer to sign a $20,000 order with a 35-cent ballpoint pen. Carry a fine pen and always keep it handy so you don't have to fumble to find it.

Source: *Adapted from David Severson, "When a Sales Pitch Won't Do,"* Training & Development Journal *(June 1985), 18–19. Copyright June 1985,* Training & Development Journal, *American Society for Training & Development. Reprinted with permission.*

Effective Behavior and Listening Principles

How salespeople behave during sales presentations and demonstrations is critical. Inappropriate behavior—as seen through the eyes of the *prospect*—can ruin even a solid presentation or demonstration. Similarly, a salesperson who shows poor listening attentiveness or frequently interrupts when the prospect is talking gives the impression of regarding the prospect's problems and needs as unimportant. The old maxim "The reason you have two ears and one mouth is that you should listen twice as much as you talk" is especially true for a salesperson. Additionally, always keep your deportment consistent with your prospect's business setting and personal values and beliefs. Most important, listen carefully and respectfully to your prospect.[7] Table 6.5 offers a list of professional behaviors that salespeople employ when making successful presentations and demonstrations. In Table 6.6, we provide important guidelines for effective listening during presentations and demonstrations. Although you may consider some of these suggestions obvious, many buyers can recount horror stories of salespeople who failed to behave in accordance with these basic guidelines and thus failed to garner sales from the buyers.

Chapter Review Question

Why are clothing and accessories important considerations in making an effective sales presentation?

ON THE FRONTLINES: THE LIFE OF A SALESPERSON

The Sales Presentation and Demonstration

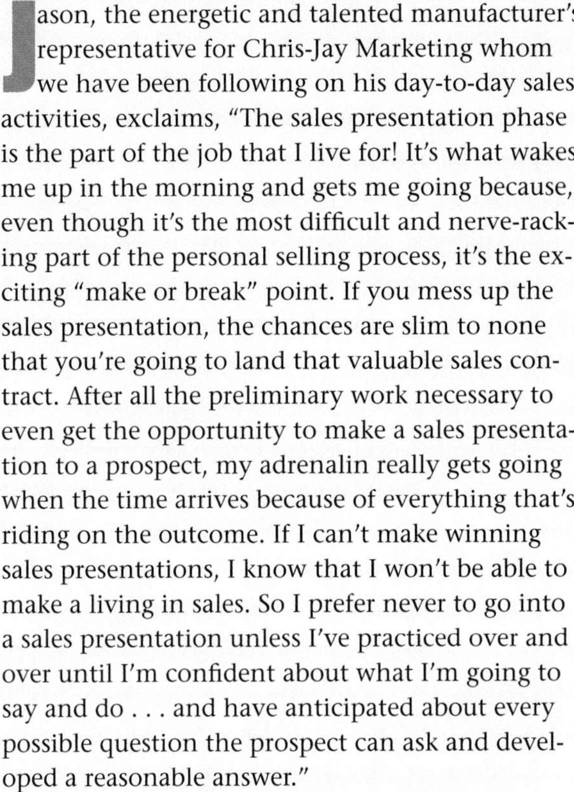

Jason, the energetic and talented manufacturer's representative for Chris-Jay Marketing whom we have been following on his day-to-day sales activities, exclaims, "The sales presentation phase is the part of the job that I live for! It's what wakes me up in the morning and gets me going because, even though it's the most difficult and nerve-racking part of the personal selling process, it's the exciting "make or break" point. If you mess up the sales presentation, the chances are slim to none that you're going to land that valuable sales contract. After all the preliminary work necessary to even get the opportunity to make a sales presentation to a prospect, my adrenalin really gets going when the time arrives because of everything that's riding on the outcome. If I can't make winning sales presentations, I know that I won't be able to make a living in sales. So I prefer never to go into a sales presentation unless I've practiced over and over until I'm confident about what I'm going to say and do . . . and have anticipated about every possible question the prospect can ask and developed a reasonable answer."

Even practicing for sales presentations gets Jason's creative juices flowing, and if he can find one of his co-workers or family members to play the part of a tough buyer, he feels his practice becomes more productive and realistic. "Of course, it's unreasonable to think that every sales presentation will go well and that I'll always win the sales contract," he explains. "But there's no denying that the more I practice my sales presentations, the higher my success ratio. While I practice, I also try out my 'arsenal' of different sales presentation strategies, so that if one isn't working for me, I can switch to another. I also practice *trial closes* to use at appropriate points in my presentation and demonstration. Speaking of the demonstration, it can be the most effective sales presentation tool of all. I always carry samples of my products to show and demonstrate. As much as possible, I try to get full customer participation in the demonstration. I learned long ago that the most effective demonstrations involve as many of the customer's senses as possible—the more they can see, touch, smell, taste, or hear a good product, the more likely they are to buy it. Sometimes, I bring along a few competitors' products to enable my prospect to make side-by-side comparisons—and this can have a strong impact on the purchase decision."

During his practice, Jason keeps in mind that his prospect may ask questions at various points in the presentation, and this is good because it shows interest and involvement. Whenever the prospect asks a question, Jason tries to be just as good a listener as he was a sales presenter a few moments before. As Jason points out, "The more involved in my sales presentation and demonstration the prospect becomes, the higher my chances of getting the sale."

On sales calls, Jason always dresses professionally and appropriately, whether he is doing a formal or informal sales presentation. Usually he wears a conservative dress suit, but sometimes, depending on the setting for the sales call, he wears more casual clothes to fit in better with the prospect's attire. Before he leaves his home or office to start his daily sales calls, Jason makes sure he isn't wearing flashy jewelry, affiliation lapel pins, or even strong cologne that might divert attention from his sales presentation. He recalls one salesperson who absentmindedly wore to a sales call a lapel pin indicating that he was a Democrat.

(continued)

Unfortunately, that prospect happened to be a local Republican party leader, and he became so upset upon seeing the lapel pin that he refused to meet with the poor salesperson, who was never able to sell anything to that prospect.

"The sales presentation is the heart of the personal selling process," explains Jason. It's my job during the sales presentation to show exactly how my products and services offer more customer benefits than my competitors' do. My presentations vary from one customer to another. Some customers like informal meetings that are laid back with open give-and-take discussion. Others like more formal PowerPoint presentations. I do my best to accommodate their presentation style preferences."

"While sales presentation strategies are important, it's even more crucial to engage the customers and get them involved. Customers need to feel they are an integral part of the presentation. And when a customer speaks, I stop and listen and never *ever* interrupt until he or she has finished. I pride myself on being a good listener. I've found that listening enhances trust. It shows that I'm patient and really want to understand my customer's problems and needs. To show that I'm intent on developing a long-term relationship with the prospect, I focus on presenting the key benefits that my customers will derive by buying products from the companies I represent. Because my sales presentation approach centers on the overall added value that my products offer over those of competitors, I seldom need to offer price discounts to make a sale. It seems that my customers readily perceive the extra value in my offerings. Also, I like to think that customers see my professionalism and dedication to serving them as the most important added value. Making sales presentations can be stressful, but the highs are fantastic and the rewards are great when everything clicks," says Jason, with a gleeful grin.

TABLE 6.5

Behavioral Guidelines for Effective Sales Presentations and Demonstrations

- Establish rapport early.
- Include in your introductory remarks questions that will grab the prospect's attention and promote involvement.
- Look for and use responsive behaviors.
- Connect prospect needs and product benefits with respected reference groups.
- Combine factual and emotional appeals.
- Assume an initial relatively firm negotiating position.
- Help prospects draw the right conclusions.
- Use humor with discretion and only where appropriate.
- Never disparage another individual or company.
- Avoid making puns, which can come off as childish.
- Never tell ethnic jokes or offensive jokes of any kind.
- Readily admit minor weaknesses in the product, because doing so increases your credibility with prospects and customers.

TABLE 6.6

KEYS TO GOOD LISTENING

- Stop, look, and listen! You cannot listen when you're talking, and you won't grasp the subtle meaning of words unless you're closely watching the prospect's body language. Wait until prospects have finished talking before you respond. The important point they're making may be in their upcoming fourth sentence, and interrupting before then will prevent you from hearing that critical information.
- Make prospects feel comfortable and uninhibited about talking freely with you by listening in a nonjudgmental way. Avoid either positively or negatively critiquing their statements; just let them know that you understand what they're saying.
- Ask nonthreatening, probing questions to clarify the prospect's comments. Doing so shows that you're listening, encourages the prospect to talk more, and helps you both to understand the communication that has taken place.
- Empathize with prospects and their problems, and, if applicable, tell them specifically how you relate to their problems. Make the prospect's needs more important than your own.
- Give prospects your full attention, both mentally and physically. Do not yawn, allow your eyes to glaze over, doodle, tap your fingers, shuffle papers, or allow your mind to wander while the prospect is talking. Continue to look and be interested.
- Keep your emotions under control. No matter what happens, keep cool. An emotional person is unlikely to hear or see clearly. Avoid arguments. Even if you win, you'll probably lose the sale.
- Make notes of major points in your discussion with the prospect at the first opportunity, probably in the car before driving to your next appointment.
- Some top salespeople send the prospect a memorandum summarizing each meeting. Before doing so, however, ask the prospect if he or she would welcome this. Unless he or she agrees, keep your notes to yourself. Of course, a thank-you note for the prospect's time is always appropriate.

SALES PRESENTATIONS TO GROUPS

Sales presentations to organizational prospects and customers must include a business strategy (also called a business plan) that explains how the product can profitably be resold or used to make other products. Organizational customers must be convinced that the overall business strategy is sound before they will buy the product. Because the purchasing decision is so important to their success, large organizational customers will often ask salespeople to make presentations to a group of company employees, including people from purchasing, accounting, marketing, production, engineering, and finance.[8] To assist you in preparing such a presentation, you may want to make a *presentation-planning checklist*. The checklist (which can be adapted for different types of presentations) will provide you with direction for your

Because purchasing decisions are important to their company's success, large organizational customers often ask salespeople to make presentations to a group.
Corbis

presentation, improve your preparation, and enhance your comfort level prior to and during the presentation. On pages 189 and 190, you will find one kind of presentation-planning checklist.

Sales Presentation Format

Salespeople succeed using many different kinds of group presentations. One popular group presentation format follows this sequence: *problem, product, benefits, evidence, summary,* and *action.* An abbreviated version of a salesperson's presentation, using this standard format, is shown on page 191.

Depending on the situation and the prospect audience, a standardized sales presentation format can often work well. However, the professional salesperson first answers three basic questions to ensure that the presentation is both appropriately tailored to (aligned with) the audience and consistent with several guidelines. Table 6.7 outlines these questions and guidelines, and we discuss them below.

TABLE 6.7

SALES PRESENTATION ALIGNMENT AND GUIDELINES FOR PROSPECT GROUPS

Questions Regarding Alignment of the Sales Presentation
1. Who is the audience? ________
2. What benefits are they seeking? ________
3. How do they prefer to communicate? ________
Guidelines for Sales Presentations
• Begin with an audience-focused statement of purpose.
• Translate the product into customer benefits.
• Energize the sales presentation and demonstration.
• Encourage interaction and participation.
• Show your commitment to customer service.
• Ask for specific action.
• Critique the sales presentation.

PRESENTATION PLANNING CHECKLIST

1. Who is the prospect?

   Company name ____________________

   Key people and their positions ____________________

   Address ____________________

   Phone number ____________________

   Fax number ____________________

   E-mail address ____________________

2. Date, time, and place of appointment:

   Date __________ Time __________ Place ____________________

3. Statements of customer problem and/or opportunity as related to our product/service offerings:

   ____

4. Major buying motives of the prospect (if known):

   ____

5. Objectives of the presentation:

   Major objectives: ____________________

   Minor objectives: ____________________

6. Preferred communication style:

   a. Amiable __________ b. Analytical __________

   c. Expressive __________ d. Driver __________

7. Important customer benefits to be stressed:

   ____

   ____

8. Evidence needed to support my claims (competitive comparisons, test results, testimonials, etc.):

   ____

   ____

9. Other information needed (terms, delivery schedules, etc.):

   ____

   ____

(continued)

PRESENTATION PLANNING CHECKLIST [CONTINUED]

10. Sales tools needed (e.g., brochures, audiovisual equipment, samples): ______________________________

____

11. To start the presentation, I will: ______________________________

____

• state objectives and approach: ______________________________

____

• establish rapport by: ______________________________

____

• attract attention, obtain interest, and transition by: ______________________________

____

12. I anticipate the following objections and will respond to them as follows:

a. objection 1: ______________________________

response: ______________________________

b. objection 2: ______________________________

response: ______________________________

13. To close the sale, I will ask for the order by:

____

____

14. To ensure customer satisfaction, I will follow up with these actions:

____

____

15. I have rehearsed the presentation to emphasize the following key customer benefits:

____

____

16. If other people from my company are involved in the presentation, we all understand our roles, as well as the roles of the others.

	Name of Person
Individual Role 1. ______________	______________
Individual Role 2. ______________	______________

17. I have planned to be flexible during the presentation and will be able to adapt my presentation if the situation warrants it. Possible adaptive strategies include:

____

Group Presentation Example

1. **Problem:** "Good morning. I'm delighted to be at Fisher-Price this morning and to have this chance to talk with you and bring you some good news. First, based on my discussions with many of you, it is my understanding that the poor adhesive quality of the glue you're currently using has been a major source of customer complaints and merchandise returns to retailers. Two of your newest toys are being recalled at a cost of several hundred thousand dollars because the glue is simply not holding. Is that essentially correct? *[Additional discussion of the problem may take place here as members of the prospect group clarify the specific nature of their collective and individual needs. Information gathered here can help the salesperson to make some adjustments in the focus of the sales presentation.]*
2. **Product:** Well, I'm delighted to report that our new product, *Fantastic Glue,* is the answer to your problem. *Fantastic Glue* is a revolutionary new adhesive recently developed and tested at our research laboratories, and it will be available next month. I've got a sample of it right here, in the bright blue tube on the table. After four years of intense effort, our research scientists developed this unbelievable product, which more than doubles the holding properties of any other industrial-strength glue on the market, and what's more, it sets up twice as fast.
3. **Benefits:** *Fantastic Glue* will completely solve your product adhesion problems, raise customer satisfaction, and increase your company's reputation for quality products. Your customer complaint department people may become as lonely as the Maytag repairman. At the same time, your company's annual profits will jump by several thousand dollars, not only from increased sales, but also because *Fantastic Glue's* fast-setting properties will make your gluing operations nearly twice as efficient, saving you hundreds of hours of employee time and labor. Equally important, you'll see a noticeable improvement in employee morale on the production line.
4. **Evidence:** Our packaging and shipping department has been using *Fantastic Glue* for the past three months now, and everybody gives it rave reviews. I know from my personal experience that *Fantastic Glue is* terrific. I've taken samples home to repair some broken toys and appliances in my own household. My wife and kids think I'm brilliant now that I can repair just about anything that gets broken. Let me prove it to you. Here's one of the broken toys returned by one of your unhappy customers. I'll just brush on a little *Fantastic Glue,* and one minute later, I'll challenge anyone to pull the two pieces apart. *[Salesperson performs the demonstration with help of prospects.]* Now, isn't that truly fantastic!
5. **Summary:** Well, there you have it. You've seen the incredible qualities and benefits yourself. *Fantastic Glue* will immediately solve your adhesive problems, stop the customer complaints about broken toys, enhance your company's reputation for quality (thereby increasing sales), improve production line morale, and dramatically improve your company's profits by making your gluing operations more time- and cost-efficient.
6. **Action:** I've got some more good news for you. As a special incentive for new buyers to try *Fantastic Glue,* we're offering a 20 percent discount with a double-your-money-back guarantee. In fact, if you order today, I'll even personally guarantee that *Fantastic Glue will* be delivered to you by this Thursday so you can start solving those gluing problems as soon as possible. How many gallons do you think you'll need? *[Salesperson takes out the order pad and pen.]*

Alignment of the Sales Presentation

Generally, the more precisely a sales presentation's content and communication style are aligned, or matched, with the audience's characteristics, desired benefits, and communication style, the more effective the presentation will be. Creating such alignment requires you to ask three crucial questions.

1. *Who Is the Prospect Audience?* Top salespeople always identify and confirm their audience before delivering their sales presentations. Some salespeople have been known to make sales presentations focused on highly technical aspects of a product, only to learn later that the audience included no engineers or technicians, only marketing and finance people. Find out what information the prospect organization requires before it will make the purchase. Until they know their prospects' characteristics and interests, even the best sales presenters can't communicate persuasively. This information should be acquired through research before the sales presentation is prepared and should be confirmed at the start of the presentation. Probably the most straightforward way to confirm the audience before you start the presentation is to ask, "It's my understanding that everyone in the room is an engineer. Is that correct?"
2. *What Benefits Are the Prospects Seeking?* Depending on their type of business or nonprofit activities and on the macroenvironment, organizations may have unique problems and needs at different stages in their life cycle. In general, however, the sales presentation should focus on the organization's primary functions. For example, a sales presentation to retailers and wholesalers needs to explain how they can profitably resell the product, and a sales presentation to industrial firms needs to focus on how the product will improve profitability in producing and marketing the buying firm's products.
3. *How Do the Prospects Prefer to Communicate?* Find out ahead of the sales presentation how the members of the prospect group communicate with each other, so you can prepare and rehearse appropriately. Several questions need to be answered: What special jargon and gestures do they use? How do they normally dress—business suits, sports coats, or blue collars? What beliefs and attitudes underlie their business relationships and decisions? What do they recognize as achievements and why? How do they regard time? Do they prefer a formal style or a more relaxed style? How is space handled? Do they sit or stand close together? Do they make frequent eye contact? How do they prefer to receive information: color transparencies, slides, flipcharts, videotapes, printed material, PowerPoint, or verbal communication? Do they prefer open, give-and-take discussions?

Group Sales Presentation Guidelines

After aligning the sales presentation content and communication style with the audience, professional salespeople generally follow seven basic guidelines.

(a) *Begin with an Audience-Focused Statement of Purpose.* Many salespeople outline their sales presentations according to *the points they want to make* to prospects. However, the most effective presentations focus on *what the audience wants to hear.* The opening purpose statement should clarify the presentation goals and approach, as noted in the following example:

> Our purpose today is to show you how ABC Company can help you solve your product quality problems. Our approach will be to show you how we solve similar problems in various industries and companies by presenting four different scenarios. Finally, we have these four goals for this presentation: (1) to illustrate our understanding of your problem, (2) to demonstrate the benefits provided by our new punch press, (3) to show how it will pay for itself within the first year of use, and (4) to explain how we will maintain and service the equipment to ensure that it remains in top working order.

(b) *Translate the Product into Prospect Benefits.* Prospects are interested in benefits or solutions to *their* problems, which are not necessarily the benefits the salesperson thinks he or she is selling. All the snazzy features and advantages of the product or service will have little impact unless you can hit the prospects' "hot buttons"—their desired benefits. If the salesperson has not yet been able to pinpoint major benefits sought by the prospect, sometimes the product demonstration will reveal which benefits prospects value most.

When emphasizing the product's benefits, you should use *specific, positive* statements, rather than general, vague statements. For example, *don't* say, "Our competitors can't do this." Instead, say, "Our product is unmatched by competition, as we have over 97 percent up time." *Don't* say, "This motor has outstanding performance." Rather, say, "This motor can turn 4500 rpms with minimum maintenance."

(c) *Energize the Sales Presentation to Make It Memorable.* A sad tie can spoil the appearance of a suit, but **SAD TIE** is an acronym memory aid to salespeople in planning ways to spice up a sales presentation, as explained on page 195. Such efforts enhance the clarity of the presentation and credibility of the seller.

SAD TIE A memory-aid acronym that stands for **S**tatistics, **A**nalogies, **D**emonstrations, **T**estimonials, **I**ncidents, and **E**xhibits, one or all of which the salesperson may use to spice up a sales presentation.,

(d) *Encourage Interaction and Participation.* In developing a relationship, nothing works better than personal give-and-take discussions. Salespeople can learn more about prospect needs and perceptions through direct discussions than from any market research technique. Essentially, such efforts are implicitly directed at taking the "pulse" of the sales presentation through prospect feedback. Learning to subtly facilitate and manage a group discussion while directing it along the sales presentation track is a talent that develops only after much role-playing or actual experience. Some salespeople try to involve prospects at various points during and after the sales presentation by asking, "Are there any questions?" Unfortunately, this approach seldom stimulates much response from the audience and does little to strengthen buyer-seller communication. A better way to obtain prospect involvement after completing part of the sales presentation is for the salesperson to ask a specific question, such as "Could you tell me how the system I've laid out might help you in your work?" or "Now, would you want one large central workstation or would a group of smaller ones best meet your needs?" If no one volunteers to answer even specific questions like these, the salesperson can direct the question in a nonthreatening way to a particular member of the buying group. For example, you might ask, "Mary, how do you think this system will fit in with your company's data processing needs?" or "Bill, how might your manufacturing plant benefit from this hydraulic pumping system?" In addition, when demonstrating the product, ask prospects to operate the product (if feasible and safe) to help familiarize them with the functioning of the product. Doing so should enhance their ability to see the benefits that they can realize from the product. Just as car salespeople ask prospects to take a test drive to "get the feel" of an automobile, prospects' participation in a demonstration can give them increased awareness of the strengths of the product under consideration, as well as how it will help their business operations.

(e) *Show Your Commitment to Customer Service.* It's important to show prospects and customers that you care about fully satisfying their business needs and that your service will continue after the sale. Explain your professional selling philosophy to them. Let them know that you want a *permanent* business relationship or partnership with them and that your success depends on their success. Telling them that you want them to be lifetime customers, not merely one-time customers, shows that you are committed to customer satisfaction and service. Make such pronouncements, however, only if you really mean them and plan to back them up with exceptional service. Paying lip service to such ideals without following through will come back to haunt you and your company. Raising customer expectations without meeting those expectations only fosters customer dissatisfaction and loss of future sales.

(f) *Ask for Specific Action.* Just as with sales presentations to individual buyers, it is necessary for salespeople to seek some kind of commitment from a group of buyers. Although salespeople should try to close a sale whenever possible, they must be prepared to seek other specific actions by prospects. Every sales call should include several possible secondary objectives in case a purchase commitment cannot be obtained. Maybe the prospects can be persuaded to use a small amount of the product on a trial basis or to schedule an appointment for another sales presentation to a larger buying committee. By accomplishing one or more of their secondary objectives, salespeople learn to view nearly every sales call as at least a partial success that furthers the prospect-seller relationship and moves closer to future mutually satisfying sales agreements. This

SAD TIE

S—*Statistics:* Business audiences are particularly receptive to a few statistics, because they use them to make their own sales pitches to their bosses. Too many numbers, however, can be confusing; so show just enough to make key points. It's best also to show the numbers in a graphical form such as a pie or bar chart.

A—*Analogies, Similes, and Metaphors:* Innovative use of *analogies, similes,* and *metaphors* can bring special life to sales presentations. Most salespeople will tell you that analogies are an effective way to win people over to your way of thinking. *Analogies* enable prospects to visualize and comprehend something complex by relating it to something different but familiar and easier to understand. For instance, talking about a billion dollars is rather vague until you tell people how many miles that many dollars would stretch if laid end to end, or how many hundred-thousand-dollar homes you could buy with that much money. *Similes* are direct comparisons preceded by the preposition *like* or *as.* For example: "An Apple computer greets you like an old friend every time you turn it on" or "Our cellular phone makes you feel as if you never left home." *Metaphors* are implied comparisons that use a word or phrase that at first seems inappropriate to create a dramatic visual image. For example: "Our new razor *skates* smoothly over your face." "The *eye* and *ear* of this lightweight camcorder will *see* and *hear* everything you do."

D—*Demonstrations:* Use actual product demonstrations or simulations to bring benefits to life for the prospect and make a memorable impression. Nothing is more impressive to prospects than seeing, feeling, touching, tasting, or smelling the product benefits. Some salespeople are so confident in their products that they believe a time-honored maxim: "If they try it, they'll buy it."

T—*Testimonials:* Support your position with expert testimony. People will be more easily persuaded if you provide testimonial support from an objective source that the prospect respects. The product testimonial doesn't have to be a direct one; it can be implied: "Did you notice that the *Today Show* uses our cordless microphones?" "Do you know that the president wears the same brand of suit?"

I—*Incidents:* Describing a relevant incident brings a point home and usually makes a lasting impression. For example, if you're selling a new heating plant system, you could describe the specific experience of a well-known and respected company that saved money using the same system.

E—*Exhibits:* An exhibit is a selling prop and can take many forms. It can be a display at a trade show, the flipchart you're using as you talk, or a model of the product. The purpose of an exhibit is to help bring the sales presentation to life and enhance the sales presentation performance. For example, if you're making a presentation to a company interested in buying laptop computers for their executives, you could show a display of different laptops used by businesspeople over the years, ranging from the early bulky models to today's miniaturized versions that you want them to buy.

perspective clearly is preferable to that of a salesperson who believes that every sales presentation must lead to a close. The attitude that a sale must be made on every call can lead salespeople to become too pushy and even rude, two outcomes sure to spell disaster with buyers.[9]

(g) *Critique the Sales Presentation.* Professional football teams review game films weekly to identify strengths and weaknesses in their previous game and prepare for the next one. Similarly, salespeople can critique every group (or single-prospect) sales presentation and prepare for the next. If other members of the seller organization attended the sales presentation, they too can help the salesperson by offering their perspectives. Here are several questions to ask in such a review:

- Was the sales presentation executed from the prospects' viewpoint?
- Which benefits seemed most important to prospects? Why?
- What product features and advantages did prospects seem most interested in?
- What did you learn about the prospects that you want to include in the next sales presentation?
- Did you attempt enough *trial closes?* How did the prospect react to each? Which ones worked best?
- Which of your sales presentation goals were achieved? Which were not achieved?
- Which presentation format did you use? How well did it work?
- Overall, what parts of the sales presentation could you have done better?

Chapter Review Questions

In context of making presentations to groups, what does the acronym SAD TIE stand for?

Define and give an example of each of the following aids for sales presentations: (a) analogies, (b) similes, and (c) metaphors.

For maximum benefit, conduct your debriefings both orally and in writing while encouraging a positive climate for candor and learning. Feedback and corrective action stimulate learning and lead to improved performance in subsequent sales presentations.

SALES PRESENTATION STRATEGIES

Several alternative presentation strategies ought to be considered in preparing effective sales presentations to achieve specific objectives. As summarized in Table 6.8, these include the stimulus-response, formula, need satisfaction, consultative problem solving, depth selling, and team selling approaches. We will briefly discuss each of these six basic sales presentation strategies. Note also that salespeople can enroll in sales presentation training programs offered by companies such as the Empowerment Group (www.empowermentgroup.com/presentation_training.html) to further develop their sales presentation skills.

TABLE 6.8

SALES PRESENTATION STRATEGIES

Strategy	Approach	Advantage or Disadvantage
Stimulus-Response	Salesperson asks a series of positive leading questions.	Customer develops habit of answering "yes," which may lead to a positive response to the closing question. Can appear as manipulative to more sophisticated prospects.
Formula	Salesperson leads the prospect through the mental states of buying (AIDA: attention, interest, desire, and action).	Prospect is led toward purchase action one step at a time, as the prospect participates in the interview. May come across as too mechanical and rehearsed to win prospect's trust and confidence.
Need Satisfaction	Salesperson tries to find the prospect's dominant but often latent buying needs; skillful listening, questioning, and use of certain image-producing words will help the sales person uncover the critical need or needs to be satisfied if the sale is to be won.	Salesperson listens and responds to the prospect while "leading" the prospect to buy; the sales person learns dominant buyer needs and motivations. Salesperson must not overlook latent needs of prospect that are not articulated.
Consultative Problem Solving	Salesperson carefully listens and asks probing questions to more fully understand the prospect's problems and specific needs and then recommends the best alternative solutions.	Through the parties working together to understand and solve problems, the salesperson forges a trustful, consultative relationship with the prospect. Salesperson and buyer negotiations focus on a "win-win" outcome and a long-run relationship.
Depth Selling	Salesperson employs a skillful mix of several sales presentation methods.	A customized mix of the best features of all of the strategies that draws on most of their advantages. Depth selling requires exceptional salesperson skill and experience.
Team Selling	Salesperson, in concert with other company personnel, sells the product/service benefits and avoids intragroup conflicts by promoting harmony. Salesperson must identify and cater to the needs of each interest group.	Team selling involves counterparts from both the buyer and seller organizations interacting and cooperating to find solutions to problems. Salesperson serves as coordinator of the buyer-seller team interactions.

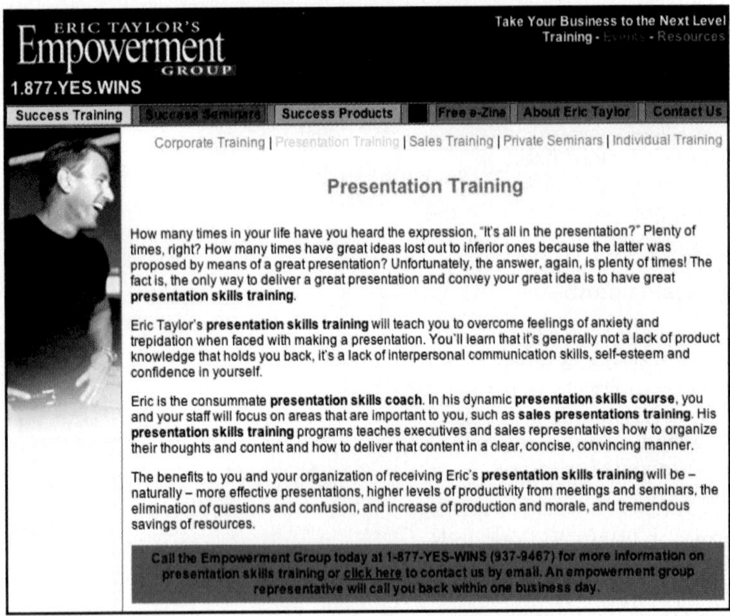

Reprinted by permission of Eric Taylor

Stimulus-Response

Stimulus-response strategies call for stimuli (selling points) to be presented in such a way as to elicit favorable responses from prospects while leading them toward the sales close. In order to obtain a series of "yes" responses from the prospect while demonstrating the product, the sales rep may ask leading questions such as "Aren't you surprised to see how smoothly and efficiently this new computerized lathe works compared to your current ones?" This sales presentation technique is widely used for training new salespeople, but it may come across as robot-like and disingenuous if rigidly followed. This approach can sometimes work for novice salespeople talking to relatively naïve prospects, but salespeople who deal with sophisticated buyers should seldom employ the stimulus-response approach, except perhaps briefly in the product demonstration to help clarify benefits for the prospects.

Formula

Formula sales presentation strategies tend to focus on the products offered rather than on the prospect's needs, but they do have the advantage of encouraging prospect involvement. *AIDA* is the name of one commonly employed formula. It tries to move prospects toward a purchase decision by sequentially progressing through four mental states: A*ttention, Interest, Desire,* and *Action*. Sales reps must capture their prospects' undivided attention and then arouse their interest by describing benefits and pointing out advantages to them, stimulate their desire for the benefits by offering proof, and finally motivate them to take prompt purchase action.

An industrial-strength vacuum cleaner salesperson calling on a large factory might make effective use of a formula sales presentation, even using the most stereotypical salesperson demonstration. First, the salesperson sprinkles sawdust or metal scrapings around the prospect's factory floor to dramatically draw the prospect's *attention*. As the dismayed plant manager's anxiety grows, the salesperson gains *interest* by saying: "Now wouldn't you like to see this mess cleaned up quickly and quietly?" Of course, the prospect's *desire* is to do exactly that and immediately, so the salesperson plugs the cord into the outlet, and the vacuum neatly cleans up all the particles. Demonstrating the benefits of the industrial vacuum cleaner usually can relieve and delight the prospect so much that the plant manager may be motivated to purchase (action) on the spot. Of course, using a little understated humor before and during such a classic salesperson's demonstration would probably go a long way toward making it successful. For example, you might say: "Before I start this demonstration, your electricity is working, isn't it?" After a "yes" answer, the salesperson continues: "Good, now you've probably never seen or heard of the demonstration I'm about to give, but it will show you just how well our industrial-strength vacuum will work in your plant."

Need Satisfaction

In applying a need satisfaction strategy, the salesperson avoids talking about the product or service until she or he has discovered the prospects' dominant needs or wants. Through skillful questioning, the salesperson encourages prospects to reveal their psychographic makeup (attitudes, interests, opinions, personality, and lifestyle) and needs. Need satisfaction strategies require the salesperson to be a patient, perceptive listener and observer of body language in order to fully understand what the prospect is saying and feeling. This approach is most appropriate when the potential purchase involves a significant economic and psychological commitment on the part of the prospect. Misreading the prospect's dominant buying motives will lose the sale, so using the need satisfaction strategy effectively calls for considerable selling practice and experience. Some dominant needs are latent and may not be articulated because of embarrassment, guilt, or unawareness, so the salesperson must "read between the lines" as the prospect describes his or her needs. A prospect may express the *manifest needs* for transportation, safety, and comfort in buying a carpooling van for the firm, but as the prospect talks, an alert salesperson may also detect a strong *latent need* for status. Unless the van satisfies this unspoken but perhaps dominant status need, the sale may fall through.

Consultative Problem Solving

The most frequently recommended and generally most successful sales presentation strategy for today's professional salespeople is *consultative problem-solving*. Consultative problem-solving sales presentations focus on the prospect's problems, *not* the seller's products. It emphasizes the partnership of buyer and seller and stresses "win-win" outcomes in negotiations, which is why most salespeople and customers see it as the *best* sales presentation method. This approach is most often used by sellers of complex technical products who seek to establish long-term relationships built on mutual trust, confidence, and respect. For example, an electronics company considering the purchase of some robots for an assembly line versus the alternative of upgrading its current manual equipment would probably prefer a problem-solving sales presentation strategy that would analyze the pros and cons of each possible solution from the buyer's perspective.

Chapter Review Question
What is the consultative problem-solving sales presentation strategy? Give an example of a selling situation where this strategy would be especially appropriate.

In applying problem-solving strategies, salespeople must make full use of their listening and questioning skills to understand the prospect company's problem and discover its precise needs. Several face-to-face meetings, telephone calls, e-mails, in-depth research, and the help of backup technical specialists may be needed to prepare a final written proposal that accurately analyzes the prospect's problems and recommends alternative solutions along with their advantages and disadvantages. Contrasted with traditional canned formula presentations, dramatic product demonstrations, or splashy multimedia shows, the consultative problem-solving approach to sales presentations is rather uncomplicated, as described by a salesperson in the *On the Frontlines* feature on page 200.

ON THE FRONTLINES

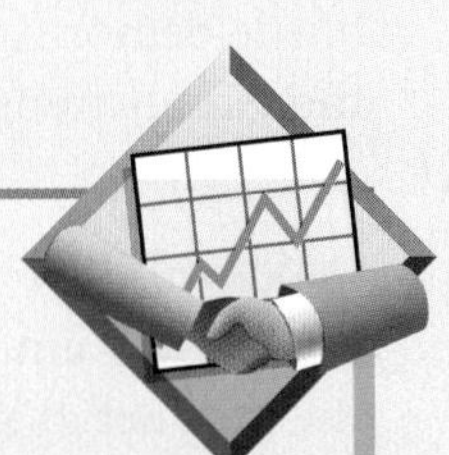

A Consultative Problem-Solving Sales Presentation

I used to think that lacking a dazzling sales presentation style worked against me, but no more. Recently, I earned my biggest commission ever, and it was the easiest sales presentation I ever made. Four competitive salespeople and I were scheduled to make a sales presentation to a local manufacturer. I'd been up against these four sales reps before, and I knew each of them would make a multimedia, show-biz type sales presentation to try for the business. Recognizing that I didn't have a high-tech sales presentation or the kind of flare to beat them at their game, I decided not to play their game at all. Instead, I spent my time trying to learn as much as I could about the prospect's problems. First, I went to the library and read about the prospect in various sources that the reference librarian helped me find. Then I talked to several noncompeting salespeople who have done business with the company. Next, I took a personal plant tour arranged by one of the plant supervisors to see how the prospect's assembly line operates. During the tour, I asked my supervisor friend and other employees I met a bunch of questions. Any question that didn't get answered to my satisfaction I wrote down in my little notebook.

On the day of the sales presentation, I didn't bring any audiovisual aids at all, just my notebook of questions and a couple of pens. After saying hello and shaking hands with the four people (from purchasing, engineering, production, and finance) who were going to hear my presentation, I opened up by asking a question: "I understand you have some problems at your Chicago assembly plant. Do you mind giving me your perspectives on the problems?" They took turns talking. As soon as they all had said everything they wanted to in response to that question, I asked another question. And it kept going like that. I'd ask a question, and they'd answer it, oftentimes providing a lot of interesting information that I wouldn't have thought to ask for. After a while, we were talking back and forth like members of the same team, working for the same company—and come to think of it, that's what we were!

They probably talked 90 percent of the time, which was fine with me because I was taking notes and gathering all the information I needed: when and why they believed the problems had started, what it would take to solve the problems, how they would go about selecting a supplier, and how the purchasing process would be set up. At the end of three hours, I summarized what I thought had been said, and they helped me clarify a few points. Then I said, "I'm confident that we can provide the right products and service to solve your problems, and I'll send you a written proposal within a week." Two weeks after receiving the proposal, one of them called to say that my company had won the contract. They didn't even quibble over price; they just told me to move ahead on the contract as fast as possible.

Later, as I got to know the four quite well, one of them told me that my sales presentation was the only one that asked for their perspectives on their company's problems. All the other sales presentations took up the entire time doing an elaborate "dog-and-pony" show that centered on the products they had to sell. As the customer put it, "They were trying to sell products; you were trying to help us solve our problems."

Depth Selling

Depth selling is a strategic mix of several sales presentation strategies. For example, a sales representative might start with an overall formula strategy, such as AIDA (attention, interest, desire, action), while using probing need satisfaction questions to discover buying motives, then turn to stimulus-response questions to encourage the prospect to think positively about the product, and finally move to the consultative problem-solving strategy to suggest alternative solutions and win the prospect's confidence. Effectively employing depth selling requires a skillful, perceptive, and flexible mastery of sales presentation strategies, so it is most often used by veteran salespeople.

Team Selling

As organizational buying functions become more centralized and buying committees more expert, team selling strategies are becoming increasingly important. Team selling is a response to the growing buyer insistence that sellers spend less time pitching products to them and more time helping them solve their problems. A team selling approach significantly increases the chances for reaching most members of the buying center.

There are two types of selling teams—core selling teams and selling centers.[10] A **core selling team** consists of assigned members of the selling firm who work together to develop and maintain particular prospects or customer relationships. The team tends to stay together for the duration of the buyer-seller relationship. A **selling center** consists of members of the selling organization assigned to a certain prospect to close a particular sales transaction. After the sale is consummated, the selling center is likely to disband. Both kinds of selling teams consist of individuals from different parts of the company brought together to marshal the resources necessary to work effectively with the customer or prospect. The strength of team selling is clear:

Core Selling Team Members of the selling firm assigned to particular prospects or customers to develop and maintain ongoing buyer-seller relationships with them.

Selling Center Members of the selling organization assigned to a certain prospect to close a particular sales transaction. After the sale is consummated, the selling center is likely to disband.

> . . . selling firms often have a great opportunity to deliver high levels of value, in both real and perceived terms, to their customers by effectively marshaling resources and expertise from across their entire enterprise. A real competitive advantage can be gained if salespeople . . . can effectively locate and deploy the expertise that may reside outside the selling organization [sales department].[11]

Depending on the organization, the customer, and the sales situation, the exact nature of team selling can vary widely. Team selling usually takes place at one of three distinct levels.[12] At the first level, team selling simply means that the field salesperson is supported closely by the branch sales manager, the district sales manager, and perhaps the national sales manager. At a second level, team selling implies that the salesperson's field efforts are closely integrated with customer-oriented efforts in other in-house departments, such as engineering, manufacturing, accounting, customer service, market research, advertising, and sales promotion. In this stage the salesperson serves as a coordinator of all company activities that impinge on the customer and constantly asks, "Where can I find the best resources to help solve a specific customer need or problem?"

IT'S UP TO YOU

You are thirty minutes into a planned sixty-minute sales presentation to a buying group in a conference room of a pesticide manufacturer. During your presentation on a new specialty chemical, you have paused several times to ask whether there are any questions, and each time all buying group members have shaken their heads "no." The room is warm, and you are concerned that you are talking too much and losing your small audience's attention. To revive them, you are thinking about pausing to tell a funny and relevant, though risqué, joke, but you are not sure how the conservative-looking prospects will react. Another option is to mention that it's very warm in the room, so perhaps it is a good time to take a five-minute break for everyone to refresh, but you're afraid that you'll lose some of your audience if you take a break. Still another way to perk up the audience might be to ask two or three people specific questions about how they plan to use the product in their respective areas of responsibility. You don't have much time to decide what to do as you can see that some members of the buying group are already glancing at their watches and beginning to stir restlessly. What are you going to do? Think fast!

Team selling strategies are important for reaching some members of the buying center.
Steve Niedorf Photography/Getty Images

At the third and highest level, all of the seller team members, whether technical, administrative staff, or managerial, work directly with their counterparts in the buyer organization. From the presidents of the two companies on down, there are open lines of communication, interaction, and cooperation between counterparts in both seller and buyer organizations. The salesperson acts as the coordinator and contact person for the buyer and sales teams, which may consist of specialists from marketing, finance, engineering, production, or research and development. Specialists from the seller team work closely with their counterparts from the buyer team to make sure that the selling team understands and responds to all facets of customer needs and problems. For instance, the traffic manager of the seller organization will coordinate product delivery with the receiving manager at the customer organization, and the seller's advertising manager may work with the buyer's advertising manager on cooperative advertising campaigns aimed at the product's ultimate consumer or user. Customer-supplier relationships are so integrated in some high-tech companies that the customer is allowed to choose preferred after-sale support team members from the supplier's organization. Being selected to provide customer service as a member of a support team is an honor that generates considerable competition among support personnel. The *It's Up to You* feature on page 202 gives you a chance to consider an impromptu decision that must often be made during sales presentations.

ADAPTIVE VERSUS CANNED SALES PRESENTATIONS

The opportunity to customize, or adapt, each presentation to individual prospects differentiates personal selling from all other promotional tools. **Adaptive selling** stresses the unique advantage that skilled salespeople have in adjusting their selling behavior to the particular prospect and selling situation.[13] Traditional salespeople usually make a relatively standard or habitual sales presentation that doesn't vary too much with different prospects or customers. But salespeople who modify their presentations in accordance with specific prospect or customer needs and behaviors are more effective than those who do not.[14] This may seem obvious, but only salespeople who are predisposed to engage in adaptive selling are likely to do so during the sales call.[15] Successful professional salespeople not only mentally prepare themselves to adapt their sales presentation, but they remain alert to opportunities to do so throughout the sales presentation and demonstration. For instance, if a buyer for Hertz's (www.hertz.com) fleet of automobiles shows more interest in safety than gas mileage, then an observant salesperson for General Motors (www.gm.com) quickly adapts the sales presentation and demonstration to emphasize the safety benefits of GM cars. Remaining adaptable, however, does not mean that the salesperson should not have a sound, basic structure for his or her sales presentation and demonstration. Some sales managers, in their efforts to improve efficiency while controlling the accuracy and ethics of the sales message, have found structured or **canned (or programmed) selling** best for some types of prospects, selling situations, and salespeople. Salespeople, however, tend to think of canned and adaptive sales presentations as polar extremes. Many believe that increasing structure decreases the professional salesperson's role in the sales presentation. Some salespeople protest, "Anybody can read a script or play a video."

Adaptive Selling Modifying each sales presentation and demonstration to accommodate each individual prospect.

Canned (or Programmed) Selling Any highly structured or patterned selling approach.

Although most salespeople prefer wide latitude and flexibility in deciding what to say and show prospects, the best sales presentations may often blend the canned and adaptive approaches.[16] In his book *Superselling*, former (before Jay Leno) "Tonight Show" host Johnny Carson's long-time sidekick Ed McMahon, who has sold everything from vegetable slicers on Atlantic City's boardwalk to countless products on television, says,

> I believe that perfecting your presentation is probably the most important work you can do now to advance your sales career. . . . I rehearsed my entire sales interview down to each lifted eyebrow

HOW ADAPTIVE ARE YOU?

Assume that you are a salesperson, and respond to each of the following statements to determine how adaptive you would be in dealing with a prospect or a customer. Use the following scale when responding to each statement:

Strongly Agree	Agree	Neither Agree nor Disagree	Disagree	Strongly Disagree
5	4	3	2	1

1. Each customer requires a unique approach. ____
2. When I feel that my sales approach is not working, I can easily change to another approach. ____
3. I like to experiment with different sales approaches. ____
4. I am very flexible in the selling approach I use. ____
5. I feel that most buyers can be dealt with in different ways. ____
6. I change my approach from one customer to another. ____
7. I can easily use a wide variety of selling approaches. ____
8. I use varied sales approaches. ____
9. It is easy for me to modify my sales presentation if the situation calls for it. ____
10. Basically, I use a different approach with most customers. ____
11. I am very sensitive to the needs of my customers. ____
12. I find it easy to adapt my presentation style to most buyers. ____
13. I vary my sales style from situation to situation. ____
14. I try to understand how one customer differs from another. ____
15. I feel confident that I can effectively change my planned presentation when necessary. ____
16. I treat each of my buyers differently. ____

Add up your scores for the sixteen questions. A score of 64 or higher indicates that your adaptability is strong; a score of 48 or less indicates that your adaptability is weak and needs work.

Source: *Adapted from Rosann L. Spiro and Barton A. Weitz, "Adaptive Selling: Conceptualization, Measurement, and Nomological Validity,"* Journal of Marketing Research *27 (February 1990): 60–61. Reprinted with permission of the American Marketing Association.*

and dropped tone. . . . There is only one way you can free your mind to give a professional, order-winning performance: You have to know your lines. . . . Without even thinking, you have to be able to adapt your presentations to the buyer and the circumstances under which you're selling. Questions such as the following should be running through your mind constantly as you work to fit what you say to . . . the person you're trying to persuade:

- How is this prospect reacting?
- Should I speed up or slow down?
- Should I get more technical or should I skip the heavy data?
- What will get this buyer excited about my product?
- What's my best close?
- Why isn't this guy smiling?[17]

While the debate between canned and adaptive approaches continues, salespeople are making increasing use of multimedia aides and computer-developed sales presentation materials. Many salespeople find that these tools enliven their sales presentations and help keep prospects interested. Moreover, they enable salespeople to present prospect-focused information efficiently and effectively, while they closely observe the prospect's reaction and appropriately adapt later parts of the sales presentation.

Occasionally, the risk of coming across too slick arises. A highly programmed, multimedia presentation to decision makers in a consumer products company may position a salesperson as a skilled professional. This same presentation to a group of conservative engineering managers at a public utility may come off as orchestrated hucksterism. It is essential for the salesperson to know the prospect's normal communication methods and styles before making a sales presentation and demonstration—and to adapt aptly to the prospects' responses. Do you think you are or will be an adaptive salesperson? Take the test on page 204 to see how adaptive you are now.

Chapter Review Question
Explain the difference between adaptive and canned sales presentations.

WRITTEN PRESENTATIONS

Whether used at the time of the verbal sales presentation or mailed as a follow-up after the sales call, a **written presentation** (also called a sales proposal or business plan) can be effective in winning sales. Written presentations force salespeople to be specific about prospect needs and ensure that the salespeople do their homework. Putting the sales presentation in writing also enables the prospect to share information with other key decision makers in the company. Written presentations, usually from ten to twenty pages long, allow the salesperson to reinforce the material presented orally and to bring in more material, such as detailed financial analyses that cannot be adequately covered in a verbal presentation. Each written sales presentation should contain the following:

Written Presentation In sales presentations to organizational prospects, the salesperson's explanation of how the prospect can profitably use the product. Also called a sales proposal or business plan.

- statement of the prospect's problem (or opportunity)
- problem solution (that is, the seller's product and related benefits for addressing the prospect's problem)
- detailed listing of the product's specifications, features, advantages, and benefits
- cost-benefit analysis (information regarding what product benefits the prospect will receive for the money spent over the life of the product)
- financial analysis of the sale (e.g., pricing, payment terms, leasing arrangements, and interest rate)
- timetable (an enumeration of the key events, such as delivery, installation, and trial period, that will occur after the prospect has agreed to make the purchase)
- written contract (order form)

TABLE 6.9

Tips for a Written Sales Presentation

- Make sure you spell all prospect company names and titles correctly. Nothing turns off prospects more than a salesperson who doesn't take time to ensure correct spelling of names and titles.
- Make the opening paragraph exciting and interesting so prospects will look forward to reading your sales proposal. (*We're delighted to tell you that our sales proposal will show how we can save your company several thousand dollars during the coming year.*)
- Be positive and upbeat in a natural, conversational writing style.
- Tailor each written sales presentation to a specific prospect or customer.
- Use a logical format along with a creative but professional look.
- Sequence benefits in the most effective order, usually in term of importance to the prospect.
- Provide proof or support for benefits (such as scientific and objective tests results, testimonials from experts or satisfied customers, and/or endorsements from authorities or celebrities)
- Use powerful action-oriented words while minimizing tentative words such as *maybe, promising, per chance, tentatively, hopeful, perhaps, likely, apt, and possible.*
- Never disparage competitors or their products and services.
- Use paragraph headings, occasional bold or italicized type, graphs, tables, charts, figures, and pictures to clarify material, add interest, and guide prospects through the narrative.
- Provide an incentive (e.g., a limited-time discount, free gift, or special services) to purchase or take other desired action (such as requesting more information) promptly.
- Personalize the proposal with a handwritten note in a postscript (P.S.).
- Double-check and proofread everything before mailing, faxing, or e-mailing.

Chapter Review Questions

List and briefly describe the basic sales presentation strategies. Which one is generally considered best for professional salespeople? Why?

Give some basic guidelines for written sales presentations.

Salespeople who think they cannot afford time out from making sales calls to write sales presentations must learn that they *are* selling when they're writing sales proposals. Persuasive written proposals can win sales. Carefully study the tips for writing effective sales presentations noted in Table 6.9.

SELLING THE LONG-TERM RELATIONSHIP

Although most customer relationship management (CRM) strategies are initiated at the top-management level, they must be implemented throughout the seller organization and beyond into buyer organizations. Investing in customer relationships offers a much greater potential payoff than almost any new investments in plants, equipment, or products. Trying to sustain competitive advantage by making improvements to existing products and/or developing new products is a frustrating game. Beyond their short life cycles, many products in any given category are so similar that customers perceive them as virtually undifferentiated commodities. Short-term leads attributable to product innovation are eroded quickly by imitation or superior technology. Therefore, it is critical to redefine the arena of competitive advantage beyond products and services to the customer relationship experience. The real payoff in today's selling world is in providing total customer experiences that encourage fully satisfying long-term relationships and customer loyalty.

While making sales presentations and demonstrations by which they hope to win an immediate sale, today's professional business-to-business salespeople must keep in mind that they also are their company's ultimate customer relationship managers and that they need to sell the long-term relationship even if they don't make this particular sale. In fact, CRM-oriented salespeople must go beyond mere "selling" to "serving" their customers much like consultants or business partners. In this role, they may occasionally advise a customer to buy a competitive product if it offers more added value than their own company's product. What's more, they need to become customer advocates who represent their customers' interests within their own companies and elsewhere. Many salespeople have great difficulty accepting this across-the-board customer-oriented perspective, even though their own companies may encourage it. Salespeople who enthusiastically carry out their companies' CRM strategies in their ongoing interactions with pros-pects and customers should reap substantial payoffs for their companies and themselves.

SUMMARY

The sales presentation and demonstration form the pivotal exchange between buyers and sellers and thus should be based on a carefully developed strategy. Although several sales presentation strategies are available, most professional salespeople use the consultative problem-solving strategy, which requires full use of their listening and questioning skills to understand the prospect's problems and needs. Consultative problem solving emphasizes the partnership of the buyer and seller. When making sales presentations and demonstrations to an individual or group (either orally or in writing), salespeople need to understand and follow some basic guidelines. In addition, they need to practice adaptive selling to enhance their effectiveness with increasingly demanding and sophisticated prospects and customers. Those sales presentations that offer the highest value-added benefits, as perceived by prospects and customers, are most likely to result in successful sales contracts. While making sales presentations and demonstrations to win immediate sales contracts, today's professional salespeople also need to "sell" the long-term relationship with customers and carry out their companies' CRM strategies.

KEY TERMS

FAB
SELLS
Value-Added Selling
SAD TIE
Core Selling Team
Selling Center
Adaptive Selling
Canned (or Programmed) Selling
Written Presentation

TOPICS FOR THOUGHT AND CLASS DISCUSSION

1. Why do you think the consultative problem-solving sales presentation is the most successful strategy for professional salespeople? What are the benefits of this strategy to the prospect or customer?
2. Name at least five special prospect categories, and describe an appropriate strategy for a sales presentation to each.
3. Which do you think is more effective for most business-to-business selling, an *oral* or a written sales presentation? Why?
4. Do you think sales presentations and demonstrations are more important for tangible products or for intangible services? Why?

INTERNET EXERCISES

1. Using an Internet search engine, find three firms that specialize in sales presentation training, and visit their websites to determine whether they use other types of sales presentation strategies in addition to those identified and described in this chapter.
2. Use Google or any other search engine to locate two examples of sales presentation strategies being demonstrated using Flash or streaming video.

PROJECTS FOR PERSONAL GROWTH

1. Contact two business-to-business salespeople and ask them about their methods of preparing sales presentations, dress style during the presentation, and demonstration techniques.
2. Research the following two industries and report on the methods and approaches that each uses to sell its products: (a) airplane manufacturers, and (b) manufacturers of household products.
3. Contact three salespeople (one who sells to manufacturers, one who sells to resellers, and one who sells to the national government) and ask them how they prepare for their sales presentations and demonstrations. Are there major differences? What similarities emerged?
4. With a classmate, take turns playing the role of a publishing company sales rep trying to sell a new textbook to a college professor who might be nicknamed "Skeptical Sid." Then prepare a *written* sales presentation to sell a textbook to the instructor of your personal selling class. Depending on how creative or cooperative your instructor is, you may want to ask him or her to play one of the prospect stereotypes described in Table 6.2.
5. Assume that you are a sales representative for a manufacturer of automatic fire sprinkler systems for commercial buildings. Outline sales presentations using each of the seven basic strategies. For each strategy, create and then describe the individual prospect or group of prospects to whom you're presenting.

ROLE-PLAY EXERCISE 6.1

Making a Sales Presentation to a Silent Procrastinator

Situation

Norman Kent is a sales representative for a camera and photography accessories manufacturer, Bodak-Ganon, that sells its products to wholesalers who, in turn, sell to various types of retail outlets. Norm has just greeted Sidney Husher, a buyer for one of the larger wholesalers in Norm's sales territory. In preparing for this sales call, Norm learned that Mr. Husher is well known for remaining totally silent during sales presentations and for asking few, if any, questions afterward. This would be fine if Mr. Husher made the decision to buy quickly after a sales presentation, but he is also a notorious procrastinator who seldom acts quickly. Looking around Mr. Husher's office, Norm notices a picture of a fish jumping out of the water and a copy of *Fly Casting* magazine on a table in the corner. Also, there is a picture of two preteen boys on Mr. Husher's desk. Mr. Husher looks to be in his midfifties, so Norm doubts that the boys are his children.

Roles

Norman Kent After working for Bodak-Ganon for several years, Norm is confident that his company makes the best nonprofessional cameras and photography accessories in the industry. Norm knows that he must get Mr. Husher to talk about his purchasing problems and needs if this sales presentation is to be successful. In addition, Norm feels that he will have to offer some special incentive for Mr. Husher to buy now.

Sidney Husher A shy and insecure man, Mr. Husher is terribly afraid of making a buying mistake, so his normal purchasing approach is to carefully compare and almost agonize over the relative benefits offered by competing suppliers before making the final purchase decision.

ROLE-PLAY EXERCISE 6.2

What Happens When a Product Breaks Down During a Demonstration?

Situation

Carol Rhein's worst nightmare has just happened! In the middle of her demonstrating a new electronic metering device that regulates fluid levels to hospital patients, the product has failed before an assembled group of hospital administrators, doctors, and nurses, and it is now showing obviously erroneous readings. If the device were in use, hooked up to a patient, a product failure of this type could cause a doctor or nurse to make incorrect adjustments in regulating the flow of a vital fluid, perhaps endangering a patient's life. Carol realizes that within a few seconds, everyone in the room will realize that the product has failed. Panic nearly overwhelms Carol's brain as she is trying to think what to do or say next.

Roles

Carol Rhein Carol has been a sales representative for Medical Support Systems, Inc., for two years, and this is the first time she has had a product fail during a product demonstration. She always checks to make sure that any product to be used in a demonstration is working correctly before she meets with the prospects or customers, and this metering device was working fine just twenty minutes before the scheduled product demonstration. Carol always carries a backup product with her, and she has one today in the large briefcase in the corner of the room.

Dr. Rajiv Hingorani Chief surgeon for Metropolitan Central Hospital and spokesperson for the assembled doctors, he will be very upset as soon as he notices this product failure. Dr. Hingorani sets very high standards for himself and others, and he always demands the highest-quality equipment for his doctors and nurses.

Alice Atwong Purchasing director for the hospital, Ms. Atwong will be very embarrassed to have all these doctors, nurses, and administrators witness a product failure, because she will fear that it will be taken to reflect on her judgment in selecting potential suppliers.

CASE 6.1 SELF-ANALYSIS OF A SALES PRESENTATION

Peter Kimball, a sales representative for United Container Company, is sitting in front of the desk of Mark Spearman, the head purchasing agent for Modern Office Equipment Company. Just after Peter finished his twenty-minute sales presentation, Mr. Spearman's secretary buzzed Spearman for an important phone call. Picking up the phone, Mr. Spearman spun his chair around so that his back was to Peter, and he is now deeply engaged in conversation with the person on the other end. While Mr. Spearman is talking on the phone, Peter reflects on his sales presentation and wonders what else he can do to convince Mr. Spearman to purchase his line of shipping containers. Modern Office Equipment Company would be a big account to land. Prior to making the sales call, Peter had carefully developed and rehearsed a sales presentation strategy. His presentation incorporated results of his research on Modern online and at his local library, as well as some perspectives he elicited from noncompeting salespeople about Mr. Spearman, an analytical person who is interested mainly in buying at the lowest price. Peter continues to think about whether or not he adequately covered the five basic objectives of his sales presentation and what he should do when Mr. Spearman hangs up the phone. Here are Peter's thoughts on each of his five sales call objectives:

1. *Build rapport.* Initially, Mr. Spearman acted low key and analytical, just as I was told he would. But I caught his interest by asking him several nonthreatening questions about his son, who I know is a football player at the University of Missouri. I think my gently probing questions put him in the right frame of mind to respond to my questions and even prompted him to ask a few of his own.
2. *Uncover problems and perceived needs.* At first, when I asked him to describe some of his major packaging problems, he claimed Modern didn't have any special packaging problems. I told him how amazing that was and that most of my other customers have a lot of packaging problems; otherwise, I'd be standing in a bread line somewhere. Hearing that, he laughed, loosened up a little, and admitted that his company occasionally experienced some "minor" problems when Modern equipment was damaged in customers' warehouses. Mr. Spearman elaborated: "Usually the damage is caused by forklift trucks cutting through our heavy-duty cardboard boxes and puncturing our equipment. Although we're really not responsible for damage in the customer's warehouse, our company philosophy is that 'the customer is always right,' so we allow customers to return any damaged equipment still in the packing box. Guess it would help if our packing boxes were made of tougher material, but we get a great price on the heavy-duty cardboard boxes."
3. *Learn how satisfied Modern is with its current supplier.* When I asked how satisfied Modern is with its current supplier, Mr. Spearman said everybody in the company seemed "satisfied," except perhaps the quality control manager who handles customer complaints about equipment. Although he didn't say so, I think Modern's major supplier is Megastar Container, because I saw some Megastar cardboard box flats outside the warehouse near where I parked my car. Mr. Spearman didn't seem interested in even talking about buying our metal containers, even though I told him that they would eliminate equipment damage in shipping or storage and that the price was only about 15 percent higher than for heavy-duty cardboard containers. Anyway, I've already put our product brochure for the metal containers on his desk. When I asked him whether he would consider changing suppliers if we could offer him a lower price for the same quality of product he was buying now, he replied that he would have to see the total sales proposal, not just the price. I'll have to prepare him a written sales proposal. Maybe I should prepare four different sales proposals, one for each quality of container we sell. That's a lot of work. Maybe Bob or Jennifer in Marketing will help me out in preparing the proposals, because I'm going to need some information from them.

(*continued*)

4. *Demonstrate that United Container has the right products to solve Modern's problems and satisfy its needs.* I gave him several brochures about our products and carefully pointed out the features and benefits of our four major packaging products. I also stressed that United takes great pride in its reputation for customer service and keeping customers satisfied. But darn it, I couldn't quickly find our latest price sheet. I must have left it on the prospect's desk at my first sales call. I probably shouldn't have left my laptop computer in the trunk of my car, either, because I know that I could go to our Intranet to find prices. But he would probably want the prices in writing anyway. Oh well, I'll send Mr. Spearman our new price sheet when I mail him the written sales proposals next week.
5. *Convince Mr. Spearman that he can trust me and that United Container Company can deliver quality products at fair prices backed up by excellent service.* I showed him a list of other companies we sell to, and he seemed impressed. I told him that I will personally service his account once a month and that I always carry a beeper that will enable him to reach me in case of an emergency. When I mentioned that our company was spending a lot of money on research to develop new environmentally safe packaging products, I must have hit his "hot button," because his eyes really lit up and he asked several questions about what we were doing. He said that he was chairing a committee on environmental issues for the Purchasing Agent Association and that the PAA was holding a regional conference in three months on the topic of environmental packaging. Mr. Spearman is going to present a paper at the conference, and Modern's vice president of marketing will be a major speaker. I asked whether our company could help him at this meeting, and he gave me some suggestions that I'll follow up on with some of our R&D people. Maybe I should ask him whether he knows about the union strike that began at Megastar yesterday. They might not even be able to deliver containers unless they have a lot more inventory than we have. Of course, I don't want to sound like I'm knocking a competitor.

Just as Peter is mulling over his last thought, Mr. Spearman finishes his phone call, spins his chair around to face him, and says, "Sorry. Now, where were we?"

Questions

1. What should Peter say and do now? How do you think Mr. Spearman will react? Why?
2. What do you think about Peter's sales presentation? What could he have done better?
3. What advice would you give Peter for capitalizing on the interest Mr. Spearman showed in environmental packaging?
4. Should Peter mention the union strike at Megastar?

CASE 6.2 WHAT MAKES HIM SO SUCCESSFUL?

CASE 6.2 "WHAT MAKES HIM SO SUCCESSFUL?" CAN BE FOUND ONLINE AT HTTP://COLLEGE.HMCO.COM/PIC/ANDERSONPS2E

CHAPTER 7

Negotiating Sales Resistance and Objections for "Win-Win" Agreements

"In successful negotiations, there should be no losers—only winners."

Anonymous

After reading this chapter, you should understand:

- Why objections and sales resistance are important to personal selling.
- How to plan for objections.
- The various forms of buyer resistance and objections.
- How to deal with prospect resistance.
- The importance of win-win negotiation outcomes.
- How to overcome objections to price.
- Techniques for negotiating resistance and objections.

INSIDE PERSONAL SELLING

Meet John Affriol of Samsung Electronics America

When prospects start to ask questions that sound like objections, John Affriol knows they are really interested in his products. Affriol is a zone sales manager for the consumer electronics group of Samsung Electronics America, a division of the South Korea–based global technology, telecommunications, and home appliance giant Samsung. He sells high-end plasma TV sets, DVD players, digital music players, camcorders, and other sophisticated products to big retailers and chain stores, who in turn sell them to the public.

If a retail buyer shows little interest in stocking a certain Samsung product, Affriol probes to find out why. Sometimes the buyer may say that the store's customers aren't interested in that category. In response, Affriol points to other retailers with a similar customer base that have sold the product successfully: "Millions of people buy this product, including some who are already your customers. You're now forcing them to go somewhere else to buy the product. Why not test to see how it will sell in your store?" He recently won over a buyer by showing that a Samsung product had unique new features that competing products lacked—and would therefore attract new customers and increase sales for that prospect.

Affriol addresses certain objections as soon as they surface—such as a retailer's reluctance to even carry a product—but when objections such as price arise, he checks all the data before responding. In either situation, however, he works to clearly understand the customer's true objection by asking questions. "I believe in not just being a reporter—simply listening to what a customer says—but in being an investigator. You really have to know your customers inside and out, getting as much information as possible to determine what will work and what won't work with each one."

In sales situations where objections boil down to price, special services, or delivery concessions, Affriol's negotiation strategy is to know the market and the customer's competitive landscape. "I talk about the after-market support we can bring, including advertising," he says. "We are very good at promoting the Samsung brand, an extra 'sell' feature to overcome an objection. Also, I talk about product quality, the company's financial stability, and building long-term relationships with our customers."

To make each sales call a win-win situation for Samsung and the prospect, Affriol always sets expectations prior to the call. "Time is very valuable for both sides these days," he notes. "First research the customer and set the agenda to figure out where you want the meeting to go. Are you presenting a new product mix, or does the prospect have a problem you can help solve? To really make it a win-win, you have to be prepared and be flexible with your presentation."

In Chapter 6, we described how to develop an effective sales presentation strategy. Armed with this knowledge, you can now deliver a "clutch" sales presentation that will clearly demonstrate how your sales solution provides greater value for your prospect. Yogi Berra, Hall of Fame baseball catcher for the New York Yankees, famously said, "It ain't over 'til it's over!" He wasn't talking about personal selling, but his quip couldn't be more apt. During a sales presentation, for example, you may generate tremendous prospect enthusiasm. You may have given an impressive presentation and demonstration. In fact, you may believe that you did everything right. But your prospect still doesn't agree to buy. Why? Because prospects rarely embrace any sales proposition wholeheartedly at first. They usually have anxieties about the purchase, so they want reassurance before making a commitment. It doesn't take long for new salespeople to learn that prospect objections and sales resistance are a normal—even welcome—part of the buying-selling process. And they must learn how to deal with it successfully.

"Without sales resistance, I wouldn't have a job," is a comment often heard from successful salespeople. They understand that if prospects put up no resistance to buying, then the first seller to reach them would make the sale, and trained salespeople wouldn't be needed at all. Most professional salespeople appreciate that a certain amount of prospect resistance indicates interest, which is a healthy way to start negotiations between buyers and sellers. Some have even called objections "the salesperson's best friends" or "rungs on the ladder of selling success" because serious negotiations seldom begin until the prospect's objections surface.

WHAT ARE BUYER OBJECTIONS AND RESISTANCE?

Objection Anything that the prospect or customer says or does that impedes the sales negotiations.

Before "nailing" your carefully planned command sales presentation, you will usually segue into a session where your prospect will pose several questions that reflect resistance or objections. With experience, salespeople learn to anticipate these questions and think "outside the selling mentality box" to provide answers from the buyer's perspective that will give the buyer confidence to make the purchase. **Objections** are simply statements, questions, or actions by the prospect that indicate resistance or an unwillingness to buy—at least not yet. Buyer objections and resistance offer both a challenge and an opportunity. Some novice salespeople let initial prospect objections so discourage them that they all but lose the sale at that point. In reality, however, chances for a sale increase when prospects raise objections. Why? Because when prospects raise objections, it usually means they are tuned into and interested in your selling proposition. Therefore, don't be discouraged when you encounter sales resistance—and don't take it personally. In the following pages of this chapter, we will show you how to negotiate prospect resistance and objections, which is stage 5 of the Personal Selling Process (see Figure 7.1).[1]

FIGURE 7.1

THE PERSONAL SELLING PROCESS

Reasons for Objections

Prospects and customers raise objections for myriad reasons. Some rationales seem logical, and others do not, as the following list will show.

- People will almost always raise objections, even if they are totally sold on the product. This action is a function of human nature. Essentially, prospects try to rationalize the decision and want information to help them do this—and besides, they don't want the salesperson to think that they are a pushover.
- The prospect may seek reassurance that the product will perform as promised. Perhaps the prospect tends to believe what you have said about the product but wants you to reaffirm your selling proposition ("A major benefit of our system is that it has only 1 percent down-time, which will minimize production line disruption").
- The prospect may have been trained to raise objections as a matter of buying technique or negotiation strategy. Just as professional buyers are trained to sell effectively, purchasing personnel are trained in buying strategies and techniques that will afford their firm the "best" buy.
- The prospect may lack the authority to buy but may cover up this fact by raising several smokescreen objections. Through effective prospect qualifying, the salesperson should encounter this situation less frequently over time.
- A few prospects will raise objections merely to be an irritant to salespeople or to have fun seeing them work for the order. In other words, these prospects seem to delight in the perceived game of negotiating with salespeople.
- An objection may actually be the prospect's appeal for assistance in justifying a decision to buy. For example, the prospect may say, "Gee, your price is very high." But the prospect may be thinking, "Tell me how my company can afford or justify spending the money to buy your clearly superior product."
- Some prospects raise objections so that they can bargain for a better deal. Regardless of how low your price might be compared to competition, some prospects are obsessed with getting an even lower price so that they can feel "victorious."
- Prospects may raise an objection because they have a bias against the salesperson's company or product type or, in rare cases, simply dislike the salesperson. For instance, the prospect may have done business with your firm years ago, may have had a bad experience, and may be determined never to buy from your firm again.

Whatever the reason for an objection, don't view sales resistance as a sign of impending failure. Although you may have your work cut out for you to overcome the prospect's sales resistance and close the sale, think of objections as a request for more information and an overall positive sign in the selling process. If you've done your homework in the first four steps of the PSP, chances are you will be able to address the prospect's objections effectively and consummate the deal.

Signs of Interest

Prospect objections usually are *positive* signs of interest and involvement in the sales presentation. As noted above, objections are often indirect ways for prospects to say that they want to know more. Professional buyers sometimes purposely make negative statements about some aspect of a product to elicit more information that they can use in defending the purchase decision up the line. For instance, a purchasing agent for a large manufacturer may say, "I like your product, but we require just-in-time (JIT) delivery to keep our costs low, and I'm afraid that your company won't be able to provide the quick response we need." Maybe the sales rep can honestly answer, "I'm glad you raised that point because we're already working with IBM (www.ibm.com) and General Electric (www.ge.com) on a JIT basis. We know that to compete in most industries today, you need fast response to customer requests, shorter lead times, lower stockouts, and less waste and scrap. That's why we exchange information with customers via computer linkups. I'm confident that you'll find our JIT system as good as any available." This sort of response should reassure the purchasing agent and dispel that potential barrier to buying. Each time a salesperson can answer a specific prospect or customer objection, another obstacle in the path to the sale is removed.

Nonverbal Resistance

Prospect or customer resistance is part of nearly every negotiation. It might not even be active resistance. Sometimes prospects show resistance through silence or through body language such as shaking their head, frowning, glancing at the time frequently, playing with their watch or some desk accessory, reading their mail while the salesperson talks, yawning or exhaling a big breath, or just looking bored, puzzled, or expressionless. When salespeople spot this passive kind of resistance, they must find some way to perk up the presentation and involve the prospect.

You can often find up-to-date, sound advice on improving the overall selling process, including negotiating sales objections and subtle kinds of resistance, in the monthly issues of *Sales and Marketing Management* magazine, described in the accompanying *Keeping Up Online* feature.

Chapter Review Question

What do we mean by "buyer objections and resistance?"

KEEPING UP ONLINE: SALES AND MARKETING MANAGEMENT (S&MM)

S&MM is one of the more popular trade publications read by salespeople and their managers. Each issue is replete with suggestions on improving one's personal selling efforts or managerial skills. Today's dynamic selling arena calls for salespeople to continually update their knowledge and capabilities and the tools in their selling repertoire. Why do you think many salespeople find it so useful? How might *S&MM* assist you now? Try to find answers to these questions by perusing the *S&MM* website at www.salesandmarketing.com.

PLANNING FOR OBJECTIONS

To deal most effectively with sales resistance, you should learn as much as you can about the prospect; then an objection is less likely to take you by surprise.[2] If you know or anticipate prospect objections, your confidence in addressing those objections will increase. And research shows that a salesperson's confidence can significantly increase customer satisfaction with sales presentations, as well as success in closing sales.[3] Therefore, one of the best ways to minimize objections is to learn what the customer's objections are likely to be *before* you begin the sales presentation and then adapt the sales presentation to cover these points.

By raising the issue during your presentation, you can pre-empt the objection. That is, you mention it and handle it before the prospect actually raises it. This puts you in a better position to control the negotiations, thereby improving your chances for making the sale. Salespeople who successfully anticipate prospect objections can soften or forestall them by including evidence, testimonials, and demonstrations in their sales presentation and subsequent negotiations.

Chapter Review Question
What steps are involved in planning for prospect objections?

Keep a Running File of the Most Typical Objections

Develop a master list of prospect objections that come up in your own experience and that of other salespeople, and classify them according to type, such as product, price, delivery, installation, service, and company. Include successful and unsuccessful ways of dealing with each objection. In sales meetings and informal discussions, tap sales colleagues' knowledge about various types of prospect resistance and successful methods for dealing with each. Somewhat like an entertainer who learns to ad lib or have a joke ready for every audience situation, the salesperson can learn a technique to defuse nearly every objection.

DIFFERENT FORMS OF OBJECTIONS

Sales resistance can be categorized into either valid or invalid objections. Salespeople need to recognize each type in negotiating with prospects or customers. Table 7.1 enumerates various forms of common valid and invalid objections that you are likely to encounter in your selling efforts. How might you respond to each? By the end of this chapter, you'll surely know!

Valid Objections

Valid objections are sincere concerns that the prospect wants addressed before he or she is willing to make the commitment to buy. In other words, valid objections are those concerns that won't go away and will prevent the sale from taking place unless the salesperson can satisfactorily handle them. They are relevant to the current buying situation and are truthful as far as the prospect knows.

Valid Objections Sincere concerns that the prospect needs addressed before he or she will be willing to buy.

TABLE 7.1

Types of Valid and Invalid Objections

	Valid Objections
Product Objections	• Product characteristics and benefits are perceived as less than ideal by the prospect. • The proposed product is not superior to the product currently being used. • Product characteristics and benefits are not competitive.
Price Objections	• Price is too high for the value offered. • Price isn't competitive. • Price exceeds the prospect's budget limitations • Discounts are inadequate. • Payment terms are out of line.
Promotion Objections	• Cooperative advertising is insufficient. • Free display merchandise is not offered. • No "push money" is provided for reseller salespeople. • No advertising support is offered.
Distribution Objections	• Delivery lead time is too long. • Minimum order size requirements are unacceptable. • Delivery arrangements are inadequate. • Questions regarding who pays transportation costs. • The salesperson's company is unwilling to provide consignment sales. • Inadequate damage and return goods policy. • Prospect's fear of being overstocked.
Capital Objections	• Required investment outlays are too high. • Customer credit rating is too low to obtain favorable interest rate for capital fund loans. • The prospect company's capital budget has not yet been approved. • Customer has cash flow problems, so is currently unable to buy capital goods.
Source Objections	• Source company's reputation is poor. • Buyer prefers a local supplier. • Buyer wants to do business with a national company. • Lingering concerns over past problems in doing business with the seller. • Buyer prefers to stick to the status quo in supplier relationships. • Vendor has a reputation for manufacturing low-quality products. • Vendor is known to be unethical.
Needs Objections	• Buyer has no need for the seller's product or service. • Buyer is satisfied with the products currently being purchased.

(*continued*)

TABLE 7.1

Types of Valid and Invalid Objections [continued]

Invalid Objections	
Latent Objections	• Buyer usually purchases from an old friend. • Prospect does not have the authority to make the purchase but is embarrassed to let the salesperson know this. • Prospect resents the salesperson making an unannounced visit. • Prospect simply doesn't like the salesperson or his or her company and doesn't want to start a business relationship.
Stalling Objections	• To put-off the salesperson for the time being or get him to leave and not return, the prospect says something like: • "Thanks for coming in, we'll get back to you if we decide to consider purchasing your products." • "Purchasing decisions are made by a buying committee, so I'll let you know if the committee decides to consider your company as a supplier."
Time Objections	• Prospect says he has to prepare for a meeting. • Prospect claims he needs time to assess the purchase specifications and requirements. • Prospect says he is just too busy to meet with the salesperson.
Unethical Objections	• Prospect does not do business with people from a particular ethnic group or religion. • Prospect makes sexual overtures to the salesperson. • Prospect solicits bribes or kickbacks.

Thus, once these valid objections are identified, they can be dealt with in a variety of ways. You are likely to be more successful if you treat most objections as valid and address them as being truthful and real, until proven otherwise. Strategies for addressing seven valid sources of sales resistance often encountered by salespersons are discussed below and summarized in Table 7.1.

Product Objections. Product objections usually concern the features, advantages, and benefits associated with a product or service. When prospects use this form of resistance to purchasing, salespeople should provide additional information to reassure them. For example, salespeople working for Sonus Networks (www.sonusnet.com) or Vonage (www.vonage.com), two companies that market products for the deployment and management of voice and data services, might demonstrate how switching from the traditional telecommunication system to a computer-based Voice-over Internet Protocol (VoIP) can save thousands of dollars per year with no reduction in reliability or loss of sound quality.

Price Objections. Price objections are the most frequently raised form of initial resistance. To counter price resistance, salespeople must show that their product or service offers the prospect higher value per dollar spent than competitive offerings. For specific suggestions on how a salesperson can successfully negotiate this form of valid objection, please refer to the section on price resistance and the related discussion on value analysis later in this chapter.

Promotion Objections. Promotion objections are commonly used as a resistance tactic when the seller is known not to promote products aggressively. To overcome this resistance, salespeople may have to offer buyers promotional allowances or cooperative advertising arrangements, special rebates, or purchase incentives. They may even have to pay "slotting allowances" to obtain retail shelf space.

Distribution Objections. Distribution objections typically involve the physical movement of products through the channels of distribution. These forms of buyer resistance include concerns about long delivery time, high delivery costs, and large-quantity stocking requirements. Although salespeople cannot control distribution, they should be well aware of their company's usual performance in this area so that they can provide prospects with realistic delivery dates and offer assurances that they will do all they can to meet prospect expectations.

Capital Objections. Capital objections generally revolve around budgetary issues that prospects give as an excuse for not purchasing products now. This resistance tends to increase with the price of the product or service. An example is the sale of commercial aircraft to American Airlines (www.aa.com) by Boeing (www.boeing.com) or Airbus (www.airbus.com). Sales of major equipment such as aircraft must include extended payment plans, lease-to-own options, and innovative credit arrangements. General Electric (www.ge.com) offers credit to its customers via its GE Financial Services subsidiary (www.ge.com/en/financial/index.htm).

Source Objections. Source objections may result from negative publicity about unethical, illegal, or inefficient business practices by the seller. Conversely, the seller company may not be well enough known for the prospect to feel comfortable purchasing from it. Source objections also can result from the prospect's loyalty to a competing firm. Here are some examples of source objections:

- "Your company is too small and too little known for me to justify buying from you to my boss."
- "Your company has a reputation for questionable ethics, and dealing with you may hurt our own company's reputation."
- "Your firm has a reputation in the market for misleading advertising and deceptive sales promotions."

A more personal source objection might be not wanting to deal with an individual salesperson who has an unethical or unprofessional reputation. Even the salesperson's inappropriate appearance or clothing can stimulate a source objection. A few salespeople, for example, have unknowingly lost a sale because of body piercings or tattoos that triggered unspoken resistance by the buyer. Ameliorating source objections is difficult, but it can be accomplished over time if you do your best to be aware of potential source objections, discuss them openly with prospects, and assure them that you and your company are working hard to remove these barriers to sales agreements.

Needs Objections. Needs objections are raised by prospects who feel they simply do not currently need or have use for the products or services being offered. Handling "no need" objections requires innovative approaches by salespeople to educate prospects on the potential benefits to be derived from purchasing their products. Frequently, a need can be created by pointing out how things can be done more effectively or efficiently. For example, you might show how your products and services can cut the prospect company's costs, increase profits, or improve employee morale.

Invalid Objections

Objections that are merely defense mechanisms used by prospects to stall, slow down, or prevent the sales process from proceeding are called invalid.[4] **Invalid objections** are typically irrelevant, untruthful, delaying, or latent reasons for the prospect's unwillingness to negotiate. They are difficult to identify and overcome because the prospect does not deal with the salesperson in a straightforward, honest manner. Instead, the prospect plays a cat-and-mouse game without considering the actual sales offering. Prospects who regularly use invalid or untruthful objections are revealing their basic insincerity —and questionable business conduct. Some salespeople prefer not to waste precious selling time calling on such disingenuous buyers. As shown in Table 7.1, there are four categories of invalid objections.

Invalid Objections Irrelevant, untruthful, delaying, or hidden reasons for not buying.

Latent Objections. Latent objections are hidden and sometimes too personal or embarrassing for the prospect to reveal, so they remain unspoken. Some of these "silent" objections include such prospect thoughts as the following:

- "I'm not going to buy from you because I always buy from my old friend Charlie."
- "I don't like your style. You come across as arrogant and patronizing."
- "You seem more interested in making a sale than in solving my problems."

Discerning latent objections is difficult because the prospect is unlikely to reveal them to the salesperson. Sometimes the salesperson can learn about the prospect's hidden objections by cultivating a relationship with a receptionist, secretary, or other employee in the firm who knows why the prospect isn't receptive. However, this can be a long-term process and may not be worth the effort, because even if the hidden reasons are identified, they will still be major obstacles to the sale.

Stalling Objections. Stalling objections are usually delaying tactics articulated by such comments as "Around here, all decisions are shared, so just leave your product literature for us to look over, and we'll get back to you if we're interested." Salespeople might try to deal with these obvious put-offs by replying as follows: "Okay, why don't you share the product literature with the rest of your team? Then, perhaps we can meet again later this week, say Friday morning around ten o'clock, so I can show you more about the specific benefits we can provide." If the prospect rejects the salesperson's proposed rescheduling of a meeting and gives additional stalling objections, then it may be a clear sign that these objections are invalid. No professional salesperson wants to give up on a prospect too soon, but, at the same time, effective and efficient use of time will determine his or her sales success. It is usually a waste of time to attempt to overcome repeated prospect objections that appear invalid.

Time Objections. Time objections are delaying tactics that usually surface in prospect statements such as "I've got to prepare for a meeting in ten minutes, so I don't have time to talk now," or "I'm just too busy for the next several weeks with a special project to meet with you." Salespeople might attempt to deal with these obvious put-offs by such replies as: "How about our getting together after your meeting, say around three o'clock, or tomorrow morning if that's more convenient for you?," or "I understand how busy you are on this special project, so how about us setting up an appointment now for right after the project completion date?" If the prospect continues to use time excuses to put the salesperson off, then these are probably invalid objections that cannot be negotiated. Thus, the prospect should be moved to a much lower sales call priority.

Unethical Objections. Unethical objections include actions or attitudes that seem unprincipled or immoral. Examples of unethical resistance to buying include excuses to avoid doing business with salespeople from a particular ethnic group or religious persuasion, use of sexual overtures, and soliciting bribes or kickbacks. It's very difficult for a salesperson to deal with a blatantly discriminatory or unethical prospect, and it may be best not to try. For example, if a female salesperson finds a potential buyer trying to "come on to her," she might wisely ask her sales manager to assign some other salesperson to that prospect. Similarly, for most salespeople, it would not be worth compromising their own personal and professional ethical standards to win an unethical prospect's business by bribery. Moreover, once a bribe has been offered and accepted, it may become necessary for a salesperson to continually increase the size of the bribe to make future sales to that customer. As we learned in Chapter 3, bribing to win sales is not only unethical but illegal.

Chapter Review Question

How can a salesperson distinguish between valid and invalid objections?

IDENTIFYING AND DEALING WITH THE PROSPECT'S KEY OBJECTION

Determining the customer's dominant or key objection is one of the most difficult and intriguing tasks that confront salespeople. Why? Because prospects often give several reasons for not buying, but it is possible that none of these is the *dominant* reason. Generally, however, one objection acts like a keystone in the buyer's "arch of resistance," as depicted in Figure 7.2. Here the key objection is the product's styling, although the buyer also objects to the price, delivery terms, service contract terms, and lack of accessories. If the sales rep confronting this particular arch of resistance can show the buyer an acceptable product style

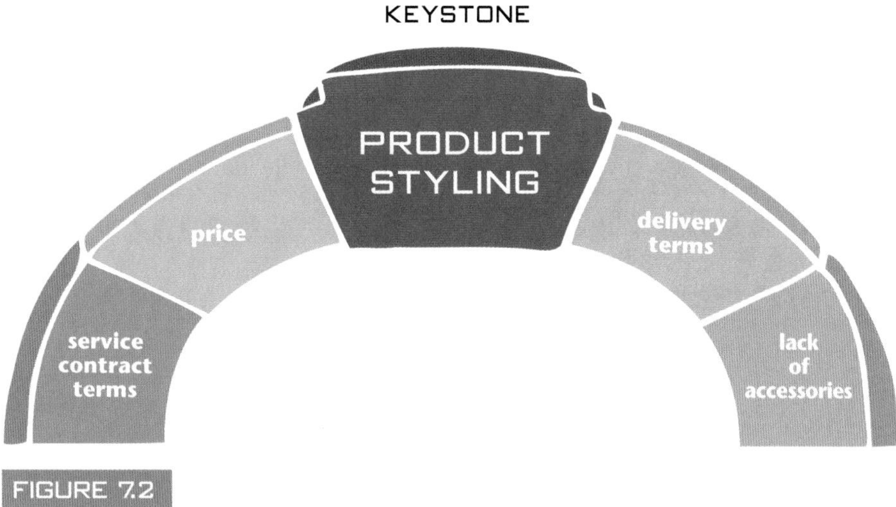

FIGURE 7.2

KEYSTONE IN THE ARCH OF RESISTANCE

and thus knock out the dominant or **keystone objection,** the other objections that make up the arch of resistance may well fall quickly thereafter.

Keystone Objection The customer's most important objection.

How can you uncover the keystone objection? One subtle way to start is by engaging the prospect in informal conversation before the sales presentation. Encourage the prospect to reveal his or her personal concerns by asking probing questions, such as the following:

- "I guess you've been involved in a lot of planning and decision making for this new installation?"
- "Have you decided exactly what you're going to need?"
- "What special features or benefits are you looking for?"
- "What are your major concerns in purchasing and installing the new equipment?"
- "Are you leaning toward any special kind of equipment or particular features?"
- "What led you to change suppliers in the past?"

When you successfully identify and resolve the buyer's key objection, you will have a powerful opportunity to resolve many or all of the other objections in short order. This is especially true if the key objection is taken care of quickly. In this case, your next statement to the buyer should be "I'm glad we resolved that issue. Now I'm confident that we can iron out these other sticking points without much difficulty." A word to the wise, however: Don't be overconfident. It takes a skilled salesperson to identify, "nail down," and resolve the key objection without allowing another, lesser objection to become the new key objection. If the negotiations threaten to take this turn, you might try reminding the buyer that you thought that the problem just resolved was the biggest one and that this or that other objection was relatively minor. Otherwise, resign yourself quickly (and as happily as possible) to starting back at square one in the negotiations. Table 7.2 outlines a process for uncovering and overcoming objections.

TABLE 7.2

Process for Uncovering and Overcoming Objections

1. Start with the Proper Attitude. An antagonistic "seller versus buyer" attitude is inappropriate. Don't view the buyer as a rival or as antagonistic when he or she raises objections. Successful salespeople welcome objections. They view objections as an indication that a purchase decision may be close at hand. After all, objections are typically raised prior to making the sale.

2. Uncover the Objection. If the objection is not stated, you must probe for the objection. You will need to determine what's going on in the buyer's mind when the selling process is being impeded but no specific objection has been raised. Start the prospect talking about reasons for not buying.

3. Clarify the Objection. You need to identify the real objection. What *really* accounts for the prospect's reluctance to make the purchase? For example, the prospect may say, "The price is too high." In relation to what is it too high? Competitive products? Budget constraints? You may want to paraphrase or repeat the objection if you're not sure you understand the objection correctly. Doing so will give you more time to think about and clarify the objection.

4. Acknowledge the Objection. In most cases, valid objections should be acknowledged ("Bill, you have raised an important point"). In doing so, you are merely telling the prospect that he or she has brought up a reasonable objection. People like to be praised; you are offering positive input to the prospect when you acknowledge the objection.

5. Handle the Objection. In most cases, your prior preparation will enable you to anticipate and promptly handle most objections. However, you should generally delay handling an objection if you encounter the following situations:

(a) *An early price objection arises.* Generally, you want to address the price issue after you have presented the product's features, advantages, and benefits so that you will be in a better position to justify the price.

(b) *Frequent, harassing objections emerge.* The prospect may just be in a bad mood that day or feel antagonistic toward your company. In such situations, it's usually best to just listen and avoid responding to unreasonable objections, because your response might lead to a confrontation with the prospect. In such situations, perhaps you can graciously excuse yourself by saying something like "I apologize, but can we make another appointment? I'm running late today, and we'll need more time to thoroughly discuss the issues you're bringing up." If the encounter thus ends on a gracious note, it is possible that productive negotiations can be conducted later, when the prospect is in a better mood.

(c) *A logical reason for discussing the objection later in the presentation exists.* Say, for example, the prospect raises an objection about delivery dates and installation service before you have even started talking about the specific product desired or investigated its availability. In such cases, you might say, "I'm confident that we'll be able to meet your requirements in those areas, but first we'll need to determine exactly which of our products will best fit your needs."

As with most areas of personal selling, it's helpful to have an overall sequential process to think about and follow. Of course, it is only seldom that the process can be followed exactly as planned. One or more steps may have to be skipped, altered, or returned to in response to prospect and customer reactions. Sometimes, you'll have to take two steps forward and one or more steps back. On a few rare occasions, you may not have to follow the process at all and

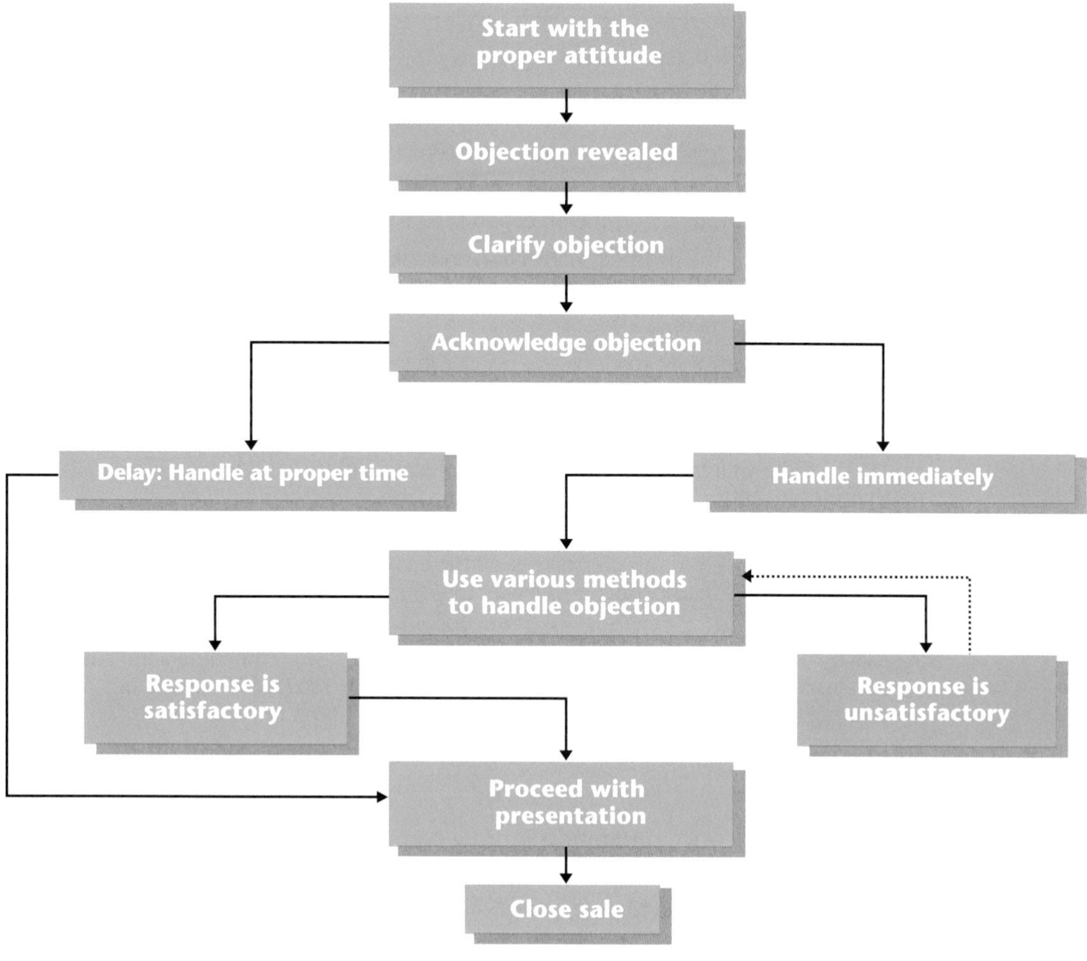

FIGURE 7.3

FLOW CHART APPROACH FOR HANDLING OBJECTIONS

can move directly to close the sale, perhaps because the customer is already presold by product literature and earlier sales calls that you've made at the company. When such a situation arises, jump over all the other intermediate steps and go right to the sales close. The steps in the sales process are merely guidelines to help you move toward your ultimate objectives. If a shorter route to your objectives opens up, be flexible and confident enough to take it. A sequential flow chart to follow in dealing with objections in shown in Figure 7.3.

Sell the Prospects on the Benefits

Prospects may use many sales resistance tactics, but by emphasizing the bundle of benefits that the prospect will derive from the product, salespersons can resolve many objections or push them into the background. Salespeople must remember to cover intangible benefits as well as tangible ones. Brand image, expertise and experience in the area, state-of-the-art technology, timely delivery, flexible credit terms, prompt installation, training assistance, and outstanding post-purchase service may be more important to some customers

TABLE 7.3

General Rules for Negotiating Objections

- Don't be defensive about objections. Welcome objections as a sign of prospect interest.
- Make sure you understand the objection before you answer it.
- Don't disparage the prospect's objection and risk deflating the prospect's ego.
- Lead the prospect to answer his or her own objection by politely asking for elaboration on the objection.
- Never argue with the prospect. You don't win sales by winning arguments.
- Don't over-answer or belabor the point in dealing with an objection and risk insulting the prospect's intelligence.
- Don't be drawn into pointless squabbles over some objection. Tell the prospect that's all the information you have at this time, and move to another benefit.
- Don't fake an answer. Admit you don't know, but promise that you'll find an answer promptly. No salesperson has all the answers. In fact, agreeing to find information for the prospect is one way to ensure a return sales call.
- Confirm your answers to objections, but don't put the prospect on the defensive by asking, "Have I fully answered your question?" This can come across as condescending and arrogant, which may cause some prospects to bring up more objections merely to try bringing you down a notch or two.

than quality or price differences among competing products. Salespeople should prepare a list of specific objections related to their products that can be offset by persuasive evidence, proof, and convincing testimony of the product's tangible and intangible value. Although stressing the product's *bundle* of specific benefits can usually overcome most objections, general rules that can help salespeople successfully negotiate prospect and customer objections are suggested in Table 7.3.

NEGOTIATING WITH PROSPECTS AND CUSTOMERS

In dealing with prospect or customer objections, the operative word is *negotiation*. Several dictionaries define *negotiation* as "mutual discussion and arrangement of the terms of a transaction or agreement." This definition implies mutual understanding, respect, and satisfaction between the negotiating parties. Negotiation does not mean manipulating or outfoxing an opponent. Instead, negotiation in professional selling means that buyers and sellers work together to reach mutually satisfying agreements and solve problems of shared interest. Thus both buyer and seller come out of the negotiation as winners, and indeed, that's the only outcome that will further a long-term relationship. In the *On the Frontlines* feature on page 228, you'll learn how Jason Smyczynski handles objections and negotiates with customers.

Negotiation Strategies

Buyers use negotiations to obtain various objectives, including lower price, higher quality, special services, concessions on delivery or payment, and increased cooperative efforts. The best way to negotiate with prospects is to draw them into creative partnerships.[5] The following are several basic strategies and tactics for moving a customer away from resistance to a problem-solving mentality.

- Take a relatively firm negotiating position initially so that when you compromise, the prospect will feel that he or she has negotiated a bargain. This approach also helps you find the lowest possible combination of price and terms acceptable to the buyer.
- Avoid making the first concession except on a minor point. Studies show that those who make the first concession tend to give away too much in each concession and usually get the worse end of the agreement.
- Keep track of the issues resolved during the discussions. Frequent recaps help confirm the steady progress being made.
- Concentrate on problem-solving approaches that satisfy the needs of both the buyer and the seller. Neither party in the negotiations should use unequal leverage or power to force an unfair solution, because that will hurt the long-term business relationship. Salespeople should always think of the lifetime value of the customer, not just the profit that can be made on any single transaction.
- Focus on issues where you and the prospect agree most. Leave the areas of widest disagreement until last. Reaching amicable agreements on several easier issues sets up a pattern for win-win negotiation and shows the salesperson's interest in working with the customer.
- Agree to a solution only after it is certain to work for both parties.

Chapter Review Question
Outline some basic negotiating strategies.

Negotiation Outcomes

Any sales negotiation has four possible outcomes: win-win, win-lose, lose-win, and lose-lose. Only the *win-win* outcome will further the business relationship and set the stage for future sales agreements, as shown in Figure 7.4.

Seller Win–Buyer Win Agreements. When both parties feel satisfied with the outcome, you have the basis for a continuing mutually beneficial relationship. **Win-win negotiations** are the *only* kind that lead to long-run success for salespeople and the only kind that professional salespeople seek. One study found that when both buyers and sellers engage in cooperative tactics (that is, seek to negotiate with open and accurate information, offer mutually advantageous concessions to each other, and respect each other's goals), deadlocks are less likely to arise and negotiation satisfaction is higher than when both parties engage in competitive (win-lose) tactics.[6]

Win-Win Negotiations
Negotiations in which both parties feel satisfied with the outcome; the only kind of negotiations that professional salespeople seek!

Seller Win–Buyer Lose Agreements. When the salesperson feels good about the agreement but the buyer is dissatisfied, the business relationship is in trouble. A buyer who feels taken advantage of may refuse to have anything more to do with the salesperson or the company he or she represents. Some disaffected buyers may also feel vindictive and seek to destroy the salesperson's relationships with other prospects and customers, perhaps through negative word-of-mouth.

ON THE FRONTLINES: THE LIFE OF A SALESPERSON

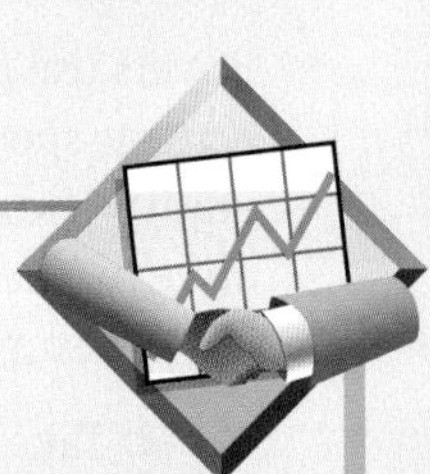

Negotiating Sales Resistance and Objections for "Win-Win" Agreements

"'Off the hook!' and 'High-five's!' Those were generally the responses I'd get from my teammates after presentations during my undergraduate years as a student. However, even with all that I learned in college, the part that made me most nervous was not the presentation itself, but handling the tough audience questions that might be thrown at me. That, I kid you not, is *the* most nerve-racking part of a sales call! No amount of training can adequately remove the fear of being 'put on the spot.' At times—even if I knew the right answer—I have tensed up and quickly blurted out an incorrect response. To sharpen my negotiation skills, one of the first things I did after taking my sales job was to enroll in a professional negotiations skills development seminar. What I learned there, and from my own experiences in sales, is that you've got to learn to anticipate the questions that may be asked. It's somewhat like anticipating what your college professors might ask on a quiz. When you've anticipated the questions, the right answers come fairly easily. I actually look forward to prospect questions now. They show that the prospect is interested, and they give me a chance to demonstrate my knowledge and professionalism. Once you've piqued prospect interest, your job becomes largely one of answering questions in a convincing manner. If you can do this, you'll usually win the sale," says Jason.

"I don't want to make it sound like dealing with objections is easy. Sales resistance can come from about a dozen different areas, like price, product, promotion, distribution, timing, budget constraints, company image, or even ethical issues. So I try to anticipate questions in all the major areas. But even when you've prepared for all the questions asked, there may still be hidden objections that the prospect never mentions. And hidden objections are by far the most difficult to overcome because you've first got to uncover them. Often, the prospect won't reveal them because they're too embarrassing. My approach is to politely ask the prospect some questions to obtain clues about who else might also have to approve the purchase or how long the firm has been purchasing from its present supplier. Answers to these gentle probes can sometimes reveal things that the buyer will never tell you directly—for example, that someone up the line has to approve all purchases of this type or that the prospect is locked-in with their current supplier. With this information, you figure out whether you can subtly go around the buyer to sell up the line or whether you should offer a one-time special incentive to try to get the prospect to switch from the long-time supplier. Some latent objections cannot be overcome in the short run, so you just have to recognize the situation and see if it's changed on subsequent sales calls."

One objection that you nearly always get right up front is about the "high price," continues Jason. "My sales presentations always focus on providing prospects the highest *value* in relation to price—never just the lowest price. But most prospects still try to negotiate the price downward. So I just keep returning to value selling by showing that my offer provides more prospect benefits for the price than competitors do, and thus my price is the best in terms of the benefits received. Usually, I need to illustrate overall value versus competitors over the life of the product, because a lot of competitors will offer a lower purchase price. It's important never to lose patience with prospects for bringing up a lot of what I call 'trial objections.' You've got to remember that their job performance depends on

(*continued*)

getting the best possible deal from you, and I have to respect where they're coming from," explains Jason.

"Over the years, I've developed some critical negotiation rules that I always follow: (1) Never disparage other competitors; (2) Never lie or mislead a customer because there is no quicker way to lose trust. And once you've lost trust, you aren't going to be able to do business; (3) Don't fake an answer. It's better to just say, 'I don't know, but I'll do some research on this issue and get back to you with the answer as soon as I can.' Prospects respect this kind of honesty because they know that no one has all the answers immediately. Also, coming back with the answer to their question often gives me a chance make another short sales presentation," states Jason.

Jason knows several techniques for negotiating buyer objections, but he says that selecting *the* appropriate negotiation strategy is highly situation- and prospect-specific and that no single strategy is more effective than another. In fact, he sometimes uses two or three different strategies with the same prospect, depending on the twists and turns that the negotiations take. "My overall negotiation strategy with all my prospects and customers has one overriding goal: to make sure that our sales agreement is viewed as fair to all parties. In sales negotiations, the only good outcomes are "win-win," because only those outcomes further the buyer-seller relationship."

Seller Lose–Buyer Win Agreements. Sometimes salespeople offer buyers an extraordinarily low price on a temporary basis in order to win an order from a new customer. They think that they'll be able to make up the profit loss on future orders from the customer. Unfortunately, an unusually low price or other one-time concession can create buyer expectations for similar "super deals" in the future. And customers may be angry if they aren't continued. Automobile manufacturers and dealers have fallen into this trap by offering cash rebates

SALESPERSON \ BUYER	Win	Lose
Win	Both the buyer and the salesperson are satisfied with the agreement, and the business relationship is in good shape. A problem-solving partnership is developing.	The salesperson is satisfied with the agreement, but the buyer is dissatisfied, and may even feel manipulated or taken advantage of, so the business relationship is in trouble.
Lose	The buyer is satisfied with the agreement, but the salesperson feels manipulated, and may reciprocate in future negotiations or reduce customer service. The business relationship is in trouble.	Both parties are dissatisfied with the agreement. Thus, the bond of trust between them may be so damaged that they are unlikely to enter into any future business agreements.

FIGURE 7.4

SALES NEGOTIATION OUTCOMES

Salespeople and customers can express their win-win frame of mind through their communication styles.
Dirk Anshulz/Getty Images

and low-interest or even no-interest loans on new cars to stimulate sales and compete with foreign competition. When they return to normal pricing strategies, customers look elsewhere for a good deal. Occasionally, prospects or customers who know that a salesperson wants their business badly will press for a "seller lose–buyer win" agreement, thinking erroneously that it will be to their long-run advantage. For instance, a buyer may assert, "I'll buy from you only if you lower your price by 10 percent" or "I don't want the free warranty program, so just reduce my price by the cost of that program" or "I'll buy your product if you throw in some free merchandise along with it." On such deals, the buyer may temporarily win the upper hand by squeezing the seller. Sellers can't stay in business by losing on each agreement, though, so they must find a way to make it back from the buyer, perhaps by cutting corners on quality or service.

Seller Lose–Buyer Lose. A "lose-lose" agreement that results in a loss for both parties leads to a deteriorating situation and the eventual end of the relationship. Occasionally, lose-lose agreements can be sustained for a while if both parties somehow believe that they are winning. For example, a shortsighted buyer may force a salesperson eager for new business to accept an unprofitable agreement. To make the agreement profitable, however, the salesperson may give the buyer's purchase low priority for delivery, neglect to inform him or her about special discounts, and generally ignore service requests. Gradually, both buyer and seller will see this relationship as a lose-lose situation and end it. In negotiating sales agreements, it all boils down to this: Both buyers and sellers are best off in the long run when they conscientiously strive to reach win-win agreements. Try your hand at creating a win-win outcome in the accompanying *It's Up to You* feature.

Chapter Review Question
Describe the four possible outcomes in any business negotiation.

IT'S UP TO YOU

You have finished your presentation to a prospect who seemed interested in and agreeable to your selling proposition. He has been smiling much of the time, and he hasn't even interrupted you or asked any questions during your presentation. Now, however, the prospect's smile turns to a blank stare and he says nothing. What do you do next?

TABLE 7.4

Specific Techniques for Negotiating Buyer Objections

Put-Off Strategies	Offset Strategies
• *I'm Coming to That*	• *Compensation or Counterbalance*
• *Pass-Off*	• *Boomerang*
Switch Focus Strategies	**Denial Strategies**
• *Alternative Product*	• *Indirect Denial*
• *Feel, Felt, Found*	• *Direct Denial*
• *Comparison or Contrast*	**Provide Proof Strategies**
• *Answer with a Question*	• *Case History*
• *Agree and Neutralize*	• *Demonstration*
• *Humor*	• *Propose Trial Use*

SPECIFIC TECHNIQUES FOR NEGOTIATING BUYER OBJECTIONS

As we noted earlier, prospects may bring up objections for many different reasons. Unless the salesperson can ease the prospect's anxieties by emphasizing benefits to be derived at minimal risk, the sale may be lost. Various methods have been developed and tested to handle prospect objections, as outlined in Table 7.4. In fact, these methods, used effectively, can sometimes lead to an immediate close or move the salesperson much closer to consummating the deal. We will briefly discuss and illustrate some of the different strategies for negotiating resistance or dealing with objections under five categories: put-off, switch focus, offset, denial, and provide proof. Note too that salespeople can enroll in comprehensive programs offered by internationally known companies such as Karass (www.karrass.com) to further enhance their negotiation skills.

Put-Off Strategies

One set of strategies for handling a prospect's objections are **put-off strategies** because they require the salesperson to delay dealing with the objection initially.

Put-Off Strategies A set of strategies for handling a prospect's objections that require the salesperson to delay dealing with the objection initially.

"I'm Coming to That". Although most objections should be answered as they are raised, some objections are best put off until later in the presentation because a premature answer may turn off prospects. "What's the price?" is a typical question that should be answered later in the sales presentation, after product benefits have been fully discussed. The salesperson can delay the exact answer to the price question by saying,

Salespeople can use various negotiating techniques to achieve "win-win" agreements.
Jose Luis Pelaez, Inc./CORBIS

> That's a good question. I think you'll be pleased by the value you'll receive for your dollars. But if you don't mind, I'll return to price in just a few minutes because there are three product-service options I need to lay out for your consideration. You'll want to make sure that one of them satisfies your particular needs before we zero in on price. Let me first briefly outline the benefits offered by the basic product package. Then I'll cover the benefits offered in the comprehensive and the deluxe product packages.

In fact, this salesperson's presentation may be so convincing that the prospect may even drop the objection later on.

Pass-Off. Salespeople cannot avoid or counter all objections or criticism of their products. Sometimes the best response to a prospect's objection is to smile and say nothing. This approach is especially appropriate if the objection is not serious or really requires no attention. In fact, the salesperson may just quietly acknowledge the objection by a nod of the head and move on in the presentation. For example, a regional buyer for a grocery store chain muttered about his dislike of the salesperson's company advertisements. Rather than seek to justify his firm's ads, the salesperson merely smiled, agreed with the buyer, and went on with his sales presentation.

Switch Focus Strategies

A second set of strategies for negotiating prospect objections relies on the salesperson's ability to switch the prospect's focus through various tactics.

Karrass, the world leader in negotiating programs. Training almost one million people worldwide. Headquartered in Beverly Hills, Calif. 323-951-7500.

Alternative Product. Some sales reps are inclined to help prospects identify the purchase criteria, such as product features, that are necessary for a purchase to take place and the products that do or don't meet those criteria. Such efforts can enhance salespeople's selling effectiveness.[7] Most times the salesperson will have more than one product alternative or model to sell. Each product will have its advantages and disadvantages compared to the others. When an objection is raised about a feature of one product, the salesperson can switch the prospect's focus to an alternative product until one is found that will satisfy the prospect. For example, one prospect was disappointed that a computer software salesperson's program could not simultaneously print an invoice and a billing statement. The salesperson addressed the objection by turning the buyer's attention to a new, higher-priced program that included the desired printing capability.

Feel, Felt, Found. A versatile technique that enables the salesperson to agree with the prospect's objection, confirm that it's a normal reaction to the product, and then disconfirm the objection over the longer run is called "feel, felt, found." For instance, a prospect may comment, "This computerized lighting system is too complex for me to operate. I'm not a very mechanical person." In response, the salesperson can say,

> I know how you *feel* because I'm not very mechanical myself. In fact, many of my customers *felt* the same way when they first saw all the gauges and buttons on this model, but they soon *found* that they only need to use three buttons to do everything most people want. The other twelve buttons are just for fine-tuning the main three operations. You'll be amazed how comfortable you'll be with all the buttons in a few weeks, and you'll be happy to have the extra options.

Comparison or Contrast. By comparing the product with another acceptable or unacceptable alternative, salespeople can often dissolve prospect resistance. For instance, a favorable comparison with other alternatives can address a prospect's objection regarding the price of a computerized credit information service: "A report from a traditional credit bureau costs ten dollars or more per name and may take days to receive. But our online service enables you to instantly obtain a complete credit report on any of more than four million people in the Delaware Valley area for less than ten cents per name."

Notice that the salesperson renders the objection neutral or inconsequential without arguing about or minimizing the prospect's concern.

Answer with a Question. This versatile approach technique separates valid objections from invalid ones or allows the salesperson to zero in on the specific reason for buyer resistance. It essentially turns the responsibility for providing an answer to the objection over to the prospect. Moreover, a question can help clarify the objection for both the buyer *and* the seller. When the salesperson asks a question, the prospect is not invited to raise another objection but, rather, is forced to address his or her own objection. For instance, a potential client might say, "I don't think your company has enough expertise or experience in accounting to audit a company the size of ours." The client representative for the accounting firm might reply, "What is it that makes you think that we don't have sufficient expertise or experience?" This response forces the prospect away from generalized resistance to a more specific objection that the rep can address.

Agree and Neutralize. In response to many objections, the salesperson can state some level of agreement and then go on to neutralize the objection. For example, a prospect may say to a salesperson for a contracting firm, "Compared to your competitors, your firm is estimating that it will take nearly twice

Using humor effectively can be a valuable way for a salesperson to defuse a tense situation with a buyer.
Corbis

as long and cost 25 percent more to complete this office building." The salesperson can say,

> Yes, you're right. That's because our completion estimates are accurate, and our cost projections include the highest-quality materials and the work of skilled professionals. If we build it, you'll never have to tell your commercial tenants about any delays in their move-in date. And you won't hear any complaints from them about the quality of the materials or the work. We do it right the first time. Our way does take a little more time and money initially, but it will save you time and money over the long run.

Essentially, this approach allows the salesperson to concede the objection and then provide more information to support his or her company's position. It offers a means for justifying the existence of the objection.

Humor. Telling a humorous story to ease the tension and defuse an objection can be an effective approach when skillfully done. A funny anecdote may relieve the uneasiness and allow the sales presentation to be continued even if the objection has not been fully addressed. Not every salesperson can tell a humorous story well, but for those who can, humor is a valuable tool.

Offset Strategies

Offset Strategies A set of strategies for dealing with objections that uses the technique of offsetting the objection with a benefit.

A third category of strategies dealing with objections uses the technique of **offset strategies**—offsetting the objection with a benefit.

Compensation or Counterbalance. Countering an objection that cannot be denied by citing an even more important buying benefit is an effective means of addressing an objection. By using this approach, the salesperson is telling the prospect that the seller's offering isn't perfect, but that its advantages far outweigh the disadvantage that the prospect has raised. For instance, a retailer may complain to a manufacturer's rep, "I don't think I'll have much success selling your *Dustlifter* hand vacuum cleaner in my store. It runs for only fifteen minutes before it has to be recharged, whereas the competitive *Quick Pickups* runs for thirty minutes before recharging." The salesperson might reply,

> That's correct, but their hand vacuum weighs twice as much as ours, so the householder's hand is under considerable strain and discomfort while using theirs. Our studies show that the typical

> person uses a hand vacuum for more than ten minutes at once only about 8 percent of the time. We decided to make it as lightweight and comfortable to use as possible, while covering more than 90 percent of the usage times. I think we made the right trade-off, don't you?

Boomerang. Turning the objection into a reason for buying, but avoiding making the prospect look simple-minded for raising the objection, is called the "boomerang" method. If you are selling anything that has a safety concern associated with it, the boomerang method is a good technique for responding to objections such as price, design, weight, or size. For instance, a Fortune 500 company CEO who wants to buy two corporate airplanes for top executive use might say, "Your airplanes cost fifty thousand dollars more than those your competitors offer." In response, the salesperson can say, "Yes, and there's an important reason for that—construction quality and safety features. Do you and your top executives really want to fly in an airplane built by the lowest bidder?"

Notice that with this response, the objection becomes the reason for making the purchase. The boomerang technique is especially useful for objections not strongly backed by facts; the objection can be defused before the facts can be marshaled to support it. Read the following *From the Command Post* about how some small high-tech companies offset their size disadvantages in competing against giant competitors.

Denial Strategies

A fourth category of techniques for dealing with prospect objections calls for denying the objection, either indirectly or directly. These strategies are often effective in responding to negative rumors about your company, products, or services.

Indirect Denial. Using this approach, the salesperson agrees with the prospect's objection but then inoffensively follows with a disclaimer. This technique recognizes that prospects and customers do not like to be contradicted; that is, they prefer to deal with salespeople who will bend a bit (just like a boxer who rolls with punches to soften the blow from the other boxer). For example, a prospect for a truck manufacturer might say, "I can't take a chance on buying from you because your truck tires have a reputation for poor quality." Using the indirect-denial method, the salesperson can answer as follows:

> You're absolutely right. We did have a quality control problem in some of our older plants about seven years ago. But now we have state-of-the-art manufacturing equipment and modern quality control procedures in all our plants. For the past three years, our truck tire quality has consistently been among the best in the business as rated by several independent research laboratories. We've regained nearly all our old customers, and we're anxious to win back your business, too. Let me show you what we have to offer.

Direct Denial. Occasionally, prospects or customers will relate some incorrect information to a salesperson as a reason for not buying. In these instances,

FROM THE COMMAND POST: CHARGE OF THE LILLIPUTIANS

High-tech companies were the business juggernauts in the 1990s. Not so any longer! A sea change has taken place. Many dot-coms have fallen by the wayside; hardware and software firms are merging, struggling, or going bust; and venture capitalists and Wall Street pundits are no longer enamored with e-commerce. Despite these phenomena, however, some companies have been able to rise above the fray and succeed despite tenuous circumstances. Surprisingly, some of these companies are Lilliputians. And not only have they held their own despite their diminutive stature in the market, but some of them have captured very large accounts.

What has led to the success of many small high-tech players? First, because they lack deep pockets, the high-tech dwarfs must "outthink" the Goliaths. Instead of relying on conventional selling approaches, their sales forces must develop close partnerships with customers by helping them improve their own profitability. Doing so typically requires a more steadfast commitment than that of their competitors to providing the highest level of customer service and understanding of their customers' businesses. Devotion to such service means that these small vendors are ever ready to serve clients at any hour of the day or night. This commitment is backed up by ensuring that all salespeople and managers include their work, home, and cell phone numbers on their business cards and invite customers to contact them at any time and anywhere.

Because they are small players on an uneven playing field dominated by giants, these little companies often make use of "guerilla" marketing tactics. For instance, to demonstrate their technological strength and product superiority to prospects and customers, they often use promotions that confront their large competitors, such as challenging a larger competitor to a competing-product contest. Thus, when small size is the objection, the Lilliputians stress small size as a reason to buy because the customer gets more personalized service and higher-quality products.

the salesperson needs to refute what the prospect has said and then explain the true situation. The ideal means of using this technique is to be earnest but not offensive. Ruffling the prospect's or customer's feathers may allow you to win the battle (by addressing the objection) but cause you to lose the war (by not closing the sale).

Many rumors, both true and false, tend to circulate about companies or industries from time to time, and some can hurt sales badly. For example, false rumors have been floated about McDonald's using worms in their hamburgers and about Procter & Gamble's corporate trademark symbolizing a satanic cult. Negative publicity about a salesperson's company or products can make sales calls particularly challenging. Today, a common rumor about a company is that of impending bankruptcy. When a salesperson is confronted with such a rumor, it's usually best to confront the rumor or accusation head-on:

> "Yes, I've heard that rumor myself, and I can assure you that there's absolutely no truth to it. Our company is in strong financial condition. In fact, to put that rumor to rest, I've taken to carrying our annual report, which shows our latest accounting audit. Here's

a copy. You'll see that a well-known accounting firm gives us a complete bill of health. In fact, the next few years should be among our best ever."

Provide Proof Strategies

The fifth category of responses to objections involves providing proof of the quality of the product by citing a case history, giving a demonstration, or letting the prospect use the product on a trial basis.

Case History. Relating the experience of another prospect who purchased the product and is now extremely satisfied with it can effectively turn objections around. Although you might present the story in various lengths or dramatizations, the bottom line will be to show how satisfied other customers are with your company's product. For example, a sales rep for an agricultural feed producer could say, "Mack Turkey Farms has seen their average bird's weight increase by nearly a pound since they started using our K240 turkey feed last year."

Demonstration. All good salespeople know their product's advantages and disadvantages versus those of competitors. A demonstration that dramatizes these major advantages is one of the best ways to overcome the prospect's various objections. A demonstration can reveal that the prospect's objection is not applicable. Salespeople using demonstrations, however, should carefully avoid unfair or deceptive product demonstrations that are mere "surrogate or false indicators" of a product's benefits. In addition to their being unethical, prospects eventually see through misleading demonstrations and lose trust in the salesperson. The professional salesperson uses only demonstrations that substantiate legitimate advantages.

Propose Trial Use. A good way to deal with many potential objections simultaneously is to propose that the buyer use the product on a trial basis for a short period. Free trial use often resolves objections, including those related to people's fears of new technology. Apple computer dealers have urged people, "Take an Apple out for a test drive. See for yourself how user-friendly a computer can be." This no-risk trial helps salespeople by enabling prospects to try out products that they might not risk buying for reasons unrelated to quality, such as the product's small market share, as in Apple's case. This technique is most appropriate for wary customers. As they use the product for a few weeks, they can determine whether the product is appropriate for them. Essentially, the trial allows the prospect to identify clearly the benefits of the product, which in some cases can show prospects a good alternative to the products they're currently purchasing or considering.[8] This method is also called the "puppy dog" close, because after trying the product, people begin to feel attached to it and are more likely to make the purchase. (Remember the puppy: "How can I pass him up after he wagged his tail so eagerly and licked my face so many times? Well, I can't!") The *On the Frontlines* feature on page 238 describes one creative use of this method.

One sure way to become a better salesperson is to learn, practice, and master the different techniques for handling buyer objections and to know in what negotiating situations to use them. Salespeople with these skills in their repertoires will win many sales that less-prepared salespeople will lose.

Chapter Review Question

Give some basic techniques for handling objections in each of the five categories discussed in the chapter.

ON THE FRONTLINES

What a Dinghy!

A boat manufacturers' rep sells pleasure boats made by several manufacturers to retailers throughout the Midwest. Like many top salespeople, he is creative in dealing with buyer objections. On one occasion, he tried to sell a yacht dealer a pontoon boat, but the dealer wasn't interested. The dealer told him, "We sell expensive yachts! No one has ever come in here and asked for a mere pontoon boat." The sales rep promptly quipped, "I bet that no one has ever come in here and asked for a haircut, either. But if you put up a barber pole, someone would!" Following this insightful comment, the sales rep convinced the dealer to display four pontoon boats—and they all sold within two weeks. Now this upscale yacht dealer is one of his biggest customers for pontoon boats.

A MAJOR NEMESIS: PRICE RESISTANCE

Prospect resistance to price is probably the most common and sometimes most difficult one for salespeople. Of course, if people only bought on the basis of price, eventually only one seller, the one with the lowest price, would remain in each product category. Most buyers, in fact, are more concerned about relative value for their money than with absolute price. Usually, a price objection means that the salesperson has not convinced the buyer of the product's value in terms of its price. Professional salespeople rarely sell on the basis of price—they sell on value.[9] One creative firm confronts price objections head-on in its sales presentations when salespeople make the following statement, "The bitterness of an inappropriate product lasts far longer than the sweetness of a giveaway price."[10]

Perceived Value A product's value from the prospect's perspective.

Value, or more accurately **perceived value,** is determined by the prospect taking what he or she perceives as the bundle of benefits offered and dividing it by the perceived price, as in this equation:

$$\text{Perceived VALUE} = \frac{\text{Perceived BENEFITS}}{\text{Perceived PRICE}}$$

The essential job of the salesperson, therefore, is to convince the prospect that the perceived benefits to be derived by the prospect *significantly* exceed the product's perceived price (which can include many intangibles, such as the inconvenience in switching to another supplier). Although every salesperson frequently hears the objection that the price is too high, prospects who make this comment can mean various things. It's the salesperson's job to sort out the real meaning of the price objection and deal with it appropriately. To find out the real reason for the price objection, the straightforward reply to a question about high price is to ask, "Why do you think the price is too high?" If

TABLE 7.5

Addressing Price Resistance

- Break the price down into *smaller installments over time.* "It costs your company only about eighty cents a day more than the competitive product—less than the price of a cup of coffee."
- Make *price–value comparisons* with competitive products. "This superb Acer mainframe computer provides all the features of the IBM for $2,500 less."
- Emphasize the product's *uniqueness.* "Our ZX-330 fax machine is the only fax available that gives you all these high-tech, high-performance features at this low price."
- Work down from higher-priced *product alternatives* to a level that the prospect finds acceptable. "You can buy the premier model at $6,300, the champion at $5,400, or the challenger model for $4,200. Which one do you think will best fit your needs?"

the objection is not merely a stalling tactic by the prospect, salespeople can address price resistance in several ways, as detailed in Table 7.5.

Value Analysis and Industrial Buyers

To deal specifically with price resistance, the industrial sales representative is always prepared to provide the industrial buyer with a **value analysis.** Sometime called value engineering or value assurance, value analysis shows how the salesperson's product is the best value for the buyer's (organization's) money.[11] It is usually a printed document that assesses a product's cost as compared to its value and is often presented as part of the sales proposal. Most industrial salespeople spend much of their time trying to provide alternative—better, cheaper, more efficient—products for their customers, and this often involves replacing a competing product. A value analysis is absolutely essential for such competitive situations. Three basic approaches to the preparation and presentation of a value analysis are (1) unit cost, (2) product cost versus value, and (3) return on investment. Let's examine each of these approaches.

Value Analysis A financial analysis, usually written, that shows how a product is the best value for the money.

Chapter Review Question

What do we mean by perceived value? How do prospects determine perceived value?

Unit Cost. A value analysis using the unit cost approach simply breaks the cost of the product down into smaller units. If you can show that your product's price per unit is lower than the competing product's price per unit, and that you offer the same or better quality, you will probably make the sale. For example, a large baking company might need a particular kind of detachable bolt that workers use to secure its large bread-cooling trays to stationary racks. These bolts are frequently replaced for safety. Currently, the buyer purchases packages of ten bolts from your competitor for $120, or $12 per unit. You know that you can beat the competitor's price by selling in larger packages, so you provide a simple value analysis showing how the buyer can obtain packages of fifty high-quality bolts for $500, or $10 per unit; seventy-five bolts for $630, or $8.40 per unit; or one hundred bolts for $700, or $7 per unit.

Product Cost versus Value. For a broader portrait of a product's value, you could prepare a value analysis that reveals the product's costs *over time.*

Returning to the preceding example, your competitor is also selling the large bakery special switches for dough mixers in its central baking facility for $55 per unit. You offer the customer a similar switch for $100. You know that the customer must replace your competitor's switch every three months, and you can prove that your switch will last three times as long. Furthermore, you know that the customer uses twelve of these switches in the baking facility at one time. Your value analysis of this situation for an eighteen-month period might look like the chart seen below.

Competitor Switches: 12 × $55 = $660

Your Company's Switches: 12 × $100 = $1,200

Elapsed Time	Competitor Company	Your Company
0 months	$ 660	$1,200
3 months	$ 660	—
6 months	$ 660	—
9 months	$ 660	$1,200
12 months	$ 660	—
15 months	$ 660	—
18 months	$ 660	$1,200
Total cost/18 months	$ 4,620	$3,600
Total customer savings with your switches		$1,020

Return on Investment. Finally, industrial buyers are interested in what percentage return on investment they can expect from the purchase of a particular product. *Return on investment* (ROI) refers to the amount of money expected from an investment over and above the original investment. Because it produces measurable results expressed as a percentage return, many companies view an industrial purchase as an investment. Say you are now trying to sell the baking company from the examples above a computer inventory and ordering system. After discussions with the buyer and plant supervisor, you and the baking company agree that computerization would save the company at least $5,000 per month in hourly wages paid to employees in the inventory and ordering systems. The monthly cost of your equipment is $4,000 per month, including full customer technical assistance and repair and replacement service. Now you can prepare a simple table to reveal the customer's potential ROI for this arrangement:

Return on Investment ($1,000/$4,000) = 25 percent per month

Value of Hourly Wages Saved	$5,000 per month
Cost of Equipment	−$4,000 per month
Customer's Cost Savings	$1,000 per month

Whether or not they are engaged in industrial selling specifically, all consultative salespeople should carry out their own value analysis programs on their own products versus those of competitors and should actively participate with their prospects and customer organizations to ensure that the calculations are correct. You should be aware that many organizations regularly perform value analysis studies on the products they buy and sell to discover ways to provide their own customers with the same basic product at a lower price, or a better product at the same price. Take time to hone your value analysis skills, and make sure your customers know that purchasing your product gives them real value for their money.

Price Resistance and "Reality"

Admittedly, your product's price can often be a selling obstacle for the buyer. And as buyers come more and more to view products as commodities, price is likely to remain a major factor in their purchase decisions. Nonetheless, professional salespeople recognize that prospects and customers often raise price objections merely to try for a better deal (even when they already know that they are being offered one) or to slow down the selling process. In fact, prospects' price resistance may well be a ploy to conceal their real reason for not buying. Therefore, through careful unveiling of the prospect's sales resistance, professional salespeople can discern how critical price is to the buyer and which selling strategy to employ to deal with that resistance successfully.[12]

Chapter Review Question

What are the three basic approaches to preparing and presenting a value analysis, and how does each approach work?

SUMMARY

Without sales resistance, there would be little need for salespeople. Prospect objections are usually positive signs of interest and involvement in the sales presentation. Uncovering and negotiating the prospect's key objection is one of the salesperson's most important and challenging tasks. Several objectives and strategies help salespeople negotiate prospect resistance. Every sales negotiation has four possible outcomes, but only the win-win outcome will further the buyer-seller relationship and encourage future negotiations.

Anticipating objections and preempting them in the sales presentation is one of the best ways to minimize objections. The most common objection is to price, which means that the salesperson has not convinced the prospect of the value of the product. Perceived value can be expressed as the ratio of the product's perceived benefits to the product's perceived price from the prospect's viewpoint. Techniques for negotiating prospect's objections can be divided into five basic categories: put-off, switch focus, offset, denial, and provide proof strategies. Value analysis can show prospects that your product offers the best value for their money.

KEY TERMS

Objections
Valid Objections
Invalid Objections
Keystone Objection
Win-Win Negotiations
Put-off Strategies
Offset Strategies
Perceived Value
Value Analysis

TOPICS FOR THOUGHT AND CLASS DISCUSSION

1. Why are objections sometimes called the salesperson's best friends? Wouldn't it be better for salespeople if prospects had no objections to buying their products?
2. Explain the concept of the buyer's "arch of resistance" and the "keystone" objection.
3. Why is the term *negotiation* appropriate for describing how the salesperson should handle prospect resistance and objections?
4. Describe some ways in which a salesperson could change the prospect's perceived value for a product.

INTERNET EXERCISES

1. Use an Internet search engine to find three firms that specialize in negotiation training. Peruse their websites to see if you can find some negotiation strategies, in addition to those discussed in this chapter, that could be used in personal selling.
2. Use Google or any other search engine to locate two examples of negotiation strategies being demonstrated using Flash or streaming video.
3. Use the Internet to find articles on negotiating sales resistance. Identify and describe some guidelines for handling objections besides those outlined in Table 7.2.

PROJECTS FOR PERSONAL GROWTH

1. Go to the Business Periodicals Index online or at your school library or do a computer search to find five articles on *business negotiation*. Read at least three of them, and then prepare a list of guidelines that a salesperson might use. In class, compare the list you developed with those developed by classmates also given the same assignment.
2. Ask four professional salespeople about their philosophies and strategies in negotiating prospect objections and resistance. Decide, on the basis of these discussions, whether they believe in win-win or win-lose outcomes in negotiating with prospects. Explain your reasons for making this judgment about each salesperson.
3. Ask three professional salespeople who each sell to different customer categories what their favorite techniques are for handling buyer resistance and objections. Do the negotiating techniques differ with the customer type? Why or why not?

ROLE-PLAY EXERCISE 7.1

Negotiating an Agreement with a Buyer Who Insists on Winning

Situation

Marilyn Boldt, a sales rep for Solex-Analog—a large semiconductor manufacturer—is negotiating with the chief buyer for National Computer Company (NCC). This buyer, Howard Logan, is such a hard bargainer that he won't agree to sign a contract unless he feels that he's gotten the best of the supplier in the negotiations. He has just demanded that Marilyn give him a whopping 25 percent discount on all NCC purchases, or he won't buy anything from Solex-Analog. If the 25 percent discount is provided, Mr. Logan will give Solex-Analog all of NCC's semiconductor business. Marilyn knows that her company can't make any profit if she agrees to a 25 percent discount, and she's quite sure that no other semiconductor supplier will offer such a large discount. While Mr. Logan continues talking,

Marilyn is thinking to herself how to respond to Mr. Logan's demand.

Roles

Marilyn Boldt Wanting the NCC contract badly, she is tempted to agree to the demands of Howard Logan, even though it will result in a "seller lose–buyer win" agreement.

Howard Logan He is such an aggressive, greedy bargainer that most salespeople hate to negotiate with him. And when they do reach the usual "seller lose–buyer win" agreement with NCC, they try to salvage a little profit on the contract by cutting some corners, usually on product quality or service.

ROLE-PLAY EXERCISE 7.2

Negotiating Prospect Resistance

Situation

For the past three years, Madeline Wooten has successfully operated her own general store out of a storefront in a small country town. Business is very good, and some regular customers come from as far as fifty miles away to purchase the beautiful handmade blankets, dresses, shawls, hats, hand tools, and sundry gifts that she sells. A large Amish population lives in the area and regularly supplies Mrs. Wooten with many handmade items. She employs two full-time people (retired women both in their 70s) during most of the year, but during the holiday period from November to January, Madeline adds two part-time employees (usually first-year college students on winter break) to help out. Sixty-eight years old, Madeline has been an entrepreneur all her life and has owned several small homemade goods businesses.

On the first day of October, Lamont Zachary, a marketing representative for the American division of a small Taiwan electronics manufacturer called Peach Company, is talking to Ms. Wooten about the possibility of buying a new, Taiwan-made computer for her business. Lamont says, "With excellent small business software programs available, like EasyBiz, you'll be able to keep track of all your business transactions with minimal labor, and you won't have to worry about computing errors." Ms. Wooten replies, "Well, I'm not too sure that my small staff and I would save much time because we've gotten used to keeping our books by hand. Also, my two full-time store employees and I don't feel comfortable around computers. None of us has one at home. Learning that EasyBiz software program sounds too complicated and time-consuming—especially with the start of our busy season only a few weeks away."

Roles

Lamont Zachary Although he had owned a computer for several years, it wasn't until last year that Lamont bought a copy of the EasyBiz program. He was pleasantly surprised, once he set it up, how easily he could keep track of all his business transactions. And he was able to finish his tax return in about half the usual time and e-mailed the completed federal and state tax forms right from his computer desktop. For the first time ever, it was almost fun keeping business records and doing his taxes—and never having to check for errors. Lamont believes that Ms. Wooten could benefit greatly from having a computer in her store and using the EasyBiz program, but he has to figure out some way to overcome Ms. Wooten's fear of computers.

Madeline Wooten Even though she is intelligent and energetic, Madeline has always been somewhat intimidated by computer hardware and software, and she has never felt the need for them. In her view, good typewriters, calculators, and ballpoint pens are all the tools that she and her small, experienced staff need to run the business. Of course, training her part-time employees during the holiday season is usually time-consuming, and they sometimes make calculating errors for which she must later reimburse customers.

CASE 7.1 LEARNING TO HANDLE PROSPECT OBJECTIONS

Rachel Glassman sips her morning coffee as she waits for the last trainee to return from the morning break. Rachel, regional sales training manager for a multinational machine tool company, is in the middle of a long and intense day of sales training for recently hired salespeople. Today's training concentrates on negotiating prospect resistance and objections. From past experience, she knows that this part of the company's five-week training program is one of the most difficult for new representatives to master. Over the years, Rachel has tried many approaches to help trainees learn negotiation strategies and tactics. One of the best approaches, she believes for two reasons, is to combine video simulations with role-playing. First, former trainees who used the videos claim that the simulations hit close to what they later experienced in real sales situations. This testimonial makes current trainees more responsive. They understand that what they are viewing will be of value to them once they are assigned to a sales territory. Second, when sales trainees role-play immediately after they view the videotapes, they practice and reinforce negotiation strategies and techniques that they have just learned.

Today Rachel is presenting some simulated selling situations in which a sales representative deals with customer resistance or objections. In the first three segments, which three trainees viewed along with Rachel before the morning break, the videos followed a representative through a sales presentation and showed how salespeople handle various types of customer objections. The last two segments, which Rachel will present to the three trainees after the break, are again vignettes of sales presentations where the salesperson encounters various types of customer resistance and objections. In these videotapes, however, at the point when the objection is raised, the tape stops and each trainee is asked to recommend a strategy or technique to deal with the situation. When all sales trainees have made a recommendation, the simulation is restarted, and the viewers observe how the representative actually handled the customer's objection.

The essence of these two videotaped situations, along with brief summaries of how the three sales trainees responded, follows.

Situation 1

A salesperson is just completing a sales presentation of a Power Spray water broom to Cecil Jergens, a purchasing agent for National Industrial Equipment. The salesperson's concluding statement is "As you have seen, Mr. Jergens, the water broom enables workers to simultaneously wash away and sweep up tough dirt and grime from factory or plant floors in minutes. At the price of $34.95 per unit, it's a tremendous bargain, and I'm sure that each one of your plant managers will want several."

"Yes, the water broom looks like a useful product," responds Mr. Jergens, "but your price is nearly three times the price of our heavy-duty industrial brooms, which do a good clean-up job. I don't see the value in paying three times as much for a product that does the same job."

TRAINEE BOB: "Mr. Jergens seems to have some hidden agenda. I think he's probably buying the industrial brooms from a friend of his whom he has dealt with for years. I don't think there's much of a chance for a sale here."

TRAINEE PETE: "Mr. Jergens still isn't convinced of the benefits of the water broom relative to its price. I think the sales rep has to restate the benefits of the water broom in terms of worker time saved, cleanliness of the plant floors in ridding them of ground-in oil and grease as well as dirt, and improved worker morale. The salesperson ought to point out that the water broom's benefits relative to its price are actually much greater than the traditional industrial broom's benefits compared to its price. Doing so will indicate to Mr. Jergens that he will receive more value for his dollars by buying the water broom.

TRAINEE ALLISON: "At three times the price of the industrial brooms, perhaps the price of the water broom is too high. I'm sure the sales rep has some room to negotiate on price, so I'd recommend of-

(continued)

fering the water broom at a lower price—say $29.95—to see how Mr. Jergens responds."

Situation 2

After making the sales presentation and demonstration, a sales representative for Tool Storage Cabinet, Inc., asks the purchasing agent for Tebbets Machining Company this question: "May I go ahead and order five of these welded steel tool chests for your plant, Mr. O'Connor, so your machinists can soon have the peace of mind that comes from knowing that their valuable tools are secure?"

"Well, I know the machinists want more secure tool chests," replies Mr. O'Connor, "but I don't think they're going to like the combination locks on the doors. They're used to using keys, and it's going to slow them down a lot to have to remember and work the combinations each time they want to open the doors of their tool chests."

TRAINEE BOB: "The engineers who designed those tool chests weren't very customer oriented. They should have known that the machinists would want access by keys instead of a combination lock. I'd go back to headquarters and tell them that we need to redesign the locking device on our tool storage chests."

TRAINEE PETE: "I'd turn this apparent disadvantage into an advantage. I think the sales rep could correctly say that the locks were purposely designed with combination locks for some well-thought-out reasons. First, keys get mislaid, lost, or stolen, and anyone with the key can open the tool chest. Combinations are not likely to be lost or stolen. Second, if a key is left at home, the machinist must return home for the key, but a combination is carried around in one's head. Third, when there is turnover in the plant, a new machinist can securely use the former employee's tool chest by merely changing the combination, rather than having to rework the entire locking device for a new key. Fourth, talented thieves can pick open key locks, but few thieves can open combination locks. By pointing out these advantages of the combination lock, I think the sales rep can overcome the prospect's objection."

TRAINEE ALLISON: "I'd tell Mr. O'Connor that I bet some of the machinists will prefer the combination lock to the key-lock tool chests, and that I'd appreciate him taking a little poll to find out. Then I'd tell him that we can provide both types of locking devices, depending on what the machinists want. If I found out later that our company didn't offer anything but the combination lock, I'd call Mr. O'Connor back and tell him that I'm sorry but I was mistaken about our selling the key-lock type. Then I'd ask for an order for the combination-lock tool chests, assuming that some of the machinists will prefer them."

Questions

1. Look at the two situations one at a time. In your opinion, which of the three sales trainees seems to be on the best track toward handling the objection in each situation? How do you think the prospect will respond to the other two sales reps' approaches in each case?
2. Which one of these sales reps would you prefer to be assigned to a territory where you were the sales manager? Why?
3. What overall advice would you give the sales reps to help them in negotiating prospect objections or resistance?
4. What do you think of the process of setting up a situation via videotape, stopping the tape to let sales trainees explain how they would deal with the situation, and then showing how the sales rep actually dealt with the situation?

CASE 7.2 NEGOTIATING PRICE WITH A TASKMASTER

CASE 7.2 "NEGOTIATING PRICE WITH A TASKMASTER" CAN BE FOUND ONLINE AT HTTP://COLLEGE.HMCO.COM/PIC/ANDERSONPS2E

CHAPTER 8

Confirming and Closing the Sale: Start of the Long-Term Relationship

After reading this chapter, you should understand:

- Why some salespeople fail to close.
- When to attempt a trial close.
- What trial closing cues are and how to make use of them.
- Key principles of persuasion in closing.
- Effective closing techniques.
- How to deal with rejection.
- What immediate post-sale activities must be performed.

"You don't close a sale, you open a relationship if you want to build a long-term, successful enterprise."

Patricia Fripp

INSIDE PERSONAL SELLING

Meet Mike Andrews of J.A. Riggs Tractor Company

Closing a deal in Mike Andrews's world "absolutely should be anticlimactic." Andrews is the corporate sales manager for J.A. Riggs Tractor Company, the Little Rock, Arkansas–based Caterpillar dealer. He sells heavy construction equipment—bulldozers, backhoes, paving equipment, and mining machines—ranging in price from $20,000 to millions of dollars. Andrews sees the close as the natural next step in the process of learning about the customer's problem and suggesting the appropriate solution. "If you have done an excellent job in qualifying the customer, developing the deal, and providing the correct recommendation," he says, "then the proposal will fit the customer's needs and he will say, 'That's exactly what I want.'"

Andrews's customers are construction companies, individual owner-operators, municipal governments, agricultural businesses, and multinational mining corporations. His prospects generally know the kind of equipment they want, so the sales discussion focuses on "what our product will do for you, versus what the competitor's product will do for you," he explains. "Each product has its unique benefits and inherent objections. The secret is to develop each benefit into value for the customer."

Dealership support is also a critical issue, because customers have a lot to lose if a million-dollar machine won't start or breaks down.

"What customers really value is how often the machine will be available to do the job that they bought it for," Andrews notes. Knowing this, he recently closed a sale involving twenty backhoe loaders by guaranteeing that if any of the machines stops operating, "we will be there in the next 24 hours and we will get it up and running."

Another element in closing a sale is the dealership's ability to deliver the equipment exactly when the customer needs it. A construction company, for example, may be forced to pay a penalty if it fails to meet the deadline for starting or completing a highway project. By understanding the customer's schedule as well as its needs, Andrews can work toward a close date that helps the customer avoid the pain of paying a penalty. "The close must be tied to relieving the customer's pain," he says. Therefore, after responding to any objections and clarifying the benefits, Andrews may remind the customer that "if we do not reserve the machine, it may not be available when you need it." This trial close adds a sense of urgency and focuses the customer on the pain of missing a deadline.

When a prospect doesn't buy, Andrews analyzes the lost sale to see where the dealership could have done a better job of qualifying, understanding needs, recommending a solution, and presenting the solution's value. This is important because prospects will have other needs in the future—needs that Riggs may be able to fill. "Most of these are not just one-time purchases," Andrews emphasizes. "These are relationships that, once established, can go on for years."

Now comes every salesperson's moment of truth. You've gone through the preceding five steps of the PSP brilliantly. Your qualified prospect has witnessed a solid sales presentation and demonstration, you've addressed all the questions that arose, you've adeptly negotiated various objections, and the prospect seems convinced of the merits of your product. Now you just have to use the right strategy to "snag" that important order—close the sale—and you can count the prospect as one of your customers. But are you ready to seize the challenge of inducing the prospect to approve the purchase? By the end of this chapter, you will be armed with the knowledge to do just that!

The **close** can be defined as those activities involved in eliciting a positive buying decision from the prospect. It should be a natural step in the sales process and should not seem forced.[1] If you have done your job effectively in the preceding five steps of the PSP, the close should evolve almost automatically. That is, the prospect's desire and enthusiasm for the product should be keen, and his or her questions or objections should have been addressed, so the time should be ripe to ask the prospect to make the purchase.

Close The stage in the selling process where the salesperson tries to obtain the prospect's agreement to purchase the product.

Although a sale is typically closed after completion of the previous five steps in the PSP, professional sales personnel *constantly* evaluate when they should close the sale. This assessment indicates whether to close the sale now or continue with the selling process. You may be able to close earlier with some prospects than with others and to close earlier in some situations than in others. Don't be surprised if a prospect indicates readiness to sign the order form before you've completely finished the five PSP stages; just go ahead and take the order. After all, your primary purpose is to make sales—not sales presentations.

A common showbiz saying is "It's easier to get on than it is to get off." This is also true in sales. The close is the final curtain. Closing is the make-or-break time of personal selling, when having some small morsel of extra knowledge or skill often makes the difference between earning and losing a commission. Only one question really matters: "Can I close this buyer?"[2]

CLOSING AND CONFIRMING THE SALE

As shown in Figure 8.1, the close is that stage in the selling process where the salesperson tries to obtain agreement from the prospect to purchase the product.[3] It's also the integral part of the selling process that confirms agreement on the details of the purchase contract. Some scholars and practitioners refer to "confirming the sale" instead of "closing the sale." In their view, *closing* incorrectly implies the end of the selling process, when in fact much hard work must follow the sale in terms of service to satisfy the customer and win repeat business. Professional salespeople realize that their job has just begun after the prospect has agreed to buy. Why? Because only attentive efforts will retain the current sale, maintain the prospect's satisfaction with the purchase, and enhance the relationship with this account (by securing additional business and referrals, for instance).

FIGURE 8.1

THE PERSONAL SELLING PROCESS

FROM THE COMMAND POST: WEB AUCTION SITES JUST KEEP ON SELLING MORE AND MORE

Web auction sites such as eBay (www.ebay.com), UBid (www.ubid.com), Amazon Auctions (www.amazonauctions.com), Sotheby's (www.sothebys.com), QXL(www.qxl.com), and TripBid (www.tripbid.com) are among cyberspace's favorite and most successful Web venues. Started chiefly to help consumers buy and sell such prosaic items as candy dispensers, books, and second-hand products, collectively they represent a gigantic channel of distribution. Web auction users buy collectibles of all kinds, in addition to clothing, sports equipment, and almost anything else that's legal. And their success has been colossal. Millions of goods change hands daily through these sites, generating billions of dollars in annual sales revenues.

Why are these sites so effective? First, they provide a convenient commerce platform on the Internet. Second, most continue to seek out additional customers, increase the offerings sold on their sites, expand into global markets, and offer users an enjoyable and exciting experience.

In efforts to thrive in cyberspace, some auction sites have moved into the business-to-business (B2B) and business-to-consumer (B2C) channels, rather than being merely a consumer-to-consumer (C2C) alternative. Businesses—whether producers, wholesalers, or retailers—can buy or sell myriad kinds of items (e.g., copiers, computers, and cars) on the websites. Even giant companies, such as IBM (www.ibm.com) and Sun Microsystems (www.sun.com), are marketing their products on auction websites. In addition, numerous businesses are using these websites to sell directly to consumers. To complement and promote all of these activities, some auction companies are advertising their business services aggressively—not only online but also via television, direct mail, and print ads—to attract larger user bases.

For many dot-coms and cyberspace firms, the road to glory has been paved with potholes and insurmountable obstacles. For Web auction companies, though, sticking close to their strengths and goals, plus adept execution, has led to amazing growth, success, and increasing aspirations.

Closing Is Part of the Ongoing Selling Process

Instead of viewing the close as the end or pinnacle of the PSP, many professional salespeople regard the close as simply a vital part of the *ongoing* selling process and buyer-seller relationship. No matter how clever the closing strategies used, the salesperson is unlikely to make the sale unless he or she has done a good job in each stage of the PSP leading up to this point. Conversely, no matter how brilliantly the salesperson has performed in the preceding stages of the PSP, the sale can still be lost unless the salesperson uses the right closing strategy and tactics.

What the Close Represents

A successful close confirms the *win-win* agreement reached with a buyer and the continuance of the buyer-seller relationship. It indicates that the salesperson has done a thorough selling job (so far) and that the buyer is pleased with his or her purchase decision (at least so far). Because of its widespread acceptance, and for convenience, we will frequently use the term *closing the sale,* but keep in mind that the close is not the end but merely a *continuation* of the selling process. Read the *From the Command Post* feature on page 249 to see how Web auction sites have been successfully closing sales again and again and again.

AVOIDING THE CLOSE

Despite the significance of closing the sale and its natural sequence in the PSP, some salespeople are reluctant to close. This happens with both experienced and inexperienced salespeople. Whatever the reason, a failure to close can abruptly end the buyer-seller relationship that had just begun. Let's look at some reasons why sales reps may fail to close.[4]

Experienced Salespeople

Some experienced salespeople become so involved in the selling process that they don't even try to close until they've finished their sales presentation and product demonstration. Such behavior can either delay the sale or result in the prospect's raising more and more objections or the salesperson's talking past the point of making a sale (so the prospect becomes "cold"). Still other veteran salespeople become so complacent about selling techniques that have worked well in the past that they avoid trying new closing methods in new selling situations. Consequently, their closings efforts become stale and ineffective.

The best salespeople are sensitive to every opportunity to close and are always shaping their closes to fit individual prospects and selling situations. This often means trying new closes, or at least old closes with new twists—both of which not only improve closing effectiveness but also help keep the selling job interesting and exciting.

New Salespeople

Some new salespeople find it extremely difficult to close sales for three basic reasons: a lack of confidence in themselves, the product, or the company; guilt about asking people to part with their money; or a general fear of failure that causes them to postpone the close as long as possible.

1. Lack of confidence is common in new salespeople who are thrust into new selling situations without adequate training. One way to help overcome this lack of confidence is to talk with other salespeople—both with those who are also new and are dealing with the same confidence problem themselves and with sympathetic veterans who can tell stories about their own shaky confidence during their first few months in sales. Sales managers understand this common problem and can usually help by providing support, information on confidence-building books and exercises,

ON THE FRONTLINES

Perseverance Pays Off

A salesperson was assigned to a territory that included a large federal government installation in a major city. This installation used about five thousand personal computers (PCs), and a major computer manufacturer seemed to have a lock on the business because the head purchasing agent preferred that brand.

On the salesperson's initial call, the head purchasing agent told him that the installation bought only the large competitor's PCs and that the salesperson would be wasting his time trying to sell any other brand. Refusing to give up, the salesperson cultivated a relationship with the head purchasing agent's assistant. The salesperson made it a point to call on the installation at least once a month, when he would teach the assistant all about PCs. After about ten months, the assistant called the salesperson and asked him to stop by the following morning. Arriving early, the sales rep met the assistant, who said that his boss had taken early retirement and that he himself was now the head purchasing manager. Before the sales rep could even congratulate him on his promotion, the newly appointed head purchasing manager asked the salesperson whether his firm's PCs met all government specifications. After checking to make sure that they did, the sales rep was delighted to hear the new head purchasing manager say, "Okay, what's the 50-PC price?"

The PC salesperson personally installed each of those 50 PCs and instructed the buyer's employees in their use. He also arranged for his company's service manager to meet with his counterpart at the installation to set up a two-day course for the repair technicians and a spare parts inventory system. Everything ran smoothly for three months, whereupon another order came in, this time for 150 PCs! Those 200 PCs enabled the salesperson to make 225 percent of his annual sales quota and were largely responsible for a key promotion in his career.

Later, the new head purchasing manager told the PC sales rep that his refusal to give up and his willingness to share information without any apparent return convinced him to put in the first order for 50 PCs. The sales rep's thorough follow-up on those PCs and the support provided by his company's service department earned the second order for 150 PCs. Success usually crowns the efforts of salespeople who never quit trying and make the most of opportunities when they appear.

and perhaps further training. In addition, having the sales manager accompany the new rep on sales calls can provide a source of comfort and confidence for the novice salesperson. In fact, the manager may be able to assist the salesperson with the close without stealing the new rep's "thunder." One computer salesperson asked his sales manager to accompany him on what would turn out to be his first sale. Both the sales manager and the salesperson attempted trial closes that eventually led to an order. After the sale, the manager and sales rep evaluated the sales call as a means of enhancing the salesperson's knowledge and confidence regarding his ability to close a sale.

2. As children, we are taught not to ask people for money—it simply isn't polite. If you harbor guilt feelings about asking people to make a commitment to purchase, those beliefs also might spring from your negative perceptions about the role of selling. Professional salespeople, however, realize that they are helping people solve problems and are performing a vital and important societal function. People spend money only when they believe the purchase will answer their needs. A sale is thus confirmation of your useful and important role in the buyer's life and livelihood.
3. Fear of feeling rejected is common in selling. Therefore, some salespeople consider the close so terribly important and dramatic that, ironically, they can never find just the right moment to make the close. Procrastination provides comfort to salespeople who fear that all their previous work in the selling process may come to naught. Fear of failure can be overcome by recognizing that few products are sold on the first sales call. Failure on a particular closing attempt certainly does not mean that the sale is irretrievably lost. There will be other opportunities. The best salespeople, however, share one winning attitude: They never give up.

Chapter Review Question
What are some reasons why some salespeople don't even attempt to close?

On the Frontlines (page 251) recounts an inspiring story about a salesperson who was so patient and persevering that when the close came, it actually took him by surprise.

THE TRIAL CLOSE

Trial Close Any well-placed attempt to close the sale; can be used early and often throughout the selling process.

There is no single best time to attempt a close. Some situations, though, almost cry out for an attempted close, as we shall see.

When to Close

Closing attempts are especially appropriate in three situations:

1. When you have completed a presentation without the prospect raising any objections, try to close. Doing so may elicit prospect objections, which you can then deal with.
2. When the sales presentation is completed and all questions and objections have been addressed, closing is logical.
3. If the buyer indicates an interest in buying the product by giving a "closing signal," the time is appropriate to close.

Professional salespeople who are prepared to close anywhere, anytime know their *ABCs—Always Be Closing.*[5] In fact, they learn to use subtle trial closes early and often throughout each stage of the selling process. Some salespeople refer to the **trial close** as a "mini-close," but when handled properly, a small trial close can quickly become the *big close*. A trial close is simply a way to see whether the prospect is ready to buy and thus ready for the close.

Chapter Review Question
When should salespeople try to close?

Let's say that a salesperson has thoroughly discussed the product features, advantages, and benefits with a prospect who seems interested in the product. The salesperson might then ask, "Should I tell our warehouse personnel to reserve a hundred units for you?" or "Would next week be a convenient time for you to take shipment?" If the prospect says yes to either question, the sale is confirmed and the trial close has been successful. But if the buyer isn't ready to place the order, the salesperson can simply resume the sales presentation and patiently wait until the buyer again seems ready to place the order—either during the same presentation or during a later sales call. Salespeople should continue with their sales presentation when they encounter such caution signs as the following:

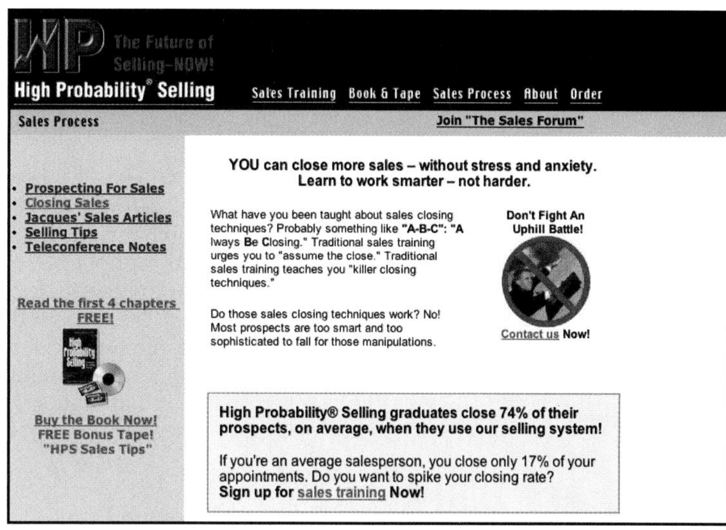

Reprinted by permission of High Probability Selling

- A trial close fails to elicit a positive response from the prospect.
- An interruption disrupts the prospect's frame of mind.
- Another objection or request for more information arises.

Salespeople can learn more about closing sales, as well as improve their sales closing performance ratio, by enrolling in skill improvement workshops offered by companies such as High Probability Selling (www.highprobsell.com/html/closing_sales.html).

Trial Closing Signals

Salespeople must learn not only *how* to close but also *when* to close, given the various "trial closing signals." A *trial closing signal* is a verbal or nonverbal indication that the customer may be ready to make the purchase. Positive *verbal* signals occur when the prospect asks specific questions about the product or says something positive about it, or when the salesperson does a good job answering a particular objection. *Nonverbal* signals occur when the prospect begins showing substantial interest in the product and in what the salesperson is saying and conveys this through positive body language. When salespeople notice a trial closing signal, they can immediately follow it up by using one of the closing techniques that we discuss later in the

Salespeople should be looking for verbal and non-verbal signals from customers that indicate it's time for a trial close.

Jeff Greenberg/PhotoEdit, Inc.

TABLE 8.1

Trial Closing Signals

Verbal Signals

When the prospect asks

- about product price, delivery, installation, or service.
- about any special discounts, deals, or special incentives to buy.
- a hypothetical question about buying: "If I do decide to buy . . . "
- who else has bought the product.
- what other customers think about the product.
- whether a special feature is included or available.
- whether the product can accomplish a particular task.
- the salesperson about one product version versus another.
- what method of payment is acceptable.

When the prospect says

- something positive about the product.
- that he or she has always wanted some special product feature.

When the salesperson

- successfully answers one of the prospect's objections.
- asks whether the prospect has any more questions and the prospect says no or is silent.

Nonverbal Signals

When the prospect

- begins closely studying and handling the product.
- tests or tries out the product.
- seems pleased by the product's performance or by some product feature.
- looks more relaxed.
- becomes more friendly.
- increases eye contact with the salesperson.
- looks over the order form or picks up the pen the salesperson has handed him or her.
- nods his or her head in agreement or leans toward the salesperson.
- begins to listen more intently to the salesperson.
- lends the salesperson a pen.
- picks up, fondles, smells, tastes, or closely studies the product.
- unconsciously reaches for his or her checkbook or wallet.

When the salesperson

- finishes the sales presentation.
- completes a successful product demonstration.
- hands the order form and a pen to the prospect.

Chapter Review Questions

What is a "trial close"? Give some examples of trial closes.

What verbal and nonverbal cues from the prospect indicate that it's time for a trial close?

chapter. Doing so often leads to an early sale. If not, just continue where you left off in the sales presentation. The verbal and nonverbal closing signals summarized in Table 8.1 should help you to recognize trial closing opportunities and to time your trial closes effectively. *It's Up to You*, on page 255, puts you in charge of a sales presentation. How would you handle the close?

IT'S UP TO YOU

You are a salesperson for a large industrial chemicals company. You arrive at a potential customer's plant just in time for an appointment with a purchasing agent, scheduled three weeks ago. You have prepared and practiced a brilliant one-hour sales presentation focusing on specific benefits that you think will overwhelm the agent and stimulate her to immediately buy $100,000 in chemicals from you. As soon as you walk into her office, the purchasing agent says, "I'm sorry, but I only have fifteen minutes to spend with you today. I've looked over your product brochures and I'm impressed. I've decided to place a $25,000 order with you." What do you do now?

PRINCIPLES OF PERSUASION IN CLOSING

In developing closing strategies for various buyer negotiating styles and buying situations, salespeople can benefit from at least a rudimentary understanding of the basic principles of persuasion, as outlined in Table 8.2. Any one or various combinations of these seven principles can be effective when used within the overall framework of a closing strategy.[6] As you read each principle, think about how you might make use of it now and when you become a salesperson.

TABLE 8.2
PRINCIPLES OF PERSUASION IN CLOSING

Consistency Principle. Prospects and customers want to be perceived as logical and consistent in thought and behavior; thus past thoughts and behaviors have a strong effect on future thoughts and behavior.

Application. When a group life insurance salesperson asks the prospect to agree on *each* of various reasons to buy group life insurance for the firm, such as the importance of financial planning for retirement, the need for a forced savings plan, or to provide family security in case of loss of income, the salesperson is building to the close using the consistency principle of persuasion. By gaining individual agreement to *each* of the advantages, the salesperson makes it harder for the prospect to turn down a group policy, because such a refusal would be inconsistent with earlier agreements.

(*continued*)

TABLE 8.2

Principles of Persuasion in Closing [continued]

Commitment Principle. Prospects' prepurchase efforts to learn about a product tend to increase their commitment to buying the product.

Application. A dealer who makes a special trip to a manufacturer's warehouse sale has taken action that is consistent with buying. The more effort the dealer makes to reach the sale, the greater the commitment effect and the higher the likelihood of buying.

Reciprocity Principle. Most cultures have a convention that if one person does something for a second person, the second person is obligated to reciprocate. Often, the reciprocated favor is even greater than the original favor.

Application. When a salesperson provides special services to a prospective account beyond "favors" extended by competitors, the salesperson is often rewarded with a large order that exceeds the value of the original service provided.

Social Validation Principle. Prospects are more likely to purchase a product when people (and companies) similar to themselves or their desired reference groups have also purchased it.

Application. Salespeople can increase the likelihood of the prospect's buying a product by providing product testimonials and stories from satisfied customers similar to the prospect and his or her reference groups.

Authority Principle. Prospects are more likely to buy from salespeople who are perceived as expert in their field.

Application. Salespeople with relevant expertise or even symbolic expertise can be effective in persuading prospects. Prospects often ascribe expertise to salespeople who look and act the part.

Scarcity Principle. As products become more scarce, they are perceived as more valuable and desirable. Thus the likelihood of persuading a prospect to buy increases if the product, the price, or the opportunity to buy are perceived as fleeting.

Application. Salespeople frequently use an "impending event" close, which consists of telling a prospect to buy now before something occurs that decreases or eliminates the availability of the product or the current price. "This low price is only good through this week, then the price goes up ten percent" or "These punch presses are so popular that this is the last one in stock."

Friendship Principle. Prospects are more easily persuaded by salespeople they like. Perhaps this is an offshoot of the consistency effect, because not to buy from a friend would be inconsistent behavior.

Application. Salespeople use this principle by ingratiating themselves with prospects. Four effective ways to promote liking are *similarity, praise, cooperation,* and *physical attractiveness.* Salespeople encourage prospects to like them by reflecting similar attitudes, backgrounds, hobbies, and lifestyles. Subtle praise or compliments are also effective. In team selling, a good-cop, bad-cop approach can be used, wherein one of the salespeople positions himself or herself as fighting for (cooperating with) the customer with a tough sales manager. Finally, salespeople try to maximize their attractiveness through grooming, dress, and personality.

Chapter Review Question

What are some principles of persuasion?

CLOSING TECHNIQUES

A wide range of basic closing strategies have been developed over the years, and the salesperson can tailor each to fit a particular prospect and his or her own personal selling style. Table 8.3 provides a reference tool for several effective closing strategies. This is not a comprehensive list, but it does introduce you to a reasonably extensive repertoire of useful ideas for closing sales, some of which will be appropriate for your selling style and for the selling situations in which you typically find yourself. However, take care not to limit yourself to just one or two different strategies. The more strategies you know and experiment with, the greater your chances for closing sales with a vast array of different buyers. When using any of these techniques, however, keep in mind that the response you receive from the prospect will determine whether you have closed the sale or whether you must continue the selling process and attempt another close later on.

The closing techniques can be categorized into five groups: clarification closes, psychologically oriented closes, straightforward closes, concession closes, and lost-sale closes.[7] Let's briefly discuss these strategies.

Clarification Closes

Clarification closes improve prospects' knowledge and understanding of the seller's offering or overcome their lack of clarity about it.

Assumptive Close. If the prospect shows a strong interest in your product, you may close the sale by expressing the assumption that he or she will purchase the product. This can be done verbally or nonverbally. These kinds of statements show a verbal assumption: "Should I alert our credit department to activate an account for you?" or "Will you verify your shipping address to make sure that the product is delivered precisely where you want it?" Taking out the order form, handing the prospect a pen and a completed order blank, or handing the product to the prospect indicates nonverbal assumption of the purchase. This technique can appear throughout the sales presentation in statements that make the purchase sound routine. For instance, a salesperson might say early on, "After you take delivery, you'll find that this product more than suits your needs." Repeating this kind of statement is likely to be reinforcing and quite persuasive, and it can seem encouraging and comforting to the prospect, thus leading to his or her favorable purchase decision. It makes the purchase seem so natural that not proceeding would seem almost illogical to the prospect.

Choice Close. Asking prospects which of two or more alternative products they prefer limits opportunities to say no. Questions that can help set up the choice close include "Which of these two chairs do you think would be more appropriate for your office staff—the Commodore model or the Executive?" "Will you want the five-year or ten-year service plan?" Sometimes referred to as the multiple options or alternative choice close, this method removes the

TABLE 8.3

Closing Techniques

Closing Techniques	Explanation
Clarification Closes	
Assumptive Close	Assume that the purchase decision has already been made so that the prospect feels compelled to buy.
Choice Close	Offer the prospect alternative products from which to choose.
Success Story Close	Tell a story about a customer with a similar problem who solved it by buying the product. Alternatively, provide satisfied customers' written or verbal testimonies supporting the product. Especially effective are endorsements from people well known and respected by the prospect.
Contingent Close	Elicit the prospect's agreement to buy if the salesperson can demonstrate the benefits promised.
Counterbalance Close	Offset an undeniable objection by balancing it with an important buying benefit.
Boomerang Close	Turn an objection around so that it becomes a reason for buying.
Future Order Close	If a prospect does not have a current need, but may have one in the future, the salesperson can ask for a commitment from the prospect to purchase at a future time.
If/When Close	Asking the prospect to provide a clarification as to *when* an order will be placed, as opposed to *if* an order will be placed.
Probability Close	Although seemingly comparable to the if/when close described above, the probability closing technique asks the prospect to assign a quantified likelihood of signing a sales contract in the near future.
Suggestion Close	Gets the prospect to accept the advice offered without giving it a great deal of thought. A salesperson could suggest that the many customers who have purchased the product have reported high levels of satisfaction, thereby suggesting that the prospect should purchase it.
Psychological Closes	
Stimulus-Response Close	Use a sequence of leading questions to make it easier for the prospect to say yes when finally asked for the order.
Minor Points Close	Secure favorable decisions on several minor points, leading to eventual purchase of the product.

(continued)

TABLE 8.3

CLOSING TECHNIQUES [CONTINUED]

Closing Techniques	Explanation
Standing Room Only (SRO) Close	Suggest that the opportunity to buy is brief because demand is high and the product is in short supply.
Impending Event Close	Warn the prospect about some upcoming event that makes it more advantageous to buy now.
Advantage Close	This variation of the impending event close emphasizes the specific advantages of making a timely decision, while still stressing a sense of immediacy.
Puppy Dog Close	Let the prospect use the product for a while and, as with a puppy, an emotional attachment may develop, leading to a purchase.
Compliment Close	Praise prospects for raising interesting and intelligent questions to flatter their egos and lead them to sign the sales order.
Reserve Advantage Close	In this slight variation of the advantage close described above, salespeople identify a number of merits for purchasing a product, but save a few to use if the prospect exhibits resistance yet again.
Dependency Close	Used to break the "choke-hold" that a competing firm has over a prospect's business by suggesting that the prospect needs an alternative supplier to reduce the risk of being dependent on one supplier.
Straightforward Closes	
Ask-for-the-Order Close	Ask for the order directly or indirectly.
Order Form Close	While asking the prospect a series of questions, start filling out basic information on the contract or order form.
Summary Close	Summarize the advantages and disadvantages of buying the product before asking for the order.
Repeated-Yes Close	This variation of the summary close requires a salesperson to pose several leading questions to which the prospect has little choice but to respond in an affirmative manner.
Benefits Close	Also a variation of the summary close, it requires the salesperson to identify and present a synopsis of the various salient benefits that the sales solution offers.
Action Close	The salesperson simply hands the prospect a pen along with the contract, and frequently the prospect, almost by reflex, will sign.

(continued)

TABLE 8.3

CLOSING TECHNIQUES [CONTINUED]

Closing Techniques	Explanation
Negotiation Close	Both the buyer and the salesperson negotiate a compromise, thus ensuring a "win-win" agreement.
Technology Close	The salesperson more impactfully and effectively summarizes key value-added benefits for the prospect by using technologies such as PowerPoint, Excel, or other multi-media tools.
Concession Closes	
Special Deal Close	Offer a special incentive to encourage the prospect to buy now.
No-Risk Close	Agree to take the product back and refund the customer's money if the product doesn't prove satisfactory.
Management Close	When salespeople do not have the authority to make the prospect's requested commitments or concessions, they can elicit the assistance of a senior sales manager who has the authority to make the necessary decisions to close the sale.
Takeaway Close	Used as an emotional fear appeal to cause anxiety that the prospect may lose out on a special deal or incentive. A salesperson could suggest that the special offer to provide an ancillary product or service free of charge is available only for another week, thereby evoking an immediate purchase.
Lost-Sale Closes	
Turnover Close	Turn the prospect over to another salesperson with a fresh approach or a better chance to make the sale.
Pretend-to-Leave Close	Start to walk away, and then "remember" another benefit or special offer after the prospect has relaxed his or her defenses.
Ask-for-Help Close	When the sale seems lost, apologize for not being able to satisfy the prospect and ask what it would have taken to secure the sale. Then offer that.

potential confusion of considering several products at once by narrowing the choice for the prospect. Furthermore, it omits products the prospect does not need and focuses on those most suitable. In essence, the approach narrows the prospect's choice of alternatives, thus making the buying situation less frightening and clearer for the prospect.

Success Story Close. Relating a story about how another one of your customers solved a similar problem with the product can reassure a prospect about buying now. A salesperson might say something like this:

> You know Al Rakowski, the purchasing agent for Superior Plumbing Supplies in Pebbleville? Well, Al was having a heck of a time getting packaging materials that would hold up in shipping some of Superior's heavier plumbing parts to customers. He tried every conceivable type of box offered by every packaging materials and container company you can name. When I heard about his problem, I told Al that I'd give him ten of our new reinforced "Tough Guy" brand containers to test by shipping Superior's most troublesome products to California and back. If our "Tough Guys" didn't hold up, I promised to pay the shipping charges. But if they did hold up, I wanted an order for five thousand. Well, when our "Tough Guys" came back looking almost brand new and the plumbing parts didn't have a mark on them, Al called me all excited and insisted on an order for ten thousand more. If you want to listen to a true believer in our "Tough Guy" containers, just give Al a call.

Contingent Close. Convincing the prospect to agree to buy if you can show that the product will do what you have said it will do is called a contingent close (or trap close). To set up this contingency, the salesperson might say, "If I can show you how your company can cut production costs by 20 percent without losing quality, will you buy?" By setting up this contingency, the salesperson has effectively closed the sale if the product claims can be substantiated.

Counterbalance Close. Prospects who raise a legitimate objection to buying the product can often be closed on that point of resistance if it can be counterbalanced with a benefit. The prospect may object, "Your company's automatic conveyor belt system is just too expensive for our warehouse operations. We'll just stay with our manual system." As a counterbalance, the salesperson might reply,

> Mr. Greenhaus, you said you were planning to add another person to your warehouse crew. How much will you pay that new employee in wages and benefits—$20,000 to $25,000? Well, our equipment costs only $14,500 fully installed, plus you'll increase warehouse productivity enough that you won't need to hire another person. You'll save over $5,000 the first year and more thereafter because our equipment won't demand a pay raise. I don't see how you can go wrong with it, do you?

Boomerang Close. In the **boomerang close,** the salesperson turns the prospect's objection or point of resistance into a reason for buying (recall Chapter 7). For instance, a prospect might remark,

Boomerang Close Turning a prospect's objection or point of resistance around so that it becomes a reason for buying.

> I like the looks and modern style of this automatic warehouse garage door, but it's so slow that it takes twice as long to open and

> close as our other warehouse garage doors. I'm afraid that our mechanics and customers will lose patience with its slowness.

The salesperson might truthfully counter,

> Yes, this new model opens and closes at about half the speed of the older models. I'm sure you know how dangerous these heavy garage doors are, and like most managers, you can probably tell some tragic stories about people being hit by them. Based on our study of these accidents over the past five years, we found that cutting the garage door speed in half would probably reduce the number of accidents by 75 percent. Warehouse managers who are using this new door say that it takes only a few days to adjust to its pace, and there hasn't been an accident reported yet. I think you'll find that the added safety more than compensates for a little slower operation.

Future Order Close. When a prospect does not currently have a need but may in the future, the salesperson can ask for a commitment to purchase at a future time. Although there is no firm guarantee for the order, the prospect's commitment provides a better indication of the likelihood of purchase, and the salesperson can ask the prospect's permission to follow up in a few weeks to inquire on the company's needs.

If/When Close. This closing technique is also used as a means of asking the prospect to make a commitment for a future order, which can indicate the probability of eventually obtaining the sale. In essence, this is accomplished by the salesperson asking the prospect to clarify *when* an order will be placed rather than *if* an order will be placed. The prospect can be informed that with this knowledge, the salesperson can "earmark" or set aside products from the current inventory to guarantee prompt delivery.

Probability Close. Although seemingly comparable to the if/when close discussed above, the probability closing technique asks the prospect to quantify the likelihood of his or her signing a sales contract in the near future. This technique indirectly elicits a commitment by asking the prospect, "What is the probability or chances out of 100 that my firm will receive the sales contract?" The prospect can be informed that with this knowledge, the salesperson can start the paperwork for manufacturing the product to reduce the lead and order cycle time, thus facilitating early delivery.

Suggestion Close. Use of this closing technique is often effective for prospects who are faced with making a selection from a wide array of products but have limited knowledge about the usage, features, advantages, and benefits that can be derived from each of the various products being considered for purchase. In these situations, the salesperson could use a suggestion close by getting the prospect to accept the advice offered without giving it a great deal of thought. For example, the salesperson could indicate that the many customers who have purchased his or her products have reported high levels of satisfaction.

Psychological Closes

These kinds of closes focus on the prospect's emotions, thus inducing a response from the prospect that is psychologically based.

Stimulus-Response Close. By steering prospects through a series of leading questions to which they almost have to answer yes, the salesperson builds a pattern of positive responses that helps the prospect make the purchase commitment. For instance, the salesperson might start with questions like: "You would like to increase the quality of your promotional brochures, wouldn't you?" or "You would like an energy-efficient air conditioning system in your office building, wouldn't you?" Then, follow with other leading questions. This approach to closing is common among inexperienced salespeople because it can be readily learned. However, because the stimulus-response closing approach is rather mechanical and requires little prospect participation except to provide positive responses, it can come off as condescending and insulting to more sophisticated buyers.

Minor Points Close. Starting with minor decisions, prospects are asked to make incrementally larger decisions until the sale is closed. Salespeople might start by asking, "Which size do you prefer?" "Do you like the stationary or the portable model?" "Are you interested in our service plan?" In answering these sequential questions, prospects develop an increasing commitment to buying the product. Focusing the prospect on minor issues/decisions is less difficult for both the salesperson and the prospect than focusing too soon on more major issues.

Standing Room Only (SRO) Close. By implying or showing that many others are interested in buying the product, a salesperson can put psychological pressure on the prospect to buy now (i.e., instill a sense of urgency). Although this may be an honest description of the competition for a high-demand product, the SRO close has sometimes been associated with questionable ethics. For example, some real estate salespeople have been known to deliberately schedule their appointments with potential buyers to overlap so that it appears that a lot of people are interested in the property. Seeing other buyers waiting to see the property can pressure prospects to make a quick decision to buy. In another situation, a salesperson may tell a buyer, "Companies have been snatching up these new cell phones the minute they lay their eyes on them. If you think your field supervisors will want them, I'd suggest you place your order now for the twenty, so I can put them on hold until Tuesday. That should give your people enough time to make up their minds, shouldn't it?" The SRO close is probably inappropriate or even unethical for most organizational selling situations, unless you can *honestly* state—and show—that the product really is in great demand. Remember: The level of trust a buyer has in a salesperson determines whether or not there will be an ongoing relationship.[8]

Impending Event Close. An early warning about a price increase, product shortage, or other event can show the prospect the advantage of buying now. Salespeople who give their customers timely information that helps them buy wisely and efficiently gain the trust and gratitude of customers. On the other hand, nothing irritates customers more than not hearing of upcoming price increases or product shortages or later finding out that they bought a product just before it went on sale. Never use the impending event close, which is also known as the doomsday close, in a dishonest, manipulative way. Salespeople who do so jeopardize all future sales to customers whom they have duped. Providing evidence of an impending event can enhance your credibility and increase the likelihood that you'll close the sale. For instance, one copier sales rep received a fax from her firm's headquarters noting that copier prices would increase at the end of the week. Seizing the opportunity, the salesperson took the fax to her prospects to alert them to the imminent price increases. As a result, several of her prospects took advantage of the lower prices by making their copier purchases prior to the week's end. By looking out for her customers, this salesperson improved her customers' trust and satisfaction with her and her company.

Advantage Close. A variation of the impending event close, this approach emphasizes specific prospect advantages for making a timely decision. Still conveying a sense of immediacy, but accentuating the positive, the salesperson may state, "The benefit of acting quickly is that your company can increase its competitiveness by buying at a lower price. Since we have inventory on hand, we can deliver the products promptly so you can start lowering your manufacturing costs."

Puppy Dog Close. Who can resist a friendly puppy dog? People who take a puppy into their home for a few days usually become so attached that they want to keep it. Similarly, when salespeople let prospects try a product in the office for a few days or weeks, they usually form an attachment that makes it difficult to return the product—hence the term **puppy dog close**. For example, an aircraft manufacturer's sales rep who has arranged for two or three trial uses of a corporate helicopter might visit the prospect's buying team afterward and say, "Well, your colleagues seem pretty pleased with our 'copter's performance. May I take that as a sign that you'd like to own the aircraft?"

Puppy Dog Close Letting the prospect try the product for a few days or weeks before buying, on the principle that most people grow attached to something they have for a while.

Compliment Close. With the compliment close, the salesperson praises the prospect for raising interesting and intelligent questions. The compliment close works especially well with those prospects who feel that they are experts and with those with large egos. Recognizing their expertise and praising them can flatter their egos and make them respond favorably by agreeing to sign the sales order.

Reserve Advantage Close. In this slight variation of the advantage close, salespeople identify a number of merits for purchasing a product but save a few for potential use if a prospect exhibits resistance yet again. For example, when facing a prospect's change of heart, a salesperson could point out that another advantage is that the firm also provides 24/7 on-site service support at no extra charge if the computer system breaks down or requires maintenance.

Dependency Close. The dependency close is used by salespersons who are attempting to break the "choke-hold" that a competing firm has on a prospect's business. In situations where a competitor has developed a long-term, close working relationship with a prospect, a salesperson might educate the prospect about the risks associated with purchasing all products from one supplier. By having an alternative supplier, the prospect will reduce risk by not depending totally on one company for supplies.

Straightforward Closes

Straightforward closes entail salespeople asking directly for the order.

The quickest way to express your nonverbal assumption of a close is to hand the prospect a pen and your purchase agreement.
Larry Williams/Corbis

Ask-for-the-Order Close. Also known as the direct appeal close or direct technique, an effective but sometimes overlooked close is simply to ask for the order in a graciously assertive way: "Let me use my laptop computer to order the product for you now so we can start solving your company's production line problems as early as next week." If you have done everything "right" in the PSP, this may be the best way to consummate the deal. One salesperson learned the importance of this close the hard way, as described in *On the Frontlines,* featured on our textbook website **http://college.hmco.com/pic/andersonPS2e.**

Online Study Center
Improve Your Grade

Order Form Close. Salespeople use verbal and nonverbal signals to gently pressure the prospect into buying. By asking the prospect a series of basic questions, such as inquiring about an address and telephone number or the correct spelling of a name, and writing the information on the contract, the salesperson leads the prospect toward the close. After the basic information is filled in, the salesperson hands the order form and a pen to the prospect and, in a friendly way, says something like "Okay, just sign on the dotted line there, please."

Summary Close. Also called the balance sheet, T-account, or Ben Franklin close (because of his rational approach to decision making), a summary close uses a simple analysis in the form of a T-graph to show the advantages and disadvantages of buying the product. It's usually best for the salesperson to assist but to let the prospect actually prepare the T-account so that it becomes the prospect's analysis, not the salesperson's. Seeing that the product's benefits far outweigh its costs usually leads the prospect to make the purchase decision. This method is particularly apt if negotiations have taken up several sales calls and many points have been addressed. Furthermore, this type of close helps offset the prospect's forgetting certain points and reinforces points that the prospect may have objected to earlier. Below is a T-graph prepared for a summary close involving the purchase of several laptop computers from a well-known manufacturer.

Notebook Computer

Advantages	**Disadvantages**
Large active-matrix LCD screen	Relatively heavy
Professional looking	No carrying case
Includes three-year warranty	
Large RAM and hard drive	
Latest software included	

Repeated-Yes Close. The repeated-yes close, which is a variant of the summary close, requires a salesperson to pose several questions to which the prospect has little choice but to respond in the affirmative. Specifically, the salesperson carefully crafts several questions, each identifying the value-added benefits that the sales solution provides. The prospect continuously responds with a "yes" to all questions leading to the final closing question: "Should we write up the order now?" This kind of close follows a formula that fairly sophisticated or experienced buyers readily pick up on, so it is seldom used for business-to-business negotiations. The repeated-yes close can make the salesperson come across as an insecure amateur following a canned selling formula, and purchasing professionals may find it insulting.

Benefits Close. A variation of the summary close, the benefits closing technique requires salespeople to present a synopsis of the various salient benefits that their sales solution provides. Because it is often difficult to memorize all the benefits of purchasing a product, the benefits close is especially suitable as the culmination of a selling process that has extended over a long period of time.

Action Close. Typically, the prospect is required to fill out an order form or sign a sales contract. Be very cautious with the terminology and how you ask for the prospect's signature on a contract because it can be misconceived as an overly aggressive attempt to "land the sale." Instead, a salesperson can simply hand the prospect a pen along with the contract, and the prospect almost by reflex will sign without either of you saying anything more at that point. If you do say something while performing the physical action, it's often best to substitute a euphemism for the word *signature:* "With your consent at the bottom of page 3, we can get the paperwork started and have the products delivered this week."

Negotiation Close. Landing a sales contract involves negotiations. The objective of the negotiation close is to find a way to ensure that both buyer and seller perceive that they are parties to a "fair deal." Both the buyer and the salesperson negotiate a compromise, thus ensuring a "win-win" agreement. For example, the salesperson could promise to expedite delivery of the products by two weeks, but in return, the prospect must agree to pay the added freight costs of using a faster logistics solution.

Technology Close. In conjunction with other closes such as the balance sheet or Ben Franklin close, salespeople can memorably and effectively summarize key value-added benefits for the prospect by using PowerPoint, Excel, or other multi-media wrap-up presentations. For example, salespeople might use Excel color charts and figures to demonstrate the economic benefits (e.g., revenue gains, cost reductions, productivity increases, market share increases, or whatever) that are likely to accrue from purchase and use of their products.

Concession Closes

When salespeople employ a concession close, they give something free to the prospect to entice her or him to make the purchase.

Special Deal Close. When the prospect remains hesitant to make the purchase commitment despite the salesperson's best efforts to close, a special deal may provide the incentive to buy now. The salesperson might declare, "If you'll agree to sign the contract, I'll call my boss to see if she'll approve delaying your first payment until January." Or "If you buy today, I'll include the one-year service contract for free." Avoid using the same concession with the same customer often; otherwise, the customer may buy the product again only if you repeat the concession offer. Also, this close requires caution. For instance, a young computer system salesperson tried to close a particular prospect by stating, "If you purchase the system today, I'll include additional memory at no extra charge." The buying committee shot back, "We don't need more memory. Just reduce the price of your system by the cost of the extra memory!"

Offering a **price discount** is a common way to close sales. Salespeople often are authorized to offer prospects and customers reductions off the standard list price for various reasons, including paying within a certain time, buying a large quantity, buying out of season, cooperating with promotional campaigns, and serving a designated function or role in the channel of distribution. Reminding prospects and customers of a price discount can often tip the balance toward closing the sale. Table 8.4 describes how different types of price discounts work.

Price Discount Any reduction off the standard list price of a product.

TABLE 8.4

PRICE DISCOUNTS

- **Cash discounts** reward buyers for paying the invoice within a specified time period. A typical offer to most organizational buyers is *2/10, net* 30. If the customer pays within ten days, 2 percent is taken off the total bill. No discount is given if the customer pays after the tenth day, and the entire amount is due within thirty days.
- **Quantity discounts** allow the buyer a lower price for purchasing in multiple units or above a certain dollar amount.
- **Non-cumulative discounts** (one-time): "I can let you have one for $530 or two for $950."
- **Cumulative discounts** (summary of annual purchases): "We offer a 4 percent discount on total sales over $5,000; for sales over $10,000, we offer a 5 percent discount."
- **Trade discounts** are given to middlemen (retailers, wholesalers, and distributors) for performing various functions for the manufacturer, such as breaking bulk, storage, financing, or transportation. "Wholesalers receive 40 percent off the list price, and retailers receive 30 percent off."
- **Seasonal discounts** are price reductions given to buyers who buy products out of season. "We're offering a 15 percent discount on all bathing suits ordered before March 15th."
- **Promotional allowances** are concessions in price given to customers who participate in a promotional campaign or sales support program. "We'll give you $2,000 on each order of one hundred to help offset your local newspaper advertising on behalf of our new line of cameras."

Source: *From* Journal of Personal Selling and Sales Management, *Vol. 19, No. 3 (Summer 1999). Copyright © 1999 by PSE National Educational Foundation. Reprinted with permission of M.E. Sharpe, Inc. All rights reserved. Not for Reproduction.*

No-Risk Close. Prospects differ widely in the degree of risk they perceive in various purchase decisions. Some professional buyers are especially fearful about making a mistake that costs their company a lot of money. One common way to alleviate the fear of making a purchase mistake is to offer prospects a money-back guarantee: They can get their money back if they are not fully satisfied with the product. A variation on this close is to let the prospect try the product with a free time-limited trial or small sample. Small trial-sized units and money-back guarantees are all methods to close sales by taking some of the risk out of buying.

Management Close. Frequently, prospects may be unconvinced to buy by the offered terms of the sale, yet remain interested to purchase if some additional conditions are met. The management close is appropriate when salespeople do not have the authority to approve the prospect's requested commitments or concessions, so they can elicit the assistance of a senior sales manager who has the authority to make the necessary decisions to close the sale.[9]

Takeaway Close. Another example of the concession close, although it could also be considered a psychological close, the takeaway close is designed to create prospect anxiety about the possibility of losing out on a special deal or incentive, thereby evoking an immediate purchase by the prospect. For example, the salesperson may say, "The special offer to install the printing press free of charge is only open for another week."

Lost-Sale Closes

When salespeople think they will lose the sale, they can still try a lost-sale close as a last-ditch effort to win the sale.

Turnover Close. In team-selling situations, when the prospect fails to respond to one salesperson's sales closing techniques, the prospect can be turned over to another salesperson with a different style and closing approach. Usually this method employs some plausible—and truthful—excuse, such as a meeting or telephone call, so that the prospect doesn't think that the first salesperson is upset with him or her. This turnover close may position the first salesperson as the all-business, unyielding negotiator, whereas the second salesperson is friendly and flexible. To make this switch in salespeople, the first salesperson might say,

> I'm sorry but I've got to run to a meeting now, but Neil Stacey—who's as knowledgeable as I am about desktop publishing systems—will give you more information and answer any questions you might have.

Pretend-to-Leave Close. When a prospect fails to respond after several trial closes, the salesperson can excuse himself or herself to do another task. Seeing the salesperson start to walk away, most prospects will let down their guard and may even feel disappointed to see the salesperson leave them. At that moment, the salesperson can suddenly turn around and come back to

ON THE FRONTLINES: THE LIFE OF A SALESPERSON

Confirming and Closing the Sale

"Exhilarated! That's how I felt when I landed my first sales order. But allow me to digress because my foray into a career in sales was a very "rocky road" and provides an important lesson of sorts. You see, before I started to make sales calls independently, I had received on-the-job training and learned crucial selling skills by accompanying my Dad, who is a master salesperson. Even after learning from the master, when initially I went out on the road alone, I experienced my own fair share of false starts. For almost three months I was not able to close a sale. Time after time I was told, NO, we are not interested, and that accompanied every excuse in the book for not buying. You have no idea how demoralizing that can be. I almost quit! But slowly and surely, I learned the nitty-gritty. Oh yeah, while I learned not to take 'NO' personally, my sales skill-set was also enhanced as I learned important negotiation strategies and closing techniques, which inevitably helped in improving my sales performance ratio," states Jason with a grin.

"Don't misunderstand. I'm not saying that closing sales is now easy for me. It is still nerve-racking and the anticipation of receiving the sales order causes a high level of anxiety that makes you fear that you'll blow the deal by saying the wrong thing in trying to close a sale. Similar to negotiating buyer objections, selecting *the* appropriate closing strategy is also highly situation- and prospect-specific in that there is *no* one single technique that's always more effective than another. However, I always gauge the prospect's readiness to buy with a trial close. This gives me an early indication of how difficult closing the deal is likely to be, and at this point, I often decide which closing technique to use. Very rarely do I use only one closing strategy—in fact, it's not unusual for me to employ a combination of two or three closing techniques, but they are all predicated on the early response I get from the prospect. It is important to bear in mind that each closing technique has its own advantages and disadvantages, so you have to be very judicious in choosing the right one or combination to seal the deal. On occasion, I have even called in the old master—my dad—to help close the sale. If I recall correctly from my college sales course, that's called a *management close*. But I'm never reluctant to ask for my dad's help to close a sale, especially one that involves a very high purchase value that our company cannot afford to lose."

"With respect to closing strategies, I have adopted some basic rules for myself. First and foremost, bear in mind that not closing a sale doesn't mean that I'm a failure. Seeing every missed sale as a personal failure has caused a lot of potentially good salespeople to leave the profession. If I don't successfully close a sale, I just review everything that happened during my presentation and the negotiations to see what I can learn from the experience so I can do better next time. My second basic rule is never to force a sale because buyers soon discover whether or not they really needed your products—and if they think you pushed products on them that they didn't need, you can kiss off that relationship and any future sales with them. All the efforts you put in over a long time to develop rapport and trust with a prospect can be destroyed in one transaction if you do something to break that bond of trust. I always try to keep in mind what's best for the long-run relationship with a prospect or customer because repeat sales and referrals to new customers are the big payoffs. I see myself as a sales professional, and I'm building relationships for the long haul."

Thinkstock/Getty Images

Ask-for-Help Close Even after the sale seems lost, the salesperson asks the prospect what could have been done to make the sale. Oftentimes, the prospect will give a previously undisclosed reason or objection, which the salesperson can then answer and secure another chance to close the sale.

Chapter Review Question

Describe as many as you can of the closing strategies discussed in the chapter.

tell the prospect about one final benefit or incentive to buy that he or she failed to mention. Catching the prospect off guard often leads to a successful close.

Ask-for-Help Close. Even after the salesperson appears to have lost the sale, another chance to close remains. At this point, salespeople can apologize to prospects for being unable to satisfy them, and then ask them what it would have taken to make the sale—the **ask-for-help close**. Thinking the salesperson has admitted defeat and merely wants to improve his or her selling skills by humbly asking for help, many prospects readily reveal their real objection at this point or what it would really have taken for them to buy. With this information, the salesperson can now deal with the real objection and offer whatever the customer says he or she wanted to close the deal.

In the *On the Frontlines* feature on page 269, you'll also learn about the various techniques and principles that Jason Smyczynski, our talented young salesperson whose daily activities we've been following, uses to close sales with his customers.

LETTING CUSTOMERS CLOSE THE SALE

Professional salespeople who strongly advocate win-win selling sometimes advise turning the tables on tradition by *letting the customer close* the sale. Most sales can't close until the prospect is ready to buy, and by that time, he or she is as eager to move ahead as the salesperson. It is in customers' best interests to close win-win problem-solving agreements quickly so they can start receiving the desired product benefits as soon as possible. As one salesperson puts it, "My hit ratio, in fact, is a lot better on major sales when I let the customer close than it used to be when I tried to trial-close him every sentence or two." When the proposed sales agreement is obviously a win-win situation, *customers* will often try to trial-close the salesperson by asking questions such as "How soon can I get the product?" or "What credit terms do you offer?"

To motivate customers to help close the sale, clearly show the product's added value in solving customer problems and increasing customer success. Successful closes depend on all the phases of the PSP from prospecting through sales presentation and resolving prospect objections. If each stage of the selling process goes well and blends smoothly with the preceding stage and the following stage, the prospect inevitably will help the salesperson close the sale.

SILENCE CAN BE GOLDEN IN CLOSING

According to some sales trainers, "Whenever you ask a closing question, shut up. The first person to speak loses." Why is it so important not to speak after asking a closing question? Because you have just hit the ball into the prospect's court, and the pressure is on the prospect to hit it back by answering your closing question and committing to the purchase. If you speak first after the closing question, the ball automatically bounces back into your court. One study found that more high-performing than low-performing salespeople use silence in closing.[10]

Now, it may sound easy just to remain silent for a few seconds, right? But this seems to be one of the hardest tasks for salespeople or anyone else. Let us say you ask this closing question: "Well, Mr. Thurstone, which model do you like better—the Mohawk or the Eagle?" If you remain silent, Mr. Thurstone is pressured to commit himself to one of the models and probably make the purchase. If you speak first, Mr. Thurstone can avoid answering. If you break the silence by saying, "Oh well, we can return to that decision later," Mr. Thurstone slips off the hook and you must set up another closing opportunity. Of course, professional salespeople avoid antagonizing the prospect by being pigheaded about using this close. If the prospect remains silent for a long time and shows no inclination to answer, then you must move on to another benefit that may lead to a different trial close.

CLOSING MISTAKES

Many sales are lost because the salesperson makes simple mistakes in the closing stage of the PSP. Every salesperson has made most types of mistakes at least once, but top professionals learn the fundamentals and make fewer mistakes than less successful salespeople. Some of the most common mistakes that hamper sale closings are outlined in Table 8.5. Read these over several times so that when your turn comes to close a sale, you'll avoid them.

TABLE 8.5

Closing Mistakes

Talking past closing signals: Salespeople can become so enamored of their sales presentation and demonstration that they don't stop until they've finished; they talk past several prospect closing signals, despite being aware of them. They then must spend more time reselling prospects.

Failing to recognize prospect buying signals: Salespeople sometimes fail to hear and see closing signals while they are making their sales presentations and demonstrations. If you miss a closing signal, the opportunity to close the sale must wait until another closing signal offers another opportunity.

Projecting a lack of confidence: Salespeople who don't believe in themselves, their products, or their companies will manifest a lack of confidence that prospects will pick up and mirror back with reluctance to buy.

Being reluctant to try trial closes on early calls: Every sales call is an opportunity to close the sale. Salespeople who make no attempt to close until the third or fourth call will often miss closing opportunities and may lose many sales to more assertive salespeople.

Inflexibility in using closing techniques: For every selling situation, the salesperson should plan alternative closing strategies in case the preferred ones don't work. Some salespeople, though, succeed with one closing technique and then fall into the habit of relying on it almost exclusively. No one closing technique is appropriate for all customers or for all times with any one customer. Professional salespeople learn to use an array of closing techniques, as the selling situation requires.

Giving up too soon: Persistence is an essential quality for the successful salesperson. Sales are rarely closed on the first sales call.

Lingering too long after the close: Generally, after a sale has been closed (the order form signed), the salesperson should make a polite but speedy exit. Lingering too long afterward can endanger a sale because the prospect may think of more objections that the salesperson cannot successfully negotiate.

Failing to practice closing skills: As with any professional, whether doctor, lawyer, entertainer, public speaker, or baseball player, the salesperson's skills can become rusty or sloppy habits can form unless considerable time is devoted to regular practice and improvement. Salespeople who rehearse the closing skills they are likely to need for each individual sales call have a significant advantage over salespeople who don't practice.

Failing to understand the need to close: Only the most naïve salesperson fails to understand that the close is an essential stage in the selling process. An outstanding sales presentation will not ensure that the buyer will buy. Unless the salesperson asks for the order through skillful use of trial closes, many sales will never be consummated.

Chapter Review Question

Outline several closing mistakes.

HOW DO YOU HANDLE SALES REJECTION?

If you simply cannot close the sale, you may well experience negative emotions. After all, you have expended effort to attain a highly desired goal but were unable to achieve it.[11] Nonetheless, you should not feel discouraged or personally rejected. Not even the best salesperson makes a sale every time. In fact, some sales success (or "hit") ratios can be markedly low, depending on the product, competition, and prospects.

No One Wins All the Time

Let's use a baseball analogy. In challenging activities such as closing sales, you can have a moderate batting average and still achieve great success. Ty Cobb stole 94 bases in 144 attempts during his best year, for a success rate of two out of every three. But it wasn't Cobb's success rate that made him a legendary figure. Another ballplayer, Max Carey, had 94 percent success one year when he stole 51 bases out of 54 tries. If Carey had kept up that ratio, he would have far surpassed Cobb's long-time record. But Carey didn't try often enough. The difference in the level of fame between Cobb and Carey points out that it's not how many times you *fail* but how many times you *try* that usually determines outstanding success.[12]

Learning from Sales Rejection

In his book *How to Master the Art of Selling*, Tom Hopkins argues that salespeople must develop positive attitudes toward sales rejection. Instead of failure, successful salespeople view rejection as:

TABLE 8.6

CONSTRUCTIVE WAYS TO DEAL WITH REJECTION

- Never equate your worth as a human being with your success or failure as a salesperson. Base your long-run opinion of yourself not on whether you win or lose, but on how honestly and fairly you play the game.
- Separate your ego from the sale. Prospects are not rejecting you personally. If a prospect doesn't buy, he or she simply believes that at this time the product fails to fit his or her needs or offer the best value for the money.
- Don't automatically assume that you or your selling skills are the problem. The prospect may be a difficult person or may be having a bad day. These conditions are not your fault.
- Move on to other prospects. When one prospect rejects your product, simply look in your prospect file for other promising prospects on whom you can call. The more prospects you have, the more confident you'll feel.
- Positively anticipate rejection, and it will not overwhelm you. Think in advance how you will respond to rejection.
- Remember that nearly all types of selling produce many more rejections than successes. Each rejection, however, tends to increase the chances of a success on the next sales call if you learn and make appropriate adjustments as needed following an unsuccessful sales experience.
- Recognize the possibility that the prospect may at this time have to refuse for various reasons, such as timing, shared decision making, or budget constraints. And realize that many prospects will feel uncomfortable revealing to you any reasons that reflect on their power.

Source: *Adapted from Tom Reilly, "Salespeople: Develop the Means to Handle Rejection,"* Personal Selling Power *(July-August 1987), 15. Reprinted with permission.*

- A learning experience that will enable you to do better next time.
- Negative but helpful feedback that will spur you to craft more creative approaches.
- An opportunity to develop a sense of humor and begin to lose your fear of future rejection.
- The motivation you need to spend more time practicing selling skills and improving performance.
- Just a part of the selling game that you must accept in order to continue to play and win.[13]

Chapter Review Question

Discuss some ways for a salesperson to deal with rejection.

Depicted in Table 8.6 are some effective means for dealing with sales rejection. Think about how you can use these right now in your everyday life and how you will employ them as a sales rep in the future. Table 8.7 shows ways to interact with a prospect who chooses not to buy from you.

TABLE 8.7

What to Do When the Prospect Doesn't Buy

Don't burn any bridges. Never show disappointment, frustration, impatience, anger, or any "sour grapes" reaction to the prospect. Future opportunities to sell the prospect are more likely to come your way if you are a good sport now.

Analyze lost sales. Review the selling process from start to finish to see what might have gone wrong or been improved upon. Be as objective as you can so that you benefit from this post-mortem.

Help the prospect shop the competition. If the prospect wants to continue to look at competitive products before buying, you can help him or her by outlining the specific criteria on which to judge the quality and overall performance of products in the category. You should, of course, have already identified your product's performance on these specific criteria for the prospect.

Call back with new information or appeals. Continue to keep the relationship alive by providing the prospect with relevant information, such as interesting articles on the industry, new-product introductions, special deals, or upcoming price changes.

Schedule another sales appointment. Arrange for another sales appointment whenever you have a new sales proposal or product in which you think the prospect might be interested.

Never give up. As long as a prospect needs your product category, don't give up on making the sale. Organizational and operational changes can quickly change buying criteria. Many long-term relationships and profitable sales arrangements have emerged after years of prospect refusals to buy.

Chapter Review Question

What should a salesperson do when the prospect doesn't buy?

IMMEDIATE POST-SALE ACTIVITIES

As we noted at the beginning of this chapter, a sale's close is not really an ending but the *continuation* of a buyer-seller relationship. Therefore, sales personnel must engage in special post-sale efforts.

Serving and Satisfying the Customer

During the immediate post-sale period, the professional salesperson has some critical activities to perform. As the following list reveals, these tasks include providing requisite service to the customer and ensuring that the customer remains satisfied with his or her purchase decision.

- Call or write within a few days to *thank* customers for their orders, reassure them about their purchases to relieve any dissonance or anxiety, and let them know that you are there to help them with any problems. Solving little problems for customers can substantially increase customer satisfaction and help further the long-run buyer-seller relationship. After a sale, some salespeople make it a practice to send customers a little "thank you" gift—including items such as candy, wine, flowers, fruit baskets, and tickets to the theater or a sports event.
- Check on your customers' orders to ensure prompt delivery. If delivery will be delayed, call the customers to warn them. Although such news is rarely welcome, customers will appreciate receiving advance warning that enables them to make appropriate adjustments in their operations.
- Contact the credit and billing department to confirm that they have the correct information on your customers' orders before sending out invoices. Few things irritate customers more than receiving and having to straighten out erroneous bills.
- Try to be present when the product is delivered to the customer. Assisting with installation and start-up will do wonders for furthering that long-run relationship. The customer will see that you are committed to providing a high level of service.
- Promptly update your customer sales records. Do so before you forget; then you'll be prepared for the next call. Include the latest sale, personnel or organizational changes, new problems and needs, purchase plans, or any other relevant developments.

Keeping the Customer Sold

After closing the sale, professional salespeople celebrate their success only a short time because they understand that keeping the customer sold can be as challenging and time-consuming as winning the order in the first place. Some salespeople draw an analogy between retaining a customer and trying to keep a lover who is continually pursued and romanced by others. You can't take either the lover or your customers for granted. You must work at pleasing

KEEPING UP ONLINE: E-MAIL

Nearly all companies today use e-mail. However, not everyone in a firm has his or her own private e-mail account. How can a salesperson send confidential messages to a person who must share an e-mail account? Although no e-mail guarantees complete confidentiality, you can ensure some degree of privacy with separate e-mail accounts. Visit the websites www.gmail.com and www.yahoo.com to see how you might organize your work e-mail to send and receive confidential messages to and from prospects and customers.

customers, making sure that they are satisfied with the current relationship, and doing everything you can to improve on it so that they are not tempted to leave you for competition. Ignoring your customers only serves to make them susceptible to competitors' efforts.[14] Even when the buyer-seller relationship matures into a partnership, the professional salesperson keeps up the tender loving care and continues to treat the customer like a new lover instead of an old spouse. Remember: Keeping your old customers is much easier and more profitable than winning new ones.

Chapter Review Question

List some immediately post-sale activities of a successful salesperson.

SUMMARY

The sales close is an integral part of the ongoing Personal Selling Process. A successful close confirms the sale and furthers the buyer-seller relationship. Salespeople should be prepared to use a trial close whenever during the selling process it is propitious to do so. Numerous verbal and nonverbal cues can alert salespeople to an opportunity for a trial close. Some salespeople fail to close because of insufficient confidence, feelings of guilt, or fear of failure. Successful closure usually takes several sales calls, so persistence pays off. Several basic principles of persuasion can be effectively applied within the framework of different closing strategies. The five basic categories of closing techniques are clarification, psychologically oriented, straightforward, concession, and lost-sale closes. No one succeeds in closing sales all the time, so salespeople must learn to deal both with rejection and with the prospect after a sale falls through. Professional salespeople have several tasks that they carry out immediately after closing a sale in order to satisfy customers fully and develop positive long-run buyer-seller relationships.

KEY TERMS

Close	Boomerang close	Price discount
Trial close	Puppy dog close	Ask-for-help close

TOPICS FOR THOUGHT AND CLASS DISCUSSION

1. Which do you think is a more appropriate term for stage 6 in the Personal Selling Process: closing the sale or confirming the sale? Why?
2. What would you say to a salesperson friend who must overcome low self-confidence, guilt, and fear of failure before attempting to close sales?
3. Which of the closing techniques in Table 8.3 do you think you would prefer to use in your professional personal selling career? Why?
4. Why is it often effective for the salesperson to be *silent* after attempting a trial close?
5. What would you do if a prospect didn't buy from you following the fifth sales call when you thought for sure you'd achieve a successful close?
6. Assume you have just made a substantial sale. What steps would you take to further the buyer-seller relationship?
7. What do we mean by "rejection"? Why are most of us so afraid of it? How do you personally cope with various types of rejection in your life?

INTERNET EXERCISES

1. Use an Internet search engine to find three firms that will train you in closing sales. What company is offering each program? Is the focus B2B selling, B2C selling, or both? What are the length and cost of each program? Where would it be held? Who's doing the training? What will the training cover that will be new?
2. Use Google or any other search engine to locate two examples of closing strategies being demonstrated using Flash or streaming video.

PROJECTS FOR PERSONAL GROWTH

1. Ask three business-to-business salespeople to explain their favorite closing strategies. Give each strategy a name. How many of them are discussed in this chapter? Do you consider any of the closes used by the three salespeople manipulative or questionable? Why?
2. Share stories with other members of your class about how you have recently used one or more of the seven basic principles of persuasion to negotiate something. Do any of your classmates have a favorite persuasion technique that they rely on most often?
3. Survey five people in different occupations about how they deal with rejection. Would these methods also apply to personal selling? Explain how.

ROLE-PLAY EXERCISE 8.1

Choosing the Best Close

Situation

Santos Perez sells luxury automobiles for Prestige Motors, a large dealership in Miami, Florida. He is demonstrating the latest model of the Infiniti automobile to Dominic Flores, owner of his own printing company. Mr. Flores is very impressed with the automobile and wants to buy it for use in his business, but he wants to know whether it's better for him to lease or buy and would like to look at the alternatives, if Mr. Perez can prepare that comparison for him. It's early on Friday evening, and Mr. Flores says that he has just stopped by on his way home from work and must hurry home for a dinner party tonight. "This weekend," he says, "my wife and I will be driving up to the University of Florida to see my oldest daughter, but I'll bring my wife in Monday evening to have a look at the Infiniti because she's a vice president of my company and will probably drive the car almost as much as I will. Anyway, I always want her approval whenever I consider buying a new car."

Roles

Santos Perez The top new-car salesperson for the Prestige Motors dealership, Santos prides himself on successfully selling a very high percentage of the prospects he negotiates with. His belief is that nearly every sale can be achieved if the closing strategy is appropriate.

Dominic Flores It seems apparent that the purchase of a new car is a decision that Mr. Flores and his wife make jointly for their business use, so she will have to be sold on the Infiniti before the sale can be confirmed.

ROLE-PLAY EXERCISE 8.2

Coping with Rejection

Situation

Carl Grimley has been a sales representative for Upton Meters, Inc., for six months. Although he has made several small sales, he has been working with the buyer for the City of North Bend for the past three months, trying to win a major contract for 10,000 parking meters. Carl was very excited about the possibility of winning this major contract and earning some substantial commissions. Although there were two other companies vying for the contract, Carl felt that his chances were excellent because he had made an all-out effort to provide a top-quality sales presentation and a written proposal at a very competitive price. This morning, Carl was shocked to hear from the city government buyer that the contract had been awarded to another company. Extremely upset, Carl called his sales manager, Grace Block, and told her the bad news. Hearing the disappointment in his voice, Grace suggested that they meet for lunch to talk over the situation.

Roles

Carl Grimley Facing the first major rejection in his young career in sales, Carl is facing a crisis that may cause him to get discouraged and quit.

Grace Block A former salesperson who understands what rejection can be like, Ms. Block knows that Carl may be at a critical decision point in his sales career, and she wants to do and say whatever she can to help Carl deal with this rejection.

CASE 8.1 TALK, TALK, TALK!

After working at Choi Company for four years as a supervisor in the shipping department, Fred Liska was recently asked whether he would like to be considered for a position on the sales force. Although he's been taking college courses at night for two years, Fred won't earn his degree for several years, so he jumped at the chance to become a sales representative for the company.

Mr. Choi, who started the company after emigrating from South Korea fifteen years ago, has always taken a special interest in Fred. He personally recommended him for sales because he thinks Fred's personality and conscientiousness will make him an ideal salesman. Although Choi Company has no formal training program for new salespeople, Fred had the opportunity to learn how to sell firsthand by spending three weeks traveling on sales calls with Pete Hayes, one of Choi Company's senior sales reps. Pete told Fred, "Just follow me around, and watch and listen. If you have any questions, save them until after each sales call."

Pete seemed to know all the people on his sales calls by their first names, and he spent as much time socializing as selling. Not once during the three weeks did he complete a full sales presentation, and he often failed to discuss some product features and benefits. Although it looked as though Pete mainly took orders instead of doing creative selling, Fred had to admit that Pete secured quite a few orders. In fact, during the three weeks, Pete received nearly every order he asked for—oftentimes even before he was halfway through a sales presentation. "Well," Fred thought to himself, "Choi does make the best instrument carts in the industry, so maybe they sell themselves."

Fred mentally rehearsed what he knew about Choi carts. They are made of sturdy welded steel with rubber-padded, nonconductive, nonslip surfaces and a heavy bottom shelf that helps protect against tipping or failing. Each cart has two swivel and two rigid rubber wheels for easy mobility while carrying up to 1,300 pounds of equipment or instruments. Attractively finished in gray enamel, the carts contain a utility drawer that can hold tools, supplies, and other small items. The price is $395.90 per cart, or $3,459 for ten.

On the first Monday after completing his three weeks of field training, Fred nervously approaches his first sales call. The prospect is Deborah Connors, purchasing agent for Scientific Laboratories, a Chicago-based firm specializing in conducting laboratory analyses for medical doctors. After introducing himself and handing Ms. Connors his business card, Fred begins his sales presentation. Because nothing is more impressive than seeing the instrument cart as it is being described, Fred has wheeled one right into Ms. Connor's office. As he is explaining some of the features, advantages, and benefits of the Choi instrument cart, Fred notices Ms. Connors moving the cart back and forth and feeling its surface. She pulls out the cart's drawer and smiles when she sees the neat little compartment trays inside. At this point, she interrupts Fred's presentation to say, "If we do decide to buy, how long will it take for delivery?"

Fred answers, "Two weeks," and continues with his sales presentation, showing several pictures of the cart being used at various types of companies.

Studying the pictures, Ms. Connors asks, "Will the Choi cart really carry 1,300 pounds? It doesn't look that strong."

Fred replies, "One of our largest customers, Metropolitan Hospital, regularly carries equipment weighing over 1,500 pounds on the carts without any problems." Fred thinks to himself, "If she doesn't quit interrupting, I'll never get through my sales presentation," but he doesn't let any irritation show and smoothly continues with the presentation and demonstration. At this point, Fred pulls out the special drawer with compartment trays and mentions that Choi is the only cart available with this feature.

Ms. Connors smiles and remarks, "Yes, I think putting those compartment trays inside the drawer is a really clever idea. I don't know how many times I've needed a test tube, some tape, or a pair of scissors when I'm carting laboratory samples and instruments from one room to another. We could keep basic supplies in those little drawers and save a lot of time and extra steps." Fred nods his head and continues to point out other features of the cart. He smiles to himself, thinking, "I'm almost done with my sales presentation. Nothing much left to talk about except the price."

Just then, Ms. Connors's secretary interrupts to say that Henry Bauman, the vice president of operations, needs to see her right away in his office. Ms. Connors excuses herself and says, "Ask my secretary to schedule another appointment with me, Fred. I know what this meeting with Mr. Bauman is about, and it's going to take the rest of my time today. Thanks for coming in."

Fred feels deflated. "Boy," he thinks, "what lousy timing. In two more minutes, I would have finished my sales presentation and started my close. I'm sure she would have placed an order when I asked for it." Dejectedly, he picks up his sales presentation materials, places them on the cart, and pushes it out to Ms. Connors's secretary's desk to schedule another appointment.

(continued)

Questions

1. Do you believe Ms. Connors would have placed an order when Fred completed his sales close? Why?
2. What do you think of Fred's sales presentation? What improvements would you suggest?
3. Could Fred have tried a trial close before Ms. Connors left for the other meeting? If so, what should he have said?
4. What advice would you give Fred for future sales calls?

CASE 8.2 SHE'S GOT PERSONALITY . . . AND A LOT MORE!

CASE 8.2 "SHE'S GOT PERSONALITY . . . AND A LOT MORE!" CAN BE FOUND ONLINE AT HTTP://COLLEGE.HMCO.COM/PIC/ANDERSONPS2E

CHAPTER 9

Following Up and Servicing the Account: Building Strategic Partnerships by Keeping Customers Satisfied and Loyal

After reading this chapter, you should understand:

- The different levels of buyer-seller interactions
- Why it's so important to keep customers.
- The concept of customer service.
- Customer service expectations, perceptions, and satisfaction.
- The importance of customer satisfaction.
- The 8Cs of customer loyalty.
- Why customer loyalty is critical for long-run profitability.
- Several important post-sale follow-up activities.

"Among businesses that thrive, merely survive, or die in the future, the critical difference will be how successful they are in achieving and maintaining customer loyalty."

Anonymous

INSIDE PERSONAL SELLING

Meet Barbara Bleiweis of Oracle Corporation

Barbara Bleiweis knows that an attentive, responsive salesperson can make a real difference for customers. As business development manager at Oracle Corporation, she is part of a sales team that sells sophisticated software for database management, online services, and other applications to government agencies and businesses. From first contact to final contract, an Oracle sale may take as long as 18 months. Throughout this period—and beyond—Bleiweis looks for every opportunity to personalize her service and add value "so customers and prospects know that I am committed to their success."

One way she builds strong relationships is by ensuring that all of the appropriate Oracle resources are available to answer questions and support the customer's needs, from the contract stage through project planning, implementation, and completion. Another way is by managing the tiniest details to smooth the way for each project's success. "Customers and prospects get my full attention," Bleiweis explains. "They appreciate that I handle even simple services such as finding a large conference room for a meeting on short notice and confirming the schedule with attendees." Her constant attentiveness reinforces the message that "I want to make sure you are satisfied with how things are going."

Because Oracle wants to create a long-term bond with its customers, the company not only trains its salespeople in customer satisfaction but also regularly conducts satisfaction surveys to obtain customer feedback and identify possible areas for improvement. Bleiweis welcomes this feedback, seeing any customer comments as opportunities to provide more service. "When customers have nothing to say, it means they believe you can't do anything more for them," she explains. When customers do have concerns, however, she tells them, "'This is what I am definitely going to do, this is what I think I can do, and this is what I definitely can't do.' I encourage customers to focus on me as someone who can help address their concerns and make a difference."

Recently, Bleiweis was part of an Oracle sales team competing for a contract to handle part of a U.S. government agency's $2 billion technology modernization program. Instead of making a highly structured, formal sales presentation, she initially focused on establishing a good rapport with agency management. "We wanted to make it a comfortable and collegial atmosphere," she remembers. Bleiweis arranged for Oracle consultants with special expertise to attend the meetings along with the Oracle sales team. As the discussions progressed from the agency's general needs to specific technical challenges that had to be overcome, the Oracle experts were able to suggest practical solutions. "Our involvement came across as constructive," she says, an involvement that solidified the relationship with Oracle.

You've closed the sale! Way to go . . . Congratulations . . . Great job! But your selling job is *not* over—in fact, far from it. Some salespeople believe that once they've closed the sale, their work with that customer is essentially done until the next time they make a sales call. Because they love the challenge and the thrill of winning sales, these salespeople tend to place little importance on post-sale follow-up efforts, preferring instead to move promptly to the exciting challenge of selling the next prospect. By neglecting current customers after the sale, however, these salespeople leave a lot of money on the table. Savvy professional salespeople know that after consummating a sale, their work with that customer is far from over if they want to go after a bigger payoff: the long-term customer loyalty that brings profitable repeat business at a relatively low cost. After the sale, top professional salespersons often shift into a higher "relationship gear" by focusing intently on providing post-sale customer service. Why? To ensure full customer satisfaction, build loyalty, and keep the customer's repeat business in order to maximize sales volume and profit over the longer run. Achieving customer loyalty has been called the Holy Grail of customer relationship management (CRM), which Kotler and Armstrong define as "the overall process of building and maintaining profitable customer relationships by delivering superior customer value and satisfaction."[1] Today's high-performing salespeople recognize the value to their companies and themselves of operating much like field customer relationship

FIGURE 9.1

THE PERSONAL SELLING PROCESS

managers. After all, salespeople are the ones who interact most frequently with customers and know the most about them, so who else in the company can do a better CRM job? Furthermore, one of the best ways to further long-term relationships with customers is through salespeople performing post-sale services that exceed customer expectations. As stressed in our previous chapters, customer service must be provided not just in the post-sale **follow-up** but *throughout* the PSP. Numerous customer complaints involve poor service, which is often the major reason for customers leaving. Excellent customer and prospect service should be a significant part of the salesperson's overall sales mission and should be regularly scheduled, just as sales calls are. In this chapter, we focus on follow-up and serving the account, stage 7 in the PSP shown in Figure 9.1— first as you should practice them during the Personal Selling Process as a whole, and then as specific post-sale activities.[2]

Follow-up Customer service provided not just after the sale is closed, but throughout the selling process.

THE NATURE OF BUYER-SELLER INTERACTIONS

As we have stressed throughout our discussions of the PSP, the overriding objective for business-to-business salespeople is to create, enhance, and maintain mutually profitable long-term relationships with their customers, leading to customer satisfaction and loyalty. As in social relationships, however, there are different levels of intensity in business relationships. Some customer relationships never get very far at all, whereas others become increasingly closer. Generally, the most successful salespeople are those who develop the highest level of quality relationships with their customers.

Levels of Buyer-Seller Interactions

In the process of conducting negotiations and transactions, buyers and sellers develop relationships with each other. Following an initial sales transaction, some of these relationships steadily improve, while others may dissipate. Oftentimes, the different post-purchase outcomes depend largely on the quality of customer service provided by salespeople and their support team. Essentially, there are three levels of buyer-seller interactions: (1) transactional selling, (2) relationship selling, and (3) strategic partnerships.

Based on a number of characteristics, these three levels can be viewed along a continuum of relationship interactions from merely transactional on the low end of the spectrum, to relationship selling in the middle, to strategic partnerships at the high end of the continuum. Tables 9.1, 9.2, and 9.3 present various characteristics that distinguish these three levels of buyer-seller interactions based on attitudinal, behavioral, and economic dimensions.

Transactional Selling. From Tables 9.1–9.3, it is easy to see that there are substantial differences in the relationship between buyers and sellers in the three interaction stages or levels. With its focus on discrete exchanges, transactional selling lies at the low end of the continuum, where buyer-seller interactions are determined primarily by short-term customer needs. Buyers and sellers reach a one-time purchase agreement without considering any future relationship. Thus the relationship may last only as long

TABLE 9.1

LEVELS OF BUYER-SELLER INTERACTIONS: ATTITUDINAL DIMENSIONS

Characteristic	Transactional Selling	Relationship Selling	Strategic Partnerships
1. Time Orientation	Short-term	Long-run	Very long-run
2. Commitment to the Ongoing Relationship	Low	High	Very high
3. Quality of the Relationship	Low	High	Very high
4. Mutual Trust	Low	High	Very high
5. Interdependence	Low	High	Very high
6. Perceived Relationship Equality	Low	Medium	Very high
7. Level of Relationship Bonding	Low	Medium to high	Very high
8. Level of Openness	Low	High	Very high
9. Level of Closeness	Low	High	Very high
10. Opportunistic Behavior	Very high	High	Low
11. Customer Service Expectations	Low	High	Very high

TABLE 9.2

Levels of Buyer-Seller Interactions: Behavioral Dimensions

Characteristic	Transactional Selling	Relationship Selling	Strategic Partnerships
1. Salesperson Objective	To sell products and services	To develop long-term relationships	To build symbiotic partnerships
2. Frequency of Customer Contact	Low	High	Very high
3. Negotiation Approach	Bargaining and competing	Collaborative	Highly collaborative
4. Mutual Cooperation	Low	High	Very high
5. Emphasis on Mutual Learning	Low	High	Very high
6. Potential for Sustained Relationship	Low	High	Very high
7. Emphasis on Shared Value Creation (e.g., new-product development)	Low	High	Very high
8. Shared Vision and Goals	Low	High	Very high
9. Level of Strategic Integration	Low	Medium to high	Very high
10. Quality of Communication	Low	High	Very high
11. Joint Problem Solving	Low	High	Very high
12. Customization of Products and Services	Low	High	Very high
13. Sales Closing Aggressiveness	Very high	Medium	Very low
14. Understanding of Buyer Needs	Low	High	Very high

as necessary to negotiate the sales transaction. There is no long-term commitment or loyalty involved. This type of selling assigns little value to understanding long-run buyer needs and expectations, satisfying customers, or achieving customer loyalty. A tacit, underlying assumption in this sales approach is that buyers and sellers negotiate in an arms-length, opportunistic manner that best advances their own interests. Interactions between buyers and sellers are much like competitive contests in which there are winners and losers. Salespeople operating with this philosophy clearly place their company's and their own interests ahead of their customers' and try to maximize revenue and/or profits on each transaction. Conversely, buyers have little interest in a long-term relationship with the seller, so they become

TABLE 9.3

Levels of Buyer-Seller Interactions: Economic Dimensions

Characteristic	Transactional Selling	Relationship Selling	Strategic Partnerships
1. Number of Transactions	Low	High	Very high
2. Monetary Value of Transactions Over Time	Low	High	Very high
3. Shared or Integrated Technology	Low	High	Very high
4. Concern for "Win-Win" Agreements	Low	High	Very High
5. Perceived Transaction Risks	High	Low	Very low
6. Mutual Profit Potential	Low	High	Very high
7. Cost of Switching Suppliers	Low	High	Very high
8. Reciprocal Buying	Low	High	Very high
9. Emphasis on Price Bargaining	High	Low	Very low
10. Level of Shared Expertise	Low	Medium to high	Very High
11. Information Sharing	Low	High	Very high
12. Level of Financial Investment in Relationship	Low	High	Very high
13. Emphasis on Customer Satisfaction	Meet some customer expectations	Meet all customer expectations	Exceed all customer expectations
14. Emphasis on Customer Loyalty (Retention)	Low	High	Very high

hard bargainers for the best possible deal. When buyers and sellers operate in this manner, there is little possibility of developing long-term relationships built on trust that lead to repeat business.

Relationship Selling. As management began to recognize that the costs of attracting new customers were significantly higher than the costs of reselling to current customers, the Personal Selling Process evolved from mere transactional selling to customer-centric relationship selling, as described in the voluminous literature on relationship marketing.[3] Along with this movement to relationship selling came a major paradigm shift in the overall marketing discipline, which, in 2004, finally compelled the American Marketing Association to officially redefine marketing as "*an organizational function and a set of processes for creating, communicating, and delivering value to customers and for managing customer relationships in ways that benefit the organization and its stakeholders.*" In contrast to the old definition, which tended to reflect seller perspectives and transactional approaches, the new definition of marketing shifts more toward customer perspectives and emphasizes relationships.[4]

Consistent with this new definition of marketing, our recurring focus throughout this book has been on developing with customers profitable long-term relationships that lead to higher customer satisfaction and loyalty. Loyal customers frequently become a company's best unpaid salespeople by referring other prospects and spreading positive "word-of-mouth" promotion.[5] To achieve and maintain customer loyalty is not easy, especially when competitors are continually upping the ante with special offers to attract your customers. It's the salesperson's commitment to providing highly satisfying customer service that is usually most influential in customer retention. Like the old banking adage that customers choose their bank for convenience but leave because of poor customer service, business customers who feel poorly served or neglected after a sales transaction are likely to start looking for alternative suppliers. Any relationship, whether social or business, requires regular attention and nurturing if it is to survive. It's a sad situation when a salesperson works long and diligently to win a sale but then foregoes potential repeat sales by neglecting customer service. Successful professional salespeople don't allow their customers to feel under serviced or neglected because they know that the highest revenue and greatest profits generally come from loyal, repeat customers. Even though there is considerable work involved in providing superior customer service, the effort and cost necessary to keep customers satisfied and loyal are usually considerably less than the effort and cost of going through the entire PSP to win a sale from a new prospect.

As shown in Tables 9.1–9.3, relationship selling has a long-term customer focus with the objective of developing cost-effective, high-value ties that generate repeat, high-frequency transactions. Characterized by high levels of trust, cooperation, and commitment to "win-win" sales solutions, relationship selling places emphasis on understanding buyer needs. Its ultimate objective is to achieve both customer satisfaction and customer loyalty by providing value-added customer service and sales support activities.

Strategic Partnerships. We've seen how relationship selling has replaced transactional selling as salespeople and their companies have recognized the value in developing profitable long-term relationships with their customers. But there is another, higher relationship level that can be achieved with customers: strategic partnerships. Strategic partnerships come about when the goals, strategies, and resources of buyers and sellers become so interconnected and intertwined that they develop an integrated, symbiotic relationship while still retaining their independent identities.[6] Using a romantic analogy, transactional selling is similar to the "dating stage," relationship selling is like the "engagement stage," and a strategic partnership best resembles a "symbiotic, cohabiting relationship" where the success of one partner enhances the success of the other. It would be misleading to use a marriage analogy in talking about strategic business partnerships because they still maintain their independent company identities. Unlike a marriage, where the partners legally become one and intend to stay together for life "in sickness and in health," strategic business partners do *not* fully merge and become a single company.

Strategic partnerships and other inter-firm collaborative arrangements have become commonplace in today's global economy. As companies increasingly specialize, they are moving away from rigid, control-based structures and adopting more flexible, relationship-based partnering arrangements that capitalize on the relative strengths of each partner. Moreover, many companies have re-engineered their business processes to create coalitions and partnerships with their customers' companies, thus developing tightly interwoven and interdependent value chains.

Completely antithetical to the highly competitive interactions among companies, strategic partnerships lie at the opposite end of the continuum and are based more on interorganizational *cooperation* than on arms-length aggressive bargaining. One of the major reasons for creating strategic partnerships is to circumvent trying to excel at performing all the complex business functions necessary to succeed in global competition. Companies that skillfully establish collaborative, strategic partnering agreements can share expertise and resources to shore up weaknesses and capitalize on strengths, thereby making both partners stronger.[7] As the traditional "old-school" transaction-oriented perspectives make their exit, strategic partnerships for managing business and customer relationships have moved to center stage. Some key characteristics of this highest form of buyer-seller relationship are shown in Tables 9.1–9.3. They include continuous, recurring exchange transactions, very high levels of communication, relationship openness, closeness, information sharing, joint problem solving, strategic integration, and mutual learning,[8] but extremely low levels of opportunistic behavior. Additionally, strategic partnerships manifest extremely high levels of collaboration (cooperation) among partners, equality, shared vision, benefits and goals, and very high levels of trust. Trust is central to developing strategic partnerships, and trust-building behaviors are discussed in chapter 12.

Forward-thinking salespersons will proactively anticipate how they can build, manage, and sustain their buyer-seller relationships well into the future.[9] To build relationship closeness and longevity successfully, salespeople must continually provide new high-value-added customer service that will not only meet but exceed customer expectations and bring about *full* customer satisfaction. As we learned earlier, totally satisfied customers are up to six times more likely to become loyal than are less satisfied, customers.[10] Once customer loyalty has been achieved, it is not such a big step to set up a buyer-seller strategic partnership. Sun Microsystems (www.sun.com) is an example of a firm that has developed strategic partnerships. Sun has developed strong brand identity and is known as a key technology provider that manufactures server hardware, workstations, and storage devices. Although it has a professional services division that provides implementation expertise for Sun products, it does not try to develop computer solutions for customers by itself. Instead, Sun salespeople partner with software vendors and system integrators; then, as a team, they provide complete technology solutions for their customers. Because Sun almost never takes a "prime contractor" role, it does not compete but cooperates with its partners.[11] Visit the website

Reprinted by permission of Ten3 Business e-Coach, www.1000ventures.com

www.1000ventures.com/business_guide/mbs_mini_partnerships.html to review articles, case studies, and slide shows on developing strategic partnerships, which will augment your understanding of this "cutting edge" business philosophy.

Having set the stage by reviewing the evolution of buyer-seller interactions and relationships, let's now turn to the roles of customer service, customer satisfaction, and customer loyalty in building successful buyer-seller relationships.

Chapter Review Question
Identify and discuss some of the key characteristics that distinguish the three levels of buyer-seller interactions.

WHAT IS CUSTOMER SERVICE?

As new-product life cycles shorten and products become increasingly like commodities across nearly all categories, customer service remains one of the best ways to differentiate your company's products and gain competitive advantage. **Customer service** is the performance of value-added activities designed to enhance and facilitate the sale and fully satisfying use of a product before, during, and after the sale. It can include a wide array of activities, such as providing product information, technical assistance, order processing, timely delivery, installation, maintenance, and repair of products ranging widely from photocopiers to printing presses to jet engines. Companies such as Dell (www.dell.com) have grown rapidly by enhancing the total customer experience through 24/7 customer support and service.

Customer Service The performance of a broad spectrum of value-added activities designed to enhance and facilitate the sale and use of a product.

When scheduling their daily sales calls, top-performing salespeople also schedule customer service activities because they know their importance to customer satisfaction and retention. High-quality customer service can be a powerful way to build goodwill and engender trust because it shows that the salesperson is not an opportunistic, self-serving, "fly-by-night operator" but a professional who nurtures a long-run relationship with the customer. Superior customer service requires salespeople to make regular service calls on customers, not to pursue additional orders but to ascertain how well purchased products and services are meeting the customers' expectations. Sometimes, a salesperson's service call can identify an opportunity to replace a customer's current supplier who is not providing satisfactory service. Following up and servicing the account is sometimes misconceived by salespeople and their companies as an expense-incurring, non-revenue-generating activity and thus something to minimize. More realistically, customer service is an investment in customer retention and future sales. Providing superior customer service is probably the most effective and efficient strategy for increasing customer satisfaction and customer loyalty, which usually translate into repeat purchases, increased revenues, and higher profits.

Service Creates Sales

Professional salespeople realize that many customers buy on the *promise* of a great product and service, but it's the actual *performance* of great service that persuades them to become repeat customers. You shouldn't promise more than you can actually deliver, because customers have long memories—especially when promises aren't kept. The Strategic Planning Institute in Cambridge, Massachusetts, through its *PIMS (Profit Impact of Market Strategy)* program, analyzed the performance of 2,600 companies over fifteen years. Its studies show that the companies that customers perceive as having the highest quality also tend to garner the highest results by almost any financial measure—sales, market share, asset turnover, or return on investment.[12]

Satisfied customers tend to be loyal and provide the stable sales base that is essential to long-term profitability. The *PIMS* database reveals that those companies rated high on customer service are able to charge an average of 9 percent more for their products and grow twice as fast as companies rated poorly.[13] A pattern of one-time buyers is a warning signal that customer expectations are going unmet.

Many industrial firms specialize in providing superb customer service. For example, superior service enables Weyerhaeuser Company's (www.weyerhaeuser.com) wood products division to charge a healthy premium for its commodity two-by-four lumber. Weyerhaeuser developed a computer system for retail home centers and lumberyards that allows homeowners to custom-design their own decks and other home building projects. Premier Farnell (www.premierfarnell.com), a distributor of industrial parts in Los Angeles, charges up to 50 percent more than competitors for every one of the 250,000 items it sells. Premier commands such premium prices through superb customer service. When a Caterpillar (www.caterpillar.com) tractor plant in Decatur, Illinois called Premier to replace a ten-dollar electrical relay that had stopped an entire production line, a Premier sales representative found the part and rushed it to the airport for a flight to St. Louis, where another Premier sales rep took it to Decatur. By 10:30 that night, the Caterpillar production was running again. This is the kind of superior service that customers are willing to pay extra for.

Training Salespeople in Customer Service

The best companies continually train, motivate, and reward their salespeople for providing superior customer service. For instance, a large seller of computerized services to health care organizations requires all of its salespeople to take three weeks of sales and customer service training each year. Service quality is often an integral part of the reward system for sales and service people, as illustrated in the *From the Command Post* feature Customer Service Pays, which can be found on our textbook website **http://college.hmco.com/pic/andersonPS2e.**

Online Study Center
Improve Your Grade

Building Long-Term Customer Relationships Through Service

Providing a high level of service to customers increases the value that products provide and can strengthen the buyer-seller relationship. After all, adept customer service sends a strong signal to customers that they committed precious company resources to the right purchase decision. Salespeople can increase the value their products provide through a variety of activities. In the *On the Frontlines: The Life of a Salesperson* feature on page 292, you'll read about Jason Smyczynski's thoughts on customer service, satisfaction, and loyalty, along with the customer service strategies he uses to forge long-term buyer-seller relationships.

Value-Added Activities. First, service-oriented salespeople can urge their companies to simplify ordering procedures for customers by online computer entry or fax-order entry, or by personally taking orders from customers. Second, a salesperson can find ways to help the customer become operational quickly and efficiently. This includes arranging for special packaging or coding on boxes; just-in-time (JIT) delivery; helping the customer receive, handle, store, or transfer products; and training the customer's staff to use the new products. For instance, Fastenal Company (www.fastenal.com), the nation's largest distributor of nuts, bolts, and similar products, operates 980 stores for factories and commercial builders. As part of its customer service, it will manage the hardware-parts inventory for its customers.[14]

Salespeople can also assist customers in producing, marketing, and distributing products to their own customers. Other services include minimizing downtime by securing replacement parts quickly and obtaining swift resolution of customer complaints. Even periodically sending customers thoughtful little reminder gifts, such as pens, calendars, notepads, and other advertising specialties with the company logo on them, or cards for special occasions, such as birthdays, wedding anniversaries, and holiday greetings, can give the salesperson a perceived service edge on competitors. Customers like to think they're appreciated, and thoughtful efforts can make a tremendous difference in their perceptions of service.

Service Differentiation. *Customer service strategy* calls for segmenting customers on the basis of their desired level of service and then identifying those service segments that can be served at a profit. Whereas market segmentation focuses on what people and organizations *need,* **customer service segmentation** focuses on what they *expect.* To segment customers effectively,

Customer Service Segmentation A strategy for grouping customers with similar service expectations into service segments and then developing a service plan for each segment.

ON THE FRONTLINES: THE LIFE OF A SALESPERSON

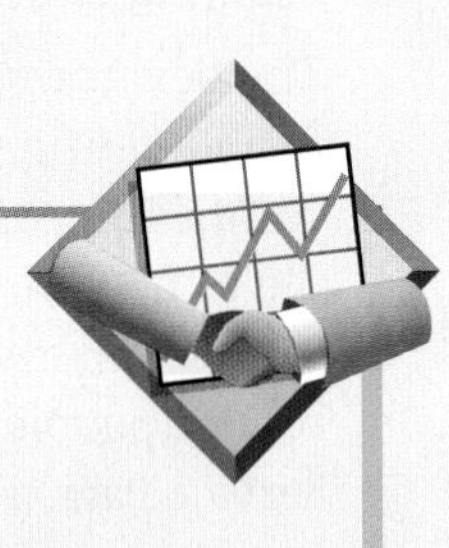

Using Customer Service to Increase Customer Satisfaction and Customer Loyalty . . . and to Build Partnerships

"One of my major personal discoveries as a fledgling salesperson was that winning or closing a sale is not the end of my relationship with that customer for a long while . . . or even the end of that transaction," declares Jason. "If handled right, the sales close can be like Captain Renault [Claude Rains] said to Rick Blaine [Humphrey Bogart] in *Casablanca*: 'the start of a beautiful relationship.' Developing fully satisfying long-term relationships with your customers so that they want to keep buying from you is the name of the game today. And the buyer-seller relationship becomes even more important and intense after the sale because that's when the customer starts assessing how the product performs, what support services you provide, and how you deal with complaints or problems. If you or your company falls down in one or more of these areas, the relationship with the customer is in jeopardy, especially if the customer has high expectations in each of these areas. Some salespeople think of customer service as a waste of their time because it keeps them from selling. I've even heard one of my sales colleagues at another company say that his sales manager wants him to cut back on customer service because it costs money and reduces profits. How short-sighted is that? I see customer service as an investment in future sales with my customer. One of the things I learned very early in my selling career is that it is a lot more expensive to find new customers than to resell to current customers. Now don't get me wrong—finding new customers is very important—but providing superior customer service takes a lot less effort and costs a lot less than going through the entire selling process with a new prospect who may or may not buy. When customers see you calling on them not just to sell something but to find out whether the products you've already sold them are performing as expected and, more important, adding to their "bottom line," they begin to view you as someone who really cares about them. From my dating days, I learned that nothing builds a relationship faster than showing someone that you care for her. Well, it's the same way in business relationships. I view customer service as one of my best sales tools. By investing in customer service now, I'll receive a big payoff down the road," Jason states emphatically.

When asked about his views on customer satisfaction and loyalty, Jason readily responds in his typical confident, animated way: "It's really competitive out there in most markets. Everybody's hustling to find new ways to sell more products—and, of course, earn higher profits. In my opinion, one of the simplest ways to increase sales is to provide exceptional customer service so that your customers become loyal repeat buyers. Then, as they succeed and grow, your sales to them keep growing, too. Every quality service you provide for your customers adds another link in the value chain that connects you closer with them. Over and over, I've seen how services that surpass customer expectations generate higher customer satisfaction and customer loyalty—and sometimes even partnerships where you and your customer work together on strategic plans and strategies. Of course, not all customers want the same high level of service, so you first need to find out what kind and how much service each of your customers wants. Then, depending on the customer's relative value or profitability to your company, you try to

(*continued*)

meet or exceed their service expectations. You can't separate customer service from company profits, so there's always a trade-off necessary to ensure that a customer that demands a high level of service will remain profitable if that service level is provided over the long run.

"Customer service is really my 'ace in the hole' when going against competitive products that often are priced lower. My customer service edge gives me confidence against any competitor. After I spell out the services that my company and I will provide the prospect, the perceived added value of my offer usually soars to the top . . . and I win the sale. After that, it's my responsibility to make sure I deliver on my promises and satisfy the customer's service expectations. As Yogi Berra said, 'It ain't over 'til it's over' . . . and it's never over when customers expect continuing exceptional customer service," winks Jason with a sheepish grin.

it is necessary to find out how much they value different levels of service and then to estimate the costs and benefits of providing the desired service. Service level expectations normally correlate closely with the dollar amount of the sale. Rolls Royce (www.rolls-roycemotorcars.com) and Mercedes (www.mercedes-benz.com) automobile manufacturers provide whatever service their customers want, including 24-hour roadside assistance. Premium-priced shipping firms such as United Parcel Service (www.ups.com) and Federal Express (www.fedex.com) provide similar kinds of high-level service.

Customer service expectations can be greatly influenced by seemingly minor visible cues, such as the personal grooming of the service providers and the quality of their uniforms; the appearance of brochures describing the service; the age and condition of service trucks and equipment; the friendliness, professionalism, and courtesy of service personnel; and the product's temporary packaging or wrapping after it has been purchased or serviced. Customers tend to have a higher opinion of a product's quality and its supporting service when special attention is paid to the service *presentation,* such as well-groomed IBM (www.ibm.com) repair technicians dressed in business suits or the expensively decorated office of a law firm. For example, after promoting a guaranteed private room and home-like environment for expectant mothers, St. Joseph's Hospital in St. Paul, Minnesota, saw obstetrics admissions jump 10 percent.

Chapter Review Question
Why should customer service markets be segmented?

Extra service cannot be stored in inventory, so some idle capacity is always required to accommodate sudden increases in demand. But service quality drops off sharply when demand considerably exceeds the theoretical capacity. Whenever customer service demands exceed capacity, salespeople should give their best customers first priority and cut back on service to less valued customers. Service organizations ranging from popular restaurants to fuel oil companies often do this by seating preferred customers first during prime dining hours, say, or supplying loyal customers first when unexpectedly cold weather increases demand for fuel oil.

Product and Service Quality

Product Quality
Perceived performance of the tangible product in satisfying customer expectations.

Quality consists of two components: product quality and service quality. **Product quality** is the degree to which the product offered performs as

Service Quality Expected and perceived quality associated with an intangible product. All activities supporting the sale, from the initial contact through the post-sale servicing, that meet or exceed customer expectations and enhance the value of a product.

promised. It is concerned with the perceived performance of the tangible product in satisfying customer expectations. **Service quality** is more difficult to define or measure, because services have unique characteristics that distinguish them from tangible products. Services are perishable, have greater variability, and are produced and consumed simultaneously, so their intangible performances, such as experience or credence, cannot be assessed until after use. For example, medical, insurance, travel, restaurant, education, and consulting services can be fully assessed only after the service is performed, and even then the evaluation can be very subjective because people perceive service performance uniquely.

Chapter Review Question

Name and define the five dimensions of customer service quality. Which one of these dimensions do customers perceive as the most important?

In general, services include all the activities that *support* the sale, from the initial contact through the post-sale servicing, and the quality of services reflects the *degree* to which these activities meet or exceed customer expectations and enhance a product or service's value. Service can include product information, technical assistance, financing, order processing, delivery, installation, maintenance and repair, parts availability, and attitudes of service personnel as perceived by prospects and customers.

Being intangible in nature, the service quality, as perceived by the buyer, can be enhanced by emphasizing attributes of services. Various studies reveal that service quality is determined by the following five dimensions:[15]

- *Reliability*—the ability to perform the desired service dependably, accurately, and consistently.
- *Tangibility*—the physical facilities, equipment, and appearance of sales and service people.
- *Responsiveness*—the willingness to provide prompt service and help customers.
- *Assurance*—employees' knowledge, courtesy, and ability to convey trust and confidence.
- *Empathy*—the provision of caring, individualized attention to customers.

Reliability Ability to perform the desired service dependably, accurately, and consistently; the single most important component of customer service.

Salesperson **reliability** is the single most important factor for about half of all customers surveyed.[16] Customers must have confidence that the expected service will be delivered accurately, consistently, and dependably. One model of service quality stresses that there are often gaps between the services that customers want and what they perceive they are receiving.[17] Therefore, it is important that salespeople readily identify any gaps between customer service expectations and their perceptions of performance—so that these gaps can be filled in promptly. Savvy salespeople ask their customers on each post-purchase sales call whether the purchased products and services are meeting expectations and, if not, what needs to be done.

Perceived Service Quality The quality of service individual customers believe they deserve and expect to receive relative to what they actually perceive receiving.

Perceived Customer Service Quality and Customer Satisfaction

In most competitive industries, producers eventually offer similar product quality, so the *real* competition boils down to service quality and, beyond this, to **perceived service quality.** FedEx (www.fedex.com) defines service as "all actions and reactions that customers perceive they have purchased."[18] Most companies have general customer service policies, but *perceived* service quality reflects the quality of service that individual customers *believe* they deserve and expect to receive relative to what they actually perceive receiving. Salespeople, as the single most important part of the company's prospect and customer service program, must be sensitive to each individual prospect's and customer's service demands and expectations.

Salespeople should be on hand when the customer's equipment order is delivered to ensure proper installation and correct usage.
Roger Tully/Getty Images

When it comes to perceived service quality, salespeople essentially must deal with four basic kinds of prospects and customers, and each type pulls them in a different direction. For simplicity, we can categorize customers as either good (profitable, cooperative) or bad (neither very profitable nor cooperative) and as either demanding or not demanding lots of service. How do you serve these four different types of customers? Here is some advice:

- *Good customer/Lots of service:* Working extra hard to please this customer should be a joy for you. But, you cannot provide so many services as to make the account unprofitable.
- *Bad customer/Lots of service:* You may eventually have to speak with your sales manager about this customer, but look to yourself first. Are you providing the wrong kinds of service to the wrong people in the organization? If the customer was once "good" and then turned "bad" (stopped buying or paying bills), find out why. You may be able to save the situation.
- *Good customer/Little service:* Nothing wrong with this situation, right? Wrong! Are you constantly monitoring the service situation with this customer, making sure that the appropriate people in the organization receive the products and services they need? Beware of complacency; competition is waiting in the wings.
- *Bad customer/Little service:* Once again, you should look to yourself first. Is the customer "bad" because you have not been providing appropriate services to the appropriate people? Speak with your sales manager about the potentially salvageable situation, too.

Rising customer service expectations and a decreasing tolerance for poor service are expected to have the greatest impact on salespeople's effectiveness in the years ahead. Service quality depends on *customer perceptions,* not on what the seller thinks. Technical Assistance Research Programs Institute (TARP) (www.tarp.com) found that on average, one out of every four customers dissatisfied with customer service switches suppliers. More than

KEEPING UP ONLINE: THE DIGITAL ROUTE TO CUSTOMER SALES AND SERVICE

Despite the financial problems that enveloped many organizations at the start of the 21st century, several companies are still successfully marketing their wares. Maybe it's not "like the good old days," but these companies have not succumbed to economic and business malaise. Instead, these companies are obtaining digital help to continue an unremitting commitment to building customer relationships and providing a high level of customer service to maintain those relationships.

Beyond serving as an additional selling tool, websites are a convenient and easy-to-use means of servicing customers. For example, websites enable customers to track the status of their orders, retrieve billing information, and obtain answers to their questions about technical problems. By giving customers direct access to such information, these websites free up salespeople to spend more time in face-to-face selling and developing closer relationships with prospects and customers.

Websites offer substantial benefits for sellers. Receiving website hits and inquiries can enhance prospecting efforts, reduce selling costs, and translate into substantial sales revenue. And, not least, employing a website as a supplemental service provider can reduce a firm's need for service personnel and technical support engineers. Digital sales and digital service are a "win-win" for both buyers and sellers. Apple Computer (www.apple.com), Hewlett-Packard (www.hp.com), Toshiba (www.toshiba.com), and Sony (www.sony.com) are examples of companies that use websites to sell their products as well as to provide a wealth of customer support information electronically.

If you were a salesperson working for Dell or IBM selling enterprise solutions to other businesses that need mid-sized to large computers and data storage servers, how would you use the Internet to find information about the different range of computers that you could offer for sale to your organizational customers? Can you demonstrate to your prospect how you can go online to order a complete enterprise solution using the Internet and determine the price for the different enterprise solutions? Can you show your prospect how to keep track of the order delivery status? How would you demonstrate that your prospect can readily find information to resolve minor problems that might arise? Try to find answers to these questions by perusing the Dell (www.dell.com) and or IBM (www.ibm.com) websites.

Chapter Review Questions

Define and explain the meaning of customer service.

What characteristics of intangible services make them diffferent from durable products?

What most influences customer perceptions of a company's overall quality?

90 percent of these unhappy customers will never again buy from that company and will tell at least nine other people about their negative experience.[19] These results suggest why many executives consider "service quality" one of their chief business concerns. Visit TARP's website (www.tarp.com), where you can find various white papers and case studies to learn more about customer satisfaction and customer loyalty.

Customers have certain overall expectations for service quality, influenced by their past experience, personal needs, advertising, and word-of-mouth information. *Customer satisfaction is generally assured when the seller meets or exceeds the customer's expectations for perceived service quality.* If a gap exists between what they expect and what they perceive they receive, (i.e., they think they are getting less than they expected), customers are usually disappointed in the quality of the service).[20]

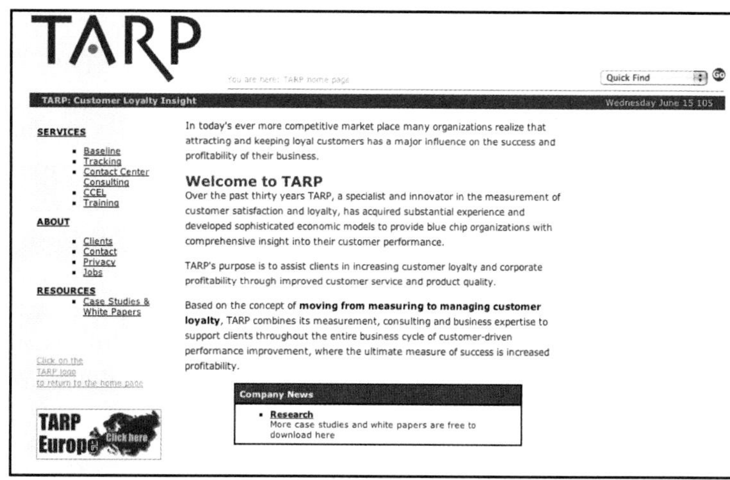

Reprinted by permission of TARP.

Derived largely from customer experiences, perceived service quality, rather than product quality or low price, is usually the *deciding factor* in customer satisfaction. Indeed, studies have shown that enhanced customer service contributes significantly to increasing customer satisfaction.[21] Poor service is typically the number-one reason for switching to competitors. Salespeople can never afford to be complacent about customer service because any service quality standard less than 100 percent may not be good enough. To appreciate quality from the dissatisfied customer's perspective, read the words of an IBM (www.ibm.com) executive: "We make 300,000 components. Don't say to me, '97 percent are okay.' Say instead, '9,000 were defective.' You don't really want 9,000 angry customers, do you?"[22] Read the *Keeping Up Online* feature on page 296 to see how the Internet can be used to enhance customer service.

Chapter Review Questions

What is the major reason why customers switch to competitors?

List some positive and some negative actions that can affect post-purchase relationships with customers.

IMPORTANCE OF CUSTOMER SATISFACTION

Consumer satisfaction is typically defined as "the result of an evaluative process that contrasts pre-purchase expectations with perceptions of performance during and after the consumption experience."[23] In other words, customer satisfaction depends on the product's perceived performance relative to a buyer's expectations. If the product's performance falls short of expectations, the customer is dissatisfied. If performance meets expectations, the customer is satisfied. If performance surpasses expectations, the customer is very satisfied or delighted.[24] Many organizations proclaim the importance of customer satisfaction to their employees. Whether espoused in speeches by top-level executives, in organizational policy manuals or credos, on office or store signage, or in company newsletters, such efforts are designed to instill in employees the belief that customers are the driving force behind their success. That is, satisfied customers lead to favorable firm and employee results. Let's take a look at how satisfied customers can affect an organization.

The Economics of Customer Satisfaction

Keeping satisfied customers is a lot cheaper than finding new ones. Studies have shown that it is five to six times more costly to attract new customers than to keep current ones. This ratio has been found to be virtually the same for online and off-line businesses. According to research conducted by the Boston Consulting Group (www.bcg.com), selling to a current customer via the Web costs about $7, compared to the $34 it costs to win a new customer.[25] Many experts contend that the major reason for a company's existence is to satisfy customers.[26] Without such satisfaction, the rest of a company's goals and efforts will be compromised, at least in the long run. Therefore, professional salespeople are constantly vigilant about keeping their customers satisfied, and they seek to satisfy their prospects as well by providing them pre-sale service to induce them to buy later on. Several compelling reasons exist for keeping profitable customers satisfied. These explanations revolve around (a) company profits, (b) the impact on the selling organization, and (c) the morale of salespeople and other company employees.

Company profits will increase through retention of profitable customers. This desired situation develops for the following reasons:

- Reducing customer defections by 5 percent can increase profitability anywhere from 25 percent to 95 percent.[27] Obtaining a new account after losing a customer is costly (remember, the cost of retaining an existing customer is about one-fifth the cost of obtaining a new customer).
- The longer a customer stays with the seller, the more the costs to service that customer tend to decrease (the learning curve of dealing with the customer becomes less steep over time).
- The seller can charge higher, even premium, prices for its products if the customer has confidence in and loyalty to the company.
- The customer provides positive, free word-of-mouth advertising for the company, thus providing the salesperson with referrals.
- The customer will increase his or her purchases over time.
- The customer purchases other products as the seller adds them to its product mix.
- The customer will pay less attention to competing brands and be less persuaded by competing offerings.[28]

Conversely, dissatisfied customers can have an extremely negative impact on companies and their salespeople because

- Dissatisfied customers are likely to switch suppliers and stop buying from the salesperson's company.
- Customers are less likely to buy again if a problem is not resolved satisfactorily.
- Customer dissatisfaction can lead to low employee morale.
- Dissatisfied customers are likely to tell other people about their bad experience. This decreases prospective customers' interest in purchasing from the salesperson's firm.
- Research shows that dissatisfied customers tell an average of eleven other people about their negative experience.[29]

Research indicates that customer dissatisfaction directly affects employee turnover. That is, the more dissatisfied customers a firm has, the less likely employees are to stay. Companies with many dissatisfied customers usually undergo higher sales force turnover than the typical industry annual average of about 20 percent. Replacing salespeople who leave increases recruitment, selection, and training costs. In addition, opportunity costs arise from lost sales during the departing salesperson's absence from his or her territory.

Types of Customers vis-à-vis Satisfaction Levels

As is now obvious, how salespeople attend to their customers strongly affects customer satisfaction and customer responses to the salespeople and their companies. Six different kinds of customers have been identified on the basis of their level of satisfaction.[30]

Loyalists. Customers who are completely satisfied and keep returning to the company are referred to as *loyalists*. These customers' needs and the performance of salespeople match up well. Thus, such customers are often the easiest to serve.

Apostles. In this loyalist camp are individuals who are extremely satisfied and whose experiences with your company far exceed their expectations; therefore, they share their strong feelings with others—and become *apostles*.

Defectors. On the downside, *defectors* are those who are neutral, quite dissatisfied, or more than dissatisfied. These individuals may have been satisfied previously but have encountered failures left uncorrected by the firm.

Vigilantes. Defectors who have had a particularly bad experience and are eager to tell others about their anger and frustration are called *vigilantes*. They actively work to undermine your company's reputation.

Mercenaries. Another customer who can make life miserable for salespeople and their companies is the *mercenary*. These customers seem to defy the satisfaction/loyalty rule. They appear to be and often say that they are highly satisfied but still have almost no loyalty. This type of customer seeks low prices, buys on impulse, looks for fashion trends, or chases something new for the sake of change. Such customers do not stay long enough in the relationship for the seller to turn a profit, so they are sometimes called "butterflies" because of their tendency to flit and flutter from one supplier to another.

Hostages. Buyers who experience the worst the seller has to offer but must grin and bear it are considered *hostages*. Companies with a monopolistic advantage often see little reason to respond to hostages. If these customers have no alternatives, why bother to correct their problems? Well, there are at least two reasons for not taking a callous or indifferent attitude toward these trapped customers. First, if the competitive environment suddenly shifts, nonresponsive companies will pay the price as their hostage customers quickly defect. Second, hostages are difficult and expensive to serve. They may be trapped, but they still take the opportunity to complain and ask for special service. Hostages can destroy company morale, and their negative impact on per-unit costs can be dramatic.

Overall, the sales rep's goal is to develop and maintain loyalists and apostles and prevent the other four kinds of customers from emerging. After all, a satisfied customer represents a bright future for the salesperson; a rankled customer can represent a nightmare.

Moving Beyond Customer Satisfaction to Customer Loyalty

It is widely recognized that customer satisfaction is essential to the success of a company. But more important than customer satisfaction is customer loyalty, which companies are increasingly seeing as the critical metric that will determine whether their business thrives, merely survives, or dies in the fierce competition ahead. Customer satisfaction and customer loyalty are not the same. Customer satisfaction is usually defined as meeting or exceeding customer expectations, but it does not ensure customer loyalty. From 60 to 80 percent of customers who leave say that they are satisfied just before leaving.[31] Customer loyalty is a more demanding metric that requires and builds on customer satisfaction. Customer loyalty can be defined *as a favorable attitude toward a brand resulting in consistent repeat purchasing of the brand over time.*[32] Thus customer loyalty includes both attitudinal and behavioral components. One study found that increasing customer retention by 5 percent could double a small firm's profitability in about ten years and could double the average Fortune 500 company's revenue growth rate almost immediately.[33]

Many online and off-line companies are focusing on customer loyalty as the key indicator of how well they're doing, because customer satisfaction has not proved reliable for several reasons, including corrupted measurement. For example, General Motors (www.gm.com) executives were early advocates of customer satisfaction surveys as they tried to stop the steady erosion of their market share to foreign car companies. Management and employee evaluations, recognition, and bonuses were based partly on statistically rigorous calculation of scores from customer satisfaction surveys. Customer satisfaction ratings improved dramatically to 90 percent or higher, but market share and profits continued to decline, and customer retention rates remained largely unchanged below 50 percent.

Unfortunately for General Motors, rewards based on customer satisfaction scores encouraged various unproductive, questionable behaviors. Some automobile dealerships played the ratings game by offering special discounts and incentives to customers who agreed to complete a survey checking "highly satisfied" in all categories. A few dealers brazenly displayed a copy of the survey form showing exactly how to mark it "properly" at the highest level. Some just threw away poor ratings from customers. Dealers also discovered that they could obtain the highest scores by surveying customers shortly after they bought a new car, when it was too early for any problems to have come to light. Finally, recent studies show that customer loyalty is not ensured unless customers consistently rate you at the highest possible level on the scale, such as 5 on a 5-point scale. In other words, 4 out of 5 is not good enough! By focusing on customer satisfaction, some companies have improved their customer retention rates, at least initially. But much of this early success has proved elusive over the longer run as competitive promises lure customers away with more attractive offers.

If customer satisfaction is not enough, what *does* drive customer loyalty?

The 8Cs of Customer Loyalty. Recent research by Srinivasan, Anderson, and Ponnavolu has identified eight factors, or the **8Cs of customer loyalty**, that appear to drive customer loyalty both online and off-line.[34] Companies can benchmark and compare their performance on these 8Cs against their past performance, managerial goals, or competitors. Salespeople, too, can evaluate their interactions with prospects and customers according to the 8Cs, as described below:

8Cs of Customer Loyalty Eight factors (customization, contact interactivity, cultivation, care, community, choice, convenience, and character) that have been found to drive customer loyalty. These 8Cs are moderated by customer trust and satisfaction.

- ***Customization***—the degree to which products, services, and the transactional environment are tailored to the individual characteristics and requirements of each customer. Each customer has his or her own unique personality and communication style (as we'll discuss in chapter 12). Savvy salespeople, for instance, often try to arrange sales calls in settings where their customers are most comfortable (be it the golf course, a good restaurant, or the ballpark), and they present products and services that best match their customers' interests (e.g., high quality, durability, low price, creative design, fast delivery, or some combination). The more you can customize your products, services, and the negotiating environment to individual customers, the more likely you are to close the sale and further the relationship.
- ***Contact Interactivity***—the extent of high-quality, mutually desired communication and interaction with customers. In personal selling, listening is more important than talking, but providing an easy flow of communication exchanges between you and your customers is essential for positive, long-run rapport. The best customer-salesperson relationships are those in which you genuinely like each other and feel comfortable speaking openly and honestly together. You might not become close friends with all your customers, but you can develop open communications and a high level of contact interactivity with each. For example, you might send regular newsletters by postal mail or e-mail to keep customers informed about upcoming price changes, inventory shortages, new products, or any other items of interest. In each newsletter, you can ask customers for feedback about their product/service needs, concerns, complaints, and opinions with respect to your performance on various criteria important to them. Take a tip from some politicians who regularly ask their constituents, "How am I doing?" Salespeople who don't solicit opinions from customers to learn about their changing perceptions are unlikely to keep their repeat business.
- ***Cultivation***—the degree to which salespeople provide customers with desired information and helpful cross-selling offers. Salespeople should proactively help customers find products and services they need and should suggest supplemental products to enhance customers' experience with their purchases. For example, when a Dell business customer purchases new laptop computers, the salesperson is trained to suggest the purchase of ancillary items such as printers, scanners, and service contracts to enhance customer use of and satisfaction with the laptops. Depending on their customers' communication preferences, salespeople can use the phone, e-mail, fax, or regular mail, as well as face-to-face

contact, to inform their accounts about new-product releases or imminent events (such as price increases and product deletion decisions) that are likely to affect the buyers. Customers appreciate cross-selling efforts when they provide helpful information about products that can support and enhance the use of their primary purchase.

- ***Care***—the extent to which a salesperson demonstrates special concern for the customer's welfare in all pre- and post-purchase interactions. Demonstrating genuine caring for customers can develop loyalty far beyond mere customer satisfaction. USAA (www.usaa.com), the giant insurance company headquartered in San Antonio, regularly shows that it cares about customers and thinks of them almost as family members. During the U.S. military's 1991 call-up for Operation Desert Storm, USAA notified its customers (mainly active-duty, reserve, and retired military people) that they could add to their life insurance before going overseas and that they should ask about reduced premiums for their car insurance if their car was not going to be driven as much while they were in the Persian Gulf. (In contrast, most other insurance companies refuse to sell life insurance without special clauses in the contracts that exempt the company from paying if a policyholder is killed in war.) By showing exceptional caring for their customers, USAA consistently achieves 97 percent customer loyalty. Salespeople who act as advisers and consultants to their customers can encourage them to remain loyal by showing authentic caring in ways that go beyond the immediate bottom line.
- ***Community***—the degree to which customers can share opinions among themselves about a company's products and services. Harley-Davidson (www.harley-davidson.com) customers, who affectionately call themselves "hogs," have bonds among their community members that act as strong deterrents to buying any other motorcycle or accessory brand. For its hundredth anniversary, Harley-Davidson sponsored a yearlong celebration for its customers, beginning with a five-continent road tour and ending with a huge party in Milwaukee for about 200,000 loyal customers. Salespeople who willingly give their customers the names of other customers (who have granted permission) to ask about the performance of their products and services can develop communities that will help past customers sell future customers. Communities of customers strengthen a common bond among salespeople and their customers even when complaints arise.
- ***Choice***—the range of desired products and services from which customers can choose. Most customers don't want to buy products from several different salespeople if they can conveniently buy everything they need from one salesperson (one-stop shopping). Even if his or her company offers only some of the products needed, a resourceful salesperson will offer to find and help deliver those other products to the customer, too. This value-added service gives customers the feeling that they can go to you for fulfillment of all their product needs, and many will gladly pay a premium for such service.
- ***Convenience***—the ease with which a customer can conduct negotiations and transactions with a seller. Customers want products and

services provided when and where needed with minimal effort on their part, and without hassles. Installation and maintenance of products and the return of flawed products must be convenient if customers are to become loyal repeat buyers. Here is another aspect of convenience: Customers want to avoid hardball negotiations with salespeople. Salespeople who see interactions with customers as contests with a clear-cut winner may win a few sales, but they will never win the long-term loyalty of customers.

- ***Character***—the image and reputation that a seller projects to customers. Some companies are fortunate enough to have a highly visible person within their companies, usually the founder, to represent them in positive ways. These people often are so likable or so well respected that they give the company a positive character, personality, or reputation. Thousands of investors around the world proudly call themselves "bogleheads" in honor of John Bogle, founder of Vanguard Group, a giant mutual fund investment firm (www.vanguard.com). They credit him personally with ensuring that Vanguard's mutual fund management costs remain the lowest in the industry. Bogle's well-known frugal ways, straight-talking personality, and reputation for integrity have helped make Vanguard the most trusted of all financial firms. Only a few people can inspire such loyalty from customers, but all salespeople can learn from Bogle's example that a favorable reputation is invaluable to sales success and long-run customer relationships.

Moderators of the 8Cs of Loyalty. The foregoing eight characteristics are so interconnected that none can be considered adequately in isolation from the others. Moreover, although the 8Cs directly affect customer loyalty, two critical moderating variables, *cumulative full customer satisfaction* and *trust,* influence their overall effectiveness. Unless businesses and their salespeople can maintain a bond of trust with customers and continuously provide full satisfaction, customer loyalty will suffer even when the 8Cs are highly positive. It's a big task, but companies and salespeople who can do all this are likely to reap a substantial payoff in long-run profitability.

Chapter Review Question

Why is customer satisfaction not the same as customer loyalty?

CUSTOMER FOLLOW-UP STRATEGIES

In order to increase customer satisfaction, enhance customer loyalty, and work toward building a strategic partnership following the sale, salespeople should consider the following service strategies:

- *Express appreciation for the customer's business.* Salespeople should be conscientious about showing genuine appreciation for their customer's business. Appreciation can be shown in many ways, from merely saying "thank you" in a sincere, enthusiastic way (in person or by telephone call, e-mail, or handwritten note) to sending the customer a useful gift, such as an address book or small calculator with the seller's logo.

- *Make sure products are delivered and installed on time.* Whenever possible, the salesperson ought to be on hand when the customer's order is delivered. By being there, the salesperson reassures the customer that he or she cares about pleasing the customer and that any potential problems will be promptly resolved. In addition, the salesperson learns to see this important aspect of service from the customer's viewpoint.
- *Assist customers with credit arrangements.* Dealing with company credit personnel can often be frustrating for customers. A salesperson who has already made it a point to establish and maintain good relationships with the credit department can serve as an effective go-between during the credit-granting process and insulate the customer from potential problems.
- *Help customers with warranty or service contracts.* When customers need repair service or must return a defective product, it's best for the salesperson to serve as the liaison with company service people. Not only will customers appreciate your saving them time and effort, but it is an opportunity to become acquainted with your company's customer service people.
- *Represent customers in solving their problems with your company.* Customers don't know your company's organization, policies, procedures, or personnel, so the best salespeople serve as their customers' advocates within the company, whether handling product repairs, exchanges, returns, or complaints. Having one contact person to take care of problems can be a tremendous relief to customers. Let your customers know that you *want* them to call you whenever they have a problem and that you will strongly represent their interests in any dispute with your company. Learning who's who in providing customer service within your company, and developing a positive personal relationship with them ahead of time, should help you avoid many bureaucratic problems in promptly obtaining service for your customers.
- *Keep customers informed.* Customers want to know about possible product shortages, price changes, upcoming sales, introduction of new products, and any other information that may affect them or their business operations. Customers will quickly lose trust in salespeople who allow surprises that adversely affect them or their businesses.
- *Ask customers about their level of satisfaction.* As we have learned, an absence of customer complaints does not indicate that they are satisfied. It is part of the professional salesperson's job to solicit customers' opinions regarding their level of satisfaction and what services they believe should improve. Even if their company also surveys overall customer satisfaction periodically, salespeople can obtain product-specific and detailed feedback information, while showing genuine concern for customers, by asking about their level of satisfaction with their products and supporting services. Sometimes the salesperson will discover that a competitor's product and service are unsatisfactory—and that creates an opportunity to replace that competitor's product.
- *Think of prospects and customers as individuals.* The best salespeople meet as many employees as possible in their customers' organizations, not just the purchasing agents and managers but all those who may influence

purchase decisions. Whenever possible, see how and by whom your products and services are used. *Selling by walking around the customer's site* is a service-oriented strategy many top salespeople use. It allows them to meet the buying organization's employees, understand their jobs, and develop personal relationships at all working levels. Morgan Stanley (www.morganstanley.com), the brokerage firm, probably expresses the customer service concept best: "*We measure success one investor [customer] at a time.*"

- *Ask customers how else you might help them.* Salespeople should regularly ask customers what other services they would like or what problems they'd like solved. For many years, DuPont Company (www.dupont.com) sold only adhesives to the shoe industry. Only after a DuPont salesperson asked Reebok International how DuPont could assist it further did DuPont come up with the idea of inserting flexible plastic tubes into the soles of Reebok's (www.reebok.com) new ERS lines. The tubes gave the sneakers a more lively, bouncy feel, and the success of the ERS lines boosted Reebok's net earnings sharply—making Reebok an even more loyal customer of DuPont.
- *Empathize with and be sensitive toward the customer.* Promptly return customer phone calls, letters, e-mails, and faxes. Also, proactively seek ways to provide extra services to the customer. Treating customers fairly, honestly, and with respect at all times will demonstrate that the customer is truly important to you. Making product and service recommendations when appropriate shows the customer that you are serving him or her like a consultant. Also, use precise language that is most meaningful to customers to enhance communication and understanding between you. Working with customers to plan a mutually profitable future together shows customers that you are a trusted partner focused on win-win solutions.

As you can see, today's professional salespeople have much to do after closing a sale if they hope to keep their customers satisfied and loyal. With this in mind, read the *It's Up to You* feature on page 306 and determine what needs to be done to rectify the situation.

Whenever possible, the salesperson should be on hand when the customer's order is delivered.
Mug Shots/Corbis

Handling Customer Complaints

Successfully handling complaints is a critical activity, and doing so can be even more important online than off-line. As Jeff Bezos, CEO of Amazon.com, puts it, "In the physical world, if I make a customer unhappy, they'll tell five friends . . . on the Internet, they'll tell 5,000."[35] Professional salespeople recognize complaints as opportunities to improve relationships with customers. Customers who complain are likely to be more satisfied in the long run than those who do not complain.[36]

IT'S UP TO YOU

In reviewing your territory's annual sales report provided by your sales manager, you notice that one of your steady customers, a large paint and wallpaper wholesaler, bought no painting or wallpaper supplies from your company during the past six months. Normally, this wholesaler places two big orders a year, one in each half of the year. You called on this customer twice during the past six months to check in and to leave some new-product information brochures. Each time, your meeting was cordial, and the buyer didn't mention any problems. You made no sales presentation either time because this customer has a direct computer hookup with your company's order-processing department, and the usual practice has been to merely replenish basic stock. The only change in the customer's organization has been the promotion of one of the senior buyers, whom you know casually, to director of purchasing.

What has probably led to the current situation with this customer? What steps should you take to rectify it?

A TARP study showed that up to 70 percent of customers who complain will buy from the seller again if their complaint is resolved satisfactorily. More than 95 percent will buy again if their complaints are resolved promptly.[37] Salespeople should be hesitant to engage in subsequent sales efforts when an existing customer problem with a prior sale has yet to be resolved. Such endeavors could lead the aggrieved customer to view the salesperson as a mere "huckster" who has little concern for the buyer. In dealing with customer complaints, sales and service people should follow the guidelines noted in Table 9.4.

Customers Who Don't Complain

As you may have guessed from our earlier discussion about the two customer types who receive little service, you cannot afford to assume that no complaints means customers are satisfied. Because few dissatisfied customers actually file a complaint, sellers do not know the true extent of customer dissatisfaction. Many unhappy customers don't go to the trouble of complaining, especially when a purchase is not expensive, and simply buy elsewhere next time. Measuring customer satisfaction with service performance is essential. Even if their companies regularly measure overall customer satisfaction, salespeople should verify their own customers' level of satisfaction with their products and services. Just as poor service by competitors will create additional sales opportunities for you, poor service on your part creates an opportunity for competitors. It's important for salespeople to continually monitor customer satisfaction and promptly address any perceptions of poor service or dissatisfaction. Read *On the Frontlines* on page 308 to see how one salesperson minimizes complaints by making sure that he meets customer expectations.

Chapter Review Questions

Do most dissatisfied customers actually complain? Why or why not?

Name some basic customer follow-up strategies.

About what percentage of customers who complain will buy again from the seller if their complaints are resolved promptly?

TABLE 9.4

Basic Rules for Handling Customer Complaints

- Anticipate customer complaints and try to resolve them before the customer expresses them.
- Listen closely and patiently to customers' complaints without interrupting.
- Never belittle a customer's complaint. Few customers actually complain, and those who do are a valuable source of feedback and information that can help improve the quality of your product and service.
- Encourage customers to talk and fully express their feelings so that they can vent their emotions.
- Don't argue with customers or take their complaints personally. You gain nothing by making a customer angry, and there is no surer way to do so than to argue over the customer's version of the complaint.
- Record the facts as the customer sees them. If you take the complaint over the telephone, let him or her know that you are carefully recording the facts without passing judgment.
- Reassure customers that you hear and understand their complaints accurately by verbally repeating the information as you record it. This repetition reassures customers about your accuracy and interest. Asking nonthreatening and nonjudgmental questions to clarify their various points can also help them to know that they are communicating successfully.
- Empathize with customers and try to see the situation from their point of view.
- Don't make excuses for service problems or criticize your firm's service personnel.
- Ask customers how they would like to have their complaint resolved instead of volunteering what you're going to do. Customers may have quite different expectations about how to solve their problem, and you may offer the wrong solution or much more than they expect. By asking customers what they want, you'll meet their expectations and not overdo it in making amends.
- Resolve problems promptly and fairly, even if that means the sale will become unprofitable.
- Thank customers for voicing the complaint. Welcome them as people who care enough to try to help you improve your products and services.
- Follow up to ensure that a customer's complaint has been resolved to his or her satisfaction.
- Keep records on all customer complaints and their outcomes so that, through analysis, you can spot patterns of problems.

CLOSING WITH THE CUSTOMER SERVICE TEAM

Although you are usually the one to ask for the prospect's business, you rarely close alone. It is important for salespeople engaged in organizational selling to work smoothly and effectively with marketing and other in-house teams in order to gain their support in cultivating the best possible relationships with

ON THE FRONTLINES

Salesperson . . . and Serviceperson

Richard Angarita, a sales rep for Rainin Instrument Company (www.rainin.com), a supplier of laboratory instruments in Woburn, Massachusetts, sold more than one hundred systems in eighteen months, at prices up to $30,000, in a territory where the previous sales rep sold only two instruments in two years. Considered a sales consultant by customers, Mr. Angarita is thoroughly familiar with the products he sells because he is both the territory's salesperson and a highly trained service technician. He sells, installs, and repairs his company's products and also trains customers how to use them. An expert at explaining product features and benefits, he quickly gains the trust of his customers by providing quality service promptly. He makes sure that the equipment will meet the customer's expectations or he won't sell it to them. After all, he's also the service technician who must resolve any later problems or complaints.

customers. If you have done your job properly, by the time you ask for the prospect's business, you will already know all the post-sale details—product availability and delivery schedules, whether or not the customer will receive credit approval, and so on. No salesperson alone can adequately provide all the services that his or her customers expect. It is necessary for salespeople to work closely with their company's customer support or service team. Customer service policies and procedures are extremely important because so many aspects of customer service cross departmental lines. Immediately before you close the sale, however, you should once again check with colleagues and friends in the (1) customer credit, (2) order-processing, and (3) product delivery teams to iron out any potential difficulties. Let's quickly describe the roles these three teams play.

Credit Team

Two natural sources of conflict arise between salespeople and credit managers. The first is essentially geographic. Credit is still a centralized function in most companies, whereas salespeople usually operate from decentralized regional offices. Beyond physical distance, some natural conflict emerges between the roles of salespeople and credit managers. Salespeople are expected to be their customers' advocates for credit approvals, whereas the credit department's job is to protect the company from entering into sales agreements with customers who are unlikely to pay.

The best salespeople actively search for ways to minimize the effects of these sources of conflict. Some companies are encouraging their credit managers to spend a week or two each year in sales territories to further their understanding of the needs of customers and salespeople. Another good approach to improving the working relationships between salespeople and customer service departments is to schedule joint training meetings. Such meetings sometimes include role-playing exercises where salespeople play the role of credit managers and credit managers play the role of salespeople in negotiations. In companies that require their salespeople to collect overdue accounts, salespeople quickly understand the problems of the credit department. Some common complaints that salespeople and credit managers express about each other are shown in Table 9.5.

TABLE 9.5

Potential Conflicts Between Credit and Sales

Credit Department Complaints About Salespeople

- Salespeople often over-commit the company.
- Salespeople approve payment delays for customers without even notifying the credit department.
- Salespeople will do almost anything to avoid refusing credit to a customer, including going around the credit department to appeal to upper management for support.
- Salespeople often argue for the profit "potential" of marginal prospects and thereby compromise the credit manager and jeopardize the company's profits.
- Salespeople sometimes write large orders for normally low-to-moderate-volume customers without obtaining a financial update or even considering that one might be needed.
- Salespeople promise special credit services that simply cannot be performed.
- Salespeople won't address even the possibility that a customer might not pay. To them, every customer is "as good as gold."

Salespeople's Complaints About the Credit Department

- The credit department doesn't explain what it needs to evaluate prospects and customers. The sales department is excluded from the policy and the process.
- Excessive demands on prospective customers weaken sales potential.
- The sales department has to "patch up" customer relationships after negative credit department contacts with customers.
- The credit department exists in a corporate ivory tower and doesn't understand the difficulty in the field.
- The credit department is too quick to condemn a customer who's past due and won't negotiate to save the account. It is too short-run oriented.
- The credit department doesn't notify salespeople in time when a customer is past due or when the account has been referred for third-party collection.
- The sales department isn't notified when a customer's credit is being reevaluated.

Source: *From* Management Review *by Nathaniel Gilbert. Copyright © 1989 by American Management Association. Reproduced with permission of American Management Association via Copyright Clearance Center.*

Order-Processing and Product Delivery Teams

The goal in designing a physical distribution system is to develop minimum-cost systems for a range of customer service levels and then provide the service level that generates the highest profits or sales minus distribution costs. Salespeople and company transportation managers must learn to appreciate the full range of policies, procedures, and activities that affect customer perceptions of service, such as complaint procedures, minimum order sizes, order cycles, inventory returns, stockouts, and promised deliveries. Salespeo-

TABLE 9.6

SOME COMMON CUSTOMER SERVICE COMPLAINTS

Order Processing and Billing
• Invoice had errors.
• Discount not taken off price.
• Name and address incorrect.
• Not notified about late shipment.
• Special instructions not followed.
• Missing paperwork.
Inventory Control, Warehousing, and Packaging
• Product out of stock.
• Wrong product sent.
• Unordered product sent.
• Product package not sealed properly.
• Damaged product sent.
• Poor-quality product shipped.
• Wrong product quantity shipped.
• Incorrect papers packaged with product.
• Packaging inadequate to protect product.
Traffic and Transportation
• Product delivered prior to date wanted.
• Product delivered too late.
• Product lost in transit.
• No tracking of delayed product.
• Requested customer routing not followed.
• Specific handling instructions ignored.
• Errors on the bill of lading.
• Delivery people left product outside in rain or snow.
• Delivery people refused to carry product inside.
• Delivery people didn't deliver invoice.

ple should cultivate good relationships with people in order processing and transportation by carefully checking customer order forms to minimize any potential misunderstandings and by keeping customer service people informed about any unique customer requirements. When salespeople show that they care about their customers by providing such extra services, the feeling becomes contagious and is usually picked up by the order-processing and transportation staff. When both salespeople and transportation managers start seeing their functions through the eyes of the customer, they begin to think differently. Frito-Lay (www.frito-lay.com) is one company that doesn't worry excessively about costs when it comes to making sure customers receive the products they need when they need them, as noted in the *From the Command Post* feature Service to Sales, which can be found on our textbook website **http://college.hmco.com/pic/andersonPS2e.**

Online Study Center
Improve Your Grade

It is unfortunate that the people responsible for order processing and product delivery often miss out on the excitement of cultivating a new customer and increasing business with an old one. If you want an excellent relationship with these important teams, you will take the time to tell managers and workers the story of a successful sale and thank them for their hard work in supporting that sale. This will give them not only a sense of excitement surrounding your closed sale, but also some specific ideas about that particular customer's order-processing and delivery expectations. Also, it will have the added benefit of making your customers especially memorable to people whom you may occasionally have to call upon for rush delivery, special delivery terms, and the like.

Just like credit managers, transportation managers can develop a customer orientation by participating with salespeople in training meetings that include interactive role-playing. Good relationships between salespeople and personnel who handle traffic and transportation, inventory control, warehousing and packaging, and sales and order service will help avoid customer complaints like those depicted in Table 9.6.

Chapter Review Question

Name three complaints that salespeople have about credit managers and three complaints that credit managers have about salespeople.

KEEPING UP WITH RISING CUSTOMER SERVICE EXPECTATIONS

In order to provide improving quality service, salespeople and their backup customer service teams must stay close to customers and their evolving expectations. Staying close to customers means keeping in mind several basic concepts.

Only Customers Can Define Customer Satisfaction

Continually soliciting customer feedback is the best way to determine what customer service is and should be. Carlson Systems (www.csystems.com), a distributor of fasteners and packaging products, asks its customers to fill out regular "report cards," rating the company from poor to excellent on such services as handling back orders or invoice errors.[38]

Nothing is ever gained by making a customer angry, and there is no surer way to do so than to dispute the customer's version of a complaint.

Christopher Bissell/Stone/Getty Images

Oftentimes, the seller's policies, systems, and procedures, not employee motivation, stand in the way of better customer service. When salespeople and other front-line people are asked for suggestions on how to serve customers better, they generally respond with numerous practical ideas. An example of a firm that understands the importance of the customer service relationship is presented in the following *From the Command Post.*

Everyone Serves a Customer

Salespeople have customers, receptionists have customers, traffic managers have customers, custodians have customers—everybody in the organization has internal customers (other employees) to serve, and all directly or indirectly serve the external customers (prospects and customers). Serving internal customers well leads to the kind of teamwork that creates synergistic results and success for the entire organization in satisfying external customers.

Customer Service Is a Partnership with the Customer

Salespeople and their companies who most consistently provide the highest-quality customer service usually have developed a partnering relationship with customers, as described in the *From the Command Post* feature on page 313.

FROM THE COMMAND POST: SERVICE-ORIENTED WHOLESALER

AmerisourceBergen (www.amerisourcebergen.com) is a drug wholesaler selling to 9,500 hospitals, regional drug chains, and independent drug stores nationwide. Its salespeople are called "consultants" to emphasize the service focus of their jobs. AmerisourceBergen's salespeople offer customers various computer programs to speed ordering and delivery. A comprehensive training program, including hands-on experience in all departments of the company as well as pharmacies, ensures that AmerisourceBergen company salespeople can implement any service program the firm offers. *Space Management,* a merchandising program based on product sales data, helps retailers keep the right products in the right place at the right time. For a monthly fee, AmerisourceBergen advises customers on product and shelf arrangement. *Compu-Phase* is a computer system for processing prescriptions, storing patient information, and updating prices. The *Good Neighbor Pharmacy* advertising program gives retailers the advertising benefits enjoyed by chains without sacrificing their local identity. AmerisourceBergen also offers financial management programs.

FROM THE COMMAND POST: BETTER SERVICE THROUGH PARTNERSHIPS

As the demand for quality service grows, many manufacturers form partnerships with just a few of their resellers—wholesalers, distributors, and retailers. Partnerships between manufacturers and "middlemen" bring cost savings through larger purchase volumes, reduced competition, and predictable markets. In addition, the usual adversarial role among channel members is replaced with one built more on trust, cooperation, and compatible goals.

To facilitate service delivery, many buyers and sellers have interconnected their computer systems. Casual Male Retail Group (CMRGinc.com), a retail chain, has linked its computers directly to Levi Strauss Company (www.levis.com). Levi Strauss now knows which of its products is selling fastest because sales data are transmitted directly from the point of sale to the manufacturer's computers. Sharing data enables Levi Strauss to anticipate CWRG's needs and make timely delivery of needed products.

CUSTOMER SERVICE QUESTIONNAIRE

Indicate the extent to which you agree with each of the statements below, using the following scale:

5-Strongly Agree; 4-Agree; 3-Neither Agree nor Disagree; 2-Disagree; 1-Strongly Disagree

1. XYZ Company insists on error-free records. ____
2. XYZ Company employees tell you exactly when services will be performed. ____
3. Employees of XYZ Company give you prompt service. ____
4. XYZ Company employees are always willing to help you. ____
5. Employees of XYZ Company are never too busy to respond to your request. ____
6. The behavior of employees of XYZ Company instills confidence in you. ____
7. You feel safe in your transactions with XYZ Company. ____
8. Employees of XYZ Company are consistently courteous with you. ____
9. Employees of XYZ Company have the knowledge to answer your questions. ____
10. XYZ Company's operating hours are convenient for you. ____
11. XYZ Company employees give you personal attention. ____
12. XYZ Company has your best interest at heart. ____
13. Employees of XYZ Company understand your specific needs. ____

The more strongly a customer agrees with each of the above statements, the greater the satisfaction with the level of service the salesperson and firm provide. Although a perfect score of 65 may be hard to achieve, the salesperson should not be complacent about a score of all 4's or a total of 52.

Source: *Copyright © 1999 by Pi Sigma Epsilon, Inc. From* Journal of Personal Selling and Sales Management, *Vol. 19, No. 3 (Summer 1999), pp. 73–82. Reprinted with permission.*

EVALUATING CUSTOMER SERVICE

Regular checkups for your customer service performance are critical to sales health. An easy way to assess how satisfied your customers are is to have them complete a brief questionnaire, such one on page 313. Such as questionnaires also can ask customers *how important* each of the service-related statements is. Those items that customers consider relatively unimportant require less service attention from the salesperson than those service-related activities that customers consider important.

SUMMARY

In the process of conducting negotiations, buyers and sellers develop relationships with each another; some of these relationships steadily improve, whereas others fade away. The quality of post-purchase attention and service provided by salespeople and their support teams usually determines the future relationship with the customer. Based on various attitudinal, behavioral, and economic characteristics, three levels of buyer-seller interactions can be identified on a commitment continuum from merely sporadic *transactions* on the low end, to long-term *relationship* in the middle, to strategic *partnerships* on the high end. Selling to current customers is much less expensive and time-consuming than trying to locate new prospects and going through the entire PSP again. So salespeople should provide exceptional post-sale customer service to ensure that profitable customers stay satisfied and loyal. Customer service has five dimensions, the most important of which is *reliability*. Service quality is determined by customer perceptions, not by what the seller thinks. The absence of customer complaints does not necessarily mean that customers are satisfied, because few dissatisfied customers actually complain. Most simply start buying from another supplier without giving you any feedback unless you specifically ask for it. Customer complaints should not be dreaded but, rather, should be recognized as opportunities to improve relationships with customers.

Customer service strategy calls for segmenting customers by the amount of service they expect and then identifying those customer segments whose service expectations can be profitably met. Salespeople need the help of the company's customer service team and internal support staff to fully satisfy customer service expectations. Salespeople and their companies who consistently provide service of the highest quality often form partner-like relationships with their customers. One thing is certain: Customer service expectations will continue to rise, and it is up to salespeople to coordinate the activities to meet these rising standards.

Sales organizations continually assess how satisfied their customers are with their service. However, customer satisfaction by itself is not enough to ensure customer loyalty. Moreover, there are multiple difficulties in accurately measuring customer satisfaction, so many companies are focusing on achieving customer loyalty, which has been called the Holy Grail of customer relationships. Eight factors (the 8Cs) that work interdependently have been identified as primary drivers of customer loyalty. By ensuring high levels of customer-perceived performance on these 8Cs, plus two critical moderator variables—customer satisfaction and trust—salespeople and their companies can more readily reach the levels of customer loyalty needed to maximize profits over the long run.

KEY TERMS

Follow-Up
Customer Service
Customer Service Segmentation
Product Quality
Service Quality
Reliability
Perceived Service Quality
8Cs of Customer Loyalty

TOPICS FOR THOUGHT AND CLASS DISCUSSION

1. What is your personal definition of customer service and what do you consider the most important dimensions of customer service?
2. How do you think customer service expectations are changing?
3. Why do you think that only a low percentage of dissatisfied customers ever complain?
4. Have you ever made a formal complaint about a product? Why? Was your complaint answered? How?
5. As a new salesperson, how would you go about gaining the cooperation of your company's customer service team in solving your customers' problems?
6. Explain this statement: "Everyone serves a customer, either an internal one or an external one."
7. How does forming a buyer-seller partnership affect customer service?
8. How do you account for the differences in level of customer service among retail store chains?

INTERNET EXERCISES

1. Using an Internet search engine, find three firms that provide training to salespeople for improving their customer service skills. Is the focus on improving customer service in B2B selling, in B2C selling, or in both? What are the length and cost of each program? Where is each held? Who does the training? What does the training cover?
2. Use Google or any other search engine to locate two examples of customer service strategies being demonstrated using Flash or streaming video.
3. Use an Internet search engine to find additional rules or techniques for handling customer complaints other than those identified in Table 9.4.
4. Use the Internet to find articles on customer satisfaction and approaches for accurately measuring it.
5. Research the Internet to find articles that describe how strategic partnerships and alliances are being used by different companies. What characteristics shown in Tables 9.1–9.3 are exemplified by the buyer-seller relationships described in these articles?

PROJECTS FOR PERSONAL GROWTH

1. (a) Ask four of your classmates to brainstorm with you about which commercial and nonprofit organizations consistently provide the best customer service. Come up with three examples of each category, and then take turns explaining the reasons for each selection. (b) Ask each of your four classmates to select two organizations that usually provide the worst customer service. Take turns explaining why. As each of your classmates gives his or her explanations, write down the key points. After everyone has finished, identify the key criteria your classmates mentioned that cause them to perceive organizations as providing the *best* and the *worst* customer service.
2. In your college library or online resources, find two articles about how companies measure business customer satisfaction and two articles about how they handle customer complaints. From the perspective of the customer, critique the methods described for handling customer complaints. As part of your critique, consider the channels of communication that both kinds of customers have for providing feedback to sellers. How effective and efficient are these channels? Finally, outline an ideal system for obtaining regular feedback on customer satisfaction and for resolving customer complaints promptly.

3. Select two area companies, and contact the customer service manager for each by telephone, e-mail, or letter. Be sure to tell the manager that you're doing a school project, because that should help you obtain responses. Ask the following questions: (a) How does your company define customer service? (b) Who is responsible for customer service? (c) How do you measure your customers' level of satisfaction with your products and services? (d) What is your general process for handling customer complaints? After obtaining this information, write your own critique of the way the two companies are dealing with these critical concerns for retention of customers.

ROLE-PLAY EXERCISE 9.1

Post-Sale Activities and Services

Situation

Jeffery Hornum, who has been selling medical equipment for General Health Corporation for nearly a year, has just made a large sale of several new sterilization machines to Washington General Hospital. After calling his wife and his sales manager to give them the good news, Jeff rewards himself with lunch at an excellent restaurant. At lunch, he begins to think about what he should do in the way of post-sale activities. Too embarrassed to ask his boss, Jeff decides to call one of his friends who works in sales at a noncompeting company to get some advice.

Roles

Jeffery Hornum Elated about making the important sale, Jeff knows that he must "keep the customer sold" by doing some post-sale activities and providing post-sale services—perhaps some immediately and some over the longer run—but he's not too sure what these should be.

Pete Mingo A senior salesperson for Zepper Corporation, producer of a line of steel lathes for precision metal manufacturers, Pete knows how important post-sale activities are, and he wants to help his young friend Jeffery.

ROLE-PLAY EXERCISE 9.2

Handling Customer Complaints

Situation

Alex Webster, a sales representative for Tectron Scientific Software (TSS) Corporation, recently sold an expensive new software program to a new account, the Biology Department of the University of Western Pennsylvania. A week after the software was installed, Alex called the department chairperson, Dr. Kim Feng, to see how the program was working out.

ALEX: Dr. Feng, this is Alex Webster from TSS. I just called to make sure that you're completely satisfied with your new TSS customized software program.

PROFESSOR FENG: Alex, I was just about to call you. Professor Denise Kriebel and two of her graduate students have complained to me that the TSS software is not working right, and they suspect there are some errors in the software program you sold us. As you know, Alex, this purchase made a huge dent in our departmental budget, and we simply can't tolerate any bugs in the software we're using for the high-precision work under our National Science Foundation research grant. Because we're under such time pressures to complete this research, we don't have much time to wait while TSS programmers figure out what's wrong. Professor Kriebel wants you to pick up this software and return our money, so we can buy your competitor's product.

ALEX: Dr. Feng, just let me talk to Professor Kriebel before you give up on the software. We've got dozens of other customers using virtually the same program, and this is the first problem we've had.

Roles

Alex Webster Tectron Scientific Software has a "no return" policy on customized software, so Alex feels he has to convince Professor Kriebel to allow him to get a technical rep out to work on the problems that she and her graduate students are encountering with the software. His first task, however, is to contact Professor Kriebel and hear her complaints. He manages to get both Professors Kriebel and Feng on a conference telephone call.

Professor Kim Feng As department chair, Dr. Feng will serve as mediator between Alex and Professor Kriebel and will be responsible for making any final decision on what to do with the software.

Professor Denise Kriebel Irate over the problems with the TSS software, she is in no mood to negotiate with Alex. She wants Dr. Feng to return the TSS software to Tectron and buy from a competitor.

CASE 9.1 ADDRESSING CUSTOMER PROBLEMS: SERVICE OR DISSERVICE?

Rob Azar is excited. Actually, he is thrilled. He has just closed a big order with an account that had stopped buying from his company. Most of the other sales reps said it couldn't be done, but Rob knew he could do it. After all, they didn't call him the "Slammer" for nothing. At the beginning of the year, Rob was promoted to account representative at Master Mailers, Inc., a mailing equipment manufacturer. Although he has been with Master Mailers only about three years, he has quickly moved up through the ranks. In fact, in his three years with the company, he has been promoted at the end of each year. Interestingly, Rob always experiences high sales at the beginning of a year, but his sales taper off toward the end of the year. This has never really concerned him because his final numbers are all that matter, and he always surpasses his sales quotas. Besides, after he "blows" through a territory, he is always promoted out of it, so the year-end drop-off isn't a problem for him.

Rob has been in his new assignment for only three months, and as usual, he is going like gangbusters. He has a city-center hospital assignment that contains both users and nonusers of his company's mailing equipment. Whereas his old territory consisted of many smaller accounts, his new territory has larger accounts that have much more potential. As a result, he must spend more time becoming acquainted with these accounts and understanding their needs.

On this particular day, Rob is pleased with himself. He has just closed a substantial order with one of his higher-potential accounts, Union Hospital, which has been buying only 20 percent of its mailing equipment from Master Mailers. Rob really went after this account, knowing there was a lot more business to be had there. The head of purchasing, Marilyn Krane, has been with the hospital for years. During the sales call, she told Rob about her reluctance to buy from him because the hospital experienced several customer service problems with Master Mailers in the past. Rob, who is known for his exceptional ability to negotiate prospect resistance and objections, convinced Ms. Krane to give his company another chance by assuring her that he would be personally responsible for the account and that Union Hospital could depend on him to promptly resolve any problems they might have with his company or its products. In reality, Rob has a team of people behind him to service the account, and if anything does go wrong, he plans to direct Ms. Krane to one of them. When Rob brings all the paperwork back to the office and receives hearty congratulations from his district sales manager, Roger Stone, he gives the order to Joan Newman, the district office administrative assistant, to process.

The following Friday, Rob learns that the mailing machine that Union Hospital ordered is in short supply. Although the usual product delivery

(*continued*)

time is five to ten working days, delivery time for this particular model has been pushed back to three to four weeks. When Rob finds out about the delay, he runs to his manager, telling him that he needs his help in securing a unit in five days for the hospital order. Mr. Stone is upset with Rob because it's standard practice for all salespeople to check on product availability before guaranteeing a delivery date. Nevertheless, he immediately calls the company's vice president of manufacturing. The vice president tells Mr. Stone that faster delivery on that particular model is impossible because of higher production priorities. Mr. Stone in turn tells Rob he has no option but to call the account promptly and explain the delay in delivery. Rob is not eager to call Ms. Krane because he knows she will be upset, and he's afraid that she may cancel the order. Besides, it is already Friday afternoon. He decides to wait until Monday to call the account, hoping that in the meantime he'll think of something.

On Monday, Rob has several sales calls to make, and before he knows it, the day is over and he still hasn't called Ms. Krane. On Tuesday morning, he receives a phone message from Ms. Krane asking for confirmation of the scheduled delivery date. Rob waits until he knows she will be out to lunch before returning her call and leaves a brief message on her voice mail saying that he will call back. For the next two days, he deliberately plays telephone tag with Ms. Krane. Finally, on Thursday, Rob knows he must let her know that the new mailing machine is not going to be delivered that Friday. Ms. Krane is angry when Rob tells her the bad news, but he calms her down by assuring her that it will be only one more week before delivery and that he will bring her a "loaner" machine on Friday morning, which he does. The next week passes and still the new equipment has not been delivered to Union Hospital. A deeply upset Ms. Krane leaves another message for Rob asking about the promised delivery, but Rob doesn't bother to return her call. He rationalizes that the hospital has the "free" use of a loaner machine, so there isn't any big problem. When the equipment is finally delivered the following week, Rob calls to make sure that it's working to the hospital's satisfaction. Ms. Krane seems calmer, but not all that happy. Rob figures he'll wait a couple of weeks for matters to settle down and then take her out to a four-star restaurant for lunch to smooth her ruffled feelings.

About two weeks later, before Rob has had a chance to invite Ms. Krane for lunch, she calls to ask his help in straightening out a billing problem. Rob suggests that they discuss it over lunch the following day. At lunch, he takes notes on the problem. It seems that Master Mailer has billed the hospital for a feature that the new mailing machine does not have. Rob explains that this is a minor problem and promises to take care of it. He takes the erroneous invoice and says he will call Ms. Krane within two days to let her know the problem has been resolved. But Rob is so busy over the next two days that he has no time to take care of the billing problem. In fact, it slips his mind until he receives another phone message from Ms. Krane asking whether the hospital's bill has been corrected. When he calls Ms. Krane back, he assures her that he is working on the problem and that it will be resolved shortly. Back in his office that day, Rob makes a point of giving the problem invoice to Joan Newman to handle. After all, he reasons, he's a sales rep, not a credit rep.

About a month later, Rob receives an urgent phone call from Ms. Krane. It seems that Master Mailers' credit department has notified Union Hospital that all its future purchases will be on a C.O.D. basis because the hospital has failed to pay its last invoice. Ms. Krane is furious, saying Union Hospital does not do business this way. After Rob apologizes, he promises that he will resolve the matter that day. Rob immediately returns to the office, and in about four hours he has the situation settled. Mr. Stone, who has heard about the problem from his secretary, asks Rob why the credit department has so mismanaged the Union Hospital account. Reluctant to explain the whole embarrassing set of circumstances, Rob puts Mr. Stone off by saying, "You know Credit's philosophy: 'The customer is always wrong.' But I got it straightened out, Boss. Got to run to another sales appointment. Talk to you later." Rob calls Ms. Krane the following morning to let her know that everything is fine and that the hospital's account is completely straightened out.

Over the next two months, Rob is extremely busy chasing down new sales. Because he hasn't heard from Ms. Krane, he assumes all is well with the Union Hospital account. Actually, he doesn't feel that comfortable calling Ms. Krane with the delivery and billing problems so fresh in her mind. By the middle of the third month, Rob calls Ms. Krane to set up another sales call, figuring that by this time, all the past problems have been put to rest and he can safely approach her for additional orders. When Rob arrives at the hospital, he is surprised to see one of his biggest competitor's mailing machines in an office. He pokes his head into the office and comments to the woman using it, "Is that a new machine?" The woman replies, "Yes, it is. We just got this machine this week and four others just like it. It's a great little machine. I really love it." Rob feels his stomach sink as he thinks about losing out on a sale of five brand new units. Boy, could he have used those commissions! He approaches Ms. Krane's office with a growing sense of discouragement about winning a larger share of Union Hospital's business.

Questions

1. Do you believe that Rob is an effective salesperson? Is he customer-service-oriented? Why or why not?
2. What customer service mistakes did Rob make in handling the Union Hospital account? What should he have done differently?
3. What should Rob have done after making his initial sale to Union Hospital?
4. What advice would you give Rob now in his efforts to win a higher share of business from Union Hospital?

CASE 9.2 A SLAM-DUNK THAT REALLY HURTS

CASE 9.2 "A SLAM-DUNK THAT REALLY HURTS" CAN BE FOUND ONLINE AT HTTP://COLLEGE.HMCO.COM/PIC/ANDERSONPS2E

CHAPTER 10

Understanding and Negotiating with Organizational Buyers

After reading this chapter, you should understand:

- Four kinds of organizational buyers.
- Roles of the members of the buying center.
- Major steps in the buying process and the three types of buying situations.
- Why, what, and how organizational markets buy products and services.
- Six negotiation styles of organizational buyers.
- Buyers' preferred relationships with salespeople.
- Decision-making styles of buyers.
- How to do business in international markets.

"Communication is a skill that you can learn. It's like riding a bicycle or typing. If you're willing to work at it, you can rapidly improve the quality of every part of your life."

Brian Tracy, author and motivational speaker

INSIDE PERSONAL SELLING

Meet Jeanne Connor-Osborn of Sikorsky Aircraft

Who needs a helicopter—and why? That's what Jeanne Connor-Osborn, a Sikorsky Aircraft sales manager, must determine when selling medical helicopters to hospitals, aircraft operators, ministries of health, and governments. Some customers are transporting victims from traffic accidents; others are flying patients to hospitals two states away. "I need to know what customers must do, down to the weight of the patients they will lift and the types of patients they will handle," says Connor-Osborn. "We recently won a contract because our competitor didn't fully understand the customer's business. We pointed out that the other aircraft didn't have the range to reach the customer's top five referral hospitals—the customer's customers—a majority of the time. Understanding the need behind the need gives you the advantage every time."

Connor-Osborn also must understand how different organizations buy. For example, the buying process of hospitals supported by state or federal funds may be regulated. Some organizations hire consultants to help develop product specifications. "Recently, we worked with a consultant who had a medical transport background but no specific aviation background," says Connor-Osborn. "Although he was well versed

regarding specific aircraft features, we had to carefully explain the effect that the combination of features would have on the helicopter's performance."

Selling to buyers in different countries is another challenge. In Japan, for example, helicopters cannot land on roads to pick up traffic victims. As another example, the Canadian government centralizes medical care for certain specialties and buys helicopters to move patients from smaller hospitals to specialty centers.

Connor-Osborn forges long-term relationships by being prepared to respond to customers' needs and concerns. Recently, she submitted a proposal to a hospital that wanted to buy two helicopters, each capable of carrying two patients and a four-person medical crew. The hospital asked Sikorsky and a competitor to make presentations. Two vice presidents, two directors, a medical specialist, and a salesperson from the competing firm arrived in a deluxe helicopter. They brought pictures of their helicopters signed by company employees and answered questions for two hours.

Connor-Osborn knew the competing helicopter was performing a similar mission at another hospital, but under less demanding requirements. Representing Sikorsky, she came alone to the meeting, toting just one cardboard box packed with presentation material. "I focused on the customer's mission," she says. "I knew which hospitals and trauma centers it served. I anticipated the board's questions and the criteria it would use to evaluate the proposals. I could even explain what would happen if they had to land at an alternative airport." Because she was thoroughly prepared, having talked in detail to the hospital's management, pilots, nurses, and mechanics about their specific concerns, she made the multi-million-dollar sale.

As a consumer, you've undoubtedly interacted with a variety of salespeople at retail stores. Some of these salespeople were probably little more than order takers who gave you almost no help, whereas others may have worked patiently with you to find just the right product or service to satisfy your needs. Perhaps you have formulated some strong views—positive or negative—about salespeople on the basis of these experiences. However, before you make up your mind about all salespeople, remember that all of these exchanges were between a salesperson and you—a consumer. Less visible to consumers, but vitally important to the business world, is personal selling that occurs predominantly between a salesperson or sales team and an organizational buyer or buying team. The end result of interchanges between a salesperson and a consumer and those between a salesperson and an organizational buyer follow the same basic Personal Selling Process (PSP), but distinct differences emerge in the sales rep's level of preparation, the nature of the interaction and negotiations, and the extent of customer service. Why? Because organizational buyers make purchases for their companies for different reasons and in more disciplined ways than consumers make purchases for themselves. Although professional buyers often do want to satisfy some *personal* objectives in making a business purchase, they must be concerned primarily with achieving their company's objectives.

As a college graduate pursuing a profession in selling or sales management, you will probably spend most of your career selling to organizations. The highest-earning salespeople sell to various types of organizations, including manufacturers, resellers, governments, and not-for-profit institutions. All of these types of organizations purchase a vast assortment of goods and services, and each has its own perspectives and procedures. In this chapter, we will discuss the buying practices and viewpoints that salespeople must understand in order to sell successfully in organizational markets.

Salespeople identify four types of organizational markets:

1. *Industrial Markets*: Also called *manufacturer* or *producer* or *business markets*, these organizations buy goods and services for the production of other products and services that are sold, rented, or supplied to other organizations and to final consumers.
2. *Reseller Markets*: These organizations (retailers, wholesalers, and industrial distributors) buy goods *to resell or rent* to other organizations and ultimate consumers.
3. *Government Markets*: These markets include federal, state, and local governmental units that buy goods and services for conducting the functions of government.
4. *Nonprofit Markets*: These markets include organizations, such as universities, colleges, hospitals, museums, libraries, and charitable institutions, that are not profit-oriented but buy goods and services for carrying out their functions.

WHAT ORGANIZATIONAL BUYERS WANT FROM SALESPEOPLE

Organizational buyers want to buy from salespeople they can trust to deliver on their promises, provide reliable service, and supply them with precise, accurate, and complete information. They expect salespeople to forewarn them about upcoming price changes, product shortages, employee strikes, delivery delays, or anything else that might affect them and their organizations. Buyers want to do business with salespeople who are truly looking out for their organization's best interests and who help them look good personally—in other words, they want a trusted, reliable consultant, business partner, and friend if possible. Indeed, research suggests that when a "commercial friendship" develops between buyers and sellers, buyers are more loyal, have greater satisfaction, and are more inclined to provide favorable word-of-mouth promotion about the seller's firm.[1]

Creating and Maintaining Long-Term Relationships

Relationships in organizational markets are critical. Instead of taking a short-run view by making as much profit as possible on each transaction, salespeople who successfully sell to organizations understand that it is a much more profitable strategy for their companies and themselves to create and nurture long-term relationships with customers. Negotiations with buyers must always be *win-win (both parties satisfy their needs)*, never *win-lose (only the seller's needs are satisfied)*. Professional salespeople do not try to win a contest or competition. In fact, you will not succeed over the long run by beating customers in negotiations. Even if you do have the power to take unfair advantage of a customer, never yield to the temptation. The lifetime value of a loyal customer is much greater than any profit from a one-time sale—no matter how large—and the buyer-seller relationship may be ended by an unbalanced outcome. Thus salespeople should focus on creating long-run relationships, not merely making short-run sales transactions. In short, they should be continually thinking about building enduring strategic partnerships with customers.

Strategic Partnerships

Strategic partnering includes all activities aimed at creating, developing, and maintaining successful exchange relationships with customers. Salespeople calling on organizational customers should make managing these relationships their main focus. It is folly for a salesperson who wishes to develop a trusting, long-lasting buyer-seller relationship to mislead or withhold information or manipulate the buyer in any way. Instead, strive to make sure that all parties are satisfied in all transactions or agreements. Relationships between buyers and sellers are more effective and long-lasting when both parties cooperate with one another, trust one another, and realize that each of them needs the other.[2] Strategic partners work together cooperatively to make each other successful.

INDUSTRIAL MARKETS

Largest and most diverse of all the organizational markets, industrial markets offer outstanding opportunities for anyone considering a professional selling career. There are more careers in industrial selling than in other kinds of selling because many more transactions occur at the business level between members of the channels of distribution. In addition, nearly all industries buy from and sell to one another in creating products for the final consumer. Thus the dollar volume of industrial marketing transactions far exceeds that in consumer markets.

North American Industry Classification System (NAICS)

One of the best basic sources for identifying new business prospects and their general requirements is the **North American Industry Classification System (NAICS)** published by the U.S. Office of Management and Budget (OMB). NAICS, which is pronounced "nakes," replaces the old Standard Indus-

North American Industry Classification System (NAICS) Covers more than 19,000 industry descriptions, used to identify new business prospects and their general product and service requirements by up to six digits of specificity.

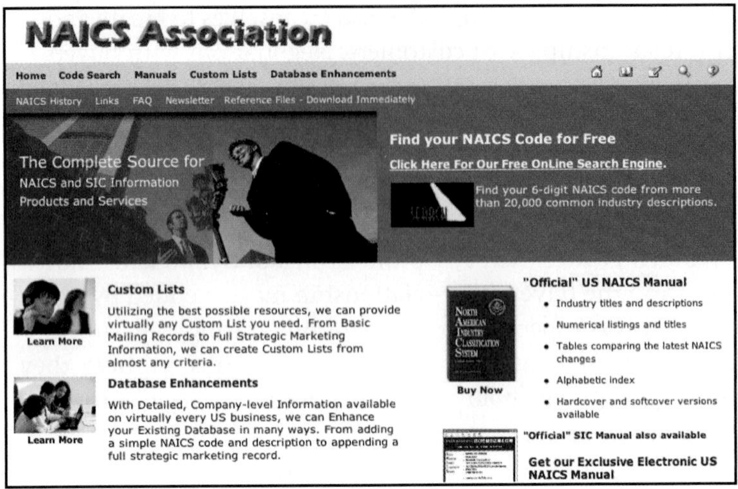

trial Classification (SIC) System and provides for standardization in reporting economic data among Mexico, Canada, and the United States. NAICS is more detailed than SIC and provides better coverage of services such as health care, entertainment, and financial institutions. As illustrated in Figure 10.1, the NAICS code starts with the broad industry category identified by two digits and then focuses more specifically on products and services with each additional digit. To learn more about industrial classification of manufacturing and service firms, visit www.naics.com.

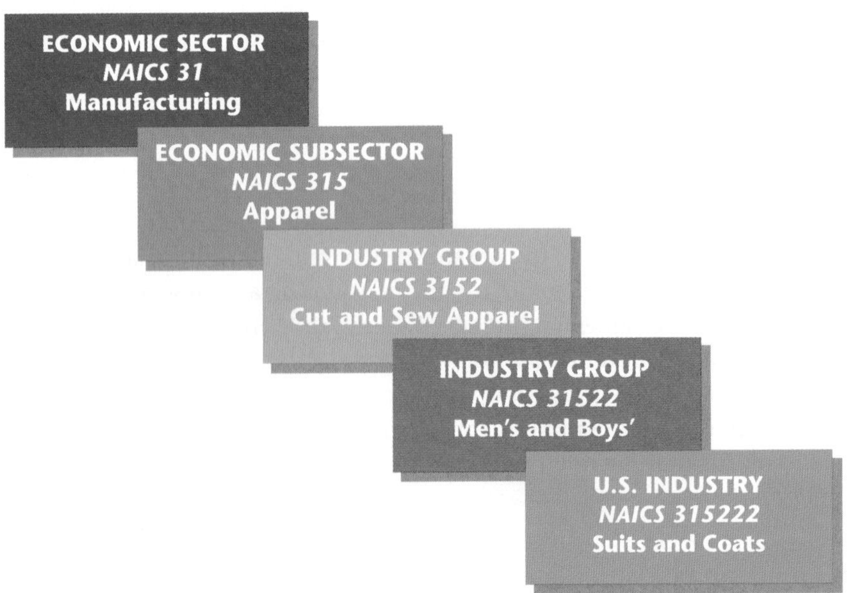

FIGURE 10.1

NORTH AMERICAN INDUSTRY CLASSIFICATION SYSTEM FOR IDENTIFYING BUSINESS PROSPECTS

TABLE 10.1

Industrial Versus Consumer Market Characteristics

Characteristic	Industrial Market	Consumer Market
Demand	Derived	Direct
	Price inelasticity	Price elasticity
	More volatile	Less volatile
	Relatively few buying centers	Many individuals or households
Buyer	Buying centers	Individual or household buyers
	Professional	Amateur
Purchasing Process	Long negotiations	Short negotiations
	Infrequent purchases	Frequent purchases
	Large order size ($ or units)	Small order size ($ or units)
	Servicing expected	Servicing not expected
	Reciprocity often demanded	No reciprocity demanded
	Often lease	Seldom lease
Marketing Mix:	Customized, more technical	Standardized, less technical
Products/Services	Formal bids	List prices
Price	Emphasis on personal selling	Emphasis on advertising
Promotion	Shorter channels	Longer channels
Distribution	Buy direct from producers	Buy through middlemen (e.g., retailers)

Industrial Market Characteristics

Industrial markets differ significantly from consumer markets in the areas of demand, buyers, purchasing process, and marketing mix, as outlined in Table 10.1. Let's briefly discuss these differences.

Derived Demand Demand created as a result of consumer demand; typical of industrial markets.

Demand. Industrial demand tends to be **derived demand**; i.e., demand for the industrial good comes from demand for a consumer good. For example, Ford Motor's (www.ford.com) demand for sheet steel from a steel manufacturer as an input in manufacturing automobiles is derived from consumer demand for Ford automobiles. If the demand for automobiles weakens, so will the demand for sheet steel to produce automobiles. Price *elasticity* of demand, i.e., the degree to which demand is sensitive to changes in price, is another characteristic of industrial demand, especially in the short run, when industrial producers find it difficult to make changes in production methods. In *consumer* markets, sometimes even a small upward change in price will have a large negative impact on consumer demand, meaning that demand is *elastic* with respect to price. In industrial markets, however, a comparatively small change in price usually has little or no impact on overall demand, meaning that demand is *inelastic* with respect to price. Finally, industrial demand is characterized by *volatility*. Because industrial goods are so affected by final consumer demand, a small change in consumer demand creates a much larger change in the demand for industrial goods and services.

Buyers. Industrial buyers tend to be geographically concentrated. About half of the nation's producers are in seven states: New York, California, Pennsylvania, Illinois, Ohio, New Jersey, and Michigan. Industrial buyers are also usually grouped into buying centers or committees, which typically include technical experts and top management. Salespeople need to be well trained and well prepared to make presentations before such groups of experts.

Purchasing Process. Industrial purchases are less frequent and normally require a longer negotiation period than consumer purchases. This is because the industrial product is generally made to order, which requires agreement on exact specifications, and because industrial buyers often require formal bids, which requires time for the seller to prepare precise cost estimates. If the product is complex and expensive, industrial organizations often buy directly from producers instead of going through industrial distributors or other middlemen. Major airlines, for example, buy their aircraft directly from manufacturers such as Boeing (www.boeing.com) or Airbus (www.airbus.com).

Reciprocity In industrial buyer-seller relationships, an informal agreement between two or more organizations to exchange goods and services on a systematic and more or less exclusive basis. In other words, "You buy from me, and I'll buy from you."

Reciprocity often figures in industrial buying. Taking our cue from the old saying "If you scratch my back, I'll scratch yours," we can define reciprocity, in the context of industrial organizations, as a *mutual exchange of benefits*. In other words, "I'll buy from you if you'll buy from me." A company that procures hardwood veneers and laminates, for example, might buy its office desks and bookcases from its biggest customer, an office furniture maker. Most such reciprocal arrangements are not backed by a formal contract, though some companies have a "trade relations" department to keep track of their reciprocal buying arrangements with various customers and suppliers. Companies that develop long-term relationships based on reciprocity have found it a beneficial competitive tool.[3] Smaller companies tend to make most use of reciprocal agreements. However, the systemic practice of reciprocity can damage morale in a company's sales force and in its purchasing department. Surveys show that most purchasing agents and salespeople dislike reciprocity because it restricts their ability to negotiate for the best terms with reciprocating partners.[4]

Finally, even though reciprocity may sound like a reasonable business practice, the Federal Trade Commission and the Justice Department's antitrust division prohibit it if it becomes anticompetitive. Contracts requiring an exclusive supplier arrangement, exclusive dealing, or tying agreement generally have been found illegal in court. Buyers must be able to show that they are obtaining competitive prices, quality, and service from suppliers with whom they engage in reciprocity.

Leasing in lieu of purchasing is a rapidly growing option in industrial organizations. Each year, U.S. companies lease billions of dollars worth of equipment, ranging from power plants and offshore drilling rigs to office copiers and forklift trucks. Company cars, computers, and machine tools that have high obsolescence are frequently leased to save capital investment funds and ensure access to the latest technology.

Marketing Mix. The many differences between industrial and consumer markets in terms of demand, buyers, and purchasing process require that companies selling to industrial organizations develop marketing mixes tailored to specific customer groups and their unique needs. Because sellers must anticipate and satisfy the changing needs of industrial customers who, in turn, are trying to satisfy the needs of their own customers, it is easy to understand why personal selling is the most important factor in their marketing mixes. Every successful company knows that the only way to sell to industrial organizations is to have salespeople who make it their job to understand their customers' organizations inside and out. For this reason, companies make major investments in training their industrial salespeople. As the role of purchasing becomes more strategic to the success of most organizations, salespeople must develop unique *value propositions* for their prospects and customers. Motorola (www.motorola.com), for example, seeks to establish relationships only with parts suppliers that can provide cutting-edge technology to increase the perceived value of Motorola's products for customers and thereby strengthen its competitive position in diverse markets. Cisco Systems enhances its value proposition by selling directly to organizational customers from its website. At any time, buyers can log on to www.ciscosystems.com and commence the buying process. In the early stages, customers can search first for specific products, specifications, prices, and lead times. Then, before making their final selections, they can try different configurations online to see how proposed changes affect prices. After ordering, buyers can go online whenever they wish to check the delivery status of their purchases and order follow-on services, parts, or product upgrades.

Chapter Review Questions

- Compare and contrast industrial markets and consumer markets.
- Explain why industrial demand is *derived* demand.
- Why are industrial markets more price inelastic and volatile than consumer markets?

The Role of the Industrial Buyer

Industrial buyers (frequently called *purchasing agents*) are buying experts for their organizations. Large companies have purchasing departments with many purchasing agents, each specializing in buying a particular product or service from various salespeople who call on them. Over the past few decades, the industrial buyer's role and responsibilities have expanded from essentially those of a clerk to those of an executive. With increasing competition worldwide, the industrial buyer has had to become a highly sophisticated career professional. Skillful purchasing, especially during times of resource shortages, is a major determinant of an organization's profitability. Thus an organization's success largely depends on its industrial buyers' ability to do the following well:[5]

Industrial Buyer The buying expert for an organization. Sometimes called the purchasing agent.

Chapter Review Question
Name the different criteria by which a company will measure the success of its purchasing agent.

- Negotiate favorable prices and purchase terms.
- Develop alternative solutions to buying problems, while keeping organizational departments informed about negotiations.
- Protect the organization's cost structure (its cost of doing business).
- Ensure reliable, long-run sources of supply.
- Maintain good relationships with suppliers.
- Manage the procurement process (reorder procedures, order expediting, order receipt, and record control).

To successfully develop and maintain long-run relationships with customers, you must keep in mind all of the foregoing goals of industrial buyers. Unless you help *them* succeed, *you* won't succeed. "Win-win" relationships are the only ones that last.

What Do Industrial Markets Buy?

Foundation Goods Goods used in the production process that do not become part of the finished product, such as fixed major machine tools and office equipment.

Entering Goods Ingredients or components that become part of the finished product, such as raw materials and semi-manufactured goods.

Facilitating Goods Goods consumed in the ongoing production process, such as maintenance and repair items.

We can develop our perspective on the industrial buying process, with its diffused buying influences and diverse products and services, by classifying goods on the basis of their relationship to the organization's production process and cost structure. Industrial buyers are interested in three basic categories of goods and services. The categories are described below, and Table 10.2 illustrates product examples.

1. **Foundation goods** are used in the production process but do not become a part of the finished product (e.g., installations, accessory equipment, office equipment).
2. **Entering goods** are components that become part of the finished product (e.g., raw materials, semi-manufactured goods, parts, manufacturing services).
3. **Facilitating goods** are goods and services consumed in the production process (e.g., maintenance and repair items, operating supplies, business services).

Airplanes are foundation goods used by airlines to provide services.
Pascal Le Segretain/Getty Images

TABLE 10.2

Classification of Industrial Goods

Foundation Goods

Installations: Items considered part of the fixed plant of the purchaser.

Examples: Large machine tools, printing presses, electric generators, elevators.

Equipment: Capital investment items not regarded as part of the fixed plant.

Examples: Motor trucks, portable tools, computers, desks.

Entering Goods

Raw Materials: Unprocessed primary materials from agriculture and other extractive industries.

Examples: Wheat, livestock, cotton, crude petroleum, iron ore, lumber.

Semi-manufactured Goods: Finished output of one manufacturer or processor that undergoes additional changes in form by another manufacturer or processor.

Examples: Sheet steel, basic chemicals, cement, textiles sold to garment manufacturers, flour sold to bakeries.

Parts: Manufactured products that can be installed as a component of larger products.

Examples: Electric motors, automobile batteries and tires (original equipment), thermostats for refrigerators.

Contract Manufacturing Services: Part of the manufacturing process contracted to an outside organization.

Examples: Dyeing, casting, cutting, or shaping services performed by a company on materials supplied by the customer.

Facilitating Goods

Maintenance and Repair Items: Quickly consumed and highly expendable items that help ensure the continued satisfactory functioning of plant and equipment.

Examples: Repair parts, lubricants, nails, cleaning materials, paint.

Operating Supplies: Items required for day-to-day operations.

Examples: Copier paper, cash register tape, pencils.

Business Services: Services provided by others, often involving the use of supplies.

Examples: Printing services, janitorial or cleaning services, business repair services, consulting or advertising services.

How Do Industrial Markets Buy?

Buying Centers. In larger organizations, it's realistic to refer to industrial purchasing operations as **buying centers,** because several people participate in purchasing decisions. A buying center consists of all people in the organization who participate in or influence the purchase decision process. This includes anyone who plays any of the following six roles in the buying process:

Buying Center In a buying organization, a group of organization members who participate in the purchase decision.

1. *Initiators:* People who first recognize or anticipate a problem that may be solved by buying a good or service.
2. *Gatekeepers:* People who control information or access to decision makers are **gatekeepers.** Purchasing agents, technical advisers, secretaries, and even telephone switchboard operators can assume this role by preventing salespeople from seeing users or deciders. In situations where sales reps cannot win over gatekeepers, they will have to find ways to subtly go around them to make sales.
3. *Influencers:* **Influencers** affect the purchase decision by helping set product and service specifications, by negotiating purchasing procedures and prices, or by providing information about evaluating alternatives. Technical specialists usually are important influencers.
4. *Deciders:* In many cases these are higher-level managers who have power to select or approve suppliers and final purchase decisions. For routine purchases, the purchasing agents are the deciders.
5. *Buyers:* People who have formal authority to order supplies and negotiate purchase terms within organizational constraints.
6. *Users:* People who will actually use the product or service purchased. Users are generally people in production, including machine operators, shop forepersons, and supervisors. Users often initiate the buying proposal and help decide product specifications.

Gatekeeper Person who controls access or flow of information to decision makers. Examples include technical advisers, secretaries, security guards, and even telephone switchboard operators.

Influencers People who can influence the purchase decision by helping set product specifications, negotiating purchasing procedures and prices, or providing information about evaluating alternatives.

Chapter Review Question

What six roles can different members of a buying center play in the industrial buying process?

Successful salespeople must know all members of the buying center and the roles they play, because each one can influence the purchasing decision. What's more, salespeople must provide each member the precise information needed to facilitate the eventual sale. Because several individuals take part in the buying process, the ultimate sale is likely to be time-consuming, so patience and diligence are required when selling to buying centers.

Some salespeople virtually move in with their large customers; i.e., they work with them on a daily basis and may set up an office nearby or even in the buyer's headquarters or factory.[6] Doing so helps them stay attuned to the multiple buying influences in order to do some multilevel, in-depth, consultative selling. Ask the salespeople in any company, "Are you, with most customers, dealing with the same purchasing agents today as you were five years ago?" Usually, the answer is no. People in the customer organization are continually changing—they may leave the company, receive a promotion to a different job, take a long vacation, retire, or become ill. Farsighted salespeople acquaint themselves with *all* possible members of the buying center to keep their relationship with the customer from depending on just one person. In other words, they don't put all their eggs in one basket (relationship).

Types of Buying Situations. Industrial buyers face a series of decisions that depend on each buying situation. Figure 10.2 illustrates three basic types of buying situations: (1) straight rebuy, (2) modified rebuy, and (3) new task buy. Purchasing agents are most influential in straight rebuys and modified rebuys, which involve, respectively, routine response and limited problem solving. But engineers are most influential in new task buying, which requires extensive problem solving.

INCREASING COMPLEXITY

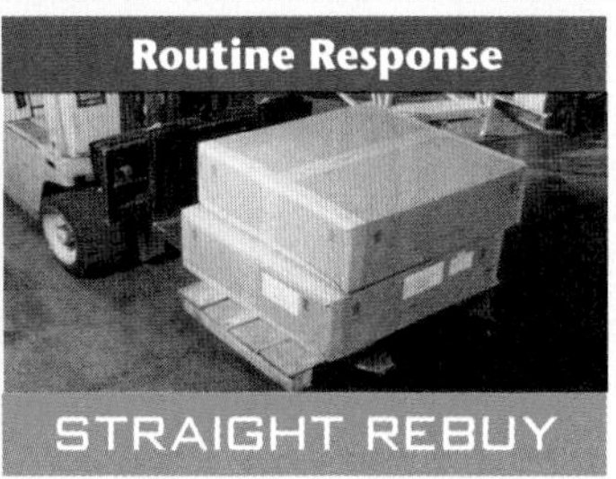

FIGURE 10.2

THREE TYPES OF INDUSTRIAL BUYING SITUATIONS

Straight Rebuy. A routine, programmable decision is a *straight rebuy,* where the buyer reorders something from a supplier on the "approved list." Examples of straight rebuys include purchases of bulk chemicals, utilities, or office supplies. Suppliers on the approved list strive to maintain product and service quality and encourage automatic-reordering systems to save the purchasing agent's time and keep out other suppliers. Suppliers not on the approved list must try to get their foot in the door by offering something new or by providing an incentive such as price discounts or greater service to obtain a small order. Once on the list, and after performing well on a small order, the salesperson can seek larger orders.

Modified Rebuy. A more complex decision process requiring more information and involving more decision participants is a *modified rebuy*. Such purchases come about when the buyer seeks a change in product specifications, prices, supplier performance, or the like. In this situation, "in" suppliers run scared trying to protect their relationship with the buyer, while "out" suppliers offer customers various inducements to switch to them. Examples of modified rebuys are consulting services and new company cars or trucks.

New Task Buy. A supplier's greatest opportunity comes when the buyer considers purchasing a product or service for the first time. Examples of a new task include the purchase of a huge installation such as a heating plant and the construction of a new building. The first-time purchase of a complex new product or service calls for the greatest amount of information and the most decision participants. Buyers must determine product specifications, price limits, delivery terms and times, service requirements, payment terms, order quantities, acceptable suppliers, and the selected supplier. As we mentioned in chapter 6 (on the sales presentation), such a process often begins with specialized sales teams of salespeople and technical specialists who make comprehensive presentations "selling the company" to the potential customer. The new task buying situation comes up rather infrequently, but it is vital that salespeople be well prepared to make their presentations for these purchase situations, because winning the contract can lead to many spin-off rebuys later on. Try resolving an organizational purchase problem in the following *It's Up to You* feature.

IT'S UP TO YOU

You recently sold an air conditioning and heating system to Beecher Company, a small manufacturer. You were even present when the system was installed. After about a month, you receive a call from Beecher. The buyer is arguing that the new system is not effective—the building is either too hot or too cold, and employees are constantly complaining about the room temperature. The buyer is demanding that the new system be removed and a better one installed at no additional cost. What is your first step? If you need further information, where will you look or whom will you ask? How will you resolve this problem?

The buying center for very expensive commercial airplanes includes senior management as well as senior pilots.
Jeff Greenberg/The Image Works, Inc.

Stages in the Buying Process. Today's industrial buyers often know much more about industrial selling behavior than the industrial salesperson knows about industrial buying behavior. Thus salespeople who fail to understand how their potential customers make their buying decisions are at a severe disadvantage. Thoroughly researching and understanding the customers' buying process is one of the selling secrets of successful salespeople. As shown in Figure 10.3, there are eight major stages in the industrial buying process: (1) recognizing the problem, (2) describing the basic need, (3) developing product specifications, (4) searching for suppliers, (5) soliciting proposals, (6) evaluating proposals and selecting suppliers, (7) setting up the order procedure, and (8) reviewing performance. Let's discuss each of these steps briefly.

Recognizing the Problem. The window of opportunity opens for alert salespeople when a business customer complains about a competitor's equipment or products, or when machines break down, supplies and inventories become low, materials are in short supply, current products or services are unsatisfactory, new equipment is being installed, or new products are under consideration. Of course, if your firm's products and services are not performing well, you must do something fast to keep the customer's business. You must remain continually sensitive to means of improving the customer's profitability by anticipating problems and alerting customers to opportunities (recall discussions about post-sale follow-up in chapter 9).

Describing the Basic Need. After recognizing the problem, the industrial buyer tries to better define the needed item's general characteristics through

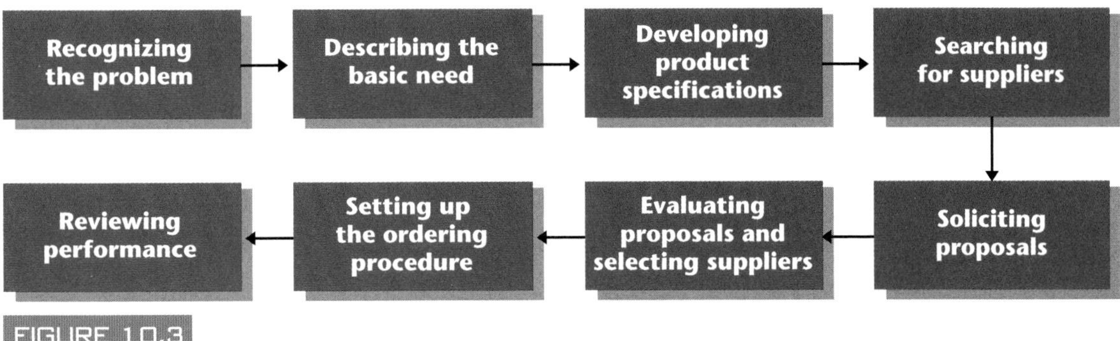

FIGURE 10.3

STAGES IN THE BUYING PROCESS

discussions with company engineers, research and development scientists, or line managers. At this stage, the buyer organization usually conducts a feasibility study to determine whether it would be better to make or to buy the item.

Developing Product Specifications. The buying organization develops detailed technical specifications to ensure that no error is made by the industrial buyer or the suppliers in providing the exact item needed. Any confusion about the exact specifications (dimensions, quality, or quantity) can result in costly manufacturing delays for the customer and lost business (rejected items) for the supplier. Many times, especially with government customers, suppliers will try to work with buyers to write tight specs designed to enable their own companies to secure the business. Most buyers, though, oppose any product specifications so rigid as to limit consideration of supplier alternatives. This is because no buyer wants to be dependent on a sole supplier unless the buyer has extreme leverage over the supplier (as would a large company whose purchases represent a major share of a small company's sales).

Searching for Suppliers. Using product specifications as the guide, the buyer tries to identify qualified potential suppliers (sometimes called *vendors*). Trade directories and recommendations from other industrial buyers are useful in this search phase. Aggressive sales organizations will probably have already solicited business from most potential customers, but unsolicited "call-ins" are still a valuable source of sales. And inside salespeople who handle these call-ins must be as well trained as outside salespeople. Beyond this, salespeople should ensure that their company and its offerings are listed in all appropriate trade directories and that the company's reputation as a supplier remains favorable. Repeat business and referrals from satisfied customers are the fastest, most reliable ways to a profitable sales operation.

Soliciting Proposals. Industrial buyers usually invite qualified suppliers to submit proposals for producing and selling the specified items. After reviewing these proposals, the buyer will solicit formal presentations by the more promising potential suppliers. Thus professional salespeople require training in researching, preparing, and presenting proposals so that they can "sell" the company as well as the technical product. In preparing and presenting sales proposals, professional salespeople keep in mind five basic decision criteria used by nearly all organizational buyers:

1. *Performance criteria:* How well will the product or service do the required job?
2. *Economic criteria:* What is the total cost associated with buying and using the product or service?
3. *Integrative criteria:* Will the supplier be flexible and responsive in working closely with us to meet our changing requirements and expectations?
4. *Adaptive criteria:* How likely is the seller to produce and deliver according to specifications and terms?
5. *Legalistic criteria*: What legal or policy parameters must be considered in buying the product or service?[7]

Evaluating Proposals and Selecting Suppliers. In reviewing the proposals before awarding a contract, industrial buying organizations evaluate the potential supplier on various criteria. These criteria vary with the size and nature of the buying organization as well as the type of product. Delivery capability, product quality, service, technical ability, and price are usually most important in buying technically complex products. In this stage, it is especially important for salespeople to keep in mind that the engineering department is usually the most influential in new task buying, whereas the purchasing department has the most influence in straight rebuys and modified rebuys.

Setting Up the Ordering Procedure. Instead of preparing a new contract for each periodic purchase order, most industrial buyers prefer *blanket contracts* that establish an open purchase arrangement over a stated period at a certain price so that reorders are routine. Computerized ordering procedures are common for staple supplies. An order is automatically printed out or e-mailed to the designated supplier whenever inventory dwindles to a specified level. Salespeople often suggest setting up blanket purchase agreements when they win an order because such an arrangement encourages single-source buying through automatic reordering.

Chapter Review Question
Name and describe the sequential stages in the industrial buying process.

Reviewing Performance. Many industrial buyers proactively and regularly contact the end-user departments in their company to obtain feedback on suppliers' performance. These performance reviews, which can be relatively

KEEPING UP ONLINE: GENERAL ELECTRIC CORPORATION

General Electric Corporation (GE) produces a wide array of different products and offers a variety of services to various markets. Visit its website *www.ge.com* and describe the different markets that its salespeople must serve. Does GE have a different sales force for each of these markets? How might GE use its website to provide customer and salesperson services during the buying process and obtain customer feedback on its performance?

casual conversations or detailed, formal ratings, shape relationships with suppliers by continuing, modifying, or terminating purchase orders. Salespeople should constantly review their own performances so that problems are "nipped in the bud." Read the *Keeping Up Online* feature on page 334 to discover how a company's website might help its customers and salespeople during the buying process.

RESELLERS

Resellers include all those intermediary organizations that buy goods for reselling or leasing to others at a profit or for conducting their own operations. Resellers serve as purchasing agents for their customers, so they buy products and brands that they think will appeal to their customers.

Kinds of Resellers

The following are three categories of resellers:

1. *Industrial distributors*, which sell to manufacturers and producers
2. *Wholesalers*, which sell to retailers
3. *Retailers*, which sell to consumers

Industrial Distributors. Industrial distributors in the United States number about 12,000, and each generates an average yearly sales volume of about $4 million. E-commerce between businesses represents more than 90 percent of the estimated $4 trillion in e-commerce sales.[8] Industrial distributors handle a variety of products: maintenance, repair, and operating (MRO) supplies; finished products of original equipment manufacturers (OEM); and tools, equipment, and machinery used in the operation of the business. There are three kinds of industrial distributors. *General-line distributors* (mill supply houses) are the "supermarkets" of industry because of the broad range of products they carry. *Specialist firms* stock a narrow line of related products, such as bearings, abrasives, and cutting tools. General-line houses have been developing specialist departments, so the difference between these two types has blurred. A third type, the *combination house*, operates like a wholesaler as well by selling to retailers and institutions in addition to manufacturers and construction firms. Industrial distributors are increasing in importance as their sales volume continues to grow more rapidly than the gross national product. Generally, salespeople who work for industrial distributors sell to manufacturers and constructions firms.

Wholesalers. Wholesaling organizations serve the buying requirements of resellers who, in turn, sell to consumers. The three basic types of wholesalers are (1) merchant wholesalers; (2) agents, brokers, and commission merchants; and (3) manufacturers' sales branches. Merchant wholesalers, often called distributors, account for more than 80 percent of all wholesalers in the United

States.[9] Salespeople who sell to retailers work for various types of *full-service* and *limited-service* merchant wholesalers (e.g., brokers, agents, or manufacturer's sales branches).

Retailers. More than 1.6 million retailers in the United States employ more than 20 million people. This number has stayed relatively constant over the past twenty-five years, whereas sales volume has quadrupled to nearly $3 trillion annually.[10]

Chain stores—centrally owned and managed groups of retail stores—account for more than one-third of all retail sales, even though they comprise less than 1 percent of all retail establishments. Despite the growing importance of chains, *single-unit, independently owned stores* remain prevalent in retailing. This ownership category accounts for more than 90 percent of all retail stores. Most retail salesclerks are little more than order takers and have traditionally been paid poor hourly wages. Only recently have a few large chains begun offering commissions on sales to all of their retail salespeople, thereby providing the incentive for them to do creative selling.

Reseller Buying Situations

Salespeople dealing with *reseller* buyers should know that resellers generally find themselves involved in three types of buying situations. Let's discuss each briefly.

New-Product Situation. The *new-product situation* arises when suppliers seek distribution for a newly developed product. Because storage and display space are always at a premium, the buyer often must determine what item to drop if the new product is to be ordered for stock. Many buyers estimate potential profit per cubic foot before making a decision. When determining whether to take on a new product, buyers typically consider such factors as profit margins, product uniqueness, seller's intended positioning and marketing plan, test market results, promotional support, and seller's reputation. Also, many supermarket chains demand "slotting allowances"—payments up front before they will make room for a new product on their shelves. Some supermarkets even demand "pay to stay" payments to keep the manufacturer's product on the shelves.

Selection of the Best Supplier. Resellers must *select the best supplier* from several when space limitations permit only one or two brands in a product category or when they require a private-label supplier for their own house brand. For example, Sears (www.sears.com) chose Whirlpool Corporation (www.whirlpool.com) to make its private-label Kenmore clothes washers, so Whirlpool has the inside track in selling its other brands of home appliances, including KitchenAid and Roper, to Sears stores.

Better Set of Terms from Current Suppliers. The third buying situation comes about when the reseller wants to obtain *a better set of terms from current suppliers*. McDonald's, the world's most successful food franchiser, decided a few years ago to buy all its food and nonfood products from one supplier. Golden State Foods Corporation (www.goldenstatefoods.com), which was supplying McDonald's (www.mcdonalds.com) burgers, buns, and potatoes, was forced to take on a line of paper products to keep McDonald's business, which accounted for 80 percent of Golden State's sales at the time.

Reseller Information Systems

Recent years have seen the rapid rise of the *professional reseller manager*, who is more scientific and information oriented than his or her predecessor. Although electronic point-of-sale (POS) systems and in-store computers began appearing in retail outlets in the early 1970s, computer software packages for efficiently managing information on inventory, purchases, cash flow, and accounts payable were slow in arriving. Installation of checkout scanners has generated an abundance of timely and specific data about consumer response. Instead of receiving monthly or bimonthly reports about how a brand is doing, retailers now receive weekly or even daily data for every item and size. They are learning precisely how a price cut, promotional coupon, store display, or quantity discount actually affects sales and profits. For example, Nestlé Foods Corporation (www.nestle.com) discovered that a combination of store displays and newspaper ads resulted in large volume increases for its chocolate drink *Quik*. Warner-Lambert, now a division of Pfizer (www.pfizer.com), found that store displays were far more effective than newspaper ads or price promotions, and its sales force now focuses on providing incentives to supermarket managers to set up in-store displays.

Computer-Assisted Buying

Today's customers place increasing value on having timely information and often award their business to the seller who provides the best information. For instance, after outfitting its salespeople with laptop computers, Evan-Picone Hosiery, a division of the Jones Apparel Group (www.jny.com/index.jsp), sharply reduced the turnaround time for receiving, manufacturing, and delivering sales orders. In addition, the company can spot fashion trends earlier now that it knows the status of every order for every product. This information has helped Evan-Picone serve its customers better and thereby win more sales.

As reseller information systems based on computerized purchasing operations increase in sophistication, the professional salesperson's job will rapidly shift toward providing buyers with detailed and comprehensive data. Some large manufacturers' sales forces have already edged ahead of the competition by providing retailer customers with individualized merchandising service. For example, salespeople for R. J. Reynolds Tobacco (www.rjreynolds.com) show retail customers various ways to increase profits by better use of display space, new merchandising techniques, and improved inventory control. See Table 10.3 for a variety of incentives that salespeople can offer to make their products more attractive to resellers.

Chapter Review Question

List, discuss, and give examples of the three types of industrial buying situations.

TABLE 10.3

INCENTIVES OFFERED TO RESELLERS

Radio Frequency Identification (RFID): Seller attaches RFIDs to products purchased, so that resellers can more easily track inventory products and reduce theft.

Point-of-Sale Inventory-Tracking Systems: Seller sets up a computerized system that automatically generates repurchase orders when inventories reach pre-designated levels.

Product Tags: Seller attaches product tags that detail the price, color, size, manufacturer, and identification number to enable resellers to track products sold.

Cooperative Advertising Allowances: Seller provides monetary assistance to help defray reseller costs for advertising seller's products.

Promotional Pricing: To attract customers, the seller authorizes reduced prices for store promotions.

Trade Margins and Allowances: Seller provides attractive cash, trade, and quantity discounts, as well as allowances for reseller product returns, merchandise exchanges, and markdowns of seller products.

Reseller Contests and Sweepstakes: Seller conducts contests and provides rewards for reseller salespeople who generate the highest sales revenue for seller's products.

Point-of-Purchase Displays: Seller provides in-store displays, glossy posters, and print advertisements.

Reseller Training Programs: Seller provides training to reseller salespersons, especially for technologically complex products that requires special know-how to sell.

In-Store Demonstrations: Seller sets up in-store demonstrations to show customers how products work and to persuade them to buy.

Slotting Allowances: Seller pays money to rent shelf space from the reseller and provide an incentive to push its products.

Just-in-Time Purchasing: To reduce carrying costs for the reseller, inventory is carried by the selling firm, which delivers goods to the reseller on short notice.

Source: *From* Marketing Management: The Millenium Edition, *10th Edition by Philip Kotler. Copyright© 2000 by Philip Kotler. Reprinted by permission of Pearson Education, Inc., Upper Saddle River, NJ.*

GOVERNMENT MARKETS

The U.S. government, 50 state governments, more than 3,000 county governments, and nearly 87,000 local governments purchase well over a trillion dollars worth of goods and services annually. Federal, state, and local government spending has grown rapidly over the years as increasing services have been provided for citizens. Total purchases in the trillions of dollars makes the United States federal government the largest customer in the world.

Sales Opportunities in Government Markets

Government markets offer opportunities for both producers and "middlemen" to sell everything from spacecraft to toothpaste—everything needed to provide citizens with such services as national defense, fire and police protection, education, health care, water, postal service, waste disposal, and public transportation. Government purchasing patterns sometimes change abruptly in response to budget constraints and the service demands of citizens, which can present a problem—or an opportunity—for sellers. The **FedBizOpps.gov** website lists federal government procurement opportunities over $25,000. Through this single portal, commercial vendors seeking federal markets for their products and services can search, monitor, and retrieve opportunities being solicited by the entire federal contracting community.

FedBizOpps.gov Website that contains all federal contracting community solicitations for purchases exceeding $25,000.

How Do Governments Buy?

Governments spend public funds derived largely from taxes, so by law, their purchases must be made on the basis of bids or written proposals from vendors. Although purchasing procedures are rigorous in order to ensure quality products and honest, efficient expenditures, selling to governments can be profitable for sellers willing to cope with some bureaucratic red tape. Government purchasing agents have the basic goal of obtaining goods and services from the lowest-cost qualified supplier. Sometimes, however, this goal comes second to such objectives as favoring small businesses, minority-owned companies, or suppliers from depressed areas.

Federal buying serves two sectors, civilian and military. For the federal government's civilian sector, the General Services Administration (GSA), through its Office of Federal Supply and Services, buys all general goods and services (such as office furniture, equipment, supplies, vehicles, and fuels) for use by other government agencies. Defense Department purchases are made by the Defense Logistics Agency (DLA) and the three military services, the army, navy, and air force. The DLA operates specialized supply centers that function as "single managers" for purchasing and distributing construction materials, electronics, fuel, personnel support, and industrial and general supplies used in common by the army, navy, and air force. In addition, each branch of the military buys to meet its specialized needs through its own supply system.

Both the GSA and the DLA function as wholesalers and resellers for other government units. Together they account for most federal contracts for goods and services, although nearly five hundred other offices in Washington have their own buying functions and procurement policies. Most states have procurement offices to help carry out these massive federal government purchasing activities. Booklets explaining the procedures to follow in selling to governments are available at state purchasing offices and at the U.S. Government Printing Office. For more information, see the following websites: www.access.gpo.gov/su_docs/ and www.access.gpo.gov/#business.

Chapter Review Question

Briefly discuss government markets. What are the two sectors for which the federal government buys? How are most government purchases made? What sources of help in dealing with the government are available?

NOT-FOR-PROFIT MARKETS

Nonprofit organizations, also called *noncommercial, nonbusiness,* and *not-for-profit* organizations, include colleges, hospitals, libraries, charities, churches, museums, and organizations such as the National Organization for Women (www.now.org), the American Association of Retired People (www.aarp.com), and the Red Cross (www.redcross.org). Too often, salespeople and their companies overlook many nonprofit organizations as prospects, perhaps thinking the opportunities for profitable sales are limited. This is a big mistake. Although nonprofit organizations themselves may not strive for profits, they can offer highly profitable opportunities for salespeople who are energetic and persistent enough to learn about the operations, goals, and problems these diverse organizations face, while keeping in mind their unique characteristics. Many nonprofit organizations use buying processes similar to those of commercial businesses and buy everything from janitorial services to automobiles. However, nonbusiness organizations do have several distinct characteristics that salespeople must keep in mind throughout the selling-buying process and the ongoing relationship. The most important of these characteristics are

Dual Management A management system in which both professional managers and specialists without managerial training run an organization, sometimes resulting in conflict. Typical of many nonprofit organizations.

- *Multiple Objectives:* Nonprofits' "bottom line" consists of multiple nonfinancial and financial goals, such as the social impact of their efforts, the number of people served, and the amount of donations or gifts received.
- *Services and Social Change:* Rather than selling a tangible product, most nonprofits distribute ideas and services to change people's attitudes and behaviors.
- *Public Scrutiny:* Their dependence on public support, their tax-exempt status, and their operation in the public interest often place nonprofit organizations under close public scrutiny.
- *Dual Management:* Management in nonprofits usually includes both professional managers and specialists without training in management (e.g., artists and other creative individuals); this **dual management** sometimes leads to conflict about organizational goals, activities, and expenditure of funds.

Chapter Review Question

What four major characteristics distinguish nonprofit markets from the three other organizational markets?

NEGOTIATING STYLES OF ORGANIZATIONAL BUYERS

In dealing with organizational buyers, salespeople must be prepared to interact with buyers who exhibit a variety of behavioral styles. Six different kinds of buyers have been identified.[11] Let's take a quick look at each.

Hard Bargainers. Some organizational buyers are *hard bargainers* who keep several suppliers competing aggressively against one another to win their business. These buyers negotiate strenuously to win every possible concession from the salesperson. They tend to see the negotiations as a contest and to use every weapon available in their effort to win. In dealing with hard bargainers, salespeople must guard against being pressured into an unprofitable agreement, because hard bargainers will readily switch to a new supplier who offers better terms next time.

Facilitators. Buyers who try to work efficiently and cooperatively with salespeople in order to reach mutually acceptable agreement are called facilitators. They understand that win-win arrangements are to each party's advantage, and most are a joy to work with.

Straight-shooters. Straight-shooters exhibit honesty and integrity throughout negotiations and refrain from pressuring the salesperson into concessions. Salespeople must avoid the temptation to take advantage of straight-shooters, because these buyers will be good long-run customers as long as they are treated fairly.

Socializers. Prospects and customers who enjoy the camaraderie of interpersonal relationships and don't want to be rushed through the sales presentation and close are known as socializers. Salespeople who stay relaxed and informal in their sales presentations and spend some time in friendly chit-chat will usually close sales with these buyers. One study found that highly sociable buyers are particularly focused on the salesperson's ability to solve their problem.[12]

Persuaders. Organizational prospects and customers who try to make their own sales presentations about the reputation and quality of their companies are considered persuaders. Sometimes persuaders simply want to tell a salesperson (who may be representing a better-known organization) that their organization deserves respect, too. Other times they are interested in convincing the salesperson that their organizations are successful and that treating them well in purchasing agreements can lead to a long-term profitable relationship. Be patient and let persuaders tell their story. Show respect for them and their organizations, and express appreciation for their business.

Considerate Buyers. Organizational purchasers who empathize with salespeople and try to work with them to reach mutually acceptable agreements are considerate buyers. These exceptional buyers are so considerate that they will frequently accept product substitutes or even compromises in the purchase agreement. Again, salespeople must never shortchange considerate buyers just because they are more flexible than, say, hard bargainers. Considerate buyers understand that a successful partnership always requires give-and-take, so take a reasonable approach to negotiations. When you have customers such as these, you are fortunate; treat them well.

Obviously, some buyers' negotiating styles will be harder to work with than others. The challenge to the professional salesperson is to work out *win-win* agreements with diverse buyer personalities.

Does the prospect in this situation look like a hard bargainer, facilitator, straight-shooter, socializer, persuader, or considerate buyer?
Walter Hodges/Corbis

BUSINESS ORIENTATION OF ORGANIZATIONAL BUYERS

Organizational buyers differ with respect to the kind of relationship they prefer to have with salespeople. We can categorize three types of customers with respect to their preferred relationship.[13] *Commercial friends* interact with salespeople like personal friends, as they share intimacy and casual conversation and engage in joint leisure activities beyond the usual sales call (e.g., attending sporting events). Such relationships tend to be long-term. *Customer co-workers* treat salespeople almost like a fellow employee and meld both personal and business aspects of the relationship. They tend to form less intimate, but still long-term, buyer-seller relationships. *Business acquaintances* maintain a formal relationship with salespeople and rely on them for economic gain. Although the association is cordial—and may even incorporate discussions of personal life—it lacks intimacy and does not entail interaction beyond the business context.

Even before the first sales call, professional salespeople should try to determine what kind of relationship their prospects and customers desire and adapt their behavior accordingly. This avoids the risk of making a first impression that the customer considers inappropriate (e.g., too chummy or too formal). Once you have done some background research, you should be able to determine what will probably be the best balance between product/service discussion and personal exchange. For instance, salespeople who spend more time discussing how their product or service can satisfy the prospect's needs and who reveal personal information about themselves have better

ON THE FRONTLINES

Buyers and Decision-Making Styles

Buyers' firms tend to have one of three kinds of *decision-making styles*—planning-oriented, entrepreneurially oriented, and bureaucratically oriented. A buyer's style influences his or her preferences for the seller's selling strategy. Therefore, the selling strategy a salesperson uses with a given customer should reflect that customer's decision-making style.

A *planning-oriented* style entails making decisions on the basis of long-run considerations, as the needs of the firm are carefully evaluated and planned. It requires detailed information and consultations with multiple departments. The *entrepreneurially oriented* style usually involves no formal policies and has one or two decision makers whose preferences and actions lead to the decision. Other company members provide little input, and decision making employs minimal technical information. A *bureaucratically oriented* style is characterized by utilization of formal rules and policies that determine information flows, activities, and interactions among company members. The information matrix in Table 10.4 suggests how salespeople should attend to each type of buyer.

TABLE 10.4

TYPE OF DECISION-MAKING STYLE

Decision-Making Style Characteristics	Planning-Oriented Style	Entrepreneurially Oriented Style	Bureaucratically Oriented Style
Nature of buyer	Large company	Smaller company	Government or nonprofit agency
Number/type of decision maker(s)	Group	One or two	Formal hierarchy
Number/type of seller(s) involved	Experts in selling firm matched with experts in buying firm	One person	Salesperson makes initial contact, and fulfillment of order and follow-up are done by support department
Decision-making time for buyer	Medium	Low	High
Decision-making procedure	Problem-solving oriented	Simple	Complex
Emphasis in sales presentation	Solution-oriented nature of the product or service	Innovative nature of the product or service	Product or service specifications and price advantages

Source: *Adapted from Arun Sharma and Rajnandini Pillai, "Customers' Decision-Making Styles and Their Preference for Sales Strategies: Conceptual Examination and an Empirical Study,"* Journal of Personal Selling and Sales Management *16 (Winter 1996): 21–33.*

interaction with prospects on an initial sales call. Furthermore, salespeople who spend more time responding to customer-provided information and questions are more likely to interact again with the buyer than sales reps who do not engage in such behavior.[14] Read *On the Frontlines* on page 342 and Table 10.4 above to further consider which selling strategy to use with buyers who exhibit different decision-making styles.

Chapter Review Question

Compare and contrast the three different types of decision-making styles used by professional buyers: the planning-oriented, entrepreneurially oriented, and bureaucratically oriented styles. How would you negotiate with buyers who exhibit each of the three styles?

INTERNATIONAL NEGOTIATIONS

As domestic markets become saturated, nearly every company is interested in increasing international sales. This is little more than wishful thinking until the company's sales representatives find global customers, build trustful relationships, and bring the global sales concept to fruition. With intensifying global competition, salespeople play major roles in helping the United States remain economically strong. Perspectives on negotiation strategies, time, desire to be liked, and the willingness to make concessions vary greatly from country to country. Therefore, U.S. salespeople who sell in overseas markets cannot be ethnocentric and assume that the U.S. way of conducting business is the only way. Rather, they must be extremely sensitive to individuals in international markets and cognizant of accepted business practices in those locales. To do otherwise is pure folly. Thus professional salespeople must be especially aware of cultural differences that they will encounter when doing business with international organizational buyers and understand how those differences will influence the buyer-seller relationship.

International Views of Negotiation

Buyers from other countries often see U.S salespeople as negotiating with a "winner-take-all" attitude. This attitude assumes that negotiation is a contest where the objective is to outwit the other side. It emphasizes bluffing, confrontation, areas of disagreement, and legalistic aspects of contracts. Europeans, by contrast, prefer to develop from the outset buyer-seller relationships that encourage win-win negotiations based on trust. Europeans want the agreement to be good not only for themselves but also for the other party. It is not that they are more principled or generous than their U.S. counterparts, but they understand clearly what is in their own long-run best interests. If an agreement is good for both parties, they acknowledge the added incentive for both parties to implement the agreement fully. Forcing the other party to accept an unfavorable agreement increases the likelihood that he or she will try to find ways to squirm out of the arrangement or to cut corners in implementing it.

International negotiators generally believe that trust and shared interests, not some complex legal contract, characterize a healthy relationship. They place more emphasis on thoroughly understanding the other negotiators and their perspectives, so they like to spend time socializing before transacting business. This knowledge provides insights that facilitate the negotiations and improve the relationship. One successful Rockwell International salesperson made seven trips to Venezuela trying to close a sale for three jet transports. He shared several four-hour lunches with the prospect, discussing everything from politics to sports, without any mention of his products or terms of sale. The prospective customer wanted to size up the U.S. sales representative before discussing business. Long, drawn-out negotiations that require socializing first are common even when U.S. companies deal with global suppliers.

Concessions

Russians and Eastern Europeans are tough negotiators because they are slow to make concessions. They realize that any concession that they could make now can also be made next week. In contrast, Americans tend to make concessions quickly when negotiations don't move right along. Cultures also differ in the importance that negotiators attach to feelings of friendship toward the other party and in their desire to create goodwill with their opponent. Russian and

Eastern European negotiators, for instance, do not seem to care about their popularity with Westerners, so it is much easier for them to be rigid, inscrutable, and unwilling to reciprocate when the other side makes a concession.

U.S. salespeople negotiating in Japan frequently have found the pace of negotiations so frustrating that they've made expensive concessions long before the Japanese are even ready to negotiate. Japanese, Middle Eastern, and Latin American negotiators generally build in a great deal of maneuvering room between their opening stance and their planned final position. Initially adopting an extreme negotiation stance is part of their strategy so that they will have room to make concessions later that will not hurt. Latin Americans, for example, assume that their opponents are also overreaching—and thus that every opening offer or asking price is highly negotiable.

Know Your Negotiating Partner

When you engage in international negotiations, make yourself aware of local customers, traditions, customs, habits, and sensitivities. More than courtesy, this is a practical way to avoid misunderstandings, enhance mutual respect, and increase the chances for success in the negotiations. In some countries, personal selling must be unobtrusive. For example, European industrial buyers dislike being seen with salespeople in public. Private areas are usually set aside at trade

ON THE FRONTLINES

Selling in Japan

Sales calls are not taken lightly in Japan. Professional salespeople never make a cold call on a Japanese prospect without a formal introduction. If a salesperson doesn't know anyone to make the introduction, he or she can contact the U.S. office of the Japanese company, call a U.S. federal or state government representative in Tokyo, or hire a consultant.

Relationships in Japan are based largely on trust. Insisting on a written contract makes a negative impression on most Japanese businesspeople. Be content to seal the initial deal with a handshake and leave signing a written contract to another meeting. Do not try to ingratiate yourself *during* a business meeting by telling a joke or using humor. Even though Japanese businesspeople may laugh heartily before or after a business meeting, and later in a social setting, their business meetings are always strictly business.

Always accept after-hours social invitations, but never bring your spouse because the Japanese business executives will not bring theirs. At dinner, let the Japanese host pick the subjects of conversation. Wait for your host's toast before you sip your drink, and always keep your neighbor's glass full. Do not brag about yourself or members of your family during conversation because Japanese etiquette is to be humble, even about your children. An old Japanese saying is "The nail that sticks up gets hammered down." To sell successfully in Japan, you must adapt your behavior to gain your prospect's respect and trust.

shows where negotiations between buyers and sellers can be conducted out of sight. France goes so far as to prohibit door-to-door selling. Before you approach customers in other countries, learn and be ready to adapt to unfamiliar behavioral rules. Read *On the Frontlines*, page 345, for some insights on selling in Japan.

Guidelines for Doing Business in International Markets

When you sell to global buyers, you may find that your typical way of selling in the domestic market is totally inappropriate. Some caveats and guidelines for doing business with organizational buyers in international settings appear in Table 10.5.

TABLE 10.5

Considerations in Doing International Business

Don't Be in a Hurry: U.S. salespeople usually want to get down to business, believing that "time is money." Rushing any negotiation generally puts salespeople at a great disadvantage and leads them to push forward without sufficient information. In other countries, U.S. salespeople must fight the temptation to try closing the sale quickly. Asian and South American cultures find our standard American directness offensive.
Understand Time: Salespeople who hope to negotiate business deals in developing nations may need to adjust their attitude toward time. Business appointments are flexible to people in most developing countries. If something comes up that's more important than business, such as a festival or a wedding, then business is postponed. In Latin countries, this proclivity is called the *mañana* (tomorrow) syndrome. In Spain, people also move at a leisurely pace. Most offices and shops close for siestas (1:30 to 4:30 P.M.), and restaurants rarely reopen until after 9 P.M. and get into full swing about 11. However, attitudes toward time may vary widely within a given country. In São Paulo, Brazil, the pace is much like that of a large city in the United States. But in Rio de Janeiro, business discussions begin only after considerable socializing and when a feeling of simpatico (warm empathy and deep understanding) has been established. People in developing countries also have a habit of "looping" their conversations. They may begin a conversation by talking about the last time they saw you or some other chitchat, then move into substantive issues concerning the business at hand—only to switch abruptly back to some social topic. This looping process is seldom a part of conversations with someone from their own country.
Continue Gathering Information: Even when well prepared, no salesperson has all the facts before negotiations begin. Some information is always missing, and some is soft information based on assumptions, opinions, or rumors. Therefore, it is important to use small talk during socializing and surrounding the negotiations themselves to obtain valuable information about your international counterparts and what issues they perceive as most important. (Inexperienced salespeople tend to think that small talk at the beginning of negotiations is merely perfunctory rather than potentially useful. Not so.)
Be Comfortable with Silence: Salespeople who try to fill any negotiating vacuum with talk can make serious mistakes. Japanese, Chinese, and Koreans use silence as a bargaining tactic when negotiating with U.S. salespeople. Because most Americans are uncomfortable with long periods of silence, they will often jump in and lower the price, just to start the conversation going again.

(continued)

TABLE 10.5

Considerations in Doing International Business (continued)

Never Be Confrontational or Argumentative: Seldom is anything gained in negotiations by losing your cool or attacking the other party. Such behavior makes it clear to the other side that you consider the negotiations a contest, not a shared partnership. Even belligerence contrived to gain a concession will be offensive to most negotiators and will seldom contribute to furthering the relationship. Always negotiate with a *buyer win-seller win* attitude and convey that feeling to international buyers.

Thoroughly Prepare Before Any Negotiations: Learn about the other parties' culture, religion, ethical standards, and social customs. Most U.S. salespeople are already at a language disadvantage in dealing with global prospects and may have to work through an interpreter. They cannot afford to neglect their homework in learning about their international prospects. Knowledge is power in any negotiation, but especially in international negotiations.

Stay Open to Different Negotiating Styles: In Western countries, specific issues are tediously negotiated. Only after agreement has been reached on each of these separate issues is an overall agreement achieved. In Japan and Russia, however, packages are negotiated first. Individual issues will be discussed in increasing detail but will not be finally decided until after agreement on the package as a whole has been reached.

Try Negotiating by the Other Side's Rule Book: Quoting a local proverb as the reason for doing something is far more likely to encourage agreement and obtain desired results. For example, when a U.S. business executive in Beijing wanted to exclude an item from a contract and met Chinese resistance because they wanted to operate on the basis of trust, the executive cited an old Chinese adage: "Man is mortal. What if one of us were to have an accident or pass away? How would our successors know what to do, in case of our absence, if we didn't leave a written record of our agreements?"

Business Etiquette in Other Cultures

U.S. salespeople must learn as much as they can about local business etiquette when negotiating in different countries. Avoiding a mistake in business etiquette can often spell the difference between successful and unsuccessful negotiations.[15] Some major issues to be aware of and sensitive to are the following:

- *Use of business cards*—Always carefully read the prospect's title aloud and treat the business card with respect. Never just thrust it into your pocket without glancing at it.
- *Use of first names*—Avoid the temptation to use first names when meeting prospects from another country; doing so can appear disrespectful. Even in the United Kingdom, people may work with one another for decades but still use last names when addressing each another.
- *Eye contact*—Excessive eye contact can come across as too aggressive in many countries. In fact, in many Arab countries, men tend to avoid looking at women, as a sign of respect, when conversing with them.
- *Understanding what "yes" means*—In some cultures, such as Japan's, a positive response often is no more than a sign of politeness indicating that you are heard. It does not imply a positive answer to your question.

- *Acceptance of gifts*—Always be careful about giving gifts to a man's wife. Always, too, make sure that any gift conveys no negative cultural meaning. For example, in Russia, giving cutlery says that "you are cutting the relationship." And in Japan, white (in flowers or any other item) connotes death.
- *Interpretation of smiling handshakes*—Even the common U.S. practice of smiling while shaking hands can suggest insincerity in some countries, such as Germany.
- *Use of one's voice*—U.S. salespeople too often speak in a loud, overly enthusiastic manner that prospects from other countries can interpret as overbearing and aggressive. Even in the United States, it is wise to adapt one's voice to the tone and level of the prospect's speech.
- *Posture and body language*—One's posture or body language can unintentionally convey offensive messages. For instance, in Arab countries, crossing your legs and showing the sole of your foot sends a negative message. In South American countries, making what people in the United States know as the "okay" sign by forming a circle of one's thumb and forefinger is tantamount to thrusting the middle finger upward.
- *Distance between buyer and seller*—While conversing with each other, people in many countries tend to stand much closer together than people in the United States do. For example, a U.S. salesperson who retreats from a Latin American prospect back into his or her comfort zone of personal space may risk offending the prospect.
- *Awareness of host country holidays*—Some U.S. salespeople have made the incredibly naïve mistake of ignoring host country holidays and thinking that the host country also celebrates U.S. holidays.
- *Use of the term "foreigners"*—Never use the term *foreigners* when selling abroad. You are the foreigner there, not they.
- *Importance of face-to-face contact*—In many countries, such as Italy, face-to-face contact and negotiations are nearly always necessary to reach successful agreements, so the telephone calls, e-mails, and faxes alone won't do the job.
- *Importance of humility and modesty*—In many countries, humility and modesty—whether sincere or not—are characteristics always displayed in public. Exhibiting arrogance or overconfidence can be counterproductive to personal selling success. Even in the United States, salespeople should not overlook the value of humility and modesty, especially when first meeting prospects.

Chapter Review Question

Provide some basic guidelines and rules of business etiquette for salespeople selling in international markets.

SUMMARY

In this chapter we discussed organizational markets and how and why they buy. We examined the three types of purchasing situations, as well as the organizational buying process. In addition, we reviewed the four major kinds of organizational buyers—industrial, reseller, government, and nonprofit organizational markets. Then we described the submarkets within each of these larger categories. Resellers include industrial distributors, wholesalers, and retailers who buy goods for reselling or leasing to others at a profit or for conducting their own operations. Government markets include the federal government and all state and local governments, which purchase goods and services in order to provide citizens with necessary services such as fire and police protection, education, and health care. Nonprofit markets, which include institutions and organizations such as colleges, hospitals, libraries, and charities, purchase goods and services in order to provide people with services, attract donations, or change public attitudes about social concerns and problems. The various roles of individual industrial buyers and industrial salespeople were also examined. Six kinds of organizational buyers were analyzed vis-à-vis their negotiation styles, three kinds of purchasers were described with respect to the kind of relationships they prefer to have with sellers, and three kinds of decision-making styles of buyers were examined. Finally, we explored doing business in international markets and considered what salespeople need to know and do to sell successfully in different cultures.

KEY TERMS

North American Industry Classification System (NAICS)
Derived Demand
Reciprocity
Industrial Buyer
Foundation Goods
Entering Goods
Facilitating Goods
Buying Center
Gatekeeper
Influencers
FedBizOpps.gov
Dual Management

TOPICS FOR THOUGHT AND CLASS DISCUSSION

1. How would you go about becoming acquainted with members of an organization's "buying center"? How would you determine which specific role each person played?
2. What do you think about the practice of reciprocity in business?
3. If you were a small business owner who wanted to obtain some federal government contracts, how would you find out how to sell to the government? Outline the steps that you would take.
4. What do you think are some of the reasons why U.S. salespeople sometimes fail when trying to negotiate contracts with prospects from other countries? What might they do to increase their success?
5. Of the four different types of organizations (manufacturers, resellers, governments, and nonprofits), which do you think you would most like to call on as a salesperson? Which would you least like to call on? Why?

INTERNET EXERCISES

1. Use the Internet to access the North American Industry Classification System (NAICS) website at www.naics.com. What are the different industrial sectors on which you can find information? Describe the type of information that is available about manufacturing and service firms in North America. As a salesperson, how would you be able to use this information?
2. Using Google or any other search engine, find guidelines (in addition to those discussed in this chapter) for doing business in international markets.
3. Use the Internet to find articles on business etiquette that salespeople should be aware of when doing business in countries whose cultural systems are very different from those in the United States.

4. Using an Internet search engine, find articles on different international negotiation approaches. Which countries do you think differ the most in their negotiation approaches?

PROJECTS FOR PERSONAL GROWTH

1. Your company's R&D department has developed a chemical compound made from corn by-products that provides airtight sealing properties when coated over various substances. R&D scientists believe that this product, tentatively named Sealatron, will have many uses in the heavy construction industry. They say it may be appropriate for a final coating on top of the outer insulation wrappings for large oil and gas pipes, power lines, and perhaps sewer and water mains. It might also be used for waterproofing the exteriors of commercial buildings. Go to your school library and use the North American Industry Classification System (NAICS) to research the potential markets for this new chemical sealant. How specifically can you define the potential markets with NAICS digits? Once you've found the level of specificity that you want, how will you use the NAICS information?
2. Assume that you sell for a small clothing manufacturer that wants to supply your company's undershirts, undershorts, and trousers to one or more of the military branches. Go to FedBizOpps.gov and see what information you can find about federal government solicitations for clothing contracts. What other websites did you visit to find more information? Keep at it until you find at least two solicitations that you believe your company could bid on. Find out how, when, and where to submit your bid.
3. Select a country (other than the United States) in which you would like to sell products and services for a U.S.-based company. What are some basic considerations and rules of etiquette that you need to know and follow in order to sell successfully in this country?

ROLE-PLAY EXERCISE 10.1

Selling a Line of Men's Clothing

Situation

Craig Larkin, a manufacturer's rep, sells men's clothing on a commission basis to large department stores. He feels that success in his line of work depends on (1) suggesting appropriate clothing styles for retailers based on what's in vogue and (2) communicating with them "on their wavelength" by identifying their personality types.

As he approaches the new men's suit buyer for a large retail department store chain, Craig notices that the buyer is an impeccably dressed and well-groomed man about 40 years old. He is wearing a Brooks Brothers suit, an expensive, conservatively striped shirt with cuffs, a classic red-striped tie, red suspenders, Johnston and Murphy tassel loafers, and bright red socks. Craig notices that he is also wearing a Lafayette College Maroon Key Club tie-pin.

Roles

Craig Larkin After working in the clothing business for eight years, Craig feels that he can "read" the personality, lifestyle, social class, and stage in the life cycle of most people by closely observing and listening to them for a few minutes. He is very skilled at adapting his approach to communication styles and personalities of different customers.

Gerald McFarland III Coming from a well-to-do family, Gerald is active in community affairs, and he likes to dress conservatively with a little flair. He feels especially confident in buying men's clothing because of his privileged upbringing.

ROLE-PLAY EXERCISE 10.2

Negotiating with a "Chiseler" Buyer

Situation

Phil Hermann sells a line of plumbing supplies for Britt-Bose Corporation to industrial distributors. Although he enjoys most aspects of his sales work, he does find it distasteful to deal with certain types of buyers. Probably the ones who irritate him the most are those he calls "chiselers," who always try to squeeze out of him every price concession they can on every purchase. Then they quickly switch to a new vendor whenever they can get a lower price.

Today, Phil is calling on one of these so-called chiseler buyers. His name is Albert Sakin, and he is the 60-year-old head buyer for Mertz Industrial Supply House. Immediately upon greeting him, Mr. Sakin says to Phil, "Well, have you got any deals to offer me? If not, you're wasting your time and mine." Phil tells Mr. Sakin that he can offer him a 15 percent discount on everything he buys this month. Mr. Sakin responds, "Well, you've got my attention, but you'd better offer a larger discount than that if you expect to beat out Sampson for my order this month. They've offered me a deal that's hard to turn down."

Phil knows that he sells higher-quality products than Sampson, and he doubts that Sampson has offered a higher discount than 15 percent. Also, he was told by Mr. Sakin's secretary, Alice Miller, that a couple of plumbing companies had called in to complain about the quality of the Sampson parts they bought from Mertz.

Roles

Phil Hermann Even though Mr. Sakin is difficult to deal with, he buys in such large quantities for Mertz that some profit can be made even when Phil offers a discount of up to 20 percent. Phil is sure that Mr. Sakin knows that Britt-Bose offers higher-quality products than Sampson. But he understands that Mr. Sakin's negotiating style is to disparage Britt-Bose products if he thinks that will help him win a larger price discount or work a better deal.

Albert Sakin Proud of his reputation as a tough negotiator, Mr. Sakin likes to play a cat-and-mouse game with salespeople. He sees every negotiation as having a winner and a loser. And he uses any technique or means he can to make sure that he's the winner.

CASE 10.1 DO I REALLY HAVE TO WORRY ABOUT ALL THESE PEOPLE?

Linda Stephens is a sales engineer for McDonnell-Cummins Company, which sells specialty chemicals, plastics, and polymer products to large consumer goods companies. After graduating from Michigan State University with a degree in chemical engineering, Linda interviewed with several companies and received three job offers. She decided to take the job as sales engineer with McDonnell-Cummins because it offered the best overall compensation package (including perks such as a new car and an expense account), as well as a career path that could lead to top management. After three months of intensive training that included classroom lectures and discussions, laboratory demonstrations of products, videotapes, lots of reading material, and several examinations, Linda feels confident of her knowledge of the company's products and believes that she is prepared to make effective sales presentations to customers.

Still, on her first sales call at the headquarters of Gamble & Simpson, a large consumer products manufacturer, she is a little apprehensive as she walks into the huge lobby and sees many other people—apparently salespeople—waiting. After she introduces herself to the receptionist and says she is here for a 9 a.m. meeting with Bill Constantin in

(*continued*)

the purchasing department, she takes her Gamble & Simpson visitor's pass and sits down in a comfortable chair to wait for Mr. Constantin. (She learned his name from the call reports that the previous sales engineer handling this account had submitted.) Within a few minutes, Mr. Constantin's secretary, Marie Doyle, comes down to the lobby to greet Linda and escort her back to Mr. Constantin's office. Marie says that Mr. Constantin can spend only about fifteen minutes with Linda because he has to prepare for an emergency meeting scheduled for 9:30 a.m. with the vice president of purchasing.

Arriving at Mr. Constantin's office, Linda introduces herself and gives Mr. Constantin her business card. Bill Constantin seems somewhat harried and preoccupied, so Linda thinks she had better forget the small talk and get down to business. Handing a packet of product brochures to Mr. Constantin, she tells him that her company will be introducing several new products over the next few months and that she wants to give him some preliminary information about them. Linda makes a short presentation on each of five new products, while Mr. Constantin listens and leafs through the brochures. Upon finishing her presentations, Linda asks whether he has any questions. Mr. Constantin replies, "Not at the moment, but I'll probably have some later when I get a chance to read the brochures and talk to some of the R&D people. Right now, I've got to get ready for my 9:30 a.m. meeting."

At that moment, Mr. Constantin's department manager, Esther Hughes, pokes her head in the door and says that she'd like to talk with Mr. Constantin after his meeting with the VP. Mr. Constantin quickly introduces Linda to Esther and leaves for his meeting. Esther was hired as purchasing manager only a month earlier, so she is still progressing up the learning curve at Gamble & Simpson. She asks Linda a few questions and requests copies of the product brochures to bring her up to date on what McDonnell-Cummins is offering. She remarks that at her previous company she bought from a competitor of Linda's firm. Ms. Hughes soon excuses herself and asks Marie if she would mind taking Linda out to the laboratory to introduce her to some of the research and development people who use the products that Mr. Constantin buys for them.

In the laboratory, Linda meets Dr. Stuart Forbes and Dr. Li Chu, two scientists who provide Mr. Constantin with detailed specifications for products they need in their work. Li Chu says that he is working on a new idea for a laundry detergent for which he needs a polymer with particular properties. He asks Linda whether her company can provide such a product. Linda admits that she isn't sure but says that she will talk to her company's R&D people and let him know as soon as possible. While in the laboratory, Linda also meets Fred Burnett, a laboratory technician who carries out most of the experiments designed by Dr. Forbes and Dr. Chu. Mr. Burnett is an uninhibited young man about Linda's age who cracks a couple of lighthearted jokes along the line of "What's a nice person like you doing in a place like this?" Finally, on the way out of the laboratory, Marie introduces Linda to the director of R&D, Dr. Leland Birsner, whose approval is required for any product requests submitted to purchasing. Dr. Birsner seems rather dour, but he is polite enough and says that he hopes Linda will keep him informed about any new products her company is developing. Taking this as her cue, Linda hands him another packet of brochures from her briefcase.

Later, while walking back to the lobby with Marie, Linda asks who will make the purchasing decision on her products. Marie responds, "Oh, lots of people have input. It's usually more of a group decision than any one person's, although the R&D director and the purchasing manager have the final say."

Leaving Gamble & Simpson, Linda is a bit overwhelmed by the possibility that all of the people she's met have input in deciding whether or not to purchase her company's products. Her first job, she decides, is to prepare an organizational chart of the Gamble & Simpson buying center to help her understand the multiple roles played by the different people. Then she will develop an overall strategy and specific tactics for developing and maintaining good relationships with all of these people.

Questions

1. In terms of buying-center roles (initiators, gatekeepers, influencers, deciders, buyers, and users), how should Linda classify each of the seven people she met at Gamble & Simpson (Marie Doyle, Bill Constantin, Esther Hughes, Dr. Stuart Forbes, Dr. Li Chu, Fred Burnett, and Dr. Leland Birsner)?
2. Which of these people do you think has the greatest influence on purchase decisions? Why?
3. What advice would you give Linda in her efforts to think up a strategy and tactics to develop and maintain good relationships with all of these buying center members?
4. Now that her first sales call is over, what should Linda do to follow up with some or all of the Gamble & Simpson people?

CASE 10.2 NOW WHAT AM I GOING TO DO?

CASE 10.2 "NOW WHAT AM I GOING TO DO?" CAN BE FOUND ONLINE AT HTTP://COLLEGE.HMCO.COM/PIC/ANDERSONPS2E

CHAPTER 11

Strategic Understanding of Your Company, Products, Competition, and Markets

An empowered organization is one in which individuals have the knowledge, skill, desire, and opportunity to personally succeed in a way that leads to collective organizational success.

Stephen R. Covey, author and consultant

After reading this chapter, you should understand:

- Why in-depth knowledge about your company, products, competition, and markets helps you become a more successful salesperson.
- How to evaluate your firm's competition.
- Various sources of information and their potential uses.
- The growing professionalism in purchasing and its impact on personal selling.
- How to keep current on product developments, competitors, and markets.

INSIDE PERSONAL SELLING

Meet Nikki Verna of Beiersdorf

To be successful, Nikki Verna must understand not only the products she sells and the needs of her customers but also what her customers' customers might want. As a national account manager for Beiersdorf AG, Verna sells two main product lines to large retailers: Curad bandages and Futuro elastic braces and supports. She builds strong relationships with her customers by helping them determine which specific Curad and Futuro products each store should carry and providing support for the retailers as they present and sell these products to consumers.

Market knowledge is critical: "If we don't know what the consumer is looking for," Verna explains, "we're not going to get our products into the store." In addition to examining broad market trends and analyzing consumers' historical buying patterns, she receives analytical reports from researchers who visit hundreds of stores to count every bandage and support product on the shelves. This kind of information reveals, for example, that bandage sales typically increase during March, April, and May as people begin spending more time outside and stock their medicine cabinets for summer cuts and scrapes.

Understanding market dynamics enables Verna to balance two key customer concerns. Retailers do not want to have large

quantities of Curad or Futuro products sitting unsold on store shelves, nor do they want to run out of a product and have consumers walk away empty-handed. For this reason, a member of Verna's team monitors each account's sales—item by item, day by day. At one retailer, for example, the goal is to have Beiersdorf products in stock 98.5 percent of the time. "If we see that a certain item is about to dip below that level," she says, "we check the inventory in each individual store and immediately restock those that are running low."

Understanding her company, products, and markets helped Verna sell Curad to a recalcitrant buyer. "We had a fantastic relationship with him on Futuro elastics," she remembers, "but he was carrying two other bandage brands and wasn't interested in carrying a third. We made at least ten sales presentations about profit opportunities, unique products, and other reasons to carry the Curad line. Yet we simply couldn't get anywhere."

Verna ultimately convinced the buyer to try a no-risk test of three Curad products as a way to demonstrate consumer interest. "We promised to take the products back if they didn't sell," she says, "but the test went very well. This retailer ended up expanding the order and now carries twelve of our items." Just as important, the buyer has even more respect for Beiersdorf as a company because "we stood behind our products, we used the facts to tell our story, and it worked."

We have certainly had a lot to say about how to sell in the past several chapters. You may feel more than ready to head out into your sales territory and become the successful salesperson you know you can be. Well, it's great that you have such confidence and eagerness. You *have* learned a lot! You now know how to find and qualify new prospects efficiently, collect valuable preapproach information, smoothly contact a customer for the first time, make a sound sales presentation, adroitly handle sales resistance, skillfully close the sale, and attend to critical post-sale activities. But as a professional salesperson, you also must be intimately familiar with the selling environment in which you'll operate; otherwise, you'll waste a lot of energy. It's time to add knowledge of your company, its products, your competitors, and target markets to make you fully prepared to start making sales calls.

Several studies have shown that more effective salespeople have richer and more interrelated knowledge about their customers and selling strategies than less effective salespeople.[1] How do salespeople acquire this knowledge? At one time, salespeople were given a price list and told, "Go make some sales calls to see if you can get some orders." With no training and little product knowledge, most of these salespeople failed miserably and soon left the company. Today, many products are complex and customer needs are diverse, so new salespeople require thorough training about their company and its products, competitors, and markets before calling on customers. Many companies provide much of this essential knowledge in formal training programs that make use of videotapes, lectures, demonstrations, role-playing sessions, computer exercises, and trainee interaction with each other and seasoned salespeople.[2]

One Fortune 500 company, for example, uses a three-tiered sales training program that extends over three or four *years*. The first tier includes two weeks of classroom and demonstration lab work in the company's modern training center. Most of the second-tier training occurs in the district sales offices, where the manager's monthly staff meetings are followed by two hours of sales training. Each district office includes a library of training modules on CD-ROMs for sales trainees' use. The third training tier takes place in the homes of the sales reps. Each rep receives a PC or workstation on which he or she completes computer-assisted homework exercises in preparation for classes at the district office. The in-home PCs are networked so that messages, such as assignments, can be broadcast simultaneously to the reps.

High-performing salespeople must have detailed knowledge about their company, the products it sells, the company's competitors, and the markets in which it operates. Armed with this valuable knowledge, salespersons are better able to develop and offer "win-win" sales solutions to their customers. Being deficient in any of these categories will lead to inefficient and ineffective selling efforts. This chapter focuses on these four areas, their importance, and how salespeople learn this requisite information.

STRATEGIC UNDERSTANDING OF YOUR COMPANY

Company history, organization, mission statement, culture, philosophies, goals, objectives, strategies, tactics, policies, and procedures are among the first subjects that sales trainees study. Companies take different approaches to teaching these basics. Some companies present this information in formal training programs, and others provide it in manuals and handouts. Whatever the approach, every salesperson needs to thoroughly understand his or her company in order to develop selling strategies and respond to customer questions knowledgeably. Let's see why.

Company History

Studying the company's history may not seem particularly interesting at first, but this knowledge provides perspectives and insights that will serve the salesperson well throughout a career. It may be intriguing to see how humbly the company began. What new sales trainee would not be inspired by the story of young Steve Jobs and Steve Wozniak? Jobs and Wozniak raised $1,300 by selling Jobs's Volkswagen bus and Wozniak's Hewlett-Packard handheld calculator and then built the first personal computer "for the rest of us" in a tiny garage.[3] Today, Apple Computer (www.apple.com) is known all over the world. Most great companies were started by one determined individual with a marvelous vision. Because a company's present business philosophy and slogans often trace back to its founder, a study of company history generally begins with the founder's life and philosophy. Usually the company's librarian or personnel manager can recommend a good book on the company and its founder. Many customers enjoy hearing the story of a company's origins, and it may help win respect for the salesperson's professional knowledge.

Reprinted from www.dnb.com with the permission of Dun & Bradstreet

Growth and Development

Another aspect of a company's history is the record of its growth in sales, market share, profits, and new products. Reading annual and quarterly reports or independent financial analysts' evaluations of the firm [such as that of Value Line (www.valueline.com), Standard and Poor's (www.standardandpoors.com), Dun & Bradstreet (www.dnb.com), or Morningstar (www.morningstar.com)] can keep you current about company growth and development and give you an advantage in closing sales. If a potential customer asks, "How's this new product been selling so far?" a knowledgeable salesperson can truthfully answer, "It's the fastest growing new product in the industry; we're barely able to keep up with orders. Your two major competitors have already placed large orders." Sharing this information not only reassures customers but also helps persuade them to make the purchase in order to keep up with competition. Without such timely knowledge, a salesperson would have to answer, "Gee, I don't know. Let me check with the home office." Most likely, the customer would delay buying until the salesperson reported back—or buy from someone else in the interim.

Company Organization

Many companies carefully maintain one or more organization charts. An organization chart provides an overview of a company's chain of command, communication flows, and overall structure. The organization chart might be anything from a single sheet of paper giving the names of company officers and executives, to an elaborate wall chart on display in the company's main boardroom or on the company's website.

New salespeople can learn a lot about the positions and unique roles

To sell successfully in dynamically changing markets, it is necessary to keep current by reading business magazines and newspapers.

Richard Hutchings/PhotoEdit

of key individuals by studying the organization chart. Most companies maintain a separate, detailed organization chart for the sales department showing the hierarchy of sales managers, sales support people, and the most important people in the sales organization: the salespeople. The way a company structures its organization chart suggests what's really important to top management. If a sales force is structured by geographic location, for example, this could suggest that management considers specific geographic markets large enough to justify special attention. A sales force structured by type of customer, however, may reflect management's concern with identifying and solving problems and issues for specific customers or customer types.

Mission Statement

Mission Statement Sets forth in writing the organization's orientation, goals, basic values, and sense of purpose.

The **mission statement** provides an understanding and feel for the organization's orientation, goals, basic values, and sense of purpose. In describing the essence of the company's business and what it seeks to accomplish, the mission statement lays out the company's vision and direction for the next ten to twenty years. It also can help motivate salespeople to extraordinary performance. For example, it is much more satisfying and challenging for salespeople to think of their jobs as helping to create cleaner, healthier, more attractive home environments for families rather than to think of themselves as merely selling home air and water filters. Newport News Shipbuilding's (nns.com) classic mission statement remains unchanged since the company's founding in 1886: *"We shall build good ships here—at a profit if we can—at a loss if we must—but always good ships."* What an inspirational message for Newport News Shipbuilding salespeople to relay to customers who ask about the quality of a ship they're planning to buy!

Culture

Culture A set of formal or informal values, norms, morals, attitudes, beliefs, customs, and behaviors that establish the code of conduct for a group of people or an organization.

Every organization has its unique culture, or operating climate. **Culture** may be defined as a set of formal or informal values, norms, morals, attitudes, beliefs, customs, and behaviors that establish the code of conduct for a group of people or an organization. A highly centralized organization run by authoritarian management will create a sales climate sharply different from that of an organization where authority is decentralized and management employs a more consultative or democratic style. Some organizations may have no one pervasive climate but, rather, various climates across departments or units.

Not only does an organization have its own culture, but the sales force within the firm may have its own culture. Although the two are related—because the company's overall culture usually sets the tone for the sales organization's culture—points of difference may arise between the two. For instance, a firm's corporate culture may be formal, but the culture within a given sales manager's selling team still might be somewhat informal as a consequence of the sales manager's leadership style. Knowledge about organizational culture is important to your success as a salesperson. It will affect your job satisfaction, performance, commitment to the firm, and motivation.[4] Thus it's a good idea for a new salesperson to size up both the organizational culture and the sales force culture quickly in order to learn what is acceptable and expected behavior.

A few coffee breaks or lunches with more experienced salespeople and staff can prove invaluable in understanding the corporate culture and sales management leadership styles.

Chapter Review Question
Why is it important for salespeople to understand their company's culture and that of the sales department? How would you suggest that a salesperson quickly learn about the culture of his or her company and department?

Goals and Objectives

Goals and *objectives* are terms often used interchangeably, and we see no value in trying to distinguish between them here. Companies generally apply one of these terms to long-run, less quantifiable targets (such as becoming the most innovative company in the industry) and the other term to short-run, quantifiable targets (such as earning a 15-percent return on investment in the next year). Good salespeople know the goals and objectives of their company, the marketing department, and each successive organizational unit (sales region, division, branch) in which they work. They use this knowledge to formulate more compatible and realistic personal goals and objectives. For instance, it would probably be unrealistic for a salesperson to forecast an increase of 30 percent in territorial sales if the company and the region's overall forecast is for a 5 percent sales decline. Awareness of the company and sales department forecasts can help keep a salesperson from making serious errors in personal sales forecasting.

Strategies and Tactics

A **strategy** is a total program of action for using resources to achieve a goal or objective. A **tactic** is a short-run, specific action that constitutes a part of the larger strategic plan. A small company might develop a sales strategy, for example, to compete against IBM (www.ibm.com) by concentrating its field sales force calls on small businesses, because IBM focuses its resources more on large companies. Sales tactics might include use of Spanish-language videotapes and brochures for sales presentations to Hispanic customers. Salespeople who understand their companies' strategies and tactics will have useful guidelines for making their own personal selling decisions in the field. In order for any organization to succeed, every member of the team needs to know the overall plan (strategy) as well as the individual tasks (tactics) to employ.[5] Company strategic success has been directly linked to salesperson effectiveness.[6]

Strategy A long-run total program of action for using resources to achieve an overall goal.

Tactic A short-run, specific action that is part of the larger strategic plan.

Policies

To ensure consistency, continuity, and expeditious organizational decisions on routine matters it is necessary to establish general rules of action called policies. *Policies* are predetermined decisions for handling recurring situations efficiently and effectively. Knowledge of company policies helps salespeople make better field decisions and better serve customers. For instance, a salesperson who is familiar with the company's policy of not shipping goods until payment has been received for the previous shipment can prevent customer embarrassment or annoyance. In order to negotiate price and terms with the buyer, the salesperson must thoroughly know the company's credit policies and credit terms. Some companies offer discounts for quantity purchases or to buyers who pay the invoice within a specified number of days.

IT'S UP TO YOU

One of your better customers has just called you to complain about the latest batch of packaging that your company delivered. It seems that the company's telephone number and address are incorrect on all the packaging. You check the order to see how such a mistake could have been made, and you notice that the customer made the mistakes in filling out the order. Your company's policy is to take back any packaging misprinted by its fault. But customers are responsible for any errors that they make in ordering, and this is clearly printed on the order form. This customer has been increasing its purchases from you by about 10 percent a year, and last year bought $17,500. The invoice price of the misprinted packaging is $1,250. What is your next move? What policy can you develop for dealing with such problems in the future?

Even the salesperson's own financial planning requires knowing whether the company's policy is to pay commissions to salespeople when the order is accepted, when the goods are shipped, or when the customer pays the invoice. Most companies pay commissions when the goods are shipped. Consider how to address the problem outlined in the accompanying *It's Up to You* feature, which pertains to an issue concerning company policy.

STRATEGIC UNDERSTANDING OF YOUR PRODUCTS

Studies consistently show that more effective salespeople have greater knowledge about their company's products.[7] Few customers will respect or buy from a salesperson who is poorly informed about the product's technical details and its application to their problems. Therefore, professional salespeople must be technically qualified and knowledgeable about their products. They must understand what their products can and cannot do for customers and how they can best be used. When salespeople feel technically deficient, they should seek intracompany experts who can supply the needed knowledge or jointly meet with prospects or customers. Salespeople who really understand their products develop a pride and confidence that shines through to prospects and helps gain their confidence and trust—and, most likely, the sale.

As product cycles shorten and technology advances at an ever-accelerating pace, salespeople must work harder to keep informed about company products. What do salespeople need to know about their products? The answer is simple—*everything*. And this is not an exaggeration. Essentially, salespeople

TABLE 11.1

Requisite Product Knowledge of Professional Salespeople

- Where does the product come from? Where is it mined, grown, assembled, or manufactured? How is it shipped to the present location? Does shipping significantly affect its quality or price?
- Who designed the product? How is the product made? What kind of machines produced it?
- How should the product be used? What are the manufacturer's recommendations regarding care and maintenance? What can be learned from other customers who have used the product? Do any special features or advantages distinguish this product from competitive products on the market?
- What kind of guarantee or warranty does the company offer on the product? What kind of repair and maintenance service does the company provide? Does the company have a service department or service centers? Where are they located?
- What happens if a product is broken in delivery? Is the customer protected? What is the procedure for returning the product if it proves unsatisfactory?

need to know how the products they sell are made, packaged, shipped, and received by the customer; unpackaged; sent to the buyer's production line; picked up; placed into the final product or adjoined to other parts; and then packaged and shipped to their customer's customers. They also need to know how the products perform. Listed in Table 11.1 are a few of the many questions that salespeople must be able to answer about their product line.

Products from the Customer's Perspective

Most products and services offer a range of functional, psychological, and sensory (sight, hearing, smell, touch, and taste) attributes. A bar of soap may become much more appealing and may satisfy a wider array of the customer's functional and psychological needs when it is conveniently and attractively shaped, contains a special moisturizing agent, gives off a pleasant scent, feels good to the touch, and has a pleasing, eye-catching wrapper. In a related fashion, earth-moving equipment becomes much more appealing to industrial buyers when it is well designed for operator use and the seller guarantees that it will be replaced or repaired within twenty-four hours of any breakdown.

It is not enough simply to explain to a customer the basic functions or general uses of a product. A customer is really looking for *personal benefits or solutions to his or her problems* before anything else. Salespeople must use their product knowledge to present products in ways that match the needs and desires of customers. Various customers may view the identical product quite differently, depending on their individual needs. Consider the following conversation between a computer salesperson and a prospective customer:

CUSTOMER: "What different types of personal computers do you sell?"

SALESPERSON: "Well, I have sold some firms personal computers (PCs) that help them manage their clients' stock and bond investments. I have sold magazine publishers PCs that streamline their efforts and get the work done in a timely fashion. Mary Jones, Inc., a public relations firm, bought several PCs to keep records on its customers and to develop creative presentations for clients. The physics department over at the university recently purchased our PCs to help faculty members analyze the statistical results of their experiments.

CUSTOMER: Wow, sounds like you sell a wide range of computers!

SALESPERSON: No. Actually, we sell just one basic PC, but people buy it for a lot of different reasons. Let's talk about the kind of help *you're* looking for.

Selling Multiple Products

The problem in obtaining full product knowledge is compounded when salespeople must handle several lines of products. A salesperson who carries five product lines has nearly five times as much work to know all the products and keep them straight. When you need a systematic way to stay informed about your products, you should consider developing, maintaining, and carrying for ready reference a simple *product knowledge worksheet,* as shown in abbreviated format in Table 11.2. You can update this worksheet and add relevant questions as you receive new questions from prospects and customers. Either a file on a laptop computer or a handwritten copy will do. In addition to the product knowledge worksheet for your own products, it's important to have a *competitive analysis worksheet,* as illustrated in Table 11.3. If the comparison will be favorable, consider using a side-by-side comparison of your products and those of leading competitors.

Interaction with Other Products

Not only must salespeople know their products thoroughly, they must also know how these products work with *other* products. For example, a customer may ask, "What color printers are compatible with this PC?" or "Does this PC come with a built-in DVD burner?" Without understanding how his or her products interact with other equipment and stack up against competitive products, the salesperson cannot reassure and inform the customer and may risk losing the sale. It is especially important for salespeople to know everything about the product and compatible ancillary equipment when they are selling a product without a well-known brand name. For instance, although Research In Motion (www.rim.com), a small, relatively unknown company, introduced the *BlackBerry*—an interactive e-mailer and pager—its salespeople were able to make it a quick success by effectively showing its superior benefits and advantages versus competitive products.

Knowledge About Product Service

Most products, whether tangibles such as mainframe computers and oil derricks, or intangibles such as group life and health insurance, require service.

TABLE 11.2

PRODUCT KNOWLEDGE WORKSHEET

Characteristics	Product A	Product B	Product C	Product D
Customer Benefits				
1.				
2.				
3.				
Features				
1.				
2.				
3.				
Advantages				
1.				
2.				
3.				
Initial Price				
Estimated Life				
Estimated Life Cycle Cost				
Size				
a. Weight				
b. Dimensions				
Installation Ease				
Required Service				
Return Policy				
Warranty				
Trade-in Allowance				
Other Characteristics				

All products eventually need servicing, repairs, changes, or replacements. For instance, companies purchasing life and health insurance for their employees need and expect advice as demographic factors and lifestyles change. Professional sales reps know what services their companies provide for each product, the costs of those services, which are most appropriate for different customers, and how they can be included in the buyer's purchase order.

STRATEGIC UNDERSTANDING OF YOUR COMPETITION

Because salespeople nearly always sell in a competitive environment, they must understand competitors' products and services almost as well as their own company's.[8] Customers will have confidence in a salesperson who can knowledgeably compare his or her own product's features and advantages with those of a competitor. This confidence, however, can be undermined if the salesperson gives in to the temptation to disparage the competition in front of customers. Negative comments such as "Our competitor's machine is pathetically slow and has one of the worst repair records on the market" often work against a salesperson who is trying to win the trust and respect of customers. It's always better to make product comparisons in positive terms: "Our tabletop copiers average about five thousand copies before you need to change the toner cartridge—nearly twice as many as any other comparable machines—and our repair record is one of the best. In fact, using an objective study by *Consumer Reports,* allow me to compare our record with those of others."

It's a good idea always to be prepared to provide objective and factual comparisons with your competitors' products and services without being negative about them. Rating sources such as *Consumer Reports* (www.consumerreports.org), ZDNet (www.reviews-zdnet.com), and Epinions (www.epinions.com) can often provide valuable assistance.

The *Thomas Register*

Thomas Register The primary source that most Fortune 500 companies use to locate suppliers. Published annually, it provides information about 189,000 manufacturers regarding product categories, specific products, names of the companies, branches, top executives and their job titles, affiliation data, and credit rating.

One of the most comprehensive and widely used sources of information about who makes what products and where they can be purchased is the *Thomas Register of National Manufacturers*. The ***Thomas Register*** is the primary resource that most Fortune 500 companies use to locate suppliers. Published annually, it provides information about 189,000 manufacturers regarding product categories, specific products, names of the companies, branches, top executives and their job titles, affiliation data, and credit rating. Available in several hardcopy volumes at most large libraries, the *Thomas Register* also is online at www.thomasregister.com, with thousands of online catalogs and links to company websites, plus millions of downloadable computer-assisted design (CAD) drawings. Salespeople who know that their products' customers are manufacturers of certain types of products can search by product, company, or brand name. For example, a salesperson who sells equipment to companies that manufacture machine lathes can type in "machine lathes" at the *Thomas Register* website and go to a Web page that lists the different types of lathes. From here the salesperson can, in a few more keyboard clicks, find the address of prospect companies, catalogs, websites, order and request-for-quotation (RFQs) forms, CAD drawings, and e-mail addresses to contact. Although used mainly by purchasing agents, savvy salespeople can effectively and efficiently use the online or off-line *Thomas Register* to locate manufacturer prospects for their products and services.

Chapter Review Question

What is the *Thomas Register*? How might salespeople use it?

Competitive Analysis Worksheet

Many professional salespeople maintain well-organized files on competitors and their offerings. They keep running files on each of their competitors—products they sell, competitive advantages and disadvantages, major customers, products that each customer buys and for what use, names of competitive salespeople, and their estimated sales volume. A salesperson can prepare a competitive analysis worksheet, like the one shown in Table 11.3, with input from customers and thus can systematically compare competitors' product and service offerings with those of his or her own company's.[9]

TABLE 11.3

COMPETITIVE ANALYSIS WORKSHEET

For each dimension below, rank our company versus competitors on a scale of 5 to 1, with 5 being the highest rank.

Product Dimension	Our Firm	Competitor A	Competitor B	Competitor C	Competitor D
Sales growth	5	4	4	3	3
Market share	4	4	3	2	2
Sales force	5	3	3	2	2
Financial strength	4	5	3	1	1
Marketing strategy	5	5	4	3	2
Marketing mix	4	4	3	2	2
Image/ reputation	5	5	4	3	2
New products	4	5	3	2	1
Product quality	5	5	3	3	3
Pricing (value)	5	4	3	3	3
Promotion	5	5	3	2	1
Installation	4	3	3	3	2
Delivery	4	4	4	3	3
Billing/ invoicing	4	4	4	4	3
Repair	5	5	4	3	3
Customer service	5	4	3	3	3

To learn about competitors, salespeople often turn to both online and off-line sources for information.
Susan Van Etten/PhotoEdit

STRATEGIC UNDERSTANDING OF YOUR MARKETS

Where are your company's present and future markets? Who are and will be its customers? Economic, technological, political-legal, cultural-social, ethical, and competitive environments are continuously changing. Companies that have prospered most over the years are those that have successfully anticipated and responded to the many dynamic changes in the macromarketing environment.

Timely customer feedback is critical to the company's response to a dynamic environment. Salespeople are supposed to be the "eyes and ears" of the company in the marketplace, but sales and marketing managers often ignore this information-gathering function of salespeople. Thus the company loses a valuable early-warning system about changing customer needs and the evolving marketing environment. Most salespeople and their companies' managers believe they know the market thoroughly. Yet overwhelming evidence indicates that they do not. Important innovations rarely come from firms currently dominant in a given industry. Numerous industry leaders have been slow to recognize technological developments that changed their markets forever, as shown in Table 11.4.

Beyond anticipating and adjusting to changes in the environment, an organization must apply marketing and sales planning to its relationships with all its influencing publics, not just customers. All of these publics (such as the financial community, suppliers, governments, employees, stockholders, and the general public) should be considered *stakeholders* in the company. Each of these publics influences the operation of sales and marketing organizations for

TABLE 11.4

Companies Slow to Recognize Opportunities in Markets They Dominated

Company or Industry	Innovative Product or Service
Parker Brothers, Mattel	Video games
Kendall (cloth diaper cleaners)	Disposable diapers
Levi Strauss	Designer jeans
Goodyear, Firestone, Goodrich	Radial tires
Swiss watchmakers	Digital watches
Anheuser Busch, Miller	Light beer
Coke, Pepsi	Diet soda and bottled water
Wine producers	Wine coolers
Eversharp, Eberhard Faber	Ballpoint pens
IBM	Microcomputers
Converse, Keds	Running shoes
Keuffel & Esser (leading manufacturer of slide rules)	Calculators

better or worse, so in developing strategies and tactics, it is necessary to consider the potential reaction of each.

Keeping Informed

Successful salespeople work at staying well informed about the industry they serve and about business in general. They regularly do their own personal market research at local university or college libraries or via the Web. They are alert to trends in, and regularly read publications about, their customers' industries. They join trade associations that publish current developments in the industry and can supply membership lists that lead to new customers. And they attend trade shows and seminars where they can interact with customers and learn more about their customers' businesses.

An abundance of information about prospects and companies is available in most college and large city libraries and over the Internet from company websites and online databases. At a library, check with the business reference librarian to learn about the many sources of company information available in hardback volumes, microfilm, or online. Sales professionals read the annual reports of their customers, their competitors, and their own companies, and they study analyses on these companies prepared by financial firms such as Dun & Bradstreet, Standard and Poor's, and Value Line. They periodically review data from *Dun & Bradstreet's Million Dollar Directory, Ward's Directory of Major U.S. Private Companies,* and the *Thomas Register of National Manufacturers.*

Business Periodicals Index A cumulative subject index that lists business articles from more than 160 periodicals.

They go to the ***Business Periodicals Index*** at a library or on the Web to find specific articles about a company, product, issue, or problem. They regularly read general business publications such as *Business Week*, the *Wall Street Journal*, *Forbes*, and *Fortune* in order to keep up with the latest in the business world and to project a more informed image to prospects and customers. They don't rely on just one source for information but, rather, try to corroborate data with various sources.

For salespeople and their managers, particularly valuable information can be found in the *Source Book of Demographics and Buying Power for Every Zip Code in the U.S.A.* (einsys.einpgh.org/MARION/ABJ-4716). It provides population, socioeconomic characteristics, buying power, and other demographic information for zip code areas throughout the United States. Each zip code area is assigned a *purchasing potential index* number based on its consumption potential across a variety of product categories. For instance, if the purchasing potential index for a certain zip code is 115 for purchase of office desks, then that zip code has a 15 percent greater potential to buy office desks than the U.S. average. Conversely, if a zip code has an index of 85 for purchasing printing machines, then its purchasing potential for that product is 15 percent below the national average. Purchasing potential information can be extremely helpful to salespeople in identifying which zip codes in their sales territories offer the best opportunities to sell their particular products and services.

A second source of useful data on an area's effective buying income is the *Survey of Buying Power* published annually in *Sales and Marketing Management* magazine (www.salesandmarketing.com/salesandmarketing/index.jsp). An overall indicator of an area's buying power is the *buying power index (BPI)*, expressed as a percent of total U.S. sales. The higher an area's BPI, the greater the ability of that market to buy general merchandise. For example, a city with a BPI of .3242 has greater potential ability to buy than a city with a BPI of only .2783. A serious limitation of the BPI is that it calculates only potential for buying general merchandise. Specific product categories require a customized BPI.[10]

After you've identified some high-potential buying areas, you might next go online to *SalesLeadsUSA* (www.SalesLeadsUSA.info) and use the free database service to search the addresses and phone numbers of more than eleven million businesses in the United States and Canada by name, type of business, NAICS code, names of key executives, and more. Sales leads can also be found at *Harris InfoSource* (www.HarrisInfo.com), which provides information on more than 350,000 companies and 600,000 key decision makers.

Online, you will find countless other valuable sources of information for salespeople. Companies that produce similar products and services often belong to industry trade associations, which means you can start at the Federal Consumer Information Center website (www.pueblo.gsa.gov/crh/trade.htm), where you will find lists of hundreds of associations, both commercial and not-for-profit, by type of activity (e.g., automobile, banking, insurance, utilities, and military) and alphabetically. At this website, you will find a brief statement about whom the association represents and what they do, along with the association's address, telephone and fax numbers, e-mail address, and website address.

KEEPING UP ONLINE: U.S. CENSUS BUREAU

The U.S. Census Bureau has an abundance of data for the entire nation. Check out the offerings at *www.census.gov*. How could a salesperson make use of these data? Do you see any problems in using these data?

When you contact an association or go to its website, you can obtain valuable prospecting information and perhaps the membership directory. Some good places to find company websites are Internet search engines such as *Yahoo's Business and Economy* (www.yahoo.com/Business and Economy/Companies), which provides links to companies in more than one hundred industry categories. Overall, the Internet is home to hundreds of searchable online databases, some free and some for a fee. Table 11.5 describes some of the information sources available to resourceful salespeople. Most of the trade directories, business guides, indexes, and government publications usually can be found in hardcopy at larger libraries, and in many cases on the Internet as well. Colleges and universities generally allow their students free access to the many Internet sources of information. Log on to the U.S. Census Bureau's website (see the above *Keeping Up Online* feature) to discover how much government information is readily available at the click of a mouse.

TABLE 11.5

SOURCES OF INFORMATION

Trade Association Directories
Encyclopedia of Associations (Gale Research Company, Detroit; library.dialog.com/bluesheets/html/bl0114.html) Provides detailed information on thousands of nonprofit membership organizations worldwide.
National Trade and Professional Associations of the United States and Labor Unions (Columbia Books, Washington, D.C.; dir.yahoo.com/Business_and_Economy/Organizations/Trade_Associations) Contains data on about 5,000 organizations, trade and professional associations, and national labor unions.
Directory of Corporate Affiliations (National Register Publishing Company, Skokie, Illinois; www.corporateaffiliations.com/Content/index.html) Cross-references more than 3,000 parent companies with their 16,000 thousand divisions, subsidiaries, and affiliates.
Business Guides
Thomas Register of National Manufacturers (www.ThomasRegister.com) Leading and most comprehensive purchasing guide to the manufacturing industry. Database includes more than 189,000 companies and 72,000 product categories. Provides comprehensive company information on 550,000 industrial distributors, manufacturers, and service companies classified in 6,000 product and service categories.

(continued)

TABLE 11.5

Sources of Information (continued)

Buyers and engineers can access supplier information through e-commerce–enabled catalogs, brochures, fax forms, line cards, and hotlinks to supplier websites. Users can negotiate and complete the entire buying/selling process online.

Reference Book of Corporate Managements (Dun & Bradstreet, New York; www.loc.gov/rr/business/duns/dunsindx.html) Identifies more than 30,000 executives who are officers and directors of 2,400 large corporations. Also at this Library of Congress website are numerous additional Dun & Bradstreet business publications.

Standard & Poor's Corporation Services (Standard & Poor's Corporation, New York; www.standardandpoors.com) Provides various services, including *Industry Surveys* (trends and projections); *Outlook* (weekly stock market letter); *Stock Guide* (monthly summary of data on 5,000 common and preferred stocks); *Trade and Securities* (monthly listing of statistics on business, finance, stocks and bonds, foreign trade, productivity, and employment).

Dun & Bradstreet Information Services (www.dnb.com) Provides the latest business news and trends, plus corporate profiles and financial information for privately held companies.

Standard & Poor's Register of Corporations (Standard & Poor's Corporation, New York; www.netadvantage.standardandpoors.com) Contains a cross section of U.S. companies and some international companies. Information includes company name and address, parent company name, NAIC codes, year started, sales, number of employees, market territory, and names of executives.

Standard Directory of Advertisers (National Register Publishing Company, Skokie, Illinois; www.bowker-saur.co.uk/Products/Business/redbooksadvertisers.htm) Offers detailed information on more than 24,000 U.S. and international advertisers who each spend more than $200,000 annually on advertising. Each listing includes advertising expenditures by media, agency, annual sales, and key contact personnel.

Indexes

Business Periodicals Index (H.W. Wilson, New York; www.silverplatter.com/catalog/wbpi.htm) Cumulative subject index listing international English-language business articles from about 600 magazines, journals, and other periodicals.

Wall Street Journal Executive Library (Dow Jones, Princeton, New Jersey; www.executivelibrary.com) Indexes of business articles published in the *Wall Street Journal* and many international newspapers, magazines, journals, and websites. Also includes many business reference sources and toolkits. Articles arranged into corporate news and general news.

CommerceNet (www.dnb.com) An index of websites for major companies, where you can find annual reports, earnings data, and product information.

Government Publications (www.access.gpo.gov/su_docs/locators/cgp)

Survey of Current Business (U.S. Department of Commerce, Bureau of Economic Analysis, Washington, D.C.) Updates 2,600 different statistical series in each monthly issue. Includes data on gross national product, national income, international balance of payments, general business indicators, employment, construction, real estate, and domestic and foreign trade.

(continued)

TABLE 11.5

Sources of Information (continued)

Monthly Catalog of United States Government Publications (Superintendent of Documents, U.S. Government Printing Office, Washington, D.C.) Lists federal publications issued each month, by agency.

Monthly Checklist of State Publications (Superintendent of Documents, U.S. Government Printing Office, Washington, D.C.) Lists state publications received by the Library of Congress.

Census Data: Provides an extensive source of information on the United States.

Bureau of the Census Catalog of Publications: An index of all Census Bureau data, publications, and unpublished materials.

- *Census of Retail Trade:* Provides data on the number of retail operations, sales, payroll, and personnel by primary metropolitan statistical areas (PMSAs), counties, and cities with populations of 2,500 or more by kind of business.
- *Census of Wholesale Trade:* Same as above but for wholesalers.
- *Census of Selected Services:* Provides data on hotels, motels, beauty parlors, and other retail service organizations.
- *Census of Housing:* Provides detailed data on various housing characteristics, including occupancy, financing, equipment, and facilities by state, metropolitan areas, and city block.
- *Census of Manufacturers:* Provides various data on manufacturers, including value added, employment, payrolls, new capital expenditures, cost of materials, and value of shipments for 450 manufacturing industries classified by geographic region and state, employment size, and type of establishment.
- *Census of Population:* Provides social and economic description of U.S. population with cross-classification of inhabitants for metropolitan statistical areas, urban areas, and all locales of 1,000 people or more.
- *Census of Agriculture:* Provides data for all farms and for farms with sales of $2,500 or more by county and state.

Internet Information Sources

Fortune 500 and Fortune Global 500 (fortune.com/fortune500 *OR* fortune.com/global500) Lists the top 500 U.S. companies and the top 500 global companies as compiled by *Fortune;* the lists can be downloaded in spreadsheet form or ordered on disk.

Hoover's Online (www.hoovers.com) This database provides brief company profiles; links from the company profile to financial statements, news, and quotes for the selected company are provided.

Encyclopedia of Associations (library.dialog.com/bluesheets/html/bl0114.html) Provides a database of 81,000 professional societies, trade associations, labor unions, cultural and religious groups, fan clubs, and other nonprofit organizations of all types.

Federal Consumer Information Center (www.pueblo.gsa.gov/crh/trade.htm) Lists the name, address, telephone number, e-mail address, and websites for hundreds of commercial and nonprofit associations by major activity and alphabetically.

Yahoo's Business and Economy (www.yahoo.com/Business_and_Economy/Companies) Yahoo, an Internet search engine, provides links to companies in more than 100 industry categories from its Companies page.

(continued)

TABLE 11.5

Sources of Information (continued)

PR Newswire (www.prnewswire.com) Offers the latest press releases on companies, industries, and executives; releases are from participating PR Newswire members.

Companies Online (companiesonline.com) Partnership between Dun & Bradstreet and Lycos provides a search engine for information on more than 100,000 public and private companies.

Dun & Bradstreet Information Services (www.dbisna.com) Includes industry data and business reference solutions, such as the *Dun & Bradstreet Million Dollar Directory,* which includes in-depth information on more than a million leading U.S. public and private businesses.

Wall Street Journal Online (www.wsj.com) Includes the *Dow Jones Interactive Publications Library,* a searchable database of articles published in more than 5,000 newspapers, newswires, magazines, trade and business journals, transcripts, and newsletters.

Lexis/Nexis (www.lexis-nexis.com) *Lexis-Nexis* is an online, full-text database that contains comprehensive information in the areas of business, news, government, finance, patents, company information, law, legislation, and other items of value to salespeople implementing the selling process. Sources include newspapers, journals, wire services, research reports, press releases, transcripts, codes, and regulations. One of the strongest features of Lexis-Nexis is that it is updated continuously throughout the day, which makes it a fantastic resource for current information. Another advantage of Lexis-Nexis is that you can access the full text of articles you are viewing and print or download that information at your computer workstation, without having to track down your information piece by piece. However, Lexis-Nexis is a complicated online service, and assistance is often required in using it. Also, you must pay for the service unless your school has purchased it for free use by students.

STAT-USA (www.stat-usa.gov/stat-usa.html) A service of the United States Department of Commerce, this website provides vital economic, business, and international trade information from hundreds of government offices and divisions.

BigYellow (www1.bigyellow.com) Find more than 16 million U.S. business telephone listings, 100 million U.S. residential telephone listings, or more than 15 million e-mail addresses from all over the world; also includes global directories.

Internet 800 Directory (www.inter800.com) Find any toll-free 800 or 888 number; this is a free service for users.

Understanding Professional Buyers

Chapter Review Question

What are some of the off-line and online sources through which salespeople can find information to help them better serve customers?

Once salespeople could rely chiefly on personal creative selling skills, but now they usually deal with professional buyers or purchasing agents who are mainly interested in the salesperson's assurance of on-time delivery, product quality, and reliable service. They want to feel sure a product will positively affect their company's profits, and they are demanding greater service and more concessions in price and curtailing the number of approved vendors for their local operating units. Professional buyers expect a salesperson not only to know their needs well but also to have keen knowledge about *their* customers' needs.[11]

Salespeople also need to know how their product is compatible with the buying organization's strategy. That is, how does the product fit in with the customer's strategy and achievement of objectives? Such knowledge can be helpful in crafting the sales presentation and in demonstrating to buyers that the salesperson's offering does more than solve a problem: It actually helps them achieve their firm's goals.

One overriding goal of most customers is higher profitability. To assist in achieving this goal, salespeople should help customers *sell through* to their own customers. This can be done in many ways, such as sharing marketing research findings, recommending promotional strategies, or helping train the employees of customers.

Professional Knowledge Is Essential. Salespeople who can demonstrate that they have studied the customer's business and understand the customer's problems in serving its own customers will have a firm foundation upon which to build a sales relationship. Such a well-grounded, long-term relationship will be based on mutual trust, cooperation, interdependence, social relationships, adaptation, and commitment.[12] Although friendliness and an outgoing personality help, professional knowledge is essential for success in sales as indicated by the major attributes that buyers want from salespeople.[13] These attributes include:

Chapter Review Question

Name the ten attributes that industrial buyers say they like in salespeople.

- Thoroughness and follow-through
- Knowledge of product line
- Willingness to go to bat for the buyer within the supplier's firm
- Market knowledge and willingness to keep the buyer informed
- Imagination in applying products to the buyers' needs
- Knowledge of the buyer's product line
- Diplomacy in dealing with operating departments
- Preparation for well-planned sales calls
- Regularity of sales calls
- Technical knowledge

Buyers Are Human, Too. Although novice salespeople sometimes think that organizations buy for purely rational reasons, remember that professional buyers are human beings with needs and motivations that cannot help but influence their purchase decisions. For instance, a corporation will seldom buy a multimillion-dollar executive airplane unless the CEO becomes personally excited about it and conveys this enthusiasm and support for the acquisition to the company's purchasing agent. In working with buyers, a perceptive salesperson can soon determine whether emotional as well as rational

Professional salespeople need an extensive knowledge base to work effectively with their increasingly demanding customers.
William Taufic/Corbis

Chapter Review Question
Why is it critical that salespeople understand their company and their company's products, competition, and markets? How might salespeople acquire this understanding?

factors might influence a purchase decision. Emotional factors can include the reward/punishment system for purchase mistakes, perceived purchase risk, buyer self-confidence, perceived image of the supplier, or the personal relationship between the salesperson and the buyer. Perceptive salespeople will make all necessary efforts to satisfy the emotional as well as the rational needs of a buyer.

SUMMARY

To be effective and efficient revenue generators, salespeople today need to keenly understand their company and their company's products, competition, and markets. Whether selling low-tech or high-tech products, salespeople must present product features, advantages, and benefits that match their customers' needs and wants. After completing the company's training program, the most successful salespeople keep up-to-date by reading professional and general business magazines and by making use of trade association directories, business guides, indexes, the Web, and government publications in searching for specific information. The roles of professional buyers for organizations are expanding dramatically, as top management comes to understand ever more clearly their impact on profitability. To keep pace with professional buyers and computerized purchasing systems, salespeople must be continuously seeking information from off-line and online sources to better serve their customers.

KEY TERMS

Mission Statement
Culture
Strategy
Tactic
Thomas Register
Business Periodicals Index

TOPICS FOR THOUGHT AND CLASS DISCUSSION

1. In what ways might the company's stakeholders, other than customers, affect personal selling?
2. If you were a new sales trainee about to start a two-week training program, what instructional methods would you prefer? Why?
3. Why do you think the role of company purchasing agents is expanding?
4. Do you think it's necessary for salespeople to know nearly as much about competitive products as they do about their own company's products? Or is it sufficient to know just the major strengths and weaknesses of competitive products? Why?
5. Why do you think so many product innovations come from smaller companies instead of the most dominant company in the industry?
6. Name some off-line and online sources that you have consulted to find information. What information were you looking for? Were you successful in finding what you needed?

INTERNET EXERCISES

1. Assume that you have just been recruited to work as a sales representative for a large company that manufactures medical devices and implants such as hip replacement joints. You need to learn about the industry and your company's competitors quickly. Using some of the appropriate resources, such as Value Line (www.valueline.com), Standard and Poor's (www.standardandpoors.com), Dun & Bradstreet (www.dnb.com), and/or Morningstar (www.morningstar.com), as well as sources of information identified in Table 11.5, conduct an industry competitive analysis by finding the following information:
   (a) Total number of medical device manufacturers
   (b) Total industry annual sales for all medical devices and implants over the last five years
   (c) Annual sales, market shares, profits, and earnings per share reported by your company's five major competitors over the last five years
   (d) Number of employees and the locations/regions of the country in which your company's five major competitors operate
   (e) Based on the information you find, describe the current industry trends.
2. As a follow-up to Exercise 1, to learn even more about your medical device and implant manufacturing company's five most significant competitors, use the websites identified in the chapter or any other sources of information to find the following information:
   (a) Company profiles
   (b) Different product lines for medical device and implants manufactured by each competitor
   (c) Strengths and weaknesses of each competitor
3. Assume that you work as a salesperson for a Fortune 500 company that manufactures copy machines. You need to learn about the industry and your company's major competitors. Using some of the appropriate resources, such as Value Line (www.valueline.com), Standard and Poor's (www.standardandpoors.com), Dun & Bradstreet (www.dnb.com), and/or Morningstar (www.morningstar.com), as well as sources of information identified in Table 11.5, conduct an industry competitive analysis by finding the following information:
   (a) Total number of copy machine manufacturers
   (b) Total industry annual sales for all copy machines over the last five years
   (c) Annual sales, market shares, profits, and earnings per share reported by your company's five major competitors over the last five years
   (d) Number of employees and the locations/regions of the country in which your company's five major competitors operate
   (e) Based on the information you find, describe the current industry trends.
4. As a follow-up to Exercise 3, to learn more about your copy machine manufacturing company's five most significant competitors, use the websites identified in the chapter or any other sources of information to find the following information:
   (a) Company profiles
   (b) Different product lines for copy machines manufactured by each competitor
   (c) Strengths and weaknesses of each competitor

PROJECTS FOR PERSONAL GROWTH

1. Contact two business-to-business salespeople and ask what their firms' policies and procedures are for:
   (a) Processing special rush orders.
   (b) Approving customer credit.
   (c) Delivering and installing products.

(d) Opening new customer accounts.
(e) Handling returned or damaged goods.

2. Ask each of the two salespeople you contacted in your work on Project 1 to describe their company's culture. Is their sales department culture different from their company's overall culture? If so, why?

3. Choose a company of interest to you, then use (a) a trade association directory, (b) a business guide, (c) an index, and (d) a government publication to learn as much as you can about the company's history, mission, organization of the sales force, products sold, markets served, and major competitors. Which source(s) proved most helpful? Write a three-page report summarizing what you discovered about the company that would be important in selling to that company.

4. Choose a favorite product or service that you have recently purchased, and then prepare a product knowledge worksheet comparing the product you bought to three competitive products you might have purchased.

ROLE-PLAY EXERCISE 11.1

Selling a Sales Training Program

Situation

Charles "Buck" Raymond is a sales manager for Farris Telecommunications, a manufacturer of a full line of facsimile machines. A four-year-old company, Farris Telecommunications does not have any formal sales training. All the marketing reps, as the salespeople are called, learn by working on the job for three weeks with a seasoned rep. Janice Tanebaum, a sales representative for Sales Training & Development Company (STD), has called on Mr. Raymond to try to sell him "STD's Professional Sales Training Program" for Farris's new salespeople.

Roles

Charles "Buck" Raymond As he often says, Mr. Raymond is a graduate of the school of hard knocks, and he has little regard for formal sales training because the real world isn't so neatly packaged. Buck wants his salespeople to be flexible enough to deal with any situation—to "go with the flow." He is convinced that just throwing his salespeople into the arena for three weeks of "on-the-job" training teaches them lessons that they'll never forget.

Janice Tanebaum Quickly recognizing "Buck" Raymond's low regard for formal sales training, Janice knows she must persuade him that salespeople need to become increasingly effective and efficient to compete in today's fiercely competitive markets. She must convince him of the benefits that his salespeople and he, as sales manager, will derive from a professional sales training program for each new salesperson—and later, perhaps, refresher training for experienced salespeople.

ROLE-PLAY EXERCISE 11.2

Selling a College Education to Consumer Prospects

Situation

Leah Parker is a 25-year-old admissions counselor in the office of enrollment management for Wallingford College, a small liberal arts school in the Midwest. Ms. Parker describes her job this way: "I'm really a field salesperson for Wallingford. My job is to call on high schools throughout the Midwest, making presentations to high school guidance counselors and student groups about the benefits of an education at Wallingford College. If I can convince students to apply to Wallingford, I've done my job. My real success, however, is measured by the number of students who actually enroll at Wallingford."

Roles

Leah Parker An alumnus of Wallingford, Leah is enthusiastic about her alma mater and can share many personal anecdotes about the special advantages and benefits of an education at a small liberal arts college like Wallingford. She realizes that she cannot appear to be merely a cheerleader for Wallingford, because the students will see through this hyperbole and dismiss much of what she tells them.

High School Students Senior high school students interested in attending college listen to Leah's short sales presentation. Then they ask her a number of questions about college life at Wallingford and the benefits and advantages of an education there compared to other colleges.

CASE 11.1 I'LL COOK HIS GOOSE

Beth Morelli was in her first year of selling business forms for Forms International. She was walking down the hall to the office of Chuck Stoner, purchasing agent for Forest Building Supply (FBS). Beth knew little about FBS, except that it was a division of a large multinational enterprise and that FBS had just opened this office two months ago. Even before Beth entered the office, she was apprehensive because she has always had difficulty approaching new accounts, especially ones she didn't know much about. But the sight of Bill Reilly made her even more concerned. Reilly, a sales representative for Troy Corporation, a major competitor of her company, had been a nemesis of hers from day one. Seeing him leave Stoner's office made Beth realize that she had a major selling job ahead of her. Beth's boss, who had covered the territory before her, had warned her about Bill Reilly. Not only had Reilly covered the same territory for six years, but he was also well liked and respected by customers. And sure enough, even though Beth felt confident that her products were superior to those of any competitor's, including Troy Corporation's, in her first three months Reilly managed to beat her out at four different accounts.

As they passed each other in the hallway, Bill Reilly greeted Beth cordially and asked, "How are things going?" Beth was always a little surprised by Reilly's friendly greeting each time they met because they were in head-to-head competition on many accounts. After a light-hearted chat, Beth excused herself so she wouldn't be late for her appointment with Stoner. Reilly called to her, "Good luck." As she walked toward Stoner's office, Beth thought, "If he wasn't such a tough competitor, I might really like Bill Reilly."

As she entered Stoner's office, Beth was pleased to see him stand up, smile, and extend his hand. Beth returned the handshake cordially.

MORELLI: Good morning, Mr. Stoner. You seem to be in a good mood.

STONER: Yes, I am. Bill Reilly just gave me two tickets to tonight's baseball game. My son's going to be thrilled.

MORELLI: Well, that's nice, but I heard there's a 50-50 chance of rain tonight.

STONER: [Looking a little annoyed] I sure hope not. What do you have to show me today?

[Beth makes her sales presentation, explaining her company's services and showing examples of her company's business forms.]

MORELLI: So, Mr. Stoner, what do you think?

STONER: Well, your products do look good, but I'm not sure they're any better than Troy's. [Beth thinks for a moment. She wants desperately to win this account.]

MORELLI: Well, Mr. Stoner, from what I've seen, I'm not sure why anyone would be interested in Troy's products. They have slow service, old-fashioned-looking products, and high prices. Our company's a lot more progressive. Troy's been having some union problems lately that have affected customer

(*continued*)

service. Did you know that Troy sent a hundred cases of business forms to Metropolitan Hospital last month, and all had the wrong address on them? Every one of them had to be returned, and for two weeks the hospital had to ration forms to keep from running out. Customers can't afford many mistakes like that, can they?

[Beth thinks to herself, "That ought to make Stoner nervous about choosing Reilly's company over mine."]

MORELLI: Mr. Stoner, if I can take an order this week, I'm authorized to give you a 10 percent discount on the entire order. How many cases of forms can I order for you?

STONER: Well, I've got to run to a 10 o'clock meeting now, but I'll get back to you when I decide. Thanks for coming in.

Before Beth could say another word, Stoner was standing up and heading out the door to his meeting. As Beth was gathering up her presentation materials, she wondered what her chances were of landing a big order.

Questions

1. How do you think Mr. Stoner perceived Beth Morelli's sales presentation?
2. What do you think Beth should have done differently? Why?
3. How would you compete with a competitive salesperson like Bill Reilly?
4. What advice would you give Beth if Mr. Stoner calls her later? What should Beth do if Mr. Stoner doesn't call her?

CASE 11.2 "GEE, WHAT COULD HAVE GONE WRONG?"

CASE 11.2 "GEE, WHAT COULD HAVE GONE WRONG?" CAN BE FOUND ONLINE AT HTTP://COLLEGE.HMCO.COM/PIC/ANDERSONPS2E

CHAPTER 12

Communicating Effectively with Diverse Customers

After reading this chapter, you should understand:

- The five modes of communication.
- The three dimensions and four levels of listening.
- The formats and types of questions.
- How to use space in the buyer-seller interaction.
- The use of body language.
- The four communication styles, sources of conflicts between them, and how to flex with different communication styles of buyers.
- How to build trust with prospects and customers.

"There are four ways, and only four ways, in which we have contact with the world. We are evaluated and classified by these four contacts: what we do, how we look, what we say, *and* how we say it.*"*

Dale Carnegie, 1888–1955, American author and trainer

INSIDE PERSONAL SELLING

Meet Ewell Hopkins of Sapient Corporation

Effective communication is the key to selling services—especially the business strategy consulting, systems design, software implementation, and research services that Ewell Hopkins sells on behalf of Sapient Corporation. As director of client relations, Hopkins needs top-notch communication skills to uncover a prospect's problems before he can begin to sell anything: "We interpret a business need, reach consensus with the client through workshops and other interviewing processes, agree on the ultimate goal, and then design a solution to meet that goal."

Hopkins considers listening more important than talking in a sales situation. "You can't learn anything when you're talking," he notes. "More important, prospects look for someone who understands their unique needs. If you start off talking, prospects will be concerned that you are not prepared to listen or understand their needs."

To probe for needs, goals, and information, Hopkins asks open-ended questions beginning with "Why . . . ?" or "How . . . ?" and explains his rationale for asking so that prospects understand where the discussion is leading.

"You don't want people wondering why you're asking the question," he stresses.

Not long ago, Hopkins met with a Canadian financial firm seeking a creative way of using technology to strengthen relations with existing customers and attract new customers for its retirement products. He had to prove that he understood the prospect's challenge and could help the prospect reach its goals. This required listening actively and empathetically to the prospect's management and its customers. "We established why customers want retirement accounts and what they liked about working with an investment provider," Hopkins says. Based on this research, the client and the Sapient team collectively came up with the idea of an interactive game to make retirement planning more appealing to the prospect's customers.

When Hopkins meets in a prospect's office, he looks around for conversation-sparking ideas. "People put things in their personal space for a reason," he observes. "You can discuss virtually anything if it's in plain view." In a group meeting, he lets the prospect's representatives sit first and notes how they position themselves versus one another: "If I bring two or three colleagues, I spread them out so my people are not all seated on one side with the prospect's people on the other side. I will intentionally sit on 'their' side."

After the sale, Hopkins closely monitors progress toward meeting deadlines and ensures that the Sapient team is fully informed about the client's needs and situation. This requires good internal and external communication. He stays in touch with the client and advises his colleagues of any special pressures or requests that affect the project. "People don't like to work in isolation," Hopkins explains. "If you explain the context and show how they fit into the big picture, people are much more motivated to do a quality job."

Are you an effective communicator? If you are, that's great! But most people require training to become good communicators. As a college student, you've probably had a lot of practice. But how good have you become at the more subtle other half of communication—that is, listening? Of course, you listen carefully in class for anything that might be on an upcoming exam. But what about outside of class? Before responding, candidly answer the following questions: Do you always carefully listen and try to fully comprehend what another person is saying? Do you "cool your jets" long enough to let the other person finish before you start speaking? Do you seldom interrupt other people while they're talking . . . and do you rarely complete their sentences for them even when they seem to be hesitating? Do you avoid anticipating or prejudging what the other person is going to say? Do you stay away from thinking about your own reply until the other person has finished talking? Are you good at putting yourself in the other person's shoes and empathizing with his or her viewpoint even when it is different from yours? Are you perceptive in picking up subtle, underlying points and body language beyond an individual's spoken words?

If you have honestly answered yes to all the foregoing questions, you are probably an excellent communicator. If you answered no to one or more, you, like most of us, could improve your overall communication skills. As indicated by the questions you answered, communicating isn't *just* about speaking clearly, audibly, articulately, or even persuasively. It involves much more. By the end of this chapter, you will not only learn what communication is and how to do it effectively, but you should also be well on your way toward becoming a better communicator—an invaluable asset for a salesperson or, for that matter, anyone in any walk of life.

Successful salespeople, like successful people in most any profession, are excellent communicators. So central is communication to successful selling and marketing that the words of Marion Harper, Jr., from many years ago are still true today:

> More and more it is becoming apparent that marketing is almost entirely communications. The product communicates; the price communicates; the package communicates; salespeople communicate to the prospect, to the trade, to management and to each other; also, prospects, dealers, management and competitors communicate.[1]

WHAT IS COMMUNICATION?

Communication is a process whereby information and understanding are conveyed between two or more people. Communication should not be confused with the related concept of promotion. **Promotion** is typically a one-way flow of information and persuasion from seller to buyer, whereas communication is a *two-way exchange*.

Communication A process in which information and understanding are conveyed in two-way exchanges between two or more people.

Promotion Typically, a one-way flow of persuasive information from a seller to a buyer.

We use five distinct modes of communication: (1) listening, (2) writing, (3) talking, (4) reading, and (5) an often overlooked means—*nonverbal* communication. Of the first four modes, the average person, unlike many salespeople, normally spends more time *listening*, as shown in Figure 12.1. Nonverbal communication, sometimes called "body language," is expressed through

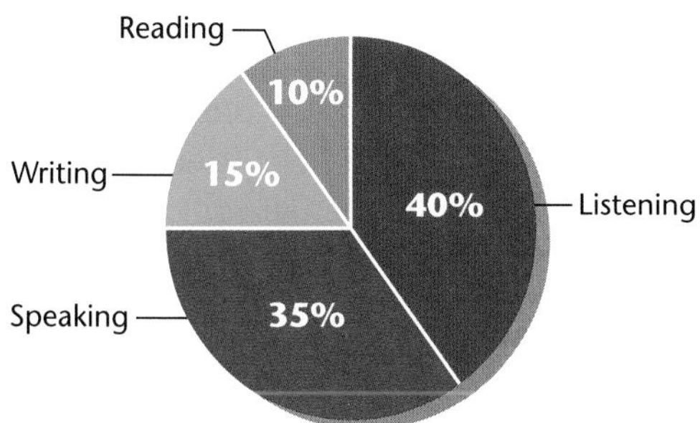

FIGURE 12.1

TIME PEOPLE SPEND IN EVERYDAY COMMUNICATION

IT'S UP TO YOU

You are in the middle of your sales presentation to a buying committee at a large company. As the presentation unfolds, you seem to be doing fairly well, and one of the prospect's representatives seems particularly interested. She is responding favorably to your questions, and, in turn, is asking you a lot of questions. What is troubling you, however, is that the prospect keeps interrupting your presentation, and you make little progress. Some of her comments pertain to questions or issues relevant to the presentation; others, however, are totally unrelated ones or ones that you will answer later in the presentation. You don't want to offend the prospect by telling her to stop interrupting, but you also want to complete a solid, informative, convincing presentation before you run out of time and some of the members of the buying committee have to leave. What is your next move? How will you conduct the rest of this call?

our bodies (face, arms, hands, legs, and posture) or our voices (rate of speech, volume, pitch, tone, accent, rhythm, emphasis, and pauses). And it has significant meaning in buyer-seller exchanges, as you will see later in the chapter.

Keen listening is especially important for salespeople. You can't learn anything about prospects and customers while you're talking. In fact, to succeed at personal selling, you must learn to be an expert listener, one who shows empathy and respect for prospects and continually strives to enhance rapport with them. Keep in mind that you, the salesperson, are not the only one with a message to communicate. Customers want you to understand them and comprehend *their* message *first*. Unfortunately, a chronic complaint of buyers is that salespeople simply do not listen to their customers. Without listening attentively to customers, solving their problems and satisfying their needs will be virtually impossible. Read *It's Up to You* and give your communication skills a try.

Chapter Review Question
Explain the difference between communication and promotion.

DEVELOPING COMMUNICATION SKILLS

Today's top professional salespeople continually increase their communication effectiveness and efficiency by improving their skills in (1) listening, (2) asking questions, (3) using space, (4) interpreting nonverbal communication, and (5) dealing with the different communication styles of different buyers. Let's discuss these skills and ways in which you can develop and use them in your sales career.

Listening

Becoming an effective listener does not mean that you must give equal attention to everything you hear. On any given day, you may hear or have the opportunity to hear an incredible quantity and variety of messages from family, friends, colleagues, subordinates, superiors, radio and television broadcasts, prospects, and customers, and from interactions with service people of all kinds—from taxi cab drivers to restaurant waiters to health care professionals. Relatively little of this barrage of messages will merit your full attention, however. Your mind processes messages of importance to you, filters those that seem irrelevant, and perhaps summarily dismisses others.

Three Dimensions of Listening. There are three dimensions of listening.[2] The first dimension is **sensing.** The most basic aspect of listening, it entails hearing words, inflection, and paralanguage (e.g., speed of speech, use of colloquialisms), as well as observing nonverbal language (e.g., body language, facial expressions). **Processing,** the second dimension, consists of operations in the salesperson's mind that give meaning to the message through understanding, interpreting, evaluating, and remembering the communication. After sensing and processing the message, salespeople engage in the third dimension, **responding** to the message. Listeners send information back to speakers indicating that the speakers' message has been received correctly. Responding assures the prospect that the salesperson has listened accurately and is encouraging the communication to continue.

Sensing The most basic aspect of listening; includes hearing words, inflection, and paralanguage (e.g., speed of speech, use of colloquialisms), as well as observation of nonverbal language (e.g., body language, facial expressions).

Processing Operations within the salesperson's mind that give meaning to the prospect's message through understanding, interpreting, evaluating, and remembering the communication.

Responding Assures the prospect that the salesperson has been listening accurately and is encouraging the communication to continue.

Levels of Listening. In addition to the foregoing three dimensions of listening, a *hierarchy* of listening involves four kinds of listening, from least effective to most effective.[3] When **marginal listening** occurs, salespeople hear words but are easily distracted and may allow their minds to wander. This flawed kind of listening can cause the salesperson to miss a key point or important material provided by the buyer.

Evaluative listening entails concentrating on what the buyer is saying but not sensing what is being said through nonverbal or subtle verbal cues. As a result, the salesperson is likely to process the buyer's message inaccurately and not understand the true meaning of the communication.

Active listening occurs when the salesperson receives a verbal and nonverbal message, processes it, and then responds to it to encourage further communication. Moreover, active listeners provide verbal and nonverbal feedback to the buyer. Salespeople who actively listen tend to use all of their senses to clearly understand the message—and they communicate their understanding to prospects.

The highest level of listening is **active empathetic listening (AEL).** With AEL, the salesperson

> . . . receives verbal and nonverbal messages, processes them cognitively, responds to them verbally and nonverbally, and attempts to assess their underlying meaning intuitively by putting [himself or herself] in the customer's place throughout.[4]

By putting yourself in the customer's shoes, you show genuine concern for your prospect. And when you show sincere concern for prospects, they are likely to respond favorably to you and your offering. Top-performing

Marginal Listening Occurs when salespeople hear the prospect's words but are easily distracted and may allow their minds to wander.

Evaluative Listening Occurs when the seller concentrates on what the buyer is saying but fails to sense what is being said through nonverbal or subtle verbal cues.

Active Listening Occurs when the salesperson receives a message, processes it, and then responds to it to encourage further communication.

Active Empathetic Listening (AEL) Highest level of listening; occurs when the salesperson receives verbal and nonverbal messages, processes them cognitively, responds to them verbally and nonverbally, and attempts to assess their underlying meaning intuitively by putting herself or himself in the customer's place throughout.

TABLE 12.1

Examples of Four Levels of Listening

Car Buyer: I'm not sure I like this car's color.

Salesperson responds with ***marginal listening:*** Let's take a test drive. [The salesperson has not really heard what the prospect was saying.]

Salesperson responds with ***evaluative listening:*** There's a classic blue one over there. Let's take a test drive. [The salesperson failed to sense what the prospect was saying because of a failure to sense the prospect's verbal and nonverbal cues.]

Salesperson responds with ***active listening:*** What is it that you dislike about the color of the car? Is there anything else you don't like about the car? [The salesperson accurately sensed verbal and nonverbal messages but failed to put himself or herself in the prospect's shoes.]

Salesperson responds with ***active empathetic listening:*** You seem to be saying that this car is not right for your company. What are the really key features that you want your car to have? We'll consider only cars that have those particular features. [The salesperson has identified with the prospect's perspective to better empathize and understand what the prospect was attempting to communicate.]

Source: *From* Journal of Personal Selling & Sales Management, *Vol.19, No.1 (Winter 1999). Copyright © 1999 by PSE National Education Foundation. Reprinted with permission of M.E. Sharpe, Inc. All rights reserved. Not for reproduction.*

salespeople are effective active empathetic listeners. An illustration of the four different levels of listening is provided in Table 12.1.

Guidelines for Effective Listening. Effective listening is an active process. As noted above, even when salespeople hear a prospect's words, they must observe body language and listen carefully for voice inflection and tone to fully understand what the words mean. The guidelines described in Table 12.2 are those that effective listeners employ.

TABLE 12.2

Guidelines for Effective Listening

- **Ask Probing Questions:** As a salesperson, your most important tool is the probing question. Probing enables you to uncover a sales opportunity. Further, questions can stimulate a need for your product and ultimately convert the prospect into a customer.
- **Paraphrase the Information You Hear:** In paraphrasing, you restate the prospect's key words for emphasis and understanding. Be careful when using this technique, however, to avoid annoying customers by echoing everything the prospect says. A confirmatory paraphrase simply restates a prospect's comment to confirm an attitude or fact. This technique can help build rapport and a climate of empathy and mutual understanding. For example, you can say, "Then, it's my understanding that you think your plant manager would like us to implement our 'just-in-time inventory response' program right away." Paraphrasing indicates to the prospect that you are attentively listening, understanding his or her concerns, and showing genuine concern for what is being said.

(continued)

TABLE 12.2

Guidelines for Effective Listening (continued)

- **Use a Leading Phrase When Appropriate:** With a leading phrase you subtly encourage prospects to reexamine and modify their views by interpreting their words to make your point. For instance, when the prospect comments, "Your product may be the best, but it is just too expensive," a good leading paraphrase might be "If I understand you correctly, you think that price is a more critical consideration than product quality." You have to be careful in using leading paraphrases because your interpretation of their words can irritate prospects. A prospect might testily retort, "I didn't say that quality is less important than a reasonable price. I said that we need both." Hearing this response, you would be wise to back off a little and reply, "I'm sorry I misunderstood. I know that you just want the best value for your company. And I assure you, Mr. Peters, that our product will be your best buy over the long run because our quality is much higher and our price is only a little higher than our competitors'."
- **Clarify the Information:** Sometimes in communicating with prospects, conversations become a little vague. It's better to seek clarification before the sale is made than after the sale is closed and corrective action is impossible. Make sure that you understand exactly why, where, when, and how the product or service is desired by asking follow-up questions to clarify your understanding. For example: "Now, let me make sure I understand exactly *when* you need the stronger steel and *where* it should be delivered. If one of our big trailer rigs dumped a load of steel in the wrong place, you'd probably come looking for me. You said to deliver one trailer load to Twelfth and Market Streets on the morning of August 31st at 7:30 A.M.—right?"
- **Use Affirmative Responses:** Salespeople can convey to prospects and customers that they are actively empathetically listening by nodding their heads, maintaining good eye contact, and making an occasional comment such as "I see," "Okay," "Yes," or "Uh-huh." Doing so informs the prospect that you are listening and allows you to acknowledge that what the prospect is saying is important to you.
- **Welcome Pauses and Silences:** Don't be fearful of long pauses or silences in communicating with prospects. Remember the old saw: "Silence is golden." A common mistake of rookie salespeople is to try to fill any gap in communication with words. Short pauses and even longer silences give both you and the prospect some time to think and to make sure that you haven't overlooked anything. Silences by the salesperson also encourage the prospect to continue talking and providing more information about the purchase decision and reasons for buying. Most prospects and customers like to talk—so let them! You will only gain from your silence (now's the time to use your listening skills!).
- **Summarize the Conversation:** At the conclusion of the sales call, it's a good idea to summarize the sales interview so that the prospect has a final chance to correct any errors or misunderstandings. Summaries demonstrate to the prospect that you have been an attentive listener throughout the selling process. This summary can also reassure the prospect that you are a thorough, conscientious, and empathetic professional.

Asking Questions

Studies have shown that the more questions salespeople ask, the more successful they are in closing sales.[5] Top salespeople know that superior selling is *less telling, more asking*. They are nearly always excellent questioners. They know exactly what information they need, so each of their questions has a

Chapter Review Questions

Outline the four levels of listening and give an example of each.

What are some guidelines to facilitate good listening?

Professional salespeople augment their communication effectiveness by using active empathetic listening.
Royalty-Free/Corbis

specific purpose. They develop questioning skills and approaches that enable them to quickly discover

- The best prospects
- The prospect's real needs
- What, when, and how the prospect buys
- Who influences the purchase decision
- What product or service benefits the prospects want
- Why prospects seem to prefer one brand over another
- How quickly the prospect wants the product
- How the prospect will pay for the order
- What kind of post-purchase service the prospect will require
- Who the competitors are and what they offer

To learn more about communicating effectively with customers and to further enhance their communication skills, salespeople can enroll in comprehensive training programs offered by firms such as Eudicor Business Communications (www.eudicor.com/products/sale_communications.html).

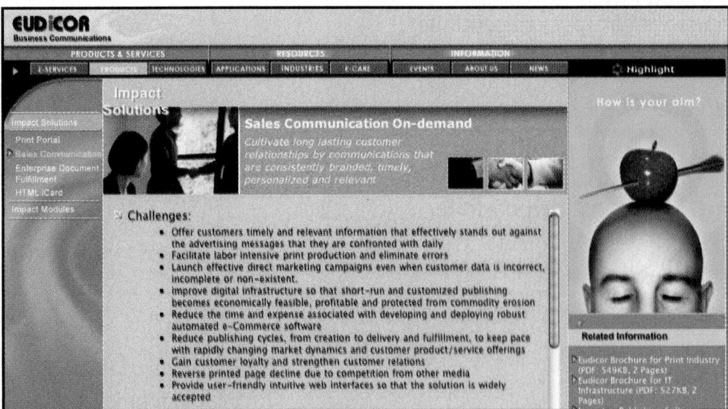

Courtesy of Eudicor Business Communications

Question Formats. Experienced salespeople use three basic question *formats*: (1) open-ended, (2) closed, and (3) semi-open questions. *Open-ended questions* usually begin with words such as *who, what, why, where, when,* and *how*. They allow prospects to answer in their own words and are best for eliciting general background or prospect feelings, confirming understanding of a comment, and probing for subconscious feelings. Open-ended questions look like these: "What kind of benefits are you seeking

KEEPING UP ONLINE: BIZJOURNALS.COM

Bizjournals.com is a daily online newspaper that provides exclusive local business intelligence in fifty-eight major U.S. markets, such as New York, Chicago, and Minneapolis–St. Paul. The access to news and information that it offers can give salespeople the competitive edge for the market or markets they choose.

Visit Bizjournals.com at www.bizjournals.bcentral.com. How might bizjournals.com help you in your sales career? How might it help you improve your communication skills with prospects and customers?

from this product?" "How do you think you'll use the product?" "Why do you believe that Brand A is better than Brand B?"

Closed questions usually can be answered directly with simple yes or no responses. They are best for ensuring that you are on the right track, confirming information, and narrowing the focus of discussion. Closed questions often begin with some form of the verbs *be, do,* or *have.* Here are some examples of closed questions: "Are your office computers networked?" "Do you think Mr. Johnson would be interested in buying laptop computers for the sales force?" "Will he be back from vacation next Monday?"

Chapter Review Question
Name the three basic question formats. What kind of response would you expect from a customer for each format?

Semi-open questions seek precise information and thus tend to have only one or a few possible answers. They help you obtain specific facts. Semi-open questions include the following: "When can we set up an appointment?" "What day do you want us to deliver the equipment?" "What's your preference—the mahogany executive desk or the walnut one?" "Do you want to pay by cash or credit?" Read the accomopanying *Keeping Up Online* feature and determine how the website it describes can assist you in formulating questions for prospects.

Types of Questions. Professional salespeople use six basic *types* of questions: **probing questions, evaluative questions, strategic questions, tactical questions, dichotomous questions,** and **multiple-choice questions.** All have different purposes and are appropriate at different times. Table 12.3 offers detailed information about these six major types of questions.

Asking the right types of questions in the right format, in the right tone, and in the right context is both an art and a science. Undoubtedly it requires practice to produce effective results over time. But just as verbal questions are critical in the sales job, so are written questions sent to prospects and customers in the form of a questionnaire. Read *From the Command Post* on page 391 to see how some companies are making increased use of cyberspace to ask important questions and obtain answers that can ultimately affect marketing and sales force efforts.

Probing Question Used to search for information when prospects and customers have difficulty articulating their precise needs.

Evaluative Question Used within the open-ended question format to stimulate prospects and customers to talk about their general or specific goals, problems, and needs.

Dichotomous Question Used to set up a clear-cut "either-or" answer for prospects and customers.

TABLE 12.3

Question Types, Purposes, Appropriate Uses, and Examples

Question Type	Purpose	When to Use	Example
I. Probing	Allows you to dig for information when prospects can't seem to articulate their needs or wants.	Any time after rapport has been established with prospect.	"Bob, what do you think the plant manager means by his comment?"
1. SILENCE	Encourages the prospect to keep talking.	Whenever you want the prospect to elaborate on his or her thoughts and feelings.	
2. CONSEQUENCE	Points out the disadvantages of continuing to use the prospect's present product.	During the early part of the sales presentation.	"Ms. Byrd, if you continue to use a dot matrix printer while other departments are using laser printers, aren't you afraid that top management will think your reports are less professional?"
3. ENCOURAGEMENT	Encourages prospect to continue talking by nodding agreement, making supporting sounds, looking interested, leaning forward, etc.	Any time you want the prospect to keep talking and expanding on something.	While nodding the head, make supporting responses such as "Yes, I see," "Go on," "Uh huh," "I didn't know that," or "Is that right?"
4. ELABORATION	Obtains more information from prospect along the same line.	Best to mix with other probes. Overuse may limit range of information obtained.	"Will you tell me a little more about the problems you're having with your current product?"
5. CLARIFICATION	Requests prospect to supply additional information on specific subject.	When you need clarification about some topic or to obtain more detailed information.	"Can you explain what you mean by that?"
6. TOPIC CHANGE	To switch topics. Must be done subtly to keep from irking prospect.	When you believe you have obtained all the information you need about a given subject.	"May I ask you a question on a somewhat different topic?"

(continued)

TABLE 12.3

Question Types, Purposes, Appropriate Uses, and Examples (continued)

7. DIRECTIVE	Aimed at obtaining facts about a focused topic.	Within your sales presentation.	"Who will be using the facsimile machine?"
8. VERIFYING	Designed to obtain prospect confirmation of information.	To verify presales call information and set the stage for further questioning.	"Are you still the purchasing agent responsible for buying truck axles?" "Do you think you'll need to buy about 5,000 axles this year?"
9. LEADING	To check for understanding, obtain feedback, or answer an unspoken question.	Use later in the sales call to determine options desired and to obtain agreement on purchase decision.	"Do I understand correctly that you prefer the upgraded model?"
10. LOADED	Emotionally charged words designed to bring out strong prospect feelings.	After rapport has been established with prospect. This can be most effective in the later stages of the sales presentation or during the close.	"Don't you think that anybody who drives a foreign car is unpatriotic?"
II. Evaluative	Open-ended questions designed to stimulate prospects to talk about their goals, problems, and needs.	To learn about the prospect's goals and what he or she thinks, feels, wants, and hopes.	"What do you think about the design for your new office?" "What are the problems with your current inventory system?"
1. DIRECT	Ask direct questions to obtain the views and opinions of prospects.	To learn about the prospect's beliefs and attitudes about the selling firm, the seller's products, the product type, and such.	"What is your opinion of this kind of product?" "How do you know about our firm?"
2. INDIRECT	Learn indirectly what the prospect thinks or feels without producing a negative reaction.	When the prospect may not want to directly express his or her thoughts and feelings.	"What do you think most people in your department will say about this new photocopier?"

(continued)

TABLE 12.3

QUESTION TYPES, PURPOSES, APPROPRIATE USES, AND EXAMPLES (CONTINUED)

III. Strategic	Allows you to continue productive questioning even when the prospect is negative.	Anytime during sales call with negative prospect to uncover underlying needs and attitudes.	"Why do you think our mainframe computer isn't in the same league with the IBM computer?"
IV. Tactical	To "hit the ball" back into the prospect's court when dealing with a tough question.	When the prospect asks a sensitive or irritating question to put you on the defensive.	"Don't you think that small businesses are as capable as large firms in providing quality service?" "Didn't virtually every business start out small?"
V. Dichotomous	"Either-or" questions that set up alternatives for prospects.	During the sales close to force an indecisive prospect to make a choice.	"Would you prefer a notebook or desktop computer?
VI. Multiple-Choice	Offer the prospect a range of choices in pushing for a purchase decision.	During the close to force a prospect to come to a decision. Offer only two or three choices to avoid confusing the prospect and delaying a decision.	"Which of the three do you want to order—the regular, large, or extra-large quantity?"

Using Space, or Proxemics

The manner in which a salesperson utilizes space with prospects and customers can dramatically influence the success of his or her buyer-seller interactions. Let's see how.

Proxemics The nature of the spatial relationships among people and objects.

Proxemics. The term **proxemics** refers to the way people use space. Salespeople need to be aware of the proxemics of every sales situation, especially with new prospective customers, because their spatial relationship to prospects has a proven impact on the outcome of the sales presentation. You must be careful about moving too close to a prospect who wants a little more

FROM THE COMMAND POST: SURVEYING CUSTOMERS VIA E-MAIL

Most marketing organizations are keenly aware of the difficulties associated with designing and administering surveys of customers. Phone and mail questionnaires can be very costly and time-consuming to create, distribute, and analyze. An increasing number of sales organizations have turned to developing and sending surveys to prospects and customers via e-mail. Why? Because e-mail offers several significant benefits: quick turnaround, increased response rates, lower costs, and faster analysis of responses.

Without requiring technical training or expensive new equipment, questionnaire design software enables salespeople to develop their own questionnaires and obtain desired feedback from prospective and current customers. Salespeople can create the survey instrument on their own computers and then distribute it instantly via e-mail to hundreds or even thousands of recipients with a mouse click or two.

Typically, respondents are instructed to go to a website containing the survey. Depending on the software, respondents may be able to respond to the questionnaire directly from the initial e-mail. As a result, completed survey responses often come back within hours instead of the days or weeks needed with traditional postal mail surveys. What's more, survey responses usually can be downloaded directly into statistical packages for speedy data analysis. Finally, with tight budget constraints, another major advantage of e-mail surveys is that there are no postage costs!

space—or too far away from a prospect who prefers a little more intimacy. The first prospect may think that you're trying to be dominating, intimidating, or even sexy. The second prospect may perceive you as standoffish or formal. Believe it or not, where you stand in the prospect's office may well be the determining factor in your winning or losing the sale.

Zones of Buyer-Seller Interaction. People in the United States appear to recognize four zones of human interaction: (1) *intimate*—for loved ones and close friends, (2) *personal*—for business acquaintances, (3) *social*—for opening most sales presentations, and (4) *public*—for selling to a group. In each situation, people are most comfortable with an appropriate distance between themselves and the persons with whom they are communicating. Prospects tend to stake out a zone or surround themselves with a "private sphere" in which they feel most comfortable.

Intimate zones are about an arm's length (roughly two feet) and are reserved for loved ones and close friends. In general, avoid entering a prospect's intimate space, because many prospects resent invasion of this space as a pushy attempt to dominate. If you're alert, you'll notice prospects recoiling when you move into their intimate space. Quickly move back when the prospect seems uncomfortable or tries to retreat.

Personal zones (two to four feet) are areas that strangers or business acquaintances are normally allowed to enter. Some prospects are even uncomfortable with new salespeople in this area. Desks or tables are often used as barriers to keep salespeople and others from coming closer than this personal zone.

Social zones (four to twelve feet) are best for most sales presentations. You should begin the sales presentation in the middle of the social distance zone, six to eight feet, in order to avoid putting the prospect on the defensive. This is especially true if you are not well known to the prospect. Later, as rapport grows, prospects may invite you into their personal space by pulling their chair closer or moving out from behind their desk. Highly successful salespeople gradually move closer to prospects as they prepare to close the sale.[6]

Public zones (more than twelve feet) are typical when a salesperson makes a presentation to a group of people. This distance is about the same as that between a teacher and students in a classroom. It is nonthreatening and allows people to feel comfortable and secure in their own territorial zones.

How a salesperson uses interpersonal physical space will have a dramatic impact on the success of the buyer-seller interaction.
Jose Luis Palaez/Corbis

Interpreting Nonverbal Communication: Kinesics, or Body Language

Much of human communication is nonverbal, even though most of us are unaware when we communicate this way. **Kinesics** is a term describing any movement in our bodies, including shifts in posture (body angle); facial expressions; eye movements; or arm, hand, and leg movements. Every movement or gesture—from a shrug of our shoulders, to crossing our legs, to the subtle wink of an eye—is a part of kinesics, or body language. Unconscious movements or changes (such as a throbbing neck muscle, heavy breathing, or a blushing face) can reveal many emotions, including tenseness, frustration, anger, and embarrassment.

Kinesics The description of bodily gestures and movements in terms of what these gestures and movements communicate to other people.

Reading Body Language. Everybody reads and uses body language to some degree. Many professional athletes are expert readers and users of body language—and this ability gives them a real competitive edge. For example, clever opponents might observe that a football quarterback slaps the center with the back of his right hand a split second before the snap. On pass plays, some linesmen will lean back with their shoulders up and hand barely touching the ground to enable them to step back and block more effectively. Centers will sometimes tighten their grip on the ball just before the snap. In baseball, players converse by body language. Catchers call pitches with their fingers, and coaches use various body language signs to tell batters to bunt or base runners to steal. Some players tip off careful observers to when they are going to try to steal by the way they crouch just before taking off, and some pitchers unconsciously display a characteristic facial expression when they are about to throw a curve ball.

Some salespeople become expert at reading body language and use this ability to determine prospects' mental states during a sales call. Prospects are always sending signals via body language. Some of the messages are obvious. For instance, when prospects start clearing off their desk or reading their mail, they are signaling that they want to end the interview. When this happens, you should acknowledge the value of the prospect's time and try to close the sale quickly. If it appears that your close won't be successful this time, ask for another appointment, thank the prospect, and make your exit. Most body language is more subtle. One highly successful salesperson claims he knows of two unmistakable clues regarding intent to buy: (1) when prospects put their fingers on their chins, they are ready to buy, and (2) when they put their hands over their mouths or on or near their noses, they are not yet ready to buy.

Sending Body Language Messages. Learning to read and use nonverbal language can also be important to sales success. In a pioneering study of nonverbal communication, Edward T. Hall predicted 74 percent of the time whether a sale would take place by observing nonverbal language only.[7] You will make better sales presentations when your nonverbal language is harmonious with your verbal expression. We have all seen speakers whose body language wasn't in harmony with their words and voice inflections. It's almost like watching a movie where the sound and the action are not synchronized.

Nonverbal messages have several channels or vehicles: (1) distance and proximity, (2) general appearance and personal hygiene, (3) body postures and movements, (4) face, (5) arms, (6) hands, (7) legs, and (8) voice characteristics. Distance and proximity were discussed above; the others are described below.

1. *General Appearance and Hygiene:* Good grooming and personal hygiene are essential to salespeople who wish to send positive messages to prospects and customers. Shined shoes, neatly pressed shirt or blouse and suit, clean and trimmed fingernails, and neatly combed hair will enhance your communication effectiveness. Clothing style, quality, and fit can say a lot about a salesperson. What you wear should be stylish, not out of date; it should appear to be of good quality; and it should complement your height and size very well. Also, most salespeople should refresh their mouths by brushing their teeth, gargling with mouthwash, or using a breath mint or spray before calling on the next customer.
2. *Body Movements:* Prospects who make side-to-side movements with their bodies are usually expressing negative feelings, perhaps anxiety and uncertainty, and prospects who move their bodies back and forth are expressing positive feelings. When prospects lean toward you, they usually are interested in what you're saying and showing a positive reaction. Prospects who lean away from you, however, are communicating negative emotions, perhaps disinterest, boredom, hesitation, wariness, or distrust.
3. *Posture:* A rigid, erect posture conveys defensiveness, and a sloppy posture suggests lack of interest or boredom. People who share the same opinion

in a group tend to unconsciously assume the same body postures. When prospects agree with you, they may imitate your body posture. This is a signal to attempt a trial close.

4. *Eyes and Facial Expressions:* Some people have "rubber faces" that openly show approval, disapproval, concern, relaxation, frustration, impatience, and the whole range of human emotions. Other people have "stone faces" that reveal little about what's going on inside their heads. Eyes are the most important features on our faces. When we are interested or excited, our pupils tend to enlarge. Magicians have long known this and use their eye-reading skills to identify which card we picked out of a deck. Jewelry salespeople are so widely known to be expert at reading people's eyes that jewelry buyers sometimes wear dark glasses so that salespeople cannot see their level of interest in different pieces!
5. *Eye Contact:* Eye contact in our culture conveys sincerity and interest, whereas avoidance of eye contact suggests insincerity and dishonesty. Long contact usually indicates rapt attention, but eye contact that lasts too long may invade the prospect's privacy and be considered threatening. People can smile with their mouths and with their eyes. In fact, unless the eyes are smiling, the person's mouth smile may be seen as insincere.
6. *Arm, Hand, and Leg Movements:* Like the maestro leading the orchestra, our arm movements express our intensity of feeling. If we wave our arms frantically, we are in distress or trying to catch someone's attention. Similarly, when we make stiff, jerky movements with our arms, we express determination or aggression. If we move our arms gracefully and slowly, we express warmth and gentleness. People from some cultures have been teased about being unable to talk without using their hands. Hand language is challenging to decipher because hand movements must be interpreted within a given situation or cultural context. People often show impatience by tapping their fingers on a desk. Clenched fists are a strongly defensive or offensive gesture. Touching the fingertips of one hand to the fingertips of the other hand to form a kind of steeple indicates dominance or weighing of alternatives. Prospects may cup their mouths with their hands to whisper a secret or cover their eyes to show embarrassment. When prospects handle a product roughly, they are suggesting that they find it of little worth. Handling a product gingerly generally indicates that they feel the product is valuable. To suggest high quality, clever salespeople often remove their products, whether knives or perfume, from fancy packages in front of prospects. Prospects who cross their legs in an open position toward the salesperson are sending a message of confidence, interest, and cooperation. But prospects who cross their legs away from a salesperson are sending a negative message.
7. *Voice Characteristics:* Voice qualities such as pitch, sound articulation, resonance, tempo, and nonlanguage sounds or vocalizations such as laughing, yawning, grunting, and expressions like *uh-uh* for "no," *uh-huh* for "yes," and *ah* or *er* for hesitation are called *paralanguage*. Salespeople need to listen for and learn to interpret the various feedback and subtle messages sent by the prospect's paralanguage. One study found that using

TABLE 12.4

SALESPERSON VOCAL QUALITIES

Voice Quality	Potential Problems
Volume	Do you speak too loudly or too softly?
Pitch	Is your voice too high or too low?
Clarity	Do you slur your words, or do you enunciate clearly?
Resonance	Is the timbre, or tone, of your voice unpleasant?
Inflection	Do you speak in a monotone, or do you use changes in inflection to emphasize points?
Speed	Do you speak too rapidly or too slowly?

a speaking rate somewhat faster than that of normal conversation leads to increased selling effectiveness.[8] Also, a salesperson's accent can influence selling effectiveness; that is, those who speak the local dialect are likely to be more successful and to be perceived as more credible than those who do not (i.e., those who "have an accent").[9]

It's a good idea to audiotape your sales presentation practice sessions so that you can critique your own voice characteristics (see Table 12.4) and nonverbal communication. Varying your speech pattern by increasing its volume or pace can help emphasize key points during your sales presentation. Speaking in a quiet voice can sometimes draw attention to your points as well. Pace your delivery in accordance with the prospect's preferences and the complexity of the presentation. You can cover easy-to-grasp material at a faster rate of speech, but slowing down at times will give emphasis to important points.

Putting It All Together

So now you see what it takes to be an excellent communicator—and thus a more effective salesperson as well. Listening, speaking, giving verbal and nonverbal signals, and receiving verbal and nonverbal cues require practice, practice, and more practice. Rome wasn't built in a day, and professional sales rep communication skills aren't either. But steadfast dedication to the concepts that we have discussed in this chapter will help you become a successful salesperson. Read *On the Frontlines* on page 397 to see how one canny salesperson used his communication skills—especially listening—to cultivate a relationship with an erstwhile gadfly of a prospect.

At the beginning of this chapter, we asked you a series of questions about how effective a communicator you thought you were. Well, now let's see how effective you *really* are. Take the following communication "test." Be objective in your response to each statement. After completing the test, you will be able to determine whether you are truly an effective communicator. Additionally, you will be able to see how to improve in areas where you might be less than effective. Good luck!

Chapter Review Questions

How would you describe the difference between proxemics and kinesics?

Describe the different dimensions of vocal quality.

What might a salesperson do to improve his or her vocal quality?

ARE YOU AN EFFECTIVE COMMUNICATOR?

Use the scale from 5 to 1, below, to respond to the statements that follow. (When responding to the statements, assume that you are involved in face-to-face interaction with another individual.)

5–Strongly Agree; 4–Agree; 3–Neither Agree nor Disagree; 2–Disagree; 1–Strongly Disagree

When I have face-to-face communication:

1. I focus only on the other person. ____
2. I try to maintain regular eye contact when the individual is talking. ____
3. My nonverbal gestures communicate that I am listening carefully. ____
4. I remain genuinely interested throughout the interaction. ____
5. I ask for more details when I do not completely understand what the individual is saying. ____
6. I paraphrase questions to make sure I understand before answering.____
7. I do not interrupt when another person is talking. ____
8. I do not change the subject frequently when communicating. ____
9. I never try to finish another speaker's sentences. ____
10. I try hard to understand fully what the individual is saying. ____
11. I respond with useful statements rather than merely replying "yes" or "no." ____
12. I offer relevant information regarding questions another person asks me. ____
13. I show eagerness and enthusiasm in my responses. ____
14. I answer all questions at the appropriate time. ____

It would be great if you scored a perfect 70 on this 14-question assessment of your communication effectiveness, but very few people do. In fact, if your self-assessment was a 70, it might be a good idea to let a friend objectively rate you on each question. Then consider how you might improve on any questions where you rated less than 5.

Source: *Adapted from Rosemary P. Ramsey and Ravipreet S. Sohi, "Listening to Your Customers: The Impact of Perceived Salesperson Listening Behavior on Relationship Outcomes,"* Journal of the Academy of Marketing Science *25 (Spring 1997): 127–137.*

COMMUNICATION STYLES

Communication Style The way a person sends and receives messages in communicating with other people.

Our prospects and customers are continuously sending us verbal and nonverbal signals about their personalities and how to communicate with them most effectively. Your capacity to correctly detect and understand the messages that buyers send you—whether verbal or nonverbal—will affect your success.[10] Your ability to respond to these specific messages rather than relying on your own predispositions or flawed beliefs about customers will influence how effective you are with buyers.[11] In addition, the stage of your relationship with the buyer (early, middle, or late), as well as the buyer's **communication style,** will influence your communication style.[12]

Because we are all mixtures of diverse personality characteristics, it may seem overly simplistic to classify everybody in a simple typology. But before

ON THE FRONTLINES

Whose Show Is This Anyway?

After earning his college degree in marketing, Marvin Gibson took a job with Universal Building Supplies, headquartered in Delaware. After a six-week training course, Marv was assigned a territory in southeast Pennsylvania notorious for one tough purchasing agent, Mike Bitters of Henderson Modular Homes (HMH). A warning from the previous salesperson in the territory unnerved Marv about calling on Mr. Bitters, even though the account had a high volume potential. The previous salesperson had been insulted by Mr. Bitters and thrown out of his office on the first sales call for "wasting his valuable time," so he never called on HMH again. He told Marv, "Mike Bitters is a domineering jerk. Nobody can sell him anything. He hasn't changed suppliers in twenty years, so there's no use even calling on him."

Marv avoided the HMH account during his first three months on the job. But one day when he was in a particularly upbeat mood, Marv decided to give the notorious Mike Bitters a try. Arriving at Henderson Modular Homes headquarters, Marv felt a lump in his throat as he asked the receptionist if he could see Mr. Bitters. The receptionist smirked and called Mr. Bitters's secretary. To his and the receptionist's surprise, Mr. Bitters would grant him exactly five minutes but not a minute more. So off Marv trotted to Mr. Bitters's office where, through a half-opened door, he saw a large, rough-featured man in his early sixties staring down at some papers. Knocking on the door, Marv said, "Mr. Bitters, I'm Marv Gibson from Universal Building Supplies. May I come in?"

"Yeah, but get straight to the point. I'm busy and don't have time to waste bullshooting with a salesman."

Glancing quickly around the office, Marv noticed a plaque on the wall to the right of Mr. Bitters' desk and blurted out without thinking, "That's an impressive plaque; what's that for?" Well, those turned out to be the magic words. Mr. Bitters launched into a story about how he had been chosen Pennsylvania's top purchasing agent five years ago and exactly what led to his selection. Marv didn't say a word for thirty minutes. He just listened intensely with a few appropriate nods of his head and "mmm's" and "huh's." At the end of the half-hour, Mr. Bitters said curtly, "I've got to go to a meeting. Leave your product brochures with my secretary." Then he got up and left without so much as a goodbye or a handshake.

Thinking he had failed like everyone else, Marv felt a little depressed as he drove home after his last sales call that night. But the next morning, to his delight, he learned that Mr. Bitters had called and placed a large order and given Marv credit for being a persuasive salesperson. After that, Marv called on Mr. Bitters regularly, and within two years, HMH had become Marv's biggest customer. According to Marv, what really won over Mr. Bitters was that "I unwittingly encouraged him to tell his own story. No other sales rep had ever shown any interest in Mr. Bitters personally. They were all too intimidated by his gruff reputation."

Source: *This story was related to one of the authors by a former student who became a successful salesperson. The names of all people and companies have been changed.*

we can begin to understand the complex personalities of our prospects and customers, we need ways to classify them.

Classifying Communication Styles

Assertiveness The degree to which a person attempts to control or dominate situations and direct the thoughts and actions of other people.

Responsiveness The level of emotions, feelings, or sociability that a person openly displays.

David Merrill, Roger Reid, Paul Mok, and Anthony Alessandra, among several other researchers, have developed taxonomies for classifying people's preponderant behavior and communication styles.[13] Most of these behavior models classify people into one of four distinct categories based on two dimensions: (1) assertiveness and (2) responsiveness. **Assertiveness** is the degree to which a person attempts to control or dominate situations and direct the thoughts and actions of other people. **Responsiveness** is the level of emotions, feelings, or sociability that a person openly displays.

Using Figure 12.2 on page 399, we can plot an individual's degree of assertiveness and responsiveness and classify him or her into one of four communication styles:[14] (1) Amiable, (2) Expressive, (3) Analytical, or (4) Driver. Let's discuss the people who use these four communication styles and how you can sell to them.

Amiables. Open, relatively unassertive, warm, supportive, and sociable people who "wear well" with others, *Amiables* are the most people-oriented of all of the four styles. As shown in the upper left-hand corner of Figure 12.2, they are high in responsiveness and low in assertive behavior. In communicating, their voices are enthusiastic and congenial, and their body language is warmly animated. Co-workers and salespeople may perceive them as compliant and easygoing because they emphasize building a trustful relationship and work at a relatively slow pace. They readily share their personal feelings and are often charming storytellers. Generally, they are deliberate in making decisions or taking action because they want to know how others feel first. Amiables prefer friendly, personal, first-name relationships with others. They dislike interpersonal conflicts so much that they will often say what others want to hear rather than what they really think. Amiables are understanding listeners and easily make and keep friends. They don't like pushy, aggressive behavior. They tend to be cooperative team players who get along with most everyone. Amiables' offices will probably be decorated in a comfortable, open, friendly style with informal seating arrangements conducive to close contact. On their desks, you'll probably find family pictures and various personal items. Family or group pictures and personal mementos are likely hanging on their office walls.

Watch out! How can you recognize that these salespeople may be pushing this buyer too much?
Eyewire, Getty Images

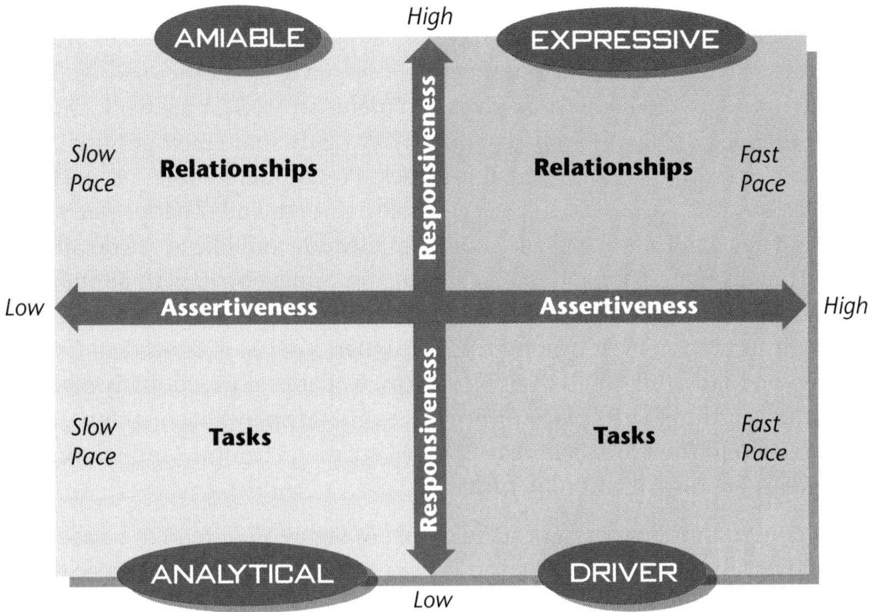

FIGURE 12.2

COMMUNICATION STYLES

Expressives. In the upper right-hand corner of Figure 12.2 are the *Expressives,* who rate high in both responsiveness and assertiveness. Enthusiastic, spontaneous, talkative, and extroverted, they work at a fast pace. They operate largely on intuition and express their views dramatically. They dislike being alone. If no one's around, they'll spend a lot of time on the telephone. Full of ideas, Expressives may daydream and chase a lot of rainbows. Their usually excellent persuasive skills enable them to excite others about their ideas. They seek approval and recognition for their accomplishments and achievements. They are usually creative and can think quickly on their feet. Uninhibited in giving verbal or nonverbal feedback, they readily share their personal feelings. They believe that success depends more on "whom you know than what you know." Expressives tend to become involved in too many activities and may not be strong on follow-through because of their impatience and relatively short attention spans. Their desks are often cluttered and disorganized. Hanging on their office walls will be awards, provocative posters, and motivational slogans. Their offices are usually decorated in an open, friendly style, and the seating arrangement invites interaction and contact.

Analyticals. *Analytical buyers,* in the lower left-hand corner of Figure 12.2, tend to be low in both assertiveness and responsiveness. Logical, controlled, and self-contained, they are not very demonstrative in their verbal or nonverbal communication. They like organization, structure, and self-discipline and work at a deliberate pace. Being systematic problem solvers who ask many detailed questions, they like sales presentations to be based on facts. Analyticals will probably be most persuaded by objective product tests conducted by independent research organizations, expert testimonials, and comprehensive warranties.

Security conscious, they prefer predictability. They want to know how a product or service works and what proof you have of its quality. Analyticals like organization and structure and dislike too much involvement with other people. They work slowly and precisely by themselves and prefer an intellectual work environment that allows them to self-actualize. They rarely share their personal feelings and are slow in giving nonverbal feedback. Precise, detail-oriented, and time-conscious, they are likely to be critical of their own and other people's performance. They exhibit a skeptical "show me" attitude and like to see details in writing. They like salespeople to be organized and professional, with all the facts at their fingertips. In their desire for information, Analyticals may keep collecting information even beyond the time when a decision is needed. Clues that help you to identify Analyticals are offices that appear functionally organized with everything in its place. Office walls often display charts, graphs, and pictures related to their job. Pictures of people are rare. Furniture and seating arrangements are formal and impersonal.

Drivers. *Drivers*, in the lower right-hand corner of Figure 12.2, tend to be assertive and unresponsive. Controlled and decisive, they operate at a fast pace and are goal-oriented in their relationships with others. Strong-willed, impatient,

TABLE 12.5

SUMMARY OF COMMUNICATION STYLES

Key Variables	Amiable	Expressive	Analytical	Driver
Communication Style	Responsive and non-assertive	Responsive and assertive	Nonresponsive and non-assertive	Nonresponsive and assertive
Pace of Communication	Slow and easy	Fast and spontaneous	Slow and systematic	Fast and decisive
Personal Focus	Human relationships	Influencing others	Analytical process	Results
Wants to Be	Liked	Admired	Correct	In charge
Wants You to Be	Pleasant	Stimulating	Precise	To the point
Decision Making Is	Participatory	Spontaneous	Deliberate	Decisive
Risk Orientation	Avoids risks	Takes risks	Calculates risks	Controls risks
Seeks	Close relationships	Recognition	Accuracy	Productivity
Office or Work Space	Personal Relaxed Friendly Informal	Stimulating Personal Cluttered Friendly	Structured Organized Functional Formal	Busy Formal Efficient Structured
Personal Appearance	Casual Conforming	Fashionable Stylish	Formal Conservative	Businesslike Functional
Achieves Acceptance by	Conformity Loyalty	Playfulness Stimulating environment	Correctness Thoroughness	Leadership Competition

(continued)

TABLE 12.5

SUMMARY OF COMMUNICATION STYLES (CONTINUED)

Key Variables	Amiable	Expressive	Analytical	Driver
Gains Security by	Close relationships	Flexibility	Preparation	Control
Wants to Maintain	Relationships	Status	Credibility	Success
You Should Support Their	Feelings	Ideas	Reasoning	Goals
Personal Fears	Confron-tation	Loss of prestige	Embarrass-ment	Loss of control
Under Tension Will	Concede Compromise	Argue Use sarcasm	Withdraw Reconsider	Confront Verbally attack
Irritated by	Insensitivity Impatience	Boredom Routine	Surprises Unpre-dictability	Inefficiency Indecision
Measures Personal Worth by	Compatibil-ity with others Depth of relationships	Acknowl-edgment Recognition Applause Compli-ments	Precision Accuracy Systematic process	Results Track record Measurable progress
Needs to Know (Benefits)	How it will affect their personal relationships	How it enhances their status Who else uses it	How to justify the purchase logically	What it does What it costs When it can be delivered
Salesperson Should Appreciate the Prospect's	Feelings	Creativity	Knowledge	Goals and achievements

tough, "take-charge" personalities, Drivers show a low tolerance for the feelings, attitudes, and advice of others. Believing that success depends on themselves, they need to control situations and people and actively seek leadership roles. They thrive on decision making and producing results. Inflexible, impatient, and poor listeners, they tend to ignore facts and figures and to rely more on their "gut feel." Clues identifying the Driver personality are desks piled high with work projects. Their offices are decorated to indicate power and control, and the walls may contain honors and achievement awards or a large planning sheet/calendar. Seating arrangements are likely to be closed, formal, and positioned for power. Some Drivers even raise their chair heights or choose extra large desks to project their dominance over others.

Although most people show characteristics of all four communication styles at least occasionally, most prospects or customers will exhibit a preponderant communication style. It is the salesperson's job to identify that style early on and to adapt the presentation accordingly. After perusing Table 12.5, which

WHAT'S YOUR COMMUNICATION STYLE?

For each of the questions below, select the answer that best describes you. Remember, there are no right or wrong answers to these questions. You're just trying to learn about your own communication style, so select the response with which you most agree, not the answer that you think is most desirable or socially acceptable.

1. Which of the following best describes how you talk with others?____
   a. slow and easygoing
   b. fast and spontaneous
   c. slowly and very precisely
   d. fast and very decisively
2. What is your usual personal focus in communicating with others?____
   a. developing warm relationships
   b. impressing them
   c. learning whether or not they know what they're talking about
   d. trying to keep the chitchat short so I don't waste too much time
3. Which do you most prefer?____
   a. being liked
   b. being admired
   c. being correct and precise
   d. being in charge
4. What is your decision-making style?____
   a. participatory
   b. spontaneous
   c. deliberate
   d. decisive
5. What do you seek most in human relationships?____
   a. friendship
   b. recognition
   c. accurate information
   d. productivity
6. What is your orientation toward risk?____
   a. I try to avoid risk.
   b. I readily take risks.
   c. I carefully calculate risk.
   d. I try to control risk.
7. How would you describe your personal appearance?____
   a. casual, conforming
   b. fashionable, stylish
   c. functional, conservative
   d. executive-like, formal
8. What does your office, apartment, or room look like? ____
   a. friendly, informal, inviting
   b. stimulating, creative, interesting, artistic
   c. organized, very functional, practical, utilitarian
   d. structured, formal, efficient, busy professional look
9. How do you try to achieve acceptance from others?____
   a. by being affable and sympathetic
   b. by being stimulating and exciting
   c. by being precise and thorough
   d. by being competitive and goal-oriented
10. Which of the following is most important to you?____
    a. relationships with others
    b. status
    c. credibility
    d. success
11. What do you most often share with other people?____
    a. feelings
    b. creative ideas
    c. reasoning process
    d. goals
12. When you're involved in a heated discussion with someone, what are you most likely to do?____
    a. compromise
    b. use sarcasm and witty remarks
    c. withdraw and re-analyze my position
    d. confront and verbally attack
13. Which of the following characteristics most irritate you?____
    a. insensitive and impatient
    b. dull and boring
    c. unpredictable and uninformed
    d. inefficient and indecisive

(continued)

14. Which of the following do you fear most?____
    a. confrontation
    b. loss of prestige
    c. embarrassment
    d. loss of control
15. How do you generally measure your personal worth?____
    a. depth of relationships with people
    b. recognition and compliments from others
    c. analytical reasoning process and accurate decision making
    d. achievements and track record for getting results
16. What do you appreciate most in other people?____
    a. friendliness
    b. creativity
    c. knowledge
    d. accomplishments
17. How would you like other people to see you?____
    a. as a good friend
    b. as creative and dynamic
    c. as knowledgeable and analytical
    d. as competitive and successful
18. How would you like people to describe you?____
    a. relaxed and pleasant
    b. exciting and stimulating
    c. precise and analytical
    d. direct and to the point
19. In social settings, what makes you feel most secure?____
    a. being congenial and empathetic
    b. being flashy and colorful
    c. being knowledgeable and scholarly
    d. being strong and powerful
20. What kind of friend would you like to be to others?____
    a. a good, trusted friend
    b. an admired, full-of-life friend
    c. a practical, scholarly friend
    d. a respected, high-achieving friend

Count how many responses you have for each letter, a, b, c, and d. The letter (a) indicates an ***amiable*** communication style, (b) an ***expressive*** style, (c) an ***analytical*** style, and (d) a ***driver*** style. The letter that you have chosen most often is probably your dominant communication style. If your responses are spread across two or more letters, your communication style is a blend of those. Once you have identified your primary communication style, check Table 12.6 to see which styles you are most and least compatible with. For example, amiables and drivers tend to make incompatible pairings, and so do expressives with analyticals.

provides a quick reference tool for the four communication styles, complete the accompanying self-assessment exercise on pages 402–403 to identify *your* communication style.

Developing Communication Style Flexibility

Pairing a salesperson and prospect with different communication styles can be tricky. Let's see how the professionals manage.

Dimensions of Communication Style. Besides differences in levels of responsiveness and assertiveness, styles may clash in terms of pace and priority. *Pace* is the speed at which a person moves. People who are high in assertiveness (Expressives and Drivers) prefer a fast pace in talking, thinking, and making decisions, whereas those who are low in assertiveness (Amiables and Analyticals) prefer a slower pace. *Priorities* identify what a person considers important. Goals, objectives, and task achievement are highest in priority for those who are low in responsiveness (Analyticals and Drivers), whereas relationships with other people are the top priority for those who are high in responsiveness

TABLE 12.6

Sources of Conflicts Between Communication Styles

Style Match-Up	Shared Dimension	Area of Agreement	Area of Conflict
Amiable with Expressive	High responsiveness	Priorities	Pace
Analytical with Driver	Low responsiveness	Priorities	Pace
Amiable with Analytical	Low assertiveness	Pace	Priorities
Expressive with Driver	High assertiveness	Pace	Priorities
Amiable with Driver	None	None	Both
Expressive with Analytical	None	None	Both

(Amiables and Expressives). Table 12.6 illustrates the types of conflicts that occur when people with different styles try to communicate.

As you can see in Table 12.6, Amiable/Driver pairings and Expressive/Analytical pairings encounter difficulties with both pace and priority when they try to communicate with each other. All other pairings of communication style, except for identical styles, must deal with either a pace or a priority problem.

Style Flexing. The many possible conflicts between salesperson and prospect communication styles illustrate the need for every salesperson to cultivate the ability to *flex* with prospect communication styles. *Style flexing* will enable you to sell to your prospects *in the way they want to be sold.* If prospects talk and move fast, you should adjust your rate of speech and movements to match theirs. If they like to take their time and engage in light conversation, relax and allow more time for the appointment. If prospects are task-oriented, shift your focus to tasks. If they are relationship-oriented, you should stress relationships, too. When you meet another person's behavioral style needs, a climate of mutual trust begins to form. As a bond of trust develops, the other person will begin to tell you what he or she really needs. Instead of a contest, you will foster a compatible, productive relationship that will probably result in a sale and a long-term customer. Table 12.7 shows flexing approaches to employ with prospects or customers who exhibit one of the four communication styles.

Chapter Review Questions

Briefly describe how you would sell to each of the four communication styles: Amiable, Expressive, Analytical, and Driver.

What do we mean by "style flexing" and why is it important to salespeople? Give an example of style flexing in a selling situation.

TABLE 12.7

Flexing with Prospect Communication Styles

Selling to Amiables

- Approach Amiables in a friendly, neighborly way with a sincere greeting and a warm handshake. Use a relaxed, informal pace to build trust, friendship, and credibility.
- Try to get to know Amiables personally. Ask nonthreatening questions about their interests and activities. Be agreeable and supportive; be professional but friendly. Show them that you genuinely like them.
- Present the product or service in a close interactive way so that you develop a good relationship. Make the demonstration meaningful and congenial.
- Deal with resistance and objections by using testimonials from other people, personal assurances, and guarantees.
- Close in a warm, reassuring way. Do not be pushy or aggressive.
- Follow up with friendly personal letters, notes, and phone calls to make sure that they are satisfied with the product or service.

Selling to Expressives

- Approach Expressives boldly by introducing yourself first and extending your hand. Tell them that you are delighted to meet them. Enthusiastically ask questions to learn about their needs, goals, and dreams.
- Ask questions that will allow them to brag a little. You can obtain clues from the pictures, trophies, awards, and interesting art objects that you are likely to see in their office.
- Show appreciation for their abilities and achievements. Compliment them on their accomplishments if you can do so sincerely.
- Present your solution with stimulating stories and illustrations that are related to them and their goals. Be confident and animated throughout your presentation and demonstration. Spice up your sales presentation with interesting stories and illustrations.
- Deal with resistance and objectives candidly and confidently.
- Close with lively appeals that provide positive support for achievement of their dreams and goals.
- Follow up by confirming the purchase in writing. Your letter should be friendly, clear, and cordial.

Selling to Analyticals

- Approach Analyticals in a gracious, genial way, but quickly move on to the task at hand.
- Be prepared to answer a series of detailed questions about the product, its use, and its performance.
- Make your sales presentation logical, objective, and deliberate, citing many facts and figures.
- Deal with resistance and objections by providing detailed analysis and research findings.

(*continued*)

TABLE 12.7

Flexing with Prospect Communication Styles (Continued)

- Close by summarizing the benefits (and drawbacks) of purchasing the product.
- Follow up with reassuring information from survey or research findings that support their purchase decisions.

Selling to Drivers

- Approach Drivers directly with a firm handshake and in a confident, businesslike manner.
- Plan your presentation to be well prepared, organized, fast paced, and to the point.
- Present your selling points clearly and directly by showing how the products and services will help them achieve their goals. Involve the prospect in a hands-on product/service demonstration.
- Deal with resistance and objections directly. Do not try to double-talk or pass over prospect concerns, because Drivers are tenacious; they go after the answers they want like pit bulls.
- Close in a straightforward, professional way by emphasizing the bottom-line results or benefits.
- Follow up by asking how well the product or service is helping them achieve their goals. Suggest additional products that may help them improve results.

COMMUNICATION AND TRUST BUILDING

A common recurring theme throughout this book has been the development of long-term buyer-seller relationships. Toward that end, the foundation of an enduring buyer-seller relationship is *mutual trust*. Trust can be defined as "one party's belief that its needs will be met in the future by actions undertaken by the other party."[15] In other words, trust is a mutual belief between the parties in a relationship that each will fulfill agreed-to obligations. Trust requires confidence in another party's reliability and integrity in situations where vulnerability and risk are often present.[16] Accordingly, we have repeatedly stressed the importance of salespeople being trustworthy in all buyer-seller interactions, just as we emphasized, in a similar vein, that being ethical in buyer-seller relationships engenders trust. Your words and actions communicate to prospects and customers how trustworthy you are or are likely to be. Saying one thing (e.g., "We always deliver on time") and then doing another (delivering the product two weeks late) violates the trust a buyer may have placed in a salesperson. Alternatively, consistent words and actions maintain or enhance a buyer's trust in the sales rep. Professional salespeople use five "trust builders" to communicate to buyers that they are deserving of trust.[17]

Candor (Words)

- Sales presentations are balanced and fair (product limitations as well as strengths are mentioned).
- What the salesperson says agrees with what the buyer knows to be true.
- The proof the salesperson uses to support statements is credible.
- Subsequent events prove the statements to be true.

Dependability (Actions)

- The salesperson's actions fulfill his or her prior (verbal) promises.
- Current actions fit a pattern of prior dependable actions by the salesperson.
- The salesperson refuses to promise what cannot be delivered.

Competence (Ability)

- The salesperson displays technical command of products and their applications.
- The salesperson has the skill, knowledge, time, and resources to follow through on promises and do what the buyer wants.
- The salesperson's words and actions are consistent with a professional image.

Customer Orientation (Intent)

- The salesperson understands the buyer's needs and places them on a par with his or her own organization's needs.
- The salesperson gives fair and balanced presentations and offers objective and verifiable statements of benefits.
- The salesperson advises or consults rather than sells (that is, doesn't push an unneeded product on a buyer).

Likableness (Personality)

- The salesperson makes efficient use of the buyer's time.
- The salesperson is courteous, polite, and congenial.
- The salesperson and buyer share and talk about areas of commonality; this extends to nonbusiness topics.

If you can put the above five trust builders into practice while flexing your communication style with that of your prospect or customer, you are well on your way toward gaining rapport and developing a long-term sales relationship.

Chapter Review Question

Give examples of five trust builders that salespeople employ when negotiating with prospects.

SUMMARY

In this chapter we examined principles and theories of communication and communication skills for the professional salesperson. After stating that listening is the most important communication skill for the salesperson to learn and practice, we described requisite communication skills for the salesperson. We discussed four levels of listening (marginal, evaluative, active, and active empathetic), three question formats (open-ended, closed, and semi-open), and six distinct types of questions (probing, evaluative, strategic, tactical, dichotomous, and multiple-choice). Proxemics (the use of space) and kinesics (nonverbal communication) were also shown to be important to selling success. We learned that the best salespeople are constantly sharpening their ability to (1) listen, (2) ask questions, (3) use space, and (4) communicate nonverbally. We also discussed how an individual's levels of assertiveness and responsiveness could be plotted in four directions, yielding four basic communication styles: (1) Amiable, (2) Expressive, (3) Analytical, and (4) Driver. Quickly comprehending each new prospect's communication style and flexing to that style will help salespeople sell to prospects and customers in the way in which they want to be sold. Finally, we described five trust builders—candor, dependability, competence, customer orientation, and likableness—that salespeople can use in buyer-seller relationships.

KEY TERMS

Communication
Promotion
Sensing
Processing
Responding
Marginal Listening
Evaluative Listening
Active Listening
Active Empathetic Listening (AEL)
Probing Question
Evaluative Question
Dichotomous Question
Proxemics
Kinesics
Communication Style
Assertiveness
Responsiveness

TOPICS FOR THOUGHT AND CLASS DISCUSSION

1. Can you think of any people—in your own life or in public life—who appear to be effective communicators? What do you think makes them so effective? How might you incorporate some of their communication techniques into your own repertoire of techniques?
2. Do you think that women tend to be better at some communication skills whereas men are better at others? Or do you believe that gender is largely irrelevant to communication skills? If you think gender differences arise in communication skills, how do you account for these differences?
3. Which do you think conveys the most accurate information—people's words or their body language? Why? Do you think you can tell more readily whether people are being honest with you by hearing their words or by reading their body language? Why?
4. Rank each of the communication modes (talking, listening, reading, writing, and body language) in terms of your own personal effectiveness using each. What has helped make you good in the highest-ranked mode and relatively weak in the lowest-ranked one? What advice do you have for a person who wants to improve in each area?
5. Are you consciously aware of your use of body language when communicating? Do you have certain mannerisms that other people have commented on? What are they? What do you think they convey in communication?
6. Which communication style do you most often use? Do you flex this style when communicating with different people? Give some examples of your own style flexing with different people (e.g., family members, friends, members of the clergy, teachers, coaches, police officers, and new acquaintances).

7. Try to think of an example of each of the four communication styles among your own family and friends. How well do these individuals reflect the different qualities listed under their primary style in Table 12.5? Do you ever notice yourself adjusting to any of these people's styles when you communicate with them? Do you get along better with some of these people than with others? After taking the test that identifies your communication style, consult Table 12.6 to see whether your two styles match up well or poorly. Do you think your communication style match-ups help explain your interpersonal relationships?
8. Which of the trust builders do you think is most important for people in learning to trust someone? Why is that one most important? How well do you generally do at trust building?

INTERNET EXERCISES

1. Use an Internet search engine to find three firms that specialize in sales communication training. What company is offering each program? Is the focus B2B selling, B2C selling, or both? What are the length and cost of each program? Where would it be held? Who is doing the training? What topics will the sales communications training cover that will be new?
2. Using Google or any other search engine, find two examples of communication styles being demonstrated using Flash or streaming video.
3. Use the Internet to find articles on salespeople whose effectiveness has been increased by their communication skills.
4. Using an Internet search engine, find examples of international nonverbal communication. Why do you think nonverbal communication varies across countries?

PROJECTS FOR PERSONAL GROWTH

1. Make a simple two-column chart on a separate piece of paper (or on your computer)—a "T" design will do. In the left-hand column list the six types of questions salespeople use, leaving plenty of space between entries. Then, in the right-hand column, put down in your own words as much information as you can about each question type—how and when to use it, the expected or desired response, and examples.
2. If your class is small enough and students are willing, ask everyone in class to classify each other student into one of the four communication styles: Amiable, Expressive, Analytical, or Driver. (Only students who are perfectly willing to have their communication styles categorized should participate.) Which style appears to be most prevalent in your class? Now discuss how a salesperson using one of the communication styles would negotiate with the students exhibiting each of the four communication styles.
3. As an experiential exercise, ask for student volunteers who believe that they know their own communication style to try to sell something, perhaps a textbook, to students with different communication styles. After observing the role-play, other students should offer their perceptions of the interaction and negotiations.

4. If you're confident enough, ask one of your classmates to give you an honest appraisal of your vocal qualities. Were you surprised by the evaluation? Why? What might you consider doing to improve your voice quality?
5. Prepare a fifteen-minute sales presentation on a product with which you are familiar. Rehearse it several times. Then, ask a friend to watch you while you give your presentation and to note positive and negative verbal and nonverbal communication. In a critique afterward, compare the effect you thought you were having to the effect your friend thought you had during the presentation. Any surprises? (If you have the resources, try doing this exercise with a video camera and then an audiotape recorder.) *With a video camera:* After taping your presentation, play it back while observing and listening to all modes of communication; then play it back with the sound off so you can analyze body language. *With an audio recorder:* Record your presentation, and then analyze your voice characteristics. Whether you make your presentation to a friend, videotape it, or merely record it, ask yourself the following questions: Do I look and sound sincere? Would I buy from myself? With respect to verbal and nonverbal communication, what do I like about my presentation? What don't I like? How might I improve my communication?
6. Over the next two days, find two people who are giving a speech or an address, whether in person or on television, and take the time to hear and watch the whole presentation. Evaluate their verbal and nonverbal communication. What advice would you give these people to improve their communication effectiveness? Do you think they made their points? What did you find convincing and/or inspiring about what they said and did? Did they look or sound at all insincere? What was basically good about their "performances," and what was basically bad about them?

ROLE-PLAY EXERCISE 12.1

Selling Executives on Speaking to a Student Marketing Association

Situation

James Fromm is vice president for programming of the Student Marketing Association at Southeastern College. His job on behalf of the organization is to call up prospective speakers and convince them to come to the college for a 45-minute presentation to students during activities hour, Wednesday afternoons from 1:00 to 1:45 p.m.

Today, Jim has just telephoned the office of Phillip Geller II, president and CEO of Geller Industries, Inc.—manufacturers of artists' supplies. Mr. Geller, who is an alumnus of Southeastern College, is widely known as a Driver-type personality. His office is about fifteen miles from the Southeastern campus, and several Southeastern alumni work for Geller Industries. On the second ring, Carol Saunders, Mr. Geller's executive secretary, answers the phone.

Roles

James Fromm Bright, articulate, and enthusiastic, Jim knows that he must quickly sell executives on the benefits of coming to Southeastern to speak to about 50 marketing students for 45 minutes. Jim usually exhibits an expressive communication style. On this call, Jim must first sell Ms. Saunders on putting him through to talk to Mr. Geller; then he must "sell" Mr. Geller on coming to campus.

Carol Saunders Although she is a nice person, Ms. Saunders initially sounds somewhat officious on the phone. Her normal communication style is analytical, and she knows that her boss gets upset if she transfers unimportant calls to him.

Phillip Geller II Rather gruff and blunt-talking, Mr. Geller does not allow his time to be wasted. Unless he sees some personal benefit from talking to the students, he will no doubt decline the invitation. His communication style is definitely that of a Driver.

ROLE-PLAY EXERCISE 12.2

Matching Conflicting Styles of Communication

Situation

Patricia Brittingham sells a line of women's cosmetics, called Eternal Youth, to upscale department stores in the New York City area. Patricia has been quite successful introducing a new perfume, Gloria Devine's Intrigue, named after a movie star. She has just been ushered into the office of Wanda Sanchez, the cosmetics buyer for Blossomgales' Department Store, and is about to greet her. Patricia has heard that Ms. Sanchez is considered one of the most professional and astute buyers in the business. As she quickly glances around the office before Ms. Sanchez gets off the phone to greet her, Pat notices that the office is very organized, formal, and functional with several charts and graphs on the walls, but no pictures of people.

Roles

Patricia Brittingham Enthusiastic, stylish, extroverted, fast-thinking, and assertive, Pat has been very successful in selling women's cosmetics in New York City. She finds that her personality works well with most people, but she does consciously shift gears when she meets someone with a contrasting communication style.

Wanda Sanchez Logical, controlled, unemotional, and very deliberate in negotiations, Ms. Sanchez generally asks many detailed questions during sales presentations to her. Unless she is given objective data, she is very skeptical about any product claims. She expects salespeople to be organized and very professional, with the facts "at the ready."

CASE 12.1 MIRROR, MIRROR ON THE WALL

Sally Blakemore is beginning her first day in the field on her job as missionary salesperson or "detail person" for Bevan-Warner Pharmaceutical Company. Having completed a three-month training program, she is now ready to call on hospitals and medical offices in the Philadelphia area to introduce and explain her company's pharmaceutical products to health care professionals. Ms. Blakemore will not directly sell or take orders for her company's product. She is called a detail person because her job is to give doctor "deciders" all the details needed to convince them to prescribe the Bevan-Warner pharmaceuticals for their patients.

As she learned in her training program, few doctors can keep up with the latest pharmaceutical products because of their hectic schedules. Most tend to rely heavily on detail people to keep them up-to-date. Sally Blakemore's job is to provide in-depth information on the chemical make-up of the product, how it interacts with other medicines a patient may be taking, and its potential side effects. To gain the trust of medical professionals, detail people must know their products thoroughly and answer questions in a straightforward, professional way. In addition, the detail person must communicate effectively with physicians with differing personalities.

On her first day of fieldwork, Sally is calling on three doctors: (1) Dr. Peter Hartman, an orthopedic surgeon, (2) Dr. Elizabeth Butterfield, a general practitioner; and (3) Dr. Janice Winer, a gynecologist. Her predecessor, who was promoted to district sales manager after three years in the field, tried to help

(continued)

Sally understand the personalities of the three physicians. Here's the way she described each one:

> *Dr. Peter Hartman* is a tall, thin man about fifty-five years old who tends to be somewhat irritable and generally preoccupied. He's definitely not Mr. Warmth. I always get the feeling in talking to him that he doesn't quite believe me. I can never keep him listening to me for more than ten minutes, and he always sits on the edge of his chair like he's ready to jump up at any time. He's got a reputation as a loner in that he doesn't socialize with any of the other doctors or nurses. His wife divorced him three years ago after they raised three children—two of whom are doctors. I think the other one is a struggling artist. With Hartman, you'll need to get straight to the point because his favorite line is "Give me the short version and nothing but the facts, please." He won't ask many questions, but he'll expect to see the research that backs up product claims; so leave him all the technical product literature you can and send him more between visits. I've found that he actually reads those reports, so it will help you on your next call to have him high up on the learning curve.
>
> *Dr. Elizabeth Butterfield* is one of the nicest, least pretentious people you'll ever meet. She's everybody's mother. Although she has a heavy load of patients every day, her spirits never seem dampened. She's always laughing and telling playful little one-liners, often about her size—she is over six feet tall and "full-figured," as they say. Her husband's a high school principal, and they have five children, ranging in age from four to twenty. Her patients love her, and so does nearly everyone else. Dr. Liz will always find fifteen or twenty minutes to see you, no matter how backed up her schedule is. I hear that she often stays in her office until ten o'clock at night seeing patients. And her nurses say she is just as upbeat at the end of the day as she is at the beginning. The thing that always amazed me is that she'll remember your name after meeting you once, and she'll remember the names of any family members you've talked about, too. She always asked how my mother was doing. It's a joy to call on her because she makes you feel that she likes, trusts, and respects you.
>
> *Dr. Janice Winer* is a super-intelligent woman, about thirty-seven years old, who I heard was number one in her medical school class. She's perpetual motion and all business. She moves fast, thinks fast, and makes decisions fast. I don't think I have ever met anyone who is more organized and efficient. Her whole office staff is the same way. You know how most doctors seem to have a lot of patients in the waiting room? Well, I've never seen more than two or three in her waiting room at any one time. At first, I thought it was because she didn't have many patients. Then her receptionist showed me her appointment book—she's booked up solid for months ahead of time, but she's simply one of those rare doctors who is nearly always ready to see you at approximately the time of your scheduled appointment. You don't waste time with her on chitchat. She'll greet you politely and then say, 'Okay, what have you got?' You can be halfway through a product presentation and she'll stop you and say, 'Okay I'm sold on it. What else do you have?' I never really got to know her personally, but I understand she got married last year to a corporate executive twenty years her senior.

Ever since listening to her colleague describe the people she will meet on her first three calls, Sally has felt anxious about whether her own personality will mesh or clash with the personalities of the three physicians. In college, her classmates used to jokingly call her "grind" because of her unwillingness to break her habit of studying at the university library every weeknight from seven to eleven. True, she graduated with a 3.8 average on a 4.0 scale, but she certainly doesn't think of herself as a grind, because she was an officer in the student marketing club and a sorority member. She saved her partying for the weekends. Thinking about how

(*continued*)

others might describe her, Sally imagines they might mention traits like quiet, reserved, intelligent, hard-working, cooperative, organized, goal-oriented, determined, and likable. "Hmmm," she thinks to herself, "I'm not sure what personality type I am. I seem to be a mixture of several types, like most people. Oh well, no use worrying any more—best to just get going."

Questions

1. How would you categorize the personalities of each of the three physicians on whom Sally will be calling?
2. What personality type is Sally?
3. Which of the physicians do you think Sally will communicate best with? Why? With which one will she have the most difficulty communicating? Why?
4. What advice would you give Sally before she calls on each physician?

CASE 12.2 HE KEEPS GOING AND GOING AND GOING

CASE 12.2 "HE KEEPS GOING AND GOING AND GOING" CAN BE FOUND ONLINE AT HTTP://COLLEGE.HMCO.COM/PIC/ANDERSONPS2E

CHAPTER 13

Managing Your Time and Your Territory

"Do the hard jobs first. The easy jobs will take care of themselves."

Dale Carnegie, 1888–1955, American author and trainer

After reading this chapter, you should understand:

- Why salespeople must be concerned about efficiency as well as effectiveness in allocating their time.
- How salespeople function as field marketing managers.
- How to use ROTI (return on time invested) to manage the territory.
- Methods for using time wisely.
- Efficient routing strategies for sales calls.
- Ways to prioritize accounts.
- How to avoid falling into time traps.

INSIDE PERSONAL SELLING

Meet Lance Perkins of GE Medical Systems

Lance Perkins is a fair-sized company all by himself. As executive account manager for General Electric's Medical Systems unit, he helps hospitals achieve goals such as cutting costs, boosting productivity, and improving quality through annual purchases of more than $25 million worth of goods (CAT scanners, x-ray equipment, and more) and services (such as repair contracts, consulting, and financing). Perkins is the main company contact for hospitals in his territory and coordinates the sales efforts of other GE specialists. If a hospital executive mentions building plans, for instance, Perkins will suggest GE Industrial Systems, "because we sell roofing, tile, even power systems for emergency generators."

In addition to meeting monthly sales goals, Perkins must progress through a series of activity milestones leading to each sale, because nine to eighteen months may pass between an initial meeting and a signed contract. GE also evaluates the leadership skills of its sales professionals. "In this sales position, you manage a lot of other people," says Perkins. "You may have ten or twelve other salespeople who are in touch with each hospital. I establish the relationship and bring in other specialty sales reps to supplement my discussions with customers."

Working on commission, Perkins learned to identify his best sales opportunities—the 20 percent of customers who account for 80 percent of his sales volume. "Fresh in the territory, it takes at least a year before you get the pulse of the market and figure out how to work smarter instead of harder," he observes. Although he initially reacted to every lead, he gradually began focusing on larger accounts, narrowing his contact list from sixty hospitals to fewer than twelve.

Perkins spends about three days a week visiting customers. The rest of the time he sets appointments, updates customer files and sales forecasts, obtains quotes, and coordinates the work of other GE specialists through e-mail, teleconferences, and meetings. Despite his busy schedule, Perkins makes cold calls every week. "Many salespeople have call reluctance," he says. "If they don't set a time to do it, they just won't do it." Without the cold calls, the milestones, and information about past sales—such as when a service contract expires—Perkins might miss potential sales.

Instead of writing call reports about customer contacts, Perkins creates "trackers," spreadsheets listing how much money each deal will generate, what milestone each deal is at, and the probability that a deal will close—and when. He constantly reviews and revises his trackers to see which sales may close in a given month and where he needs more support from other GE personnel. Managing his time and his territory, says Perkins, "is really like running a business and trying to figure out what the cash flow will be."

As a student, you have almost total control over how you spend your time. Although professors put demands on you, you still can prioritize your preparation time. After all, no one is really forcing you to do everything at once. And although you may not have as much free time as you'd like, you have tremendous discretion over how to spend that time. Generally, you choose what activities and pursuits you want to do and when you want to do them. Well, believe it or not, so do many salespeople!

SELF-MANAGEMENT

Unlike people in most jobs where performance is usually judged subjectively by a boss, a professional salesperson's performance is much more objectively measured and depends mainly on personal abilities and how well he or she manages a sales territory. Few jobs demand more self-management than professional selling. Self-management, where boss and worker are the same person, can be more challenging than management by superiors who provide various kinds of feedback to keep you on track and motivated. As your own manager, you must decide what to do, and how and when to do it. You set the daily performance standards—whether high or low—for yourself. You decide whether to be hard-driving or complacent, whether to be customer service–oriented or indifferent, whether to use modern technology, and, in the long run, whether to succeed or fail.

Some salespeople have even worked out a system of rewards and punishments to motivate their own behavior. For example, if they successfully sell a new account, they may buy themselves a nice gift or take the afternoon off to play golf. On the other hand, if they fail to accomplish some task on time, they may punish themselves by working overtime that night on paperwork.[1] Whatever method you use to motivate yourself, your success as a professional salesperson will be greatly affected by how effectively and efficiently you manage your time and your sales territory.

EFFECTIVENESS AND EFFICIENCY

Effectiveness Results-oriented focus on achieving selling goals.

Efficiency Cost-oriented focus on making the best possible use of the salesperson's time and efforts.

Successful salespeople understand that their success depends not only on their effectiveness but also on their efficiency. **Effectiveness** is *results-oriented* and focuses on achieving goals (e.g., sales revenue or profitability). **Efficiency** is *cost-oriented* and focuses on expending minimum time, effort, and resources on tasks (e.g., number of miles driven or expenses incurred). The combination of effectiveness and efficiency produces sales success, as depicted by the following formula:

Effectiveness + Efficiency = Sales Success

Time is a precious, nonexpandable resource. Consequently, salespeople must work to optimize their use of this precious commodity. One national study of nearly 10,000 sales representatives showed that they spend 33 percent of their time in face-to-face selling, 20 percent in travel, 16 percent in phone selling, 16 percent in account service and coordination, 10 percent in administration, and 5 percent at internal company meetings (see Figure 13.1).[2]

Although spending one-third of their time in face-to-face selling may not seem impressive, this is a higher percentage than many other studies have found. Perhaps growing professionalism among salespeople and increased use of the latest telecommunication tools have contributed to greater face-to-face selling time.

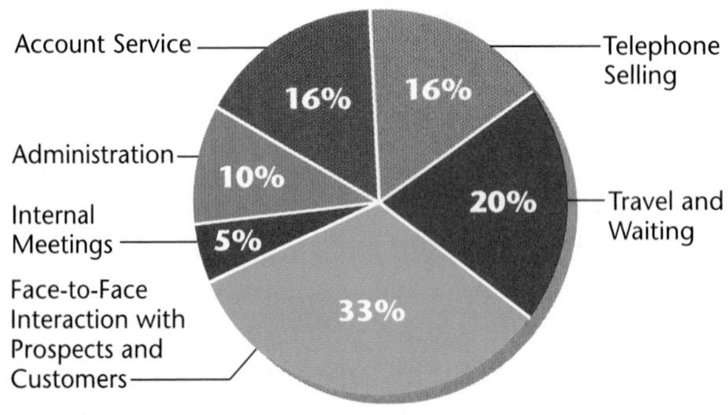

FIGURE 13.1

HOW SALESPEOPLE SPEND THEIR TIME

The extent of face-to-face selling time can have a tremendous impact on a salesperson's effectiveness and efficiency. Assuming the typical salesperson works 40 hours per week and takes a two-week vacation, salespeople who spend 25 percent of their time in face-to-face selling have just 500 hours a year (40 hr/week × .25 × 50 weeks/yr = 500 hr) in which to sell. Those salespeople whose efficiency allows them 33 percent face-to-face selling time have 660 hours a year (40 × .33 × 50 = 660), or 160 hours more, to achieve selling goals. Table 13.1 on page 418 shows, given each of these assumptions, the worth of an hour of the salesperson's time at different earning levels. For a salesperson earning $100,000 a year, each hour of selling time costs more than $200 if only 25 percent of the time is spent in face-to-face selling. That cost drops to $152 an hour if selling time is increased to 33 percent. Thus it's obvious that increased efficiency pays off substantially for a salesperson.

The most successful salespeople are the best prepared to make maximum use of their limited face-to-face selling time with prospects. Effective salespeople tend to possess the following characteristics:

- Their product knowledge, competitive knowledge, and face-to-face selling skills are excellent.
- They serve as clearinghouses of information, advisers, relationship builders, problem solvers, customer advocates, and deal makers.
- They use their influence to work closely with both internal staff and customers. Because salespeople generally have no subordinates, they must work through others over whom they have little or no direct control. Influencing others to change their priorities and interrupt their schedules is a major part of the sales job.
- They understand that providing customer service is as important as making the sale. Therefore, they do not abdicate responsibility for installation, implementation, and service to technical support staff. They continue to maintain a close post-sale relationship that their customers find valuable.

Put your time- and relationship-management skills to work when you read the accompanying *It's Up to You* feature.

Chapter Review Questions

Define and distinguish between the terms *effectiveness* and *efficiency*.

How do salespeople actually spend their time?

IT'S UP TO YOU

Your district manager calls you Wednesday evening and says he wants to work with you over the next two days as you make each of your sales calls. Last week, you scheduled four 2-hour sales calls on both Thursday and Friday of this week, so your appointment book is filled. However, two of these accounts, one on each day, are notorious for canceling out at the last minute. You are fearful of this happening while your boss is working with you, and you are trying to decide how to avoid two hours of idle time each day in case of last-minute cancellations. What, if anything, should you say to your boss? What is your next move?

TABLE 13.1

What Is One Hour of Selling Time Worth?

Earnings	Approximate Worth of One Hour	
	25% of Time Face-to-Face (500 Hours/Year)	33% of Time Face-to-Face (660 Hours/Year)
$ 40,000	$ 80	$ 61
50,000	100	76
60,000	120	91
70,000	140	106
80,000	160	121
90,000	180	136
100,000	200	152
150,000	300	227
200,000	400	303
300,000	600	455
400,000	800	606
500,000	1,000	758

SALES ACTIVITIES

Judging on the basis of a study of nearly 1,400 salespeople from fifteen manufacturing industries, salespeople spend their time carrying out ten basic activities, as seen in Table 13.2. Depending on the industry, the prospects or customers, the products, and the situation, though, these activities vary in importance. Therefore, you will want to determine what weight to assign to each of these activities in your given market environment and set your time priorities accordingly.

What's Your Job Description?

Beyond understanding the general activities of salespeople, you need to know the exact performance expectations for your specific job assignment. One of the first tasks for a new salesperson should be to obtain a copy of his or her job description and make sure that it is current and accurate by verifying the description with the sales manager. If you don't know what is expected, you will find it impossible to set meaningful time priorities. Figure 13.2 on page 419 shows a typical job description for a salesperson.

In addition to a current job description, salespeople need to know what they are expected to achieve during a given time period. Salespeople and their

TABLE 13.2

BASIC ACTIVITIES OF SALESPEOPLE

Basic Activities	Examples of Tasks Involved
Selling Process	Search out leads; prepare sales presentations; make sales calls; negotiate resistance.
Working with Orders	Process orders; expedite orders; handle shipping problems.
Servicing the Product	Test equipment; provide training; supervise installation.
Managing Information	Disseminate and gather information from customers; provide feedback to superiors.
Servicing the Account	Take inventory; set up point-of-purchase displays; stock shelves.
Attending Conferences or Meetings	Attend sales meetings; set up and staff exhibits at trade shows.
Training/Recruiting	Recruit new sales reps; train new sales reps.
Entertaining Customers	Take clients to dinner, golfing, to stage plays.
Traveling Out of Town	Travel overnight to sales appointments.
Working with Distributors	Establish and maintain relationships with distributors; extend credit; collect past-due accounts.

Source: *Adapted from William C. Moncrief, "Selling Activity and Sales Position Taxonomies for Industrial Salesforces,"* Journal of Marketing Research *(August 1986): 261–270.*

sales manager should mutually agree on what is to be accomplished and then establish explicit time-based objectives, such as quotas for sales calls, unit sales, and new customers during the quarter. Knowing what must be accomplished by a certain date will help you better manage your territorial activities and will help reduce the stress of uncertainty about your role and performance. After all, how will you know where you're going and whether or not you've arrived if you haven't established the destination?

Chapter Review Question
What are the basic activities of salespeople?

Salespeople as Field Marketing Managers

For many companies, the modern professional selling job has evolved into that of *field marketing manager* for a sales territory. Today's salespeople have more responsibilities than ever before, and they must fill many roles. They are largely their own bosses in their sales territories, working with groups of people over whom they have little control and who often impose conflicting demands and expectations on them. For example, customers may expect salespeople to help them obtain extended credit on purchases, while the company accounting department is putting pressure on them to collect overdue accounts. Salespeople today perform many functions similar to those of marketing or sales managers, as illustrated in Table 13.3. They are involved in analyzing customer problems, setting sales objectives, doing financial analyses,

SALES REPRESENTATIVE

Position: District Sales Representative

Reports to: Regional Sales Manager

Division: Food Processing Machinery

Purpose of Position: To sell and/or lease all manufactured and agency equipment and parts in the assigned territory and/or to assigned customers, and assist on national account promotions and sales.

POSITION RESPONSIBILITIES

1. Manage territory to create and maintain an environment for customers or potential customers to buy, use, and recommend products from our company.
2. Call regularly on major, unpenetrated accounts to build future business.
3. Complete studies and quotations, make technical and sales presentations, close sales and leases, draw sales contracts and other sales documents on machinery, and obtain parts orders.
4. Maintain representation and liaison between customers and all departments within our company to gain and maintain a high level of acceptance in our customers' organizations.
5. Work with Customer Service and other departments to ensure prompt and adequate service to customers to include using sound business judgment in handling pricing problems, pressures for concessions, and difficult negotiations.
6. Monitor competitive market posture to advise on necessary redesign of equipment, modification of pricing policy, or similar changes as may be indicated.
7. Assist the Credit Department in establishing customer's financial condition.
8. Maintain expenses at a prudent level and evaluate entertainment and conference expenditures to ascertain their potential to generate sales.
9. Implement aggressively all divisional product line promotional programs.
10. Manage time and utilize available resources to provide adequate coverage to customers.
11. Assist management in preparing accurate sales forecasts, quotas, and financial reports.

POSITION REQUIREMENTS

1. B.S. degree (Engineering, Technical, or Business)
2. One or more years experience in the food industry
3. Willing to relocate

FIGURE 13.2

POSITION DESCRIPTION

coordinating members of a selling and customer service team, educating or training customers in the proper use of products, and controlling their own activities and time to maximize productivity.

As field marketing managers, salespeople research the needs of their prospects and customers, analyze evolving markets to spot opportunities for

TABLE 13.3

THE SALESPERSON'S MANAGEMENT AND MARKETING ACTIVITIES

Management Activities	
Problem Analysis	Analyzing customer problems that can be solved by the salesperson's products or services.
Objectives Setting	Establishing sales volume, market share, and customer service levels needed in a territory to ensure a strong competitive position.
Financial Analysis	Evaluating the impact a customer's purchase will have on that customer's financial health.
Supervision and Coordination	Working with others in the salesperson's own firm to answer questions, supply information to prospects, provide customer service, and coordinate efforts of a company selling team.
Training	Educating buyers in the proper and productive use of products sold by the salesperson.
Controlling	Reviewing time allocations to different prospects, customers, territories, and various tasks to determine how to become more productive.
Marketing Activities	
Research	Investigating prospect and customer needs and recommending product changes or new-product ideas.
Market Analysis	Determining the size and needs of various market segments. Continually searching for new market opportunities.
Sales Forecasting	Predicting sales volume for different customer groups and individual accounts to help allocate selling time.
Buyer Behavior	Studying the buying process to become more effective in adjusting to different motivational and behavioral needs of prospects and customers.
Marketing Strategy	Understanding the overall marketing strategy of customers in order to assess the impact of purchases on their inventory, distribution, product development, pricing, sales, and profits. Helping customers profitably "sell through" to their customers.
Information Systems	Using telecommunications technology to supply and access data needed in the salesperson's competitive efforts as the interface between buyers or sellers.

Source: *Adapted from Thomas R. Wotruba and Edwin K. Simpson,* Sales Management: Text and Cases *(Boston: PWS-Kent, 1992).*

KEEPING UP ONLINE: RADVISION

Radvision specializes in video networking products such as videoconferencing. Visit Radvision's website at *www.fvc.com* to examine Radvision's offerings. How could a company's salespeople use these services to improve their time and territory management?

new products and new customers, forecast sales for their territories, continually study buyer behavior to keep in touch with changing market segments, devise marketing strategies to help customers improve their profitability, and use central information systems to keep themselves and customers informed. In contrast to sales or marketing managers, however, salespeople are responsible for managing only their own activities, not those of other people in a sales force or marketing department.

Return on Time Invested

Return on Time Invested (ROTI) The designated return achieved, calculated by dividing the result achieved by the amount of time spent to accomplish that result.

Return on time invested (ROTI) is a financial concept that can help salespeople spend their time more profitably with prospects and customers. To calculate ROTI, salespeople divide the result achieved by the amount of time spent to accomplish that result (that is, result achieved/time). The *result* can be measured in various ways, such as dollar sales to a customer, profits on a certain product category, or new customers won. For example, if a salesperson spends sixty hours in preparing a sales call, making a sales presentation, and providing service to a customer who orders $90,000 worth of products, the ROTI is $90,000 (the result achieved) divided by 60 hours (the time spent), or $1,500. Another salesperson who invests 30 hours of time to make a sale of $25,000 has an ROTI of $833. The higher the ROTI, the better the salesperson's performance. Salespeople must keep accurate hourly records to know their ROTI for different activities, customers, and products. Although this may sound like tedious record keeping, it takes only a few minutes a day to record this information, and ROTI calculations can help salespeople manage their time more effectively and efficiently. Simple *sales call planning and results* sheets can be completed each week and then filed in folders or put on a computer for later analysis. Read the accompanying *Keeping Up Online* feature to discover excellent tools for saving time.

Chapter Review Questions

Why is a job description important to a salesperson?

Identify the major *management* and *marketing* activities of salespeople.

Describe the concept of return on time invested (ROTI).

SETTING PRIORITIES

Setting priorities is essential. Salespeople who don't set priorities often work on relatively minor tasks first because these are the easiest to complete and provide the feeling of accomplishment. Priorities should be related to specific objectives to be accomplished over a certain time period, such as a year, quarter, month, or week. Once you have determined your selling objectives, order them according to their importance and assign a date for their completion.

Salespeople who don't set priorities often work on relatively minor tasks first, deferring more important tasks.
Photo Disc

Three Axioms in Personal Selling

Top-performing salespeople always set priorities in their work; they recognize the truth of three axioms: (1) Parkinson's Law, (2) the concentration principle, and (3) the iceberg principle. Let's briefly discuss each of these.

Parkinson's Law Work expands to fill the time allotted to it.

Parkinson's Law. The axiom that work tends to expand to fill the time allotted for its completion is known as **Parkinson's Law.** For example, if you have eight hours to write a sales proposal, you will probably take that much time to complete the task. But if you had only four hours to write the proposal, you would somehow manage to complete it within that time.

Concentration Principle Most sales, costs, and profits come from a relatively small proportion of customers and products; also known as the 80–20 rule.

Concentration Principle. Often called the 80-20 rule, the **concentration principle** says that most of your sales, costs, and profits come from a relatively small proportion of your customers and products. For example, a large cosmetics producer markets its products in more than fifty countries, but only eight countries account for 86 percent of the company's sales and for 90 percent of its profits. Also, about 20 percent of its sales reps account for more than half of its sales.[3] A pharmaceutical company increased its sales 250 percent over four years by eliminating sales calls on 330,000 small accounts in order to concentrate on 70,000 major ones.[4] Later in this chapter, you'll see how you can determine which of your accounts are more important than others—and thus deserve more of your attention and effort.

Iceberg Principle Analogous to an iceberg, most sales problems are hidden beneath the surface of overall positive sales totals.

Iceberg Principle. Analogous to an iceberg that shows only 10 percent of its mass above the water, many sales problems can remain hidden beneath the surface of overall positive sales totals—the **iceberg principle.** That is, *total* company or sales office sales do not reveal a complete picture of the effectiveness and efficiency of sales operations. For instance, *total* sales could be increasing dramatically, yet *certain* territories, products, or classes of customers may be "bleeding red ink" and proving to be serious profit drains. As a result, many sales managers analyze sales, costs, and profitability reports by territory, product, customer, and salesperson. Salespeople should not hesitate to ask their sales managers for detailed analyses relevant to their territories. If this information is unavailable to you, perhaps you can develop your own analyses on products and customers within your territories.

Performance Measures

All salespeople want to know how well they're doing. Having this information helps you determine how far you are from your goals and what you need to do to reach them. For example, you may need to reset some priorities. Applying several *quantitative* and *qualitative* standards is better than relying on a single performance measure, such as sales volume, because you will obtain a more complete picture of your performance. For instance, if you emphasize only keeping sales and service expenses low, you may find sales revenue and profits adversely affected.

Quantitative measures, such as dollar or unit sales volume or net profit by product or customer, affect sales or expenses directly and usually can be measured objectively. *Qualitative measures,* such as the salesperson's product knowledge, customer relationships, or ethical behavior, have a more indirect and longer-run impact on sales and expenses and thus must be evaluated on a more subjective basis.

Most prospects and customers place more importance on qualitative measures of salesperson performance than on quantitative measures. For instance, prospects and customers prefer to interact with salespeople who are effective listeners, can address questions and issues well, don't waste time, and have strong communication skills.

Another way to look at sales activities is as efforts and results. *Sales efforts* include selling activities, such as the number of sales calls made on potential new accounts, or nonselling activities, such as the number of service calls, displays set up, collections made, or customer complaints handled. *Sales results* include measurable outcomes, such as the number of orders obtained, average dollar amount of orders, percent of quota achieved, and gross margin by product or customer type. Table 13.4 shows quantitative measures of a salesperson's selling efforts and selling results. Let's discuss two important kinds of salesperson performance measures: sales quotas and customer reviews of performance.

Sales Quotas. Derived from sales forecasts, sales quotas provide performance objectives and motivational incentives for salespeople. They are usually stated in terms of dollar or unit volume, and sales managers rely heavily on them as standards for appraising the performance of individual salespeople.[5] To spur themselves on to greater performance, some top-performing salespeople establish even higher quotas—inspirational quotas—for themselves that exceed those assigned by their sales manager. If your company does not assign you specific quotas, you should establish your own goals or quotas for various performance measures in your territory. Here are four types of quotas that salespeople ought to consider: (1) *sales volume quotas,* such as dollar or unit sales; (2) *financial quotas,* such as gross margin, net profit, or expenses; (3) *activity quotas,* such as number of sales calls made or number of dealer training sessions given; and (4) *combination quotas,* which include both financial and activity goals. It is important to have activity quotas as well as financial quotas, because meeting activity quotas can continue to motivate salespeople who fail to meet financial quotas.[6]

One problem in using quotas in business-to-business selling is that sales may rely on the efforts of several people, including telemarketers, inside salespeople, or even a selling team. When several people influence sales,

TABLE 13.4

Quantitative Measures of Salesperson Performance

Personal Selling Efforts	Personal Selling Results
Sales Calls: • Number of calls on current customers. • Number of calls on new prospects. • Number of sales presentations. • Number of sales demonstrations. • Selling time versus nonselling time. • Call frequency ratio per customer type.	Orders: • Number of orders obtained. • Number of orders canceled by customers. • Average order size (dollars or units). • "Batting average" (orders÷sales calls).
Selling Expenses: • As percent of sales volume. • As percent of sales quota. • Average per sales call. • By customer type. • By product category. • Direct selling expense ratios. • Indirect selling expense ratios.	Sales Volume: • Dollar sales. • Unit sales. • Percent of sales quota obtained. • Sales by customer category. • Sales by product type. • Market share.
Customer Service: • Number of service calls. • Number of customer complaints. • Percent of sales (units÷dollars) returned. • Delivery cost per unit sold. • Displays set up. • Delivery cost per unit sold. • Average time spent per call.	Margins: • Gross margin for territory. • Net profit for territory. • Gross margin by customer and product. • Net profit by customer and product.
	Customer Accounts: • Number of new accounts. • Number of lost accounts. • Number of overdue accounts. • Dollar amount of accounts receivable. • Collections from accounts receivable. • Percent of accounts sold.

many companies use team or group quotas and split commissions on some predetermined basis among group members. It is important for salespeople to understand clearly how and when commissions will be distributed in order to avoid disputes later.[7] Most companies pay commissions after orders are *shipped,* but some pay when orders are *received* and others not until orders are *paid.*

Periodic review of sales performance measures is critical to the success of an organization.
Lisette Le Bon/SuperStock

Customer Reviews of Performance. Increasingly, customers are conducting annual reviews of supplier performance. Salespeople should ask for an annual evaluation of their performance by customers and should participate in this review process at a special meeting. Obtaining feedback from customers is one of the most effective ways to keep from losing touch with them. Staying on top of your customers' needs and your performance in satisfying them demonstrates your commitment to the firm. The more committed you are to an account, the more satisfied the account is likely to be, and the less likely it is to switch suppliers.[8]

ACCOUNT AND TERRITORY MANAGEMENT

Sales Territory A control unit that contains customer accounts.

A **sales territory** is a control unit that contains customer accounts. Most salespeople are assigned a geographic control unit such as a state, county, zip code area, city, or township because these are the bases for a great deal of government census data and other market information. Other market factors such as buying habits and patterns of trade flow can also define territories.[9] Companies establish sales territories to ensure comprehensive market coverage, facilitate sales planning and control, increase sales, keep selling costs low, reduce travel time, improve salesperson rewards and morale, strengthen customer relations, and coordinate selling with other marketing functions.[10] With escalating selling costs, territory management is becoming increasingly important.[11]

Once the geographic control unit has been established, the next step is to analyze the customers and prospects in the territory on the basis of their sales potential. Accounts must first be identified by name. Many sources provide this information. Computerized directories represent one of the most effective sources for identifying customers quickly. The Yellow Pages Online website (www.yellowpages.com) contains a huge database of U.S. and international businesses by name, mailing address, and phone numbers. Read the *Keeping Up Online* feature on page 427, and think about how the Yellow Pages Online website can help your selling.

Chapter Review Question

Name at least five *quantitative and five qualitative* measures of salesperson performance.

KEEPING UP ONLINE: INSTANT YELLOW PAGES

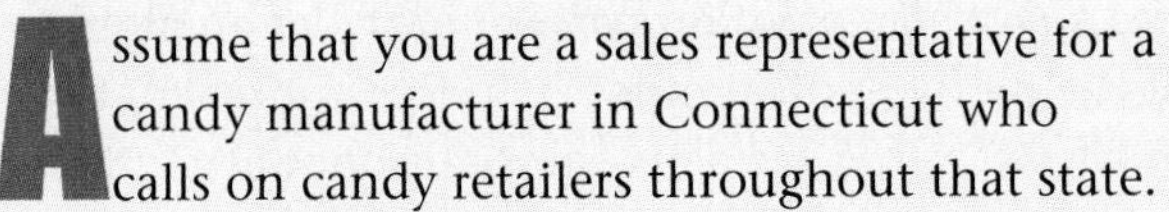

Assume that you are a sales representative for a candy manufacturer in Connecticut who calls on candy retailers throughout that state. How might you improve your effectiveness and efficiency by using yellowpages.com to identify prospects?

Salespeople can also use company records of past sales, trade directories, professional association membership lists, directories of corporations, publishers of mailing lists, trade books and periodicals, chambers of commerce, federal, state, and local governments, and personal observation. Once you've identified potential accounts, the next step is to estimate the total sales potential for all accounts in each geographic control unit. After you make those sales estimates, classify the accounts according to their annual buying potential. Those with the highest sales potential can be designated category A accounts and assigned the largest share of your time. Next, classify the average potential accounts as category B. Finally, those accounts with very little sales potential can be labeled category C. Now you can decide which accounts to make sales calls on and which to contact by telephone, e-mail, or direct mail. As illustrated in Figure 13.3, the concentration principle is usually evident after customers are ranked by sales potential. Here, customers in category A (20 percent) account for about 70 percent of the sales volume, category B (25 percent) accounts for 23 percent of sales, and category C (55 percent) accounts for only 7 percent of sales. Many companies use computer programs to assist their salespeople with account analysis, planning, and control.

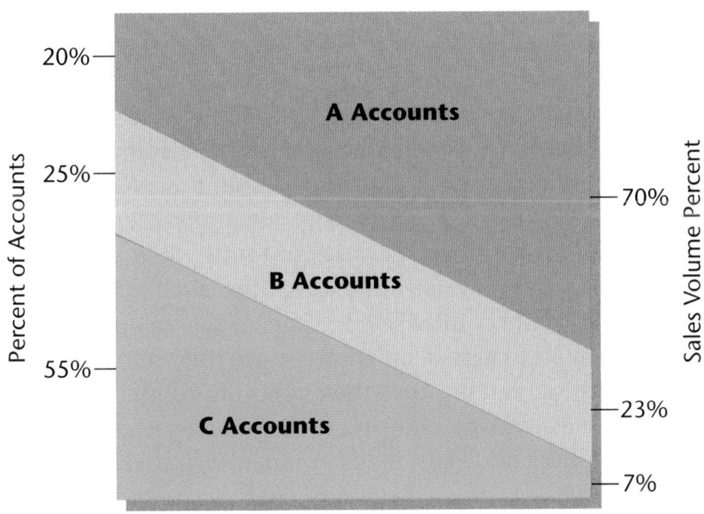

FIGURE 13.3

RANKING CUSTOMERS ACCORDING TO THE CONCENTRATION PRINCIPLE

Portfolio Analysis Approach

Many organizations still refrain from helping their salespeople with computerized mathematical models because these models are so complex. Also, not every sales call can be accurately programmed because of the diverse variables that affect success and failure. A *portfolio analysis approach* provides an alternative to the analytical rigor of the mathematical models. In this approach, the sales call strategy is based on the account's attractiveness. Account attractiveness depends on two dimensions: account opportunity and strength of position. The label Account Opportunity refers to the prospect's need and ability to purchase the product; the label Strength of Position refers to the strength of the selling firm's position with the prospect.[12] Presented in Figure 13.4 is a portfolio analysis approach. Segment 1 represents what most companies call a key account. Segment 2 would be considered a potential customer or prospect. Segment 3 is a stable account, and Segment 4 represents a weak account. This kind of matrix enables salespeople to set calling priorities among their accounts and to establish sales call strategies for them.

Note that the above approach involves the salesperson's assigning a *generalized* assessment concerning the attractiveness of an account. An alternative approach to determining how valuable an account is uses *quantitative* information by considering (1) the present profit contribution of a customer and (2) the customer's potential profit contribution. Once this determination is made for all accounts, each account can be positioned into one of four quadrants:

- High present profit contribution and high potential profit contribution (desirable accounts)
- High present profit contribution and low potential profit contribution (developed accounts)
- Low present profit contribution and high potential profit contribution (developing accounts)
- Low present profit contribution and low potential profit contribution (undesirable accounts)

The analysis will suggest the value of each account and help you decide which ones merit attention and which do not.[13] Following the portfolio analysis, you are now prepared to undertake the next phase of account management—territorial routing.

Territorial Routing
Devising a travel plan or pattern to use when making sales calls.

Territorial routing is devising a plan or pattern to use when making sales calls. The primary goal is to minimize nonselling time (such as time spent traveling and waiting) and maximize selling time for salespeople.[14] A well-designed routing system also helps salespeople reduce their selling costs, improve their territory coverage, and improve their communication with sales managers, customers, or others who, by knowing their routing pattern, can more easily locate them on short notice. In many companies, individual salespeople still route themselves because they know their territories and customers best.

Depending on the geographic distribution and number of prospects and customers, routing systems can be quite complex. A basic pattern can be made simply by locating all the accounts on a map and determining the optimal

STRENGTH OF POSITION / ACCOUNT OPPORTUNITY

	Strong	Weak
High	**SEGMENT 1** **Attractiveness** Accounts are very attractive, since they offer high opportunity and the sales organization has a strong position. **Sales Call Strategy** Accounts should receive a high level of sales calls, since they are the sales organization's most attractive accounts.	**SEGMENT 2** **Attractiveness** Accounts are potentially attractive, since they offer high opportunity, but sales organization currently has weak position with accounts. **Sales Call Strategy** Accounts should receive a high level of sales calls to strengthen the sales organization's position.
Low	**SEGMENT 3** **Attractiveness** Accounts are somewhat attractive, since sales organization has strong position, but future opportunity is limited. **Sales Call Strategy** Accounts should receive a moderate level of sales calls to maintain the current strength of the sales organization's position.	**SEGMENT 4** **Attractiveness** Accounts are very unattractive since they offer low opportunity and since sales organization has weak position. **Sales Call Strategy** Accounts should receive minimal level of sales calls and efforts should be made to selectively eliminate or replace personal sales calls with phone sales calls, direct mail, or e-mail.

FIGURE 13.4

ACCOUNT ANALYSIS

order in which to visit them and the fastest route to take. Before developing a routing plan, you must decide how many calls to make each day, decide how frequently to call on each class of customer, determine the distance to each account, and choose what method of transportation you will use. With this information, you can locate present and potential customers on a map of the territory. In the past, accounts were often identified on a map by marking their location with felt-tip pens or using different colors of pushpins for each account category. Today, salespeople can use various computer software programs to obtain a complete routing plan in minutes. The overall objective in developing a routing path is to minimize backtracking and crisscrossing, thereby saving time.

Several professional optimization software programs are available to design routing paths for various sales territories. For example, see the following six websites: AlignStarV3 (www.alignstar.com); TerrAlign 4 (www.terralign.com/terralign4.htm); BusinessMAP4 (www.hallogram.com/mappro/businessmap.html); Sage CRM MME (www.prior-analytics.com/solutions/sagecrm/sagecrm.html); NetSuite CRM+ (www.netsuite.com/netcrm/products/crm_plus/sfa_territory_tracking.shtml); and RouteView Pro

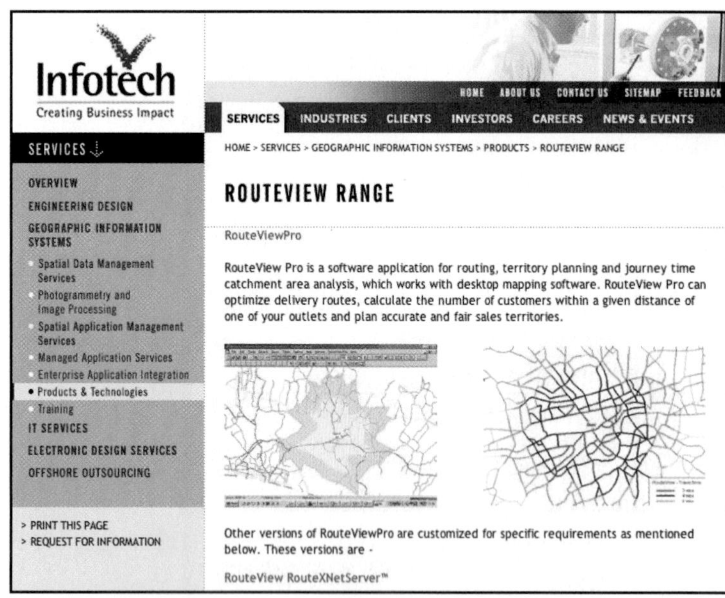

Reprinted by permission of Infotechsw.com

(infotechsw.com/launch/services/rv.html). More specifically, salespeople and their sales managers can work together with a program like RouteView Pro to optimize sales call routes, calculate the number of customers within a given distance, and develop equitable sales territories. Salespeople also can enhance their territory management skills by enrolling in Web-based seminars offered by well-known companies like Siebel Systems (www.crmondemand.com/training_support/training_webseminars.jsp).

Routing Patterns

Depending on the sales territory's size and shape, routing patterns are commonly straight or circular. With a *straight-line* route, the salesperson starts at the office and makes calls in one direction until he or she reaches the end of the territory. *Circular patterns* start at the office and move in a circle of stops until the salesperson ends up back at the office. Two less common and more complex route patterns are the hopscotch and the cloverleaf. With *hopscotch* patterns the salesperson starts at the farthest point from the office and hops back and forth, calling on accounts on either side of a straight line back to the office. For speed, the salesperson may fly to the outer limits of his or her territory and then drive back calling on customers. On the next trip the salesperson would go in another direction in the territory. Used when accounts are concentrated in specific parts of the territory, a *cloverleaf* route is similar to a circular pattern, but rather than covering an entire territory, the route circles only part of a territory. The next trip is an adjacent cloverleaf, and the pattern continues until the entire territory is covered. The hopscotch and cloverleaf patterns are depicted in Figure 13.5.

In the "outer ring" approach to routing, shown in Figure 13.6, the salesperson first draws an outer ring around the customers to be called on. Then, those customers inside the ring are connected to the outer ring route using angles that are as obtuse as possible. The general principles underlying this "outer ring" approach to routing include the following:

- Customers in close proximity to each other should be visited in direct succession.
- Sales calls should be made along the way to eliminate sharp angles in the route.
- Avoid using the same route to and from a customer, because retracing your steps is the most acute angle of all.
- Routes already traveled should not be crossed.
- Daily travel routes should be as nearly circular as possible.[15]

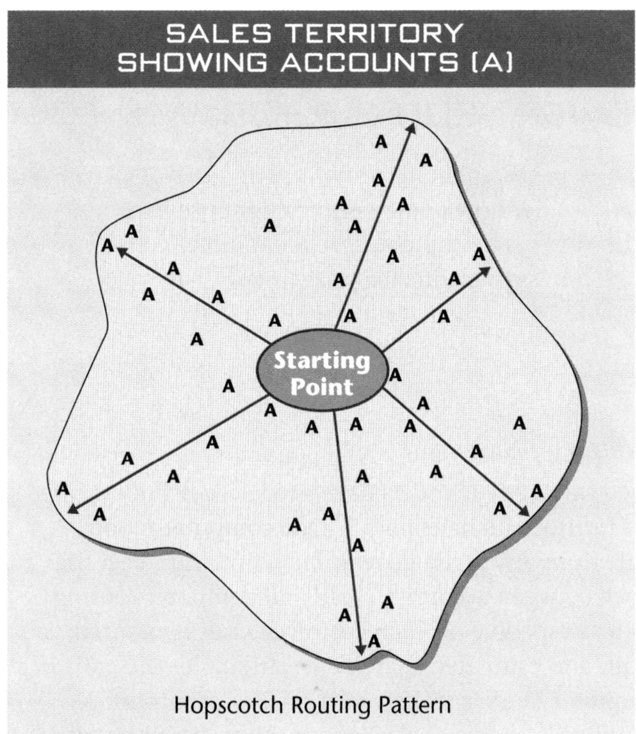

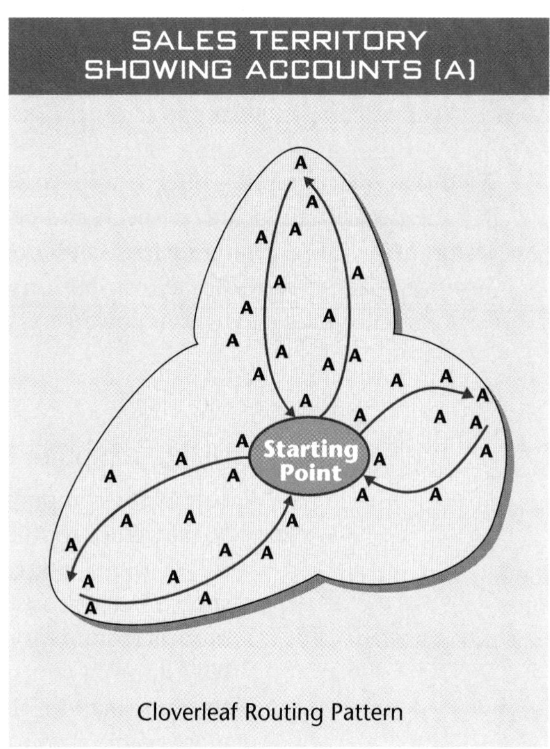

FIGURE 13.5

HOPSCOTCH AND CLOVERLEAF ROUTING PATTERNS

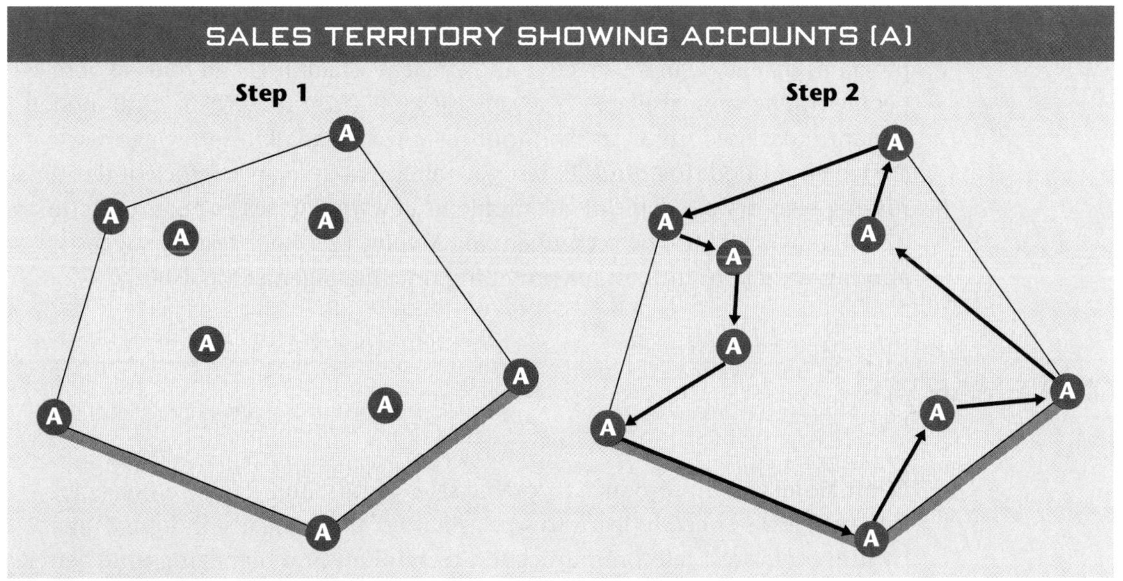

FIGURE 13.6

"OUTER RING" ROUTING PATTERN

KEEPING UP ONLINE: EMPOWER GEOGRAPHICS

Empower Geographics offers a website at which salespeople can locate prospects and customers on maps using criteria such as sales, driving distance, markets served, lead distribution, or work load. Investigate www.empowergeo.com/pages/about_territory.htm and consider how a salesperson might use such maps to improve efficiency and effectiveness in territory management.

Using Computer Programs in Routing

Numerous computer-based interactive models have been successfully applied to sales force routing and territory management.[16] One computer model, called *nearest-city,* can start from any given geographic point and select the shortest, least-cost distance between accounts. Nearly all computer routing models require input from salespeople on each customer's sales potential, call length, profit contribution, and estimated share penetration. On the basis of this information, the computer models realign sales territories into more manageable account groupings and route sales reps in terms of call frequencies, travel time, and length of call.

With the help of sophisticated software programs, you can quickly and conveniently develop your own optimal routing and scheduling strategies on your computer. In recent years, more elaborate sales force automation models have become available from companies such as Siebel Systems (www.siebel.com), which sells *enterprise relationship management* (ERM) software to direct and monitor sales, customer service, and call center relationships with prospects and customers. In the years ahead, comprehensive mathematical models and software programs that allow more effective and efficient scheduling and routing of salespeople will become available. You can see some current mathematical models and formulas used in salesperson routing at www.nada.kth.se/~viggo/www compendium/node104.html. To test your ability to develop an efficient territorial routing plan, try out some of the problems at www.courses.psu.edu/mktg/mktg 220rso3/qwrap.htm. The accompanying *Keeping Up Online* feature suggests another website of interest for providing time management assistance.

WORKING SMARTER

Effort alone will not produce favorable sales results. To increase efficiency, salespeople also need to learn to work smarter.[17] Two means of doing this are by using the latest telecommunication technology and managing time better.

Using the Latest Technology

As discussed in chapter 2, salespeople have at their disposal a wealth of technological advances in hardware and software to assist them in performing their job more efficiently and effectively. The experiences of diverse companies already attest to the value of laptop, handheld computers, PDAs, and multi-function camera cell phones to their salespeople and customers—and who knows what exciting technologies will be available in the future? To help in managing territories, completing paperwork, and gaining more face-to-face selling time, one pharmaceutical firm equipped its salespeople and sales managers with notebook computers. Now the company's salespeople can obtain information for their thousands of physician customers in a few seconds. Administrative tasks are taking about 20 percent less time, and reports are more accurate. The firm estimates that every 1 percent boost in a rep's effectiveness increases revenue by $6.7 million per year.

At a life insurance company, salespeople use their handheld computers to determine instantly how different options can change the cost of a prospect's insurance policy. Prior to the availability of computer analyses, such calculations took days or even weeks. At a large oil company, advances in computer software have largely freed field sales reps from administrative functions, resulting in sales productivity gains of 15 to 20 percent. Salespeople for the marketing services group of a large data processing firm are saving an average of 4.4 hours per week on various sales-related tasks and meeting customers' information needs faster. A steel manufacturer estimated a 20 to 25 percent reduction in clerical errors after its salespeople began submitting orders via e-mail. And salespeople at an electronics manufacturer are using the latest

FROM THE COMMAND POST: IT'S ALL IN THE PALM OF MY HAND

BlackBerrys (www.rim.com) and other multi-function handheld telecommunication devices have become indispensable in the selling arena. Few sales personnel today would be caught without one. Their potential for increasing sales productivity is almost limitless. In fact, without one, a salesperson may well be bereft of crucial information and the means with which to close a sale, provide customer service, or execute customer reorders. Depending on their device's configuration, sales reps can scan their products' UPC bar codes, align the device with their PCs, and e-mail purchase orders to company headquarters instantly, whenever and wherever they want. No longer do salespeople need to incur long delays while playing "phone tag" with their sales managers and other support people to obtain or send critical information.

Handheld high-tech devices have significantly decreased the time required to place orders, transfer them to company headquarters, and enter them into the supplier's accounting software. Some companies have cut the amount of time once needed to perform these activities by almost 99 percent! Not only is ordering time expedited, but salespeople now have more time to spend on building customer relationships. And because multi-function handheld devices are becomingly increasingly user-friendly, salespeople can quickly become attuned to their features and advantages, thus minimizing the former "learning curve" disadvantages of adopting new technology.

technology to gain two to three extra hours a week in selling and servicing time. Many other organizations have experienced significant improvements in budgeting and controlling expenses through computer software developments. Read how some firms have expedited their sales reps' capabilities in *From the Command Post* on page 433.

Paperwork can be a dreaded and time-consuming chore for salespeople who aren't good time managers.
Tony Freeman/Photo Edit

Managing Time Better

Many organizations provide their sales reps with training in time management. Nonetheless, some salespeople find many excuses for using time inefficiently.[18]

Excuses About Time. Some salespeople are chronically late, disorganized, and generally inefficient in using time. Part of the problem is often the person's attitude toward time and the acceptance of excuses for its inefficient use. Some of the most excuses most commonly offered are listed in Table 13.5.

Paperwork. One of the most dreaded and time-consuming tasks of salespeople is handling their *paperwork*. Like other sales-related activities, paperwork ought to be scheduled on the salesperson's daily or weekly planning calendar. Some companies put the 200 to 700 pages of memos, newsletters, brochures, reports, announcements, and other sales-related materials sent to salespeople each week onto audiotapes. The tapes are recorded according to topics, so salespeople can choose exactly what they want to hear.

Customer Service. Another time-consuming but important activity is providing *customer service*. Although it is hard to predict *which* customers will want *what* services *when*, salespeople must recognize that customer service is a regular part of their jobs and needs to be scheduled like any other activity. The following suggestions may assist you in focusing your customer service activities:

- Segment your customers according to costs and the potential profits that could accrue from providing them with superior service.
- Remember that all customer contacts, whether through telephone operators, receptionists, secretaries, delivery and repair personnel, or customer service people, shape the perceptions of your company's service. Try to encourage all these people who have contact with customers and prospects to treat them well.
- Continually stress the importance of customer service to people in your company, and reinforce this attitude by your own actions.
- Design and use measures of service effectiveness, such as the percentage of on-time deliveries, the length of time it takes to repair a product, and the level of customer satisfaction.

TABLE 13.5

Excuses for Poor Time Management

- **Insufficient time:** There is always enough time to accomplish essential tasks. A salesperson who believes that he or she has insufficient time can usually overcome the problem by reassessing priorities for daily activities. Some tasks can be postponed or delayed indefinitely.
- **Too many demands on my time:** Learning to say no is probably the most important timesaving technique you can learn. Letting other people preempt your priorities with their own allows them to control your time. Whenever someone places an unexpected demand on your time, ask yourself: Is this unplanned activity more important than what I had planned to do with this time? If it isn't, give a courteous but brief explanation of why you cannot comply with the request.
- **I can do it better myself:** Some salespeople have such a need for control and perfection that they waste time doing unimportant tasks that could be delegated to others. Ask yourself whether such tasks are the best use of your time. If someone else can do minor tasks well enough for you, you gain more time to spend on important projects.
- **If I only had more time each day:** Everyone has the same 24 hours each day, but some people learn how to use those hours more efficiently. Working more hours every day produces mental and physical fatigue that can be counterproductive to overall performance.
- **I don't have time to plan:** The old saying "If you want something done, ask a busy person" illustrates the importance of planning the use of one's time. People who achieve a lot have learned how to manage their time by skillful planning.
- **I can't find time to work on big projects:** Because many complex projects cannot be finished quickly, people tend to let them go until they can find large blocks of time. Schedule at least an hour every day to work on major projects so that you do not procrastinate and face panic later when the deadline draws near.
- **Unexpected problems disrupt my plans:** Whenever the unexpected occurs, ask yourself the key question: Is this more important than what I had planned to do at this time? If it isn't, don't do it.
- **If only I could work faster:** Most people make mistakes when they hurry. When you lack the time to do everything on your list, setting priorities is the key: Do high-priority tasks and ignore tasks with low priority.
- **It's better to do small tasks first:** This is the exact opposite of what the best time managers do. Create the habit of doing your most important tasks early in the day before minor tasks crowd them out.

The professional salesperson must learn to work smarter instead of harder. The following *On the Frontlines* suggests how salespeople can do exactly that!

Time Traps. Many salespeople undermine their own efficiency by falling into daily traps that waste their time. The most successful salespeople learn how to avoid time traps so that they make the most of each hour and each day. Some of the most common time traps are identified in Table 13.6 on page 437.

ON THE FRONTLINES

A Prosaic High-Tech Selling Tool

Most salespeople want to stand out from the pack, excel, and be recognized as among the best in their field. In this high-tech age, there are manifold ways of achieving this goal. One means that is sometimes overlooked, perhaps because it is so commonplace today, is e-mail.

E-mail can be an efficient and effective means of selling, but using it requires careful attention. Otherwise, it can become just another selling tool—and not a particularly useful one at that. Prospects and customers are flooded with myriad e-mail missives day in and day out, many of which they do not read or even open. Nevertheless, well-crafted e-mail messages can be an extremely valuable weapon in the selling battle. Several means of ensuring the effectiveness of your e-mail messages are available.

The accuracy of the database must be checked. Names and addresses, as well as any other pertinent information purchased from the database provider (e.g., company size, nature of industry, and names of contact people) must be correct. Prior notification to your e-mail provider is also important, so that your e-mails will not be automatically blocked as "spam." Otherwise, precious promotional dollars and efforts will be wasted on e-mails that never reach a legitimate prospect or customer.

Additionally, e-mail lists need to be segmented to enhance financial return. E-mail prospects who have earlier shown an interest in your company's offerings should receive specially tailored information or discounts that customers on the more general e-mail list do not receive. Just as segmentation works for marketing products and services to target markets, it is also beneficial for providing customer service with technical support updates and advance notice of new-product introductions. Once an e-mail distribution list has been completed, the campaign should be thoroughly evaluated and tested. After the e-mails are sent, an evaluation can help determine the effectiveness and efficiency of your e-mail efforts. For instance, the tests can provide information on the number of e-mail messages sent, delivered, opened, examined, and forwarded successfully, as well as the addresses from which the message was bounced back and the reason for this. With such feedback, the e-mail lists can be "cleaned up" until they largely contain only qualified prospects and customers.

For those salespeople who work for companies that offer quality products or services and emphasize customer service, e-mail sales activities may be just the extra medicine required to achieve renewed sales health.

A Plan for Each Day. Every salesperson can benefit from preparing a daily to-do list of projects and tasks ranked into A, B, and C categories of importance. Work first on all the A priorities until no more work on them can be done; then move on to the B categories, and finally work on the C category tasks. Although the A items are likely to be complex or long-term projects, use the *Swiss cheese* approach to punch little holes in such tasks at every opportunity because they are your top priority. For example, if one of your A priorities is preparing a sales proposal for a large client, take every opportunity to work on that report during your day, perhaps by looking up a reference or doing a few

TABLE 13.6

The Box of Time Traps

- Calling on unqualified or unprofitable prospects.
- Insufficient planning for each day's activities.
- Poor territorial routing and travel plans.
- Making too many cold calls.
- Taking long lunch hours and too many coffee breaks.
- Making poor use of waiting time between appointments.
- Spending too much time entertaining prospects and customers.
- Not using modern telecommunication equipment, such as a cell phone, beeper, portable fax machine, and computer.
- Doing tasks that could be delegated to a staff person or to automated equipment.
- Failing to prioritize work.
- Doing work that isn't a part of the job description.
- Procrastinating on major projects or on contacting high-potential prospects, resulting in redundant preparation and paperwork.
- Inefficient handling of paperwork and disorganized record keeping.
- Putting too many documents into a pending file, so that you wind up handling each sheet of paper several times as you look through the pending file periodically.
- Failing to break up huge, long-range goals into small, currently manageable tasks.
- Ending workdays early, especially on Friday afternoons.
- Failing to insulate yourself from interruptions on sales calls or while doing paperwork.
- Letting sales meetings and discussions veer too far off course.
- Conducting unnecessary meetings, visits, and phone calls.
- Socializing excessively during or between sales calls.
- Allowing other people to preempt your priorities with their own.

Chapter Review Question

What are the classic time traps into which salespeople can fall?

calculations. By doing a small piece of this major project every day, you will complete it before you know it. Follow these tips in your daily planning:

- Outline your daily tasks and activities.
- Arrange them in A-B-C priority order.
- Work on the A priorities until you can do no more, then work on the B priorities, and finally address the C priorities.
- Delegate as many tasks as you can.
- Control interruptions.
- Don't let other people preempt your priorities.

Steps to Manage Your Time More Effectively. Although experts on time management have suggested numerous guidelines, most seem to agree on the following steps:

- *Accomplish one major objective each day:* Pick one important task and concentrate on completing it. If you develop this habit, it will prevent you from filling up your day with low-priority activities.
- *Each weekday afternoon, write down your schedule for the next day:* Committing your schedule to writing will force you to think carefully about your plan. It will help you set realistic deadlines and motivate you to accomplish the plan, as well as achieve any call quotas and sales goals that have been set for you. Use a daily schedule sheet that covers each hour like the one shown in Figure 13.7.
- *On Friday afternoon, plan your schedule for the following week:* By the middle of Friday afternoon, you have a good idea of what you've accomplished—or failed to accomplish—that week. The pressure has eased, so you can think clearly. It's the ideal time to decide what you need to accomplish the following week. This tactic allows you to mentally rehearse your schedule over the weekend so that you'll have a psychological head start Monday morning. When you arrive at the office, you'll hit the ground running.
- *Reduce one time-waster each week:* You can never quit wasting time altogether, but you can waste less of it. For example, by closing your door to concentrate on writing or reading reports, you can reduce time lost to drop-in visitors.

DAILY SCHEDULE DATE ______

Hours	Appointments/Activities
8:00	
9:00	
10:00	
11:00	
12:00	
1:00	
2:00	
3:00	
4:00	
5:00	
Evening Hours	

FIGURE 13.7

DAILY SCHEDULE SHEET

- *Concentrate on keeping meetings shorter and more productive:* As Peter Drucker says in *The Effective Executive*, "Meetings are by definition a concession to deficient organization. For one either meets or one works. One cannot do both at the same time." You can, however, take steps to keep meetings manageable. Mail out an agenda to meeting participants; put a suggested time limit beside each item on the agenda, and stick to it; start and end the meeting on time; and take five minutes at the end of a meeting to summarize decisions and who will be responsible for what.
- *Concentrate on high priorities:* Salespeople must learn to work on high-priority projects first, even when only a little can be accomplished on the project that day, before switching to lower-priority tasks.
- *Spend your time as though you had to buy it:* If you look at your time as a precious asset like gold, that costs you money to use up, you'll learn to use it more productively.
- *Stop procrastinating:* Change your "do-it-later" habit into a "do-it-now" habit. Some salespeople delay work on large projects until they can find large blocks of time. But this approach can cause them to leave their most important projects until the last minute when they are forced to finish them quickly and poorly.
- *Schedule some personal time every day:* The best way to obtain personal time is to schedule it in your daily appointment book so that it's protected from intrusions. Listen to music, read a book, talk with friends and family, or go for a long walk. Personal time is not a luxury or something to postpone until you can fit it into your schedule. It's a requirement for maintaining a healthy balance and control in your life.
- *Good intentions are not enough:* As the old saying goes, "The road to hell is paved with good intentions," so stop talking about how you're going to manage your time better and start doing it now.[19]

Few, if any, human beings have ever reached optimal effectiveness and efficiency or maintained them for long. Nevertheless, salespeople should keep careful track of how they use their time each day so that they can find ways, even small ways, to increase their number of productive hours. Such continuous efforts can soon pay off in higher sales and greater income.

Chapter Review Questions

Give some guidelines for better time management.

What are some steps that salespeople can take to manage their time better?

SUMMARY

Top-performing salespeople are usually efficient and effective managers of their territories. Operating much like field marketing managers, they try to maximize their return on time invested (ROTI). They understand the various quantitative and qualitative measures of performance and conduct regular reviews of their own performance with their individual customers. They use the most efficient account analysis and routing plans, sometimes developed by sophisticated computer programs. They are excellent time managers who learn ways to work smarter by utilizing the latest technology and by avoiding the classic time traps that plague less effective salespeople.

KEY TERMS

Effectiveness
Efficiency
Return on Time Invested (ROTI)
Parkinson's Law
Concentration Principle
Iceberg Principle
Sales Territory
Territorial Routing

TOPICS FOR THOUGHT AND CLASS DISCUSSION

1. Why are salespeople described as operating like field marketing managers? Do you believe that this is an accurate representation of the typical field salesperson? Explain.
2. Do you think that most job descriptions for salespeople accurately reflect their current duties and responsibilities? Why?
3. Pick a routine task in your life and map out a plan for improving your efficiency and effectiveness in accomplishing it.
4. How do time traps disrupt your time management? How can you avoid these traps?
5. What techniques do you use to plan, organize, and set priorities in your daily activities? Do you use the "Swiss cheese" approach for large or complex projects? Give an example of how you might do this.
6. Do you allow other people to frequently preempt your priorities in use of your time by substituting something that is of high priority to them? Give an example. How might you deal with future situations where someone wants you to accept his or her priority for time use instead of yours?

INTERNET EXERCISES

1. Use an Internet search engine to find three firms that specialize in sales territory management training. What are the length and cost of each program? Where would it be held? Who's doing the training? What topics will the sales territory management training cover that will be new?
2. Using Google or any other search engine, find two examples of sales territory management training being demonstrated using Flash or streaming video.
3. Use the Internet to find articles on salespeople whose effectiveness has been increased by their improved skills in time and sales territory management.
4. Search the Internet to find additional tips for managing your time. What time management suggestions did you find advocated?
5. Use the Internet to find examples of quantitative and qualitative metrics that are used to evaluate the performance of salespeople (in addition to those identified in Table 13.4). What inferences can you make about how your performance might be assessed if you were to embark on a career in sales? What activities might you emphasize to ensure a high performance rating and, in the process, a successful career?
6. Using an Internet search engine, find software that can be used to chart efficient territorial routing patterns. What are some of the different types of territorial routing patterns that can be developed?

PROJECTS FOR PERSONAL GROWTH

1. Contact three salespeople and ask them how they plan, organize, and prioritize their daily activities. Mention that you are a student working on a class project. Evaluate their approaches in terms of ROTI.

2. Classify four of your student friends on the basis of your perceptions of their effectiveness and efficiency. Then ask these student friends these two questions: (a) "What techniques do you use to plan, organize, and set priorities in your daily activities?" and (b) "What *time traps* are most responsible for wasting your time each day?" Compare your friends' answers with your prior classification of them. Any surprises?

3. For the coming week, write down how you spend each hour of the seven days. At the end of the week, compute approximately how much of your time you used productively and how much you wasted. Draw up a plan for better managing your time, and use it throughout a second week. At the end of this second week, evaluate whether or not you obtained more productive time. If so, what made the difference?

4. Go to the library or use electronic sources and find three current articles on managing a sales territory. Summarize them and report what you learned to your classmates.

ROLE-PLAY EXERCISE 13.1

Working Smarter

Situation

Dave Greco is about to complete his fifth year of working as a sales representative for BecoPlastics Company, a manufacturer of various household products made from plastics. Dave works as hard as anyone on the sales force, but his sales record seems to have reached a plateau during the past two years, and this year he is concerned that his total sales may even decline. Dave is very upset by his lack of sales growth because company sales are climbing steadily, and many BecoPlastics salespeople are enjoying excellent sales increases in their territories.

It's frustrating for Dave not to see his long hours on the job pay off. He prides himself on being one of BecoPlastics' most customer-relations-oriented and service-oriented salespersons. For example, even when he knows that a customer isn't interested in buying anything that month, Dave still tries to make a friendly in-person call to drink a cup of coffee and discuss how things are going, and he handles all his customer service problems himself. In company-wide surveys of customers, Dave's customers tend to be the most satisfied. Unfortunately, each year some of Dave's customers move or go out of business, so his total number of customers is steadily declining. Today, Dave was stunned to receive a memo from his sales manager, Peter Bilodeau, expressing some concerns about Dave's sales performance and asking him to come in tomorrow for an early-morning meeting.

Roles

Dave Greco Extremely well liked and respected by his customers, Dave works long hours, but his efforts don't seem to be paying off in higher sales. Yet he spends more time than any other company salesperson maintaining customer relations, and his customers are the most satisfied in the company.

Peter Bilodeau An experienced salesperson who has been a sales manager for four years, Mr. Bilodeau wants to help Dave work smarter, not just harder.

ROLE-PLAY EXERCISE 13.2

Tallying Time Traps

Situation

Gene Childs is a salesperson for an industrial gasket manufacturer. His company is rotating all members of its sales force through a two-day course in time management. Gene was in the first group selected, and after completing the second day of the course this Friday afternoon, he stops in to his favorite pub to unwind with a couple of beers before heading home for dinner. Two other salespeople he knows are already in the pub talking and drinking. With a boisterous greeting, Gene walks over and joins them. After talking about sports for a while, Gene shifts the discussion to the course he's just completed and challenges his friends with this question: "Bet you each a beer that you two together can't name twenty time-wasting traps that most salespeople fall into each day."

Roles

Gene Childs Having recently completed the time management course, Gene wants to show off a bit. There are more than twenty time wasters that afflict salespeople, depending on the salesperson and the selling job, but he thinks it will be hard for his rather self-satisfied sales colleagues to come up with even twenty.

Joe Grisi A grocery products salesperson for a large food manufacturer, Joe has been selling for eight years. He doesn't think he wastes much time, but he knows salespeople who do, and he accepts Gene's challenge.

Steve Bandy Senior sales engineer for a machine tool company, Steve prides himself on using his workday effectively, but he feels confident that he can think of at least twenty ways that other salespeople waste their time. He readily accepts Gene's challenge, too.

CASE 13.1 TIME IS NO OBJECT

Steve Burbank and his fiancée, Diane Boutilier, had shared a gloriously long weekend of sunbathing, swimming, boating, and gambling in Atlantic City, New Jersey. While driving back to New York City late that evening, Steve thought about how fortunate he was, at age twenty-six, to have a pretty, fun-loving fiancée and a great job that gave him a lot of independence. Steve had accepted the job with Pearson Machine Tools after graduating from the State University of New York with a degree in marketing. His first year with Pearson had been spent in training—learning about the machine tools and different customer needs. With a guaranteed salary of $48,500 for the first year and no sales pressure, Steve had enjoyed the training even though he didn't take some of it too seriously. After all, training programs always give the theoretical approach, while the real work is different—or so he thought.

Only a month ago Steve had been assigned to his own territory and on Monday would begin his first long field trip. Arriving home that evening, Steve felt mellow but tired, and he had fallen asleep without setting his alarm clock for 7:00 A.M. as he had planned in order to catch an 8:30 A.M. flight to Boston. Steve had learned about the "hopscotch" routing pattern in training, and he was going to use it this week to fly to the farthest point of his territory and then rent a car and make sales calls on the way back home.

Although he missed his 8:30 A.M. flight to Boston, Steve caught another flight about an hour later. Arriving in Boston around 10:30 A.M., he rented a car at the airport, checked into a convenient motel, and started telephoning the four accounts he planned to call on that day. After getting a busy signal on each of his first three calls, Steve decided to just drive over to the first customer's

(continued)

office, which was only twenty minutes away. On the drive over, he realized that he should have set up precise appointments for each of his customers before leaving on this trip, but he had sent out postcards the previous week informing them that he would be calling on them sometime this week.

11:00 A.M. Upon announcing his business purpose to the receptionist at his first account's office, Steve was shocked to learn that the purchasing agent, Burt Haywood, had suffered a mild heart attack two days ago and was in the hospital. No one had yet been assigned to handle Mr. Haywood's work. After expressing his sympathy and good wishes for Mr. Haywood's quick recovery, Steve decided to go to lunch because it would be nearly noon before he could make it across midday traffic to his second account.

11:30 A.M. Because he was on an expense account, Steve picked out one of the better restaurants nearby but had a fifteen-minute wait for a table. After being seated, he ordered a cocktail and the restaurant's special broiled lobster lunch. Although expensive, it was delicious, and Steve was in a better mood now, especially after a second cocktail.

1:15 P.M. Arriving at Simpson's Electronics Company, Steve found three other salespeople waiting in the reception area for Robin Wolfe, the purchasing manager. Taking a seat, Steve chatted pleasantly with Mr. Wolfe's secretary and then began reading the latest copy of *Sports Illustrated,* which he had in his briefcase. Steve always took magazines with him on sales calls to help make the waiting time go faster.

1:45 P.M. Mr. Wolfe's secretary ushered Steve into Mr. Wolfe's office, where the two engaged in light conversation. "Well, I didn't expect to see you today, Steve. How have you been?"

"Fine, Mr. Wolfe, how about yourself? Guess you saw the Lakers and 76ers basketball game on television last night. It was quite a contest. I love to see L.A. and Philadelphia play." After discussing the game for another 10 minutes, Steve asked whether Mr. Wolfe was ready yet to replace that old punch press they had talked about over the phone three weeks ago. To his dismay, Steve learned that Mr. Wolfe had bought a new machine from one of Pearson's biggest competitors, who was offering a 15 percent discount special this month. Greatly disappointed, Steve blurted out, "We've got a 20 percent discount special on our best model punch press all this month. It's the one we talked about."

"I'm sorry, Steve," replied Mr. Wolfe, "but I didn't get any promotional literature from you, so I didn't know about it. The guys in the foundry would have preferred your machine. With all the business we give you Steve, I should think you'd want to keep me better informed about upcoming deals."

"I was going to mail the promotional pieces out last week, but since I was coming down to see you this Monday, I didn't think it would be necessary," responded Steve.

2:30 P.M. Really upset about missing out on a $65,000 order, Steve consoled himself with a candy bar and a soft drink before calling on his last two accounts for the day. On the first call, he learned that Louise St. Germain—the head buyer at Crown Laboratories—had started her vacation today and wouldn't be back for two weeks. Someone was filling in for her, but that person didn't have authority to buy equipment—only supplies and maintenance items.

2:45 P.M. Telephoning his last account for the day, Steve was relieved to hear that Ken Endicott was in and would see him as soon as Steve arrived. It was only a five-minute drive, so Steve took a short coffee break.

3:15 P.M. Upon arrival, Steve and Mr. Endicott exchanged friendly greetings and light banter for a few minutes; then Mr. Endicott's secretary buzzed him. Mr. D'Arcy, the vice president of purchasing, wanted to see him immediately. Apologizing for the interruption, Mr. Endicott left but told Steve to relax and that he would probably be back within half an hour. Again Steve took out his magazine to read.

4:00 P.M. Mr. Endicott returned and told Steve that he had an emergency project to do for his boss but that he would be glad to see Steve early tomorrow morning. Although Steve had another customer scheduled for tomorrow morning, he said that would be fine and waved goodbye.

(*continued*)

4:10 P.M. Leaving Mr. Endicott's office, Steve was feeling down because it hadn't been a good day. It was already past four o'clock, so he decided against trying to reach any more customers for the day. Instead, he drove back to his motel for a quick nap before dinner. Tomorrow had to be a better day!

Questions

1. How would you evaluate Steve Burbank's management of his time and territory?
2. What would you recommend to help him improve his effectiveness and efficiency?
3. How might Pearson's training program have better prepared Steve for managing his territory?

CASE 13.2 WORKING SMARTER . . . OR JUST HARDER?

CASE 12.2 "WORKING SMARTER . . . OR JUST HARDER?" CAN BE FOUND ONLINE AT HTTP://COLLEGE.HMCO.COM/PIC/ANDERSONPS2E

CHAPTER 14

Starting Your Personal Selling Career

After reading this chapter, you should understand:

- Some of the many benefits in a personal selling career.
- Various online and off-line sources of sales jobs.
- What companies are looking for in new salespeople.
- How you may be screened for a personal selling job.
- Reasons why some candidates for sales jobs are rejected.
- Questions often asked in an interview.
- How to use the PSP to find a good job in personal selling.
- Various suggestions for preparing your résumé and cover letter.

"It is not the technical skills, hard knowledge or intelligence that makes fast track selling professionals effective in their jobs. Most of the time, it is their superior skill in handling people that propels their career, boosts productivity and ensures their job satisfaction."

Dan Brent Burt, American business writer

INSIDE PERSONAL SELLING

Meet Tere Blanca de Ulloa of Codina Realty Services

College graduates starting a career in personal sales need perseverance, discipline, and good communication skills, says Tere Blanca de Ulloa, a senior vice president at Codina Realty Services Inc., ONCOR International. As her company's most productive salesperson, de Ulloa sells and leases commercial real estate and land in Miami-Dade County, Florida. She represents owners of office buildings and land as well as tenants looking for office space. Over the years, she has found that prospective salespeople can learn effective sales techniques but often "need to polish their verbal and written communication skills," she says.

De Ulloa took a job in banking after graduating from the University of Miami with a concentration in international finance and marketing. Eighteen months later, she returned to school for a graduate degree. "The M.B.A. program gave me an overview of all the business disciplines and developed my writing and presentation skills," she says.

Then de Ulloa moved to San Diego and, at the suggestion of friends, pursued jobs in sales. Visiting the University of San Diego campus, she spotted a note on a bulletin board: "Seeking people for positions with Burroughs Corporation [now

Unisys Corporation]." De Ulloa applied, was hired, and began selling computer products to distributors after a week of sales training. Selling for Burroughs "was a terrific experience, and I developed my sales skills," she remembers. Seeking more diversity in sales contacts and wanting to apply disciplines she learned in graduate school, she looked into commercial real estate, where "each deal and client is different and finance skills are important, especially when handling investment properties."

Returning to Miami, de Ulloa was hired by Coldwell Banker Commercial Real Estate, completed its training program, and remained with the firm for about two years. The president of Codina Realty Services recruited de Ulloa when he began expanding the company fourteen years ago. Codina typically recruits through referrals, seeking candidates who have some sales experience—even in a different field. People who want to work in sales must be "absolutely hungry for the job," observes de Ulloa. "Selling is tough because you get negative reinforcement at first. When you are cold calling, the way most salespeople start, you hear 'no' from a lot of people. If you don't have discipline and perseverance, the job will not work out."

Her advice to students considering a sales career? Gain some experience in your chosen field before you graduate. "Get an internship in a company and industry that interest you," she suggests, "and try to work with the sales teams by helping with research, presentations, or marketing materials." Although an internship may not be easy to find, de Ulloa points out that successfully getting such a position demonstrates the kind of discipline and perseverance every sales professional needs.

Congratulations, you've done it! You have persevered through thirteen chapters of learning about a career in personal selling, and now you're ready to start looking for that entry-level sales position. The good news is that the very tools and skills that you've just acquired can help you effectively and efficiently look for a job and sell yourself to an employer. That's how flexible the Personal Selling Process is!

YOUR CAREER IN SALES

If you are interested in following a career path that promises you a wealth of opportunities when you graduate, we strongly suggest a job in professional selling, especially in business-to-business sales. As the critical link between a firm and its customers, successful salespeople consult with customers to better understand their businesses and problems, so that they can offer the best combination of products and services to satisfy their customers' needs. As the ultimate revenue generators, salespeople are critical to the well-being of their companies and to their country's economy in global competition. Unless products and services are profitably sold, companies cannot stay in business and their employees will lose their jobs. Thus, in many ways, every business and nearly everyone—from customers to employees—depend on the success of salespeople.

Besides its importance to revenue generation, professional personal selling offers a career opportunity that can be personally satisfying as well as financially rewarding for highly motivated men and women. Demand for sales jobs is expected to grow by 10 to 20 percent through the year 2012,[1] and a recent study reported that the average annual income across all levels of salespeople is over $100,000. For entry-level salespersons with between 0 and 3 years of sales experience, the average earnings were approximately $50,000.[2] What's more, opportunities for advancement are excellent, and the benefits are exceptional. Also, unlike a lot of jobs where you are evaluated somewhat subjectively by a superior, job performance in sales can be measured more objectively. Your career choice will play a major role in determining not only your income but also your lifestyle, success, and personal happiness. A career in sales, more than most other career options, offers an attractive, well-rounded combination of these important "quality of life" elements. As we noted in chapter 1, a sales career offers many benefits:

- high earnings potential
- job freedom and independence
- special perquisites such as a company car, company credit card, club memberships, and incentives for superior performance
- opportunities to travel and entertain customers on an expense account
- continuous job challenge and excitement
- tax deductions for home offices and other expenses not covered by the company
- opportunities to meet and interact with new and diverse people
- recognition within the company because top salespeople are the highly visible "superstars" who directly generate revenues that keep the company financially healthy. In fact, it's often said that everyone's job depends on how well salespeople do their jobs.
- fast-track opportunities for promotion all the way to the top of an organization
- jobs for diverse types of individuals with varied backgrounds and personalities to match up with diverse prospects and customers
- high mobility, because good salespeople are always in demand
- opportunities to contribute to a healthy, growing economy by solving problems and making a real difference in your customers' and your own company's "bottom line"
- multiple career paths in professional selling, sales management, or marketing management

Chapter Review Question
List some of the major benefits of a sales career.

Career Path Options

Do you remember, from chapter 1, the three major career paths branching out from personal selling? You usually begin your sales career as a sales trainee for a few weeks or months. Then you become a sales representative with a territory of your own to manage. After a few years in the field, you may have an opportunity to make a career choice: (a) professional selling, (b) sales management, or (c) marketing management. If you choose the *professional selling* path, your first promotion after *salesperson* typically will be to *senior sales representative.* After several years in this job, you may be promoted to *master sales representative.* Then, top-performing master sales reps are promoted to *national account executive* or *key account executive* with responsibility for selling to a few major customers, such as DuPont, Procter & Gamble, or Wal-Mart.[3]

If you choose the *sales management* route, you'll probably advance from *salesperson* to *sales supervisor* and then to *sales manager* at the branch, district, zone, division, or regional level.[4] From this point, you may be promoted to *national sales manager* or *vice president of sales.* The foregoing are all line sales management jobs. Another way to move into management is through the sales staff side. Staff people are needed at every sales organizational level and may hold positions in sales planning, sales promotion, sales recruiting, sales analysis, or sales training. For example, you might serve as a *sales analyst,* a *sales training manager,* or an *assistant to the sales manager.* Although people in sales management staff positions have no line authority over the sales force, they may hold impressive titles, such as *assistant national sales manager,* and they often switch over to top positions in line management.

Following success in field selling, another alternative open to a salesperson is the *marketing management* career path. This path often starts with promotion to *product or brand manager* for a product category such as Pillsbury's Hungry Jack biscuits or Procter & Gamble's Colgate toothpaste. As a product or brand manager, you're like a president of a company within a larger company. The product manager is accountable for whatever happens to Colgate toothpaste, whether good or bad, because he or she is responsible for marketing it successfully. Success in product management may lead to promotion to *director of product management* and then to *vice president of marketing* and maybe even *president and CEO.*

Chapter Review Question

What are your basic career options after serving as a successful salesperson for a few years?

Sources of Sales Jobs

Companies recruit salespeople through various *internal* and *external* sources.[5] Among the most widely used *internal sources* are employee newsletters, bulletin board announcements, and *employee referral programs,* which may offer employees a "finder's fee" to recommend potential salespeople. Current salespeople and purchasing agents are especially good sources because they know what sales jobs demand, and they hear about salespeople who are discontented and about to leave. Sometimes the company will announce to all employees that they are looking for people interested in transferring into sales. If too few qualified and interested people emerge from among present employees, the company will use *external sources* such as newspaper advertisements, employment agencies, colleges and universities, career conferences or job fairs, and professional organizations. People interested in sales careers should make a habit of reading the daily *newspapers* covering the areas in which they would like to work. The *Wall Street Journal* is a good source of quality sales jobs across the world.

Trade journals offer information on specific types of sales jobs and often have an employment section. If you have an interest in working in a particular industry, you can use a general search engine such as www.google.com to find the name of the key trade journal for that industry and then ask your college's business reference librarian to locate the current copy for you. *Private employment agencies* can sometimes help you locate sales jobs, but some charge a fee of up to 20 percent of your first year's earnings. Employers, not job seekers, will pay the agency fee for higher-caliber sales jobs. Sales Consultants (www.mriscs.com) is one of many international employment agencies that specialize in finding quality sales and marketing people. On the Internet, you can find all kinds of general job websites covering diverse job openings in the United States and around the world, as well as websites that specialize in sales jobs. Don't neglect the general websites; nearly all of them have separate listings for many sales jobs. At most of these sites, you can review job openings in the exact city or area of the country in which you'd like to work. Moreover, you can prepare and post your résumé and then send it to specific companies or even broadcast it to many companies. Some websites will send you an e-mail when a job opening appears that matches your job specifications. Some sites provide helpful *personal assessment tools*. After you complete an online self-assessment questionnaire and submit it online, you'll shortly receive a personal analysis and advice by e-mail on how to develop your sales skills further. You can even compare salaries for different jobs in various markets online. Serving as the bridge between company recruiters and individual job seekers, websites are continuously upgrading their services. Several general and specialized websites to peruse for sales jobs are identified in Table 14.1 on page 450. For example, visit one of the more popular websites at www.jobs4sales.com.

College and university campuses are most likely to be used by large companies with sales trainee programs. Campus recruiters usually do not expect you to have sales experience, and many companies even *prefer* college students who have not learned the bad selling habits that many experienced salespeople pick up. Campus placement centers can help you in setting up interviews, preparing your résumé, and providing facilities for meeting with company representatives.

Job fairs provide an excellent opportunity for students to submit their résumés and discuss career opportunities with representatives of several companies.
Viviane Moos/Corbis

TABLE 14.1

General Job Websites

www.monster.com—Contains hundreds of thousands of job listings in all fields and links to related job sites globally, including home pages of companies.

www.marketingjobs.com—Lists sales, marketing, and advertising/public relations jobs, provides direct links to companies with openings, and offers ideas and helpful books on finding employment.

www.careercity.com—Allows you to search 4 million job openings and provides links to 27,000 U.S. companies. Also has free résumé posting and comprehensive salary surveys for all fields.

www.usajobs.opm.gov—Includes a résumé builder and e-mail notification of jobs that match your criteria.

www.ajb.dni.us—(America's Job Bank)—Provides information on more than a million jobs in all fields at all levels. Allows you to create and post your résumé online.

www.diversitylink.com—Lists job opportunities from employers seeking minority candidates.

www.eop.com—Home page of Equal Opportunity Publications. Specializes in identifying job opportunities and career fairs for minority or physically challenged candidates.

www.minoritiesjobbank.com—Hosted by *Black Collegian* magazine, it offers a job and résumé bank for companies interested in a diversified workforce. Provides valuable career and specific job information to African Americans, Hispanic Americans, Asian Americans, Native Americans, and women.

www.philanthropy-journal.org—Presents a job bank for people looking for employment with nonprofit organizations.

www.espan.com—Has about 10,000 job listings that you can search by job title, company, and state. You can also post your résumé.

www.americanjobs.com—Allows you to post and send résumés free to potential employers.

www.careerpath.com—Contains classified employment ads from more than twenty large city newspapers and many smaller ones.

www.resweb.com—Offers a job data bank of more than 200,000 listings and free posting of your résumé.

www.careerweb.com—Alerts you via e-mail to job openings that match your qualifications; also includes a salary calculator and career fair information.

www.careertips.com—For those who want to pursue employment or education outside the United States.

www.nytimes.com/pages/jobs/index.html—Contains jobs listed in the *New York Times.*

www.hoovers.com—Offers various search tools such as sales development assessment questionnaires. This subscription service charges a monthly fee, although many parts of the site are free.

http://jobs.internet.com—Specializes in high-tech jobs.

http://jobs.guardian.co.uk—Has job openings in the United Kingdom.

www.overseasjobs.com—Contains international jobs.

www.bilingual-jobs.com—Is for those who speak English plus another language and are interested in working with other cultures within the United States or internationally.

Websites Specializing in Sales Jobs

www.salesjobs.com

www.nationjob.com/marketing

www.marketingjobs.com

http://sales.monster.com

www.topsalespositions.com

www.bizwiz.com/salesjobs

www.jobs4sales.com

www.nasp.com

www.sellingjobs.com

www.salesengineer.com

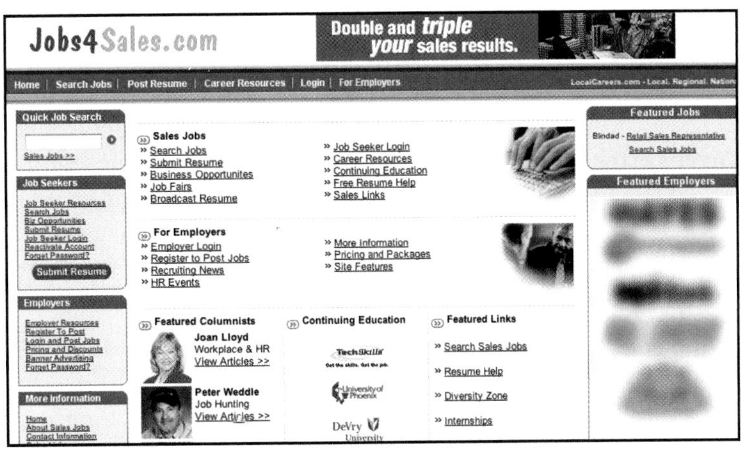

Reprinted by permission.

Cooperative education programs, offered at universities such as Drexel, Northeastern, and Cincinnati, enable undergraduate students to balance their regular classes with paid employment in their desired career field prior to graduation. A pioneer in cooperative education, Drexel has operated its cooperative education programs since 1919. Over 1,500 businesses, government agencies, and institutions located throughout the world "cooperate" with Drexel in offering students paid full-time work experience related to their college studies. Drexel's academic year is based on four terms, each three months long. Students alternate two terms of classroom study with two terms (six months) of full-time co-op employment. By working a year during the educational process, students learn what it's really like in their chosen career field, earn money to help pay for tuition when they return to school, and build impressive résumés. Students who perform well usually receive job offers, upon graduation, from the company they worked with on co-op.

Cooperative Education Programs Students combine their college studies with paid work in their career field of interest during two 6-month co-op cycles with one or more of several thousand participating companies. Students often pay for their own college education with money earned in these co-op jobs. Three universities—Drexel, Northeastern, and Cincinnati—are best known for their cooperative education programs.

Sales internship programs, offered by such companies as Procter & Gamble (www.pg.com) and Automatic Data Processing (www.adp.com), are also gaining popularity. Although you can learn much in an intern program, you usually earn no money. *Job fairs* bring hundreds of employers and job seekers together in one location for mini-interviews and for students to circulate their résumés. One organizer of job fairs, *Career Concepts,* conducts job fairs in eleven cities and charges the participating companies a fee. Professional associations, such as local chapters of the *American Marketing Association* (www.ama.org) and *Sales and Marketing Executives International* (www.smei.com), encourage students to join and interact with salesperson members. Contacts made at the meetings of such associations often lead to sales jobs. The *Marketing News,* a biweekly newspaper for AMA members, reports on the marketing profession and describes job openings in a regular section called "The Marketplace." You can learn about sales jobs from a variety of other sources, including employers, professors, friends, acquaintances, and relatives, so keep your résumé up-to-date and stay alert to all opportunities.

Sales Internship Programs Unpaid study-work programs offered to college students by several companies—for example, Procter & Gamble and Automatic Data Processing—where students learn about career opportunities.

WHAT COMPANIES LOOK FOR IN NEW SALESPEOPLE

Individual companies in different industries, large and small, look for diverse qualities in their sales recruits. At one large company, the personnel director noted, "We search for individuals who are intelligent, quick learners, problem solvers. We don't look for specific academic backgrounds. We've hired some music majors, because they have very logical minds."

Chapter Review Question

Name some online sources (websites) of sales jobs.

Cover Letter Letter that accompanies a résumé and is designed to induce employers to read the enclosed résumé. Oftentimes used by college students and others to identify the position they're applying for if they prefer not to put a job objective on their résumé.

Some companies like to hire college athletes because of their competitive drive and ability to work as a team member. It seems that every company has its own idea about what makes a successful salesperson; so learn as much as you can about the type of person a particular company likes to hire before taking an interview or even sending your résumé and **cover letter.** Clues about the type of sales candidates a company seeks can often be found in annual reports and magazine articles about the company. In general, successful sales candidates tend to have the following characteristics:

Self-Motivation

- able to explain why they selected sales as a career path
- exhibit and communicate high energy levels, indicating:
  - ability to work long and hard without discouragement
  - track record of setting and achieving meaningful goals
  - capacity to initiate action and influence events rather than being passive observers
- express thoughts and ideas clearly and directly
- organize thoughts logically
- ask insightful questions about the company
- listen attentively

Interpersonal Skills

- interact comfortably in a friendly fashion with diverse types of people in different situations
- have persuasive ability to win the confidence of others
- are flexible and adaptable to new situations
- can handle rejection and disappointments without losing confidence or effectiveness

Planning/Organizing Skills

- can establish realistic short-run and long-run objectives
- can set priorities among tasks
- can develop clear strategies to achieve objectives
- can make sound judgments and decisions based on facts[6]

Chapter Review Question

What general qualities do companies usually look for in salespeople?

HOW COMPANIES SCREEN YOU FOR A SALES JOB

Companies use a great variety of selection tools, techniques, and procedures to select candidates for their sales forces. Most companies use initial screening interviews, application forms, in-depth interviews, reference checks, physical examinations, and tests. Many firms rely heavily on application forms and job interviews, and they base most final hiring decisions on successful personal interviews—first a screening interview and then a final, in-depth interview with the sales manager to whom you will report.

Screening Interviews

The initial screening interview is the first hurdle that you must clear to be seriously considered for a sales job. You can prepare for this initial screening

TABLE 14.2

Questions Often Asked in a Screening Interview

- Why do you want to work for our company?
- What do you know about our company?
- Give me some reasons why we should hire you.
- What are your major strengths?
- What are your major weaknesses?
- What were your extracurricular activities in college?
- Were you an officer or leader of any organizations in college?
- Where do you see yourself in five years? In ten years?
- How would your friends describe you? Are they right?
- What is your greatest accomplishment to date? Why?
- What is your greatest failure to date? Why?
- Why do you think you would be a good salesperson?
- Try selling me something you see on my desk.
- What was your best subject in college? Why?
- What was your worst subject in college? Why?
- How much do you expect to earn your first year in sales with us?
- What would you like to tell me about yourself that isn't on your résumé?

by anticipating questions you might be asked and mentally preparing your response to each. Among countless questions that interviewers may ask, see how you would answer the typical ones listed in Table 14.2. In terms of employment laws, **protected groups** are people who are distinguished by special characteristics such as their race, color, ethnicity, national origin, religion, gender, age (over forty), disability, or veteran status. These particular groups are protected under federal antidiscrimination law, which mandates that people in one of these protected groups not be discriminated against in any aspect of employment, whether hiring, promotion, training, discipline, pay, or termination. State laws may protect other groups, such as individuals in certain age groups, people who smoke, and individuals with a particular sexual orientation.

Protected Groups In terms of employment laws, protected groups are people distinguished by special characteristics such as race, color, ethnicity, national origin, religion, gender, age (over forty), disability, or veteran status. These particular groups are protected under federal antidiscrimination law, which mandates that people in one of these protected groups not be discriminated against in any facet of employment—including hiring, promotion, training, discipline, pay, or termination.

Any questions asked of these protected categories of people must not have the effect of limiting job opportunities for them.[7] As shown in Table 14.3 on page 454, many questions are illegal to ask a candidate in a job interview.[8]

Employers' concerns about women becoming pregnant and taking maternity leave or having to be absent from work to take care of a sick child make female applicants for sales jobs especially subject to illegal questions by interviewers. Some potential employers have been known to use subtle means to obtain answers to illegal questions. For example, one sales manager admits that he usually takes female sales applicants out to a fine restaurant for dinner

TABLE 14.3

Questions that Interviewers Cannot Legally Ask

Subject	Illegal Questions
Age	How old are you? What is your birth date? When did you graduate from high school?
Appearance	How much do you weigh? How tall are you? What is your race or ethnic background? What is your gender?
Marital Status, Family, and Lifestyle	What is your marital status? Have you ever been divorced? Are you living with anyone? Do you plan to get married? What does your spouse do? Do you have any children? Do you plan to have children (or any more children)? Who will take care of your children while you work? What is your sexual orientation? What is your religion?
Medical	What is your medical history? Do you smoke? Do you have, or have you ever had, a drug problem? Do you have AIDS? Have you ever been treated by a psychologist or psychiatrist? Do you have a physical disability? How many days of work each year did you miss on your last job?
Military	What type of military discharge do you have? What branch of the military did you serve in? Did you receive an honorable discharge?
Home	Do you rent or own a home? Do you live in an apartment or a house? Do you have a mortgage?
National Origin	What is your native language? What is your place of birth? How did you acquire the ability to read, write, or speak a foreign language?

and then casually begins discussing his own family and how his responsibilities to them sometimes impinge on his work. In a relaxed atmosphere, this indirect approach usually causes people to open up and reveal protected information. Many women have lost job opportunities because they've talked too freely about their personal plans and the problems of raising children while pursuing a career. Finally, some company interviewers will simply ask illegal questions that put women in a no-win situation. Even though you need not answer any question unrelated to job performance, refusing to answer the illegal inquiries may alienate the interviewer and cause you to lose the job for some contrived reason.

Rationalizing that interviewers who ask unlawful questions don't deserve to be answered truthfully, some women simply lie. A divorced mother of two children, one of whom is severely handicapped, says, "Even though I'm a very reliable worker, I knew if I told the truth, I wouldn't get the job, and I needed this job badly. So I said I wasn't married—which was true—and I had no intention of having children—which is sort of true because certainly I don't plan to have any more children. I got the job. I figured that my kids were none of their business, so it didn't matter what I told them. Once I was hired, what could they do?"[9]

Chapter Review Question

Give some examples of questions that interviewers cannot ask members of protected groups.

Screening Tools and Tests

Selection tools and techniques frequently help employers spot poor candidates and identify highly qualified candidates. Most candidates, however, fall between these extremes, so the screening tools serve largely as supplements to managerial judgment in the selection process. Consultants that study salespeople, such as Boston-based McBer & Co. and Charles River Consulting, can usually predict who will fail at selling but cannot reliably predict which salesperson will do best. Nevertheless, you will probably be thoroughly analyzed, tested, and evaluated as a candidate for a sales job, especially by larger companies.

Testing. Various tests help companies increase the probability of selecting good salespeople, reduce sales force turnover, and increase sales productivity. Testing employees and job applicants had its heyday in the 1950s. Companies gathered information on prospective workers through psychological profiles, employment histories, criminal records and personal data, and tests. Use of tests in the selection of salespeople was widespread until the late 1960s. Shifting values in the 1960s and 1970s brought about the Federal Equal Employment Opportunity guidelines, which restricted employee testing unless the test could be shown to be a scientifically valid selection tool that didn't discriminate against specific racial or social groups. After passage of the Civil Rights Act in 1964, pre-employment testing of applicants dropped from about 80 percent of companies to only about 25 percent because of complaints that tests had been used to discriminate against members of minority groups.

Testing is not illegal if the questions and procedures are relevant to job performance. Small and medium-sized companies are less likely to use testing because they lack the specialized experts and employee numbers to substantiate the validity of their tests. Although most sales managers rely more heavily on the personal interview than on any other tool in selecting new salespeople, you may be asked to take one or more of several basic types of tests: (1) intelligence, (2) knowledge, (3) vocational interest, (4) sales aptitude, (5) personality, (6) polygraph, (7) attitude and lifestyle, (8) drug use, and (9) presence of the AIDS virus.

Intelligence Tests. Designed to measure the individual's ability to think and to be trained, intelligence tests include vocabulary, math, and logic questions. Scoring high on these tests still may not win you the job. Some companies have found that those who score above a certain level tend to become bored on the job, whereas those who score below a certain level have difficulty doing the job. Intelligence tests help sort out these people and thereby reduce costly salesperson turnover.

Knowledge Tests. These tests attempt to gauge how much an applicant knows about a certain market, product, service, or sales technique. Results can indicate what type and level of initial training program may be appropriate.

Vocational Interest Tests Tests designed to measure how closely an applicant's interests match the interests of other people who have successfully performed a particular job.

Vocational Interest Tests. **Vocational interest tests** attempt to measure how closely an applicant's interests match the interests of other people who have successfully performed the job. Interests are believed to be strong indicators of motivation, and a few firms have found positive relationships between interest test scores and selling success.

Sales Aptitude Tests. These tests measure an individual's innate or acquired social skills and sales ability. Numerous sales aptitude tests are available, including *Diagnostic Sales Intelligence Tests, Empathy Test, General Sales Aptitude Section of Aptitude Tests for Occupations,* and *Sales Aptitude Checklist.* Applicants for some high-tech companies are required to take an *Informational Processing Aptitude Test* to determine whether they have the ability to learn technical information.

Personality Tests. There are many complex aspects of personality, including values, social adjustment, emotional stability, temperament, and personal behavior patterns. Personality tests represent an attempt to measure the behavioral attributes believed to be important to success in selling, such as assertiveness, initiative, extroversion, and sensitivity to others. Several Fortune 500 companies use personality assessment programs to evaluate and make promotion decisions on current employees.

Yankee Gas (www.yankeegas.com), an oil and gas firm, claims to have significantly cut its high turnover rate by using a personality assessment test. Test takers are asked to review a list of phrases and adjectives, such as *life of the party, sympathetic,* and *aggressive* and to then answer two questions: "Which of these adjectives describes how you think you are expected to act by others?" and "Which of these adjectives describes who you really are?"[10]

Personality Dynamics, Inc. (PDI), a management consulting and testing firm, believes that personality has more to do with successful selling than other factors such as experience and training. PDI compares potential salespeople's answers on 179 questions such as the following:

1. If the following activities paid the same compensation and carried equal status, which would you choose? (a) representing clients in court, (b) performing as a concert pianist, (c) commanding a ship, or (d) advising clients on electronic problems.
2. Among these statements, which best describes you? (a) I don't need to be the focus of attention at parties, (b) I have a better understanding of what politicians are up to than most of my associates, or (c) I don't delay making decisions that are unpleasant.[11]

Personality tests have shown their effectiveness in the hiring of top salespeople. For instance, the financial services industry found that people who scored in the extremely high ranges of emotional intensity, recognition motivation, and assertiveness scales of the *Comprehensive Personality Profile*

(CPP) earned nearly three times as much in commissions as individuals scoring in the lowest ranges on these same scales.[12]

Polygraph Tests. Sometimes called the lie-detector test, the polygraph measures blood pressure, heartbeat, respiration, and skin reaction in response to questions as indicators of personal honesty. Because of concern about its validity,[13] federal law now severely restricts the use of polygraph testing in hiring, except for a few jobs that directly affect public safety or national security.

Attitude and Lifestyle Tests. **Attitude and lifestyle tests** became quite popular in the early 1990s because of the emergence of drug abuse as a major problem in the workplace and legislation that restricted the use of polygraph tests. Their primary purpose is to assess honesty and spot drug abusers. Typical test questions may ask how often the applicant drinks alcoholic beverages or daydreams or probe the applicant's opinions about drug use.

Attitude and Lifestyle Tests Tests that seek to assess honesty and spot drug abusers. These tests first appeared in the late 1980s when drug abuse became a major problem in the workplace and legislation restricted the use of polygraph tests.

Drug and AIDS Tests. The U.S. Chamber of Commerce estimates that drug and alcohol abuse among workers costs employers tens of billions of dollars each year in lost productivity, accidents, higher medical claims, increased absenteeism, and theft of company property to support drug habits. Today, more than 80 percent of major U.S. companies test current and prospective employees for illicit drug use. Employers are likely to require job seekers and present employees to submit samples of urine or blood for analysis. Workers are protected from surprise tests unless evidence indicates a problem or they hold high-risk jobs.

With companies afraid of wrongful-discharge lawsuits and of liability for faulty products, drug tests and other types of testing are finding increasing use as a personnel management tool. More than one-third of companies surveyed have a targeted enforcement program with surveillance, search, and detection tactics to identify abusers and dealers. Estimates are that from 4 to 10 percent of employees in any company have a substance abuse problem serious enough to merit treatment.[14] Chevron Corporation (www.chevron.com) carried out anonymous drug testing and found that about 30 percent of all job applicants and 20 percent of their employees tested positive for illegal drugs. Many large companies use urine tests to identify drug abusers among applicants or employees. As part of routine physical exams, some also check current employees and job applicants for diseases such as AIDS. Critics of drug testing argue that it violates constitutional protection against unreasonable search and seizure and invades an individual's privacy. Also, they express doubts about the accuracy of the tests, because large error rates can cause innocent people to be classified as drug abusers. Drug tests can be administered only after the company makes a job offer that is contingent on a negative test results.[15]

Personal Interviews

Many recruits will successfully pass screening interviews and testing, but the most important and final hurdle in being hired is the in-depth personal interview. Table 14.4 on page 458 shows some negative factors that frequently cause candidates for sales jobs to be rejected.

Chapter Review Question

Describe several screening tools used by employers.

TABLE 14.4

POSSIBLE REASONS FOR REJECTING SALES CANDIDATES

• Poor appearance	• Evasiveness in answering questions
• Weak interpersonal skills	• Obvious naiveté or gullibility
• Lateness for interview with no excuse	• Cynical attitude
• Poor application form or résumé	• Weak sense of humor
• Lack of goals or career plan	• Low moral standards
• Poor academic record	• Radical views
• No extracurricular activities	• Intolerance or prejudice
• Inability to express self clearly	• Evidence of wasted time
• Insufficient enthusiasm	• Poor personal hygiene
• Lack of confidence	• Laziness
• Unreasonable expectations	• Lack of ethics
• Immaturity	• Inability to accept criticism
• Tactlessness	• Dislike for schoolwork
• Discourteousness	• Arrogant attitude
• Criticisms of past employers	• Unhappy marriage
• Lack of vitality	• Poor relationship with parents
• Limp handshake	• Social ineptitude
• Unhappy social life	• Overemphasis on money
• Narrow interests	• Poor body language
• Failure to ask questions about the job	• Failure to thank interviewers for their time

Chapter Review Question

Job applicants are sometimes their own worse enemies. What are some possible reasons for rejecting job applicants?

SELLING YOURSELF TO A PROSPECTIVE EMPLOYER

With your personal services as the "product," you must convince prospective employers that they should buy your services over those of other potential candidates for the sales job. All the steps of the Personal Selling Process apply: (1) prospecting for potential employers, (2) planning your approach, (3) approaching with your résumé and cover letter, (4) making your sales presentation and demonstrating your qualifications in a personal interview, (5) negotiating resistance or persuading the employer that you are the best candidate for the job, (6) attempting to close the sale by enthusiastically asking for the job, and (7) following up to thank the prospective employer for the interview and to reinforce a positive impression. In *each* of the stages of this process of selling yourself, you should be looking for feedback from the interviewer's body language and voice inflections or tone.

A personal interview is the most popular technique for selecting salespeople.
Photo Disc

Prospecting for an Employer

After learning all about what you have to sell (your knowledge, skills, abilities, interests, motivations, and goals) and identifying the type of job you think you'd like, you might begin your Personal Selling Process by looking at the American Marketing Association's MarketingPower.com website. At this site, you'll find recommended articles and books to help you in your career planning. Probably the most famous and most widely read job-hunting book is *What Color Is Your Parachute?,* which provides insightful advice about nearly every aspect of looking for a job and planning your career. It is revised virtually every year by its author, Richard H. Bolles, so it's always up to date. Go to JobHuntersBible.com to learn more about this exceptional book, which is available in most libraries.

Sources of information about prospective employers include their annual reports (found in your college library and usually online), the annual *American Marketing Association* membership directory (company listings), telephone directories of cities where you'd like to live and work, and classified sections of the *Wall Street Journal* (online.wsj.com) or hundreds of city newspapers, which you'll find at www.onlinenewspapers.com. Before contacting a particular company, first look at its annual report, which can be useful but overly sanguine. Then find a more objective financial evaluation of the company. Two excellent sources of financial information about publicly traded companies are *Value Line* (www.valueline.com) and *Standard & Poor's* (www.standardandpoors.com). Don't hesitate to ask the business reference librarian if you need help. If you are researching only a few companies, you can obtain a list of articles on each from the *Business Periodicals Index* (BPI), which all college libraries have in hard copy and most make available online to their students free of charge. Again, check with your college's business reference librarian to find off-line and online sources.

College Placement Office. At your college placement office, find out which companies will be interviewing on campus on what dates, and then sign up for interviews with those companies that seem to best match your job skills and requirements. Usually, the college placement office has several books, pamphlets, or files that will give you leads on other prospective employers that are not interviewing on campus that term. Although campus interviews are convenient, competition can be stiff to obtain the interview time slots available with each company. Moreover, students seldom are offered a job without follow-up interviews with more senior managers at company headquarters. These headquarters interviews may take a full day or more and may involve long-distance trips, so you will need to schedule your interviewing time carefully.

Job hunting can be expensive. Printing your résumé, typing cover letters, buying envelopes and stamps, making long-distance telephone calls, incurring travel expenses, and purchasing a new suit or two will require a sizable outlay of money. Although most companies eventually reimburse you for all expenses incurred on a company visit, they seldom pay in advance. Reimbursement can take several weeks.

Networking. According to Forrester Research, about 40 percent of all successful job searches come from networking.[16] People you already know or will meet can help you find a good job. You can cultivate all kinds of people as part of your networks, including any or all of the following: family members, friends, relatives, co-workers, past employers, teachers and professors, fellow students, and service providers such as your family doctor, dentist, lawyer, realtor, or insurance agent. Give each of them a copy of your résumé, tell them the kind of job you're looking for, and then periodically follow up to let them know you're still looking. Of course, you don't want to become a nuisance, but most understand what you're going through and will want to help as much as they can.

When you receive referrals from your networking, use your source as an introduction to the potential employer. For example:

> Hello, Mr. Peterman, my name is Bruce Hopkins. Our mutual friend Chuck Addison suggested I call you about interviewing with your company for a sales job. First, let me convey Chuck's good wishes to you and your family. He said that you and he worked in the same sales office at IBM about ten years ago and that I should tell you that he's now nearly a scratch golfer. And if you believe that, he's got a piece of swamp land he wants to sell you. But the reason for my call, Mr. Peterman, is that Chuck said you were a great guy and that you might be able to help me obtain an interview.

Just as in a sales call, it's always an advantage to have a referral, because it turns a cold call into a warm call. Even if referrals don't have a job opportunity for you, ask whether they might help you with another referral. Sometimes, you can keep going from referral to referral until you make the sale—that is, win the job.

You might even try some networking online by using a website such as the *National Association of Sales Professionals* (www.nasp.com), which includes a registry of member sales representatives—many of whom allow direct e-mail access to them. Approaching any of these sales professionals (whom you've never met) via e-mail will require diplomacy and sincerity—not a shotgun approach to looking for a job. Perhaps you could ask some of them for advice about starting your sales career.

Employment Agencies. Although many employment agencies receive fees from employers for providing good job candidates, others charge job seekers (sometimes thousands of dollars or up to 20 percent of the first year's salary) for helping them find jobs. Make sure you fully understand the fee arrangement before signing up with an employment agency. Some employment agencies may not be worth your time or money because they use a programmed approach to helping you write your résumé and cover letter and to prospect for potential employers. Potential employers have seen these "canned" formats and approaches so many times that your personal advertisement (your résumé and cover letter) will appear almost indistinguishable from others.

The Hidden Job Market. Up to 90 percent of available jobs may neither be advertised nor reach employment agency files,[17] so creative resourcefulness often pays off in finding the best jobs in the **hidden job market**. Consider every reasonable source for leads. Sometimes your professors, deans, college administrators, or classmates can give you names and contact persons at companies looking for new graduates. Do not be reluctant to let other people know that you're looking for work. Classmates, friends, and business associates of your family can often help—if not directly, then at least by serving as an extra pair of eyes and ears alert to job opportunities for you.

Hidden Job Market About 90 percent of available jobs are never advertised and never reach employment agency files, so job applicants must be creative and resourceful in competing for these jobs.

Planning Your Approach

After identifying potential employers looking for people with your abilities and interests, you need to prepare a *résumé* (or personal advertisement) for yourself. An excellent source of help in preparing your résumé is MarketingPower.com, where you'll find American Marketing Association recommendations regarding articles (e.g., "Components of a Winning Resume" and "Ten Resume Mistakes," both by Peter Newfield) and books (e.g., *The Adams Resume Almanac,* by Bob Adams Publishers, and *Resumes for Higher Paying Positions,* by Cory J. Schulman). Of course, you can find scores of other articles on résumé preparation listed in the *Business Periodicals Index,* and there are numerous books on résumés in your college library, your college bookstore, commercial bookstores, and city libraries. Find two or three that communicate in the style you prefer, and then let them guide you in writing the first draft of your résumé.

Preparing Your Résumé. Your résumé should focus on your achievements to date, your educational background, your work experience, and your special abilities and interests. If you know what job you want (such as sales representative for a consumer products company), you may put your *job objective* near the top of your résumé. If you're unsure what job you want or if you wish to send out the same résumé for several different jobs, then you can describe your job objective in your *cover letter.*

No one format is correct for your résumé. Three basic formats are widely used: (1) chronological, (2) functional, and (3) combined. Using the chronological approach, you would present your schooling, employment, achievements, and activities in order, starting with the most recent. The functional approach places primary emphasis on your accomplishments, skills, and strengths instead of on your chronological history. Using the combined approach, you would stress your skills first and then follow with your employment history, which may or may not be directly related to the job for which you're applying.

No matter which résumé format you use, a little tasteful creativity can help differentiate your résumé from countless look-alike résumés (this is similar to product differentiation in marketing). Most résumés of new college graduates are only one page long, but you may go to a second page if you have something important to present. One student so blindly followed the one-page résumé rule that he left off having served as an army officer—a fact that is usually viewed very positively by prospective employers, especially if the applicant had leadership responsibilities or gained valuable work experience. To find ideas for preparing your résumé and posting it on the Internet, check out www.marketingingjobs.com and www.collegegrad.com.

Track Record of Achievement. Some students make the mistake of merely listing their job responsibilities with different employers, without indicating what they accomplished on the job. When looking for a job, students must remember that employers are looking for a *track record of achievement,* and you must distinguish yourself from those who may have had the same assigned job responsibilities but performed poorly. If you made a positive contribution on a job, say so on your résumé—in quantitative terms if possible. Examples:

- Reorganized office files to reduce staff searching time by nearly 20 percent
- Named employee of the month
- Awarded $500 for an innovative customer service suggestion
- Increased sales in my territory by 10 percent
- Received a 15 percent raise after three months on the job
- Promoted to assistant store manager after four months

If your work experience is minimal, consider a "functional" résumé where you emphasize your special skills (e.g., organizational, interpersonal, or leadership) and personal attributes (e.g., resourcefulness, perseverance, and goal orientation). But be sure to give supporting evidence or examples of these skills and attributes whenever you can. An example of a succinct résumé is provided in Table 14.5.

References. Note that the sample résumé shown in Table 14.5 does not include the usual "References furnished upon request" at the bottom. All employers know this, and such obvious statements just take up valuable space on your résumé. When potential employers do ask for recommendations, you are probably close to being hired, so assist those who will write your letters of

TABLE 14.5

Sample Résumé

CATHERINE JAMES

4111 Sandy Drive
Ocean View, MD 21758
(301) 898-0001 Telephone
(301) 898-0000 Fax
semajc@hotmail.com

Job Objective: Salesperson for a high-tech company

Education

Drexel University, Philadelphia, Pennsylvania

Earned B.S., with honors, in Marketing Management (June 2006). Dean's List last three semesters. Overall GPA = 3.4/4.0

Activities and Honors

Vice President, Beta Gamma Sigma (business administration honorary for top 10 percent of class); Treasurer, Phi Omega Chi Sorority; varsity women's basketball team, 2003–2006; advertising manager for student newspaper, *Drexel Triangle.* Selected to *Who's Who Among American College Students, 2005–2006.*

Work Experience

Summer 2005—Telemarketing Sales Supervisor, Gibson Kitchens, Inc.

Supervised a telemarketing sales team of seven people contacting homeowners about remodeling their kitchens. Increased sales 25 percent over previous summer's record.

Summer 2004—Assistant Sales Representative, Reynolds Food Company.

Traveled with sales representative throughout northern Maryland territory. Set up displays, inventoried stocks, and restocked store shelves. Received cash bonus when sales in our territory were highest in the company during June–August.

Summer 2003—Field Salesperson, Carver Towels, Inc.

Sold $25,400 in bathroom and kitchen towels door-to-door in Baltimore, Maryland, area. Selected to "Carver Achiever Club" for meeting sales quota three straight months.

Hobbies and Interests

Golf, tennis, jogging, and reading biographies

recommendation for you. You can obtain reference letters from current or former employers, professors, members of the clergy, or any other "established" adult who can attest to your personal qualities, skills, and achievements. Before giving a potential employer the names of any references, make sure you have received their permission to list them as a reference for you. Today, references are often contacted by e-mail or telephone; however, some companies still prefer to have two or three letters of recommendation for you in their files. To help busy people in writing a recommendation or serving as a reference for you, give each a copy of your résumé and cover letter, and provide answers for the basic questions that most employers will ask, such as the following:

- How long and under what circumstances have you known the candidate?
- In what percentile (25th, 50th, 75th, 95th, 99th) would you rank this candidate in terms of the following qualities: interpersonal skills, writing ability, speaking ability, listening ability, goal orientation, maturity, energy level, adaptability, resourcefulness, willingness to cooperate with others, and integrity? *[Rating yourself will help the individual if he or she doesn't interact enough with you to evaluate some of these qualities. You can explain that you thought that he or she would appreciate your own appraisal!]*
- What do you see as the candidate's major strengths and abilities?
- In which areas do you think the candidate could use more development?
- What is your overall assessment of the candidate's likelihood of succeeding as a business-to-business salesperson for our company?
- What other comments might you add that could help us in evaluating the qualifications and potential of this candidate?

[Perhaps you can suggest something unique here that isn't normally asked in standardized recommendation forms. For example, you can provide an example of your dedication and "quick-study" abilities by explaining how you worked with Habitat for Humanity in Mexico one summer and learned conversational Spanish by studying the language in the evening and speaking it during the day.]

Electronic Résumés
Many large companies now use computer software to receive, sort, store, and retrieve résumés from job applicants, so that they can later scan thousands of résumés in a matter of minutes to find the best candidates for a job opening.

Chapter Review Questions
Why are electronic résumés increasingly used to match up job seekers and employers?

Electronic Résumés. Many large companies now use computer software to receive, sort, store, and retrieve **electronic résumés** from job applicants so that they can later scan thousands of résumés in a matter of minutes to find the best candidates for a job opening. For instance, a company may need a woman who is fluent in English and Chinese, with an undergraduate chemical engineering degree, and two or more years of experience working in mainland China, to open up a new sales office there. Candidates who match these requirements can be found quickly in the company's database of résumés. Thus it's important that your résumé include key words associated with your education, work experience, skills, achievements, personal qualities, and interests. Some websites will ask you to select the key words for your qualifications and for the type of employment you're seeking. You can post your résumé for employers at most of the websites listed near the beginning of this chapter. Before posting your résumé to any website, go to MarketingPower.com and use some of the resources offered there, such as a *free* résumé evaluation.

Posting your résumé online can be a great job search advantage because it extends the life of your résumé before potential employers. Instead of being filed away or thrown away, résumés are now placed in large company data banks for two years or more of potential retrieval when a job opening becomes available. If you're interested in a particular company, go to its website to see whether it has an online résumé submission process. Of course, many colleges and universities are now putting their graduating students' résumés online for potential employers to scan.

Cover Letters. Every time you send your résumé to a prospective employer, you should accompany it with a *cover letter* to induce employers to read your enclosed résumé. The typical cover letter is reviewed by the addressee for only a few seconds, so you need to make your key points powerfully and succinctly—so that they almost jump out at the reader. In preparing your cover letter, keep the following basic guidelines in mind.

Many companies receive, sort, store, and retrieve electronic résumés from job applicants.
David Sachs/Getty Images

- Address your letter to a specific person by name (not just a job title or position).
- Clearly identify the position you're applying for, where you found out about it (e.g., which website or publication), and why you are interested in that position.
- Keep your focus on what you can do for the company, not on what you want from the company.
- Look for a special tie-in (e.g., you're a long-time user of the company's products) that indicates one reason why you are particularly interested in working for this company.
- Do not overuse self-centered words, such as *I, me,* and *my.*
- Avoid starting too many sentences with *the.*
- Keep your language conversational, not overly stiff and formal.
- Include any follow-up action you plan to take—such as a telephone call or e-mail—and when you'll be calling or e-mailing. *(Some students are uncomfortable about this, but gracious assertiveness is usually respected.)*
- Thank the addressee for considering you for the position and say that you look forward to hearing from him or her.
- Sign the letter with a medium point pen in black or blue ink.
- Fold your letter neatly, leaving about an inch border at the top, so that it can easily be unfolded by the addressee.
- Make your letter less than a page long, print it on high-quality paper, and mail it in a business-size envelope of similar quality.
- To cut down on competition, consider sending your résumé to fast-growing smaller companies (e.g., the ones ranked and described at least annually in *Inc.* magazine) instead of limiting yourself to the well-known giant companies to which students graduating from schools all over the world send their résumés.

Chapter Review Question
What is the purpose of a cover letter? Cite some guidelines for preparing and sending a cover letter.

Together, your cover letter and résumé are your direct-mail selling piece and personal advertisement to win a job interview. Although you must not be dishonest or even hyperbolic about stating your accomplishments, you cannot afford to be modest either, because most potential employers scan résumés in twenty seconds or less. Your résumé must stand out in a positive way from the thousands of others that most companies receive each year. Some Fortune 500 companies receive thousands of résumés each week from job applicants, and most are discarded readily because they don't make a strong, positive impression. Creative formats, clever envelopes, or innovative enclosures have helped some job applicants' résumés be selected for further consideration. But résumé formats that are too bizarre usually merit only a chuckle before they're discarded.

In writing your cover letter, keep in mind your goal of convincing the prospective employer to grant you an interview. Therefore, you must express yourself in terms of the employer's interests, not just your own. You are answering the question "Why should we hire you?" You may need to send a letter with your résumé enclosed to a hundred or more companies to obtain five to ten interviews, so do not be discouraged if you receive encouraging replies from only a few companies. You'll probably need only a few interviews and just one job offer to start your career.

Review some of the publications and sources mentioned under the heading "Prospecting for an Employer" on page 459, and ask your business reference librarian to show you other sources where you can learn about the prospective employer so that you can tailor your cover letter effectively. Remember, the employer is thinking in terms of his or her company needs, not yours. A sample cover letter is provided in Table 14.6 on page 467.

Making Your Approach

You can approach prospective employers by mail, by telephone, or in person. A personal contact within the company who can arrange an interview for you will enable you to avoid competing head-on with the many other candidates looking for a job with the company.

Most students start their approach in the traditional way, by mailing their résumé and cover letter to the company's recruiting department. Unless your résumé matches a particular need at that time, however, it will probably be filed away for possible future reference or simply discarded. Some students send their letter by express mail or address it to a key line executive (e.g., Mr. Sanford Biers, Vice President of Marketing), with *personal* written on the envelope. They believe that bypassing the company's personnel office will increase the likelihood of their cover letter and résumé being read by someone with authority to hire. A senior executive may forward your résumé without comment to personnel, where it might receive special attention because it came down from the top. Who knows, maybe you're the boss's niece? Some executives will like your chutzpah and tell personnel to schedule you for an interview, although others may resent your attempt to beat the system and reject you from consideration.

Giving Your Sales Presentation and Demonstration

Your personal sales presentation will occur during the interview with the prospective employer's recruiting team. You'll want to make a positive impression on everyone you encounter in the company—even while waiting in the lobby for an interview. Sometimes managers ask their receptionists and secretaries for their opinions of you. Your friendliness, courtesy, professional demeanor, personal habits, and even the magazines you choose to read while waiting can be positive or negative. It will not impress your potential

TABLE 14.6

SAMPLE COVER LETTER

May 19, 2006

Catherine James
4111 Sandy Drive
Ocean View, MD 21758

Ms. Elizabeth Burton
Sales Manager
Sampson Office Furniture Company
141 Market Avenue
Philadelphia, PA 19106

Dear Ms. Burton:

For nearly thirty years, my father has been buying Sampson chairs, desks, and filing cabinets for his law office. So I know firsthand what high-quality products you sell. My career interest is in sales, and I would rather work for Sampson than any other company.

This June, I graduate from Northern Maryland State University with a B.A. in marketing management, and I would like to apply for a job as a sales representative with your company. After successfully working in sales during all three of my summer jobs, I have learned that my interests and abilities are well suited for professional selling. My college course electives (*Personal Selling, Sales Management, Public Speaking, Business Writing, and Public Relations*) have been carefully selected with my career objective in mind. My extracurricular activities in sports and campus organizations have also helped prepare me for working with a variety of people and competitive challenges.

Will you grant me an interview so that I can show you that I'm someone you should hire for your sales team? I'll call you next Monday afternoon to arrange an appointment at your convenience.

I look forward to meeting you.

Sincerely,

Catherine James

Enclosure: Résumé

employer if you read a popular magazine such as *People* or *Sports Illustrated*. Better to be observed reading something more professional, such as *Business Week, Fortune,* or the *Wall Street Journal*.

Even if calamity befalls you, conduct yourself with class and good humor. One graduating student who was interviewing with a company spilled coffee on her light-colored suit during her first interview of the day. But she conducted herself with such aplomb throughout the rest of the day, even though her clothes were visibly stained, that the company hired her. Her ability to handle such an awkward situation confidently and pleasantly impressed all of the company executives with whom she interviewed.

During the interview, go beyond mere responses to the interviewer's questions. Ask some sensible questions of your own to indicate to the interviewer that you are alert, energetic, and sincerely interested in the job. The personal interview is your opportunity to persuade the prospective employer that you should be hired. To use a show business analogy, you will be on stage for only a short time (during the personal interview), so present an honest but positive image of yourself. You will find it easier to be alert and enthusiastic if you imagine that you are being interviewed on television. A little anxiety can be positive, but be careful not to let this "television interview" scenario make you too nervous to do your best. It's a good idea to anticipate and prepare general answers to questions frequently asked by interviewers, such as those noted in Table 14.7.

Sometimes interviewers will ask you to *demonstrate* your communication abilities by writing a timed essay about your life or to "sell something" (such as a desk stapler) to them. Others may deliberately ask you off-the-wall or hostile questions to see how you respond. Interviewers at one Fortune 500 company routinely ask candidates for sales jobs simple math questions (such as "What's 8 percent of eighty-five?") to see whether they can think under pressure. Another favorite technique of some interviewers is to ask questions like "If you could be any kind of fruit, what would it be and why?" They are probably more interested in observing how candidates respond to the unexpected than in assessing creativity or sense of humor (although these can't hurt).

Microsoft Corporation is known for asking seemingly off-the-wall questions during interviews to observe a candidate's thinking process: "How many piano tuners are there in Chicago?" "About how many manhole covers do you think there are in Manhattan?" "If I dropped a ten-pound bowling ball off the side of a ship in the deepest part of the Pacific Ocean, about how long would it take to hit bottom?" Interviewers aren't looking for a precise answer to these questions, and they certainly won't be impressed if you make some wild guess. Instead, they want you to walk through your problem-solving approach, because what they are really interested in discovering about you is how well you analyze and solve problems. For example, with regard to how many piano tuners are in Chicago, you should first estimate (if you don't know) how many people live in Chicago, one of the three or four largest cities in the United States. Then, about how many households would this population probably represent? Next, approximately what percent of these households would have a piano that's played regularly, and about how often would these pianos be tuned? Next you'd want to make an assumption as to how many pianos can be tuned by one skilled person in a normal working day. After gathering all the relevant facts, you can use simple math to produce a ballpark estimate of the number of piano tuners in Chicago. As a capstone, you might say, "Finally, I'd go to the phonebook and count how many piano tuners were listed." Just remember to keep calm and confident during any unorthodox interviewing approaches (even if the interviewer becomes hostile), and you will come off well.

On aptitude and psychological tests, many experts say that it isn't difficult to "cheat" if you are able to "play the role" and answer like the type of person that the company is looking to hire. The so-called safe approach in most personality and preference (interest) tests is to avoid extreme positions on anything not clearly associated with the job you're applying for. However, it is probably in your long-run best interests to be honest in your responses so that you create no unrealistic expectations that you cannot fulfill. It is just as important that you create a true impression and avoid beginning your sales career with a company that isn't right for you.

TABLE 14.7

Questions Frequently Asked in Interviews

- Why do you want to work for our company?
- Tell me what you know about our company.
- Tell me about yourself—your strengths, weaknesses, and career goals.
- Is any member of your family a professional salesperson? If so, what does she or he sell?
- Why do you want to start your career in sales?
- In three minutes, persuade me that we should hire you.
- What extracurricular activities do you participate in at college?
- What leadership positions do you hold or have you held?
- What benefits have you derived from participation in extracurricular activities that will help you in your career?
- Where do you see yourself within our company in five years? In ten years? Twenty years?
- What is your ultimate career goal?
- What do you consider your greatest achievement to date?
- What has been your biggest failure to date?
- What is your favorite subject in school? Why?
- Are you willing to travel and possibly relocate?
- How would your friends and associates describe you?
- How would you describe yourself?
- What do you like most about selling?
- What do you like least about selling?
- If we hire you, how soon can you start work?
- What is the minimum pay you would accept to work in our company?

Chapter Review Question
List some questions frequently asked by interviewers.

As a checklist for preparing for the interview, make sure you have done all of the following things:

- Find out the time and place of the interview and make sure you know how to get there. If driving, use one of the websites that provides driving directions from one address to another, e.g., maps.yahoo.com or www.mapquest.com.
- Learn the interviewer's name and how to pronounce it.
- Research the company before the interview.
- Have at least three good questions to ask during the interview.
- Make sure that you dress appropriately for the job for which you're interviewing.
- If you're going for a luncheon interview, do not order anything sloppy (such as spaghetti or soup) that could spill on your clothes. If you're

unsure about which fork to use first, wait until your host has picked up the silverware and take your cue from him or her.

Dealing with Resistance and Objections

Sometimes interviewers will bluntly ask, "Why should we hire you?" This requires you to think in terms of the employer's needs and to present your major "selling points" or customer benefits. Other interviewers may bring up reasons why you are not the ideal candidate: (a) "We're really looking for someone with a little more experience" or (b) "We'd like someone with a more technical educational background" or (c) "We need someone to start work within two weeks." These kinds of statements are similar to *objections* or requests for additional information. In other words, the interviewer is saying: "Convince me that I shouldn't rule you out for this reason."

To overcome such objections, you might respond to each along the following lines: (a) "I've had more than a year's experience working with two different companies during my cooperative education jobs, and I worked part-time with a third company all during college. I'm a fast learner and I adapted well to each of the three companies. I believe that my varied working experience is equivalent to three or four years of experience with the same company"; (b) "Although I didn't choose to earn a technical undergraduate degree, I've taken several technical courses in college, including basic engineering courses, chemistry, physics, and two years of math, so I have a blend of technical and managerial education. I'm confident that I can quickly learn whatever is necessary technically to do the job"; (c) "Well, I do have one more term of school, so I couldn't start full-time work in two weeks, but perhaps we could work out an arrangement where I could work part-time during the evenings or on weekends until I graduate."

Chapter Review Question

What are some typical objections that interviewers cite as contributing to their not considering a job applicant for a job? How might you respond to each of these objections?

Good salespeople do not allow an objection to block a sale. Providing reasonable solutions or alternative perspectives can often overcome employer resistance and objections—or at least allow room for further negotiation toward a compromise solution.

Confirming the Agreement or Receiving the Job Offer

Although it is not likely that a prospective employer will offer you a job right on the spot, you should nevertheless let the interviewer know that you definitely want the job and are confident that you will do excellent work for the employer. You'll need to use your best judgment as to whether or not to use other closing techniques, such as the *summary close* or *standing-room-only* close. For example, with the summary close, you can summarize those of your strong points that match up with the company's needs to reinforce in the interviewer's mind that you are right for the job. The standing-room-only close (where you let the prospective employer know that you have other job offers and will need to make a decision within a limited time) may be appropriate when you sense that the employer is impressed with you and needs a little push to offer you the job now rather than interviewing more candidates. This puts the ball in the prospective employer's court to come up with a good offer quickly or risk losing you to another company.

Following Up

Within a few days after any job interview, whether you want the job or not, business courtesy requires you to write thank-you letters to interviewers. In this letter, you can reinforce the positive impression you made in the interview and again express your strong interest in working for the company. If you don't hear back from the company about the job within a few weeks, it may be appropriate to write another letter expressing your continuing interest in the job and asking for a decision so that you can consider other options if necessary. As a possible reason for this follow-up letter, you might mention something you have achieved since the interview, more fully answer one of the interviewer's questions, or perhaps send a newspaper or magazine article of interest. A well-written, gracious follow-up letter gives you a chance to make a stronger impression on the interviewer, while exhibiting several positive personal qualities such as initiative, written communication skills, sensitivity to others' feelings, and awareness of business protocol. A checklist for sending follow-up letters is provided in Table 14.8.

TABLE 14.8

Checklist for Follow-Up Letters

After an Interview:

- Express your thanks for the interviewer's time and courteous treatment.
- Provide answers to any questions that you couldn't answer during the interview—for example, your exact college graduation date.
- Clarify any misconceptions.

To Accept the Job:

- Confirm your acceptance of the job, even if you have already done so by telephone or in person.
- Restate your understanding of the employment agreement—for example, the day and time to start the job, the job title, the salary, and other important aspects of the agreement.

To Turn Down a Job Offer:

- Express thanks for the offer, and indicate that you were impressed with the company and the people you met, including the interviewers.
- Graciously decline the offer and give an acceptable reason.
- Extend good wishes for the future to the company and its employees.

When the Company Turns You Down for a Job:

- Never show that you're upset or angry.
- Politely express your regret that no job is currently available for you.
- Ask whether you might be considered for future employment with the company.
- Ask for advice on how you can improve your qualifications to better fit the company's criteria for hiring new employees.

YOUR EARLY SALES CAREER

Even though you want to choose a company that you will stay with throughout your working life, it is only realistic to recognize that you will probably work for more than one company during your career. If you are not fully satisfied with your job or company during the first few years, remember that you are building experience and job knowledge that will increase your abilities and marketability for future job opportunities. Stay on top of the rapidly changing sales field by becoming a member of *Sales and Marketing Executives-International* (www.smei.org), where you can interact with other professionals across industries. When you join SMEI, you gain access to its Executive Library at www.smei.org/msmindex.cfm, where there are thousands of articles about sales and marketing, as well as a great deal of sales-related statistics and news.

Always keep a positive outlook and do the best you can in every job assignment, and your chances for new opportunities will come. Do not be too discouraged by mistakes that you may make in your career. Nearly every highly successful person has made and continues to make many mistakes. View these mistakes largely as *learning experiences,* and they will have less impact on your confidence. Believe that you can probably do whatever you make up your mind to do—because it's true. Best wishes to you for a successful and satisfying sales career!

SUMMARY

You can use your knowledge of the Personal Selling Process to make that first big sale: selling your personal services to an employer. With a college degree, you offer much to potential employers, so use your selling strategies and skills to make them aware of the benefits you offer to their company. Preparing your résumé and drafting an effective cover letter are major initial steps in selling your services. Use all the help available online and offline from books, articles, and associates to evaluate your cover letter and résumé; then fine-tune them.

Either in your cover letter or your résumé, identify the position or job you're seeking. Many potential employers receive hundreds, if not thousands, of résumés every week, so you are less likely to obtain an interview if you leave it to the potential employer to figure out what job in their company your qualifications would fit best. Instead, most will simply discard your résumé and go on to those that do indicate a job objective. When your résumé is at the quality level you want, it's a good idea to post it online, where potential employers can find it. Because employers use key words for their job opening to match with key words identifying your qualifications, the key words you choose to describe your credentials and desired job are critical.

When you have successfully sold yourself via your cover letter and résumé, you will receive some invitations for job interviews. In preparation for these job interviews, make sure you have a basic sales presentation on why you want to work for the company and what benefits you're offering. Prepare and rehearse your general answers to the typical questions that interviewers ask, but also prepare for some of the seemingly off-the-wall questions they may ask to observe how you go about solving difficult problems.

Practice your interviewing strategy and tactics with a friend, and ask for honest feedback about how to improve. Before, during, and after the job interview, make sure you are courteous and considerate in all interactions with gatekeepers (e.g., guards, secretaries, and administrative assistants) or anyone else you meet at the company, especially interviewers. Your behavior is always being closely observed when you are interviewing. For example, what you read and how you behaved while waiting in the reception area will probably be noticed by a secretary or security guard who may later be asked what he or she thought about you. Exhibit a gracious and friendly but professional demeanor even while waiting for your first interview. Although you're on stage throughout the interviewing process, try to stay relaxed and confident.

After the interview, gracious follow-ups in writing or by telephone, or both, will reinforce your desire for the job, allow you to add important information not covered in the interview, and show that you understand business etiquette. Few job applicants receive a job offer after every interview, but you will substantially improve your chances for success if you carefully follow each of the personal selling steps and use your sales skills. Good luck, we're pulling for you!

KEY TERMS

Cooperative Education Programs	Cover Letter	Vocational Interest Tests	Hidden Job Market
Sales Internship Programs	Protected Groups	Attitude and Lifestyle Tests	Electronic Résumés

TOPICS FOR THOUGHT AND CLASS DISCUSSION

1. If you post your résumé online, the websites often ask you to provide key words that will help potential employers looking for people with your qualifications. Come up with five key words that best describe your qualifications for a sales job.
2. How might you positively differentiate your cover letter and résumé from the thousands of others posted online or sent through the mail to prospective employers?
3. What activities would make you thoroughly prepared for a job interview at a company for which you'd like to sell?
4. Have you ever been turned down for a job? For what reason do you think you were turned down?
5. Why do you think that most graduating college students from around the world tend to overlook sending their cover letters and résumés to smaller companies? What do you think are the advantages and disadvantages in working for a small company?
6. If you were hiring new college graduates to become salespeople for a company that you owned, what criteria would you use to select candidates?
7. What screening tools do you think would be most effective in selecting candidates for sales jobs?

INTERNET EXERCISES

1. Use an Internet search engine to find additional advice on how to embark on and manage a successful career in selling.
2. Get an early start on charting your career. Using an Internet search engine, peruse some of the websites identified in Table 14.1 to find

examples of sales job openings, job descriptions, and salary potential. Identify the different categories of sales careers you found.

3. Use the Internet to find information on sales job postings and on the current and future career trends in the industry that you would like to work in. What does your research indicate about sales job opportunities? Should you pursue your sales career only in the industry in which you would like to work or modify it to include other sales fields?

PROJECTS FOR PERSONAL GROWTH

1. Prepare three different cover letters to accompany your résumé, and ask several of your friends and a professor to pick out the best one. Ask them why they chose that one.
2. Prepare your résumé using each of the three formats: chronological, functional, and combined. Which of the three formats do you think will be most effective in obtaining your desired job? Ask two professors to pick out the résumé format they consider best for you to (1) mail to prospective employers and to (2) post online. Did they choose the same format for each? If not, ask them why they chose a different format for each channel.
3. Ask one of your friends to help you rehearse interviewing for a sales position. Tell your friend first to ask you challenging and even off-the-wall questions; then ask him or her to put you on the defensive or raise objections to hiring you. Analyze your performance with your friend to determine how you might have done better.

ROLE-PLAY EXERCISE 14.1

Selling Yourself in the Job Interview

Situation

Steve Ko, a second-generation Asian American, is interviewing for a job as a missionary salesperson with Purity Products, Inc., a pharmaceutical manufacturer that sells and promotes its products to wholesalers, pharmacies, hospitals, and medical practices. Mr. Ko is receiving his degree in chemistry from a large northwest state university in four months, and he has heard from professors and others that personal selling is one of the best ways to make a great deal of money, especially for someone with a technical degree.

Roles

Steve Ko Extroverted and confident in a very palatable way, Steve thinks he would enjoy missionary sales because there is no emphasis on selling products and he believes he could talk comfortably with professionals such as doctors and pharmacists. As he understands it, all he must do is influence the decision to buy or recommend his company's pharmaceuticals by educating physicians, pharmacists, and wholesale buyers about his company's products. Steve wants to make sure that missionary selling will be right for him. His father and mother have already expressed disappointment that he is considering sales; they had hoped he would become a chemist or physician. Even if he decides later that he doesn't want the job, Steve wants to do his best to make a good impression.

Donald Montgomery District sales manager for Purity Products, Donald believes that he can tell whether someone will be good in sales no more than fifteen minutes into an interview. He asks very pointed questions to get at candidates' attitudes, perceived strengths and weaknesses, overall self-concepts, long- and short-run goals, and personality type.

ROLE-PLAY EXERCISE 14.2

How Do You Keep Motivated?

Situation

After graduating from college, Jean Hieber has been a sales rep for a curtain rod and fixtures manufacturer for about five months. In the past two months, she has become increasingly frustrated and depressed because she is working very hard but achieving only average sales success in her New England sales territory. When traveling her territory overnight, she seems to become especially melancholy after dinner when she goes back to her hotel room and watches television or listens to radio music. Jean and her fiancé, an architect, expect to be married in another year when both their careers have stabilized. Jean is concerned that she may want to change jobs before that time and that this will probably delay their wedding date. This morning, while waiting in the office of a prospect, Jean met Ben Kolberg, a sales rep for a line of paint products. They talked for several minutes and agreed to meet for dinner tonight, because they were both staying in the same hotel. Ben impressed Jean as being very nice and as someone who really loves his job. Perhaps, she thought, Ben could give me some tips on how to keep one's morale and motivation high.

Roles

Jean Hieber Like a lot of new salespeople, Jean is off to what she thinks is a slow start in sales. Her morale is faltering, and she doesn't seem to know how to perk up her spirits and empower herself to have a positive outlook. At dinner, she plans to ask high-spirited Ben a lot of questions about what he does each day to motivate himself.

Ben Kolberg Ben's friendly, enthusiastic, and confident attitude is obvious to everyone he meets. He seems to have some special inner strength or insight that makes him feel good about himself, about other people, and about his work. Ben has noticed that Jean seems a little down in the dumps, and he thinks he can help. A married man with two beautiful preschool children, Ben truly enjoys life and his work, and he sincerely wants to help others whenever he can.

CASE 14.1 DEVELOPING STRATEGIES TO OBTAIN A GOOD JOB

Aaron Shipley expects to earn his degree in marketing from the University of Florida about five months from now. Aaron has earned close to a B average during his last two years in college after earning mostly Cs during his freshman and sophomore years. His grades suffered somewhat during the first two years because Aaron tried out for the baseball team, and the sport demanded a lot of his time. Although he made the varsity team as a pitcher, he was hit by a broken bat and suffered a bad bone chip in his arm during the next-to-last game of his sophomore year. After several months of treatment, the doctor told Aaron that he should stop playing baseball in order to avoid the risk of doing permanent damage to his arm. Aaron was depressed for several months until he met Amata Ventura, a bright, pretty, and personable woman who sat beside him in personal selling class during the first term of his junior year. After they dated for a few months, Aaron and Amata both felt that they had met the one they wanted to marry. With Amata supporting him, Aaron really began to focus on earning good grades. They both earned As in the personal selling class, and Aaron thought it might be a good way to start his business career. Amata wanted to try advertising.

(*continued*)

Now, although he was born and raised in New York City, Aaron wants a job near San Francisco after graduation because he fell in love with the city after visiting it on spring break two years ago. Amata, who lives in Miami, thinks it would be great to live in California, too. Only months away from graduation, Aaron is busy preparing his résumé and cover letter to send to prospective employers. Amata has already prepared her résumé and cover letter and has had two interviews with prospective employers.

Aaron is discussing his résumé with Amata over coffee at the local Starbucks and asks her advice.

AARON: Amata, do you think it would make sense for me to put some subtle hints that I'm African-American on my résumé?

AMATA: Sure, Aaron, I think it could help. A lot of companies still don't seem to have many African-American managers, and some even advertise that they're looking for minority candidates. Under activities on your résumé, you could include that you were vice president of the Campus African-American Club, and you could also mention your coordination of last year's Dr. Martin Luther King, Jr. Day activities.

AARON: Yeah, guess you're right. I'll make sure I add those items to my résumé. But, what about you? You're a member of a minority group, too.

AMATA: I think it's pretty obvious that I'm Hispanic-American by my last name, don't you? Even my first name, Amata, is Spanish. Of course, I'm a double minority because I'm also a woman, in case you haven't noticed.

AARON: Believe me, I've noticed.

AMATA: You know that stuff we learned in our personal selling class about our being members of protected groups? Well, in both of my interviews so far, I've been asked illegal questions. Right after shaking hands at my first interview, the interviewer said, "What a pretty name? What nationality is that?" That was okay, because I wanted her to know that I'm from Central America. But later, she asked me if I had a boyfriend and whether we planned to marry soon.

AARON: Well, what did you say?

AMATA: I told her the truth, Aaron, that I had a boyfriend and that we were planning to marry this summer.

AARON: I'm not sure that was wise, Amata.

AMATA: Well, I didn't want to lie, especially if I might wind up taking a job at the company.

AARON: Have they gotten back to you yet?

AMATA: No, they haven't. It's been almost three weeks now, and I really wanted that job.

AARON: Amata, I'm afraid you lost that job opportunity when you told the interviewer that you and I were going to be married soon.

AMATA: I had no choice. If I had told her that she was asking illegal questions, I'm sure that would have just upset her, and I would have lost the job anyway. Some "protection" I have! Interviewers can ask me anything they want, and I have no options in responding except to lie—and you know that's not me, Aaron.

AARON: I know, Honey. That's one reason I love you so much. There's nothing dishonest or deceitful about you. But frankly, if they ask me illegal questions in my interviews, I'm going to give them the answers that will help me get the job. Amata, what happens if an interviewer asks if I've ever been arrested? Do you think I'm going to admit that I was arrested at sixteen for underage drinking and using a false I.D.? No way. That would probably kill my chances for the job. If interviewers are going to play the interviewing game illegally, then I have the right to be dishonest.

AMATA: Aaron, who wants a job that you have to lie to interviewers to get?

AARON: Well, I do, if it's in California! Once I'm hired, I can probably put in a few words to the right person to get you hired, too. Then we'll be working together. Wouldn't that be great? Imagine driving in to work together each day.

AMATA: I don't know, Aaron. It's seems like that would be starting off on the wrong foot for a new job. They may find out later that you lied.

AARON: Yeah, but it'll be too late then. And they'll soon see that I'm a top performer, so they're going to be happy they hired me—and you. They'll be calling us the dynamic duo. Okay, let's not worry about it now, Amata. Let me buy you lunch at your favorite restaurant.

Questions

1. What do you think about Amata's responses to the illegal questions about future marriage plans asked by the interviewer? Why would an interviewer ask such illegal questions? Do you think that many employers ask illegal questions during interviews? Will Amata's unwillingness to lie help or hurt her in securing a job? Why?
2. What do you think about Aaron's plans to give the interviewers the answers they want in order to win the job? Do you think giving false answers to questions during pre-employment interviews will hurt Aaron later, after he's hired? Why?
3. What would you do if an interviewer at a company for which you wanted to work asked you an illegal question? What if the question was "Have you ever been arrested?" and you had had an experience similar to Aaron's with the police?
4. What options does an interviewee have when an interviewer asks illegal questions?
5. Is it more difficult for women than for men to be honest in an interview when illegal questions are asked? Why?

CASE 14.2 A TALE OF THREE "BROTHERS"

CASE 14.2 "A TALE OF THREE 'BROTHERS'" CAN BE FOUND ONLINE AT HTTP://COLLEGE.HMCO.COM/PIC/ANDERSONPS2E

NOTES

Chapter 1

[1] *Marketing News* (September 15, 2004): 16.

[2] For an interesting discussion about what personality characteristics are related to college students' perceptions of selling task attractiveness, see Charles D. Stevens and Gerrard Macintosh, "Personality and Attractiveness of Activities Within Sales Jobs," *Journal of Personal Selling & Sales Management* 23 (Winter 2002-2003): 23–38.

[3] Frederick Reichheld and Earl Sasser, Jr., "Why Satisfied Customers Defect," *Harvard Business Review* (November-December 1995): 88.

[4] For more perspectives, see: Patricia J. Daugherty, Theodore P. Stank, and Alexander E. Ellinger, "Leveraging Logistics/Distribution Capabilities: The Effect of Logistics Service on Market Share," *Journal of Business Logistics* 19 (1998): 35–51; Eric R. Blume, "Customer Service: Giving Companies the Competitive Edge," *Training & Development Journal* (September 1988): 25; Frederick F. Reichheld, Robert G. Markey, Jr., and Christopher Hopton, "The Loyalty Effect—The Relationship Between Loyalty and Profits," *European Business Journal* (2000): 134–139; Srini S. Srinivasan, Rolph Anderson, and Kishore Ponnavolu, "Customer Loyalty in E-Commerce: An Integration of Its Antecedents and Consequences," *Journal of Retailing* 78 (2002): 41–50; Rolph Anderson and Srini S. Srinivasan, "E-Satisfaction and E-Loyalty: A Contingency Framework," *Psychology and Marketing*, 20 (2003): 122–138.

[5] For an interesting discussion about the development of selling as a profession, see Jon M. Hawes, Anne K. Rich, and Scott M. Widmier, "Assessing the Development of the Sales Profession," *Journal of Personal Selling & Sales Management* 24 (Winter 2004): 27–37.

[6] John T. Molloy, *Molloy's Live for Success* (New York: Bantam Books, 1983), p. 87.

[7] www.sellingpower.com/magazine/abstract/v25n3_abstract.asp (April 20, 2005).

[8] Rolph Anderson, "Personal Selling and Sales Management in the New Millennium," *Journal of Personal Selling and Sales Management* 16 (Fall 1996): 17–32.

[9] See Gilbert A. Churchill, Neil M. Ford, Steven W. Hartley, and Orville C. Walker, "The Determinants of Salesperson Performance: A Meta-Analysis," *Journal of Marketing Research* 22 (May 1985): 117.

[10] "Thriving on Order," *INC.* (December 1989): 49.

[11] Thomas N. Ingram, Keun S. Lee, and George H. Lucas, "Commitment and Involvement: Assessing a Salesforce Typology," *Journal of Academy of Marketing Science* 19 (Summer 1991): 187–197.

[12] Philip Kotler and Gary Armstrong, *Principles of Marketing* 10th ed. (Englewood Cliffs, N.J.: Prentice-Hall, 2004), p. 16.

[13] F. G. "Buck" Rodgers, *The IBM Way: Insights into the World's Most Successful Marketing Organization* (New York: Harper & Row, 1985).

[14] Alan J. Dubinsky, Lawrence B. Chonko, Eli P. Jones, and James A. Roberts, "Development of a Relationship Selling Mindset: Organizational Influencers," *Journal of Business-to-Business Marketing* 10 (No. 1, 2003): 1–30; Robert Saxe and Barton A. Weitz, "The SOCO Scale: A Measure of the Customer Orientation of Salespeople," *Journal of Marketing Research* 19 (August 1982): 343–351; Michael R. Williams and Jill S. Attaway, "Exploring Salespersons' Customer Orientation as a Mediator of Organizational Culture's Influence on Buyer-Seller Relationships," *Journal of Personal Selling and Sales Management* 16 (Fall 1996): 33–52.

[15] Gary L. Hunter, "Information Overload: Guidance for Identifying When Information Becomes Detrimental to Sales Force Performance," *Journal of Personal Selling & Sales Management* 24 (Spring 2004): 91–100.

[16] Michael A. Humphreys and Michael R. Williams, "Exploring the Relative Effects of Salesperson Interpersonal Process Attributes and Technical Product Attributes on Customer Satisfaction," *Journal of Personal Selling and Sales Management* 16 (Summer 1996): 47–57; Charles H. Schwepker, "Customer-Oriented Selling: A Review, Extension, and Directions for Future Research," *Journal of Personal Selling & Sales Management* 23 (Spring 2003): 151–171.

[17] Lawrence Crosby, Kenneth Evans, and Deborah Cowles, "Relationship Quality in Services Selling: An Interpersonal Influence Perspective," *Journal of Marketing* 54 (July 1990): 68–81; Devon Johnson and Kent Grayson, "Cognitive and Affective Trust in Service Relationships," *Journal of Business Research* 58 (April 2005): 500–507.

[18] Kotler, 2000.

[19] William C. Moncrief, "Selling Activity and Sales Position Taxonomies for Industrial Salesforces," *Journal of Marketing Research* 23 (August 1986): 261–270.

[20] For an alternative view of the seven-step selling process, see William C. Moncrief and Greg W. Marshall, "The Evolution of the Seven Steps of Selling," *Industrial Marketing Management* 34 (2005): 13–22.

[21] Richard E. Plank and David A. Reid, "The Mediating Role of Sales Behaviors: An Alternative Perspective of Sales Performance and Effectiveness," *Journal of Personal Selling and Sales Management* 14 (Summer 1994): 43–56.

[22] Frederick Reichheld and Earl Sasser, Jr., "Why Satisfied Customers Defect," *Harvard Business Review* (November-December 1995): 88; Frederick F. Reichheld, Robert G. Markey, Jr., and Christopher Hopton, "The Loyalty Effect—The Relationship Between Loyalty and Profits," *European Business Journal* (2000): 134–139.

[23] James L. Heskett, Thomas O. Jones, Gary W. Loveman, W. Early Sasser, Jr., and Leonard A. Schlesinger, "Putting the Service-Profit Chain to Work," *Harvard Business Review* (March-April 1994): 165–166; Rebecca Piirto Healt, "Loyalty for Sale: Everybody's Doing Frequency Marketing—But Only a Few Companies Are Doing It Well," *Marketing Tools* (July 1997): 65; Kenneth Carlton Cooper, "The Relational Enterprise," *Customer Relationship Management* (July 2002): 42–45.

[24] Stephanie Bernardo, Elizabeth Meryman, Hanna Rubin, and Judith D. Schwartz, "Superstars of Selling," *Success!* (November 1984): 34–35.

[25] Amy Sallee and Karen Flaherty, "Enhancing Salesperson Trust: An Examination of Managerial Values, Empowerment, and the Moderating Influence of SBU Strategy," *Journal of Personal Selling & Sales Management* 23 (Fall 2003): 299–310.

[26] Steven P. Brown and Robert A. Peterson, "The Effect of Effort on Sales Performance and Job Satisfaction," *Journal of Marketing* 58 (April 1994): 70–80; Steven P. Brown, William L. Cron, and John W. Slocum, "Effects of Trait Competitiveness and Perceived Intraorganizational Competition on Salesperson Goal Setting and Performance," *Journal of Marketing* 62 (October 1998): 88–98.

[27] Sean Dwyer, Orlando Richard, and C. David Shepherd, "An Exploratory Study of Gender and Age Matching in the Salesperson Prospective Customer Dyad: Testing Similarity-Performance Predictions," *Journal of Personal Selling and Sales Management* 18 (Fall 1998): 55–69.

[28] Leslie M. Fine and Sarah Fisher Gardial, "The Effects of Self-Monitoring and Similarity on Salesperson Inferential Processes," *Journal of Personal Selling and Sales Management* 10 (Fall 1990): 7–16.

[29] F. B. Evans, "Selling as a Dyadic Relationship—A New Approach," *American Behavioral Scientist* 6 (May 1963): 76–79. Other studies supporting Evans's results include M. S. Gadel, "Concentration by Salesmen on Congenial Prospects," *Journal of Marketing* 28 (April 1964): 64–66; Arch G. Woodside and J. W. Davenport, Jr., "The Effect of Salesman Similarity and Expertise on Consumer Purchasing Behavior," *Journal of Marketing Research* 11 (May 1974): 198–202; Edward A. Riordan et al., "The Unsold Prospect: Dyadic and Attitudinal Determinants," *Journal of Marketing Research* 14 (November 1977): 530–537; Lawrence A. Crosby, Kenneth R. Evans, and Deborah Cowles, "Relationship Quality in Services Selling: An Interpersonal Influence Perspective," *Journal of Marketing* 54 (July 1990): 68–81.

[30] J. David Lichtenthal and Thomas Tellefsen, "Toward a Theory of Business Buyer–Seller Similarity," *Journal of Personal Selling and Sales Management* 21 (Winter 2001): 1–14.

[31] Herbert M. Greenberg and Jeanne Greenberg, "Job Matching for Better Sales Performance," *Harvard Business Review* (September-October 1980): 128–133; Robert J. Zimmer and Paul S. Hugstad, "A Contingency Approach to Specializing Industrial Sales Force," *Journal of Personal Selling and Sales Management* 1 (Spring/Summer 1981): 27–35.

[32] William A. Cron, Alan J. Dubinsky, and Ronald E. Michaels, "The Influence of Career Stages on Components of Salesperson Motivation," *Journal of Marketing* 52 (January 1988): 78–92.

[33] Alan J. Dubinsky, Roy D. Howell, Thomas N. Ingram, and Danny N. Bellenger, "Salesforce Socialization," *Journal of Marketing* 50 (October 1986): 192–207.

Chapter 2

[1] For more insights on sales force automation, see Michael Fielding, "Four Technologies That B-to-B Marketers Can Leverage Now," *MarketingNews* (May 1, 2005): 13–14; Stephen Baker and Heather Green, "Blogs Will Change Your Business," *Business Week* (May 2, 2005): 56–67; Updated from Rolph E. Anderson, "Personal Selling and Sales Management in the New Millennium," *Journal of Personal Selling and Sales Management* 16 (Fall 1996): 17–32; Cheri Speier and Viswanath Venkatesh, "The Hidden Minefields in the Adoption of Sales Force Automation Technologies," *Journal of Marketing* 66 (July 2002): 98–111; Devon S. Johnson and Sundar Bharadwaj, "Digitization of Selling Activity and Sales Force Performance: An Empirical Investigation," *Academy of Marketing Science Journal* 33 (Winter 2005): 3–18.

[2] C. Murphy and M. Hayes, "Tag Line: Wal-Mart Put a Date on RFID Implementation: January 2005," *Information Week* (June 16, 2003): 18–20.

[3] For varied perspectives, see Alma Mintu-Wimsatt and Jule B. Gassenheimer, "The Problem Solving Approach of International Salespeople: The Experience Effect," *Journal of Personal Selling and Sales Management* 24 (Winter 2004): 19–25; Christopher B. Clott, "Perspectives on Global Outsourcing and the Changing Nature of Work," *Business and Society Review* 109 (June 2004): 153–170; Victoria D. Bush and Thomas N. Ingram, "Building and Assessing Cultural Diversity Skills: Implications for Sales Training," *Industrial Marketing Management* 30 (January 2001): 65; Victoria D. Bush, Greg Rose, Faye Gilbert, and Thomas N. Ingram, "Managing Culturally Diverse Buyer–Seller Relationships: The Role of Intercultural Disposition and Adaptive Selling in Developing Intercultural Communication Competence," *Journal of the Academy of Marketing Science* 29 (Fall 2001): 391–404; Kenneth R. Evans, Roberta Schultz, and David Good, "Intercultural Interaction Strategies and Relationship Selling in Industrial Markets," *Industrial Marketing Management* 28 (November 1999): 589–599.

[4] L. Mark Rivers and Jack Dart, "The Acquisition and Use of Sales Force Automation by Mid-Sized Manufacturers,"

Journal of Personal Selling and Sales Management 19 (Spring 1999): 59–73.

[5] Walter S. Mossberg, "Tiger Leaps Out in Front," *Wall Street Journal* (April 28, 2005): B1, B3.

[6] *Sales & Marketing Management*, "How Technology Is Changing Business Travel," (June 2001): 68.

[7] SellingPower.com, *Incentives Newsletter,* September 27, 2001.

[8] http:///www,gartber,cin/5_about/press_room/pre20010313a.html: "Worldwide Business-to-Business Internet Commerce to Reach $8.5 Trillion in 2005"; http://www.clickz.com/stats/sectors/b2b/article.php/475401: Michael Pastore, "To B2B or Not to B2B? That Is the Question."

[9] Stephen Baker and Heather Green, "Blogs Will Change Your Business," *Business Week* (May 2, 2005): 56–67; Michael Fielding, "Four Technologies That B-to-B Marketers Can Leverage Now," *Marketing News* (May 1, 2005): 13–14; http://learn-what-is-a-blog.blogspot.com/; http://nebogroup.com/services/business_blogging/

[10] Michael Fielding, "Four Technologies That B-to-B Marketers Can Leverage Now," *Marketing News* (May 1, 2005): 13–14.

[11] http://www.webex.com/pr/pr192.html, 4/29/2005: "WebEx Communications Services Selected by AstraZeneca for Multimedia Web Meetings"; http://www.webex.com/services/sales-center.html, 4/29/2005: "In Sales, Time Is Money."

[12] George J. Avlonitis and Despina A. Karayanni, "The Impact of Internet Use on Business-to-Business Marketing," *Journal of Business Research* 29 (September 2000): 441–459.

[13] Michael Fielding, "Four Technologies That B-to-B Marketers Can Leverage Now," *Marketing News* (May 1, 2005): 13–14.

[14] Julie Bennett, "Selling Technology Can Be a Taxing Task and Top Salespeople Are Tough to Find," *Wall Street Journal* (April 5, 2005): B7.

[15] Ibid.

[16] Don Peppers, "Banking on Strong Customer Relationships," *Inside 1to1* (March 16, 2000): www.1to1.com/publications.

Chapter 3

[1] William A. Stimson, "A Deming-Inspired Management Code of Ethics," *Quality Progress* (February 2005): 67–68.

[2] Kim McMurtry, "e-Cheating: Combating a 21st Century Challenge," *Technological Horizons in Education Journal Online*, http://www.thejournal.com/magazine/vault/articleprintversion.cfm?aid=3724 (November 2001).

[3] Erin Anderson and Barton A. Weitz, "Determinants of Continuity in Conventional Industrial Channel Dyads," *Marketing Science* 8, 4 (Fall 1989): 310–323.

[4] Amy Sallee and Karen Flaherty, "Enhancing Salesperson Trust: An Examination of Managerial Values, Empowerment, and the Moderating Influence of SBU Strategy," *Journal of Personal Selling and Sales Management* (Fall 2003): 23, 299–311.

[5] Clarke L. Caywood and Gene R. Laczniak, "Ethics and Personal Selling: *Death of a Salesman* as an Ethical Primer," *Journal of Personal Selling and Sales Management* 5 (August 1986): 81–88.

[6] "Firms Making Ethics a Part of Corporate Life," *Mobile Register* (April 16, 1995): 6F.

[7] Carl McDaniel and Robert Gates, *Contemporary Marketing Research*, 2nd ed. (Cincinnati, OH: South-Western, 1993): 223–226.

[8] Michele Marchetti, "Whatever It Takes," *Sales & Marketing Management* (December 1997): 29–38.

[9] Sergio Roman and Salvador Ruiz, "Relationship Outcomes of Perceived Ethical Sales Behavior: The Customer Perspective," *Journal of Business Research*, 58 (April 2005): 439–445.

[10] J. Brock Smith and Donald W. Barclay, "The Effects of Organizational Differences and Trust on the Effectiveness of Selling Partner Relationships," *Journal of Marketing* 61 (January 1997): 3–21.

[11] Thomas R. Wotruba, "A Comprehensive Framework for the Analysis of Ethical Behavior, with a Focus on Sales Organizations," *Journal of Personal Selling and Sales Management* 10 (Spring 1990): 30.

[12] Alan J. Dubinsky, Rajan Nataraajan, and Wen-Yeh Huang, "The Influence of Moral Philosophy on Retail Salespeople's Ethical Perceptions," *Journal of Consumer Affairs* 38 (Winter 2004): 297–319.

[13] Joseph A. Bellizzi and Ronald W. Hasty, "The Effects of a Stated Organizational Policy on Inconsistent Disciplinary Action Based on Salesperson Gender and Weight," *Journal of Personal Selling and Sales Management* 21 (Summer 2001): 199–206; Shelby D. Hunt and Arturo Z. Vasquez-Parraga, "Organizational Consequences, Marketing Ethics, and Salesforce Supervision," *Journal of Marketing Research* 30 (February 1993): 78–90.

[14] G. A. Churchill, N. M. Ford, and O. C. Walker, *Sales Force Management* (Chicago: Irwin, 1997), 63.

[15] Alan Dubinsky, Marvin Jolson, Ronald Michaels, Masaaki Kotabe, and Chae Un Lim, "Ethical Perceptions of Field Sales Personnel: An Empirical Assessment," *Journal of Personal Selling and Sales Management* 12 (Fall 1992): 9–21.

[16] For additional perspectives, see Frederick Trawick, John Swan, and David Rink, "Industrial Buyer Evaluation of the Ethics of Salespersons' Gift-Giving, Value of the Gift, and Customer vs. Prospect Status," *Journal of Personal Selling and Sales Management* 9 (Summer 1989): 31–37.

[17] Jeff Gammage and Karl Stark, "Under the Influence," *Inquirer Magazine* (March 10, 2002): 10.

[18] Betsy Cummings, "Do Customers Hate Salespeople?" *Sales & Marketing Management* (June 2001): 44–51.

[19] biz.yahoo.com/ap/050506/vioxx.html?.v=6; For a detailed account, see: www.democrats.reform.house.gov/features/vioxx/documents.asp; Catherine Arnst, "When Patients Say: Don't Ban My Drug," *Business Week* (April 25, 2005): 40–41; John Carey, "Side Effects of the Drug Scares," *Business Week* (March 7, 2005): 42–44; John Carey, "The Vioxx Fallout on the Hill," *Business Week* (February 7, 2005): 47; John Carey, "How to Prevent Another Vioxx," *Business Week* (December 13, 2004): 42.

[20] Edward C. Baig, "Progress in Online Privacy, But Critics Say Not Enough," *Business Week Online*, www.businessweek.com (May 13, 1999).

[21] Nick Wingfield, "A Marketer's Dream: The Internet Promises to Give Companies a Wealth of Invaluable Data About Their Customers. So Why Hasn't It?" *Wall Street Journal*, interactive.wsj.com (December 7, 1998).

[22] Dubinsky et al., 1992.

[23] Ajay K. Kohli and Bernard J. Jaworski, "The Influence of Coworker Feedback on Salespeople," *Journal of Marketing* 58 (October 1994): 82–94.

[24] "Discrimination Because of Sex Under Title VII of the Civil Rights Act of 1964 as Amended: Adoption of Final Interpretive Guidelines," U.S. Equal Employment Opportunity Commission Part 1604, *Federal Register* (November 10, 1980).

[25] Sexual harassment does not occur solely between employees in the same organization; it also occurs between buyers and sellers. See Leslie M. Fine, C. David Shepherd, and Susan L. Josephs, "Insights into Sexual Harassment of Salespeople by Customers: The Role of Gender and Customer Power," *Journal of Personal Selling and Sales Management* 19 (Spring 1999): 19–34.

[26] Betsy Cummings, "An Affair," *Sales & Marketing Management* (August 2001): 50–57.

[27] For more insights on sexual harassment issues, see Cathy Owens Swift and Russell L. Kent, "Selling and Sales Management in Action-Sexual Harassment: Ramifications for Sales Managers," *Journal of Personal Selling and Sales Management* 14 (Winter 1994): 77–87; Leslie M. Fine, C. David Shepherd, and Susan L. Josephs, "Sexual Harassment in the Sales Force: The Customer Is NOT Always Right," *Journal of Personal Selling and Sales Management* 14 (Fall 1994): 15–30.

[28] Banning K. Lary, "Why Corporations Can't Lock the Rascals Out," *Management Review* (October 1989): 51–54.

[29] Ken Grant, David Cravens, George Low, and William Moncrief, "The Role of Satisfaction with Territory Design on the Motivation, Attitudes, and Work Outcomes of Salespeople," *Journal of the Academy of Marketing Science* 29 (Spring 2001): 165–178.

[30] Thomas E. DeCarlo and Thomas W. Leigh, "Impact of Salesperson Attraction on Sales Managers' Attributions and Feedback," *Journal of Marketing* 60 (April 1996): 47–66.

[31] Lucette B. Comer, J. A. F. Nicholls, and Leslie J. Vermillion, "Diversity in the Sales Force: Problems and Challenges," *Journal of Personal Selling and Sales Management* 18 (Fall 1998): 1–20.

[32] For other perspectives on ethical and moral judgments by salespeople, see Lawrence B. Chonko, John F. Tanner, Jr., and William A. Weeks, "Ethics in Salesperson Decision Making: A Synthesis of Research Approaches and an Extension of the Scenario Method," *Journal of Personal Selling and Sales Management* (Winter 1996): 35–52; and Richard Tansey, Gene Grown, Michael Hyman, and Lyndon Dawson, Jr., "Personal Moral Philosophies and the Moral Judgment of Salespeople," *Journal of Personal Selling and Sales Management* (Winter 1994): 59–76.

[33] Alan R. Andreasen, "Revisiting the Disadvantages: Old Lesson and New Problems," *Journal of Public Policy and Marketing* (Fall 1993): 270–275; Judith Bell and Bonnie Maria Burline, "In Urban Areas: Many More Still Pay More for Food," *Journal of Public Policy and Marketing* (Fall 1993): 268–270.

[34] *The Economist* (April 22, 2000): 67.

[35] Sean Valentine and Tim Barnett, "Ethics Code Awareness, Perceived Ethical Values, and Organizational Commitment," *Journal of Personal Selling and Sales Management*, 23 (Fall 2003): 359–368.

[36] Dubinsky et al., 1992.

[37] William A. Weeks, Terry W. Loe, Lawrence B. Chonko, and Kirk Wakefield, "The Effect of Perceived Ethical Climate on the Search for Sales Force Excellence," *Journal of Personal Selling and Sales Management* 24 (Summer 2004): 199–214.

[38] "Executives Are Surveyed on Bribery," *Wall Street Journal* (May 15, 2002): A12.

Chapter 4

[1] Al Ries and Jack Trout, *Marketing Warfare* (New York: McGraw-Hill, 1997).

[2] Jay Conrad Levinson, *Guerrilla Marketing : Secrets for Making Big Profits from Your Small Business*, 3d ed. (Boston: Houghton Mifflin, 1998); Jay Conrad Levinson and Seth Godin, *The Guerrilla Marketing Handbook* (Boston: Houghton Mifflin, 1994).

[3] Thomas Ginsberg, "Glaxo Seeks Cease-Fire in 'Arms Race' in Sales," *Philadelphia Inquirer* (February 11, 2005), C1.

[4] Bernard M. Bass, "Personal Selling and Transactional/Transformational Leadership," *Journal of Personal Selling and Sales Management* 17 (Summer 1997): 19–28.

[5] William C. Moncrief and Greg W. Marshall, "The Evolution of the Seven Steps of Selling," *Industrial Marketing Management* 34 (2005): 13–22.

[6] For discussions of prospecting methods not included here, see Alan J. Dubinsky, "A Factor Analytic Study of

the Personal Selling Process," *Journal of Personal Selling and Sales Management* 1 (Fall/Winter 1980–1981): 26–33; Sean Dwyer, John Hill, and Warren Martin, "An Empirical Investigation of Critical Success Factors in the Personal Selling Process for Homogeneous Goods," *Journal of Personal Selling and Sales Management* 20 (Summer 2000): 151–159.

[7] Marvin A. Jolson, "Prospecting by Telephone Prenotification: An Application of the Foot-in-the-Door Technique," *Journal of Personal Selling and Sales Management* 6 (August 1986): 39–42.

[8] George A. Norris, "We Asked Our Readers to Respond to This Question: How Do You Get Qualified Referrals?" *Advisor Today* 96 (October 2001): 92.

[9] Tricia Campbell, "What's a Referral Worth to You?" *Sales & Marketing Management* (September 1997): 103.

[10] Sarah Lorge, "The Best Way to Prospect," *Sales & Marketing Management* (January 1998): 80.

[11] "Leads Are a Terrible Thing to Waste," *Sales & Marketing Management* (August 1997): 108.

[12] John Nemac, "How to Use Referrals to Generate Greater Sales," *The American Salesman* 45 (January 2000): 10–13.

[13] Bradley S. O'Hara, "Evaluating the Effectiveness of Trade Shows: A Personal Selling Perspective," *Journal of Personal Selling and Sales Management* 13 (Summer 1993): 67–77.

[14] Generating Electronic Sales Leads," *Sales & Marketing Management* (August 1996): 93.

[15] Anonymous (2002), "What Is CRM?" http://www.destinationcrm.com/articles/default.asp?ArticleID=1747; William G. Zikmund, Raymond McLeod, Jr., and Faye W. Gilbert, *Customer Relationship Management: Integrating Marketing Strategy and Information Technology* (New York: Wiley, 2003); Jill Dyche, *The CRM Handbook: A Business Guide to CRM* (Reading, Mass: Addison Wesley Professional, 2002); Arthur Middleton Hughes, *The Customer Loyalty Solution* (New York: McGraw-Hill, (2003); Glen Urban, *Digital Marketing Strategy: Text and Cases* (Englewood Cliffs, N.J.: Prentice-Hall, 2004); Ronald Swift, *Accelerating Customer Relationships: Using CRM and Relationship Techniques* (Englewood Cliffs, N.J.: Prentice-Hall PTR, 2001); Roland T. Rust, Katherine Lemon, and Das Narayandas, *Customer Equity Management* (Englewood Cliffs, N.J.: Prentice-Hall, 2005).

[16] Melinda Nykamp, "CRM: What It's Really All About," *The Customer Differential* (2001): 1–11.

[17] "Virtual Prospecting," *Business Week*, Industrial-Technology Edition, Spring 2001; Jill Dunman, "Striking Gold," *Customer Relationship Management* (November 2001): 59–60.

[18] Sean Dwyer, John Hill, and Warren Martin, "An Empirical Investigation of Critical Success Factors in the Personal Selling Process for Homogenous Goods," *Journal of Personal Selling and Sales Management* 20 (Summer 2000): 151–159.

[19] Marvin A. Jolson and Thomas R. Wotruba, "Prospecting: A New Look at This Old Challenge," *Journal of Personal Selling and Sales Management* 12 (Fall 1992): 59–66.

[20] Lee Iacocca with William Novak, *Iacocca: An Autobiography* (New York: Bantam Books, 1984), pp. 39–40.

Chapter 5

[1] William C. Moncrief and Greg W. Marshall, "The Evolution of the Seven Steps of Selling," *Industrial Marketing Management* 34 (2005): 13–22.

[2] Adapted in part from Charles Futrell, *Fundamentals of Selling: Customers for Life Through Service*, 9th ed. (New York: McGraw-Hill/Irwin, 2006).

[3] Arun Sharma, "The Persuasive Effect of Salesperson Credibility: Conceptual and Empirical Examination," *Journal of Personal Selling and Sales Management* 10 (Fall 1990): 71–80.

[4] Jon M. Hawes, Kenneth E. Mast, and John E. Swan, "Trust-Earning Perceptions of Sellers and Buyers," *Journal of Personal Selling and Sales Management* 9 (Spring 1989): 1–8.

[5] Lucette B. Comer and Tanya Drollinger, "Active Empathetic Listening and Selling Success: A Conceptual Framework," *Journal of Personal Selling and Sales Management* 19 (Winter 1999): 16–17.

[6] Don Beveridge, "The Seeds of Success," *Industrial Distribution* (July 1999): 78.

[7] Marvin A. Jolson, "Prospecting by Telephone Prenotification: An Application of the Foot-in-the-Door Technique," *Journal of Personal Selling and Sales Management* 6 (August 1986): 39–42.

[8] Douglas M. Lambert, Howard Marmorstein, and Arun Sharma, "The Accuracy of Salespersons' Perceptions of Their Customers: Conceptual Examination and Empirical Study," *Journal of Personal Selling and Sales Management* 10 (Winter 1990): 1–9.

[9] Willem Verbeke and Richard P. Bagozzi, "Sales Call Anxiety: Exploring What It Means When Fear Rules a Sales Encounter," *Journal of Marketing* 64 (July 2000): 88–101.

[10] Betsy Cummings, "Do Customers Hate Salespeople?" *Sales & Marketing Management* (June 2001): 50.

[11] Oscar W. DeShields Jr., Ali Kara, and Erdener Kaynak, "Source Effects in Purchase Decisions: The Impact of Physical Attractiveness and Accent on Salespersons," *International Journal of Research in Marketing* (February 1996): 89–101.

[12] Tony L. Henthorne, Michael S. LaTour, and Alvin J. Williams, "Initial Impressions in the Organizational Buyer-Seller Dyad: Sales Management Implications," *Journal of Personal Selling and Sales Management* 12 (Summer 1992): 57–66.

[13] Alan J. Dubinsky, "A Factor Analytic Study of the Personal Selling Process," *Journal of Personal Selling and Sales Management* 1 (Fall/Winter 1980–1981): 26–33.

[14] "If You Get Lemons, . . .," SellingPower.com, *Most Memorable Sale* (October 19, 2001).

[15] Carolee Boyles, "3-D Show and Tell," Selling Power.com, *Sales Management Newsletter* (October 16, 2001).

[16] Robert B. Cialdini, "Harnessing the Science of Persuasion," *Harvard Business Review* 79 (October 2001): 72–79.

[17] Jennifer M. George, "Salesperson Mood at Work: Implications for Helping Customers," *Journal of Personal Selling and Sales Management* 18 (Summer 1998): 23–30.

[18] Peter Schulman, "Applying Learned Optimism to Increase Sales Productivity," *Journal of Personal Selling and Sales Management* 19 (Winter 1999): 31–37.

[19] Wainright, G. R. and David Bird, *Teach Yourself Body Language* (New York: McGraw-Hill, 2003), http://www.careerbuilder.com/JobSeeker/CareerBytes/1104dolooksmatter.htm?cbRecursionCnt=1&cbsid=de0cad2875a3487fa1d66580e81ce227-166920203-rp-1.

[20] Maxwell Maltz, *Psycho-Cybernetics* (Englewood Cliffs, N.J.: Prentice-Hall, 1960): 116.

Chapter 6

[1] For a discussion about how salespeople adapt their communication style to the buyer's style, see Morgan P. Miles, Danny R. Arnold, and Henry W. Nash, "Adaptive Communication: The Adaptation of the Seller's Interpersonal Style to the Stage of the Dyad's Relationship and the Buyer's Communication Style," *Journal of Personal Selling and Sales Management* 10 (Winter 1990): 21–27.

[2] Ron D'Andrea, "Executing Profitable Sales Negotiations: Selling Value, Not Price," *Industrial and Commercial Training,*" 37 (2005): 18–24.

[3] Michael A. Humphreys and Michael R. Williams, "Exploring the Relative Effects of Salesperson Interpersonal Process Attributes and Technical Product Attributes on Customer Satisfaction," *Journal of Personal Selling and Sales Management* 16 (Summer 1996): 47–57.

[4] Thomas A. Stewart, "A Satisfied Customer Isn't Enough," *Fortune* (July 21, 1997): 112–113; Thomas O. Jones and W. Earl Sasser, Jr., "Why Satisfied Customers Defect," *Harvard Business Review* (November-December 1995): 88–99.

[5] Louis E. Boone and David L. Kurtz, *Contemporary Marketing,* 12th ed. (Mason, Ohio: Thomson South Western, 2006); Leonard Berry, "Relationship Marketing of Services—Growing Interests, Emerging Perspectives," *Journal of the Academy of Marketing Science* 23 (Fall 1995): 236–245; Mary Jo Bitner, "Building Service Relationships: It's All About Promises," *Journal of the Academy of Marketing Science* 23 (Fall 1995): 246–251; Christian Gronroos, "Relationship Marketing: The Strategy Continuum," *Journal of the Academy of Marketing Science* 23 (Fall 1995): 252–254; Jagdish N. Sheth and Atul Parvatiyar, "Relationship Marketing in Consumer Markets: Antecedents and Consequences," *Journal of the Academy of Marketing Science* 23 (Fall 1995): 255–271; Richard P. Bagozzi, "Reflections on Relationship Marketing in Consumer Markets: Antecedents and Consequences," *Journal of the Academy of Marketing Science* 23 (Fall 1995), 272–277; Robert A. Peterson, "Relationship Marketing and the Consumer," *Journal of the Academy of Marketing Science* 23 (Fall 1995): 278–281; B. A. Weitz, and S. D. Jap, "Relationship Marketing and Distribution Channels," *Journal of the Academy of Marketing Science* 23 (Fall 1995): 305–320; J. R. Nevin, "Relationship Marketing and Distribution Channels: Exploring Fundamental Issues," *Journal of the Academy of Marketing Science* 23 (Fall 1995): 327–334.

[6] Anthony Alessandra, James Cathcart, and Phillip Wexler, *Selling by Objectives* (Englewood Cliffs, N.J.: Prentice-Hall, 1988), p. 206.

[7] Lucette Comer and Tanya Drollinger, "Active Empathetic Listening and Selling Success: A Conceptual Framework," *Journal of Personal Selling and Sales Management* 19 (Winter 1999): 15–29.

[8] For a description of the buying and selling tasks involved in making a sale to a buying team, see Dawn R. Deeter-Schmelz and Rosemary Ramsey, "A Conceptualization of the Functions and Roles of Formalized Selling and Buying Teams," *Journal of Personal Selling and Sales Management* 15 (Spring 1995): 47–60.

[9] Betsy Cummings, "Do Customers Hate Salespeople?" *Sales and Marketing Management* (June 2001): 44–51.

[10] Mark A. Moon and Gary M. Armstrong, "Selling Teams: A Conceptual Framework and Research Agenda," *Journal of Personal Selling and Sales Management* 14 (Winter 1994): 17–30.

[11] Mark Moon and Susan Forquer Gupta, "Examining the Formation of Selling Centers: A Conceptual Framework," *Journal of Personal Selling and Sales Management* 17 (Spring 1997): 40.

[12] Moon and Armstrong, 1994.

[13] Susan Del Vecchio, James Zemanek, Roger McIntyre, and Reid Claxton, "Updating the Adaptive Selling Behaviors: Tactics to Keep and Tactics to Discard," *Journal of Marketing Management* 20 (2004): 859–876; Barton Weitz, Harish Sujan, and Mita Sujan, "Knowledge, Motivation, and Adaptive Behavior: A Framework for Improving Selling Effectiveness," *Journal of Marketing* (October 1986): 174–191.

[14] Jerry R. Goolsby, Rosemary L. Lagace, and Michael L. Boorom, "Psychological Adaptiveness and Sales Performance," *Journal of Personal Selling and Sales Management* 12 (Spring 1992): 51–66.

[15] Stephen S. Porter and Lawrence W. Inks, "Cognitive Complexity and Salesperson Adaptability: An Exploratory Investigation," *Journal of Personal Selling and Sales Management* 20 (Winter 2000): 15–21.

[16] Marvin A. Jolson, "Canned Adaptiveness: A New Direction for Modern Salesmanship," *Business Horizons* 32 (January-February 1989): 7–12.

[17] Ed McMahon, *Ed McMahon's Superselling* (Englewood Cliffs, N.J.: Prentice-Hall, 1989), 22–26.

Chapter 7

[1] For perspectives on how the PSP continues to evolve, see William C. Moncrief and Greg W. Marshall, "The Evolution of the Seven Steps of Selling," *Industrial Marketing Management* 34 (2005): 13–22.

[2] Thomas Wood-Young, "Three's a Charm," SellingPower.com, *Sales Management Newsletter* (October 1, 2001).

[3] Kenneth R. Evans, Robert E. Kleine, Timothy D. Landry, and Lawrence A. Crosby, "How First Impressions of a Customer Impact Effectiveness in an Initial Sales *Encounter," Journal of the Academy of Marketing Science* 28 (Fall 2000): 512–526.

[4] Marvin A. Jolson, "Broadening the Scope of Relationship Selling," *Journal of Personal Selling and Sales Management* 17 (Fall 1997): 75–88.

[5] For an interesting perspective on how to develop creative partnerships, see, for example, two articles by David T. Wilson, "An Integrated Model of Buyer-Seller Relationships," *Journal of the Academy of Marketing Science* 23 (Fall 1995): 335–345; and "Deep Relationships: The Case of the Vanishing Salesperson," *Journal of Personal Selling and Sales Management* 20 (Winter 2000): 53–61.

[6] Joe F. Alexander, Patrick L. Schul, and Denny E. McCorkle, "An Assessment of Selected Relationships in a Model of the Industrial Marketing Negotiation Process," *Journal of Personal Selling and Sales Management* 14 (Summer 1994): 25–39.

[7] Judy A. Wagner, Noreen M. Klein, and Janet E. Keith, "Selling Strategies: The Effects of Suggesting a Decision Structure to Novice and Expert Buyers," *Journal of the Academy of Marketing Science* 29 (Summer 2001): 289–306.

[8] Julie T. Johnson, Hiram C. Barksdale, and James S. Boles, "The Strategic Role of the Salesperson in Reducing Customer Defection in Business Relationships," *Journal of Personal Selling and Sales Management* 21 (Spring 2001): 123–134.

[9] Ron D'Andrea, "Executing Profitable Sales Negotiations: Selling Value, Not Price," *Industrial and Commercial Training,"* 37 (2005), 18–24.

[10] Jolson 1997, 84.

[11] Robert W. Haas, *Business Marketing,* 6th ed. (Cincinnati, Oh.: South-Western College Publishing, 1995).

[12] Don Beveridge, "Overcoming Price Objections," *Industrial Distribution* (February 1999): 94; Andy Cohen, "Don't Succumb to Price Pressures," *Sales and Marketing Management* (March 2001): 14.

Chapter 8

[1] Joan Leotta, "Effortless Closing," *Selling Power* (October 2001): 28–31.

[2] Ed McMahon, *Ed McMahon's Superselling* (New York: Prentice-Hall, 1989): 113–114.

[3] For additional perspectives on closing sales, see William C. Moncrief and Greg W. Marshall, "The Evolution of the Seven Steps of Selling," *Industrial Marketing Management* 34 (2005): 13–22.

[4] For an interesting discussion about how salespeople view their failures, see Gordon J. Badovick, Farrand H. Hadaway, and Peter F. Kaminski, "Attributions and Emotions: The Effects on Salesperson Motivation After Successful vs. Unsuccessful Quota Performance," *Journal of Personal Selling and Sales Management* 12 (Summer 1992): 1–11.

[5] Joseph P. Vaccaro, "Best Salespeople Know Their ABC's (Always Be Closing)," *Marketing News* (March 28, 1988): 10.

[6] For an interesting and easy-to-understand discussion about persuasion's use in industry, see Robert B. Cialdini, "Harnessing the Science of Persuasion," *Harvard Business Review* 79 (October 2001): 72–79.

[7] Alan J. Dubinsky, "A Factor Analytic Study of the Personal Selling Process," *Journal of Personal Selling and Sales Management* 1 (Fall/Winter 1980–1981): 26–33.

[8] Annie H. Liu and Mark P. Leach, "Developing Loyal Customers with a Value-Adding Sales Force: Examining Customer Satisfaction and the Perceived Credibility of Consultative Salespeople," *Journal of Personal Selling and Sales Management* 21 (Spring 2001): 147–156.

[9] Joan Leotta, "The Management Close," *Selling Power* (November/December 2001): 26–28.

[10] Sean Dwyer, John Hill, and Warren Martin, "An Empirical Investigation of Critical Success Factors in the Personal Selling Process for Homogeneous Goods," *Journal of Personal Selling and Sales Management* 20 (Summer 2000): 151–159.

[11] Steven P. Brown, William L. Cron, and John W. Slocum, "Effects of Goal-Directed Emotions on Salesperson Volitions, Behavior, and Performance: A Longitudinal Study," *Journal of Marketing* 61 (January 1997): 39–50.

[12] Tom Hopkins, *How to Master the Art of Selling* (New York: Warner Books, 1982): 87–93.

[13] Based on Tom Hopkins, *How to Master the Art of Selling* (New York: Warner Books, 1982): 87–93.

[14] Michael J. Dorsch, Les Carlson, Mary Anne Raymond, and Robert Ranson, "Customer Equity Management and Strategic Choices for Sales Managers," *Journal of Personal Selling and Sales Management* 21 (Spring 2001): 157–166.

Chapter 9

[1] Philip Kotler and Gary Armstrong, *Principles of Marketing,* 10th ed. (Upper Saddle River, NJ: Prentice-Hall, 2004): 16.

[2] For additional perspectives on the evolution of the PSP stage of follow-up and servicing the account, see William C. Moncrief and Greg W. Marshall, "The Evolution of the Seven Steps of Selling," *Industrial Marketing Management* 34 (2005): 13–22.

[3] For additional perspectives on relationship marketing, see Christian Gronroos, "The Relationship Marketing Process: Communication, Interaction, Dialogue, Value," *Journal of Business & Industrial Marketing* 19, 2 (2004): 99–113; James Boles, Thomas Brashear, Danny Bellenger, and Hiram Barksdale, Jr., "Relationship Selling Behaviors: Antecedents and Relationship with Performance," *Journal of Business & Industrial Marketing* 18, 2/3 (2003): 141–162; Sally Rao and Chad Perry, "Thinking About Relationship Marketing: Where Are We Now? *Journal of Business & Industrial Marketing* 17, 7 (2002): 598–614; Leonard Berry, "Relationship Marketing of Services—Growing Interests, Emerging Perspectives," *Journal of the Academy of Marketing Science* 23 (Fall 1995): 236–245; Mary Jo Bitner, "Building Service Relationships: It's All About Promises," *Journal of the Academy of Marketing Science* 23 (Fall 1995): 246–251; Christian Gronroos, "Relationship Marketing: The Strategy Continuum," *Journal of the Academy of Marketing Science* 23 (Fall 1995): 252–254; Jagdish N. Sheth and Atul Parvatiyar, "Relationship Marketing in Consumer Markets: Antecedents and Consequences," *Journal of the Academy of Marketing Science* 23 (Fall 1995): 255–271; Richard P. Bagozzi, "Reflections on Relationship Marketing in Consumer Markets: Antecedents and Consequences," *Journal of the Academy of Marketing Science* 23 (Fall 1995): 272–277; Robert A. Peterson, "Relationship Marketing and the Consumer," *Journal of the Academy of Marketing Science* 23 (Fall 1995): 278–281; B. A. Weitz and S. D. Jap, "Relationship Marketing and Distribution Channels," *Journal of the Academy of Marketing Science* 23 (Fall 1995): 305–320; J. R. Nevin, "Relationship Marketing and Distribution Channels: Exploring Fundamental Issues," *Journal of the Academy of Marketing Science* 23 (Fall 1995): 327–334.

[4] For more perspectives on changing the definition of marketing, see the comprehensive coverage provided in *Marketing News* (September 15, 2005).

[5] Rolph Anderson and Srini Srinivasan, "E-Satisfaction and E-Loyalty: A Contingency Framework," *Psychology and Marketing* 20 (February 2003): 123–138.

[6] Eli Jones, Lawrence B. Chonko, and James A. Roberts, "Creating a Partnership-Oriented, Knowledge Creation Culture in Strategic Sales Alliances: A Conceptual Framework," *Journal of Business & Industrial Marketing* 18, 4/5 (2003): 336–352; Michael K. Rich, "Requirements for Successful Marketing Alliances," *Journal of Business & Industrial Marketing* 18, 4/5 (2003): 447–456.

[7] P. Rajan Varadarajan and Margaret H. Cunningham, "Strategic Alliances: A Synthesis of Conceptual Foundations," *Journal of the Academy of Marketing Science,* 23 (Fall 1995): 282–296; George S. Day, "Advantageous Alliances," *Journal of the Academy of Marketing Science,* 23 (Fall 1995): 297–300.

[8] Fred Selnes and James Sallis, "Promoting Relationship Learning," *Journal of Marketing* 59 (July 2003): 80–107.

[9] Das Narayandas and V. Kasturi Rangan, "Building and Sustaining Buyer-Seller Relationships in Mature Industrial Markets," *Journal of Marketing* 68 (July 2004): 63–77; Sameer Kumar, Richard Bragg, and Dan Creinin, "Managing Supplier Relationships," *Quality Progress* 36 (September 2003): 24–30; Manohar Kalwani and Narakesari Narayandas, "Long-Term Manufacturer-Supplier Relationships: Do They Pay Off for Supplier Firms?" *Journal of Marketing* 59 (January 1995): 1–16.

[10] Thomas A. Stewart, "A Satisfied Customer Is Not Enough," *Fortune* (July 21, 1997): 112–113.

[11] "Strategic Partnerships," www.giantstepsmts.com/partnerships.htm.

[12] Leonard L. Berry, A. Parasuraman, and Valarie A. Zeithaml, "The Service-Quality Puzzle," *Business Horizons* (September-October 1988): 35–43;

[13] Eric R. Blume, "Customer Service: Giving Companies the Competitive Edge," *Training & Development Journal* (September 1988): 25.

[14] Dan Morse, "Hardware Distributor Sticks to Nuts-and-Bolts Strategy," *Wall Street Journal,* (July 3, 2001): B2.

[15] Leonard L. Berry, A. Parasuraman, and Valarie A. Zeithaml, "The Service-Quality Puzzle," *Business Horizons* (September-October 1988): 35–43; A. Parasuraman, Valarie A. Zeithaml, and Leonard L. Berry, "SERVQUAL: A Multiple-Item Scale for Measuring Consumer Perceptions of Service Quality," *Journal of Retailing* 64 (1988): 12–40; Valarie A. Zeithaml, A. Parasuraman, and Leonard L. Berry, *Delivering Quality Service* (New York: The Free Press, 1995).

[16] Berry et al., 1988;

[17] For in-depth discussion of the Gap Model of Service Quality, see Valarie A. Zeithaml and Mary Jo Bitner, *Services Marketing* (New York: McGraw-Hill, 2000).

[18] Christopher H. Lovelock, *Managing Services: Marketing, Operations, and Human Resources* (Englewood Cliffs, N.J.: Prentice-Hall, 1988): 263–264.

[19] *Business Week* (March 12, 1990): 90–91; Joan C. Szabo, "Service + Survival," *Nation's Business* (March 1989): 16–21.

[20] Valarie A. Zeithaml, Leonard L. Berry, and A. Parasuraman, "The Nature and Determinants of Customer Expectations of Service," *Journal of the Academy of Marketing Science* (Winter 1993): 1–12; Rolph E. Anderson, "Consumer Dissatisfaction: The Effect of Disconfirmed Expectations on Perceived Product Performance, *Journal of Marketing Research* (February 1973): 36–42.

[21] Vikas Mittal, Wagner A. Kamakura, and Rahul Govind, "Geographic Patterns in Customer Service and Satisfaction: An Empirical Investigation," *Journal of Marketing* 68

(July 2004): 48–62; Carol J. Emerson and Curtis M. Grimm, "Buyer-Seller Customer Satisfaction: The Influence of the Environment and Customer Service," *Journal of Business & Industrial Marketing* 14 (1999): 403–415.

22 Tom Peters, *Thriving on Chaos* (New York: Knopf, 1987): 103.

23 Roland T. Rust and Richard L. Oliver, "Service Quality: Insights and Managerial Implications from the Frontier." In *Service Quality: New Directions in Theory and Practice,* ed. Roland T. Rust and Richard L. Oliver (London: Sage, 1994), pp. 1–19; Richard L. Oliver, "A Cognitive Model of the Antecedents and Consequences of Satisfaction Decisions," *Journal of Marketing Research* 17 (November 1980): 460–469; Richard L. Oliver, "Measurement and Evaluation of Satisfaction in Retail Settings," *Journal of Retailing* 57 (Fall 1981): 25–48.

24 For alternative definitions of customer satisfaction, see Joan L. Giese and Joseph A. Cote, "Defining Consumer Satisfaction," *Academy of Marketing Science Review* (2000): 1–24; Philip Kotler and Gary Armstrong, *Principles of Marketing,* 10th ed. (Upper Saddle River, N.J.: Prentice-Hall, 2004): 17; Charles W. Lamb, Joseph F. Hair, Jr., and Carl McDaniel, *Marketing,* 7th ed. (Mason, Ohio: Thomson, 2004): 11.; Kevin Cacioppo, "Measuring and Managing Customer Satisfaction," *Quality Digest,* (September 2000); www.qualitydigest.com/sept00/html/satisfaction.html.

25 *Business Week* (July 3, 2000): 72.

26 Christian Homburg, Nicole Koschate, and Wayne D. Hoyer, "Do Satisfied Customers Really Pay More? A Study of the Relationship Between Customer Satisfaction and Willingness to Pay," *Journal of Marketing* 68 (April 2005): 84–96; E. U. Bond III and Ross L. Fink, "Customer Satisfaction and the Marketing-Quality Interface," *Journal of Business & Industrial Marketing* 18 (2003): 204–218; Jeanne Rossomme, "Customer Satisfaction Measurement in a Business-to-Business Context: A Conceptual Framework," *Journal of Business & Industrial Marketing* 18 (2003): 179–195; Shaun McQuitty, Adam Finn, and James B. Wiley, "Systematically Varying Consumer Satisfaction and Its Implications for Product Choice," *Academy of Marketing Science Review* (2000): 1–16; Carol J. Emerson and Curtis M. Grimm, "Buyer-Seller Customer Satisfaction: The Influence of the Environment and Customer Service," *Journal of Business & Industrial Marketing* 14 (1999): 403–415; Ralf Schellhase, Petra Hardock, and Martin Ohlwein, "Customer Satisfaction in Business-to-Business Marketing: The Case of Retail Organizations and Their Suppliers," *Journal of Business & Industrial Marketing* 15 (2000): 106–121.

27 Frederick Reichheld and Earl Sasser, Jr., "Why Satisfied Customers Defect," *Harvard Business Review* (November-December 1995): 88.

28 For more insights about loyal customers, see Frederick Hong-kit Yim, Rolph E. Anderson, and Srinivasan Swaminathan, "Customer Relationship Management: Its Dimensions and Effect on Customer Outcomes," *Journal of Personal Selling and Sales Management,* 24 (Fall 2004): 263-278; V. Kumar and Dinish Shah, "Building and Sustaining Profitable Customer Loyalty for the 21st Century," *Journal of Retailing* 80, 4 (2004): 317–330; David W. Wallace, Joan L. Giese, and Jean L. Johnson, "Customer Retailer Loyalty in the Context of Multiple Channel Strategies," *Journal of Retailing* 80, 4 (2004): 249–263; Lloyd C. Harris and Mark M. H. Goode, "The Four Levels of Loyalty and the Pivotal Role of Trust: A Study of Online Service Dynamics," *Journal of Retailing* 80, 2 (2004): 139–158.

29 Weld F. Royal, "Cashing In on Companies," *Sales & Marketing Management* (May 1995): 88–89.

30 Thomas O. Jones and W. Earl Sasser, "Why Satisfied Customers Defect," *Harvard Business Review* (November-December 1995): 88–99.

31 Frederick F. Reichheld, Robert G. Markey, Jr., and Christopher Hopton, "The Loyalty Effect – The Relationship Between Loyalty and Profits," *European Business Journal* (2000): 134–139.

32 For alternative definitions of customer loyalty, see V. Kumar and Dinish Shah, "Building and Sustaining Profitable Customer Loyalty for the 21st Century," *Journal of Retailing* 80, 4 (2004): 317–330; Richard L. Oliver, "Whence Consumer Loyalty?" *Journal of Marketing,* 63 (1999): 33–44; James F. Engel and Roger D. Blackwell, *Consumer Behavior* (New York: The Dryden Press, 1982); Jacob Jacoby, "Brand Loyalty: A Conceptual Definition," in *Proceedings of the American Psychological Association,* (Washington, DC: American Psychological Association, 1971), pp. 655–656.

33 Geoffrey Brewer, "The Customer Stops Here," *Sales & Marketing Management* (March 1998): 30–36.

34 Srini Srinivasan, Rolph Anderson, and Kishore Ponnavolu, "Customer Loyalty in E-Commerce: An Exploration of Its Antecedents and Consequences," *Journal of Retailing* 78 (2002): 41–50; Rolph Anderson and Srini Srinivasan, "E-Satisfaction and E-Loyalty: A Contingency Framework," *Psychology and Marketing* 20 (February 2003): 123–138; Frederick Hong-kit Yim, Rolph E. Anderson, and Srinivasan Swaminathan, "Customer Relationship Management: Its Dimensions and Effect on Customer Outcomes," *Journal of Personal Selling and Sales Management* 24 (Fall 2004): 263–278; Richard L. Oliver, "Whence Consumer Loyalty?" *Journal of Marketing,* 63 (1999): 33–44.

35 Zoltan Poleretzky,(1999), "The Call Center & E-Commerce Convergence," *Call Center Solutions,* 7, 17, (January): 76.

36 Dhruv Grewal and Arun Sharma, "The Effect of Salesforce Behavior on Customer Satisfaction: An Interactive Framework," *Journal of Personal Selling and Sales Management* 11 (Summer 1991): 13–23.

37 *Business Week* (March 12, 1990): 90–91.

38 *Business Week* (January 8, 1990): 33, 86.

Chapter 10

[1] Linda L. Price and Eric J. Arnould, "Commercial Friendships: Service Provider–Client Relationships in Context," *Journal of Marketing* 63 (October 1999): 38–56.

[2] J. Brock Smith and Donald W. Barclay, "Selling Partner Relationships: The Role of Interdependence and Relative Influence," *Journal of Personal Selling and Sales Management* 19 (Fall 1999): 21–40.

[3] J. Carlos Jarillo and Howard H. Stevenson, "Cooperative Strategies: The Payoffs and the Pitfalls," *Long Range Planning* (February 1991): 64–70.

[4] F. Robert Finney, "Reciprocity: Gone But Not Forgotten," *Journal of Marketing* (January 1978): 54–59.

[5] F. Robert Dwyer and John F. Tanner, *Business Marketing: Connecting Strategy, Relationships, and Learning,* 3rd ed. (New York: McGraw-Hill Irwin, 2006).

[6] David T. Wilson, "Deep Relationships: The Case of the Vanishing Salesperson," *Journal of Personal Selling and Sales Management* 20 (Winter 2000): 53–61.

[7] Dwyer and Tanner, 2006.

[8] Charles W. Lamb, Jr., Joseph F. Hair, Jr., and Carl McDaniel, *Marketing,* 8th ed. (Cincinnati, Ohio: South-Western, 2006): p. 186.

[9] *1997 Economic Census* (Washington, D.C.: U.S. Census Bureau, January 21, 2000): 7–24.

[10] Ibid., 424; Bureau of the Census, *Statistical Abstract of the United States* (Washington, D.C.: U.S. Government Printing Office, 2000): 543–544.

[11] Alan J. Dubinsky and Thomas N. Ingram, "A Classification of Industrial Buyers: Implications for Sales Training," *Journal of Personal Selling and Sales Management* 1 (Fall-Winter 1981–1982): 46–51.

[12] Gene Brown, Unal O. Boya, Neil Humphreys, and Robert E. Widing, "Attributes and Behaviors of Salespeople Preferred by Buyers: High Socializing vs. Low Socializing Industrial Buyers," *Journal of Personal Selling and Sales Management* 13 (Winter 1993): 25–33.

[13] John E. Swan, Cathy Goodwin, Michael A. Mayo, and Lynne D. Richardson, "Customer Identities: Customers as Commercial Friends, Customer Coworkers or Business Acquaintances," *Journal of Personal Selling and Sales Management* 21 (Winter 2001): 29–37.

[14] Richard S. Jacobs, Kenneth R. Evans, Robert E. Kleine, and Timothy D. Landry, "Disclosure and Its Reciprocity as Predictors of Key Outcomes in an Initial Sales Encounter," *Journal of Personal Selling and Sales Management* 21(Winter 2001): 51–61.

[15] P. Christopher Earley and Elaine Mosakowski, "Cultural Intelligence," *Harvard Business Review* 82 (October 2004): 139–146; Jared Wade, "The Pitfalls of Cross-Cultural Business," *Risk Management* 51, 3 (March 2004): 38–42; Sunanta Chaisrakeo and Mark Speece, "Culture, Intercultural Communication Competence, and Sales Negotiation: A Qualitative Research Approach," *Journal of Business and Industrial Marketing* 19, 4/5 (2004): 267–293; Mohammad Elahee and Charles M. Brooks, "Trust and Negotiation Tactics: Perceptions About Business-to-Business Negotiations in Mexico," *Journal of Business and Industrial Marketing* 19, 6 (2004): 397–404; Danny Ertel, "Getting Past Yes: Negotiating As If Implementation Mattered," *Harvard Business Review* 82 (November 2004): 60–68; John L. Graham and N. Mark Lam, "The Chinese Negotiation," *Harvard Business Review* 81 (October 2003): 82–91; James K. Sebenius, "The Hidden Challenge of Cross-Border Negotiations," *Harvard Business Review* 80, 3 (March 2002): 4–12; Jensen J. Zhao, "The Chinese Approach to International Business Negotiation," *Journal of Business Communication* 37 (July 2002): 209–237; Alex Sharland, "The Negotiation Process as a Predictor of Relationship Outcomes in International Buyer-Supplier Arrangements," *Industrial Marketing Management* 30 (2001): 551–559; Alma Mintu-Wimsatt and Jule B. Gassenheimer, "The Moderating Effect of Cultural Context in Buyer-Seller Negotiation," *Journal of Personal Selling and Sales Management* 20, (Winter 2000): 1–9; Bruce Money, "International Multilateral Negotiations and Social Networks," *Journal of International Business Studies* 29, 4 (1998): 695-710; "International Business Negotiations," *Journal of International Business Studies* 29, 4 (1998): 661–772; A. Rao and S. Schmidt, "A Behavioral Perspective on Negotiating International Alliances," *Journal of International Business Studies* 29, 4 (1998): 665–693; C. Tinsley, and Madan Pillutla, "Negotiating in the United States and Hong Kong," *Journal of International Business Studies* 29, 4 (1998): 711–727.

Chapter 11

[1] Siew Meng Leong, Paul S. Busch, and Deborah Roedder John, "Knowledge Bases and Salesperson Effectiveness: A Script-Theoretic Analysis," *Journal of Marketing Research* 26 (May 1989): 164–178; Harish Sujan, Mita Sujan, and James R. Bettman, "Knowledge Structure Differences Between More Effective and Less Effective Salespeople," *Journal of Marketing Research* (February 1988): 81–86; Steven P. Schnaars, *Megamistakes: Forecasting and the Myth of Rapid Technological Change* (New York: Macmillan, 1989).

[2] For a discussion of factors that might influence the effectiveness of a sales training program, see Alan J. Dubinsky, "Some Assumptions About the Effectiveness of Sales Training," *Journal of Personal Selling and Sales Management* 16 (Summer 1996): 67–76.

[3] Robert F. Hartley, *Marketing Successes* (New York: Wiley, 1985).

[4] Donald W. Jackson, Stephen S. Tax, and John W. Barnes, "Examining the Salesforce Culture: Managerial Applications and Research Propositions," *Journal of Personal Selling and Sales Management* 14 (Fall 1994): 1–14.

[5] For an interesting perspective on how the sales force assists the firm in implementing its business strategy, see Madhubalan Viswanathan and Eric Olson, "The Implementation of Business Strategies: Implications for the

Sales Function," *Journal of Personal Selling and Sales Management* 12 (Winter 1992): 45–58. Also, for further topics related to the role of the sales force in strategic issues, see an entire issue of *Journal of Personal Selling and Sales Management* 21 (Spring 2001).

[6] Artur Baldauf, David Cravens, and Nigel Piercy, "Examining Business Strategy, Sales Management, and Salesperson Antecedents of Sales Organization Effectiveness," *Journal of Personal Selling and Sales Management* 21 (Spring 2001): 109–122.

[7] Harish Sujan, Mita Sujan, and James R. Bettman, "Knowledge Structure Differences Between More Effective and Less Effective Salespeople," *Journal of Marketing Research* (February 1988): 81–86.

[8] For additional perspectives on understanding competition, see Ahmet H. Kirca, Satish Jayachandran, and William O. Bearden, "Market Orientation: A Meta-Analytic Review and Assessment of Its Antecedents and Impact on Performance," *Journal of Marketing* 69 (April 2005): 24–41; Dirceu Tornavoi de Carvalho and Peggy Cunningham, "Market Orientation, Corporate Culture and Business Performance," *Journal of the Academy of Marketing Science* 33 (Spring 2005): 238–241; Anita M. McGahan, "How Industries Change," *Harvard Business Review* 82 (October 2004): 86–94; George Stalk, Jr., and Rob Lachenauer, "Five Killer Strategies for Trouncing the Competition," *Harvard Business Review* 82 (April 2004): 62–71; Enrique Bigne, Ines Kuster, and Francisco Toran, "Market Orientation and Industrial Salesforce: Diverse Measure Instruments," *Journal of Business and Industrial Marketing* 18, 1 (2003): 59–81.

[9] For an alternative approach to evaluating competition, see Alvin C. Burns, "Generating Marketing Strategy Priorities Based on Relative Competitive Positions," *Journal of Consumer Marketing* 3 (Fall 1986): 49–56.

[10] "Survey of Buying Power," *Sales and Marketing Management* (Summer 2000).

[11] Daniel C. Smith and Jan P. Owens, "Knowledge of Customers' Customers as a Basis of Sales Force Differentiation," *Journal of Personal Selling and Sales Management* 15 (Summer 1995): 1–15.

[12] David T. Wilson, "An Integrated Model of Buyer-Seller Relationships," *Journal of the Academy of Marketing Science* 23 (Fall 1995): 335–345.

[13] Alvin J. Williams and John Seminerio, "What Buyers Like from Salesmen," *Industrial Marketing Management* 14 (May 1985): 76.

Chapter 12

[1] Marion Harper, Jr., "Communications Is the Core of Marketing," *Printers' Ink* (June 1, 1962): 53.

[2] Lucette B. Comer and Tanya Drollinger, "Active Empathetic Listening and Selling Success: A Conceptual Framework," *Journal of Personal Selling and Sales Management* 19 (Winter 1999): 15–29; C. David Shepard, Stephen Castleberry, and Rick Ridnour, "Linking Effective Listening with Salesperson Performance: An Exploratory Study," *Journal of Business & Industrial Marketing* 12 (1997): 315–332; Stephen Castleberry and C. David Shepard, "Effective Interpersonal Listening and Personal Selling," *Journal of Personal Selling and Sales Management* 19 (Winter 1993): 35–50; Rosemary P. Ramsey and Ravipreet S. Sohi, "Listening to Your Customers: The Impact of Perceived Salesperson Listening Behavior on Relationship Outcomes," *Journal of the Academy of Marketing Science* 25 (Spring 1997): 127–137.

[3] Comer and Drollinger (1999): 17–19.

[4] Comer and Drollinger (1999): 18–19.

[5] Camille P. Schuster and Jeffrey E. Davis, "Asking Questions: Some Characteristics of Successful Sales Encounters," *Journal of Personal Selling and Sales Management* (May 1986): 17.

[6] John T. Molloy, *Live for Success* (New York: Perigord Press, 1981).

[7] Wilbur Schramm, *The Process and Effects of Mass Communications* (Urbana: University of Illinois Press, 1954): 3.

[8] Robert A. Peterson, Michael P. Cannito, and Stephen P. Brown, "An Exploratory Investigation of Voice Characteristics and Selling Effectiveness," *Journal of Personal Selling and Sales Management* 15 (Winter 1995): 1–15.

[9] John Tsalikis, Oscar DeShields, and Michael LaTour, "The Role of Accent on the Credibility and Effectiveness of the Salesperson," *Journal of Personal Selling and Sales Management* 11 (Winter 1991): 31–41.

[10] Patricia Knowles, Stephen Grove, and Kay Keck, "Signal Detection Theory and Sales Effectiveness," *Journal of Personal Selling and Sales Management* 14 (Spring 1994): 1–14.

[11] Fred W. Morgan and Jeffrey J. Stoltman, "Adaptive Selling—Insights from Social Cognition," *Journal of Personal Selling and Sales Management* 10 (Fall 1990): 43–54.

[12] Morgan P. Miles, Danny R. Arnold, and Henry W. Nash, "Adaptive Communication: The Adaptation of the Seller's Interpersonal Style to the Stage of the Dyad's Relationship and the Buyer's Communication Style," *Journal of Personal Selling and Sales Management* 10 (Winter 1990): 21–27.

[13] See David W. Merrill and Roger H. Reid, *Personal Styles and Effective Performance, The Tracom Corporation* (Radnor, Penn.: Chilton, 1981); Paul Mok, *Communicating Styles Technology* (Dallas, Tex.: Training Associates Press, 1982); Larry Wilson, *Social Styles Sales Strategies* (Eden Prairie, Minn.: Wilson Learning Corporation, 1987); Anthony Alessandra, Phil Wexler, and Rick Barrera, *Non-Manipulative Selling* (Englewood Cliffs, N.J.: Prentice-Hall, 1987).

[14] For more in-depth explanation of communication styles, see Anthony Alessandra, Phil Wexler, and Rick Barrera, *Non-Manipulative Selling* (Englewood Cliffs, N.J.: Prentice-Hall, 1987); J. Ingrasci, "How to Reach Buyers in Their Psychological Comfort Zones," *Industrial Marketing* (July 1981): 60–64; Anthony J. Alessandra and Phillip

S. Wexler with Jerry D. DeenHugh, *Non-Manipulative Selling* (San Diego, Calif.: Courseware, 1979).

15 Erin Anderson and Barton A. Weitz, "Determinants of Continuity in Conventional Industrial Channel Dyads," *Marketing Science*, 8 (Fall 1989): 310–323.

16 Amy Sallee and Karen Flaherty, "Enhancing Salesperson Trust: An Examination of Managerial Values, Empowerment, and the Moderating Influence of SBU Strategy," *Journal of Personal Selling and Sales Management* (Fall 2003): 23, 299–311.

17 Richard E. Buehrer, "The Fundamentals of Business-to-Business Sales and Marketing," *Journal of Business & Industrial Marketing* 19, 7 (2004): 496–497; Karen Norman Kennedy, Jerry R. Goolsby, and Eric J. Arnould, "Implementing a Customer Orientation: Extension of Theory and Application," *Journal of Marketing* 67 (October 2003): 67–81; Enrique Bigne, Ines Kuster, and Francisco Toran, "Market Orientation and Industrial Salesforce: Diverse Measure Instruments," *Journal of Business & Industrial Marketing* 18, 1 (2003): 59–81; Jodie Conduit and Felix T. Mavondo, "How Critical Is Internal Customer Orientation to Market Orientation?" *Journal of Business Research* 51 (2001): 11–24; Stephen X. Doyle and George Thomas Roth, "The Use of Insight Coaching to Improve Relationship Selling," *Journal of Personal Selling and Sales Management* 12 (Winter 1992): 59–64.

Chapter 13

1 For a discussion about different tools that salespeople can use to manage themselves effectively, see Daniel Sauers, James Hunt, and Ken Bass, "Behavioral Self-Management as a Supplement to External Sales Force Controls," *Journal of Personal Selling and Sales Management* 10 (Summer 1990): 17–28.

2 "How Salespeople Spend Their Time," *Sales & Marketing Management* (January 1990): 39.

3 Paul Markovits, "Direct Selling Is Alive and Well," *Sales & Marketing Management* (August 1988): 76–79.

4 Robert F. Vizza and T. E. Chambers, *Time and Territorial Management for the Salesman* (New York: Sales Executives Club of New York, 1971), p. 97; Renee Zymanski, "A Matter of Time," *Selling Power* (October 2001): 80–82; William Kendy, "Time Management," *Selling Power* (July 2001): 34–36.

5 For a discussion about how sales executives and sales managers perceive quotas, see David J. Good and Robert W. Stone, "Attitudes and Applications of Quotas by Sales Executives and Sales Managers," *Journal of Personal Selling and Sales Management* 11 (Summer 1991): 57–60.

6 For an in-depth analysis of performance indicators that sales managers use to evaluate their salespeople, see Donald W. Jackson, John L. Schlachter, and William G. Wolfe, "Examining the Bases Utilized for Evaluating Salespeople's Performance," *Journal of Personal Selling and Sales Management* 15 (Fall 1995): 57–66.

7 A discussion of salespeople's reactions to their achieving or not achieving their quota can be found in Gordon J. Badovick, Farrand J. Hadaway, and Peter F. Kaminski, "Attributions and Emotions: The Effects of Salesperson Motivation After Successful and Unsuccessful Quota Performance," *Journal of Personal Selling and Sales Management* 12 (Summer 1992): 1–12.

8 For an interesting perspective on rewarding sales personnel for generating a high level of customer satisfaction, see Arun Sharma, "Customer Satisfaction–Based Incentive Systems: Some Managerial and Salesperson Considerations," *Journal of Personal Selling and Sales Management* 17 (Spring 1997): 61–70.

9 For an examination of the impact of territory on salesperson performance, see Bruce Pilling, Naveen Donthu, and Steve Hanson, "Accounting for the Impact of Territory Characteristics on Sales Performance: Relative Efficiency as a Measure of Salesperson Performance," *Journal of Personal Selling and Sales Management* 19 (Spring 1999): 35–45.

10 Emin Babakus, David W. Cravens, Mark Johnston, and William C. Moncrief, "Examining the Role of Organizational Variables in the Salesperson Job Satisfaction Model," *Journal of Personal Selling and Sales Management* 16 (Spring 1996): 33–46.

11 For an interesting discussion about sales territory alignment and realignment, see Andris A. Zoltners and Sally E. Lorimar, "Sales Territory Alignment: An Overlooked Productivity Tool," *Journal of Personal Selling and Sales Management* 20 (Summer 2000): 139–150.

12 Raymond W. LaForge, Clifford E. Young, and B. Curtis Hamm, "Increasing Sales Productivity Through Improved Sales Call Allocation Strategies," *Journal of Personal Selling and Sales Management* 3 (November 1983): 53–59.

13 Alan J. Dubinsky, "Customer Portfolio Analysis," in *Advances in Business Marketing,* ed. Arch G. Woodside (Greenwich, Conn.: JAI Press, 1986), pp. 113–139.

14 Andy Cohen, "Process," *Sales & Marketing Management* (September 1998): 71–78.

15 For a review of various routing models, see Wade Ferguson, "A New Method for Routing Salespersons," *Industrial Marketing Management* (April 1980): 171–178.

16 Ibid.

17 For alternative suggestions about how to work smarter rather than harder, see Harish Sujan, "Smarter versus Harder: An Exploratory Attributional Analysis of Salespeople's Motivation," *Journal of Marketing Research* 23 (February 1986): 41–49; Harish Sujan, Barton A. Weitz, and Mita Sujan, "Increasing Sales Productivity by Getting Salespeople to Work Smarter," *Journal of Personal Selling and Sales Management* 10 (August 1990): 9–19.

18 For other perspectives on time management, see Donald N. Sull and Dominic Houlder, "Do Your Commitments Match Your Convictions?" *Harvard Business Review* 83 (January 2005): 82–91; Michael C. Mankins, "Stop Wasting Valuable Time," *Harvard Business Review* 82

(September 2004): 58–65; Steven Berglas, "Chronic Time Abuse," *Harvard Business Review* 82 (June 2004): 90–97; Anonymous, "How Busy Are You?" *Harvard Business Review* 80 (October 2002): 132.

19 Thomas J. Quirk, "The Art of Time Management," *Training* (January 1989): 59–61.

Chapter 14

1 *Occupational Outlook Handbook,* 2004–05 (Washington, D.C.: Bureau of Labor Statistics, U.S. Department of Labor, 2004); and "Occupational Employment Projections to 2012," *Monthly Labor Review* (Washington, D.C.: Bureau of Labor Statistics, U.S. Department of Labor, February 2004).

2 "The 2004 Compensation Survey," *Sales and Marketing Management* 156 (May 2004): 28–35.

3 For an examination of hiring practices of key account executives, see Thomas R. Wotruba and Stephen B. Castleberry, "Job Analysis and Hiring Practices for National Account Marketing Positions, *Journal of Personal Selling and Sales Management* 13 (Summer 1993): 49–66.

4 Some reasons for and results of hiring and promoting individuals in selling and sales management can be found in Shankar Ganesan, Barton Weitz, and George John, "Hiring and Promotion Policies in Sales Force Management: Some Antecedents and Consequences," *Journal of Personal Selling and Sales Management* 13 (Spring 1993): 15–26.

5 For an interesting discussion of where firms might obtain their most profitable salespersons, see Rene Y. Darmon, "Where Do the Best Sales Force Profit Producers Come From?" *Journal of Personal Selling and Sales Management* 13 (Summer 1993): 17–30.

6 For more insights, see Timothy J. Trow, "The Secret to a Good Hire: Profiling," *Sales and Marketing Management* (May 1990): 44–55.

7 Theresa Donahue Egler and Jennifer G. Velez, "Your Hiring Practices Could Put You to the Test," *HR Magazine* (March 1997): 126; Laura M. Litvan, "Thorny Issues in Hiring," *Nation's Business* (April 1996): 34; Julia Lawlor, "Highly Classified," *Sales and Marketing Management* (March 1995): 76–85.

8 For an examination of discrimination in sales force recruitment, see C. David Shepherd and James C. Heartfield, "Discrimination Issues in the Selection of Salespeople: A Review and Managerial Suggestions," *Journal of Personal Selling and Sales Management* 11 (Fall 1991): 67–77; Lucette B. Comer, J. A. F. Nichols, and Leslie J. Vermillion, "Diversity in the Sales Force: Problems and Challenges," *Journal of Personal Selling and Sales Management* 18 (Fall 1998): 1–20; Greg W. Marshall, Miriam B. Stamps, and Jesse N. Moore, "Preinterview Biases: The Impact of Race, Physical Attractiveness, and Sales Job Type on Preinterview Impressions of Sales Job Applicants, *Journal of Personal Selling and Sales Management* 18 (Fall 1998): 21–38; Eli Jones, Jesse Moore, Andrea Stanaland, and Rosiland Wyatt, "Salesperson Race and Gender and the Access and Legitimacy Paradigm: Does Difference Make a Difference?" *Journal of Personal Selling and Sales Management* 18 (Fall 1998): 71–89;

9 Arthur Eliot Berkeley, "Job Interviewers' Dirty Little Secret," *Wall Street Journal* (March 20, 1989): A14.

10 "Can You Pass the Job Test?" *Newsweek* (May 5, 1986): 46–53.

11 Richard Nelson, "Maybe It's Time to Take Another Look at Tests as a Sales Selection Tool?" *Journal of Personal Selling and Sales Management* 7 (August 1987): 33–38; Sara Delano, "Improving the Odds for Hiring Success, Inc. (June 1983): 145-147.

12 Larry L. Craft, "The Career Life Insurance Agent," *Research Brief 96-1*, CraftSystems, Inc., (September 1996): 12-14.

13 Kenneth A. Kovach, "The Truth About Employers' Use of Lie Detectors," *Business and Society Review* (Spring 1995): 65–69.

14 "Firms Debate Hard Line on Alcoholics," *Wall Street Journal* (April 13, 1989): B1.

15 Michael P. Cronin, "This Is a Test," *Inc. Online* (August 1993): 64.

16 Joan Raymond, "The Jaws of Victory," Newsweek (March 18, 2002): 38P.

17 Tom Jackson and Davidyne Mayless, The *Hidden Job Market* (New York: Quadrangle Books, New York Times Book Company, 1976): pp. 95–122.

8Cs of Customer Loyalty—Eight factors (customization, contact interactivity, cultivation, care, community, choice, convenience, and character) that have been found to drive customer loyalty. These 8Cs are moderated by customer trust and satisfaction. (9)

Active Empathetic Listening (AEL)—Highest level of listening; occurs when the salesperson receives verbal and nonverbal messages, processes them cognitively, responds to them verbally and nonverbally, and attempts to assess their underlying meaning intuitively by putting herself or himself in the customer's place throughout. (12)

Active Listening—Occurs when the salesperson receives a message, processes it, and then responds to it to encourage further communication. (12)

Adaptive Selling—Modifying each sales presentation and demonstration to accommodate each individual prospect. (6)

Approach—The first face-to-face contact with the prospect. (5)

Ask for Help Close—Even after the sale seems lost, the salesperson asks the prospect what could have been done to make the sale. Oftentimes, the prospect will give a previously undisclosed reason or objection, which the salesperson can then answer and secure another chance to close the sale. (8)

Assertiveness—The degree to which a person attempts to control or dominate situations and direct the thoughts and actions of other people. (12)

Attitude and Lifestyle Tests—Tests that seek to assess honesty and spot drug abusers. These tests first appeared in the late 1980s when drug abuse became a major problem in the workplace and legislation restricted the use of polygraph tests. (14)

Augmented Product—Complete bundle of benefits offered by a product, including its core function, various enhancing characteristics, and supplemental benefits and services. (1)

Boomerang Close—Turning a prospect's objection or point of resistance around so that it becomes a reason for buying. (8)

Business Defamation—Any action or utterance that slanders, libels, or disparages a competitor, causing the competitor financial damage, lost customers, unemployment, or lost sales. (3)

Business Libel—Unfair and untrue statements made about a competitor *in writing* (usually a letter, sales literature, advertisement, or company brochure), damaging the competitor's reputation or the personal reputation of an individual in that business. (3)

Business Periodicals Index—A cumulative subject index that lists business articles from more than 160 periodicals. (11)

Business Slander—Unfair and untrue *oral* statements made about competitors that damage the reputation of the competitor or the personal reputation of an individual in that business. (3)

Buying Center—In a buying organization, a group of organization members responsible for making purchases. (10)

Canned (or Programmed) Selling—Any highly structured or patterned selling approach. (6)

Centers of Influence—Individuals or groups of people whose opinions, professional activities, and lifestyles are respected among people in the salesperson's target markets. (4)

Close—The stage in the selling process where the salesperson tries to obtain the prospect's agreement to purchase the product. (8)

Cold Call—Initial face-to-face contact with a prospect who is not expecting the salesperson to call. (5)

Cold Calling—Approaching or calling a business without an appointment for the purpose of prospecting or selling. (4)

Collusion—An illegal arrangement in which competing sellers agree to set prices, divide up markets or territories, or act to the detriment of a third competitor. (3)

Communication—A process in which information and understanding are conveyed in two-way exchanges between two or more people. (12)

Communication Style—The way a person sends and receives messages in communicating with other people. (12)

Concentration Principle—Most sales, costs, and profits come from a relatively small proportion of customers and products; also known as the 80–20 rule. (13)

Cooperative Education Programs—Students combine their college studies with paid work in their career field of interest during two 6-month co-op cycles with one or more of several thousand participating companies. Students often pay for their own college education with money earned in these co-op jobs. Three universities — Drexel, Northeastern, and Cincinnati — are best known for their cooperative education programs. (14)

Core Selling Team—Members of the selling firm assigned to particular prospects or customers to develop and maintain ongoing buyer-seller relationships with them. (6)

Cover Letter—Letter that accompanies a résumé and is designed to induce employers to read the enclosed résumé. Oftentimes used by college students and others to identify the position they're applying for if they prefer not to put a job objective on their résumé. (14)

Culture—A set of formal or informal values, norms, morals, attitudes, beliefs, customs, and behaviors that establish the code of conduct for a group of people or an organization. (11)

Customer-Benefit Approach—An approach whereby the salesperson offers the prospect a specific benefit that can be realized from using the salesperson's product. (5)

Customer-Oriented Selling—Focus on identifying customers' needs and engaging in selling and servicing behaviors that help build and maintain a high level of customer satisfaction and loyalty in the long run. (1)

Customer Relationship Management—A business strategy designed to augment revenues and increase the profitability of companies by better understanding their customers' needs and buying behaviors—and, in that process, developing a stronger relationship with their customers. (4)

Customer Service—The performance of a broad spectrum of value-added activities designed to enhance and facilitate the sale and use of a product. (9)

Customer Service Segmentation—A strategy for grouping customers with similar service expectations into service segments and then developing a service plan for each segment. (9)

Data Mining—Using statistical tools, such as decision trees, cluster analysis, and regression analysis, to detect relevant customer purchase patterns between and among variables in a database. (2)

Data Mining—A procedure that uses statistical software to mine volumes of data to identify "hidden" interrelationships among buyers and the products they purchase, along with associated complementary products. (4)

Data Warehouse—Corporate-wide database built from information systems already in place in the company. (2)

Database Marketing—Computerized analysis of sales transaction databases to identify customer purchase patterns and profiles to better serve target markets. (2)

Derived Demand—Demand created as a result of consumer demand; typical of industrial markets. (10)

Dichotomous Question—Used to set up a clear-cut "either-or" answer for prospects and customers. (12)

Direct Marketing—Selling alternatives that bypass or partially substitute for field salespeople, including *direct mail, telemarketing, teleselling, kiosks, facsimile,* and *electronic mail.* (2)

Door-to-Door Canvassing—Knocking on doors in a commercial area without an appointment to locate prospects. (14)

Dual Management—A management system in which both professional managers and specialists without managerial training run an organization, sometimes resulting in conflict. Typical of many nonprofit organizations. (10)

Effectiveness—Results-oriented focus on achieving selling goals. (13)

Efficiency—Cost-oriented focus on making the best possible use of the salesperson's time and efforts. (13)

Electronic Résumés—Many large companies now use computer software to receive, sort, store, and retrieve résumés from job applicants, so that they can later scan thousands of résumés in a matter of minutes to find the best candidates for a job opening. (14)

Endless Chain—A classic method of prospecting in which the salesperson simply asks recent prospects for further prospect referrals. (14)

Entering Goods—Ingredients or components that become part of the finished product, such as raw materials and semi-manufactured goods. (10)

Ethics—Moral code of conduct and principles that govern individuals and societies in determining what is right or wrong. (3)

Evaluative Listening—Occurs when the seller concentrates on what the buyer is saying but fails to sense what is being said through nonverbal or subtle verbal cues. (12)

Evaluative Question—Used within the open-ended question format to stimulate prospects and customers to talk about their general or specific goals, problems, and needs. (12)

Exclusive Dealing—Agreements in which a manufacturer or wholesaler grants one dealer exclusive rights to sell a product in a certain trading area and insists that the dealer not carry competing lines. Illegal under the Clayton Act. (3)

Extranets—Corporate networks that allow communication between a company and selected customers, suppliers, and business partners. (1)

FAB—A memory-aid acronym that stands for a product's **F**eatures, **A**dvantages, and **B**enefits that will appeal most to a salesperson's customer. (6)

Facilitating Goods—Goods consumed in the ongoing production process, such as maintenance and repair items. (10)

FedBizOpps.gov—Website that contains all federal contracting community solicitations for purchases exceeding $25,000. (10)

Follow-up—Customer service provided not just after the sale is closed, but throughout the selling process. (9)

Foundation Goods—Goods used in the production process that do not become part of the finished product, such as fixed major machine tools and office equipment. (10)

Gatekeeper—Person who controls access or flow of information to decision makers. Examples include technical advisers, secretaries, security guards, and even telephone switchboard operators. (10)

Hidden Job Market—About 90 percent of available jobs are never advertised and never reach employment agency files, so job applicants must be creative and resourceful in competing for these jobs. (14)

Hostile Environment—A pattern of sexual behavior that makes the job so unpleasant that the victim's work is adversely affected. (3)

Iceberg Principle—Analogous to an iceberg, most sales problems are hidden beneath the surface of overall positive sales totals. (13)

Industrial Buyer—The buying expert for an organization. Sometimes called the purchasing agent. (10)

Influencers—People who can influence the purchase decision by helping set product specifications, negotiating purchasing procedures and prices, or providing information about evaluating alternatives. (10)

Intranets—Internal corporate networks that allow salespeople and other employees within a company to obtain information and communicate with each other. (1)

Invalid Objections—Irrelevant, untruthful, delaying, or hidden reasons for not buying. (7)

Keystone Objection—The customer's most important objection. (7)

Kinesics—The description of bodily gestures and movements in terms of what these gestures and movements communicate to other people. (12)

Lead—Anything—a name, address, or telephone number—that points to a potential prospect. (4)

Marginal Listening—Occurs when salespeople hear the prospect's words but are easily distracted and may allow their minds to wander. (12)

Marketing Information System (MIS)—Any systematized, continuous process of gathering, sorting, analyzing, evaluating, and distributing market information. An MIS can be particularly helpful to salespeople in obtaining new leads and prospects. (4)

Mission Statement—Sets forth in writing the organization's orientation, goals, basic values, and sense of purpose. (11)

Missionary Selling—Educating, building goodwill, and providing services to customers who prescribe or recommend products for their patients, clients, or customers (e.g., doctors and dentists) by giving them samples and information about products and services (such as new pharmaceuticals and medicines to prescribe or recommend for their patients). (1)

NAME—An abbreviation for the process of qualifying a lead in terms of *need* for the product, *authority* to buy, *money* to buy, and overall *eligibility* to buy. (14)

Networking—Meeting others in social or business settings to talk informally, establish rapport, and build relationships with people who can be contacted later for referrals or as potential prospects. (4)

North American Industry Classification System (NAICS)—Covers more than 19,000 industry descriptions, used to identify new business prospects and their general product and service requirements by up to six digits of specificity. (10)

Objection—Anything that the prospect or customer says or does that impedes the sales negotiations. (7)

Offset Strategies—A set of strategies for dealing with objections that uses the technique of offsetting the objection with a benefit. (7)

One-to-One Marketing—A philosophical change from the traditional approach of looking at customers as a mass market to viewing customers as individuals. One-to-one marketing seeks to sell more products to fewer (selected) customers, rather than more products to more customers. (2)

Order Creating—The process of identifying prospective buyers, providing them with information, motivating them to buy, confirming the sale, and following up after the sale has been made to ensure customer satisfaction. Trade, technical, and creative salespeople all do order creating in varying degrees. (1)

Order Supporting—The process of having minimal involvement in sales generation but instead providing assistance to customers. (1)

Order Taking—Processing routine orders or reorders for products that have been sold previously to the buying firm. (1)

Parkinson's Law—Work expands to fill the time allotted to it. (13)

Perceived Service Quality—The quality of service individual customers believe they deserve and expect to receive relative to what they actually perceive receiving. (9)

Perceived Value—A product's value from the prospect's perspective. (7)

Personal Selling Process (PSP)—The seven interacting, overlapping stages that every salesperson, no matter what the product or service being sold, must carry out. (1)

Personal Selling Process (PSP)—Also the seven-stage process of professional personal selling, from prospecting and qualifying prospects to following up and servicing customers. (4)

Preapproach—The approach-planning stage of the selling process. (5)

Prenotification—The use of an in-person cold call, a direct mailing, or a telephone call to send a strong signal to the prospect that the salesperson would like to schedule a sales call appointment. (5)

Price Discount—Any reduction off the standard list price of a product. (8)

Price Fixing—Two or more competing sellers conspiring to set or maintain uniform prices and profit margins. (3)

Probing Question—Used to search for information when prospects and customers have difficulty articulating their precise needs. (12)

Processing—Operations within the salesperson's mind that give meaning to the prospect's message through understanding, interpreting, evaluating, and remembering the communication. (12)

Product Disparagement—False or deceptive comparisons or distorted claims *made during or after a sales presentation* about a competitor's products, services, or properties. These statements are considered defamatory *per se.* (3)

Product Quality—Perceived performance of the tangible product in satisfying customer expectations. (9)

Professional Salesperson—Salesperson who sees a sales career as a true profession for which he or she must be well educated, well prepared, and thoroughly professional in order to negotiate successfully with professional buyers. (1)

Promotion—Typically, a one-way flow of persuasive information from a seller to a buyer. (12)

Prospect—A lead that has been qualified as a definite potential buyer. (4)

Prospecting—First step in the PSP, wherein salespeople find leads and qualify them on four criteria: need, authority, money, and eligibility (NAME) to buy. (1)

Prospecting—Also the process of searching for leads—people and organizations that might need your product—and then qualifying them as prospects or potential customers. (4)

Protected Groups—In terms of employment laws, protected groups are people distinguished by special characteristics such as race, color, ethnicity, national origin, religion, gender, age (over forty), disability, or veteran status. These particular groups are protected under federal antidiscrimination law, which mandates that people in one of these protected groups not be discriminated against in any facet of employment—including hiring, promotion, training, discipline, pay, or termination. (14)

Proxemics—The nature of the spatial relationships among people and objects. (12)

Puppy Dog Close—Letting the prospect try the product for a few days or weeks before buying, on the principle that most people grow attached to something they have for a while. (8)

Push Technology—Combination of data warehousing and e-mail to retrieve and send relevant information to prospects and customers. (2)

Put-Off Strategies—A set of strategies for handling a prospect's objections that require the salesperson to delay dealing with the objection initially. (7)

Quid Pro Quo Harassment—A person in authority's demand for sexual favors from an employee in exchange for a job advantage, such as being hired or promoted. (3)

Random-Lead Searching—Generation of leads by randomly calling on organizations. Sometimes called "blind" searching. (14)

Reciprocity—In industrial buyer-seller relationships, an informal agreement between two or more organizations to exchange goods and services on a systematic and more or less exclusive basis. In other words, "You buy from me, and I'll buy from you." (10)

Reliability—Ability to perform the desired service dependably, accurately, and consistently; the single most important component of customer service. (9)

Responding—Assures the prospect that the salesperson has been listening accurately and is encouraging the communication to continue. (12)

Responsiveness—The level of emotions, feelings, or sociability that a person openly displays. (12)

Return on Time Invested (ROTI)—The designated return achieved, calculated by dividing the result achieved by the amount of time spent to accomplish that result. (13)

SAD TIE—A memory-aid acronym that stands for **S**tatistics, **A**nalogies, **D**emonstrations, **T**estimonials, **I**ncidents, and **E**xhibits, one or all of which the salesperson may use to spice up a sales presentation. (6)

Sales Internship Programs—Unpaid study-work programs offered to college students by several companies—for example, Procter & Gamble and Automatic Data Processing—where students learn about career opportunities. (14)

Sales Megatrends—Major behavioral, technological, and managerial trends that influence how salespeople perform their jobs. (2)

Sales Territory—A control unit that contains customer accounts. (13)

Seeding—Prospect-focused activities, such as mailing pertinent news articles, carried out several weeks or months before a sales call. (5)

Selective-Lead Searching—Application of systematic strategies to generate leads from predetermined target markets. (14)

Selling Center—Members of the selling organization assigned to a certain prospect to close a particular sales transaction. After the sale is consummated, the selling center is likely to disband. (6)

SELLS—A memory-aid acronym: **S**how your product's key features; **E**xplain its major advantages; **L**ead into specific benefits for the prospect; **L**et the prospect do most of the talking; and **S**tart a trial close, and use more throughout the presentation. (6)

Sensing—The most basic aspect of listening; includes hearing words, inflection, and paralanguage (e.g., speed of speech, use of colloquialisms), as well as observation of nonverbal language (e.g., body language, facial expressions). (12)

Service Quality—All activities supporting the sale, from the initial contact through the post-sale servicing, that meet or exceed customer expectations and enhance the value of a product. (9)

SMART—A method of setting sales call objectives that are **S**pecific, **M**easurable, **A**chievable, **R**elational, and **T**emporal. (5)

SPIN—A selling technique that enables the salesperson to identify a prospect's major needs quickly. The acronym stands for **S**ituation, **P**roblem, **I**mplications, and **N**eeds payoff. (5)

Spotters—People who work in jobs where they meet many other people and who can help salespeople obtain business leads. Also called "bird dogs." (4)

Strategy—A long-run total program of action for using resources to achieve an overall goal. (11)

Survey Approach—An approach whereby the salesperson asks the prospect to answer a few survey questions, the responses to which establish quickly whether the prospect has a need for the salesperson's product. (5)

Tactic—A short-run, specific action that is part of the larger strategic plan. (11)

Telemarketing—Use of telephone by support staff to help salespeople identify prospects, gather information, and answer inquiries. (2)

Teleselling—Conducting the entire personal selling process via telephone. (2)

Territorial Routing—Devising a travel plan or pattern to use when making sales calls. (13)

Territory Blitz—An intensified version of door-to-door canvassing in which several salespeople join efforts to call on every organization in a given territory or area. (4)

Thomas Register—The primary source that most Fortune 500 companies use to locate suppliers. Published annually, it provides information about 189,000 manufacturers regarding product categories, specific products, names of the companies, branches, top executives and their job titles, affiliation data, and credit rating. (11)

Tie-In—An often-illegal seller's requirement that a customer purchase an unwanted product along with the desired product. (3)

Trade Selling—Creative field service to wholesale and distributor customers, such as expediting orders, taking reorders, restocking shelves, setting up displays, providing in-store demonstrations, and distributing samples to store customers. (1)

Trial Close—Any well-placed attempt to close the sale; can be used early and often throughout the selling process. (8)

Valid Objections—Sincere concerns that the prospect needs addressed before he or she will be willing to buy. (7)

Value Added Selling—Providing customers extra or added-value benefits over those offered by competitors. (6)

Value Analysis—A financial analysis, usually written, that shows how a product is the best value for the money. (7)

Vocational Interest Tests—Tests designed to measure how closely an applicant's interests match the interests of other people who have successfully performed a particular job. (14)

Wheel of Personal Selling—Depiction of the seven stages of the PSP as a continuous cycle or wheel carried out by professionals in the field of sales. (1)

Win-Win Negotiations—Negotiations in which both parties feel satisfied with the outcome; the only kind of negotiations that professional salespeople seek! (7)

Written Presentation—In sales presentations to organizational prospects, the salesperson's explanation of how the prospect can profitably use the product. Also called a sales proposal or business plan. (6)

NAME/AUTHOR INDEX

C

D

T

U

ORGANIZATION INDEX

SUBJECT INDEX

Q

R

FOR STUDENTS

ANDERSON ONLINE STUDY CENTER

This student website provides additional information, guidance, and activities that will help enhance the concepts presented in this text. The site offers students ACE Self-Testing, Ready Notes, Flash Cards, Web Resources, Learning Objectives, Outlines, and Company Links. In addition, the site will feature links to important job and career sites.